COMPUTATIONAL FINANCE

COMPUTATIONAL FINANCE

Numerical Methods for Pricing Financial Instruments

George Levy

ELSEVIER

BUTTERWORTH
HEINEMANN

AMSTERDAM   BOSTON   HEIDELBERG   LONDON   NEW YORK   OXFORD
PARIS   SAN DIEGO   SAN FRANCISCO   SINGAPORE   SYDNEY   TOKYO

Butterworth-Heinemann
Elsevier
Linacre House, Jordan Hill, Oxford OX2 8DP
200 Wheeler Road, Burlington, MA 01803

First published 2004

British Library Cataloguing in Publication Data
A catalogue record for this book is available from the British Library

Library of Congress Cataloguing in Publication Data
A catalogue record for this book is available from the Library of Congress

ISBN 0 7506 5722 7

For information on all Elsevier Butterworth-Heinemann publications
visit our website at www.bh.com

Typeset by Integra Software Services Pvt. Ltd, Pondicherry, India
www.integra-india.com
Printed and bound in The Netherlands

To Kathryn

Contents

Preface

It was in late 1995 to early 1996 (shortly after the birth of his first daughter Claire) that the author first began to read the currently available finance books in order to write C/C++ financial software. However, apart from the book *Options Futures and Other Derivatives* by John Hull, he found very little information of practical help and had to trawl through the original journal articles in the Bodleian library for more information. Even then much information on how to implement and test various models was not included.

The current book aims to provide practical information on basic computational finance. In addition many statistical, financial, and numerical results are derived so that the reader does not need to consult a large number of other books. It should be mentioned that many of the code excerpts assume that the reader has access to NAG Ltd numerical libraries. However, for those who are not so fortunate, equivalent C/C++ software is provided on the accompanying CD ROM.

The book is divided into three parts. Part I considers the type of interfaces to financial functions that can be created using the Microsoft Windows environment. In particular it deals with the use of Dynamic Link Libraries (DLLs) and ActiveX components from languages such as Visual Basic, VBScript, VB.NET, and C#. The author considers that one of the main developments in technical computing over the past ten years has been the emergence of technologies that permit the rapid development of easy to use interfaces to complex functions. At the mouse click of a virtual button complicated computations can be performed.

Part II of the book is concerned with the mathematics of option pricing, and covers computational methods for vanilla options and also simple barrier options. In many cases more exotic options (that for example include complex barriers, lockout periods, rebates, etc.) can be created from these by using them as building blocks. Most of this material can be understood using basic college mathematics and its presentational style is inspired by Numerical Recipies, for instance see Press *et al.* (1992).

Finally Part III of the book deals with financial econometrics and the modelling of volatility. Although the main emphasis is on GARCH, Levy processes, and stochastic volatility models are also considered.

From an historical point of view the finite-difference methods used in Part II have their origin in the numerical weather forecasting techniques proposed by Lewis Richardson between 1910 and 1930, see Richardson (1910) and Richardson and Gaunt (1927). These were later developed by Phyliss Nicolson (Girton College Cambridge) and John Crank in the 1940s, and their method is known as the

Crank–Nicolson finite-difference method. GARCH time series methods can trace their roots to earlier work in the 1920s concerned with AR processes. We could continue by discussing the history of Gaussian processes, Levy distributions, etc. However, the reader can read about this elsewhere.

It should be mentioned that this is not a book about how to use and trade in various financial derivatives. In fact the author does not have this experience, and books such as John Hull are a good introduction to this subject.

I would like to take this opportunity to thank my wife Kathryn for putting up with the extra time that a book such as this requires.

I would also like to thank the series editor, Dr Steven Satchell, for his very useful advice concerning the structure of the book, and Mike Cash of Butterworth-Heinemann for his support throughout the project.

In addition I gratefully acknowledge the Risk Waters Group for allowing PDF versions of several journal articles to be placed on the CD ROM.

George Levy
Benson 2003

Part I

Using Numerical Software Components within Microsoft Windows

Chapter 1

Introduction

This part of the book describes a variety of Microsoft technologies that enable software developers to deploy their numerical/financial functions within Microsoft Windows. It would be impossible in such a short space to provide a comprehensive description of Microsoft Windows. One of the reasons is that Microsoft regularly brings to market new and improved products. For instance in 2002 Microsoft launched its release version of .NET; this had been previously available in the form of Beta 1 and Beta 2 releases. This product includes the languages VB.NET, an updated version of Visual Basic, and C#. The main purpose of .NET is to facilitate the easy deployment of *Web Service* component software over the Internet. Currently (October 2002) the full MSDN documentation and help system (with information on .NET) takes well over 1 Gbyte of computer disc space. Voluminous books have also been written on various aspects of .NET such as: VB.NET, C#, XML, and XSL, and these can be consulted as required. Here we can only aim at providing a short introduction to the use of Microsoft technology for numerical computation. In order to combat information overload we will try here to convey the maximum *essential* information in the minimum space. To achieve this we will adopt the strategy of supplying well commented code excerpts from real (working) Microsoft projects. It is intended that these code excerpts can be used as templates for the creation of computational finance components. Additional material, including documentation, complete source code and ready to use Microsoft projects can be found on the CD ROM which accompanies this book.

Before embarking on a more detailed description of various Microsoft languages and applications it would be sensible to try and gain an overview of the Microsoft Windows environment and consider the possible benefits to be gained from using it for software development.

To a large extent the Microsoft Windows environment is all about the Visual user-interface. The replacement of command line, DOS based, programming by Microsoft Windows heralded an explosion in the use of computers. Esoteric DOS commands (understood by only a few) gave way to the simple interactive user-interface. Here the user can control a program by (for example) clicking Windows buttons with the mouse and entering values into Windows textboxes. The enormous advantage of this approach (now used by nearly all computational software) is that the user is shielded from complicating factors such as the operating system and the underlying computer languages. All the user needs to do is to enter the correct data and click the appropriate button; the answer then appears on the screen.

Using Windows software can now be made as easy as turning on the television or playing a video player. However, as with the *real button* on the television or video player remote control, the *virtual button* of a Windows application can conceal a great deal of underlying technology. The purpose of this part of the book is to provide information concerning the type of Windows software that may be invoked when a Windows *event* (such as a mouse click) occurs.

We will consider the ways in which numerical and financial *components* can be incorporated into various Windows applications. Here we take the term numerical and financial *component* to mean a self-contained computational object which, given certain inputs, will return various computed results. The inputs and computed results can be single values (*scalars*), one-dimensional arrays (*vectors*), two-dimensional arrays (*matrices*), or higher dimensional arrays. The components described here are designed to be used in *mixed language* applications. This means that the component is created using a computationally efficient language such as C/C++ or Fortran, and resides in either a Windows *Dynamic Link Library* (DLL) or *COM ActiveX Control*. It is then used from another (interface) language such as Visual Basic, which *wraps* it and provides the Visual interactive interface seen by the user. If the components are to be accessible from the complete range of Microsoft languages it is good programming practice to restrict their data types to the very basic C/C++ types such as `real`, `double`, and `long` (Fortran types REAL, DOUBLE PRECISION, and INTEGER) which have equivalents in all the other Microsoft languages. It should be noted that, in C++, seemingly innocent structures, strings and character parameters can be particularly difficult (if not impossible) to deal with.

The topics covered here include:

- DLL creation using Visual C++.
- Calling C and Fortran routines from Visual Basic, VB.NET, and C#.
- Using ActiveX and COM components from Visual Basic, Internet Web pages, Excel, and Delphi.
- Scripting ActiveX components on Internet Web pages using VBScript and JScript.
- XML and transformation using XSL.

The section on XML data representation and transformation was included because it provides an introduction to viewing data (or computed results) with the Web browser Internet Explorer 6. In Chapter 6 we show how the use of XSL style sheets permits an XML file to be transformed into a HTML file. This tranformation can be accomplished automatically when the XML file is loaded into a Web browser (for example by double clicking the XML file with a mouse). By using different XSL files it is thus possible to obtain different views of the numeric values contained within an XML file. For example it may be considered appropriate to generate both a *tabular view* which gives columns of numeric values, and also a *report view* which contains fewer numbers and contains graphical plots that summarize the information.

Information is given on how to call components from Visual Basic, Delphi, VB.NET, and C#. In addition we show how numeric components can be used from within Windows applications such as Excel and Internet Explorer.

As previously mentioned we will not consider in any detail the construction of the Visual interface; this information can be readily found in the large selection of Microsoft Windows books that are currently available. We will also concentrate on the mixed language use of numeric components. This means that although all the examples in this part of the book could have been written in Visual C++, they use a variety of Windows languages such as Visual Basic, VBScript, Delphi, etc.

In practical terms this means that the creation of a computational finance application is a two-step process:

- The creation of the numerical/finance component, using a computationally efficient language such as Visual C++ or Visual Fortran.
- The construction of the application framework and user-interface using Microsoft languages such as Visual Basic, VB.NET, C#, etc.

This separation leads to a natural division of labour. The numerical components are created by an expert mathematician/numerical analyst (with limited knowledge of languages such as C++, Visual Basic, etc.) and the construction of the Visual interface is performed by a computer programmer (with limited numerical knowledge) who is expert in the more complex features of the language chosen for developing the application's visual interface. For example a numerical analyst may create an option pricing component using Visual C++. A computer programmer may then incorporate this component into a variety of applications such as: Web-based services using VB.NET or C#, spreadsheet applications using Excel, or stand-alone PC applications using Visual Basic, Delphi, etc.

Finally here are just a few remarks concerning the style of the book.

Small example applications have been included in the areas of statistics, linear algebra, financial derivative pricing, portfolio optimisation, and numerical optimisation.

Also some of the examples refer to the NAG C library DLL and also the NAG Fortran DLL. However, the techniques used in these examples can easily be applied to calling functions from other, user-defined, Windows DLLs.

Care has been taken to make all the computer code as simple as possible. We don't (intentionally) try to be clever; the main consideration is that the code works. Readers can always modify the code to suit their needs and preferences.

Finally some people may find the style rather terse compared to the coverage given in other books. This is intentional, since there is so much the information presented will be limited to the minimum required to obtain working software. The book has been written from the author's experience that:

A page of working (and well commented) computer code is worth a hundred pages of explanation.

In spite of all these caveats it is hoped the reader will find the information in the following sections both instructional and useful reference material.

Chapter 2

Dynamic Link Libraries (DLLs)

The Microsoft Windows environment is constructed so that virtually all applications make calls to Dynamic Link Libraries (DLLs). These DLLs may contain system library routines provided by a particular computer vendor or may be customized third party DLLs which provide specialized functions (e.g. graphical, mathematical, text processing, etc.). Section 2.1 shows how DLLs written in C/C++ can be used from Visual Basic and VBA. Sections 2.2 and 2.3 provide information on calling C/C++ DLLs and Fortran DLLs from VB.NET and C# respectively. As previously mentioned the examples given will mainly focus on the use of the NAG C Library DLL and the NAG Fortran Library DLL. However, the information provided is quite general and can be used to interface to a C or Fortran DLL.

2.1 VISUAL BASIC AND EXCEL VBA

The aim of this section is to provide a brief overview of how to use Dynamic Link Library functions from Visual Basic 6 (and earlier), and also from Visual Basic for applications, that is VBA within Microsoft Excel, etc. More detailed information on this subject can be found in Levy (1998), and we will refer to the NAG C library functions mentioned in that report.

2.1.1 Visual Basic types

First we need to consider the Visual Basic data types required to match those that occur in the routine argument lists of a (32-bit) C/C++ DLL. A brief summary of the fundamental types is given in Table 2.1 .

In Visual Basic all enumeration variables corresponding to enumeration variables within a C DLL should be declared as type Long. Furthermore a Visual Basic

Table 2.1 Correspondence between Visual Basic types and those of Fortran 77 and C

Visual Basic	C	Fortran 77	Size in bytes
Byte or String*1	char	CHARACTER*1	1
Long	long	INTEGER	4
Long	int	LOGICAL	4
Single	float	REAL	4
Double	double	DOUBLE PRECISION	8

variable of type long which has the value 0 is taken as FALSE by the C DLL function; if it has the value is 1 it is TRUE.

We now illustrate this in C Code excerpt 2.1 below.

```
#define Nag_RK_method_start 53
#define Nag_IncludeMean_start 281
typedef enum {FALSE, TRUE} Boolean;
typedef enum {Nag_MeanInclude=Nag_IncludeMean_start, Nag_MeanZero} Nag_IncludeMean;
typedef enum {Nag_RK_2_3=Nag_RK_method_start, Nag_RK_4_5, Nag_RK_7_8} Nag_RK_method;
Nag_IncludeMean mean;
Nag_RK_method rk;
Boolean printit, stopit;
mean = Nag_MeanZero;
mean = Nag_MeanInclude;
printit = TRUE;
stopit = FALSE;
rk = Nag_RK_7_8;
rk = Nag_RK_2_3;
```

Code excerpt 2.1 C code containing enumeration types

By default, enumerators in a given C enumeration type declaration start at zero and increase by 1 as the declaration is read from left to right. However, if a given enumerator is assigned a value then subsequent enumerators continue the progression from the assigned value. The Visual Basic code corresponding to Code excerpt 2.1 is given below.

```
Dim mean As Long
Dim rk As Long
Dim printit As Long
Dim stopit As Long
mean = 282
mean = 281
printit = 1
stopit = 0
rk = 55
rk = 53
```

Code excerpt 2.2 The Visual Basic corresponding to Code excerpt 2.1

If a C DLL function contains a structure in its parameter list then it is necessary to declare the equivalent structure in Visual Basic. We will now illustrate this with the NAG C library error structure (of type NagError) which is used in nearly all of the NAG C library functions. The definition of this type is given in Code excerpt 2.3.

```
typedef struct {
  int code;
  long print;
  char message [512];
  void (*handler)(char*, int*, char*);
  long errnum;
} NagError;
```

Code excerpt 2.3 The declaration of the type NagError, used in the NAG C library

The corresponding Visual Basic user-defined type (UDT) is given in Code excerpt 2.4; it can be seen that the pointer to the handler function has been replaced by a structure member of type Long.

```
Type NagErrorType
  code As Long
  printm As Long
  Message(511) As String *1
  handler As Long
  errnum As Long
End Type
```

Code excerpt 2.4   The Visual Basic declaration of a UDT corresponding to `NagError` in Code
excerpt 2.3

2.1.2   Function declarations

The C DLL routines are declared in Visual Basic by using the following syntax:

```
Declare Function "name" Lib "library name" Alias "decorated name" (arguments)_
As return type
```

for a C function which returns a value (of type `double` or `long`), and

```
Declare Sub "name" Lib "library name" Alias "decorated name" (arguments)
```

for a C function which returns void. The 'decorated name' is generated from the DLL
routine name using the following convention. An underscore (_) is prefixed to the
routine name. The name is followed by the at-sign (@) character, followed by the
number of bytes in the argument list. For instance the NAG C library DLL routines
`g01aac` and `f02wec` have the function prototypes

```
#define DllExport __declspec(dllexport)
extern DllExport void __stdcall g01aac(long n, double x[],double wt[], long *nvalid,
  double *xmean, double *xsd, double *xskew, double *xkurt,
  double *xmin, double *xmax, double *wsum, NagError *iflag);

extern DllExport void __stdcall f02wec(long m, long n, double *a, long tda, long ncolb,
  double *b, long tdb, Boolean wantq, double *q, long tdq, double *sv, Boolean wantp,
  double *pt, long tdpt, long *iter, double *e, long *info, NagError *iflag);
```

require Visual Basic declaration statements of the form

```
Declare Sub g01aac Lib "nagcd.dll" Alias "_g01aac@48" (ByVal n As Long, _
  x As Double, wt As double, nvalid As Long, xmean As Double, _
  xsd As Double, xskew As Double, xkurt As Double, xmin As Double, _
  xmax As Double, wsum As Double, iflag As NagErrorType)

Declare Sub f02wec Lib "nagcd.dll" Alias "_f02wec@72" (ByVal m As Long, _
  ByVal n As Long, a As Double,ByVal tda As Long, ByVal ncolb As Long, _
  b As Double, ByVal tdb As Long, ByVal wantq As Long, q As Double, _
  ByVal tdq As Long, sv As Double, ByVal wantp As Long, pt As Double, _
  ByVal tdpt As Long, iter As Long, e As Double, info As Long, iflag As NagErrorType)
```

Code excerpt 2.5   The Visual Basic declaration statements for the NAG C library functions
`g01aac` and `f02wec`

In C, pointers are used to pass arguments by reference (e.g. `double *xsd, long
*nvalid, double x[ ]`, etc.); here the notation [ ] is used to denote an array
argument. When arguments are passed by value in C the syntax type variable name
(e.g. `long n, double x`, etc.) is used. In Visual Basic, by default, all arguments are
passed by reference; the keyword `ByVal` is required to pass an argument by value. In C

all pointers are 4 bytes long. This means that the function g01aac, in which the first parameter (of type Long) is passed by value and the remaining parameters are passed by reference, has a total byte count of 48 bytes; giving rise to the decorated name '_g01aac@48'. In a similar manner the function f02wec, which has 18 parameters of 4 bytes each, has a total byte count of 72 and the decorated name '_f02wec@72'.

2.1.3 Null pointers

Many C routines make use of null pointers to indicate that an argument is to be ignored and default action is to be taken. For example the NAG C library routine g01aac has a pointer argument wt which allows the routine to perform statistical computations involving weighted data. If this argument is set to the null pointer then unweighted calculations are performed; all the weights are assumed to be 1. In Visual Basic this can be accomplished by declaring g01aac as shown in Code excerpt 2.6, where the declaration wt As Long (instead of wt As double) has been used to allow this argument to be used as a pointer.

```
Declare Sub g01aac Lib "nagcd.dll" Alias "_g01aac@48" (ByVal n As Long, _
    x As Double, ByVal wt As Long, nvalid As Long, xmean As Double, _
    xsd As Double, xskew As Double, xkurt As Double, xmin As Double, _
    xmax As Double, wsum As Double, iflag As NagErrorType)
```

Code excerpt 2.6   A Visual Basic declaration statement which allows a null pointer to be used for the parameter wt in the NAG C library function g01aac

The routine calls

```
Call g01aac(n, x(0), ByVal 0&, nvalid, xmean, xsd, xskew, xkurt, xmin, xmax, wsum, iflag)
```

and

```
Call g01aac(n, x(0), 0, nvalid, xmean, xsd, xskew, xkurt, xmin, xmax, wsum, iflag)
```

are now both valid and result in unweighted calculations being performed.

2.1.4 Function parameters

In contrast to C, Visual Basic procedures are not allowed to have function arguments. This limitation creates a problem when using and declaring DLL routines that require function parameters such as the objective function for numerical optimization routines. A solution to this problem is the creation of an auxiliary DLL to provide a convenient interface wrapper for both the objective function and optimization routine. Another way around this problem is to use ActiveX COM components as illustrated in Chapters 5 and 6.

2.1.5 Two-dimensional array parameters and storage order

In Visual Basic care must be taken when using one- and two-dimensional arrays. This is because the array indices start at zero (unless Option Base is used to define a different start index) and continue to the *maximum indices* specified in the array declaration. This means that:

```
Dim a(5) ' declares an array which holds 6 elements: a(0),...a(6)
Dim b(3,2) ' declares an array which holds 9 elements:
    b(0,0) b(0,1) b(0,2) b(1,0) b(1,1) b(1,2)
    b(2,0) b(2,1) b(2,2) b(3,0) b(3,1) b(3,2)
```

The *leading* dimension of array b is therefore 4, and the trailing dimension of b is 3. In Visual Basic multidimensional arrays are *stored by columns* (as in Fortran) rather than *stored by rows*, which is the C convention. (Note: In Sections 2.2 and 2.3 we will see that this situation has now been reversed in VB.NET and C# which both store multidimensional arrays using the C convention; that is by rows.) This means that care must be taken when a DLL routine has matrix (two-dimensional array) parameters. For example, assume that a 3 by 2 matrix

11	12
21	22
31	32

is stored in a Visual Basic two-dimensional array a in the natural manner, as in the following code fragment.

```
Dim a(2, 1) As Double
a(0, 0) =11
a(1, 0) =21
a(2, 0) =31
a(0, 1) =12
a(1, 1) =22
a(2, 1) =32
```

The array a consists of 6 elements stored in column order, as follows:

    11   21   31   12   22   32.

However, routines in a C DLL follow the convention that two-dimensional arrays are stored in row order. Suppose the array a were passed to a C routine (for instance the NAG C library DLL routine f02wec, as in the SVD example in Section 2.1.6)

```
Call f02wec(3, 2, a(0, 0), · · · ·)
```

where the first two arguments specify the number of rows and columns in the matrix. The routine would treat the array as representing a 3 by 2 matrix stored in row order

11	21
31	12
22	32

which is not the intended matrix A. One solution (which is used in Sections 2.1.6 and 2.1.7) is to store the matrix in a one-dimensional array `al`, with the element `al(i,j)` stored in `al(( i − 1)* tda + j − 1)`, where `tda` is the trailing dimension of the matrix (in this case 2).

```
Dim al(5) As Double
Dim tda As Long
tda = 2
al(0) = 11
al(1) = 12
al(2) = 21
al(3) = 22
al(4) = 31
al(5) = 32
Call f02wec(3, 2, al(0), tda ·  ·  ·  ·)
```

Another solution is to store the transpose of the matrix A in a two-dimensional array `at`, with `tda` now being the leading dimension of the array `at`

```
Dim at(1, 2) As Double
Dim tda As Long
tda = 3
at(0, 0) = 11
at(0, 1) = 21
at(0, 2) = 31
at(1, 0) = 12
at(1, 1) = 22
at(1, 2) = 32
Call f02wec(3, 2, at(0, 0), tda, ·  ·  ·  ·)
```

The Visual Basic array `at` can be larger than is needed to store the 2 by 3 matrix AT; in order that the C routine accesses the correct array elements it is essential that `tda` is set to the correct value.

```
Dim at(3, 5) As Double
Dim tda As Long
 ·  ·  ·
Call f02wec(3, 2, at(0, 0), tda, ·  ·  ·  ·)
```

2.1.6   Singular value decomposition example

In this example we use the NAG C Library DLL `f02wec` routine to perform a singular value decomposition (SVD) within Visual Basic.

Briefly the SVD of a matrix consists of the following factorization:

$$A = U\Sigma V^T$$

where A is the original matrix, Σ is the diagonal matrix of singular values, U is the matrix containing the left hand singular vectors, and V is the matrix containing the right hand singular vectors. The information obtained from an SVD (see G Golub) can be very valuable and, for example, can be used to perform principal component analysis or least squares regression; both of which have important applications in computational finance.

Here we give the DLL function two Visual Basic function declarations. The function `f02wec_full` is used to calculate both the singular values and also the left and right singular vectors of a matrix A; it also requires the declaration of 'dummy' arrays for certain array arguments that are not referenced. The function f02wec_ptr is used to calculate the singular values only, and contains the declarations ByVal q As Long, ByVal b As Long and ByVal pt As Long within its argument list. This enables assignment of null pointers to these arguments and thus avoids the use of 'dummy' array arguments when the routine is called. The example also illustrates how data is assigned to the input array a; note tda is the second (trailing) dimension of the matrix A.

The following two Visual Basic declaration statements for the C library function f02wec are used:

```
Declare Sub f02wec_full Lib "nagcd.dll" Alias "_f02wec@72"(ByVal m As Long, _
  ByVal n As Long, a As Double,ByVal tda As Long, ByVal ncolb As Long, _
  b As Double, ByVal tdb As Long, ByVal wantq As Long, q As Double ,_
  ByVal tdq As Long, sv As Double, ByVal wantp As Long, pt As Double, _
  ByVal tdpt As Long, iter As Long,e As Double, info As Long, _
  iflag As NagErrorType)
```

which requires all the parameters to be supplied, and

```
Declare Sub f02wec_ptr Lib "nagcd.dll" Alias "_f02wec@72" (ByVal m As Long, _
  ByVal n As Long, a As Double, ByVal tda As Long, ByVal ncolb As Long, _
  ByVal b As Long, ByVal tdb As Long, ByVal wantq As Long, ByVal q As Long, _
  ByVal tdq As Long, sv As Double, ByVal wantp As Long, ByVal pt As Long, _
  ByVal tdpt As Long, iter As Long, e As Double, info As Long, _
  iflag As NagErrorType)
```

which allows the use of null pointers for the parameters b , q, and pt.

```
Static a(m*n-1) As Double
Static a2(m*n-1) As Double
Static q(m*n-1) As Double
Static sv(m-1) As Double
Static pt(0) As Double
Static e(m-1) As Double
Static dum(0) As Double
Dim iflag As NagErrorType
iflag.code=0
iflag.printm=1
ncolb=0
tda=n
For i=0 To m-1
  For j=0 To n-1
    Input #2, a(i * tda+j)
    a2(i * tda+j) =a(i * tda+j)
  Next j
Next i
tdb=0
tdpt=0
tdq=n
wtp=1  ' set wantp to TRUE
wtq=1  ' set wantq to TRUE
' calculate the singular values and also the left and right singular vectors
Call f02wec_full(m, n, a2(0), tda, ncolb, dum(0), tdb, wtq, q(0), tdq, sv(0), _
  wtp, pt(0),tdpt, iter, e(0), info, iflag)
tdq=0
wtp=0  ' set wantp to FALSE
wtq=0  ' set wantq to FALSE
' only calculate the singular values, call f02wec_ptr with 3 null pointers
Call f02wec_ptr(m, n, a(0), tda, ncolb, ByVal 0&, tdb, wtq, ByVal 0&, tdq, _
  sv(0), wtp, ByVal 0&, tdpt, iter, e(0), info, iflag)
```

Code excerpt 2.7   Illustrating the use of null pointers within Visual Basic when calling the singular value decomposition function f02wec from the NAG C library

We now give an example of calling a numerical optimization function from Visual Basic.

2.1.7 Numerical optimization example

Since many financial problems involve some form of optimal decision process it is useful to show how to call numerical optimization software from Visual Basic. We will illustrate this by showing how to use the NAG C Library DLL function e04nfc; full documentation at the NAG website, http://www.nag.co.uk. The example we will consider here is taken from Bunch and Kaufman (1980) and consists of estimating the vector x that will minimize the quadratic function:

$$f(x) = c^T x + \frac{1}{2} x^T H x$$

where:

$$c = (7.0, 6.0, 5.0, 4.0, 3.0, 2.0, 1.0, 0.0)^T \text{ and}$$

$$H = \begin{pmatrix} 1.69 & 1.00 & 2.00 & 3.00 & 4.00 & 5.00 & 6.00 & 7.00 \\ 1.00 & 1.69 & 1.00 & 2.00 & 3.00 & 4.00 & 5.00 & 6.00 \\ 2.00 & 1.00 & 1.69 & 1.00 & 2.00 & 3.00 & 4.00 & 5.00 \\ 3.00 & 2.00 & 1.00 & 1.69 & 1.00 & 2.00 & 3.00 & 4.00 \\ 4.00 & 3.00 & 2.00 & 1.00 & 1.69 & 1.00 & 2.00 & 3.00 \\ 5.00 & 4.00 & 3.00 & 2.00 & 1.00 & 1.69 & 1.00 & 2.00 \\ 6.00 & 5.00 & 4.00 & 3.00 & 2.00 & 1.00 & 1.69 & 1.00 \\ 7.00 & 6.00 & 5.00 & 4.00 & 3.00 & 2.00 & 1.00 & 1.69 \end{pmatrix}$$

subject to the bounds:

$$-1.0 \le x_1 \le 1.0$$
$$-2.1 \le x_2 \le 2.0$$
$$-3.2 \le x_3 \le 3.0$$
$$-4.3 \le x_4 \le 4.0$$
$$-5.4 \le x_5 \le 5.0$$
$$-6.5 \le x_6 \le 6.0$$
$$-7.6 \le x_7 \le 7.0$$
$$-8.7 \le x_8 \le 8.0$$

and the general constraints:

$$-x_1 + x_2 \ge -1.00$$
$$-x_2 + x_3 \ge -1.05$$
$$-x_3 + x_4 \ge -1.10$$
$$-x_4 + x_5 \ge -1.15$$
$$-x_5 + x_6 \ge -1.20$$
$$-x_6 + x_7 \ge -1.25$$
$$-x_7 + x_8 \ge -1.30$$

The initial point is taken as:

$$x_0 = (-1.0, -2.0, -3.0, -4.0, -5.0, -6.0, -7.0, -8.0)^T$$

An example of using the function `e04nfc` from Visual Basic is given in Code excerpt 2.8 below.

```
Static n, i, j As Long
Static tda As Long
Static tdh As Long
Static x() As Double
Static a() As Double
Static h() As Double
Static cvec() As Double
Static bl() As Double
Static bu() As Double
Static objf As Double
Static nmax As Long
Static nclin As Long
Static ncnlin As Long
Static qphess_ptr As Long
Static options_ptr As Long
Dim iflag As NagErrorType

n = 8           ' Set the number of variables
nclin = 7       ' Set the number of linear constraints
tda = n
tdh = n
ReDim a(nclin * n)
ReDim bu(30)
ReDim x(n)
ReDim bl(30)
ReDim cvec(10)
ReDim h(100)
For i = 0 To nclin - 1           ' Loop on the number of linear constraints
  For j = 0 To n - 1             ' Loop on the number of variables
    a(i * tda + j) = 0#          ' Initialise the array a
  Next j
Next i
For i = 0 To nclin - 1           ' Loop on the number of linear constraints
  a(i * tda + i) = -1#           ' Set the elements of the constraint matrix a
  a(i * tda + i + 1) = 1#
  bl(n + i) = -1# - 0.05 * i     ' Set the lower bound of the linear constraint
  bu(n + i) = 1E+20              ' Set the upper bound of the linear constraint
Next i
For j = 0 To n - 1              ' Loop on the number of variables
  bl(j) = -(j + 1) - 0.1 * j    ' Set the lower bounds
  bu(j) = j + 1                 ' Set the upper bounds
  cvec(j) = 7 - j              ' Set the elements of the vector c
Next j
For i = 0 To n - 1
  For j = i + 1 To n - 1
    h(i * tdh + j) = Abs(i - j)
  Next j
  h(i * tdh + i) = 1.69
Next i
iflag.code = 0
qphess_ptr = 0                  ' Use a null pointer for the Hessian
options_ptr = 0                 ' Use a null pointer for theoptimization options structure
x(0) = -1#                      ' Set the initial estimates for x
x(1) = -2#
x(2) = -3#
x(3) = -4#
x(4) = -5#
x(5) = -6#
x(6) = -7#
x(7) = -8#
Call e04nfc(n, nclin, a(0), tda, bl(0), bu(0), cvec(0), h(0), tdh, _
  qphess_ptr, x(0), objf, options_ptr, 0, iflag)
MsgBox "optimum objf = " & objf   ' Output (to the screen) the ' value of the objective function
MsgBox " The solution is:"
```

```
For i = 0 To 7    ' Output (to the screen) the individual elements of the solution vector
  MsgBox "x(" & i & ") = " & x(i)
Next i
End Sub
```

Code excerpt 2.8   Illustrating how the NAG C library numerical optimization function e04nfc can be used from Visual Basic

The optimization routine e04nfc is designed to output useful information to the file e04nfce.r. This files contains information such as the optimization settings, and also the Lagrange multipliers and value of the objective function and solution vector x^* at the computed minimum. It can be seen from Exhibit 2.1 that, at the computed minimum, the solution vector is

$$x^* = (-1.0, -2.0, -3.05, -4.15, -5.30, 6.0, 7.0, 8.0)^T$$

and the value of objective function is -621.4878

```
Parameters to e04nfc
====================
Linear constraints ................... 7        Number of variables .................. 8

prob.......................... Nag_QP2          start ......................... Nag_Cold
ftol...........................1.05e-008        reset_ftol ........................... 5
rank_tol.......................1.11e-014        crash_tol .................... 1.00e-002
fcheck............................... 50        max_df ............................... 8
inf_bound.....................1.00e+020         inf_step ..................... 1.00e+020
fmax_iter............................ 75        max_iter ............................ 75
hrows................................. 8        machine precision ............. 1.11e-016
min_infeas..................... FALSE
print_level.............. Nag_Soln_Iter
outfile..................... e04nfce.r

Memory allocation:
state........................... Nag
ax.............................. Nag           lambda ........................... Nag


Results from e04nfc:
====================
Itn  Jdel  Jadd    Step    Ninf   Sinf/Obj    Bnd  Lin  Nart  Nrz   Norm Gz

 0    0     0    0.0e+000    3   2.3550e+001    5    0    3    0   1.73e+000
 1   2 U   10 L  4.0e+000    2   1.9600e+001    4    1    3    0   1.41e+000
 2   4 U   12 L  7.8e+000    1   1.1750e+001    3    2    3    0   1.00e+000
 3   6 U   14 L  1.2e+001    0   0.0000e+000    2    3    3    0   0.00e+000


Itn 3 -- Feasible point found.

 3    0     0    0.0e+000    0   8.6653e+002    2    3    2    1   1.52e+002
 4    0     9 L  1.0e-001    0   4.9824e+001    2    4    2    0   0.00e+000
 5   2 A   11 L  4.5e-001    0  -5.6227e+002    2    5    1    0   0.00e+000
 6   1 A    6 U  6.0e-011    0  -5.6227e+002    3    5    0    0   0.00e+000
 7  14 L    7 U  1.3e-001    0  -6.2149e+002    4    4    0    0   0.00e+000


Final solution:

    Varbl  State     Value      Lower Bound   Upper Bound   Lagr Mult    Residual

 V   1     LL   -1.00000e+000  -1.0000e+000  1.0000e+000   3.045e+002  0.000e+000
 V   2     FR   -2.00000e+000  -2.1000e+000  2.0000e+000   0.000e+000  1.000e-001
 V   3     FR   -3.05000e+000  -3.2000e+000  3.0000e+000   0.000e+000  1.500e-001
 V   4     FR   -4.15000e+000  -4.3000e+000  4.0000e+000   0.000e+000  1.500e-001
 V   5     FR   -5.30000e+000  -5.4000e+000  5.0000e+000   0.000e+000  1.000e-001
 V   6     UL    6.00000e+000  -6.5000e+000  6.0000e+000  -6.100e-001  0.000e+000
 V   7     UL    7.00000e+000  -7.6000e+000  7.0000e+000  -2.442e+001  0.000e+000
 V   8     UL    8.00000e+000  -8.7000e+000  8.0000e+000  -3.423e+001  0.000e+000
```

	LCon	State	Value	Lower Bound	Upper Bound	Lagr Mult	Residual
L	1	LL	−1.00000e+000	−1.0000e+000	None	2.129e+002	−2.220e−016
L	2	LL	−1.05000e+000	−1.0500e+000	None	1.315e+002	2.220e−016
L	3	LL	−1.10000e+000	−1.1000e+000	None	6.443e+001	2.220e−016
L	4	LL	−1.15000e+000	−1.1500e+000	None	1.779e+001	−4.441e−016
L	5	FR	1.13000e+001	−1.2000e+000	None	0.000e+000	1.250e+001
L	6	FR	1.00000e+000	−1.2500e+000	None	0.000e+000	2.250e+000
L	7	FR	1.00000e+000	−1.3000e+000	None	0.000e+000	2.300e+000

Exit after 7 iterations.

Optimal QP solution found.

Final QP objective value = −6.2148783e+002

Exhibit 2.1   The file e04nfce.r which contains information concerning the numerical optimization performed by e04nfc

2.2   VB.NET

In this section we will give details of how to call (and use) Fortran DLLs and C DLLs from VB.NET. Since VB.NET is very similar to Visual Basic, many of the concepts have already been dealt with in Section 2.1. We will therefore concentrate on the important differences (from a numerical view) between Visual Basic Version 6 and VB.NET (also known as Visual Basic Version 7). A brief summary of some important types in VB.NET is displayed in Table 2.2.

We will now list, and briefly comment on, the main differences between VB.NET and Visual Basic. They are as follows:

- All array indicies must start at zero. This means that Option Base 0|1, which was available in Visual Basic (Version 6) can no longer be used in VB.NET. Also the number of elements in an array is the same as in Visual Basic. If an array called mya is declared using Dim mya(8) it will have 9 elements; these are mya(0),... mya(8). (Note: In VB.NET Beta 1, this was not so. If mya was declared using Dim mya(8) would contain the 8 elements mya(0),...mya(7).) This means that the number of elements in VB.NET multi-dimensional arrays (such as matrices) is the same as that described in Section 2.1 for Visual Basic.
- Multidimensional arrays are stored in row order, rather than column order as was the case for Visual Basic. This means that it is now necessary to perform a transpose operation when using passing matrices to Fortran DLL functions; where matrices are stored in column order.
- It is not possible to alter the number of dimensions of an array by using a ReDim statement. For example this means that the two-dimension array mya

Table 2.2   Correspondence between VB.NET types and those of Fortran 77 and C

VB.NET	C	Fortran 77	Size in bytes
Integer	long	INTEGER	4
Integer	int	LOGICAL	4
Single	float	REAL	4
Double	double	DOUBLE PRECISION	8

must be declared as `Dim mya(,)` before it can be allocated using a statement such as `ReDim mya(4,3)`. In Visual Basic it was possible to declare the array as `Dim mya( )`, and then allocate it as a two-dimensional array using `ReDim mya(4,3)`.

- In contrast to Visual Basic, VB.NET and C# do not allow fixed length strings to be declared within UDTs (that is structures). This means that it is no longer possible to define a type that correponds to the NAG C Library type `NagErrorType`, see Section 2.1.1. We will show two ways around this problem. The first is to use a null pointer argument; see Code excerpt 2.9. The second method is to wrap the original C DLL function within another C function which uses an integer parameter to flag errors; see Code excerpts 2.11 and 2.13.
- The type corresponding to a 4 byte integer is `Integer`; in Visual Basic the type was `Long`.

We will now illustrate these language features by describing the computer code contained within a VB.NET project which performs some numerical computations. The example used here is a VB.NET project (Figure 2.1) that computes the singular value decomposition of a given matrix by calling either the NAG Fortran Library DLL function F02WEF, or the NAG C Library DLL function f02wec. The visual user-interface of this project is very simple, and is similar to that shown in Figure 2.2 for the C# example application of Section 2.3. We use radio button controls to choose between the NAG Fortran Library and the NAG C Library.

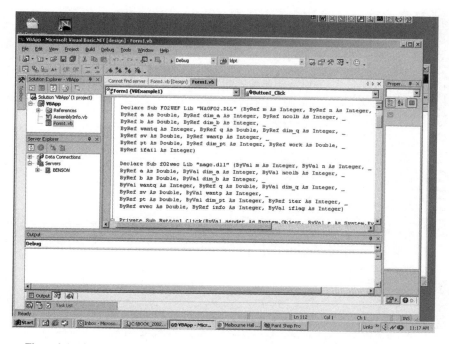

Figure 2.1 A view of the VB.NET example project corresponding to Code excerpt 2.9

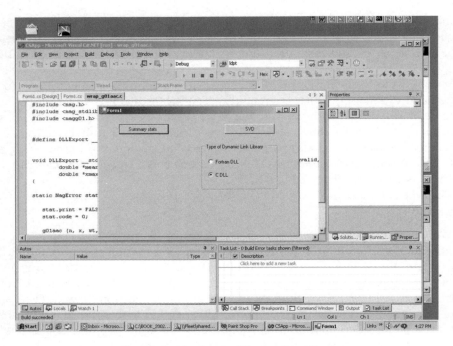

Figure 2.2   Running the C# example application

```
Public Class Form1
  Inherits System.Windows.Forms.Form
  Public use_c_dll As Boolean
#Region " Windows Form Designer generated code "
      .   .   .
#End Region
      .   .   .
  Declare Sub F02WEF Lib "NAGF02.DLL" (ByRef m As Integer, ByRef n As Integer,_
  ByRef a As Double, ByRef dim_a As Integer, ByRef ncolb As Integer,_
  ByRef b As Double, ByRef dim_b As Integer,_
  ByRef wantq As Integer, ByRef q As Double, ByRef dim_q As Integer,_
  ByRef sv As Double, ByRef wantp As Integer,_
  ByRef pt As Double, ByRef dim_pt As Integer, ByRef work As Double,_
  ByRef ifail As Integer)

  Declare Sub f02wec Lib "nagc.dll" (ByVal m As Integer, ByVal n As Integer,_
  ByRef a As Double, ByVal dim_a As Integer, ByVal ncolb As Integer,_
  ByRef b As Double, ByVal dim_b As Integer,_
  ByVal wantq As Integer, ByRef q As Double, ByVal dim_q As Integer,_
  ByRef sv As Double, ByVal wantp As Integer,_
  ByRef pt As Double, ByVal dim_pt As Integer, ByRef iter As Integer,_
  ByRef evec As Double, ByRef info As Integer, ByVal iflag As Integer)

  Private Sub Button1_Click(ByVal sender As System.Object, ByVal e As System.EventArgs) Handles Button1.Click

    Dim a1(,), q(1), sv(), pt(,), b(1), work() As Double
    Dim dim_a, dim_q, dim_b, dim_pt, m, n As Integer
    Dim i, j, ncolb, iflag, wantp, wantq, lwork As Integer
    Dim iter, info As Integer
    Dim evec() As Double
    Dim out_text As String

    FileOpen(2, "c:\BOOK_2002\SVD_DATA.TXT", OpenMode.Input) ' Open the input data file
    If use_c_dll Then   ' Open the C DLL results file
      FileOpen(1,"c:\BOOK_2002\VBF02WEC_RESULTS.txt", OpenMode.Output)
      PrintLine(1, "VB.NET Singular Value Decomposition Example:Using C DLL function f02wec")
    Else  ' Open the Fortran DLL results file
```

```
      FileOpen(1, "c:\BOOK_2002\VBFO2WEF_RESULTS.txt", OpenMode.Output)
      PrintLine(1, "VB.NET Singular Value Decomposition Example: Using Fortran DLL function FO2WEF")
    End If
    ' This example performs a singular value decomposition of a m x n matrix A using either the
    ' NAG Fortran function FO2WEF or the NAG C function f02wec.
    ' The singular values, left singular vectors and right singular vectors are output to a file.
    ' When the C function f02wec is used the left hand singular vectors are output in the array a1,
    ' and the transpose of the right hand singular vectors are output in the array pt.
    ' When the Fortran function FO2WEF is used the transpose of left hand singular vectors are output in the
    ' array a1, and the right hand singular vectors are output in the array pt.
    Input(2, m)  ' Input the number of rows of matrix A
    Input(2, n)  ' Input the number of columns of matrix A
    ' Note: The code assumes that m > n
    PrintLine(1)
    PrintLine(1)
    ReDim sv(n)  ' Allocate an array to hold the singular values
    If use_c_dll Then  ' Using the C DLL so storage is in row order
      ReDim a1(m, n)  ' Allocate the m x n matrix a1 to represent matrix A
      ReDim pt(n, n)
      dim_a = UBound(a1, 2) + 1  ' Set the trailing (second) dimension of matrix a1
      dim_pt = n + 1  ' Set the dimension of pt
    Else  ' Using the Fortran DLL so storage is in column order
      ReDim a1(n, m)  ' Allocate the n x n matrix a1, to represent the transpose of matrix A
      ReDim pt(n, n)
      dim_a = UBound (a1, 2) + 1 'Set the leading (first dimension) of matrix A.
                                 ' This is the trailing (second) dimension of matrix a1 (the ' transpose of
                                 ' matrix A)
      dim_pt = n + 1  ' Set the dimension of pt
    End If
    dim_b = 1
    dim_q = 1
    wantq = 1  ' Set WANTQ to TRUE
    wantp = 1  ' Set WANTP to TRUE
    ncolb = 0  ' Don't want to include a B matrix
    For i = 0 To m - 1  ' Loop on the row index
      For j = 0 To n - 1  ' Loop on the column index
        If use_c_dll Then
          Input(2, a1(i, j))  ' Input matrix A
        Else
          Input(2, a1(j, i))  ' Input the transpose of matrix A
        End If
      Next j
    Next i
    If use_c_dll Then  ' Use the NAG C DLL
      iflag = 0
      ReDim evec(m)
      Call f02wec(m, n, a1(0, 0), dim_a, ncolb, b(0), dim_b, wantq, q(0),_
      dim_q, sv(0), wantp, pt(0, 0), dim_pt, iter, evec(0), info, iflag)
    Else  ' Use the NAG Fortran DLL
      lwork = n * n + 4 * (n - 1)
      ReDim work(lwork)  ' Allocate the required workspace array
      Call FO2WEF(m, n, a1(0, 0), dim_a, ncolb, b(0), dim_b, wantq, q(0),_
      dim_q, sv(0), wantp, pt(0, 0), dim_pt, work(0), iflag)
    End If
    out_text = "The singular values are:"
    i = 0
    Do While i < n  ' Form a string containing all the singular values
      out_text = out_text & " " & sv(i)
      i = i + 1
    Loop
    PrintLine(1, out_text)  ' Output the text
    PrintLine(1)  ' Output a blank line
    PrintLine(1)
    PrintLine(1, "Left-hand singular vectors:")
    PrintLine(1)
    For i = 0 To m - 1  ' Loop on the row index
      out_text = ""
      For j = 0 To n - 1  ' Loop on the column index
        If use_c_dll Then
          out_text = out_text & " " & a1(i, j)  ' Output a1
        Else
          out_text = out_text & " " & a1(j, i)  ' Output the transpose of a1
        End If
      Next j
      PrintLine(1, out_text)  ' Output the text
    Next i
```

```
PrintLine(1)
PrintLine(1, "Right-hand singular vectors:  ")'
PrintLine(1)
For i = 0 To n − 1   ' Loop on the row index
  out_text = ""
  For j = 0 To n − 1   ' Loop on the column index
    If use_c_dll Then
      out_text = out_text & " " & pt(j, i)   ' Output the transpose of pt
    Else
      out_text = out_text & " " & pt(i, j)   ' Output pt
    End If
  Next j
  PrintLine(1, out_text)   ' Output the text
Next i
FileClose(2)
FileClose(1)
End Sub
Private Sub RadioButton1_CheckedChanged(ByVal sender As System.Object, ByVal e As System.EventArgs)
    Handles RadioButton1.CheckedChanged
  use_c_dll = False   ' Set the flag which indicates use of the NAG Fortran DLL
End Sub
Private Sub RadioButton2_CheckedChanged(ByVal sender As System.Object, ByVal e As System.EventArgs)
    Handles RadioButton2.CheckedChanged
  use_c_dll = True   ' Set the flag to indicate use of the NAG C DLL
End Sub
End Class
```

Code excerpt 2.9   A VB.NET program that computes the singular value decomposition by calling either the NAG Fortran DLL function F02WEF, or the NAG C library DLL function f02wec. The call to f02wec uses a null pointer for the last parameter, which in C is declared as NagErrorType*

In Code excerpt 2.9 we demonstrate the declaration of two-dimensional VB.NET arrays, and their use by Fortran and C DLLs. When a C DLL is used the arrays a1 and pt are declared with the statements ReDim a1(m, n) and ReDim pt(m, n); if a Fortran DLL is called we declare the *transposed* arrays using ReDim a1(n, m) and ReDim pt(n, m). The C DLL function f02wec is passed the second (or trailing) dimension of the arrays a1 and pt, which is $n + 1$ for both arrays. The Fortran DLL function F02WEF is passed the first (or leading) dimension of the transposed arrays a1 and pt, which again is $n + 1$ for both arrays.

```
5,   3
  2.0,    2.5,    2.5
  2.0,    2.5,    2.5
  1.6,   −0.4,    2.8
  2.0,   −0.5,    0.5
  1.2,   −0.3,   −2.9
```

Exhibit 2.2   The data file used by the example VB.NET code in Code excerpt 2.9

```
VB.NET Singular Value Decomposition Example: Using Fortran DLL function F02WEF

The singular values are: 6.56155281280883 3 2.43844718719117

Left-hand singular vectors:

    0.6011367037189      −0.196116135138183     −0.316501382272552
    0.601136703718901    −0.196116135138184     −0.316501382272552
    0.416640015914854     0.156892908110547      0.694115057121718
    0.168785003427989    −0.392232270276368      0.563618194145345
   −0.274211682173158    −0.86291099460801       0.0138769140799509
```

Right-hand singular vectors:

```
0.469353355287439    -0.784464540552737     0.405367503009068
0.432351700290912    -0.196116135138183    -0.880119576417897
0.769921707146889     0.588348405414552     0.247116811872794
```

Exhibit 2.3   The results computed by the example VB.NET code in Code excerpt 2.9

2.3   C#

In this section we provide examples of calling Fortran DLLs and C DLLs from C#. A summary of some important data types used by C# is given in Table 2.3.

We will begin by mentioning some of the features of C# connected with mixed language programming.

- In C# if the array mya is declared using double [ ] mya = new double [8]; it will have 8 elements; these are mya [0] , ... mya [7].
- The elements of multidimensional arrays are stored in row order, as is the case for VB.NET and C.
- When a DLL function is called from C# it is necessary to explicitly state which parameters are to be passed by reference; the others are taken as being passed by value. This means that the NAG C DLL function f02wec should be called as follows (see Code excerpt 2.12 for more detail):

```
double [] evec = new double[m] ;
iflag = 0; // Set iflag to zero so use the NAG C library with default error handling.
// This means that, if an error occurs, the C DLL will output a message
    f02wec (m, n, ref a[0], dim_a, ncolb, ref b[0], dim_b, wantq, ref q[0], dim_q, ref sv[0], wantp,
    ref pt [0], dim_pt, ref iter, ref evec[0], ref info, iflag); // Note iflag is passed by value here
```

This should be compared to the equivalent VB.NET code, where the following will suffice:

```
iflag = 0
Call f02wec (m, n, a1(0, 0), dim_a, ncolb, b(0), dim_b, wantq, q(0),_
            dim_q, sv(0), wantp, pt(0, 0), dim_pt, iter, evec(0),info, iflag)
```

- As previously mentioned in Section 2.2, C# does not allow fixed length strings to be declared within UDTs (that is structures). This means that it is no longer possible to define a type that correponds to the NAG C Library type NagErrorType. Here we illustrate how to overcome this problem by wrapping the original C DLL function within another C function which uses an integer parameter to flag errors; see Code excerpt 2.13.

Table 2.3   Correspondence between C# types and those of Fortran and C

C#	C	Fortran 77	Size in bytes
int	long	INTEGER	4
int	int	LOGICAL	4
float	float	REAL	4
double	double	DOUBLE PRECISION	8

A C# example application, which calls the Fortran DLL functions G01AAF and F02WEF, and also the C DLL functions g01aac and F02wec, is shown in Figure 2.2.

When the button labelled SVD is clicked the function button3_Click is executed and either the NAG Fortran DLL function F02WEF or the NAG C DLL function f02wec is used to compute the singular value decomposition. When the button labelled 'Summary stats' is clicked then the function button1_Click is executed and either the NAG Fortran DLL function G01AAF or the wrapped C DLL function g01aac_wrapped, see Code excerpt 2.13, is used to calculate summary statistics such as mean, standard deviation, etc. The C# code for this example is shown in Code excerpts 2.10 to 2.12.

```
using System;
    .   .   .
namespace App2
{
  public class Form1 : System.Windows.Forms.Form
  {
    Boolean use_c_dll;
    private System.Windows.Forms.Button button1;
    private System.Windows.Forms.Button button3;
    private System.Windows.Forms.GroupBox groupBox1;
    private System.Windows.Forms.RadioButton radioButton1;
    private System.Windows.Forms.RadioButton radioButton2;
    private System.ComponentModel.Container components = null;
    public Form1()
    {
      InitializeComponent();
    }
        .   .   .
    private void InitializeComponent()
    {
      use_c_dll = true;
      this.button1 = new System.Windows.Forms.Button();
      this.button3 = new System.Windows.Forms.Button();
      this.groupBox1.SuspendLayout();
      this.SuspendLayout();
      // button1
      //
      this.button1.Location = new System.Drawing.Point(48,24);
      this.button1.Name = "button1";
      this.button1.Size = new System.Drawing.Size(120, 24);
      this.button1.TabIndex = 0;
      this.button1.Text = "Summary stats";
      this.button1.Click += new System.EventHandler(this.button1_Click);
        .   .   .
    }
        .   .   .
    [STAThread]
    static void Main()
    {
      Application.Run(new Form1());
    }
    [DllImport("NAGG01.DLL")]
    public static extern void G01AAF(ref int n, ref double x,
        ref int iwt, ref double wt, ref double xmean, ref double s2, ref double s3,
        ref double s4, ref double xmin, ref double xmax, ref double wsum, ref int iflag);

    [DllImport("NAGF02.DLL")]
    public static extern void F02WEF(ref int m, ref int n, ref double a, ref int lda, ref int ncolb,
        ref double b, ref int ldb, ref int wantq, ref double q, ref int dim_q,
        ref double sv, ref int wantp, ref double pt, ref int ldpt, ref double work, ref int iflag);

    [DllImport("nagc.dll")]
    public static extern void f02wec(int m, int n, ref double a, int tda, int ncolb, ref double b, int ldb,
        int wantq, ref double q, int tdq, ref double sv, int wantp, ref double pt, int tdpt, ref int iter,
        ref double evec, ref int info, int iflag);
```

```
[DllImport("nagc.dll")]
public static extern void g01aac (int n, ref double x, int wt, ref int nvalid, ref double xmean,
    ref double s2, ref double s3, ref double s4, ref double xmin, ref double xmax, ref double wsum,
    int iflag);

[DllImport("wrapper.dll")]
public static extern void g01aac_wrapped (int n, ref double x, int wt, ref int nvalid, ref double xmean,
    ref double s2, ref double s3, ref double s4, ref double xmin, ref double xmax, ref double wsum, ref int iflag);
public bool get_token(ref string the_string, char delim, ref int str_ptr, ref string the_token)
{
    string str_token;
    str_token = " ";
    while (( str_ptr < the_string.Length) && (the_string[str_ptr] == delim))
    {
        ++str_ptr;
    }
    if (str_ptr >= the_string.Length)
    {
        str_ptr = 0;
        return false;
    }
    while ((str_ptr < the_string.Length) && (the_string[str_ptr] != delim))
    {
        str_token = str_token + the_string[str_ptr];
        ++ str_ptr;
    }
    the_token = str_token;
    return true;
    }
}
```

Code excerpt 2.10 A fragment of C# code which illustrates how the Fortran DLL functions G01AAF and F02WEF, and C DLL functions g01aac, g01aac_wrapped, and f02wec should be declared in C#

```
private void button1_Click(object sender, System.EventArgs e)
{
    double xmin = 0.0, xsd = 0.0, xskew = 0.0, xkurt = 0.0;
    double wsum = 0.0, xmax = 0.0, xmean = 0.0;
    int iflag = 1, iwt = 0, len, n1, i, buf_ptr, dummy = 0, nvalid = 0;
    string token = " ";
    char delim;
    string NextLine, filename;
    if (use_c_dll) // Set the results file name for the NAG C DLL
    {
        filename = @"c:\BOOK_2002\CSG01AAC_RESULTS.TXT";
    }
    else // Set the results file name for the NAG Fortran DLL
    {
        filename = @"c:\BOOK_2002\CSG01AAF_RESULTS.TXT";
    }
    // Open the input and output files
    FileStream fs_in = new FileStream (@"c:\BOOK_2002\STATS_DATA.TXT", FileMode.Open,
        FileAccess.Read, FileShare.None);
    StreamReader sr = new StreamReader(fs_in, Encoding. ASCII);
    StreamWriter sw = new StreamWriter(filename, false, Encoding.ASCII);
    NextLine = sr.ReadLine(); // Read a line from the input file, and store it in the string NextLine
    len = NextLine.Length;
    delim = ' ';
    buf_ptr = 0;
    get_token(ref NextLine, delim, ref buf_ptr, ref token); // Extract the number of data points from the
                                                            // string NextLine
    n1 = int.Parse(token);
    double [] x = new double[n1]; // Allocate the array x, which will contain the data
    double [] wt = new double[n1]; // Allocate the array wt, which will contain the weights
    NextLine = sr.ReadLine(); // Read a line from the input file, and store it in the string NextLine
    buf_ptr = 0;
    i = 0;
    while (i < n1) // Load the data into the array x[]
    {
        if (get_token(ref NextLine, delim, ref buf_ptr, ref token))
            // Extract the data values from the string NextLine
        {
            x[i] = double.Parse(token); // Assign the data value
            ++i;
        }
    }
```

```
    else NextLine = sr.ReadLine(); // Read another line from the input file
}
buf_ptr = 0;
i = 0;
while (i < n1) // Load the weights into the array wt[]
{
    if (get_token(ref NextLine, delim, ref buf_ptr, ref token))
        // Extract the weight values from the string NextLine
    {
        wt[i] = double.Parse(token); // Assign the value of the weight
        ++ i;
    }
    else NextLine = sr.ReadLine(); // Read another line from the input file
}
if (use_c_dll) // Use the NAG C DLL
{
    iflag = 0; // Use the wrapped NAG C DLL function
    g01aac_wrapped (n1, ref x[0], dummy, ref nvalid, ref xmean, ref xsd, ref xskew,
                ref xkurt, ref xmin, ref xmax, ref wsum, iflag);
    if (iflag != 0){ // Check that the function has returned without error
    MessageBox.Show("An error using g01aac_ wrapped:iflag = "+ iflag.ToString()); // Output an error
                                                                // message
    }
}
else // Use the NAG Fortran DLL
{
    G01AAF(ref n1, ref x[0], ref iwt, ref wt[0], ref xmean, ref xsd, ref xskew,
        ref xkurt, ref xmin, ref xmax, ref wsum, ref iflag);
}
if (use_c_dll) // Output the file header for the NAG C DLL
{
    sw.WriteLine("C# example summary statistics results: using the wrapped C library DLL function
        g01aac_wrapped");
}
else // Output the file header for the NAG Fortran DLL
{
    sw.WriteLine("C# example summary statistics results: using Fortran library DLL function F02WEF");
}
sw.WriteLine(" ");
sw.WriteLine("no valid cases = " + iwt.ToString());
sw.WriteLine("mean = "+ xmean.ToString());
sw.WriteLine("mean = >> {0,10:F3} << ",xmean);
sw.WriteLine("standard deviation = >> {0,10:F3} << ",xsd);
sw.WriteLine("skewness = >> {0,10:F3} << ",xskew);
sw.WriteLine("kurtosis >> {0,10:F3} << ",xkurt);
sw.WriteLine("minimum = >> {0,10:F3} <<",xmin);
sw.WriteLine("maximum = >> {0,10:F3} <<",xmax);
sw.WriteLine("sum of weights = >> {0,10:F3} <<",wsum);
sr.Close();
sw.Close();
}
```

Code excerpt 2.11   A fragment of C# code that computes summary statistics by either calling the Fortran
DLL function G01AAF, or the C DLL function g01aac_wrapped

In these code excerpts we show how both vectors and matrices are declared and
passed to Fortran and C DLL functions. Here matrices are declared as one-dimensional arrays and the elements are stored either in row order (if a C DLL function is
to be called) or column order (when a Fortran DLL function is used).

```
    private void button3_Click(object sender, System. EventArgs e)
    {
// Here we perform a singular value decomposition of an m × n matrix A
// using either the NAG Fortran function F02WEF or the NAG C function f02wec.
// The singular values, left singular vectors and right singular vectors are output to a file.
// The left hand singular vectors are output in the array a, and the
// transpose of the right hand singular vectors are output in the array pt.
```

```csharp
// When the NAG Fortran DLL is used matrix elements are stored in
// column order, and when the NAG C Library is used matrix elements are stored in row order.
double [] q = new double[1];
double [] b = new double[1];
int dim_a = 0, dim_q = 0, dim_b = 0, dim_pt = 0, m = 0;
int n = 0, iflag = 1, i, ncolb = 0, j;
int wantp, wantq, buf_ptr;
double [] work = new double[1000]; // Allocate a fixed size workspace
string NextLine, token = " ";
string filename = " ";
char delim;
int info = 0, iter = 0;

  if (use_c_dll) // Using the NAG C DLL
  {
    filename = @"c:\BOOK_2002\CSF02WEC_RESULTS.TXT"; // Set the results file name for the NAG C DLL
  }
  else // Using the NAG Fortran DLL
  {
    filename = @"c:\BOOK_2002\CSF02WEF_RESULTS.TXT"; // Set the results file name for the NAG Fortran DLL
  }
  // Open the input and output files
  StreamWriter sw = new StreamWriter(@filename,false, Encoding.ASCII);
  FileStream fs_in = new FileStream (@"c:\BOOK_2002\SVD_DATA.TXT", FileMode.Open, FileAccess.Read,
      FileShare.None);
  StreamReader sr = new StreamReader(fs_in, Encoding. ASCII);
  NextLine = sr.ReadLine(); // Read a line from the input file
  delim = ','; // Set the delimiter to be used when parsing the data
  buf_ptr = 0;
  get_token(ref NextLine, delim, ref buf_ptr, ref token); // Extract the number of rows m of matrix A
  m = int.Parse(token); // Assign the number of rows
  get_token(ref NextLine, delim, ref buf_ptr, ref token);
  n = int.Parse(token); // Assign the number of columns
  double [] sv = new double[n]; // Allocate a vector to hold the singular values
  double [] a = new double[n*m]; // Allocate a vector to hold the elements of the matrix A
  double [] pt = new double[n*n]; // Allocate a vector to hold the matrix pt
  buf_ptr = 0;
  if (use_c_dll) // Use the NAG C DLL
  {
    dim_a = n; // Set the trailing (second) dimension of the matrix A
    dim_b = 1;
    dim_q = m;
  }
  else // Use the NAG Fortran DLL
  {
    dim_a = m; // Set the first (leading) dimension of matrix A
    dim_b = 1;
    dim_q = m;
  }
  dim_pt = n;
  wantq = 1; // set WANTQ to TRUE
  wantp = 1; // set WANTP to TRUE
  ncolb = 0;
  for (i = 0; i < m; ++i) // Loop on the row index
  {
    buf_ptr = 0;
    NextLine = sr.ReadLine(); // Read another line from the input file
    for (j = 0; j < n; ++j) // Loop on the column index
    {
      get_token(ref NextLine, delim, ref buf_ptr, ref token); // Get the current data element
      if (use_c_dll) // Using the C DLL
      {
        a[i*dim_a + j] = double.Parse(token); // Store elements in row order
      }
      else // Using the Fortran DLL
      {
        a[i + j * dim_a] = double.Parse(token); // Store elements in column order
      }
    }
  }
  buf_ptr = 0;
  sr.ReadLine(); // Read another line from the input file
  if (use_c_dll) // Use the NAG C DLL
  {
    double [] evec = new double[m];
```

```
    iflag = 0; // Set iflag to zero so use the NAG C library with default error handling.
              // This means that, if an error occurs, the C DLL will output a message
    f02wec(m, n, ref a[0], dim_a, ncolb, ref b[0], dim_b, wantq, ref q[0], dim_q, ref sv[0], wantp,
        ref pt[0], dim_pt, ref iter, ref evec[0], ref info, iflag); // Note iflag is passed by value here
}
else // Use the NAG Fortran DLL
{
    F02WEF(ref m, ref n, ref a[0], ref dim_a, ref ncolb, ref b[0], ref dim_b, ref wantq, ref q[0],
        ref dim_q, ref sv[0], ref wantp, ref pt[0], ref dim_pt, ref work[0], ref iflag);
}
if (use_c_dll) // Output the file header for the NAG C DLL
{
    sw.WriteLine("C# example SVD results: using C library DLL function f02wec");
}
else // Output the file header for the NAG Fortran DLL
{
    sw.WriteLine("C# example SVD results: using Fortran library DLL function F02WEF");
}
sw.WriteLine(" ");
sw.WriteLine();
sw.WriteLine("The Singular Values are:");
sw.WriteLine();
for (i = 0; i < n; ++i) // Loop on the number of singular values
{
    sw.Write("{0,10:F4}",sv[i]);
}
sw.WriteLine(" ");
sw.WriteLine(" ");
sw.WriteLine("Left-hand singular vectors");
sw.WriteLine(" ");
for (i = 0; i < m; ++i) {// Loop on the row index
  for (j = 0; j < n; ++j) {// Loop on the column index
    if (use_c_dll)
    {
      sw.Write("{0,10:F4}",a[i*dim_a + j]); // Output the elements in row order
    }
    else
    {
      sw.Write("{0,10:F4}",a[i + j*dim_a]); // Output the elements in column order
    }
  }
  sw.WriteLine(" "); // Output a blank line
}
sw.WriteLine(" ");
sw.WriteLine("Right-hand singular vectors");
sw.WriteLine(" ");
for (j = 0; j < n; ++j) {// Loop on the column index
  for (i = 0; i < n; ++i) {// Loop on the row index
    if (use_c_dll)
    {
      sw.Write("{0,10:F4}",pt[i*dim_pt + j]); // Output the elements in row order
    }
    else
    {
      sw.Write("{0,10:F4}",pt[i + j * dim_pt]); // Output the elements in column order
    }
  }
  sw.WriteLine(" "); // Output a blank line
}
sr.Close();
sw.Close();
}
```

Code excerpt 2.12   A fragment of C# code that computes a singular value decomposition by either calling the Fortran DLL function F02WEF, or the C DLL function f02wec

			24						
193.0	215	112.0	161.0	92.0	140.0	38.0	33.0	279.0	249.0
473.0	339.0	60.0	130.0	20.0	50.0	257.0	284.0	447.0	52.0
67.0	61.0	150.0	2200.00						
1.0	1.0	1.0	1.0	1.0	1.0	1.0	1.0	1.0	1.0
1.0	1.0	1.0	1.0	1.0	1.0	1.0	1.0	1.0	1.0
1.0	1.0	1.0	1.0						

Exhibit 2.4   The data file used by Code excerpt 2.11

C# example summary statistics results: using the wrapped C library DLL function g01aac_wrapped

```
no valid cases = 0
mean =  254.25
mean = >> 254.250 <<
standard deviation = >> 433.536 <<
skewness = >> 3.895 <<
kurtosis >> 14.666 <<
minimum = >> 20.000 <<
maximum = >> 2200.000 <<
sum of weights = >> 24.000 <<
```

Exhibit 2.5 The results computed by Code excerpt 2.11

C# example SVD results: using Fortran library DLL function F02WEF

The Singular Values are:

```
  6.5616      3.0000      2.4384
```

Left-hand singular vectors

```
  0.6011     -0.1961     -0.3165
  0.6011     -0.1961     -0.3165
  0.4166      0.1569      0.6941
  0.1688     -0.3922      0.5636
 -0.2742     -0.8629      0.0139
```

Right-hand singular vectors

```
  0.4694     -0.7845      0.4054
  0.4324     -0.1961     -0.8801
  0.7699      0.5883      0.2471
```

Exhibit 2.6 The results computed by Code excerpt 2.12

Wrapping the NAG C DLL function:

```cpp
#include <nag.h>
#include <nag_stdlib.h>
#include <nagg01.h>

#define DLLExport__declspec(dllexport)

void DLLExport__stdcall g01aac_wrapped (long n, double x[], double wt[], long *nvalid, double *mean,
  double *xsd, double *xskew, double *xkurt, double *xmin, double *xmax, double *wsum, long *iflag)
{
static NagError stat;
  stat.print = FALSE;
  stat.code = 0;
  g01aac (n, x, wt, nvalid, mean, xsd, xskew, xkurt, xmin, xmax, wsum, &stat);
  *iflag = stat.code;
}
```

Code excerpt 2.13 The C++ DLL wrapper for the function g01aac

Chapter 3

ActiveX and COM

3.1 INTRODUCTION

Here we show how Microsoft ActiveX and COM technology can be used to solve mathematical problems within the Windows environment. It is intended as a general introduction to the subject and shows how to use ActiveX components rather than create them.

To call a DLL routine directly from Visual Basic requires detailed knowledge of both the routine's arguments and also the manner in which they are passed to the Visual Basic calling program. It is therefore essential that users have access to all the relevant documentation. This approach also has the following disadvantages.

- Currently there are certain restrictions on the use of DLL routines, for instance they cannot be incorporated into an HTML Web page.
- DLLs are not in the spirit of Microsoft's object-based approach to programming and do not make use of this technology.
- They must be called using low level program statements and cannot be accessed interactively or visually.

By using an Excel Add-In (as shown in Part II, Section 9.3.4) to provide a higher level user-interface to the underlying DLL it is possible to alleviate some of the difficulties previously mentioned. However, it should be mentioned that:

- Not all versions of Excel are compatible.
- There is still the issue of how potential users are to access routines from Visual Basic, Delphi, PowerPoint, etc.
- The underlying framework of the Excel user-interface cannot be changed (since it was created by Microsoft) and can appear rather tedious for routines with large argument lists, etc.

So what is the natural interface to use within Microsoft Windows? Ideally what is needed is an easy-to-use interface that would allow all routines to be called from every Microsoft product. In fact such an interface does already exist: the Component Object Model (COM). It is used by Microsoft, Inprise, Digital Equipment Corporation, and many other companies.

Microsoft has also created the COM-based technologies of ActiveX and OLE to allow Microsoft users the ability to interact with their environment. All the mathematical software described here could have been deployed using custom (user-defined) COM interfaces. However these non-standard COM interfaces would then require separate documentation and would not automatically integrate into Microsoft products such as Visual Basic, Visual C++, etc. To avoid these problems only the standard Automation interface IDispatch (see Section 3.2) will be considered here. The IDispatch COM interface allows ActiveX components to be easily used from languages such as Visual Basic, VBScript, and Inprise Delphi. It also permits easy incorporation of mathematical software into Excel, Word, PowerPoint, Access, and HTML Web pages. ActiveX components can also be used from Visual C++, Visual J++, and Visual Fortran.

Some of the advantages of ActiveX components are:

- They can be used by the complete range of Microsoft products and also by other Windows software such as Inprise Delphi.
- They support drag and drop technology and so can easily be incorporated into an application.
- The properties, methods, and events of a given ActiveX component can be viewed using the Microsoft (Inprise) Object Browser.
- Their object-based C++ technology can be used to provide simple user-interfaces to otherwise complicated routines.

The last point refers to the complete range of C++ class/object-based technology. This includes optional arguments with default values, data/information hiding within the object, object initialisation via constructors, and the properties, methods, and events supported by an object.

This section gives a brief outline of the basic principles of COM and how ActiveX controls are accessed from Visual Basic and Visual C++ using the IDispatch interface (also called dispinterface for short). There is not space to fully explain everything mentioned in this section, but comprehensive information can be obtained from the available literature on COM and ActiveX, see the computing references at the end of the book.

ActiveX controls are DLL servers that need to be registered in the Windows Registry before they can be dynamically linked to by a client. Every registered ActiveX control has a unique class identifier (CLSID) which allows a client to load it from the DLL in which it resides and create an instance of the component.

ActiveX controls are COM objects that usually have a visual user-interface and also support a variety of interfaces including those that allow Automation and events.

Automation allows an ActiveX control's properties and methods to be accessed programmatically from a language such as Visual Basic or C++, and is implemented using the IDispatch COM interface. Event-handling for events such as Single (Double) Click is implemented using COM interfaces such as IConnectionPoint and IConnectionPointContainer.

Since the main purpose of the components described here is to perform numeric calculations they only need a restricted visual user-interface, and will therefore be called primitive ActiveX components. In fact a control that maintains an on-screen window has to manage messages for the window and is therefore slower than a windowless control. These primitive controls are ideal for use as numeric engine components since their limited visual user-interface will not interfere with the user-interface of the application into which they are embedded. Mathematical applications with sophisticated user-interfaces can therefore readily be constructed through the incorporation of primitive ActiveX components.

3.2   THE COM INTERFACE IDISPATCH

All COM components are derived (in the C++ sense) from an interface called IUnknown. The definition for IUnknown is as follows:

```
interface IUnknown
{
  virtual HRESULT__stdcall QueryInterface(const IID& iid, void** ppv) = 0;
  virtual ULONG__stdcall Addref() = 0;
  virtual ULONG__stdcall Release() = 0;
};
```

It contains the three virtual functions QueryInterface, Addref, and Release. The function QueryInterface is used to find out whether an object supports a given interface and, if possible, return a pointer to it. For example an ActiveX control used from within Visual Basic could call QueryInterface to return a pointer to the IDispatch interface. The functions Addref and Release maintain a reference count on the interface of a component and use this to implement memory management. When the reference count reaches zero the component deletes itself from memory.

The definition of the IDispatch interface is:

```
interface IDispatch : IUnknown
{
  HRESULT GetTypeInfoCount(UINT* pctinfo);
  HRESULT GetTypeInfo(UNIT iTInfo,
                      LCID lcid,
                      ITypeInfo** ppTInfo);
  HRESULT GetIDsOfNames(const IID& riid,
                        LPOLESTR* rgszNames,
                        UINT cNames,
                        LCID lcid,
                        DISPID* rgDispId);
  HRESULT Invoke (DISPID dispIdMember,
                  const IID& riid,
                  LCID lcid,
                  WORD wFlags,
                  DISPPARAMS* pDispParams,
                  VARIANT* pVarResult,
                  EXCEPINFO* pExcepInfo,
                  UINT* puArgErr)
};
```

The functions GetTypeInfoCount and GetTypeInfo are used to obtain information concerning the methods and properties of the component from its type library (see Section 3.2).

The function GetIDsOfNames converts the Visual Basic name of an Automation object's properties and methods into a numeric identifier called the DISPID of the property or method.

The function Invoke uses the DISPID to run a given property or method and also passes it the required arguments in a structure of type DISPPARAMS.

3.3 TYPE LIBRARIES

Type libraries are compiled versions of an Object Description Language (ODL) file or an Interface Definition Language (IDL) file. They provide information about the interfaces, methods, properties, and arguments of a COM component and are used by the Visual Basic Object Browser to interactively display this information.

An excerpt (the complete source is given in Appendix A) from the ODL file for the example control NAGDBS.ocx (see Chapter 4) is given below in Code excerpt 3.1.

```
// NAGDBS.odl : type library source for ActiveX Control project.
// This file will be processed by the Make Type Library (mktyplib) tool to
// produce the type library (NAGDBS.tlb) that will become a resource in
// NAGDBS.ocx.

  helpstring("Dispatch interface for NAGDBS Control"), hidden ]
  dispinterface_DNAGDBS
  {
    properties:
      //{{AFX_ODL_PROP(CNAGDBSCtrl)
      [id(1)] METHODTYPE method;
      [id(2)] EXTYPE extype;
      [id(3)] double sigma;
      [id(4)] long numsteps;
      [id(5)] double intrate;
      [id(6)] double dividends;
      [id(7)] double curval;
      [id(8)] double optval;
      [id(9)] double strike;
      [id(10)] PUTCALLTYPE putcall;
      [id(11)] double maturity;
      [id(DISPID_CAPTION), bindable, requestedit] BSTR Caption;
      [id(DISPID_BACKCOLOR), bindable, requestedit] OLE_COLOR BackColor;
      [id(DISPID_FORECOLOR), bindable, requestedit] OLE_COLOR ForeColor;
      //}}AFX_ODL_PROP
    methods:
      //{{AFX_ODL_METHOD(CNAGDBSCtrl)
      [id(12)] void Calculate();
      [id(13)] void greeks(double* greekvals);
      //}}AFX_ODL_METHOD
  };
```

Code excerpt 3.1   Fragment of the ODL file for the ActiveX component NAGBS.ocx used in Chapter 4

Figure 3.1 shows the Visual Basic Object Browser using the type library NAGDBS.tlb to interactively display the properties and methods of the component contained in NAGDBS.ocx.

3.4 USING IDISPATCH

The use of the IDispatch interface can be illustrated by considering the following three line Visual Basic program:

```
Dim NAGDBS1 As Object
Set NAGDBS1 = CreateObject("NAGDBS.NAGDBSCtrl.1")
NAGDBS1.curval = 111.0
```

This program creates an instance of a COM component called NAGDBS1 and assigns a floating-point number to the property curval.

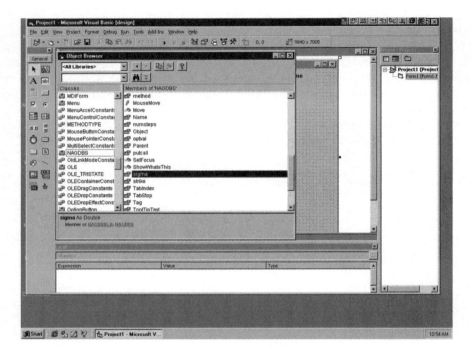

Figure 3.1   The Object Browser displaying properties and methods

The equivalent C++ code for these Visual Basic statements will now be described.

The client first needs to retrieve the component's class identifier (CLSID) from the Windows Registry. This is achieved by using the routine `CLSIDFromProgID` as follows:

```
// Initialise the OLE Library
HRESULT hr = OleInitialise(NULL);

// Get The CLSID for the application
wchar_t progid[] = L"NAGDBS.NAGDBSCtrl1.1";
CLSID clsid;
::CLSIDFromProgID(progid, &clsid);
```

Once the CLSID has been obtained `CoCreateInstance` can be used to both create an instance of the component and also return a pointer (`pDispatch`) to its `IDispatch` COM interface.

```
IDispatch* pDispatch = NULL;
::CoCreateInstance(clsid, NULL, CLSCTX_INPROC_SERVER,
                 IID_IDispatch, (void**)&pIDispatch);
```

This approach avoids an extra call to `QueryInterface` for retrieval of the `IDispatch` interface pointer. The `DISPID` of the property `curval` is then obtained so that `curval` can be accessed using `IDispatch::Invoke`. This is achieved by using the `IDispatch` function `GetIDsOfNames` as follows:

```
DISPID dispid;
OLECHAR* name = L"curval";
PIDispatch->GetIDsOfNames(IID_NULL,            // Must be IID_NULL
                          &name,               // Name of the function
                          1,                   // Number of names
                          GetUserDefaultLCID(), // Localisation info
                          &dispid);            // Dispatch ID
```

Now that the `DISPID` for `curval` has been obtained the assignment statement in the last line of the Visual Basic Program will be discussed. Here the `IDispatch` function `Invoke` runs the function `curval` using its `DISPID` and passes it the required arguments in a structure of type `DISPPARAMS`.

The steps in Visual C++ are as follows:

Initialize a variable of type `VARIANT` and assign the value 111.0 to it.

```
VARIANTARG varg;
::VariantInit(&varg);      // Initialise the VARIANT
varg.vt = VT_R8;           // Type of VARIANT data, in this case a double
varg.dblVal = 111.0;       // Set the value of the variant to 111.0
```

Now fill in the `DISPPARAMS` structure

```
DISPPARAMS param;
param.cArgs = 1            // One argument
param
.rgvarg = &varg;           // Pointer to argument
param.cNamedArgs = 0;      // No named arguments
param.rgdispNamedArgs = NULL;
```

Finally the function `curval` can be run by using `Invoke` as follows:

```
hr = pIDispatch->Invoke(dispid,
                        IID_NULL,
                        GetUserDefaultLCID(),
                        DISPATCH_METHOD,
                        &param,
                        NULL,
                        NULL,
                        NULL);
```

The use of `IDispatch::Invoke` to access a component's properties and methods is called run-time binding because the argument types are only checked at run-time. All the example ActiveX controls in this book use the `IDispatch` interface in this manner even though it is not as efficient as using a dual interface (which can access functions directly through the vtbl.

3.5   ACTIVEX CONTROLS AND THE INTERNET

Small scale numerical Internet applications can easily be constructed using the capabilities of Web-based scripting languages such as JavaScript, JScript, or VBScript.

However, the use of the Internet for medium to large numerical applications is still a matter for research.

The traditional method of solving these problems is by creating Fortran or C applications which make underlying calls to numerical library subroutines. Although this approach may have the advantages of speed/efficiency it is not based on current Internet technology. A direct consequence of this is that attempts to access such applications from the Internet may suffer from a variety of limitations such as:

- Inability to directly access individual mathematical subroutines.
- Solution is not integrated into the user's system.
- Limited interactive features.

Here we are concerned with the use of ActiveX components, within the Microsoft Windows environment, to solve medium scale numerical problems on HTML Web pages. These Web pages may either be stored on a computer's local disk or reside on a remote machine to which there is access via the Intranet or Internet. The Web pages considered here contain HTML and either VBScript or JScript. They are interpreted by means of the Web browser Internet Explorer.

We will now give some of the advantages and disadvantages of ActiveX controls from within HTML Web pages.

Advantages:

- Interactive modelling over the Internet.
- Web page VBScript can be pasted into other Microsoft products such as Visual Basic or Excel and used with little or no modification.
- A Web page can be downloaded from the Internet and used to create a working local model which can then be placed back on the Internet.
- Web page models can be easily changed by altering the VBScript code. This would be particularly useful for models where an appropriate CGI script is either not currently available or has restricted access.
- Since ActiveX components can be created using C++ it is not necessary to rewrite complicated numerical algorithms.

Disadvantages:

- Microsoft Windows specific.
- A potential lack of efficiency for large-scale numerical problems. This is because all computations are carried out on the user's local machine, and also VBScript/ JScript code is interpreted at run-time by the Web browser.

ActiveX components are therefore expected to be beneficial for small/medium sized mathematical models which require an interactive user-interface.

3.6   USING ACTIVEX COMPONENTS ON A WEB PAGE

This section gives brief details on using ActiveX components from within an HTML Web page. ActiveX controls can easily be placed on a Web page by using an interactive tool called ActiveX Control Pad.

Once the control has been placed onto the Web page it is referenced using the information contained in an HTML object tag. The object tag HTML source code for a Microsoft command button is given below:

```
<OBJECT ID="CommandButtonRed" WIDTH=44 HEIGHT=26
  CLASSID="CLSID:D7053240-CE69-11CD-A777-00DD01143C57">
    <PARAM NAME="Caption" VALUE="Red">
    <PARAM NAME="Size" VALUE="2540;846">
    <PARAM NAME="FontCharSet" VALUE="0">
    <PARAM NAME="FontPitchAndFamily" VALUE="2">
    <PARAM NAME="ParagraphAlign" VALUE="3">
</OBJECT>
```

It can be seen that the unique class identifier for all Microsoft command buttons is D7053240-CE69-11CD-A777-00DD01143C57, and that this particular one, which is referred to in VBScript/JScript as CommandButtonRed, has the caption Red written on it. The size of the component when viewed using a Web browser is controlled by the values of WIDTH and HEIGHT. If an ActiveX control has no interactive user-interface then it is only accessed via its language user-interface and can be made invisible by setting WIDTH and HEIGHT to appropriately small values.

Calling the properties and methods of ActiveX controls on an HTML Web page is similar to using them from other Microsoft products such as Excel, Visual Basic, etc. However, there are slight differences depending on whether VBScript or JScript is used within the Web page. We will now illustrate this using an ActiveX graphical component called Plot 1. Code excerpt 3.2 illustrates this using VBScript, and Code excerpt 3.3 gives the equivalent JScript code.

```
<HTML>
<HEAD>
<TITLE>VBScript GARCH modeller demonstration</TITLE>
</HEAD>
<BODY>
<SCRIPT LANGUAGE="VBScript">
<!__
Sub Calculate__GARCH__Click()
  .  .  .
'plot the modelled volatility
 Plot1.BrushColor 11,224,230
 Plot1.PenColor 0, 0, 255
 Plot1.PenWidth =1
 Plot1.text "The modelled GARCH variance",40, bot_pos1 +5
End Sub
Sub Clean_Click()
  Plot1.Clear
End Sub
-->
</SCRIPT>
```

Code excerpt 3.2 Scripting an ActiveX component's properties and methods using VBScript

The corresponding JScript code is now given:

```
<HTML>
<HEAD>
<TITLE>JScript GARCH modeller demonstration</TITLE>
```

```
</HEAD>
<BODY>
<SCRIPT LANGUAGE="JScript">
<!--
  function Calculate_GARCH_Click() {
    . . .
// plot the modelled volatility
  Plot1.BrushColor (11,224,230);
  Plot1.PenColor (0, 0, 255);
  Plot1.PenWidth=1;
  Plot1.text ("The modelled GARCH variance", 40,bot_pos1 +5);
}

function Clean_Click(){
  Plot1.Clear();
}
-->
</SCRIPT>
```

Code excerpt 3.3   Scripting an ActiveX component's properties and methods using JScript, the program corresponds to the VBScript in Code excerpt 3.2

Since ActiveX component technology is based on C++, calls to complicated numerical routines can be simplified through the use of properties, methods, events, object initialization via constructors, data/information hiding within the object, and also optional arguments that take default values.

ActiveX components can be used by the entire range of Microsoft products, from PowerPoint to Internet Web browsers, and also by other Windows products such as Inprise Delphi. It has been shown that it is easy to script ActiveX components on a Web page and that models developed in this way can be easily modified on a local machine and placed on the Internet when appropriate.

Some of the advantages of using ActiveX models on Web pages are:

- VBScript on a Web page can be converted into working Visual Basic code with only minor modifications. Therefore a Web page ActiveX mathematical model can easily be incorporated into Microsoft products such as Microsoft Visual Basic, Microsoft Excel, Microsoft Access, etc.
- Since Microsoft Web browsers are supplied free of charge VBScript or JScript models can be developed at no extra cost (as long as the required ActiveX components are freely available).
- ActiveX components can be created using Visual C++, which means complex mathematical models can be developed with existing numerical software.

Possible disadvantages include:

- ActiveX components are Microsoft Windows specific, and so cannot be used within UNIX.
- There could be a lack of computational efficiency which may become important for certain types of large or complex problems.

From an historical perspective mathematical modelling using ActiveX components and Web script is very similar to the more traditional method of writing Fortran or C programs. Here Fortran or C source code written by the developer is used instead of Web script to call numerical routines (the equivalent of the ActiveX components) from the appropriate Fortran or C numerical Library. The major differences in the approach outlined here are that:

- The model is easy to construct because it is made up of numeric ActiveX components with a simple language user-interface.
- Although an ActiveX component may have been created using Visual C++, its native language is not relevant when it is called via its `IDispatch` COM interface. This means that its properties and methods can be accessed directly from VBScript and JScript, and it is not necessary to purchase a Visual C++ compiler.
- General-purpose libraries can be replaced by self-contained ActiveX components.

Through the creation of the necessary ActiveX components and HTML Web script, the majority of numerical models implemented in traditional languages such as Fortran, C, or C++ could be placed on Web pages.

Chapter 4

A financial derivative pricing example

The financial derivative pricing control was chosen to illustrate a control that gives similar importance to both its language and interactive user-interfaces. Its properties can be set interactively at design-time and have associated events, properties and methods. This control was created using Visual C++ and calculates the value of a financial derivative (option) by solving the Black–Scholes partial differential equation, see Part II for more detail. The interface for the control is described by its ODL file which is given in the Appendix A.1. The control is contained in the file NAGDBS.ocx, and its instance in this Visual Basic example is called NAGDBS1.

It is acknowledged that a commerical version of this software would require:

- Comprehensive documentation, both printed and as Help file information.
- Sophisticated interactive design-time and language user-interfaces.

This example is therefore merely provided as a guide to show what is possible using ActiveX and should not be regarded as a definitive statement on what constitutes a good user-interface.

4.1   INTERACTIVE USER-INTERFACE

The interactive user-interface includes Property values that can be set using the Microsoft Properties Window and also Events. Figure 4.1 shows how the background colour of the control can be set interactively at design-time.

Here the ActiveX control uses an event to initiate computation at run-time. No calculations are performed until the control has been clicked by the mouse, as shown in Figure 4.2.

Once the control has been clicked the subroutine NAGDBS1_Click() is invoked and computations are performed; see Figure 4.3. The source code within NAGDBS1_Click() is given below in Section 4.2.

4.2   LANGUAGE USER-INTERFACE

When the control NAGDBS1 is placed on the user's form, Visual Basic will automatically provide the following template code:

```
Private Sub NAGDBS1_Click()

End Sub
```

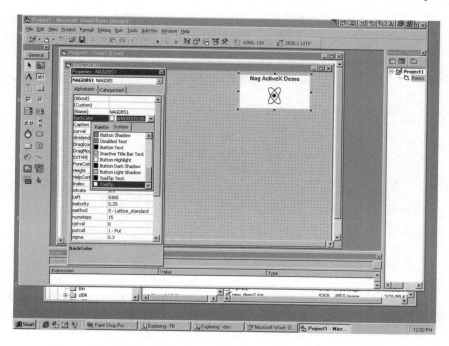

Figure 4.1　Selecting the background colour of the control at design-time

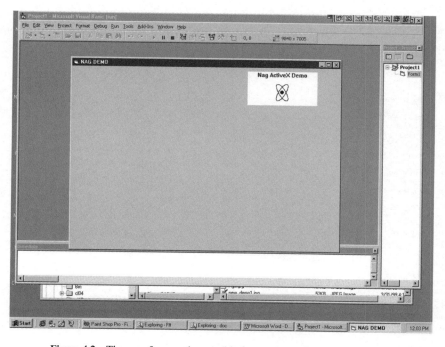

Figure 4.2　The user form and control before computations are performed

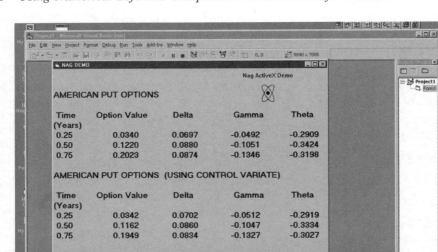

Figure 4.3   The user form after calculations have been performed

This subroutine is run whenever the control NAGDBS1 is clicked by the user's mouse. Here the subroutine contains the following code:

```
Private Sub NAGDBS1_Click()

  Dim greeks(3) As Double
  Dim S0 As Double
  Dim r As Double
  Dim q As Double
  Dim sigma As Double
  Dim T As Double
  Dim x As Double
  Dim maturity As Double
  Dim i As Long

  x = 8#
  S0 = 10#
  r = 0.1
  sigma = 0.3
  q = 0.06
  Font.Bold = True
  Font.Size = 14
  Print " "
  Print " "
  Print "AMERICAN PUT OPTIONS "
  Print " "
  Print " Time    Option Value   Delta    Gamma     Theta"
  Print "(Years) "
  NAGDBS1.putcall = 1      ' A put option
  NAGDBS1.curval = S0      ' The current asset value
  NAGDBS1.strike = x       ' The strike price
```

```
NAGDBS1.dividends = q        ' The continuous dividend yield
NAGDBS1.method = 0           ' Use the standard lattice
NAGDBS1.numsteps = 10        ' The number of time steps
NAGDBS1.intrate = r          ' The risk free interest rate
NAGDBS1.extype = 1           ' An american option
NAGDBS1.sigma = sigma        ' The volatility
' Construct a table of option values and greeks for different maturities
For i = 1 To 3
  T = i * 0.25
  NAGDBS1.maturity = T       ' The maturity, in years
  NAGDBS1.Calculate          ' Do the calculations
  opt_val = NAGDBS1.optval   ' Get the value of the option
  NAGDBS1.greeks greeks(0)   ' Get the calculated hedge statistics (greeks)


  ' Now output the results in tabular format
  Print " "; Format(T, "#0.00"),  Format(opt_val, "#0.0000"),_
    Format(greeks(0), "#0.0000"),  Format (greeks(1), "#0.0000"),_
    Format(greeks(2), "#0.0000")
Next i
Print " "
Print "AMERICAN PUT OPTIONS (USING CONTROL VARIATE) "
Print " "
NAGDBS1.extype = 2              ' An option, calculated using the control variate method
Print " Time     Option Value    Delta    Gamma    Theta"
Print "(Years) "
' Construct a table of options values and greeks for different maturities
For i = 1 To 3
  T = i * 0.25
  NAGDBS1.maturity = T       ' The maturity in years
  NAGDBS1.Calculate          ' Do the calculation
  opt_val = NAGDBS1.optval    ' Get the value of the option
  NAGDBS1.greeks greeks(0)' Get the calculated hedge statistics (greeks)
  ' Now output the results in tabular format
  Print " "; Format(T, "#0.00"),  Format(opt_val, "#0.0000"), _
    Format(greeks(0), "#0.0000"),  Format (greeks(1), "#0.0000"), _
    Format(greeks(2), "#0.0000")
 Next i
End Sub
```

Code excerpt 4.1   The Visual Basic code used to compute American option values

The code illustrates that the properties NAGDBS1.putcall, NAGDBS1.curval, NAGDBS1.sigma, etc. are used to set up the values for the problem. The method NAGDBS1.calculate is then used to perform the required calculations, and option values and greeks are returned via the property NAGDBS1.optval and method NAGDBS1.greeks respectively. It can be seen from the output in Figure 4.3 that using NAGDBS1.extype = 1 and NAGDBS1.extype = 2 results in slightly different option values and hedge statistics (greeks). This is because here the partial differential equation is approximated using a lattice with only ten time steps. The most accurate values are expected to be those calculated using the Control Variate method. This method uses the analytic value of the corresponding European option to adjust the answers returned by the lattice. However, as the number of time steps is increased the results from both methods should converge.

4.3   USE WITHIN DELPHI

Views of the Delphi project at design-time and run-time are shown in Figures 4.4 and 4.5 respectively.

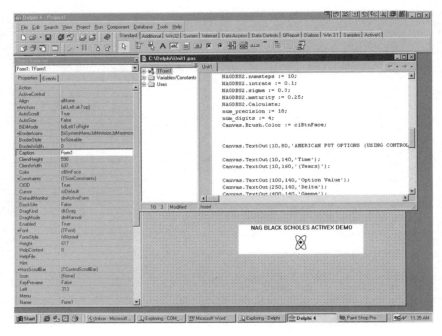

Figure 4.4   The derivative control NAGDBS2 on TForm1

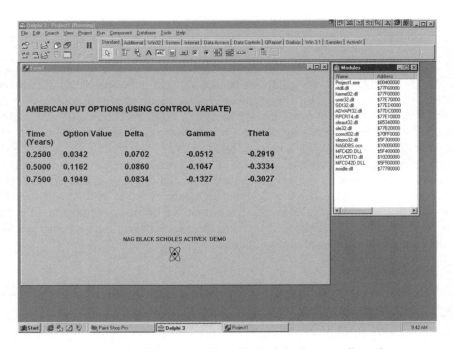

Figure 4.5   The Delphi application with the derivative control's results

Excerpts from the Delphi source code are given below.

```
procedure TForm1.FormClick(Sender: TObject);
var
  greeks: Array[1..5] of double;
  T: double;
  i: integer;
  opt_val: double;
  num_precision: integer;
  num_digits: integer;
  pos: integer;
  val1: String;
begin
  NAGDBS2.putcall :=1;           {A put option}
  NAGDBS2.curval :=10.0;         {The current value of the asset}
  NAGDBS2.strike :=8.0;          {The strike price for the option}
  NAGDBS2.dividends :=0.06;      {The continuous dividend yield}

  Canvas.TextOut(10,80, 'AMERICAN PUT OPTIONS (USING CONTROL VARIATE)');
  Canvas.TextOut(10,140, 'Time');

  for i :=1 To 3 Do
    Begin
      T := i*0.25;

      NAGDBS2.maturity := T;       {Set the maturity of the option, in years}
      NAGDBS2.Calculate;           {Do the calculation}
      NAGDBS2.greeks(greeks[1]);   {Get the hedge statistics, the greeks}
      opt_val := NAGDBS2.optval;   {Get the option value}
      val1 := FloatToStrF(T,ffFixed,num_precision,num_digits);
      Canvas.TextOut(10,pos,val1);
      val1 := FloatToStrF(opt_val,ffFixed,num_precision,num_digits);
      Canvas.TextOut(100,pos,val1);
      val1 := FloatToStrF(greeks[1],ffFixed,num_precision,num_digits);
End;
end;
end;
```

Code excerpt 4.2   The Delphi code used to compute American option values, this can be compared with the equivalent Visual Basic code given in Code excerpt 4.1

It can be seen that the option values and hedge statistics computed within Delphi are identical to those obtained (see Figure 4.3) using Microsoft Visual Basic.

Chapter 5

ActiveX components and numerical optimization

In this section we provide two illustrative examples of using numerical optimization components on a Web page. The 'Ray tracing example' performs a complicated numerical optimization involving the minimization of an integral, while the 'Portfolio allocation example' solves the classic Markowitz portfolio selection problem.

5.1   RAY TRACING EXAMPLE

It is hoped that reader will not think it too indulgent of the author to place this example in a book on mathematical finance and Windows. However, this demonstration (although nothing to do with financial modelling) does illustrate the computational power and flexibility that a numerical optimization ActiveX control, here referred to as OPTIM, allows within an HTML Web page. The optimization component could equally well have been used to demonstrate portfolio optimization, GARCH modelling, etc.

This example plots the path that a ray of light takes in a non-uniform refractive medium. Here there is a choice of three different colours and a non-uniformity (decay) parameter can also be selected. The Web page is constructed using three customized ActiveX components and standard Microsoft controls such as command buttons, labels, and textboxes. The three customized ActiveX components are:

1. A nonlinear numerical optimization control, OPTIM.
2. A graphical plotting control, GRAPH.
3. An integration control, INTG.

The ray tracing problem is modelled by finding the light path which minimizes the integral $\int n(r, \omega)dr$ where $n(r, \omega)$ is the spatial/frequency dependent refractive index. A fairly basic model is used here: the light path is assumed to follow a general cubic, which means that there are only four unknown coefficients to be determined. The width of the refractive medium is taken to be 2.5 units and the non-uniformity is assumed to be caused by radial density variation from the centre of the white ball in Figures 5.2 and 5.3. The amount of non-uniformity is controlled by changing the user-specified density decay parameter. Here we consider four rays of light (which can be either red, blue, or green) that start from different heights on the left hand side of the medium, and all pass through the point (0,2.5) on the right hand side of the diagram.

The problem is solved here by using numerical optimization with constraints in conjunction with numerical integration. This means that the call to the integration control, INTG, is nested within the objective function ofthe optimization control, OPTIM. Two user-defined functions are therefore required: a user-defined objective function and a user-defined integrand.

Excerpts from the VBScript used for this demonstration are now given, the complete source code is supplied on the CD ROM which accompanies the book. The properties and methods of each control will not be discussed in detail, since these can be worked out from the context in which they occur in the VBScript code.

The VBScript controlling the selection of the light colour is as follows:

```
Sub CommandButtonBlue_Click()
  red_color = 0
  green_color = 0
  blue_color = 255
  frequency = 7.0
End Sub
```

Here the frequency and RGB plot colour is set to that corresponding to blue light when the command button labelled 'Blue' is clicked. Computations are performed when the 'Calculate' button is clicked and the subroutine CommandButton1_ Click() is run. VBScript excerpts from CommandButton1_Click() are given in Code excerpt 5.1 below.

```
Sub CommandButton1_Click()
  Dim bl(100) ' holds the upper constraints
  Dim bu(100) ' holds the lower constraints
  Dim loc_x(100)
  Dim g(100)
  Dim a(100)
  Dim n, nclin, ncnlin, tda, num_vars
  Dim y_old, y_new, x_old, x_new
  Dim i, j, k, dx, xtemp, canvas_height, canvas_width, x_start, y_start
    tda = 3
    nclin = 1
    n = 3     ' number of variables
    ncnlin = 0
    num_vars = n
    num_pts = 51     ' number of data points to plot
    . . .
  ' on the first call initialise the plotting area
    if (first_call = 1) then
      GRAPH.BrushColor 230,240,255
      GRAPH.PenColor 0,0,0
      GRAPH.PenWidth = 3
      GRAPH.text "Rays that minimise the optical path integral",x_start,y_start +20
      GRAPH.Rectangle x_start,20,x_start+337,y_start
      GRAPH.circle 468,y_start,10
      first_call = 0
    end if
    i = 0
  For i = 0 To 3     ' loop over the vertical start position of the ray
    y_shift = i     ' set the vertical position
  ' set the initial estimates of the coefficients of the cubic
      loc_x(0) = 0.000001
      loc_x(1) = 0.000001
      loc_x(2) = 0.000001
  ' set the bounds and constraints
    For k = 0 To num_vars - 1
      bl(k) = -10.0
      bu(k) = 10.0
    Next
    bl(num_vars) = -y_shift
    bu(num_vars) = -y_shift
    tda = 3
```

```
         a(0) = 2.5 * 2.5 * 2.5
         a(1) = 2.5 * 2.5
         a(2) = 2.5
         atmospheric_factor = TextBox1.Value    ' set the atmospheric decay factor
         if (atmospheric_factor <> " ") then    ' check that the decay factor has been set
           ' perform the numerical optimization
           OPTIM.optimize n, nclin, ncnlin, a(0), tda, g(0), loc_x(0), bl(0), bu(0)
           OPTIM.getvars loc_x(0), n ' load the optimal cubic coefficients into loc_x
           ' work out the optimal path of the ray
                   . . .
           do_plot() ' now plot the optimal path
         end if
     Next
 End Sub
```

Code excerpt 5.1   The VBScript code for the subroutine `CommandButton1_Click`

It can be seen that numerical optimization is performed by the optimize method of the ActiveX component `OPTIM`. The user-defined objective function to be minimized is contained in the routine `OPTIM_Objfunction()`. The complete source code for this routine is given below

```
Sub OPTIM_Objfunction()
  ' The function to optimize.
  ' Note : The numerical quadrature ActiveX component INTG is called to evaluate the path integral
    Dim x(100)
    Dim obj_val, num_vars, a, b
    Dim result, numintervals, val, i
      num_vars = 3
      obj_val = OPTIM.Objval
      OPTIM.getvars x(0), num_vars
      numintervals = num_pts
      a = 0.0
      b = 2.5
      For i = 0 To num_vars − 1
        params(i) = x(i)
      Next
      INTG.integrate a, b, numintervals    ' evaluate the path integral
      val = INTG.answer                    ' assign the path integral to val
      obj_val = val
      OPTIM.Objval = obj_val               ' make OPTIM_Objfunction return the value of the path integral
      OPTIM.setvars x(0), num_vars
End Sub
```

Code excerpt 5.2   Illustrating the use of VBScript to define the objective function that the ActiveX
numerical optimization component, `OPTIM`, will minimize

The optical path length (to be minimized) is calculated by using the integrate method of the numerical quadrature component `INTG`. The path integral between $a = 0$ and $b = 2.5$ is calculated using 51 intervals. The user-defined integrand is specified in the following routine:

```
Sub INTG_Integrand()
  ' This routine is used by INTG to evaluate the path integral
  ' It specifies the spatial and frequency dependence of the refractive index
    Dim y, x, grad
    Dim rindex, opt_path, temp, factor, n_o

    x = INTG.getx   ' set the frequency dependency of the refractive index
    n_o = 10.0 * (1.0 − 0.12 * frequency)
    y = params(0) * x * x * x + params(1) * x * x + params(2) * x + y_shift
    grad = params(0) * x * x * 3.0 + params(1) * x * 2.0 + params(2)
    temp = y * y + (1.25 − x) * (1.25 − x)
    factor = Sqr(temp)
  ' the spatial dependence of the refractive index
```

```
rindex = n_o * Exp(-factor * atmospheric_factor)
rindex = rindex + 1.0
temp = 1.0 + grad * grad
opt_path = rindex * Sqr(temp)
value = opt_path
INTG.getfunval = value
End Sub
```

Code excerpt 5.3   Illustrating the use of VBScript to define the integrand that the ActiveX numerical quadrature component, `INTG` will integrate

The optimal rays are plotted using the subroutine `do_plot()`.

```
Sub do_plot()
   ' use the ActiveX control GRAPH to plot the optimal ray
   GRAPH.PenColor red_color, green_color, blue_color
   GRAPH.PenWidth = 2
   GRAPH.Getdata num_pts, x_pos(0), y_pos(0)
End Sub
```

Code excerpt 5.4   The VBScript that plots the results by calling the ActiveX component GRAPH

Figure 5.1 shows the Web page before any computations are performed. Illustrative results of the ray tracing are presented in Figures 5.2 and 5.3, and indicates that the model behaves as expected. The results of the ray tracing (not presented here in full) show that the model behaves as expected. For a given decay factor, red light is deviated more than blue. Also at sufficiently high decay factors and

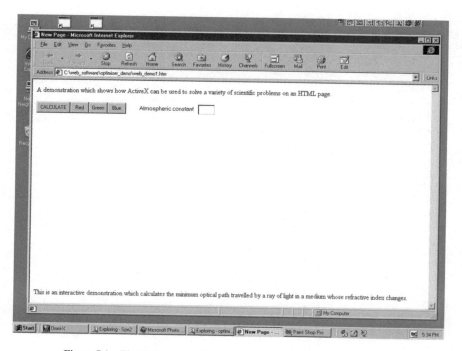

Figure 5.1   The Web page before any calculations have been performed

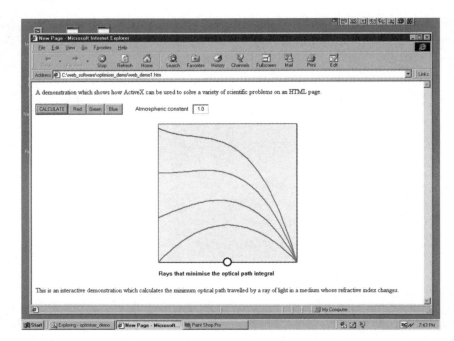

Figure 5.2   Plot of optimal red rays, the decay factor is 1

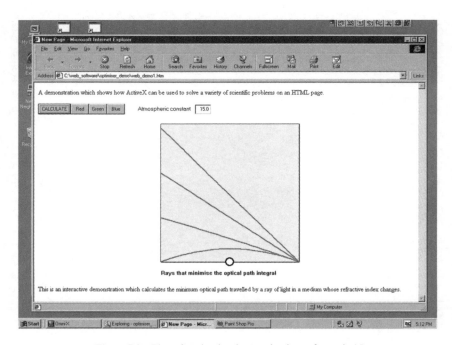

Figure 5.3   Plot of optimal red rays, the decay factor is 15

radial distances the refractive index is effectively unity. This leads to more uniformity in the medium and less curvature in the light ray. It should be mentioned that it would be easy, within a Web browser, to edit the user-defined integrand (within the source of the Web page) so as to model different spatial distributions of the refractive index, or even change the optimization and plot settings to model completely new problems.

5.2 PORTFOLIO ALLOCATION EXAMPLE

This demonstration considers an optimal portfolio selection problem, see Markowitz (1989) and Markowitz (1994), of the type:

minimize $V = X^T C X$

subject to the following constraints:

$$E = \mu X, \quad \sum_{i=1}^{n} X_i = 1, \quad L_i < X_i < U_i, \quad i = 1, \ldots, n$$

where E is the expected portfolio return, V is the portfolio risk, μ is the vector of expected asset returns, C is the covariance matrix, X is the vector of assets, and L_i, U_i are the respective lower and upper bounds on the ith asset.

Here we provide a further example of using the numerical optimization component to solve the Markowitz portfolio optimization problem.

Figure 5.4 shows the Web page before any computations are performed, and Figure 5.5 displays typical results.

The complete code is given in the **CD ROM** which accompanies the book.

```
<HTML>
<HEAD>
<TITLE>VBScript demonstration of Markowitz optimization on a web page</TITLE>
</HEAD>
<BODY>
<SCRIPT LANGUAGE="VBScript">
<!--
       .   .   .
Sub CommandButton1_Click()
       .   .   .
   nclin = 2        'number of linear constraints
   n = 4            'number of variables
   ncnlin = 0       'number of nonlinear constraints
       .   .   .
   num_pts = 15
   For i = 0 To num_pts - 1 ' Calculate the points on the efficient frontier
     portfolio_return(i) = 0.01 + 0.006*i ' Set the required portfolio return
     bl(n + 1) = portfolio_return(i)
     bu(n + 1) = portfolio_return(i)

     a(6) = asset_returns(2)
     a(7) = asset_returns(3)
     ' perform the numerical optimization
     OPTIM.optimize n, nclin, ncnlin, a(0), tda, g(0), loc_x(0), bl(0), bu(0)
     OPTIM.getvars loc_x(0), n    ' load the optimal portfolio into loc_x
     portfolio_risk(i) = OPTIM.Objval
     x_pos(i) = x_start + portfolio_risk(i)*20000
     y_pos(i) = y_start - portfolio_return(i)*2000
   Next
   GRAPH.text "Return       Risk",50,15
   For i = 0 To num_pts - 1  ' print the values
     GRAPH.text CStr(portfolio_return(i)),50,40+i*20
     GRAPH.text CStr(portfolio_risk(i)),120,40+i*20
```

```
  Next
  do_plot()    ' now plot the frontier
End Sub

Sub OPTIM_Objfunction()
' The function to optimize.

  For i = 0 To num_vars - 1
    For j = 0 To num_vars - 1
      risk = risk+covar(i,j)*X(i)*X(j)
    Next
  Next
  obj_val = risk
  OPTIM.Objval = obj_val    ' Return the value of the risk
  OPTIM.setvars x(0), num_vars
End Sub
-->
</SCRIPT>
A demonstration of the Markowitz Efficient Frontier Program on an HTML Web page.
<p> </p>

<OBJECT ID="OPTIM" WIDTH=1 HEIGHT=1
  CLASSID="CLSID:9D4EB275-06E5-11D3-AD10-0060087ED9F1">
    <PARAM NAME="_Version" VALUE="65536">
    <PARAM NAME="_ExtentX" VALUE="35">
    <PARAM NAME="_ExtentY" VALUE="35">
    <PARAM NAME="_StockProps" VALUE="0">
</OBJECT>

<p></p>
This is demonstration calculates the Markowitz minimum risk portfolio for 4 assets.
</BODY>
</HTML>
```

Code excerpt 5.5   VBScript code fragments for the portfolio optimization problem

Figure 5.4   Web page before numerical optimization has been performed

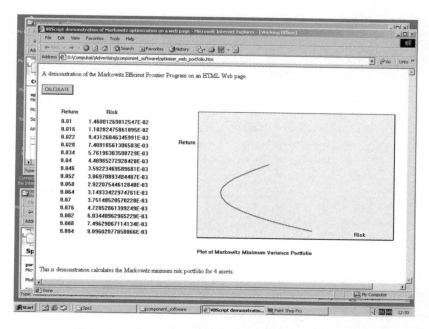

Figure 5.5 Web page showing the computed efficient frontier

5.3 NUMERICAL OPTIMIZATION WITHIN MICROSOFT EXCEL

Microsoft Excel is widely used in the finance community, and there are many situations where numerical optimization needs to be performed on the data contained within an Excel spreadsheet. Numerical optimization involves the minimization (or maximization) of a specified objective function. It is often helpful to monitor the progress of the optimization using a print function which outputs intermediate values such as:

- The major iteration count.
- The number of minor iterations required by the feasibility and optimality phases of the QP subproblem.
- The step taken along the computed search direction. On reasonably well behaved problems the unit step will be taken as the solution is approached.
- The intermediate solution vector.
- The value of the augmented Lagrangian merit function at the current iterate. This will usually decrease at each iteration. As the solution is approached it will converge to the value of the objective function at the solution.
- The Euclidean norm of the projected gradient. This will be approximately zero in the neighbourhood of a solution.

In this example we illustrate the use of an ActiveX optimization component which permits users to specify both their objective function and print function using the version of Visual Basic (VBA) within Excel (see Figure 5.6). Although this approach is slower than

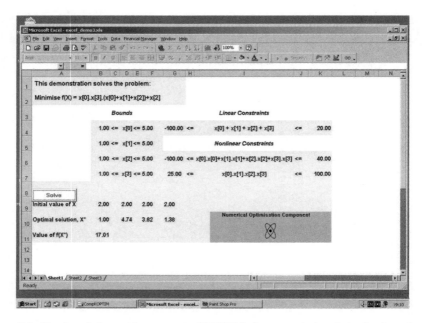

Figure 5.6   Excel worksheet with component OPTIM1 before numerical optimization is performed

coding everything in C++ it is far more convenient, and it is still possible to solve optimization problems involving several hundred variables in a few seconds.

Here the objective function is called my_objfun, and the print function printit. The variable bounds and the upper and lower constraints can be easily changed by altering the contents of the appropriate Excel spreadsheet cells. When the button Solve1 is clicked the Visual Basic subroutine Solve1_click() is run and input data such as the initial values and the upper and lower constraints, are read from the spreadsheet. The numerical optimization is then performed and the intermediate output, Figure 5.7, and computed results are written to the appropriate Excel worksheet.

Illustrative fragments from the Visual Basic code are given in Code excerpt 5.6 below.

```
Private Sub Solve1_Click()
  Dim x() As Double
  Dim bl() As Double
  Dim bu() As Double
  Dim g() As Double
    .  .  .
    ' Input the initial values and bounds from the spreadsheet
    For i = 0 To n − 1
      x(i) = Cells(8, 2 + i).Value   ' Initial values for X variables
      bl(i) = Cells(2, 2 + i).Value  ' Lower bounds for X variables
      bu(i) = Cells(3, 2 + i).Value  ' Upper bounds for X variable
  Next i
    .  .  .
  objname = "my_objfun"
  full_objname = ActiveWorkbook.Name & "!" & objname

' Set the name of the print function
  OPTIM1.printfun_funname "printit"

' Set the objective function name
  OPTIM1.objfun_funname full_objname
```

```
' Call the optimizer
  OPTIM1.optimize n, nclin, ncnlin, a(0), tda, g(0), x(0), bl(0), bu(0)
  objfun_value = OPTIM1.objf ' get the value of the objective function

' Output the X variable values for the optimal solution
  For i = 0 To n - 1
    Cells(10, 2 + i).Value = x(i)
  Next i
  Cells(11, 2).Value = objfun_value ' Output the optimal value of the objective function
End Sub

Sub my_objfun(num_variables As Long)
  ' The objective function - any valid Visual Basic code is allowed
  objective_value = x(0)*x(3)* (x(0)+x(1)+x(2)) +x(2)
End Sub

Sub printit(n As Long, it_maj_prt As Long, sol_prt As Long, maj As Long, mnr As Long,_
    step As Double, nfun As Long, merit As Double, violtn As Double, norm_gz As Double,_
    cond_hz As Double, x_ptr As Long)
  ' The user-defined print function. The user can decide the format in which any of
  ' the twelve arguments to printit are to be output.
  Dim xp() As Double
  ReDim xp(n)
    . .  . .
    If (it_maj_prt) Then ' A major iteration
    .Cells(Row, 1).Value = maj ' The major iteration count
    .Cells (Row, 2).Value = mnr ' The number of minor iterations of the QP subproblem
    .Cells (Row, 3).Value = Format(step, "0.00E+00") 'The step length along the
                                                      'search direction
      For i = 0 To n - 1  ' Output the current X variable values
        .Cells(Row, 4 + i).Value = Format(xp(i), "##.00")
      Next i
    ' Output the value of the augmented Lagrangian merit function at the current point.

End Sub
```

Code excerpt 5.6   Fragments of Visual Basic code which illustrate how to call the ActiveX numerical optimization component OPTIM1 from Excel

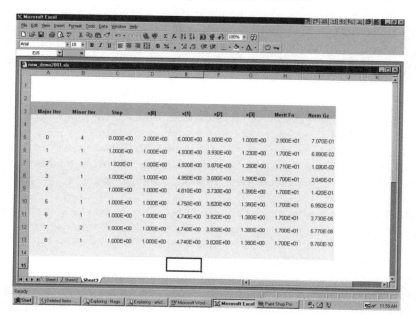

Figure 5.7   Excel; intermediate (monitoring) information from component OPTIM1 as numerical optimization is performed

Chapter 6

XML and transformation using XSL

6.1 INTRODUCTION

When numeric computation is performed it is necessary to decide on how the input data and output results will be presented. One approach is for the input data and output results to be contained in simple text files; for instance as comma separated values (CSV). This may have the advantages of simplicity and compact file size for large data sets. There may also be other benefits; for instance CSV files can be directly read into Microsoft Excel. However, this approach has the following disadvantages:

- The files are unstructured, and their contents cannot be *easily* checked to ensure that they are valid. Possible errors include: a numeric value is not within the required range, a floating point number is where an integer number should be, a string is where a floating point number should be, etc.
- It is not *easy* to *transform* the files. For instance it may be necessary to generate a specified subset of the information contained in a file or to visualize its contents graphically.
- The files cannot be *directly* viewed as Internet Web pages.

Of course many *non-standard* solutions to these problems can be found, if there are sufficient resources to create the necessary computer programs.

In order to address these issues the World Wide Web Consortium (W3C) provided the specification for an *Extensible Markup Language* (XML). In this section we discuss how XML files can be used for the structured storage and retrieval of information.

XML files can be directly viewed as Web pages. They can also have their contents validated by using an appropriate *schema*, and can be *automatically* (as they are loaded into the Web browser) transformed into HTML by using an *Extensible Stylesheet Language* (XSL) file.

Here we provide an example of a financial application in which both stock market data and financial analysis information (based on numerical optimization) are contained in a single XML file. The example application uses two XSL files: one displays the stock market data as a table of share prices, the other shows a summary report based on the financial analysis information.

6.2   XML

An XML file contains *tagged* values; the XML elements. A simple XML element is represented as:

```
<TAG>VALUE</TAG>
```

For example a share priced at 170.0 pence and with an annual return of 0.1 could be tagged as follows:

```
</PRICE>170.0</PRICE><RETURN>0.1</RETURN>
```

This format is not very useful because we haven't provided the name of the share. This can be achieved by using an XML element containing an *attribute*. An XML element with an attribute is represented as:

```
<TAG1 ATTRIBUTE=VALUE1><TAG2>VALUE2</TAG2></TAG1>
```

For example if *BT.A* shares are priced at 170.0 pence, with annual return of 0.1, and *BP* shares are priced at 440.0 pence, with an annual return of 0.18, then this can be tagged as:

```
<ITEM SHARE="BT.A"></PRICE>170.0</PRICE><RETURN>0.1</RETURN></ITEM>
<ITEM SHARE="BP"></PRICE>440.0</PRICE><RETURN>0.18</RETURN></ITEM>
```

This technique can be used to describe all the information contained in an XML file. As an example let us consider an XML file that contains daily information concerning the prices and annual returns of nine shares. The file is also assumed to contain the results of analysis which give the average annual returns and optimal holdings (based on portfolio optimization).

In Code excerpt 6.1 we give an outline of the structure of the XML file `stockmarket_data.xml`, which is used to contain this information. It can be seen that:

- All the information is contained within the XML element STOCK_DATA.
- The XML element STOCK_DATA is composed of the XML elements ALL_DATA and PORTFOLIO_ANALYSIS, which hold the complete share data and portfolio analysis results respectively.
- All the portfolio analysis results are contained in the XML element PORTFOLIO_ANALYSIS which is made up of several PORT_ITEM elements.
- All the stock market data is held in the XML element ALL_DATA. This element is made up of DATA_REC XML elements; one for each day of stock market data. The DATA_REC element is in turn composed of two XML elements: the single element DAY, which gives the day of the month, and an ITEM element for each share, to store the daily price and *current* annual return.

```
<STOCK_DATA>
 <ALL_DATA>
   <DATA_REC>
     <DAY>1</DAY>
     <ITEM SHARE=string><PRICE>real</PRICE><RETURN>real</RETURN></ITEM>4
       .   .   .
   </DATA_REC>


 </ALL_DATA>}
 <PORTFOLIO_ANALYSIS>
   <PORT_ITEM SHARE=string FULL_NAME=string><AVERAGE_ RETURN>real</AVERAGE_RETURN>
       <OPTIMAL_HOLDING>real</OPTIMAL_HOLDING></PORT_ITEM>
           .   .   .


 </PORTFOLIO_ANALYSIS>
</STOCK_DATA>
```

Code excerpt 6.1   The overall structure of the file `stockmarket_data.xml` used to contain both share prices information and portfolio analysis results. String values are denoted by string and floating point numbers are denoted by real

In Code excerpt 6.2 we give a more complete code fragment of the XML file `stockmarket_data.xml` to show in more detail the information that is actually stored. It can be seen that the XML file makes reference to the schema file `stockmarket_data.xdr`. This file specifies the allowed XML elements, the order the elements occur in the file, and also the permitted data types contained within the XML elements.

```
<?xml version='1.0'?>
<!-- This file contains stock market data, and the results of portfolio optimization -->
<?xml-stylesheet type="text/xsl" href= "report_style.xsl"?>
<STOCK_DATA xmlns="x-schema:stockmarket_data.xdr">
  <ALL_DATA>
    <DATA_REC>
      <DAY>1</DAY>
      <ITEM SHARE="BT.A"><PRICE>170.50</PRICE><RETURN>0.10</RETURN></ITEM>
      <ITEM SHARE="OOM"><PRICE>31.73</PRICE><RETURN>0.20</RETURN></ITEM>
      <ITEM SHARE="ISYS"><PRICE>62.15</PRICE><RETURN>0.01</RETURN></ITEM>
      <ITEM SHARE="VOD"><PRICE>87.15</PRICE><RETURN>0.099</RETURN></ITEM>
      <ITEM SHARE="BP"><PRICE>440.10</PRICE><RETURN>0.18</RETURN></ITEM>
      <ITEM SHARE="LGEN"><PRICE>91.70</PRICE><RETURN>0.089</RETURN></ITEM>
      <ITEM SHARE="HSBA"><PRICE>673.13</PRICE><RETURN>0.096</RETURN></ITEM>
      <ITEM SHARE="BARC"><PRICE>392.23</PRICE><RETURN>0.08</RETURN></ITEM>
      <ITEM SHARE="SHEL"><PRICE>398.75</PRICE><RETURN>0.24</RETURN></ITEM>
    </DATA_REC>



          .   .   .


  </ALL_DATA>
  <PORTFOLIO_ANALYSIS>
    <PORT_ITEM SHARE="BT.A" FULL_NAME="BT Group"><AVERAGE_RETURN>0.09</AVERAGE_RETURN>
        <OPTIMAL_HOLDING>0.01</OPTIMAL_HOLDING></PORT_ITEM>
    <PORT_ITEM SHARE="OOM" FULL_NAME="Mmo2"><AVERAGE_RETURN>0.10</AVERAGE_RETURN>
        <OPTIMAL_HOLDING>0.05</OPTIMAL_HOLDING></PORT_ITEM>
    <PORT_ITEM SHARE="ISYS" FULL_NAME ="Invensys"><AVERAGE_RETURN>0.12</AVERAGE_RETURN>
        <OPTIMAL_HOLDING>0.06</OPTIMAL_HOLDING></PORT_ITEM>
    <PORT_ITEM SHARE="VOD" FULL_NAME="Vodaphone Group"><AVERAGE_RETURN>0.20</AVERAGE_RETURN>
        <OPTIMAL_HOLDING>0.05 </OPTIMAL_HOLDING></PORT_ITEM>
    <PORT_ITEM SHARE="BP" FULL_NAME="BP Plc"><AVERAGE_RETURN>0.20</AVERAGE_RETURN>
        <OPTIMAL_HOLDING>0.28</OPTIMAL_HOLDING></PORT_ITEM>
    <PORT_ITEM SHARE="LGEN" FULL_NAME="Legal and General Group"><AVERAGE_RETURN>0.11
        </AVERAGE_RETURN><OPTIMAL_HOLDING>0.12</OPTIMAL_HOLDING></PORT_ITEM>
```

```
<PORT_ITEM SHARE="HSBA" FULL_NAME="HSBC Holdings"><AVERAGE_RETURN>0.13</AVERAGE_RETURN>
    <OPTIMAL _HOLDING>0.13</OPTIMAL_HOLDING></PORT_ITEM>
<PORT_ITEM SHARE="BARC" FULL_NAME="Barclays"><AVERAGE_RETURN>0.14</AVERAGE_RETURN>
    <OPTIMAL_HOLDING>0.05</OPTIMAL_HOLDING></PORT_ITEM>
<PORT_ITEM SHARE="SHEL" FULL_NAME="Shell Transport"><AVERAGE_RETURN>0.21</AVERAGE_RETURN>
    <OPTIMAL_HOLDING>0.25</OPTIMAL_HOLDING></PORT_ITEM>
</PORTFOLIO_ANALYSIS>
</STOCK_DATA>
```

Code excerpt 6.2   Fragment of the XML file `stockmarket_data.xml` containing both share prices information and portfolio analysis results. The file uses the schema contained in `stockmarket_data.xdr` and the XSL in `report_style.xsl`

More detail concerning schema are given in Section 6.3 below.

6.3   XML SCHEMA

As previously mentioned the structure and contents of an XML file can be checked by using an appropriate schema. There are many different schemas available, here we will consider the XML Data Reduced (XDR) schema that is supported by Microsoft Internet Explorer 6. Some of the commonly used data types supported by this schema are:

- **r4**: a four byte real number.
- **i1**: a single byte signed integer.
- **i4**: a four byte signed integer.
- **u1**: a single byte unsigned integer.
- **string**: character data.

The schema for the XML file `stockmarket_data.xml` is given below. Here both the contents and attributes of XML the elements are defined. XML attributes are defined by using the `AttributeType` tag. For example the following line:

```
<AttributeType name="SHARE" dt:type="string"required="yes"/>
```

defines a character string attribute `SHARE`.

The contents of an XML element are defined by using the `ElementType` tag. This can take the form of a single line, for example:

```
<ElementType name="DAY" content="textOnly"dt:type ="i4" />
```

defines the XML element `DAY`, which takes a four byte signed integer. It is also possible to define more complex XML elements. For instance:

```
<ElementType name="ITEM" content="eltOnly">
  <attribute type="SHARE"/>
  <element type="PRICE"/>
  <element type="RETURN"/>
</ElementType>
```

Here the keyword content="eltOnly" means that the XML element ITEM is only permitted to contain previously defined XML elements. In this example ITEM is defined to have a character string attribute called SHARE, and contain the XML elements PRICE and RETURN; in that order.

The complete XDR schema for the XML file stockmarket_data.xml is given in Code excerpt 6.3 below.

```
<?xml version="1.0"?>
<!-- This is the validation file stockmarket_data.xdr -->
<Schema xmlns="urn:schemas-microsoft-com:xml-data" xmlns:dt="urn:schemas-microsoft-com:datatypes">
  <ElementType name="DAY" content="textOnly" dt:type="i4" />
  <ElementType name="PRICE" content="textOnly" dt:type="r4" />
  <ElementType name="RETURN" content="textOnly" dt:type="r4" />
  <AttributeType name="SHARE" dt:type="string" required="yes"/>
  <AttributeType name="FULL_NAME" dt:type="string"/>
  <ElementType name="AVERAGE_RETURN" content="textOnly" dt:type="r4" />
  <ElementType name="OPTIMAL_HOLDING" content="textOnly" dt:type="r4" />
  <ElementType name="ITEM" content="eltOnly">
    <attribute type="SHARE"/>
    <element type="PRICE"/>
    <element type="RETURN"/>
  </ElementType>
  <ElementType name="PORT_ITEM" content="eltOnly">
    <attribute type="SHARE"/>
    <attribute type="FULL_NAME"/>
    <element type="AVERAGE_RETURN"/>
    <element type="OPTIMAL_HOLDING"/>
  </ElementType>
  <ElementType name="DATA_REC" content="eltOnly">
    <element type="DAY"/>
    <element type="ITEM"/>
  </ElementType>
  <ElementType name="ALL_DATA" content="eltOnly" order="many">
    <element type="DATA_REC"/>
  </ElementType>
  <ElementType name="PORTFOLIO_ANALYSIS" content="eltOnly">
    <element type="PORT_ITEM"/>
  </ElementType>
  <ElementType name="STOCK_DATA" content="eltOnly" order="seq">
    <element type="ALL_DATA"/>
    <element type="PORTFOLIO_ANALYSIS"/>
  </ElementType>
</Schema>
```

Code excerpt 6.3   The XDR schema file, stockmarket_data.xdr, used by the XML file stockmarket_data.xml

Once we have defined the schema the XML file can be validated using it. In Figure 6.1 we show the validation error caused when stockmarket_data.xml contains following invalid XML:

```
<DAY>1.1</DAY>
<ITEM SHARE="BT.A"><PRICE>170.50</PRICE><RETURN>0.10</RETURN></ITEM>
<ITEM SHARE="OOM"><PRICE>31.73</PRICE><RETURN>0.20</RETURN></ITEM>
```

Here the contents of the XML element DAY, which should be a four byte integer, have instead been replaced by a floating point number.

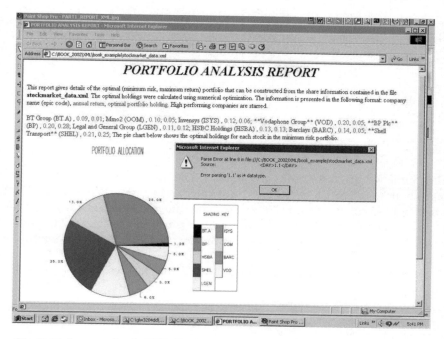

Figure 6.1   Validation error for the XML file `stockmarket_data.xml`; the value for DAY should be an integer but the XML file contains the floating point number 1.1 instead

6.4   XSL

In this section we will briefly describe the Extensible Stylesheet Language (XSL), and show how it can be used to *transform* XML files into HTML files. The transformation from XML to HTML occurs dynamically as the XML file is loaded into a Web browser, and is achieved by interpreting the contents of an associated XSL file. This means the manner in which information contained in single XML file is displayed within a Web browser entirely depends on the associated XSL file. We will now describe a few of the features of XSL. It contains the usual features that one might expect, for instance there is:

Iteration through a list of items using `<xsl:for-each>` and variable assignment using `<xsl:variable>`.

```
<xsl:for-each select="stock_xdr:ITEM">
  <xsl:variable name="v1" select="@SHARE" />
  <xsl:variable name="v2" select="stock_xdr:PRICE" />
  . . .
</xsl:for-each>
```

Sets the variable v1 to the value of the attribute SHARE and the variable tt v2 to the value contained in the child element PRICE.

Selection from a set of alternatives using `xsl:choose`, output the value of a variable `xsl:value-of`, and evaluating expressions using `test`.

```xsl
<xsl:choose>
  <xsl:when test="$return &lt; 0.10">
    <td bgcolor="pink" align="center"><xsl:value-of select="$price"/>
    </td>
  </xsl:when>
  <xsl:when test="$return &gt; 0.20">
    <td bgcolor="yellow" align="center">
      <font color="red">*<xsl:value-of select="$price"/>*</font>
    </td>
  </xsl:when>
  <xsl:otherwise>
    <td bgcolor="yellow" align="center"><xsl:value-of select="$price"/>
    </td>
  </xsl:otherwise>
</xsl:choose>
```

Here if the variable `return` is less than 0.1 then the background colour of the cell is set to pink to indicate a bad share, but if value of `return` is greater than 0.2 then the background colour of the cell is set to yellow and red stars are output to indicate that this is a good share. If the value of `return` is between 0.1 and 0.2 then the code contained in the `<xsl:otherwise>` clause is executed and the background colour is just set to yellow.

It is also possible to create procedures in XSL, for instance:

```xsl
<xsl:template name="OUTPUT_ELEMENT">
  <xsl:param name="share"/>
  <xsl:param name="price"/>
  <xsl:param name="return"/>

  <xsl:choose>
    <xsl:when test="$return &lt; 0.10">
      <td bgcolor="pink" align="center"><xsl:value-of select="$price"/>
      </td>

    <xsl:otherwise>
      <td bgcolor="yellow" align="center"><xsl:value-of select="$price"/>
      </td>
    </xsl:otherwise>
  </xsl:choose>
</xsl:template>
```

defines an XSL procedure called OUTPUT_ELEMENT with parameters `share`, `price`, and `return`. It can be called using the following syntax:

```xsl
<xsl:call-template name="OUTPUT_ELEMENT">
  <xsl:with-param name="share" select="$v1"/>
  <xsl:with-param name="price" select="$v2"/>
  <xsl:with-param name="return" select="$v3"/>
</xsl:call-template>
```

where, for instance, the parameter `price` is given the value of the XSL variable v2; the variables v1, v2, and v3 are assumed to have been set earlier in the code.

6.5   STOCK MARKET DATA EXAMPLE

In this section we give an example of how the contents of an XML file can be displayed in very different ways depending on the XSL stylesheet used. We will only provide short code excerpts; the complete code for this example is provided on the CD ROM.

The XML file used here is called `stockmarket_data.xml` and has been mentioned earlier in Sections 6.2 to 6.4. This file contains the daily prices and annual returns for nine shares. We assume that the data has been processed by a numerical optimizer which has computed an optimal (Markowitz minimum risk/maximum return) portfolio of these shares, and that the results of these computations have been written to the XML file. As shown in Code excerpt 6.2, the portfolio analysis results are stored between the XML tags ⟨PORTFOLIO_ANALYSIS⟩ and ⟨\PORTFOLIO_ANALYSIS⟩.

Here we will use two different XSL files to visualize the XML file either as data in tabular form (Figure 6.2) or as a report file (Figure 6.3), in which summary information concerning the optimal portfolio is shown.

The XSL stylesheet used to create the report view of the XML data file is shown below in Code excerpt 6.4. All the stock market data is matched using the XSL statement ⟨xsl:template match=" stock_xdr:DATA_REC "⟩, and (because we are only interested summary information) produces no output. By contrast the XSL command ⟨xsl:template match= "stock_xdr:PORTFOLIO_ANALYSIS"⟩ matches the portfolio analysis results and creates the HTML output seen in Figure 6.3.

```
<xsl:stylesheet version="1.0" xmlns:xsl="http://www.w3.org/1999/XSL/Transform "
    xmlns:stock_xdr="x-schema:stockmarket_data.xdr">
 <xsl:template match="/">
  <HTML>
  <head>
  <title>PORTFOLIO ANALYSIS REPORT</title>
  </head>
  <body>
  <xsl:apply-templates />
  The pie chart below shows the optimal holdings for each stock in the minimum risk portfolio. <p></p>
  <embed src="report_pie.svg" width="500" height="5000" name="SVGEmbed" type="image/svg-xml"
      pluginspage="http://www.adobe.com/svg/viewer/install/" />
  </body>
  </HTML>
 </xsl:template>

 <xsl:template match="stock_xdr:PORTFOLIO_ANALYSIS">
  <h1 align="center"><i>PORTFOLIO ANALYSIS REPORT</i></h1>
  This report gives details of the optimal (minimum risk, maximum
  return) portfolio that can be constructed from the
  share information contained in the file
  <b>stockmarket_data.xml</b>. The optimal holdings were calculated using numerical optimization.
  The information is presented in the following format:
  <font color="blue">company name (epic code) </font>,
  <font color="green">annual return </font>,
  <font color="red">optimal portfolio holding </font>.
  High performing companies are starred. <p></p>

  <xsl:for-each select="stock_xdr:PORT_ITEM">
   <xsl:variable name="v1" select="stock_xdr:AVERAGE_RETURN" />
   <xsl:if test="$v1 &gt; 0.19"> <b><font color="red">**</font></b></xsl:if>
   <font color="blue"><xsl:value-of select="@FULL_NAME"/><xsl:if test="$v1 &gt; 0.19"><b>
   <font color="red">**</font></b></xsl:if>(<xsl:value-of select="@SHARE"/>) </font>,
   <font color="green"><xsl:value-of select="stock_xdr:AVERAGE_RETURN"/></font>,
   <font color="red"><xsl:value-of select="stock_xdr:OPTIMAL_HOLDING"/></font>;
  </xsl:for-each>
 </xsl:template>

 <xsl:template match="stock_xdr:DATA_REC">
  <!-- DO NOT OUTPUT ANY STOCK DATA IN THIS STYLE SHEET-->
 </xsl:template>

</xsl:stylesheet>
```

Code excerpt 6.4 The XSL file `report_style.xsl` used to transform the XML file `stockmarket_data.xml` into the report view shown in Figure 6.3

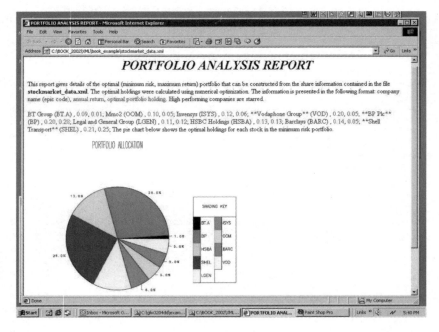

DAILY STOCK PRICE DATA FOR THE TRADING DAYS IN AN IMAGINARY MONTH. SHARES WITH ANNUAL RETURNS OF LESS THAN 10 PERCENT ARE IN PINK CELLS. THOSE WITH ANNUAL RETURNS GREATER THAN 20 PERCENT HAVE STARS NEXT TO THEM, AND ARE HIGHLIGHTED IN RED

DAY	BT.A	OOM	ISYS	VOD	BP	LGEN	HSBA	BARC	SHEL
1	170.50	31.73	62.15	87.15	440.10	91.70	673.13	392.23	*398.75*
2	173.50	32.75	64.24	88.25	*449.90*	90.81	669.13	392.12	*399.72*
3	171.50	31.79	62.21	89.10	*451.10*	91.01	671.09	392.50	*398.70*
4	171.23	34.51	63.10	85.14	452.11	93.76	674.12	393.43	395.74
5	173.54	32.76	62.24	89.45	*451.46*	92.71	673.40	390.35	397.65
6	171.30	30.75	64.30	89.27	*451.90*	91.68	672.11	391.98	*399.81*
7	168.40	28.95	64.35	89.41	449.23	91.61	675.10	392.42	*400.12*

Figure 6.2　The tabular view of the XML data file `stockmarket_data.xml` displayed using the Web browser Internet Explorer 6; the XSL style sheet is available on the CD ROM

Figure 6.3　The report view of XML data file `stockmarket_data.xml` displayed using the Web browser Internet Explorer 6; the XSL style sheet is given in Code excerpt 6.4

The report view also includes a Scalable Vector Graphics (SVG) pie chart `report_pie.svg` to display the portfolio composition. Here the SVG graphics were viewed by installing the Adobe SVG Viewer, which can be freely downloaded from `http://www.adobe.com/svg/`.

The XSL statement for including the SVG graphic is:

```
<embed src="report_pie.svg" width="500" height="5000" name="SVGEmbed" type="image/svg-xml"
    pluginspage="http://www.adobe.com/svg/viewer/install/"/>
```

where the image source is specified by using the `src` attribute, and the size of the image is controlled via `width` and `height` attributes.

Chapter 7

Epilogue

7.1 WRAPPING C WITH C++ FOR OO NUMERICS IN .NET

7.1.1 Introduction

A common software requirement is for code written in one computer language to be used by software developed in a different computer language. For instance it may be necessary to access C functions from a .NET or Java application. Here we show how existing C software can be wrapped in C++ and thus made easily accessible from .NET languages such as C# and VB.NET, see Levy (2003). Although our discussions will be concerned with the NAG C library, the method is quite general and can be applied to other C software. We illustrate the technique by considering four NAG C library numeric routines, which have applications in computational finance. These functions are:

- NAG function s15abc; the cumulative normal distribution which is used in analytic option pricing formulae, such as the Black–Scholes equation, see Black and Scholes (1973).
- NAG function f02aac; eigenvalue computation. This has applications in multi-factor models, including interest-rate models, and time series, see Rebonato (1998) and Levy (2003).
- NAG function d01ajc; numerical integration, which has applications in risk analysis, see Hull (1997).
- NAG function e04dgc; numerical optimization. This can be used to compute optimal portfolios, see Markowitz (1994).

For more details concerning these functions see NAG Ltd (2003).

7.1.2 COM, .NET assemblies and managed C++

Microsoft COM already enables the creation of numeric components which can be used by the complete range of Windows programming languages, see Levy (2001). In fact COM objects can be used within .NET.

However, from a software developer's point of view, wrapping C code in COM C++ classes has the disadvantage that there is a lot of *visible Microsoft COM baggage* that needs to be carried around. This has the effect of obscuring the code and also making it difficult to implement the C++ classes on UNIX platforms. Another limitation is that the classes contained within a COM object cannot be used to create other derived classes.

The recent introduction of .NET *assemblies* has now substantially improved this situation. Briefly, the classes in an assembly can be coded in any of the .NET languages and then used by any other .NET language. It is thus possible to create assemblies in *managed C++* that provide class wrappers for C routines, and then use these from C# and VB.NET software, see Challa and Laksberg (2002).

Code excerpt 7.1 shows the ANSI function prototypes of our four NAG C functions. The managed C++ code used to create an assembly that wraps the C functions is displayed in Code excerpt 7.2. We have called this assembly `naglib`, and it defines the namespace `NAGLIB` and the managed class `NAG_FUNCTIONS` which provides functions to access native C routines contained within the DLL 'nagc'. The Code excerpt 7.2 is only meant for illustrative purposes and is not intended to be a statement of good programming practice. However, we have included some useful features such as flagging errors and setting default parameter values via the constructor `NAG_FUNCTIONS()`.

```
/* declaration of function pointer E04DGC_FUN */
typedef void (*E04DGC_FUN) (long, double *, double *, double *, Nag_Comm *);

/* declaration of function pointer D01AJC_FUN */
typedef double (*D01AJC_FUN) (double);

/* declaration of function prototypes */
void e04dgc (long n, E04DGC_FUN objfun, double x[], double *objf, double grad[],
             Nag_E04_Opt *options, Nag_Comm *user_comm, NagError *fail);

void f02aac (long n, double *a, long tda, double *r, NagError  *fail);

void d01ajc (D01AJC_FUN f, double a, double b, double epsabs, double epsrel, long max_num_subint,
             double *result, double *abserr, Nag_QuadProgress *qp, NagError *fail);

double s15abc (double x, NagError *fail);
```

Code excerpt 7.1 The ANSI function pointers and function prototypes for the NAG C routines. The types `Nag_Comm`, `NagError`, `Nag_E04_Opt`, and `Nag_QuadProgress` are declared in the header file `nag_types.h` which is included in the header file `nag.h`

```
extern "C" {
 #include <stdio.h>
 #include <nag.h>
 #include <nag_stdlib.h>
}

#using <mscorlib.dll>
using namespace System::Runtime::InteropServices;
using namespace System;

namespace NAGLIB {

 public __delegate double INTEGRAND_FUN_TYPE(Double x);
 public __delegate void OBJ_FUN_TYPE (Int32 n, double *x, double *objf, double *g, Int32 comm);

 [DllImport("nagc")]
  extern "C" void e04dgc (Int32 n, OBJ_FUN_TYPE *f, Double *x, Double *objf,
                          Double *g, Nag_E04_Opt *options, Int32 comm, NagError *flag);
 [DllImport ("nagc")]
  extern "C" void e04xxc (Nag_E04_Opt *options);
 [DllImport ("nagc")]
  extern "C" void d01ajc (INTEGRAND_FUN_TYPE *f, Double a, Double b,
                          Double epsabs, Double epsrel, Int32 max_num_subint, Double* result,
                          Double *abserr, Nag_QuadProgress *qp, NagError *flag);
 [DllImport ("nagc")]
  extern "C" void f02aac (Int32 n, Double *a, Int32 tda, Double *r, NagError *eflag);
```

```
[DllImport ("nagc")]
extern "C" Double s15abc(Double x);

public __gc class NAG_FUNCTIONS
{
  public:
    Double QUADRATURE_epsabs;
    Double QUADRATURE_epsrel;
    Int32 QUADRATURE_max_subint;

    NAG_FUNCTIONS()
    { // the constructor: set default values
      QUADRATURE_epsabs = 0.0;
      QUADRATURE_epsrel = 0.0001;
      QUADRATURE_max_subint = 200;
    }

    void REAL_SYMM_EIGEN (Int32 n, Double *a, Int32 tda, Double *r, Int32 *flag)
    {
      NagError eflag;
      INIT_FAIL(eflag);
      f02aac(n, a, tda, r, &eflag);
      *flag = (Int32)eflag.code;
    }
    Double CUM_NORM (Double x) {
      return s15abc(x);
    }
    void OPTIMIZE (Int32 n, Double *x, Double *g, Double *objf, Int32 *flag, OBJ_FUN_TYPE *the_fun)
    {
      NagError eflag;
      Nag_E04_Opt options;

      INIT_FAIL (eflag);
      e04xxc (&options);
      options.print_level = Nag_NoPrint;
      options.list = 0;
      options.verify_grad = Nag_NoCheck;
      e04dgc(n, the_fun, x, objf, g, &options, (Int32)0, &eflag);
      *flag = (Int32)eflag.code;
    }
    void QUADRATURE (Double a, Double b, Double *result, Double *abserr, Int32 *flag, INTEGRAND_FUN_TYPE *the_fun)
    {
      Nag_QuadProgress qp;
      NagError eflag;

      INIT_FAIL(eflag);
      d01ajc(the_fun, a, b, QUADRATURE_epsabs, QUADRATURE_epsrel, QUADRATURE_max_subint, result, abserr,
          &qp, &eflag);
        *flag = (Int32)eflag.code;
    }
};
}
```

Code excerpt 7.2 The managed C++ code used to create the assembly `naglib` which contains the namespace NAGLIB, and wraps the NAG C library functions in the class NAG_FUNCTIONS

It can be seen that the code is *almost* standard C++ and (in constrast to the equivalent COM approach) could easily be ported to UNIX platforms. We will now consider each non-standard C++ (that is Microsoft specific) feature in turn.

Importing Dynamic Link Library (DLL) functions

The NAG C library routines used are contained in a DLL called 'nagc'. Here each function is imported into the C++ project by name; for instance:

```
[DllImport ("nagc")]
extern "C" Double s15abc(Double x);
```

is used to import the function `s15abc`, which computes the cumulative normal distribution.

Managed and unmanaged code

The directive `__gc` indicates that the code is managed and memory is allocated on the garbage collected (GC) heap; unmanaged code is indicated by `__nogc`.

The data types Double and Int32

In Code excerpt 7.2 the .NET data types `Double` and `Int32` have been used so that the assembly can be accessed by both C# and VB.NET code.

All managed .NET code, written in VB.NET, C#, and C++, is compiled to the same intermediate language (IL) code. In order to permit interoperability within .NET there is a common type system (CTS) which standardizes the basic data types across all languages.

A summary of the .NET data types corresponding to the C++ types `double` and `long` is given in the Table 7.1.

Delegates

In the case of numerical integration and optimization a user-defined function, or *call-back function*, needs to be passed as a parameter to the NAG C library routine. This is achieved in .NET by declaring a delegate with the same *signature* (that is return type and parameter types) as the callback function. For example

```
public __delegate double INTEGRAND_FUN_TYPE(Double x);
```

declares the delegate `INTEGRAND_FUN_TYPE` with a signature corresponding to functions that return a `Double` and have a single `Double` parameter passed by value. This delegate is used by the numerical integration routine `d01ajc` for defining the integrand. It can be seen that the declaration of a delegate is similar to the declaration of a function prototype with the additional words `public (or private)` and `__delegate`. Also the declaration and use of delegates in Code excerpt 7.2 has similarities with the declaration and use of function pointers in Code excerpt 7.1. A more complicated delegate example is:

```
public __delegate void OBJ_FUN_TYPE (Int32 n, double *x,double * objf, double *g, Int32 comm);
```

Table 7.1 The correspondence between data types used by
C++, C#, VB.NET, and the .NET CTS

C++	C#	VB.NET	CTS	Size in bytes
long	int	Integer	Int32	4
double	double	Double	Double	8

which declares the delegate OBJ_FUN_TYPE, with a signature that applies to subroutines (that is a functions which return void) with parameters of type Int32 and double *. As can be seen, here it was found necessary to use double * instead of the more general Double *. This delegate is used by the numerical optimization routine e04dgc for specifying the objective function to be minimized.

7.1.3　Accessing the assembly naglib from C#

In this section we show how the previously described assembly naglib can be accessed from a C# console project created using Visual Studio .NET. The C# code is presented in Code excerpt 7.3 and a screen view of the project is shown in Figure 7.1.

It can be seen that the C# code defines the two classes DCLASS and RUNIT.

DCLASS is derived from the class NAG_FUNCTIONS and supplies the definitions for the callback functions used by the member functions OPTIMIZE and QUADRATURE.

The class RUNIT only contains the member function Main. This function is run by the example console application, and all the computations are performed by a single numeric object (called tt) of type DCLASS.

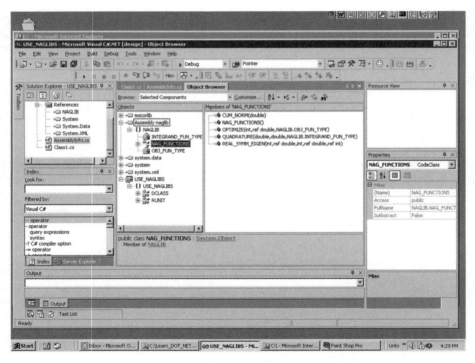

Figure 7.1　A view of the C# example project. The Object Browser displays the assembly naglib, the namespace NAGLIB, the delegates INTEGRAND_FUN_TYPE, and OBJ_FUN_TYPE, and also the member functions of the class NAG_FUNCTIONS: CUM_NORM, OPTIMIZE, QUADRATURE, and REAL_SYMM_EIGEN

```
using System;
using System.Runtime.InteropServices;
using NAGLIB;

namespace USE_NAGLIBS
{
  class DCLASS : NAG_FUNCTIONS
  {
    public unsafe void objfun (Int32 n, Double *x, Double *objf, Double *g, Int32 comm)
    {
      Double ex1, x1, x2;

      ex1 = Math.Exp(x[0]);
      x1 = x[0];
      x2 = x[1];
      *objf = ex1*(4.0*x1*x1 + 2.0*x2*x2 + 4.0*x1*x2 + 2.0*x2 + 1.0);
      g[0] = 4.0*ex1*(2.0*x1 + x2) + *objf;
      g[1] = 2.0*ex1*(2.0*x2 + 2.0*x1 + 1.0);
    }
    public Double the_integrand_c (Double x)
    {
      Double pi = Math.PI;
      Double val;

      val = (x*Math.Sin(x*30.0)/1.0-x*x/(pi*pi*4.0));
      return val;
    }
  }
  class RUNIT
  {
    static unsafe void Main(string[] args)
    {
      Int32 tda = 4, n = 4, n2 = 2, j, flag = 0;
      Double [] r = new Double [30];
      Double [] x2 = new Double [2];
      Double [] g = new Double [2];
      Double a1, b1, objf = 0.0, abserr = 0.0, the_answer, x;
      Double [,] a = new Double[n,n];
      DCLASS tt = new DCLASS();
      x = -1.0;
      the_answer = tt.CUM_NORM(x);
      Console.WriteLine ("The value of the cumulative normal = {0,8:F4}", the_answer);
      INTEGRAND_FUN_TYPE myfun_c = new INTEGRAND_FUN_TYPE(tt.the_integrand_c);
      OBJ_FUN_TYPE myobjfun = new OBJ_FUN_TYPE (tt.objfun);

      a1 = 0.0;
      b1 = Math.PI*2.0;
      flag = 0;
      the_answer = 0.0;
      tt.QUADRATURE (a1, b1, ref the_answer, ref abserr, ref flag, myfun_c);
      Console.WriteLine ("The integral (default maximum number of subintervals) = {0,8:F6}", the_answer);
      flag = 0;
      tt.QUADRATURE_max_subint = 3;
      tt.QUADRATURE (a1, b1, ref the_answer, ref abserr, ref flag, myfun_c);
      Console.WriteLine ("The integral (maximum number of subintervals set to 3) = {0,8:F6}", the_answer);

      x2 [0] = -1.0;
      x2 [1] = 1.0;
      n2 = 2;
      flag = 0;
      tt.OPTIMIZE (n2, ref x2 [0], ref g [0], ref objf, ref flag, myobjfun);
      Console.Write ("The optimization solution vector is:");
      for (j = 0; j < 2; ++j) {
        Console.Write("{0,8:F4}", x2 [j]);
      }
      Console.WriteLine();
      Console.WriteLine ("The value of the objective function is: {0,8:E4}",objf);

      flag = 0;
      //first row
      a[0,0] = 0.5;
      a[0,1] = 0.0;
      a[0,2] = 2.3;
      a[0,3] = -2.6;
      // second row
      a[1,0] = 0.0;
      a[1,1] = 0.5;
```

```
a[1,2]=-1.4;
a[1,3]=-0.7;
// third row
a[2,0]=2.3;
a[2,1]=-1.4;
a[2,2]=0.5;
a[2,3]=0.0;
//fourth row
a[3,0]=-2.6;
a[3,1]=-0.7;
a[3,2]=0.0;
a[3,3]=0.5;
tt.REAL_SYMM_EIGEN(n, ref a[0,0], tda, ref r[0], ref flag);
Console.Write("The Eigenvalues are:");
for (j=0; j<=3; ++j){
  Console.Write ("{0,8:F4}", r[j]);
}
Console.WriteLine();
}
}
}
```

Code excerpt 7.3   Example C# code which uses the assembly `naglib` in a C# console application

```
The value of the cumulative normal = 0.1587
The integral (default maximum number of subintervals) =-2.303835
The integral (maximum number of subintervals set to 3) =-3.168259
The optimization solution vector is : 0.5000-1.0000
The value of the objective function is: 2.7457E-014
The Eigenvalues are:-3.0000-1.0000 2.0000 4.0000
```

Code excerpt 7.4   The output from Code excerpt 7.3

We will now briefly discuss some of the important features of the code, for more information on C# see Robinson *et al.* (2001).

General points

The assembly containing the namespace NAGLIB is accessed with the statement using NAGLIB; which occurs on the third line of the C# code listing.

We use Math.PI to return the value of π, Math.Sin(x) to compute sin(x), and Math.Exp(x) to evaluate exp(x). These functions are members of the class Math which is contained in the namespace System.

The keyword unsafe

This directive is necessary because C# does not *really support* pointers. The keyword unsafe allows us to use pointers and thus easily pass scalars and arrays by reference to the managed C++ class NAG_FUNCTIONS contained in the namespace NAGLIB.

Declaring numeric objects and using simple member functions

The statement DCLASS tt = new DCLASS() creates a numeric object tt with the type of the derived class DCLASS. Since DCLASS was derived from NAG_FUNCTIONS it allows access not only to the public member functions objfun and the_integrand_c, but also the public member functions of NAG_FUNCTIONS: CUM_NORM, OPTIMIZE, QUADRATURE, and REAL_SYMM_EIGEN. This means that we can compute the cumulative normal distribution, and perform eigenvalue computations by using statements of the form:

```
the_answer = tt.CUM_NORM(x);
flag = 0;
// first row
a[0,0] = 0.5;
a[0,1] = 0.0;
  .   .   .
// fourth row
a[3,0] = -2.6;
a[3,1] = -0.7;
a[3,2] = 0.0;
a[3,3] = 0.5;
tt.REAL_SYMM_EIGEN(n, ref a[0,0], tda, ref r[0], ref flag);
```

We note that the keyword ref is used to pass the address of a[0, 0], r[0], and flag to the member function REAL_SYMM_EIGEN.

Using numeric objects with member functions requiring delegates

We will now consider how to call the numerical integration function QUADRATURE. This is achieved using the following C# statement:

```
INTEGRAND_FUN_TYPE myfun_c = new INTEGRAND_FUN_TYPE (tt.the_integrand_c);
```

to declare (and also define) the delegate myfun_c, of type INTEGRAND_FUN_TYPE, which corresponds to the user-defined function the_ integrand_c contained in the derived class DCLASS. The next step is to pass the appropriate parameters to the function tt.QUADRATURE; for example:

```
a1 = 0.0;
b1 = Math.PI*2.0;
flag = 0;
the_answer = 0.0;
tt.QUADRATURE(a1, b1, ref the_answer, ref abserr, ref flag, myfun_c);
```

The method of calling the numerical optimization member function is very similar. For instance in the example code we use:

```
OBJ_FUN_TYPE myobjfun = new OBJ_FUN_TYPE (tt.objfun);
x2[0] = -1.0;
x2[1] = 1.0;
n2 = 2;
flag = 0;
tt.OPTIMIZE(n2, ref x2[0], ref g[0], ref objf, ref flag, myobjfun);
```

The initial parameter estimates and computed optimal values are contained in the array x2. The estimated gradient at the solution point is returned in the array g and the parameter objf contains the value of the minimized objective function.

7.1.4   Accessing the assembly `naglib` from VB.NET

Here we illustrate how the assembly `naglib` can be used from VB.NET; for more details on VB.NET see Barwell *et al.* (2002).

The assembly `naglib` can be used from VB.NET in a similar manner to that described for C#. This is illustrated below in Code excerpt 7.5.

```
Imports System
Imports System.Runtime.InteropServices
Imports NAGLIB

Module Module1

  Public Class DCLASS
    Inherits NAG_FUNCTIONS

    Public Function the_integrand_c (ByVal x As Double) As Double
      Dim pi As Double
      Dim val As Double

      pi = Math.PI
      val = (x * Math.Sin(x * 30) / 1 - x * x / (pi * pi * 4))
      Return val
    End Function
  End Class

  Sub Main()

    Dim x, the_answer As Double
    Dim flag, j, tda, n As Integer
    Dim a(,), r(), a1, b1, abserr As Double
    Dim tt As New DCLASS()
    Dim myfun As New INTEGRAND_FUN_TYPE(AddressOf tt.the_integrand_c)

    a1 = 0
    b1 = Math.PI * 2
    flag = 0
    tt.QUADRATURE(a1, b1, the_answer, abserr, flag, myfun)
    Console.WriteLine("The integral (default number of subintervals) = {0,8:F4}", the_answer)
    tt.QUADRATURE_max_subint = 3
    flag = 0
    tt.QUADRATURE(a1, b1, the_answer, abserr, flag, myfun)
    Console.WriteLine ("The integral (number of subintervals set to 3) = {0,8:F4}", the_answer)

    x = -1
    the_answer = tt.CUM_NORM(x)
    Console.WriteLine("The value of the cumulative normal = {0,8:F4}", the_answer)

    flag = 0
    n = 4
    tda = n
    ReDim r(n - 1)
    ReDim a(n - 1, n - 1)
    'first row
    a(0, 0) = 0.5
    a(0, 1) = 0
    a(0, 2) = 2.3
    a(0, 3) = -2.6
    'second row
    a(1, 0) = 0
    a(1, 1) = 0.5
    a(1, 2) = -1.4
    a(1, 3) = -0.7
    'third row
    a(2, 0) = 2.3
    a(2, 1) = -1.4
    a(2, 2) = 0.5
    a(2, 3) = 0
    'fourth row
    a(3, 0) = -2.6
    a(3, 1) = -0.7
    a(3, 2) = 0
    a(3, 3) = 0.5
```

```
tt.REAL_SYMM_EIGEN(n, a(0, 0), tda, r(0), flag)
Console.Write("The Eigenvalues are:")
For j = 0 To n - 1
  Console.Write ("{0,8:F4}", r(j))
Next j
Console.WriteLine()
End Sub

End Module
```

Code excerpt 7.5   Example of using the numeric objects from VB.NET

```
The integral (default number of subintervals) = -2.3038
The integral (number of subintervals set to 3) = -3.1683
The value of the cumulative normal = 0.1587
The Eigenvalues are: -3.0000 -1.0000 2.0000 4.0000
```

Code excerpt 7.6   The output from Code excerpt 7.5

7.1.5   Conclusions

We have shown how to wrap C code in a managed C++ assembly, which can then be used from within either a C# or VB.NET project.

A major benefit of this approach over COM is that the managed C++ wrapper code can with little effort, be used on UNIX platforms. In addition, unlike COM, it is possible to create C# or VB.NET derived classes from the managed C++ (base) classes.

As more software supports .NET (for example Excel 2003 will) the future of OO numerics in .NET looks increasingly promising.

7.2   FINAL REMARKS

In this part of the book we have discussed various ways in which the Windows environment can be used to develop financial software. The creation of DLLs and their incorporation into Visual Basic, VB.NET, C#, and Excel has been considered. We have also described how numeric ActiveX components, with primitive visual user-interfaces, can be used from within Visual Basic, Delphi, and HTML Web pages. In addition examples of how XML, XSL, and SVG can be used to represent and display financial information from within a Web browser have been given.

With so many choices now available a software developer needs to carefully consider which is the most appropriate technology to use for a particular task. In making this decision the relative importance of the following will need to be made: the user-interface, computational speed, Internet access, speed of development, software portability, and the computer language(s) to use.

More information on these subjects can be found in the citations provided in the computing bibliography at the end of the book.

Part II

Pricing Assets

Chapter 8

Introduction

8.1 AN INTRODUCTION TO OPTIONS AND DERIVATIVES

In general, an option (also called a derivative, or contingent claim) is a contract whose value depends on the *future* values that specified underlying quantities take over a given time span. One use of options is as a means of providing insurance against certain events which *may happen* in the future. For instance an airport, which wants to insure against climatic risk, takes out a weather option. The contract for this option may pay out a given amount of cash when the outside temperature either exceeds or goes below certain prescribed levels.

This part of the book is concerned with financial options; that is options that are based on the future value of various financial quantities that can be determined from the financial markets. A *put* option is an agreement to sell an asset in the future for a fixed price *the strike price*, and a *call* is an agreement to buy an asset in the future for a given price. Furthermore *European options* can only be exercised at option maturity, whereas *American options* have greater *flexibility* and can be exercised at *any time* up to option maturity.

Here we will discuss options whose value depends on the future prices of various stocks and shares; these are called equity options. There are many different types of equity options, see Hull (1997) for more detail.

If we want to buy or sell an equity option it is very important to determine its *fair* value today. This will depend on the expected future values of the underlying stock values, based on our current (and historical) information.

To do this it is necessary to model how the stock value changes with time. In Part II of this book we will consider valuation models that are based on the assumption that the asset price can be described by Brownian motion. In Part III we consider more complex time series models for the asset price changes.

We will mainly be concerned with vanilla put and call options, however we do provide some detailed coverage of barrier options. In most cases it should not be too difficult to value more exotic options by modifying the supplied code.

We will consider the following computational methods for pricing options:

- Analytic methods and analytic approximations.
- Finite-difference lattices.

- Finite-difference grids.
- Simulation: Monte Carlo, using pseudorandom and quasirandom numbers.

We will discuss Brownian Motion and derive the Black–Scholes formula which is used for pricing European options. We will also derive formulae for the value of some commonly used European barrier options.

The value of a standard vanilla option depends on:

- The volatility of the underlying stock.
- The time to maturity.
- The strike price.
- The riskless interest rate.
- The dividends.
- Current value of the stock.

In the Black–Scholes setting the asset prices are assumed to follow a lognormal process. This means that the logarithm of the asset prices has a Gaussian distribution, and the asset returns can be modelled as a Brownian process.

8.2 BROWNIAN MOTION

Brownian motion is named after the botanist Robert Brown who used a microscope to study the fertilization mechanism of flowering plants. He first observed the random motion of pollen particles (obtained from the American species *Clarkia pulchella*) suspended in water, and wrote:

> The fovilla or granules fill the whole orbicular disk but do not extend to the projecting angles. They are not spherical but oblong or nearly cylindrical, and the particles have manifest motion. This motion is only visible to my lens which magnifies 370 times. The motion is obscure yet certain (Robert Brown, 12 June 1827; see Ramsbottom, 1932)

It appears that Brown considered this motion no more than a curiosity (he believed that the particles were *alive*) and continued *undistracted* with his botanical research. The full significance of his observations only became apparent about eighty years later when it was shown, Einstein (1905), that the motion is caused by the collisions that occur between the pollen grains and the water molecules. In 1908 Perrin, see Perrin (1909), was finally able to confirm Einstein's predictions experimentally. His work was made possible by the development of the ultramicroscope by Zsigmondy and Siedentopf in 1903. He was able to work out from his experimental results and Einstein's formula the size of the water molecule and a precise value for Avogadro's number. His work established the physical theory of Brownian motion and ended the skepticism about the existence of atoms and molecules as actual physical entities. Many of the fundamental properties of Brownian motion were discovered by Levy (1939, 1948), and the first mathematically rigorous treatment was provided by Wiener (1923, 1924). Karatzas and Shreve (1988) is an excellent text book on the theoretical properties of Brownian motion, while Shreve *et al.* (1997) provides much useful information concerning the use of Brownian processes within finance.

Brownian motion is also called a *random walk*, a Wiener process, or sometimes (more poetically) the *drunkards walk*.

In formal terms a process $Z = (Z_t : t \geq 0)$ is (one-dimensional) Brownian motion if:

(i) Z_t is continuous, and $Z_0 = 0$
(ii) $Z_t \sim N(0, t)$
(iii) The increment $dZ_{dt} = Z_{t+dt} - Z_t$ is normally distributed as, $dZ_{dt} \sim N(0, dt)$, so $E[dZ_{dt}] = 0$ and $Var(dZ_{dt}) = dt$. The increment dZ_{dt} is also independent of the history of the process up to time t.

From (iii) we can further state that, since the increments dZ_{dt} are independent of past values Z_t, a Brownian process is also a *Markov* process. In addition we shall now show that Brownian process is also a Martingale process.

In a Martingale process P_t, $t \geq 0$, the conditional expectation $E(P_{t+dt}|\mathcal{F}_t) = P_t$, where $\mathcal{F}_t$ is called the *filtration* generated by the process and contains the information learned by observing the process up to time t. Since for Brownian motion we have

$$E(Z_{t+dt}|\mathcal{F}_t) = E((Z_{t+dt} - Z_t) + Z_t|\mathcal{F}_t) = E(Z_{t+dt} - Z_t) + Z_t = E(dZ_{t+dt}) + Z_t = Z_t$$

where we have used the fact that $E[dZ_{t+dt}] = 0$. Since $E(Z_{t+dt}|\mathcal{F}_t) = Z_t$, the Brownian motion Z is a Martingale process.

We will now consider the Brownian increments over the time interval dt in more detail. Over the time interval dt we have:

$$dX_{dt} = dZ_{dt} \tag{8.1}$$

where dZ_{dt} is a random variable drawn from a normal distribution with mean zero and variance dt, which we denote as $dZ_{dt} \sim N(0, dt)$. Equation 8.1 can also be written in the equivalent form:

$$dX_{dt} = \sqrt{dt}\,\epsilon \tag{8.2}$$

where ϵ is a random variable drawn from a *standard* normal distribution (that is a normal distribution with zero mean and unit variance), and we use the notation $\epsilon \sim N(0, 1)$.

Equations 8.1 and 8.2 give the incremental change in the value of X over the time interval dt for *standard* Brownian motion.

We shall now generalize these equations slightly by introducing the extra (*volatility*) parameter σ which controls the variance of the process. We now have:

$$dX_{dt} = \sigma dZ_{dt} \tag{8.3}$$

where $dZ_{dt} \sim N(0, dt)$, and $dX_{dt} \sim N(0, \sigma^2 dt)$. Equation 8.3 can also be written in the equivalent form:

$$dX_{dt} = \sigma\sqrt{dt}\,\epsilon_i, \quad \epsilon_i \sim N(0, 1) \tag{8.4}$$

or equivalently

$$dX_{dt} = \sqrt{dt}\, \epsilon_i', \quad \epsilon_i' \sim N(0, \sigma^2) \tag{8.5}$$

We are now in a position to provide a mathematical description of the movement of the pollen grains in water observed by Robert Brown in 1827. We will start by assuming that the container of water is perfectly level. This will ensure that there is no drift of the pollen grains in any particular direction. Let us denote the position of a particular pollen grain at time t by X_t, and set the position at $t = 0$, X_0, to zero. The statistical distribution of the grain's position, X_T, at some later time $t = T$, can be found as shown below.

We divide the time T into n equal intervals $dt = T/n$. Since the position of the particle changes by the amount $dX_i = \sigma\sqrt{dt}\, \epsilon_i$ over the ith time interval dt, the final position X_T is given by:

$$X_T = \sum_{i=1}^{n} \left(\sigma\sqrt{dt}\, \epsilon_i \right) = \sigma\sqrt{dt} \sum_{i=1}^{n} \epsilon_i$$

Since $\epsilon_i \sim N(0, 1)$, by the Law of Large numbers, see Appendix F.1, we have that the expected value of position X_T is:

$$E[X_T] = \sigma\sqrt{dt}\, E\left[\sum_{i=1}^{n} \epsilon_i \right] = 0$$

The variance of the position X_T is:

$$Var[X_T] = Var\left[\sigma\sqrt{dt} \sum_{i=1}^{n} \epsilon_i \right] = \sigma^2\, dt\, Var\left[\sum_{i=1}^{n} \epsilon_i \right] \tag{8.6}$$

Using the fact that $Var[\epsilon_i] = 1$ and that

$$Var\left[\sum_{i=1}^{n} X_i \right] = \sum_{i=1}^{n} Var[X_i],$$

see Appendix F.3, we have:

$$Var[X_T] = \sigma^2 dt \sum_{i=1}^{n} Var[\epsilon_i] = \sigma^2\, dt \sum_{i=1}^{n} 1 \tag{8.7}$$

which gives:

$$Var[X_T] = \sigma^2 n\, dt = T\sigma^2 \tag{8.8}$$

So, at time T, the position of the pollen grain, X_T is distributed as $X_T \sim N(0, T\sigma^2)$.

If the water container is not perfectly level then the pollen grains will exhibit drift in a particular direction. We can modify Equation 8.4 to take this into account as follows:

$$dX_{dt} = \mu dt + \sigma\sqrt{dt}\, \epsilon, \quad \epsilon_i \sim N(0, 1) \tag{8.9}$$

or equivalently

$$dX_{dt} = \mu dt + \sigma dZ_t, \quad dZ_t \sim N(0, dt) \tag{8.10}$$

where we have included the *constant* drift μ. Proceeding in a similar manner to that for the case of *zero drift* Brownian motion we have:

$$X_T = \sum_{i=1}^{n} \left(\mu dt + \sigma \sqrt{dt}\, \epsilon_i \right) = \mu \sum_{i=1}^{n} dt + \sigma \sqrt{dt} \sum_{i=1}^{n} \epsilon_i = \mu T + \sigma \sqrt{dt} \sum_{i=1}^{n} \epsilon_i$$

which gives

$$E[X_T] = E\left[\mu T + \sigma \sqrt{dt} \sum_{i=1}^{n} \epsilon_i \right] = \mu T + \sigma \sqrt{dt} E\left[\sum_{i=1}^{n} \epsilon_i \right] = \mu T$$

The variance of the position X_T is:

$$Var[X_T] = Var\left[\mu T + \sigma \sqrt{dt} \sum_{i=1}^{n} \epsilon_i \right] = Var\left[\sigma \sqrt{dt} \sum_{i=1}^{n} \epsilon_i \right]$$

Here we have used the fact (see Appendix F.3) that $Var[a + bX] = b^2 Var[X]$, where $a = \mu T$, and $b = 1$. From Equations 8.6 to 8.8 we have:

$$Var[X_T] = Var\left[\sigma \sqrt{dt} \sum_{i=1}^{n} \epsilon_i \right] = T\sigma^2$$

So, at time T, the position of the pollen grain, X_T is distributed as $X_T \sim N(\mu T, T\sigma^2)$.

8.3 A BROWNIAN MODEL OF ASSET PRICE MOVEMENTS

In the previous section we showed how Brownian motion can be used to describe the random motion of small particles suspended in a liquid. The first attempt at using Brownian motion to describe financial asset price movements was provided by Bachelier (1900). This however only had limited success because the *significance* of a given *absolute* change in asset price depends on the original asset price. For example a £1 increase in the value of a share originally worth £1.10 is much more *significant* than a £1 increase in the value of a share originally worth £100. It is for this reason that asset price movements are generally described in terms of *relative* or percentage changes. For example if the £1.10 share increases in value by 11 pence and the £100 share increases in value by £10, then both of these price changes have the same significance, and correspond to a 10 per cent increase in value. The idea of relative price changes in the value of a share can be formalized by defining a quantity called the *return*, R_t, of a share at time t. The return R_t is defined as follows:

$$R_t = \frac{S_{t+dt} - S_t}{S_t} = \frac{dS_t}{S_t} \tag{8.11}$$

where S_{t+dt} is the value of the share at time $t + dt$, S_t is the value of the share at time t, and dS_t is the change in value of the share over the time interval dt. The percentage return R^*, over the time interval dt is simply defined as $R^* = 100 \times R_t$.

We are now in a position to construct a simple Brownian model of asset price movements, further information on Brownian motion within finance can be found in Shreve *et al.* (1997).

The asset *return* at time t is now given by:

$$R_t = \frac{dS_t}{S_t} = \mu dt + \sigma dZ_t, \quad dZ_t \sim N(0, dt) \tag{8.12}$$

or equivalently:

$$dS_t = S_t \mu dt + S_t \sigma dZ_t \tag{8.13}$$

The process given in Equations 8.11 and 8.12 is termed *Geometric Brownian Motion*; which we will abbreviate as GBM. This is because the relative (rather than absolute) price changes follow Brownian motion.

We will now use Ito's lemma (see Section 8.4) which allows us to write down the process followed by the function $\phi(S, t)$, if the asset price S follows GBM. Ito's formula states, see Equation 8.21, that:

$$d\phi = \left(\mu S \frac{\partial \phi}{\partial S} + \frac{\partial \phi}{\partial t} + \frac{\sigma^2 S^2}{2} \frac{\partial^2 \phi}{\partial S^2} \right) dt + \frac{\partial \phi}{\partial S} \sigma S dZ$$

where $d\phi$ denotes the increment in the function $\phi(S, t)$ over the time interval dt. This means that if we choose $\phi(S, t) = \log(S)$, then we have:

$$\frac{\partial \phi}{\partial S} = \frac{\partial \log(S)}{\partial S} = \frac{1}{S}, \quad \frac{\partial^2 \phi}{\partial S^2} = \frac{\partial}{\partial S} \left(\frac{\partial \log(S)}{\partial S} \right) = \frac{\partial}{\partial S} \left(\frac{1}{S} \right) = -\frac{1}{S^2}$$

$$\frac{\partial \phi}{\partial t} = \frac{\partial \log(S)}{\partial t} = 0$$

Therefore if we let $Y = \log(S)$ we have:

$$dY = \log\left(\frac{S_{t+dt}}{S_t} \right) = \log(S_{t+dt}) - \log(S_t) = \left(\mu - \frac{\sigma^2}{2} \right) dt + \sigma dZ, \quad dZ \sim N(0, dt)$$

or equivalently

$$dY \sim N\left(\left\{ \mu - \frac{1}{2}\sigma^2 \right\} dt, \sigma^2 dt \right)$$

If we now substitute the riskless interest rate, r, for the drift in the asset price, μ, we obtain the following two equations:

$$\log\left(\frac{S_{t+dt}}{S_t} \right) = \left(r - \frac{\sigma^2}{2} \right) dt + \sigma dZ, \quad dZ \sim N(0, dt) \tag{8.14}$$

and

$$dY \sim N\left(\left\{ r - \frac{1}{2}\sigma^2 \right\} dt, \sigma^2 dt \right) \tag{8.15}$$

We have therefore shown that if the asset price follows GBM, then the logarithm of the asset price Y follows standard Brownian motion. Another way of stating this is that, over the time interval dt, the change in the logarithm of the asset price is a Gaussian distribution with mean $(r - \sigma^2/2)dt$ and variance $\sigma^2 dt$.

This is a very important result and will be referred to in later sections of the book.

8.4 ITO'S LEMMA IN ONE DIMENSION

In this section we will derive Ito's formula, a more rigorous treatment can be found in Shreve (1988).

Let us consider the stochastic process X:

$$dX = adt + bdZ = adt + b\sqrt{dt}\,\epsilon, \quad \epsilon \sim N(0,1), \quad dZ \sim N(0, dt) \tag{8.16}$$

where a and b are constants. We want to find the process followed by a function of the stochastic variable X, that is $\phi(X, t)$. This can be done by applying a Taylor expansion, up to second order, in the two variables X and t as follows:

$$\phi^* = \phi + \frac{\partial\phi}{\partial X}dX + \frac{\partial\phi}{\partial t}dt + \frac{1}{2}\frac{\partial^2\phi}{\partial X^2}dX^2 + \frac{1}{2}\frac{\partial^2\phi}{\partial t^2}dt^2 + \frac{\partial\phi}{\partial X\partial t}dX\,dt \tag{8.17}$$

where ϕ^* is used to denote the value $\phi(X + dX, t + dt)$, and ϕ denotes the value $\phi(X, t)$. We will now consider the magnitude of the terms dX^2, $dX\,dt$, and dt^2 as $dt \to 0$. First

$$dX^2 = (adt + b\sqrt{dt}\,\epsilon)(adt + b\sqrt{dt}\,\epsilon) = a^2 dt^2 + 2ab\,dt^{3/2}\,\epsilon + b^2 dt\epsilon^2$$

then

$$dX\,dt = adt^2 + b\,dt^{3/2}\,\epsilon$$

So as $dt \to 0$, and ignoring all terms in dt of order greater than 1, we have:

$$dX^2 \sim b^2 dt\,\epsilon^2, \quad dt^2 \sim 0, \quad \text{and} \quad dX dt \sim 0$$

If we now replace dX^2 by its expected value $E[dX^2]$ we then have:

$$dX^2 \sim E[dX^2] = E[b^2 dt\,\epsilon^2] = b^2 dt E[\epsilon^2] = b^2 dt$$

where we have used the fact that, since $\epsilon \sim N(0, 1)$, the variance of ϵ, $E[\epsilon^2]$, is by definition equal to 1. Using these values in Equation 8.17 and substituting for dX from Equation 8.16, we obtain:

$$d\phi = \frac{\partial\phi}{\partial X}(adt + bdZ) + \frac{\partial\phi}{\partial t}dt + \frac{b^2}{2}\frac{\partial^2\phi}{\partial X^2}dt \tag{8.18}$$

where $d\phi = \phi^* - \phi$. This gives Ito's formula

$$d\phi = \left(a\frac{\partial\phi}{\partial X} + \frac{\partial\phi}{\partial t} + \frac{b^2}{2}\frac{\partial^2\phi}{\partial X^2} \right)dt + \frac{\partial\phi}{\partial X}b\,dZ \qquad (8.19)$$

In particular if we consider the Geometric Brownian process:

$$dS = \mu S dt + \sigma S dZ \qquad (8.20)$$

where μ and σ are constants then substituting $X = S$, $a = \mu S$, and $b = \sigma S$ into Equation 8.19 yields:

$$d\phi = \left(\mu S\frac{\partial\phi}{\partial S} + \frac{\partial\phi}{\partial t} + \frac{\sigma^2 S^2}{2}\frac{\partial^2\phi}{\partial S^2} \right)dt + \frac{\partial\phi}{\partial S}\sigma S dZ \qquad (8.21)$$

Equation 8.21 describes the change in value of a function $\phi(S, t)$ over the time interval dt, when the stochastic variable S follows GBM. This result has very important applications in the pricing of financial derivatives. Here the function $\phi(S, t)$ is taken as the price of a financial derivative, $f(S, t)$, that depends on the value of an underlying asset S, which is assumed to follow GBM. In Section 9.3 we will use Equation 8.21 to derive the (Black–Scholes) partial differential equation that is satisfied by the price of a financial derivative.

8.5   ITO'S LEMMA IN MANY DIMENSIONS

We will now consider the *n*-dimensional stochastic process:

$$dX_i = a_i dt + b_i\sqrt{dt}\,\epsilon_i = a_i dt + b_i dZ_i, \quad i = 1,\dots,n \qquad (8.22)$$

or in vector form:

$$d\mathcal{X} = \mathcal{A}dt + \mathcal{B}\sqrt{dt}\,\mathcal{E} = \mathcal{A}dt + \mathcal{B}d\mathcal{Z} \qquad (8.23)$$

where $\mathcal{A}$ and $\mathcal{B}$ are *n* element vectors respectively containing the constants, a_i, $i = 1,\dots,n$ and b_i, $i = 1,\dots,n$. The stochastic vector $\mathcal{X}$ contains the *n* stochastic variables X_i, $i = 1,\dots,n$, the vector $\mathcal{E}$ contains the *n* shocks ϵ_i, $i = 1,\dots,n$, and the vector $d\mathcal{Z}$ contains the *n* shocks $\sqrt{dt}\,\epsilon_i$, $i = 1,\dots,n$.

We will assume that the random vector $\mathcal{E}$ is drawn from a multivariate normal distribution with zero mean and covariance matrix C. That is we can write:

$$\mathcal{E} \sim N(0, C) \quad \text{and} \quad d\mathcal{Z} \sim N(0, dt\,C)$$

Since the diagonal elements of C are all unity

$$C_{ii} = E[\epsilon_i^2] = 1, \quad i = 1,\dots,n$$

the matrix C is in fact a *correlation matrix* with off-diagonal elements given by:

$$C_{ij} = E[\epsilon_i\,\epsilon_j] = \rho_{i,j}, \quad i = 1,\dots,n, \quad j = 1,\dots,n, \quad i \neq j$$

where ρ_{ij} is the correlation coefficient between the *i*th and *j*th variates.

As in Section 8.4 we want to find the process followed by a function of the stochastic vector $\mathcal{X}$, that is the process followed by $\phi(\mathcal{X}, t)$. This can be done by applying any n-dimensional Taylor expansion, up to second order, in the variables $\mathcal{X}$ and t as follows:

$$\phi^* = \phi + \sum_{i=1}^{n} \frac{\partial \phi}{\partial X_i} dX_i + \frac{\partial \phi}{\partial t} dt + \frac{1}{2}\sum_{i=1}^{n}\sum_{j=1}^{n} \frac{\partial^2 \phi}{\partial X_i \partial X_j} dX_i dX_j + \frac{1}{2}\frac{\partial^2 \phi}{\partial t^2} dt^2$$

$$+ \sum_{i=1}^{n} \frac{\partial \phi}{\partial X_i \partial t} dX_i dt \tag{8.24}$$

where ϕ^* is used to denote the value $\phi(\mathcal{X} + d\mathcal{X}, t + dt)$, and ϕ denotes the value $\phi(\mathcal{X}, t)$. We will now consider the magnitude of the terms $dX_i dX_j$, $dX_i dt$, and dt^2 as $dt \to 0$. Expanding the terms $dX_i dX_j$ and $dX_i dt$ we have:

$$dX_i dX_j = (a_i dt + b_i \sqrt{dt}\,\epsilon_i)(a_j dt + b_j \sqrt{dt}\,\epsilon_j)$$

$$\therefore dX_i dX_j = a_i a_j dt^2 + a_i b_j\, dt^{3/2}\epsilon_j + a_j b_i\, dt^{3/2}\epsilon_i + b_i b_j\, dt\epsilon_i \epsilon_j$$

$$dX_i dt = a_i dt^2 + b_i dt^{3/2}\epsilon_i \tag{8.25}$$

So as $dt \to 0$, and ignoring all terms in dt of order greater than 1, we have:

$$dX_i dt \sim 0 \quad \text{and} \quad dX_i dX_j \sim b_i b_j dt\epsilon_i \epsilon_j$$

If we now replace $dX_i dX_j$ by its expected value $E[dX_i dX_j]$ we then have:

$$E[dX_i dX_j] = E[b_i b_j dt\epsilon_i \epsilon_j] = b_i b_j dt = E[\epsilon_i \epsilon_j] = b_i b_j \rho_{ij} dt$$

where ρ_{ij} is the correlation coefficient between the ith and jth assets.

Using these values in Equation 8.24, and substituting for dX_i from Equation 8.22, we obtain:

$$d\phi = \sum_{i=1}^{n} \frac{\partial \phi}{\partial X_i}(a_i dt + b_i dZ_i) + \frac{\partial \phi}{\partial t} dt + \frac{1}{2}\sum_{i=1}^{n}\sum_{j=1}^{n} b_i b_j \rho_{ij} dt \frac{\partial^2 \phi}{\partial X_i \partial X_j} \tag{8.26}$$

where we have used $d\phi = \phi^* - \phi$. This gives Ito's n-dimensional formula:

$$d\phi = \left\{ \frac{\partial \phi}{\partial t} + \sum_{i=1}^{n} a_i \frac{\partial \phi}{\partial X_i} + \frac{1}{2}\sum_{i=1}^{n}\sum_{j=1}^{n} b_i b_j \rho_{ij} \frac{\partial^2 \phi}{\partial X_i \partial X_j} \right\} dt + \sum_{i=1}^{n} \frac{\partial \phi}{\partial X_i} b_i dZ_i \tag{8.27}$$

In particular if we consider the GBM:

$$dS_i = \mu_i S_i dt + \sigma_i S_i dZ_i, \quad i = 1, \ldots, n$$

where μ_i is the constant drift of the ith asset and σ_i is the constant volatility of the ith asset, then substituting $X_i = S_i$, $a_i = \mu_i S_i$, and $b_i = \sigma_i S_i$ into Equation 8.27 then yields:

$$d\phi = \left\{ \frac{\partial \phi}{\partial t} + \sum_{i=1}^{n} \mu_i S_i \frac{\partial \phi}{\partial S_i} + \frac{1}{2} \sum_{i=1}^{n} \sum_{j=1}^{n} \sigma_i \sigma_j S_i S_j \rho_{ij} \frac{\partial^2 \phi}{\partial S_i \partial S_j} \right\} dt$$

$$+ \sum_{i=1}^{n} \frac{\partial \phi}{\partial S_i} \sigma_i S_i dZ_i \qquad (8.28)$$

Chapter 9

Analytic methods and single asset European options

9.1 INTRODUCTION

A European option taken out at current time t gives the owner the right (but no obligation) to do *something* when the option *matures* at time T. This could for example be the right to buy or sell stocks at a particular *strike* price. The option would of course only be exercised if it was in the owner's interest to do so. For example a single asset European *vanilla put* option, with strike price E and *expiry* time T, gives the owner the right at time T to sell a particular asset for E. If the asset is worth S_T at maturity then the value of the put option at maturity, known as the *payoff*, is thus $\max(E - S_T, 0)$. By contrast a single asset European vanilla *call* option, with strike price E and expiry time T, gives the owner the right at time T to buy an asset for E; the payoff at maturity for a call option is $\max(S_T - E, 0)$.

The owner of an American option has the right (but no obligation) to exercise the option *at any time* from current time t to option maturity. These options are more difficult to value than European options because of this extra flexibility. Even the *simple* single asset American vanilla put has no analytic solution and requires finite-difference or lattice methods to estimate its value. Many European options on the other hand take the form of a *relatively easy* definite integral from which it is possible to compute a closed form solution. The valuation of multiasset European options, dependent on a large number of underlying assets, is more complicated but can conveniently be achieved by using Monte Carlo simulation to compute the required multidimensional definite integral.

The expected *current value* of a single asset European vanilla option will depend on the current asset price at time t, S, the duration of the option, $\tau = T - t$, the strike price, E, the riskless interest rate, r, and the probability density function of the underlying asset price at maturity, $p(S_T)$. The fair price (expected current value) of a vanilla call is thus:

$$c(S, E, \tau, r, p(S_T)) = \exp(-r\tau)E[\max(S_T - E, 0)] \tag{9.1}$$

$$= \exp(-r\tau) \int_{-\infty}^{\infty} p(S_T) \max(E - S_T, 0) dS_T \tag{9.2}$$

and that of the put is:

$$p(S, E, \tau, r, p(S_T)) = \exp(-r\tau)E[\max(E - S_T, 0)] \tag{9.3}$$

$$= \exp(-r\tau)\int_{-\infty}^{\infty} p(S_T)\max(E - S_T, 0)dS_T \tag{9.4}$$

It can be seen from Equations 9.1 to 9.4 that the fair price of a European option is its payoff, at time T, discounted by the riskless interest rate, r, to current time t.

Since we assume that r is constant throughout the duration of the option and also that the underlying asset has a given distribution (usually lognormal), we will denote the value of a European vanilla call option by $c(S, E, \tau)$, and that of a European put option by $p(S, E, \tau)$.

In this section we will consider:

- The put–call parity relationship for European options.
- The differential equation obeyed by single asset and multiasset European options.
- The Black–Scholes option pricing formula for a single asset European option.
- The pricing formulae for some European barrier options.

The notation used will be that which we have previously outlined.

9.2   PUT–CALL PARITY

9.2.1   Discrete dividends

Here we consider single asset European put and call options, and derive the following relationship between their values in the presence of cash dividends:

$$c(S, E, \tau) + E\exp(-r\tau) + D = p(S, E, \tau) + S \tag{9.5}$$

where D is the *present value* of the dividends that are paid during the life of the option. That is:

$$D = \sum_{k=1}^{n} D_k \exp(-r(t_k - t))$$

with D_k the kth cash dividend paid at time t_k; the other symbols have already been defined in the section introduction.

This result can be proved by considering the following two investments:

Portfolio A

One European call, $c(S, E, \tau)$, and cash of value $E\exp(-r\tau) + D$.

Portfolio B

One European put, $p(S, E, \tau)$, and one share of value S.

At option maturity, time T, the value of the call and put are $c(S_T, E, 0)$ and $p(S_T, E, 0)$ respectively; also at time T the value of the dividends paid during the life of the option is $D\exp(r\tau)$.

We now consider the value of both portfolios at option maturity, time T, under all possible conditions.

If $S_T \geq E$

Portfolio A is worth:

$$\max(S_T - E, 0) + \exp(r\tau)\{E\exp(-r\tau) + D\} = S_T - E + E + D\exp(r\tau)$$
$$= S_T + D\exp(r\tau)$$

Portfolio B is worth:

$$\max(E - S_T, 0) + S_T + D\exp(r\tau) = 0 + S_T + D\exp(r\tau) = S_T + D\exp(r\tau)$$

If $S_T < E$

Portfolio A is worth:

$$\max(S_T - E, 0) + \exp(r\tau)\{E\exp(-r\tau) + D\} = 0 + E + D\exp(r\tau) = E + D\exp(r\tau)$$

Portfolio B is worth:

$$\max(E - S_T, 0) + S_T + D\exp(r\tau) = E - S_T + S_T + D\exp(r\tau) = E + D\exp(r\tau)$$

We have therefore shown that under all conditions the value of portfolio A is the same as that of portfolio B.

9.2.2 Continuous dividends

Here we consider single asset European put and call options, and derive the following relationship:

$$c(S, E, \tau) + E\exp(-r\tau) = p(S, E, \tau) + S\exp(-q\tau) \tag{9.6}$$

where q is the asset's continuous dividend yield that is paid during the life of the option. The result can be proved by considering the following two investments:

Portfolio A

One European call, $c(S, E, \tau)$, and cash of value $E\exp(-r\tau)$.

Portfolio B

One European put, $p(S, E, \tau)$, and one share of value $S\exp(-q\tau)$.

At option expiry, time t, the value of the call and put are $c(S_T, E, 0)$ and $p(S_T, E, 0)$ respectively. Also, if the value of the share at time t is denoted by S, the combined value of shares and dividends at time T is $S\exp(q\tau)$. Note that q is treated in a similar manner to the continuously compounded riskless interest rate r.

As in Section 9.2.1 we will now consider the value of portfolios A and B at time T under all possible conditions:

If $S_T \geq E$

Portfolio A is worth:

$$\max(S_T - E, 0) + \exp(r\tau)E\exp(-r\tau) = S_T - E + E = S_T$$

Portfolio B is worth:

$$\max(E - S_T, 0) + S_T\exp(-q\tau)\exp(q\tau) = 0 + S_T = S_T$$

where $S_T\exp(-q\tau)\exp(q\tau)$ is the combined value of the shares and dividends at option maturity.

If $S_T < E$

Portfolio A is worth:

$$\max(S_T - E, 0) + \exp(r\tau)E\exp(-r\tau) = 0 + E = E$$

Portfolio B is worth:

$$\max(E - S_T, 0) + S_T\exp(-q\tau)\exp(q\tau) = E - S_T + S_T = E$$

We have therefore shown that under all conditions the value of portfolio A is the same as that of portfolio B.

9.3   VANILLA OPTIONS AND THE BLACK–SCHOLES MODEL

9.3.1   The option pricing partial differential equation

In this section we will derive the (Black–Scholes) partial differential equation that is obeyed by options written on a single asset.

Previously, in Sections 8.4 and 8.5, we derived Ito's lemma, which provides an expression for the change in value of the function $\phi(X, t)$, where X is a stochastic variable. When the stochastic variable, X, follows GBM, the change in the value of ϕ was shown to be given by Equation 8.21. Here we will assume that the function $\phi(S, t)$ is the value of a financial option and that the price of the underlying asset, S, follows GBM.

If we denote the value of the financial derivative by f, then its change, df, over the time interval dt is given by:

$$df = \left(\mu S\frac{\partial f}{\partial S} + \frac{\partial f}{\partial t} + \frac{\sigma^2 S^2}{2}\frac{\partial^2 f}{\partial S^2}\right) dt + \frac{\partial f}{\partial S}\sigma S dZ, \quad dZ \sim N(0, dt)$$

The discretized version of this equation is:

$$\Delta f = \Delta t\left(\mu S\frac{\partial f}{\partial S} + \frac{\partial f}{\partial t} + \frac{\sigma^2 S^2}{2}\frac{\partial^2 f}{\partial S^2}\right) + \frac{\partial f}{\partial S}\sigma S dZ, \quad dZ \sim N(0, \Delta t) \tag{9.7}$$

where the time interval is now Δt and the change in derivative value is Δf.

If we assume that the asset price, S, follows GBM we also have:

$$\Delta S = \mu S\Delta t + \sigma S\Delta Z, \quad \Delta Z \sim N(0, \Delta t) \tag{9.8}$$

where μ is the constant drift and the definition of the other symbols is as before. Let us now consider a portfolio consisting of -1 derivative and $\partial f/\partial S$ units of the underlying stock. In other words we have gone *short* (that is sold) a derivative on an asset and have $\partial f/\partial S$ stocks of the (same) underlying asset. The value of the portfolio, Π, is therefore:

$$\Pi = -f + \frac{\partial f}{\partial S} S \tag{9.9}$$

and the change, $\Delta\Pi$, in the value of the portfolio over time Δt is:

$$\Delta\Pi = -\Delta f + \frac{\partial f}{\partial S}\Delta S \tag{9.10}$$

Substituting Equations 9.7 and 9.8 into Equation 9.10 we obtain:

$$\Delta\Pi = -\left(\mu S\frac{\partial f}{\partial S} + \frac{\partial f}{\partial t} + \frac{1}{2}\sigma^2 S^2 \frac{\partial^2 f}{\partial S^2}\right)\Delta t - \sigma S\Delta Z\frac{\partial f}{\partial S} + \frac{\partial f}{\partial S}\{\mu S\Delta t + \sigma S\Delta Z\}$$

$$\therefore \Delta\Pi = -\mu S\Delta t\frac{\partial f}{\partial S} - \Delta t\frac{\partial f}{\partial t} - \frac{1}{2}\Delta t\sigma^2 S^2 \frac{\partial^2 f}{\partial S^2} - \sigma S\Delta Z\frac{\partial f}{\partial S}$$

$$+ \mu S\Delta t\frac{\partial f}{\partial S} + \sigma S\Delta Z\frac{\partial f}{\partial S} \tag{9.11}$$

Cancelling terms we obtain:

$$\Delta\Pi = -\Delta t\left\{\frac{\partial f}{\partial t} + \frac{1}{2}\sigma^2 S^2 \frac{\partial^2 f}{\partial S^2}\right\} \tag{9.12}$$

If this portfolio is risk neutral then it grows at the riskless interest rate, r and we have:

$$r\Pi\Delta t = \Delta\Pi$$

So we have that:

$$r\Pi\Delta t = -\Delta t\left\{\frac{\partial f}{\partial t} + \frac{1}{2}\sigma^2 S^2 \frac{\partial^2 f}{\partial S^2}\right\} \tag{9.13}$$

Substituting for Π and we obtain:

$$r\Delta t\left(f - S\frac{\partial f}{\partial S}\right) = -\Delta t\left\{\frac{\partial f}{\partial t} + \frac{1}{2}\sigma^2 S^2 \frac{\partial^2 f}{\partial S^2}\right\} \tag{9.14}$$

On rearranging we have:

The Black–Scholes partial differential equation

$$\frac{\partial f}{\partial t} + S\frac{\partial f}{\partial S} + \frac{1}{2}\sigma^2 S^2 \frac{\partial^2 f}{\partial S^2} = rf \tag{9.15}$$

Let us now consider put and call options on the same underlying asset. If we let c be the value of a European call option and p that of a European put option then we have the following equations:

$$\frac{\partial p}{\partial t} + S\frac{\partial p}{\partial S} + \frac{1}{2}\sigma^2 S^2 \frac{\partial^2 p}{\partial S^2} = rp \tag{9.16}$$

and

$$\frac{\partial c}{\partial t} + S\frac{\partial c}{\partial S} + \frac{1}{2}\sigma^2 S^2 \frac{\partial^2 c}{\partial S^2} = rc \tag{9.17}$$

If we now form a linear combination of put and call options, $\Psi = a_1 c + a_2 p$, where both a_1 and a_2 are constants, then Ψ also obeys the Black–Scholes equation:

$$\frac{\partial \Psi}{\partial t} + S\frac{\partial \Psi}{\partial S} + \frac{1}{2}\sigma^2 S^2 \frac{\partial^2 \Psi}{\partial S^2} = r\Psi \tag{9.18}$$

We will now prove that Ψ satisfies Equation 9.15.

First we rewrite Equation 9.15 as:

$$\frac{\partial(a_1 c + a_2 p)}{\partial t} + S\frac{\partial(a_1 c + a_2 p)}{\partial S} + \frac{1}{2}\sigma^2 S^2 \frac{\partial^2(a_1 c + a_2 p)}{\partial S^2} = r(a_1 c + a_2 p) \tag{9.19}$$

and use the following results from elementary calculus:

$$\frac{\partial(a_1 c + a_2 p)}{\partial t} = a_1 \frac{\partial c}{\partial t} + a_2 \frac{\partial p}{\partial t}$$

$$\frac{\partial(a_1 c + a_2 p)}{\partial S} = a_1 \frac{\partial c}{\partial S} + a_2 \frac{\partial p}{\partial S}$$

and

$$\frac{\partial^2(a_1 c + a_2 p)}{\partial S^2} = a_1 \frac{\partial^2 c}{\partial S^2} + a_2 \frac{\partial^2 p}{\partial S^2}$$

If we denote the left hand side of Equation 9.15 by LHS, then we have:

$$\text{LHS} = a_1 \left\{ \frac{\partial c}{\partial t} + S\frac{\partial c}{\partial S} + \frac{1}{2}\sigma^2 S^2 \frac{\partial^2 c}{\partial S^2} \right\} + a_2 \left\{ \frac{\partial p}{\partial t} + S\frac{\partial p}{\partial S} + \frac{1}{2}\sigma^2 S^2 \frac{\partial^2 p}{\partial S^2} \right\} \tag{9.20}$$

We now use Equations 9.13 and 9.14 to substitute for the values in the curly brackets in Equation 9.19, and we obtain:

$$\text{LHS} = a_1 rc + a_2 rp \tag{9.21}$$

which is just the LHS of Equation 9.21; so we have proved the result. It should be noted that this result is also true for American options, since they also obey the Black–Scholes equation.

The above result can be generalized to include a portfolio consisting of n single asset options. Here we have:

$$\Psi = \sum_{j=1}^{n} a_j f_j, \quad j = 1, \ldots, n$$

where f_j represents the value of the jth derivative and a_j is the number of units of the jth derivative. To prove that Ψ follows the Black–Scholes equation we simply partition the portfolio into sectors whose options depend on the same underlying asset. We then proceed as before by showing that the value of each individual sector obeys the Black–Scholes equation and thus the value of the complete portfolio (the sum of the values of all the sectors) obeys the Black–Scholes equation. It should be mentioned that this result applies for both American and European options and it doesn't matter whether we have bought or sold the options.

In Section 10.3.2 we will use the fact that the difference between the value of a European option and the equivalent American option obeys the Black–Scholes equation. We can see this immediately by considering the following portfolios that are long in an American option and short (that is have sold) a European option:

$$\Psi^p = P - p, \quad \Psi^c = C - c$$

where P and C are the values of American put and call options. Ψ^p and Ψ^c both obey the Black–Scholes equations, and are the respective differences in value of American/European put options and American/European call options.

9.3.2 The multiasset option pricing partial differential equation

In this section we will derive the multiasset (Black–Scholes) partial differential equation that is obeyed by options written on n assets. Proceeding as in Section 9.3.1 we will use the n-dimensional version of Ito's lemma to find the process followed by the the value of a multiasset financial derivative. We will denote the value of this derivative by $f(S, t)$, where S is a n element stochastic vector containing the prices of the underlying assets, S_i, $i = 1, \ldots, n$. If we assume that S follows n-dimensional GBM then the change in the value of the derivative, df, is (see Section 8.5, Equation 8.28) given by:

$$df = \left\{ \frac{\partial f}{\partial t} + \sum_{i=1}^{n} \mu_i S_i \frac{\partial f}{\partial S_i} + \frac{1}{2} \sum_{i=1}^{n} \sum_{j=1}^{n} \sigma_i \sigma_j S_i S_j \rho_{ij} \frac{\partial^2 f}{\partial S_i \partial S_j} \right\} dt + \sum_{i=1}^{n} \frac{\partial f}{\partial S_i} \sigma_i S_i dZ_i \quad (9.22)$$

The discretized version of this equation is:

$$\Delta f = \left\{ \frac{\partial f}{\partial t} + \sum_{i=1}^{n} \mu_i S_i \frac{\partial f}{\partial S_i} + \frac{1}{2} \sum_{i=1}^{n} \sum_{j=1}^{n} \sigma_i \sigma_j S_i S_j \rho_{ij} \frac{\partial^2 f}{\partial S_i \partial S_j} \right\} \Delta t + \sum_{i=1}^{n} \frac{\partial f}{\partial S_i} \sigma_i S_i \Delta Z_i \quad (9.23)$$

where the time interval is now Δt and the change in derivative value is Δf.

Let us now consider a portfolio consisting of -1 derivative and $\partial f / \partial S_i$ units of the ith underlying stock. In other words we have gone *short* (that is sold) a derivative that depends on the price, $S_i, i = 1, \ldots, n$, of n underlying assets, and have $\partial f / \partial S_i$ units of the ith asset. The value of the portfolio, Π, is therefore:

$$\Pi = -f + \sum_{i=1}^{n} \frac{\partial f}{\partial S_i} S_i \quad (9.24)$$

and the change, $\Delta \Pi$, in the value of the portfolio over the time interval Δt is:

$$\Delta \Pi = -\Delta f + \sum_{i=1}^{n} \frac{\partial f}{\partial S_i} \Delta S_i \quad (9.25)$$

Since the stochastic variables $S_i, i = 1, \ldots, n$ follow n-dimensional GBM the change in the ith asset price, ΔS_i over the time interval Δt is given by:

$$\Delta S_i = \mu_i S_i \Delta t + \sigma_i S_i \Delta Z_i, \quad i = 1, \ldots, n \quad (9.26)$$

where $\Delta Z_i = \epsilon_i \sqrt{\Delta t}$ and, as in Section 8.5, we write:

$$E[\epsilon_i^2] = 1, \quad i = 1, \ldots, n$$

and

$$E[\epsilon_i \, \epsilon_j] = \rho_{i,j}, \quad i = 1, \ldots, n, \quad j = 1, \ldots, n, \quad i \neq j$$

Substituting Equations 9.23 and 9.26 into Equation 9.25 we obtain:

$$\Delta\Pi = -\left\{ \frac{\partial f}{\partial t} + \sum_{i=1}^{n} \mu_i S_i \frac{\partial f}{\partial S_i} + \frac{1}{2} \sum_{i=1}^{n} \sum_{j=1}^{n} \sigma_i \sigma_j \rho_{ij} S_i S_j \frac{\partial^2 f}{\partial S_i \partial S_j} \right\} \Delta t$$

$$- \sum_{i=1}^{n} \sigma_i S_i \Delta Z_i \frac{\partial f}{\partial S_i} + \sum_{i=1}^{n} \frac{\partial f}{\partial S_i} \{ \mu_i S_i \Delta t + \sigma S_i \Delta Z_i \}$$

$$\therefore \Delta\Pi = -\sum_{i=1}^{n} \mu_i S_i \Delta t \frac{\partial f}{\partial S_i} - \Delta t \frac{\partial f}{\partial t} - \frac{1}{2} \Delta t \sum_{i=1}^{n} \sum_{j=1}^{n} \sigma_i \sigma_j \rho_{ij} S_i S_j \frac{\partial^2 f}{\partial S_i \partial S_j}$$

$$- \sum_{i=1}^{n} \sigma_i S_i \Delta Z_i \frac{\partial f}{\partial S_i} + \sum_{i=1}^{n} \mu_i S_i \Delta t \frac{\partial f}{\partial S_i} + \sum_{i=1}^{n} \sigma_i S_i \Delta Z_i \frac{\partial f}{\partial S_i} \tag{9.27}$$

Cancelling terms we obtain:

$$\Delta\Pi = -\Delta t \left\{ \frac{\partial f}{\partial t} + \frac{1}{2} \sum_{i=1}^{n} \sum_{j=1}^{n} \sigma_i \sigma_j \rho_{ij} S_i S_j \frac{\partial^2 f}{\partial S_i \partial S_j} \right\} \tag{9.28}$$

If this portfolio is to grow at the riskless interest rate, r we have:

$$r\Pi\Delta t = \Delta\Pi$$

So from Equation 9.28 we have that:

$$r\Pi\Delta t = -\Delta t \left\{ \frac{\partial f}{\partial t} + \frac{1}{2} \sum_{i=1}^{n} \sum_{j=1}^{n} \sigma_i \sigma_j \rho_{ij} S_i S_j \frac{\partial^2 f}{\partial S_i \partial S_j} \right\} \tag{9.29}$$

Substituting for Π and we obtain:

$$r\Delta t \left\{ f - \sum_{i=1}^{n} S_i \frac{\partial f}{\partial S_i} \right\} = -\Delta t \left\{ \frac{\partial f}{\partial t} + \frac{1}{2} \sum_{i=1}^{n} \sum_{j=1}^{n} \sigma_i \sigma_j \rho_{ij} S_i S_j \frac{\partial^2 f}{\partial S_i \partial S_j} \right\} \tag{9.30}$$

Rearranging Equation 9.30 gives:

The *n*-dimensional Black–Scholes partial differential equation

$$\frac{\partial f}{\partial t} + \sum_{i=1}^{n} S_i \frac{\partial f}{\partial S_i} + \frac{1}{2}\sum_{i=1}^{n}\sum_{j=1}^{n} \sigma_i \sigma_j \rho_{ij} S_i S_j \frac{\partial^2 f}{\partial S_i \partial S_j} = rf \qquad (9.31)$$

9.3.3 The Black–Scholes formula

In this section we will derive the Black–Scholes formula for pricing European put and call options on a single asset which follows GBM. The approach we will adopt here is to first derive an expression for the value of a European call option, and then use the put/call parity relationships of Section 9.2 to obtain the value of the corresponding European put option. If we denote the current time by t and the expiry time of the option by T, then the duration of the option is $\tau = T - t$. Since the asset is assumed to follow GBM we can use a discretized version of Equations 8.14 and 8.15 in Section 8.3 to write:

$$\log\left(\frac{S_{t+\Delta t}}{S_t}\right) \sim N\left(\left\{r - \frac{1}{2}\sigma^2\right\}\Delta t, \sigma^2 \Delta t\right) \qquad (9.32)$$

Here we use the following notation:

$$\Delta t = \tau, \quad S_t = S, \quad \text{and} \quad S_{t+\Delta t} = S_T$$

where S is the asset value at the current time t, and S_T is the asset value at option maturity. We will now introduce the variable X which we define as follows:

$$X = \log\left(\frac{S_T}{S}\right) \quad \text{or equivalently} \quad S_T = S \exp(X)$$

From Equation 9.32 we have that

$$X \sim N((r - \sigma^2/2)\tau, \sigma^2 \tau)$$

The probability density function of X, $f(X)$, is thus the Gaussian:

$$f(X) = \frac{1}{\sigma\sqrt{\tau}\sqrt{2\pi}}\exp\left(-\frac{(X - (r - \sigma^2/2)\tau)^2}{2\sigma^2 \tau}\right)$$

The value of a European call option, $c(S, E, \tau)$, with strike price E, is the expected value of the option's payoff at maturity discounted to the current time by the riskless interest rate r. That is:

$$c(S, E, \tau) = \exp(-r\tau)E[S_T - E]$$

This can be rewritten in terms of the probability density function of S_T as follows:

$$c(S, E, \tau) = \exp(-r\tau) \int_{S_T = E}^{\infty} f(S_T)(S_T - E)dS_T \tag{9.33}$$

Instead of integrating over values of S_T, as above, we will use $S_T = S \exp(X)$ and then integrate over X. Equation 9.33 then becomes:

$$c(S, E, \tau) = \frac{\exp(-r\tau)}{\sigma\sqrt{\tau}\sqrt{2\pi}} \int_{X = \log(E/S)}^{\infty} (S\exp(X) - E)$$

$$\times \exp\left(-\frac{(X - (r - \sigma^2/2)\tau)^2}{2\sigma^2\tau}\right) dX \tag{9.34}$$

where we have used $S\exp(X) = E$, giving $X = \log(E/S)$, to obtain the lower limit of the integral. This integral is evaluated by splitting it into the two parts:

$$c(S, E, \tau) = I_A - I_B \tag{9.35}$$

where

$$I_A = \frac{S\exp(-r\tau)}{\sigma\sqrt{\tau}\sqrt{2\pi}} \int_{X = \log(E/S)}^{\infty} \exp(X) \exp\left(-\frac{\{X - (r - \sigma^2/2)\tau\}^2}{2\sigma^2\tau}\right) dX \tag{9.36}$$

and

$$I_B = \frac{E\exp(-r\tau)}{\sigma\sqrt{\tau}\sqrt{2\pi}} \int_{X = \log(E/S)}^{\infty} \exp\left(-\frac{\{X - (r - \sigma^2/2)\tau\}^2}{2\sigma^2\tau}\right) EdX \tag{9.37}$$

To evaluate these integrals we will make use of the fact that the univariate cumulative normal function $N_1(x)$ is:

$$N_1(x) = \frac{1}{\sqrt{2\pi}} \int_{u = -\infty}^{x} \exp\left(-\frac{u^2}{2}\right) du$$

by symmetry we have $N_1(-x) = 1 - N_1(x)$ and

$$\frac{1}{\sqrt{2\pi}} \int_{x}^{\infty} \exp\left(-\frac{u^2}{2}\right) du = \frac{1}{\sqrt{2\pi}} \int_{-\infty}^{-x} \exp\left(-\frac{u^2}{2}\right) du = N_1(-x)$$

We will first consider I_B, which is the easier of the two integrals.

$$I_B = \frac{E\exp(-r\tau)}{\sigma\sqrt{\tau}\sqrt{2\pi}} \int_{X = \log(E/S)}^{\infty} \exp\left(-\frac{\{X - (r - \sigma^2/2)\tau\}^2}{2\sigma^2\tau}\right) dX$$

If we let $u = (X - (r - \sigma^2/2)\tau)/\sigma\sqrt{\tau}$ then $dX = \sigma\sqrt{\tau}du$. So

$$I_B = \frac{E\exp(-r\tau)\sigma\sqrt{\tau}}{\sigma\sqrt{2\pi}\sqrt{\tau}} \int_{u = k_2}^{\infty} \exp\left(-\frac{u^2}{2}\right) du$$

where the lower integration limit is $k_2 = (\log(E/S) - (r - \sigma^2/2)\tau)/\sigma\sqrt{\tau}$.

We therefore have:

$$I_B = E \exp(-r\tau) N_1(-k_2)$$

(9.38)

We will now consider the integral I_A.

$$I_A = \frac{S \exp(-r\tau)}{\sigma\sqrt{\tau}\sqrt{2\pi}} \int_{X=\log(E/S)}^{\infty} \exp(X) \exp\left(-\frac{\{X - (r - \sigma^2/2)\tau\}^2}{2\sigma^2\tau}\right) dX$$

Rearranging the integrand:

$$I_A = \frac{\exp(-r\tau)}{\sigma\sqrt{\tau}\sqrt{2\pi}} \int_{X=\log(E/S)}^{\infty} \exp\left(-\frac{\{X - (r - \sigma^2/2)\tau\}^2 - 2\sigma^2\tau X}{2\sigma^2\tau}\right) dX$$

(9.39)

Expanding the terms in the exponential:

$$\{X - (r - \sigma^2/2)\tau\}^2 - 2\sigma^2\tau X = X^2 - 2\{(r - \sigma^2/2)\tau\}X + \{(r - \sigma^2/2)\tau\}^2 - 2\sigma^2\tau X$$

$$= X^2 - 2\{(r + \sigma^2/2)\tau\}X + \{(r - \sigma^2/2)\tau\}^2$$

$$= \{X - (r + \sigma^2/2)\tau\}^2 + \{(r - \sigma^2/2)\tau\}^2 - \{(r + \sigma^2/2)\tau\}^2$$

which results in:

$$\{X - (r - \sigma^2/2)\tau\}^2 - 2\sigma^2\tau X = \{X - (r + \sigma^2/2)\tau\}^2 - 2\sigma^2 r\tau^2$$

(9.40)

Substituting Equation 9.47 into the integrand of Equation 9.45 we have:

$$\exp(X) \exp\left(-\frac{\{X - (r - \sigma^2/2)\tau\}^2}{2\sigma^2\tau}\right) = \exp(r\tau) \exp\left(-\frac{\{X - (r + \sigma^2/2)\tau\}^2}{2\sigma^2\tau}\right)$$

The integral I_A can therefore be expressed as:

$$I_A = \frac{S \exp(r\tau) \exp(-r\tau)}{\sigma\tau\sqrt{2\pi}} \int_{X=\log(E/S)}^{\infty} \exp\left(-\frac{\{X - (r + \sigma^2/2)\tau\}^2}{2\sigma^2\tau}\right) dX$$

If we let $u = (X - (r + \sigma^2/2)\tau)/\sigma\sqrt{\tau}$ then $dX = \sigma\sqrt{\tau}du$. So

$$I_A = \frac{S\sigma\sqrt{\tau}}{\sigma\sqrt{2\pi}\sqrt{\tau}} \int_{u=k_1}^{\infty} \exp\left(-\frac{u^2}{2}\right) du$$

where the lower limit of integration is $k_1 = (\log(E/S) - (r + \sigma^2/2)\tau)/\sigma\sqrt{\tau}$.
We therefore have:

$$I_A = SN_1(-k_1)$$

(9.41)

Therefore the value of a European call is:

$$c(S, E, \tau) = SN_1(-k_1) - E \exp(-r\tau) N_1(-k_2)$$

which gives the usual form of the Black–Scholes formula for a European call as:

The Black–Scholes formula for a European call

$$c(S, E, \tau) = SN_1(d_1) - E\exp(-r\tau)N_1(d_2) \qquad (9.42)$$

where

$$d_1 = \frac{\log(S/E) + (r + \sigma^2/2)\tau}{\sigma\sqrt{\tau}} \quad \text{and}$$

$$d_2 = \frac{\log(S/E) + (r - \sigma^2/2)\tau}{\sigma\sqrt{\tau}} = d_1 - \sigma\sqrt{\tau} \qquad (9.43)$$

To gain some insight into the meaning we will rewrite the above equation in the following form:

$$c(S, E, \tau) = \exp(-r\tau)\{SN_1(d_1)\exp(r\tau) - EN_1(d_2)\} \qquad (9.44)$$

The term $N_1(d_2)$ is the probability that the option will be exercised in a risk-neutral world, so that $EN_1(d_2)$ is the strike price multiplied by the probability that the strike price will be paid. The term $SN_1(d_1)\exp(r\tau)$ is the expected value of a variable, in a risk neutral world, that equals S_T if $S_T > E$ and is otherwise zero.

The corresponding formula for a put can be shown using put–call parity, see Section 9.2, to be:

The Black–Scholes formula for a European put

$$p(S, E, \tau) = E\exp(-r\tau)N_1(-d_2) - SN_1(-d_1) \qquad (9.45)$$

where

$$d_1 = \frac{\log(S/E) + (r + \sigma^2/2)\tau}{\sigma\sqrt{\tau}} \quad \text{and}$$

$$d_2 = \frac{\log(S/E) + (r - \sigma^2/2)\tau}{\sigma\sqrt{\tau}} = d_1 - \sigma\sqrt{\tau} \qquad (9.46)$$

or equivalently, using $N_1(-x) = 1 - N_1(x)$ we have

$$p(S, E, \tau) = E\exp(-r\tau)\{1 - N_1(d_2)\} - S\{1 - N_1(d_1)\} \qquad (9.47)$$

The inclusion of continuous dividends

The effect of dividends on the value of a European option can be dealt with by assuming that the asset price is the sum of a riskless component involving known dividends that will be paid during the life of the option, and a risky (stochastic) component; see Hull (1997).

As dividends are paid the stock price is reduced by the same amount, and by the time the European option matures, all the dividends will have been paid leaving only the risky component of the asset price.

This means that, in the case of a continuous dividend yield q, European put/call options can be priced using Equations 9.42 and 9.45 but with S replaced by $S\exp(-q\tau)$.

This results in:

The Black–Scholes formula with continuous dividends

$$c(S,E,\tau) = S\exp(-q\tau)N_1(d_1) - E\exp(-r\tau)N_1(d_2) \tag{9.48}$$

and the corresponding formula for a put can be shown (using put–call parity) to be:

$$p(S,E,\tau) = E\exp(-r\tau)N_1(-d_2) - S\exp(-q\tau)N_1(-d_1) \tag{9.49}$$

or equivalently, using $N_1(-x) = 1 - N_1(x)$, we have

$$p(S,E,\tau) = E\exp(-r\tau)\{1 - N_1(d_2)\} - S\exp(-q\tau)\{1 - N_1(d_1)\} \tag{9.50}$$

where

$$d_1 = \frac{\log(S/E) + (r - q + \sigma^2/2)\tau}{\sigma\sqrt{\tau}} \quad\text{and}$$

$$d_2 = \frac{\log(S/E) + (r - q - \sigma^2/2)\tau}{\sigma\sqrt{\tau}} = d_1 - \sigma\sqrt{\tau}$$

The above values of d_1 and d_2 are obtained by simply substituting $S = S\exp(-q\tau)$ into Equation 9.43 as follows:

$$d_1 = \frac{\log(S\exp(-q\tau)/E) + (r + \sigma^2/2)\tau}{\sigma\sqrt{(T-t)}} = \frac{\log(S/E) - q\tau + (r + \sigma^2/2)\tau}{\sigma\sqrt{\tau}}$$

$$d_2 = \frac{\log(S\exp(-q\tau)/E) + (r - \sigma^2/2)\tau}{\sigma\sqrt{\tau}} = \frac{\log(S/E) - q\tau + (r - \sigma^2/2)\tau}{\sigma\sqrt{\tau}}$$

The inclusion of discrete dividends

Here we consider n discrete cash dividends $D_i, i = 1,\ldots,n$, paid at times t_i, $i = 1,\ldots,n$ during the life of the option. In these circumstances the Black–Scholes formula can be used to price European options, but with the current asset value S reduced by the present value of the cash dividends.

This means that instead of S we use the quantity S_D which is computed as

$$S_D = S - \sum_{i=1}^{n} D_i\exp(-rt_i)$$

where r is the (in this case constant) riskless interest rate. The formulae for European puts and calls are then

$$c(S, E, \tau) = S_D N_1(d_1) - E \exp(-r\tau) N_1(d_2) \tag{9.51}$$

$$p(S, E, \tau) = E \exp(-r\tau)\{1 - N_1(d_2)\} - S_D\{1 - N_1(d_1)\} \tag{9.52}$$

where

$$d_1 = \frac{\log(S_D/E) + (r + \sigma^2/2)\tau}{\sigma\sqrt{\tau}} \quad \text{and}$$

$$d_2 = \frac{\log(S_D/E) + (r - \sigma^2/2)\tau}{\sigma\sqrt{\tau}} = d_1 - \sigma\sqrt{\tau} \tag{9.53}$$

In Section 10.2.3 we give results for perpetual European options.

The greeks

Now that we have derived formulae to price European vanilla puts and calls it is possible to work out their partial derivatives (hedge statistics). We will now merely quote expressions for the Greeks (hedge statistics) for European options. Here the subscript c refers to a European call, and the subscript p refers to a European put. Complete derivations of these results can be found in Appendix C.

Gamma

$$\Gamma_c = \frac{\partial^2 c}{\partial S^2} = \Gamma_p = \frac{\partial^2 p}{\partial S^2} = \exp(-q\tau)\frac{n(d_1)}{S\sigma\sqrt{\tau}} \tag{9.54}$$

Delta

$$\Delta_c = \frac{\partial c}{\partial S} = \exp(-q\tau)N_1(d_1), \quad \Delta_p = \frac{\partial p}{\partial S} = \exp(-q\tau)\{N_1(d_1) - 1\} \tag{9.55}$$

Theta

$$\Theta_c = \frac{\partial c}{\partial t} = q\exp(-q\tau)SN_1(d_1) - rE\exp(-r\tau)N_1(d_2) - \frac{Sn(d_1)\sigma\exp(-q\tau)}{2\sqrt{\tau}}$$

$$\Theta_p = \frac{\partial p}{\partial t} = -q\exp(-q\tau)SN_1(-d_1) + rE\exp(-r\tau)N_1(-d_2) - \frac{Sn(d_1)\sigma\exp(-q\tau)}{2\sqrt{\tau}} \tag{9.56}$$

Rho

$$\rho_c = \frac{\partial c}{\partial r} = E\tau N_1(d_2), \quad \rho_p = \frac{\partial p}{\partial r} = -E\tau N_1(-d_2) \tag{9.57}$$

Vega

$$V_c = \frac{\partial c}{\partial \sigma} = V_p = \frac{\partial p}{\partial \sigma} = S\exp(-q\tau)n(d_1)\sqrt{\tau} \tag{9.58}$$

where $n(x) = (1/\sqrt{2\pi})\exp(-x^2/2)$.

We now present, in Code excerpt 9.1, a computer program to calculate the Black–Scholes option value and Greeks given in Equations 9.54 to 9.57. The routine uses the NAG C library macro X02AJC to identify whether the arguments are too small, and also the NAG C library function s15abc to compute the cumulative normal distribution function.

```
void black_scholes(double *value, double greeks[], double s0, double x,
                   double sigma, double t, double r, double q, Integer put, Integer *iflag)
{
/* Input parameters:
   = = = = = =

   s0            - the current price of the underlying asset
   x             - the strike price
   sigma         - the volatility
   t             - the time to maturity
   r             - the interest rate
   q             - the continuous dividend yield
   put

   Output parameters:
   = = = = =

   value         - the value of the option
   greeks[]      - the hedge statistics output as follows: greeks[0] is gamma, greeks[1] is delta
                   greeks[2] is theta, greeks[3] is rho, and greeks[4] is vega
   iflag         - an error indicator

*/
   double one=1.0,two=2.0,zero=0.0;
   double eps,d1,d2,temp,temp1,temp2,pi,np;
   eps = X02AJC;
   if( (x < eps) || (sigma < eps) || (t < eps) ) { /* Check if any of the the input
                                                       arguments are too small */
      *iflag = 2;
      return;
   }
   temp = log(s0/x);
   d1 = temp+(r-q+(sigma*sigma/two))*t;
   d1 = d1/(sigma*sqrt(t));
   d2 = d1-sigma*sqrt(t);
   /* evaluate the option price */
   if (put==0)
      *value = (s0*exp(-q*t)*s15abc(d1) - x *exp (-r *t) *s15abc (d2));
   else
      *value = (-s0*exp(-q*t)*s15abc(-d1)
               + x*exp(-r*t)*s15abc (-d2));
   if (greeks){/* then calculate the greeks */
      temp1 = -d1*d1/two;
      d2 = d1-sigma*sqrt(t);
      pi = X01AAC;
      np = (one/sqrt(two*pi)) * exp(temp1);
      if (put==0) { /* a call option */
        greeks[1] = (s15abc(d1))*exp(-q*t); /* delta */
        greeks[2] = -s0*exp(-q*t)*np*sigma/(two*sqrt(t))
                    + q*s0*s15abc(d1)*exp(-q*t) - r*x*exp(-r*t) *s15abc (d2);/* theta */
        greeks[3] = x*t*exp(-r*t)*s15abc(d2); /* rho */
      }
      else { /* a put option */
        greeks[1] = (s15abc(d1) - one)*exp(-q*t); /* delta */
        greeks[2] = -s0*exp(-q*t)*np*sigma/(two*sqrt(t)) -
                    q*s0*s15abc(-d1)*exp(-q*t) + r*x*exp(-r*t)*s15abc (-d2); /* theta */
        greeks[3] = -x*t*exp(-r*t)*s15abc(-d2); /* rho */
      }
      greeks[0] = np*exp(-q*t)/(s0*sigma*sqrt(t)); /* gamma */
      greeks[4] = s0*sqrt(t)*np*exp(-q*t); /* vega */
   }
   return;
}
```

Code excerpt 9.1 Function to compute the Black–Scholes value for European options

Table 9.1   European put: option values and greeks. The parameters are: $S = 100.0$, $E = 100.0$, $r = 0.10$, $\sigma = 0.30$, $q = 0.06$

τ	Value	Delta	Gamma	Theta	Vega	Rho
0.100	3.558	−0.462	0.042	−16.533	12.490	−4.971
0.200	4.879	−0.444	0.029	−10.851	17.487	−9.860
0.300	5.824	−0.431	0.024	−8.298	21.204	−14.663
0.400	6.571	−0.419	0.020	−6.758	24.241	−19.377
0.500	7.191	−0.408	0.018	−5.698	26.832	−24.004
0.600	7.720	−0.399	0.016	−4.909	29.100	−28.544
0.700	8.179	−0.390	0.015	−4.292	31.118	−32.997
0.800	8.582	−0.381	0.014	−3.792	32.935	−37.364
0.900	8.940	−0.373	0.013	−3.377	34.585	−41.646
1.000	9.260	−0.366	0.012	−3.025	36.093	−45.843

Table 9.2   European call: option values and greeks. The parameters are: $S = 100.0$, $E = 100.0$, $r = 0.10$, $\sigma = 0.30$, $q = 0.06$

τ	Value	Delta	Gamma	Theta	Vega	Rho
0.100	3.955	0.532	0.042	−20.469	12.490	4.929
0.200	5.667	0.544	0.029	−14.724	17.487	9.744
0.300	6.996	0.552	0.024	−12.109	21.204	14.451
0.400	8.121	0.558	0.020	−10.508	24.241	19.054
0.500	9.113	0.562	0.018	−9.387	26.832	23.557
0.600	10.007	0.566	0.016	−8.539	29.100	27.962
0.700	10.826	0.569	0.015	−7.863	31.118	32.271
0.800	11.584	0.572	0.014	−7.305	32.935	36.485
0.900	12.290	0.574	0.013	−6.832	34.585	40.608
1.000	12.952	0.576	0.012	−6.422	36.093	44.640

It can be seen in Tables 9.1 and 9.2 that the values for gamma and vega are the same for both puts and calls. We can also demonstrate that the option values are consistent by using put–call parity.

$$c(S, E, \tau) + E \exp(-r\tau) = p(S, E, \tau) + S \exp(-q\tau)$$

For example when $\tau = 1.0$, we have $c(S, E, \tau) = 12.952$ and $P(S, E, T) = 9.260$. So: $c(S, E, \tau) + E \exp(-r\tau) = 12.952 + 100 \times \exp(-0.1) = 103.436$ and $p(S, E, \tau) + S \exp(-q\tau) = 9.260 + 100 \times \exp(-0.06) = 103.436$.

9.3.4   Historical and implied volatility

Obtaining the best estimate of the volatility parameter, σ, in the Black–Scholes formula is of crucial importance. There are many different approaches to volatility estimation. These include:

- Historical estimation
- Implied volatility
- Time series methods.

Here we will consider both historical and implied volatility estimation. Part III of this book deals with the more complex issues connected with time series volatility estimation.

Historical volatility

In this method we calculate the volatility using $n+1$ historical asset prices, $S_i, i = 0, \ldots, n$, and we assume that the asset prices are observed at the regular time interval, $d\tau$. Since the asset prices are assumed to follow GBM, the volatility is computed as the *annualized* standard deviation of the n continuously compounded returns, $u_i, i = 1, \ldots, n$, where

$$S_i = S_{i-1} \exp(u_i) \quad \text{or} \quad u_i = \log\left(\frac{S_i}{S_{i-1}}\right)$$

We already know, see Section 8.3, Equation 8.15, that the expected standard deviation of the asset returns over the time interval is $\sigma\sqrt{d\tau}$. This means that we obtain the following expression for $\hat{\sigma}$, the estimated volatility

$$\hat{\sigma}\sqrt{d\tau} = \sqrt{\frac{1}{n-1}\sum_{i=1}^{n}(u_i - \bar{u})^2} \tag{9.59}$$

or

$$\hat{\sigma} = \sqrt{\frac{1}{(n-1)d\tau}\sum_{i=1}^{n}(u_i - \bar{u})^2} \tag{9.60}$$

The estimated standard error in $\hat{\sigma}$ is, see for example Hull (1997), given by

$$\hat{\sigma}_{std} = \hat{\sigma}\sqrt{\frac{1}{2(n-1)}} \tag{9.61}$$

A computer program to perform these calculation is given below in Code excerpt 9.2.

```
void hist_vol(double *sigma, double *err, double data[], Integer n, double dt, Integer *ifail)
{

/*Input parameters:
  == == == == ==
  data[]    - the data, which consists of n asset prices
  n         - the number of data points
  dt        - the (constant) time spacing between the data points (in years)


  Output parameters:
  == == == == ==
  sigma     - the computed historical volatility
  err       - the standard error in the volatility estimate sigma
  iflag     - an error indicator
*/

#define DATA(I) data[(I)-1]

  double mean=0.0, sum=0.0;
```

```
double temp,tn;
Integer i;

for(i = 2; i <= n; ++i)
  mean = mean + log(DATA(i))-log(DATA(i-1));
  mean = mean/(double)(n-1);

for(i = 2; i <= n; ++i) {
  temp = log(DATA(i))-log(DATA(i-1));
  sum = sum + (temp-mean)*(temp-mean);
}
sum = sum/(double)(n-2);
*sigma = sqrt(sum/dt);
tn = (double)(2*(n-1));
*err = *sigma/sqrt(tn);
return;
}
```

Code excerpt 9.2 Function to compute the historical volatility from asset data

Implied volatility

The implied volatility of a European option is the volatility which, when substituted into the Black–Scholes formula, yields the market value quoted for the same option.

The routine provided in Code excerpt 9.2 uses Newton's method to calculate the implied volatility for a European option from its market price. We will now illustrate this technique for a European call option with market value opt_value. The implied volatility, σ, is then that value which satisfies:

$$K(\sigma) = c(S, E, \tau, \sigma) - \mathtt{opt\_value} = 0$$

where $c(S, E, \tau, \sigma)$ represents the value of the European call and the other symbols have their usual meaning.

From Newton's method we have:

$$\sigma_{i+1} = \sigma_i - \frac{F(\sigma_i)}{F'(\sigma_i)}$$

where

$$F'(\sigma_i) = \frac{\partial F}{\partial \sigma} = \frac{\partial c(S, E, \tau, \sigma)}{\partial \sigma} = \mathcal{V}_c$$

Therefore the iterative procedure is

$$\sigma_{i+1} = \sigma_i - \frac{c(S, E, \tau, \sigma) - \mathtt{opt\_value}}{\mathcal{V}_c}$$

where σ_0 is the initial estimate, and σ_{i+1} is the improved estimate of the implied volatility based on the ith estimate σ_i. Termination of this iteration occurs when $ABS(\sigma_{i+1} - \sigma_i) < \mathtt{tol}$, for a specified tolerance, $\mathtt{tol}$.

It can be seen that as $\sigma \to 0, d_1 \to \infty, d_2 \to \infty$ and, from Equation 9.58 we have $\mathcal{V}_c \to 0$. Under these circumstances Newton's method fails.

The same procedure can be used to compute the implied volatility for a European put, in this can we just replace $c(S, E, \tau, \sigma)$ by $p(S, E, \tau, \sigma)$, the value of a European put; from Equation 9.58 $\mathcal{V}_c = \mathcal{V}_p$.

```
void implied_volatility(double value, double s0, double x, double sigma[],
                        double t, double r, double q, Integer put, Integer *iflag)
{
```

```
/* Input parameters:
   = = = = = =

   value     - the current value of the option
   s0        - the current price of the underlying asset
   x         - the strike price
   sigma[]   - the input bounds on the volatility: sigma[0], the lower bound and, sigma[1], the upper bound
   t         - the time to maturity
   r         - the interest rate
   q         - the continuous dividend yield
   put       - if put is 0 then a call option, otherwise a put option

   Output parameters:
   = = = = = =

   sigma[]   - the element sigma[0] contains the estimated implied volatility
   iflag     - an error indicator
*/
   double zero=0.0;
   double fx, sig1, sig2;
   double val,tolx;
   double temp,eps,epsqrt,temp1,v1;
   Integer max_iters, i, ind, ir;
   double greeks[5],c[20],sig,vega;
   Boolean done;
   eps = X02AJC;
   tolx = eps;
   epsqrt = sqrt(eps);
   if(put == 0)
     temp1 = MAX(s0*exp(-q*t)-x*exp(-r*t),zero);        /* a call option */
   else
     temp1 = MAX(x*exp(-r*t)-s0*exp(-q*t),zero);        /* a put option */
   v1 = FABS(value-temp1);
   if (v1 <= epsqrt){
     *iflag = 3;                                         /* the volatility is too small */
     return;
   }
   *iflag = 0;
   i = 0;
   max_iters = 50;
   done = FALSE;
   sig = sigma[0];                                       /* initial estimate */
   val = value;
   while ((i < max_iters) && (!done)){                   /* Newton iteration */
     black_scholes(&val,greeks,s0,x,sig,t,r,q,put,iflag); /* compute the Black-Scholes option value, val */
     vega = greeks[4];                                    /* and vega. */
     sig1 = sig - ((val - value)/vega);                  /* compute the new estimate of sigma
                                                             using Newton's method */
     done = (tolx > FABS ((sig1 - sig)/sig1));           /* check whether the specified accuracy has been
                                                             reached */
     sig = sig1;                                          /* up date sigma */
     ++i;
   }
   sigma[0] = sig1;
   return;                                               /* return the estimate for sigma */
}
```

Code expert 9.3   Function to compute the implied volatility of European options

If the implied volatility of American options is required, the procedure is exactly the same. However, instead of using the Black–Scholes formula to compute both the option value and *Vega*, we use a binomial lattice to do this. The use of binomial lattices to obtain option prices and the Greeks is described in Section 10.4.

Below, in Code excerpt 9.4, is provided a simple test program which illustrates the use of the function `implied_volatility`; the results are presented in Table 9.3.

```
double X, value, S, sigma[2], sigmat, T, r, q;
long i, ifail, put;
ifail          = 0;
```

```
S               = 10.0;
X               = 10.5;
r               = 0.1;
sigmat          = 0.1;
q               = 0.04;
put             = 0;
printf (" Time option value implied volatility (Error)\n");
for(i = 1;i < 6; ++i){
  T = (double)i*0.5;
  black_scholes(&value,NULL,S,X,sigmat,T,r,q,put,&flag);
  sigma[0] = 0.05;
  sigma[1] = 1.0;
  implied_volatility(value,S,X,sigmat,T,r,q,put,&flag);
  printf("%8.4f  %15.4f  %15.4f (%8.4e)\n",T,value,sigma[0], FABS(sigmat-sigma[0]));
  sigmat = sigmat + 0.1;
}
```

Code excerpt 9.4   Simple test program for function `implied_volatility`

9.3.5   Pricing options with Microsoft Excel

In this section we show how the Visual Basic within Excel can be used to create powerful derivative pricing applications based on the Black–Scholes formula. We will explain how Excel's Visual Basic can be used to create an application that prices a selection of simple European put and call options at the press of a button.

In Section 9.3.3 we derived the Black–Scholes formula:

$$c(S, E, \tau) = SN_1(d_1) - e^{-r\tau}EN_1(d_2) \text{ and } p(S, E, \tau) = -SN_1(-d_1) + e^{-r\tau}EN_1(-d_2)$$

where

$$d_1 = \frac{\log(S/E)(r - \sigma^2/2)\tau}{\sigma\sqrt{\tau}} = d_1 - \sigma\sqrt{\tau}$$

where S is the current value of the asset and σ is the volatility of the asset, and

$$N_1(x) = \frac{1}{\sqrt{2\pi}} \int_{-\infty}^{x} e^{-x^2/2}dx$$

The univariate cumulative standard normal distribution, $N_1(x)$, can be evaluated in Excel by using its built in function NORMDIST. The definition of this function is as follows:

NORMDIST(x, mean, standard_dev, cumulative)

This function returns the normal cumulative distribution for the specified mean and standard deviation.

Table 9.3   Calculated option values and implied volatilities from Code excerpt 9.4

Time (in years)	Option value	True σ	Error in estimated σ
0.5	0.1959	0.1	2.7756×10^{-16}
1.0	0.8158	0.2	2.2204×10^{-16}
1.5	1.5435	0.3	3.8858×10^{-16}
2.0	2.3177	0.4	5.5511×10^{-17}
2.5	3.1033	0.5	1.1102×10^{-16}

Function parameters

x, is the value for which you want the distribution; mean, is the arithmetic mean of the distribution; standard_dev, is the standard deviation of the distribution; cumulative, is a logical value that determines the form of the function. If cumulative is TRUE, NORMDIST returns the cumulative distribution function; if FALSE, it returns the probability density function.

If mean = 0 and standard_dev = 1, NORMDIST returns the standard normal distribution.

This function can be used to create the following Visual Basic function to calculate European option values within Excel.

```
Function bs_opt(S0 As Double, _
  ByVal X As Double, sigma As Double, T As Double, _
  r As Double, q As Double, ByVal putcall As Long) As Double

' Visual Basic Routine to calculate the value of
' either a European Put or European Call option.

  Dim temp As Double
  Dim d1 As Double
  Dim d2 As Double
  Dim SQT As Double
  Dim value As Double

  temp = Log(S0 / X)
  d1 = temp + (r − q + (sigma * sigma / 2#)) * T
  SQT = Sqr(T)
  d1 = d1 / (sigma * SQT)
  d2 = d1 − sigma * SQT

  If (putcall = 0) Then    ' a call option
    value = S0 * Exp(−q * T) * WorksheetFunction.NormDist (d1, 0#, 1#, True)_
      −WorksheetFunction.NormDist(d2, 0#, 1#, True) * X * Exp(−r * T)

  Else    ' a put option
    value = −S0 * Exp(−q * T) * WorksheetFunction.NormDist(−d1, 0#, 1#, True) + _
      X * WorksheetFunction.NormDist(−d2, 0#, 1#, True) * Exp(−r * T)
  End If

  bs_opt = value

End Function
```

Code excerpt 9.5   Visual Basic code to price European options using the Black–Scholes formula

Once the function has been defined it can be accessed interactively using the Paste Function facility within Excel as shown in Figure 9.1.

The function bs_opt can also be incorporated into other Visual Basic code within Excel. To illustrate, if the following Visual Basic subroutine is defined:

```
Private Sub MANY_EUROPEANS_Click()

Dim i As Long
Dim putcall As Long
Dim S0 As Double
Dim q As Double
Dim sigma As Double
Dim T As Double
Dim r As Double

q = 0#
T = 1.5
```

```
r = 0.1
sigma = 0.2

For i = 1 To 22

  S0 = Sheet1.Cells(i + 1, 1).value
  X = Sheet1.Cells(i + 1, 2).value
  putcall = Sheet1.Cells(i + 1, 3).value
  Sheet1.Cells(i + 1, 4).value = bs_opt(S0, X, sigma, T, r, q, putcall)

Next i

End Sub
```

Code excerpt 9.6   Visual Basic code that uses the function `bs_opt`

When the button labelled 'CALCULATE OPTIONS' is clicked, the values of 22 European options will be calculated using the data in columns 1–3 on worksheet 1. This is shown in Figures 9.2 and 9.3.

The cumulative standard normal distribution can also be used to provide analytic solutions for a range of other *exotic* options such as: Barrier options, Exchange options, Lookback options, Binary options, etc. A quick reference guide of the formulae for various options is included in Appendix B.

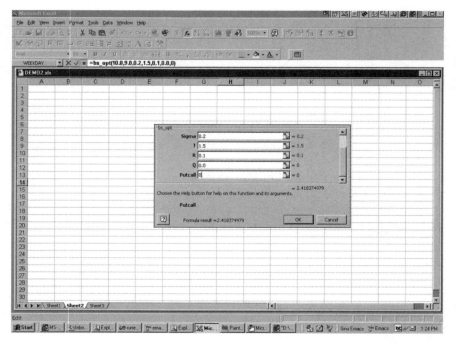

Figure 9.1   Using the function `bs_opt` interactively within Excel. Here a call option is priced with the following parameters: $S = 10.0$, $X = 9.0$, $q = 0.0$, $T = 1.5$, $r = 0.1$, and $\sigma = 0.2$

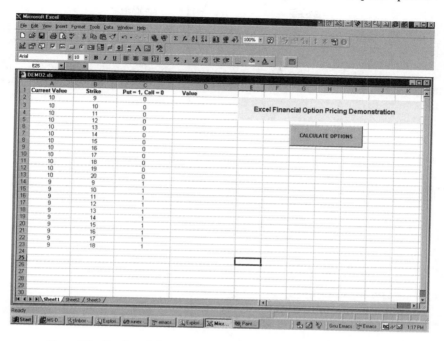

Figure 9.2 Excel worksheet before calculation of the European option values

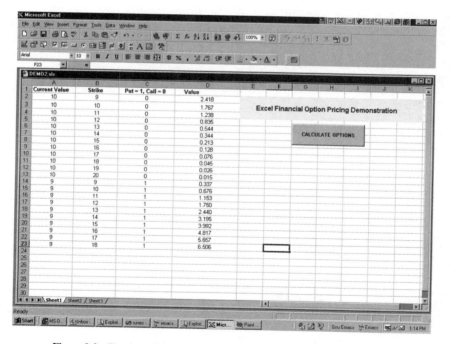

Figure 9.3 Excel worksheet after calculation of the European option values

9.4   BARRIER OPTIONS

9.4.1   Introduction

Barrier options are derivatives where the payoff depends on whether the asset price reaches a given barrier level, *B*. *Knockout options* become worthless (cease to exist) if the asset price reaches the barrier, whereas *knockin options* come into existence when the asset price *hits* the barrier. We will consider the following single asset barrier options:

- *Down and out call*: A knockout vanilla call option, value $c_{do}(S, B, E, \tau)$, which ceases to exist when the asset price reaches or goes below the barrier level.
- *Up and out call*: A knockout vanilla call option, value $c_{uo}(S, B, E, \tau)$, which ceases to exist when the asset price reaches, or goes above the barrier level.
- *Down and in call*: A knockin vanilla call option, value $c_{di}(S, B, E, \tau)$, which comes into existence when the asset prices reaches or goes below the barrier level.
- *Up and in call*: A knockin vanilla call option, value $c_{ui}(S, B, E, \tau)$, which comes into existence when the asset price reaches or goes above the barrier level.

Since the following expressions must be true:

$$c(S, E, \tau) = c_{uo}(S, B, E, \tau) + c_{ui}(S, B, E, \tau) \tag{9.62}$$

$$c(S, E, \tau) = c_{do}(S, B, E, \tau) + c_{di}(S, B, E, \tau) \tag{9.63}$$

we need to only derive expressions for both the knockout options, and then use the above equations to calculate the value of the corresponding knockin options.

The notation that we will use is as follows: *E* is the strike price, *S* is the current value of the asset, *B* the barrier level, the symbol *t* represents the current time, *T* represents the time at which the option matures and $\tau = T - t$, the duration of the option. The symbol *s*, with constraint $t \leq s \leq T$, is any intermediate time during which the option is alive.

9.4.2   Down and out call

If we consider Brownian motion (with zero drift) $X_s \sim N(0, (s - t)\sigma^2)$, $t \leq s \leq T$ which starts at $X_t = 0$ and, after time $\tau = T - t$, ends at the point $X_T = X$ then (e.g. Freedman, 1983) the probability density function for this motion not to exceed the value $X = b$ (where $b > 0$) during time τ is given by:

$$f(b \geq X_s^{\max}, X) = \Omega \sqrt{\frac{2}{\pi}} \exp\left(\frac{2b(X - b)}{\sigma^2 \tau}\right) \exp\left(-\frac{X^2}{2\sigma^2 \tau}\right) \tag{9.64}$$

where for convenience we have used $\Omega = (2b - X)/\sigma^3 \tau^{3/2}$, and $X_s^{\max} = \max(X_s, t \leq s \leq T)$.

Since X_s is Brownian motion without drift, and volatility σ then $-X_s$ is identical Brownian motion. Therefore by substituting $X \rightarrow -X$, and $b \rightarrow -b$ in the above equation we obtain:

$$f(b \leq X_s^{\min}, X) = -\Omega \sqrt{\frac{2}{\pi}} \exp\left(\frac{2b(X - b)}{\sigma^2 \tau}\right) \exp\left(-\frac{X^2}{2\sigma^2 \tau}\right) \tag{9.65}$$

where we have used $X_s^{\min} = \min(X_s, t \le s \le T)$. Equation 9.65 is the probability density function of $-X_s$ staying above the value $X = b$, where $b < 0$. These results can be generalized to include drift (e.g. Musiela and Rutkowski, 1998, p. 212), so that $X_s \sim N((r - \sigma^2/2)(s-t), \sigma(s-t))$, for $t \le s \le T$. We now have the following results:

$$f(b \ge X_s^{\max}, X) = \Omega\sqrt{\frac{2}{\pi}}\exp\left(\frac{2b(X-b)}{\sigma^2\tau}\right)\exp\left(-\frac{(X-(r-\sigma^2/2)\tau)^2}{2\sigma^2\tau}\right) \tag{9.66}$$

$$f(b \le X_s^{\min}, X) = -\Omega\sqrt{\frac{2}{\pi}}\exp\left(\frac{2b(X-b)}{\sigma^2\tau}\right)\exp\left(-\frac{(X-(r-\sigma^2/2)\tau)^2}{2\sigma^2\tau}\right) \tag{9.67}$$

A European down and out barrier option with maturity τ and a barrier at $X = B$ will cease to exist (become worthless) if at any time $X_s \le B$, for $t \le s \le T$. The probability density function that the barrier option will continue to exist at time T if the end point is X is therefore:

$$f(X > B) = -\sqrt{\frac{2}{\pi}}\int_{b=\log(B/S)}^{b=x}\Omega\exp\left(\frac{2b(X-b)}{\sigma^2\tau}\right)$$
$$\times\exp\left(-\frac{\{X-(r-\sigma^2/2)\tau\}^2}{2\sigma^2\tau}\right)db \tag{9.68}$$

or

$$f(X > B) = -\sqrt{\frac{2}{\pi}}\exp\left(-\frac{\{X-(r-\sigma^2/2)\tau\}^2}{2\sigma^2\tau}\right)$$
$$\times\int_{b=\log(B/S)}^{b=X}\Omega\exp\left(\frac{2b(X-b)}{\sigma^2\tau}\right)db \tag{9.69}$$

where we have integrated over all possible values of b (i.e. $B < b < X$) that keep the option alive. Recalling that:

$$-\int_{b=\log(B/S)}^{b=X}\Omega\exp\left(\frac{2b(X-b)}{\sigma^2\tau}\right)db = \int_{b=\log(B/S)}^{b=X}\frac{(X-2b)}{\sigma^3\tau^{3/2}}\exp\left(\frac{2b(X-b)}{\sigma^2\tau}\right)db$$

and noting that:

$$\frac{\partial}{\partial b}\exp\left(\frac{2b(X-b)}{\sigma^2\tau}\right) = \frac{2(X-2b)}{\sigma^2\tau}\exp\left(\frac{2b(X-b)}{\sigma^2\tau}\right)$$

we have:

$$\int_{b=\log(B/S)}^{b=X}\frac{2(X-2b)}{\sigma^2\tau}\exp\left(\frac{2b(X-b)}{\sigma^2\tau}\right)db = \left[\exp\left(\frac{2b(X-b)}{\sigma^2\tau}\right)\right]_{b=\log(B/S)}^{b=X}$$
$$= \left\{1 - \exp\left(\frac{2\log(B/S)(X-\log(B/S))}{\sigma^2\tau}\right)\right\}$$

So the value of the option is given by:

$$f(X > B) = \frac{1}{\sigma\sqrt{\tau}\sqrt{2\pi}} \exp\left(-\frac{\{X - (r - \sigma^2/2)\tau\}^2}{2\sigma^2\tau}\right)$$

$$\times \left\{1 - \exp\left(\frac{2\log(B/S)(X - \log(B/S))}{\sigma^2\tau}\right)\right\}$$

This integral is evaluated in Appendix G.1; here we merely state the result.

Down and out call option

$$c_{do} = S\left(N_1(d_1) - N_1(d_4)\left(\frac{B}{S}\right)^{2r/\sigma^2+1}\right)$$

$$- E\exp(-r\tau)\left(N_1(d_2) - N_1(d_3)\left(\frac{B}{S}\right)^{2r/\sigma^2-1}\right) \qquad (9.70)$$

where S is the current asset value, E the strike price, B the barrier level, σ the volatility, r the riskless interest rate, τ the duration of the option, and:

$$d_1 = \frac{\log(S/E) + (r + \sigma^2/2)\tau}{\sigma\sqrt{\tau}}, \quad d_2 = \frac{\log(S/E) + (r - \sigma^2/2)\tau}{\sigma\sqrt{\tau}},$$

$$d_3 = \frac{\log(B^2/SE) + (r - \sigma^2/2)\tau)}{\sigma\sqrt{\tau}}, \quad \text{and} \quad d_4 = \frac{\log(B^2/ES) + (r + \sigma^2/2)\tau}{\sigma\sqrt{\tau}}$$

In Code excerpt 9.7 below we provide the function `bs_opt_barrier_downout_call` which uses Equation 9.70 to price a down and out European call option. This routine will be used in Sections 10.6.3 and 10.6.6 to measure the accuracy achieved by using various finite-difference grid techniques to solve the Black–Scholes equation.

```
void bs_opt_barrier_downout_call(double *value, double barrier_level,
    double s0, double x, double sigma, double t, double r, Integer *iflag)
{
/* Input parameters:
   = = = = = = = =
   barrier_level  -  the level of the barrier
   s0               -  the current price of the underlying asset
   x                -  the strike price
   sigma            -  the volatility
   t                -  the time to maturity
   r                -  the interest rate

Output parameters:
= = = = = = = =
   value            -  the value of the option
   iflag            -  an error indicator
*/
   double one=1.0,two=2.0,zero=0.0;
   double eps,temp,temp1,temp2,a,b,d1,d2,d3,d4,d5,d6,d7,d8;
   double fac;
```

```
eps = X02AJC;
  if(x < eps) {/* then strike price (X) is too small */
    printf ("ERROR X is too small \n");
    return;
  }
  if (sigma < eps){/* then volatility (sigma) is too small */
    printf ("ERROR sigma is too small \n");
    return;
  }
  if (t < eps){/* then time to expiry (t) is too small */
    *ifail = 3;
    printf ("ERROR option maturity is too small \n ");
    return;
  }
  if (barrier_level == 0){printf ("ERROR barrier must be > zero \n");

    fac = sigma*sqrt(t);
    temp1 = -one+(two*r/(sigma*sigma));
    temp2 = barrier_level/s0;
    a = pow(temp2,temp1);
    temp1 = one+(two*r/(sigma*sigma));
    b = pow(temp2,temp1);
    if (x > barrier_level){
      d1 = (log(s0/x)+(r+0.5*sigma*sigma)*t)/fac;
      d2 = (log(s0/x)+(r-0.5*sigma*sigma)*t)/fac;
      temp =(s0*x)/(barrier_level*barrier_level);
      d7 = (log(temp)-(r-0.5*sigma*sigma)*t)/fac;
      d8 = (log(temp)-(r+0.5*sigma*sigma)*t)/fac;

      temp1 = s0*(s15abc(d1)-b*(one-s15abc(d8)));
      temp2 = x*exp(-r*t)*(s15abc(d2)-a*(one-s15abc(d7)));
      *value = temp1-temp2;
    }
    else{/* x <= barrier_level */
      d3=(log(s0/barrier_level)+(r-0.5*sigma*sigma)*t)/fac;
      d6= (log(s0/barrier_level)-(r-0.5*sigma*sigma)*t)/fac;
      d4 = (log(s0/barrier_level)+(r+0.5*sigma*sigma)*t)/fac;
      d5 = (log(s0/barrier_level)-(r+0.5*sigma*sigma)*t)/fac;

      temp1 = s0*(s15abc(d3)- b*(one-s15abc(d6)));
      temp2= x*exp(-r*t)*(s15abc(d4)-a*(one-s15abc(d5)));
      *value = temp1-temp2;
    }
  return;
}
```

Code excerpt 9.7   Function to compute the value for European down and out call options

9.4.3   Up and out call

Here we will obtain an expression for an *up and out* European call option in a similar manner to that used in Section 9.3.5 for the down and out European call option. A European up and out barrier option with maturity τ and a barrier at $X = B$ will cease to exist (become worthless) if at any time $X_s \geq B$, for $t \leq s \leq T$. The probability density function that the barrier option will continue to exist at time T if the end point is X is therefore:

$$
f(X < B) = \sqrt{\frac{2}{\pi}} \int_{b=X}^{B=S \exp(b)} \Omega \exp\left(\frac{2b(X-b)}{\sigma^2 t}\right)
$$

$$
\times \exp\left(-\frac{\{X-(r-\sigma^2/2)\tau\}^2}{2\sigma^2 \tau}\right) db \tag{9.71}
$$

or

$$f(X < B) = \sqrt{\frac{2}{\pi}} \exp\left(-\frac{\{X - (r - \sigma^2/2)\tau\}^2}{2\sigma^2\tau}\right)$$

$$\times \int_{b=X}^{b=\log(B/S)} \Omega \exp\left(\frac{2b(X-b)}{\sigma^2\tau}\right) db \tag{9.72}$$

where as in Section 9.3.5 we have used $\Omega = (2b - X)/\sigma^3\tau^{3/2}$ and have integrated overall possible values of b (i.e. $B > b > X$) that keep the option alive. Recalling that:

$$\int_{b=X}^{b=\log(B/S)} \Omega \exp\left(\frac{2b(X-b)}{\sigma^2\tau}\right) db = \int_{b=X}^{b=\log(B/S)} \frac{(2b - X)}{\sigma^3\tau^{3/2}} \exp\left(\frac{2b(X-b)}{\sigma^2\tau}\right) db$$

and noting:

$$-\frac{\partial}{\partial b}\exp\left(\frac{2b(X-b)}{\sigma^2\tau}\right) = \frac{2(X - 2b)}{\sigma^2\tau}\exp\left(\frac{2b(X-b)}{\sigma^2\tau}\right) \tag{9.73}$$

we have:

$$\int_{b=X}^{b=\log(B/S)} \frac{2(2b - X)}{\sigma^2\tau}\exp\left(\frac{2b(X-b)}{\sigma^2\tau}\right) db = \left[-\exp\left(\frac{2b(X-b)}{\sigma^2\tau}\right)\right]_{b=X}^{b=\log(B/S)}$$

$$= \left\{1 - \exp\left(\frac{2\log(B/S)(X - \log(B/S))}{\sigma^2\tau}\right)\right\}$$

Therefore:

$$f(X < B) = \frac{1}{\sigma\sqrt{\tau}\sqrt{2\pi}}\sqrt{\frac{2}{\pi}}\exp\left(-\frac{\{X - (r - \sigma^2/2)\tau\}^2}{2\sigma^2\tau}\right)$$

$$\times \left\{1 - \exp\left(\frac{2\log(B/S)(X - \log(B/S))}{\sigma^2\tau}\right)\right\} \tag{9.74}$$

We will now derive the formula for an up and out call option when $E < B$. In fact if $E > B$ then the option is worthless, since at the current time t the call option's payout, $\max(S_t - E, 0) = 0$, and if $S_t > E$ then the option will be knocked out.

$$c_{uo} = \frac{\exp(-r\tau)}{\sigma\sqrt{\tau}\sqrt{2\pi}}\int_{X=\log(E/S)}^{\infty} \{S\exp(X) - E\}f(X < B)dX \tag{9.75}$$

Taking into account the fact the option becomes worthless when $S\exp(X) > B$, (i.e. $X > \log(B/S)$) we have:

$$c_{uo} = \frac{\exp(-r\tau)}{\sigma\sqrt{\tau}\sqrt{2\pi}}\int_{X=\log(E/S)}^{\log(B/S)} \{S\exp(X) - E\}f(X < B)dX \tag{9.76}$$

This integral is evaluated in Appendix G.2, and the value of the up and out call option c_{uo} is:

Up and out call option

$$c_{uo} = \{N_1(k_7) - N_1(k_8)\}S\left(\frac{B}{S}\right)^{2r/\sigma^2+1}$$

$$- \{\exp(-r\tau)N_1(k_5) - N_1(k_6)\}E\left(\frac{B}{S}\right)^{2r/\sigma^2-1}$$

$$+ S\{N_1(k_2) - N_1(k_1)\} - E\exp(-r\tau)\{N_1(k_4) - N_1(k_3)\} \qquad (9.77)$$

where S is the current asset value, E the strike price, B the barrier level, σ the volatility, r the riskless interest rate, τ the duration of the option, and:

$$k_1 = \frac{\log(E/S) - (r + \sigma^2/2)\tau)}{\sigma\sqrt{\tau}}, \qquad k_2 = \frac{\log(B/S) - (r + \sigma^2/2)\tau}{\sqrt{\tau}}$$

$$k_3 = \frac{\log(E/S) - (r - \sigma^2/2)\tau}{\sigma\sqrt{\tau}}, \qquad k_4 = \frac{\log(B/S) - (r - \sigma^2/2)\tau}{\sigma\sqrt{\tau}}$$

$$k_5 = \frac{\log(ES/B^2) - (r - \sigma^2/2)\tau)}{\sigma\sqrt{\tau}}, \qquad k_6 = \frac{\log(S/B) - (r - \sigma^2/2)\tau)}{\sigma\sqrt{\tau}}$$

$$k_7 = \frac{\log(ES/B^2) - (r + \sigma^2/2)\tau}{\sigma\sqrt{\tau}} \quad \text{and} \quad k_8 = \frac{\log(S/B) - (r + \sigma^2/2)\tau}{\sigma\sqrt{\tau}}$$

Chapter 10

Numeric methods and single asset American options

10.1 INTRODUCTION

In Chapter 9 we discussed single asset European options and the analytic formulae which can be used to price them. Here we will consider the valuation of single asset American style options using both numeric methods and analytic formulae; in addition we will discuss the use of numerical techniques to value certain European options. The coverage in this section is as follows:

- Analytic methods applied to perpetual European and American options.
- Analytic approximation techniques for the valuation of American options.
- Binomial lattice techniques used for the valuation of American and European options.
- The valuation of American and European vanilla and barrier options using finite-difference grids.
- The valuation of American options via Monte Carlo simulation.

It should be mentioned that although much of the discussion here concerns the valuation of vanilla European and American puts and calls, the techniques used can be modified without much difficulty to include more exotic options with customized payoffs and early exercise features.

10.2 PERPETUAL OPTIONS

10.2.1 The perpetual American put

Here we derive the value, $P(S, E)$, for a perpetual American put with strike price E on an asset of current value S. This option can be exercised at any time, and so there is no expiry date. Since the option is perpetual its payoff is time independent (see Merton (1973)) and the Black–Scholes equation reduces to the following second order ordinary differential equation:

$$\frac{\sigma^2 S^2}{2}\frac{d^2 V}{dS^2} + (r - q)S\frac{dV}{dS} - rV = 0 \tag{10.1}$$

where as usual S is the asset price, V is the option value, σ is the volatility of the asset, r is the riskless interest rate and q is the continuous dividend yield.

If we substitute $S = \exp(X)$ we then have:

$$\frac{dV}{dS} = \frac{dV}{dX}\frac{dX}{dS} = \exp(-X)\frac{dV}{dX}$$

$$\frac{d^2V}{dS^2} = \frac{dX}{dS}\frac{d}{dX}\left\{\frac{dV}{dX}\exp(-X)\right\} = \exp(-2X)\frac{d^2V}{dX^2} - \frac{dV}{dX}\exp(-2X)$$

Substituting the above results into Equation 10.1 we obtain:

$$\frac{\sigma^2\exp(2X)\exp(-2X)}{2}\left\{\frac{d^2V}{dX^2} - \frac{dV}{dX}\right\} + (r-q)\exp(X)\exp(-X)\frac{dV}{dX} - rV = 0$$

$$\frac{\sigma^2}{2}\frac{d^2V}{dX^2} + \left\{(r-q) - \frac{\sigma^2}{2}\right\}\frac{dV}{dX} - rV = 0$$

So

$$\frac{d^2V}{dX^2} + \left\{\frac{2(r-q)}{\sigma^2} - 1\right\}\frac{dV}{dX} - \frac{2r}{\sigma^2}V = 0 \tag{10.2}$$

Equation 10.2 is a homogeneous equation with constant coefficients, so we can look for solutions of the form $V = \exp(mX)$. This gives:

$$m^2 + \left\{\frac{2(r-q)}{\sigma^2} - 1\right\}m - \frac{2r}{\sigma^2} = 0 \tag{10.3}$$

which can be solved to yield:

$$m_1 = \frac{1}{2}\left\{\frac{-2(r-q)}{\sigma^2} + 1\right\} + \frac{1}{2}\sqrt{\left\{\frac{2(r-q)}{\sigma^2} - 1\right\}^2 + \frac{8r}{\sigma^2}} \tag{10.4}$$

and

$$m_2 = \frac{1}{2}\left\{\frac{-2(r-q)}{\sigma^2} + 1)\right\} - \frac{1}{2}\sqrt{\left\{\frac{2(r-q)}{\sigma^2} - 1\right\}^2 + \frac{8r}{\sigma^2}} \tag{10.5}$$

The general solution to Equation 10.2 is therefore:

$$V(X) = A_1\exp(m_1X) + A_2\exp(m_2X) \tag{10.6}$$

However, since we are solving Equation 10.1 we would like the solution in terms of the asset price S. So re-substituting $S = \exp(X)$, and using the fact that $\exp(aX) = \exp(X)^a$, we obtain:

$$A_1\exp(m_1X) = A_1(\exp(X))^{m_1} = A_1S^{m_1}$$

and

$$A_2\exp(m_2X) = A_2(\exp(X))^{m_2} = A_2S^{m_2}$$

The general solution of Equation 10.2 as a function of S is therefore:

$$V(S) = A_1 S^{m_1} + A_2 S^{m_2} \tag{10.7}$$

If we assume that $(2(r - D)/\sigma^2) > 1$ then $m_1 > 0$ and $m_2 < 0$. (Note: When $(2(r - D)/\sigma^2) < 1$, $m_1 < 0$ and $m_2 > 0$.)

For the perpetual American put as $S \to \infty$ we have $P(S, E) \to 0$. This means that the coefficient A_1 in Equation 10.7 must be zero, and $P(S, E) = A_2 S^{m_2}$. Suppose we decide that we will exercise the option when $S \leq S^*$, where S^* is termed the *critical value of S*, then the payoff (which is positive) at $S = S^*$ will be

$$P(S^*, E) = E - S^* \tag{10.8}$$

This gives

$$P(S^*, E) = A_2(S^*)^{m_2} = E - S^* \tag{10.9}$$

Solving for A_2 gives:

$$A_2 = \frac{E - S^*}{(S^*)^{m_2}} \tag{10.10}$$

So we have:

$$P(S, E) = (E - S^*)\left(\frac{S}{S^*}\right)^{m_2} \tag{10.11}$$

We are now going to find the value of S^* which maximizes the option value at any time before exercise. Differentiating Equation 10.11 and setting the value to zero we have:

$$\frac{\partial}{\partial S^*}\left\{(E - S^*)\left(\frac{S}{S^*}\right)^{m_2}\right\} = \frac{1}{S^*}\left(\frac{S}{S^*}\right)^{m_2}\{-S^* - m_2(E - S^*)\} = 0$$

and

$$-S^* - m_2(E - S^*) = 0, \quad \text{so} \quad S^* = \frac{E}{1 - 1/m_2}$$

So substituting into Equation 10.10 results in:

$$A_2 = \frac{-1}{m_2}\left\{\frac{E}{1 - 1/m_2}\right\}^{1 - m_2}$$

When there are no dividends, $q = 0$, we have from Equation 10.5 that

$$m_2 = \frac{1}{2}\left\{\frac{-2r}{\sigma^2} + 1\right\} - \frac{1}{2}\sqrt{\left\{\frac{2r}{\sigma^2} - 1\right\}^2 + \frac{8r}{\sigma^2}} \tag{10.12}$$

but

$$\left\{\frac{2r}{\sigma^2} - 1\right\}^2 + \frac{8r}{\sigma^2} = \left(1 + \frac{2r}{\sigma^2}\right)^2$$

Therefore

$$m_2 = \frac{1}{2}\left\{-\frac{2r}{\sigma^2} + 1 - \frac{2r}{\sigma^2} - 1\right\} \quad \text{and} \quad m_2 = \frac{-2r}{\sigma^2} \tag{10.13}$$

Substituting for m_2 and A_2 in Equation 10.9 we thus obtain the value for a perpetual American put without dividends as:

$$P(S, E) = \frac{\sigma^2 S^{-2r/\sigma^2}}{2r}\left\{\frac{E}{1 + (\sigma^2/2r)}\right\}^{1+(2r/\sigma^2)} \tag{10.14}$$

see Merton (1973), Equation 52, p. 174.

10.2.2 The perpetual American call

Here we derive the value, $C(S, E)$, for a perpetual American call with strike price E on an asset of current value S. For the perpetual American call as $S \to 0$ we have $C(S, E) \to 0$. In the previous section we mentioned that $m_2 < 0$ which means that the $A_2 S^{m_2} \to \infty$ as $S \to 0$. Thus if Equation 10.7 is to yield a finite solution for the perpetual American call we must set $A_2 = 0$ and look for solutions of the form:

$$C(S, E) = A_1 S^{m_1}$$

The payoff for the call option is $\max(S - E, 0)$, so when $S^* = S$ we have:

$$C(S^*, E) = S^* - E = A_1 (S^*)^{m_1} \tag{10.15}$$

and

$$A_1 = \frac{(S^* - E)}{(S^*)^{m_1}} \tag{10.16}$$

This gives

$$C(S, E) = (S^* - E)\left(\frac{S}{S^*}\right)^{m_1} \tag{10.17}$$

As in Section 10.2.1 we find the value S^* which maximizes the option value by differentiating Equation 10.17 w.r.t. S^* and setting the value to zero. This yields:

$$\frac{\partial}{\partial S^*}\left\{(E - S^*)\left(\frac{S}{S^*}\right)^{m_1}\right\} = \frac{1}{S^*}\left(\frac{S}{S^*}\right)^{m_1}\{S^* - m_1(S^* - E)\} = 0$$

and

$$S^* - m_1(S^* - E) = 0, \quad \text{so} \quad S^* = \frac{E}{1 - 1/m_1} \tag{10.18}$$

Now using $A_1 = (S^* - E)/(S^*)^{m_1}$ we obtain

$$A_1 = \frac{E\{1/(1 - 1/m_1) - 1\}}{E^{m_1}\left\{(1 - 1/m_1)(1 - 1/m_1)^{m_1 - 1}\right\}}$$

$$= \frac{1}{E^{m_1 - 1}}(1 - 1 + 1/m_1)(1 - 1/m_1)^{m_1 - 1}$$

$$A_1 = \frac{1}{m_1}\left(\frac{1 - 1/m_1}{E}\right)^{m_1 - 1} = \frac{1}{m_1}\left(\frac{E}{1 - 1/m_1}\right)^{1 - m_1} \tag{10.19}$$

Therefore the value of the perpetual American call option is:

$$C(S, E) = \frac{1}{m_1}\left(\frac{E}{1 - 1/m_1}\right)^{1 - m_1} S^{m_1} \tag{10.20}$$

When there are no dividends, $q = 0$, we have from Equation 10.4 that

$$m_1 = \frac{1}{2}\left\{\frac{-2r}{\sigma^2} + 1\right\} + \frac{1}{2}\sqrt{\left\{\frac{2r}{\sigma^2} - 1\right\}^2 + \frac{8r}{\sigma^2}} \tag{10.21}$$

but

$$\left\{\frac{2r}{\sigma^2} - 1\right\}^2 + \frac{8r}{\sigma^2} = \left(1 + \frac{2r}{\sigma^2}\right)^2 \tag{10.22}$$

so substituting into Equation 10.21 we obtain

$$m_1 = \frac{1}{2}\left\{-\frac{2r}{\sigma^2} + 1 + \frac{2r}{\sigma^2} + 1\right\} = 1 \tag{10.23}$$

Setting $m_1 = 1$ in Equation 10.18 we thus find that $S^* = \infty$. Therefore from Equation 10.16:

$$A_1 = \frac{(S^* - E)}{(S^*)^{m_1}} = \frac{(S^* - E)}{(S^*)} = 1 \tag{10.24}$$

This means that the value of a perpetual American call with zero dividends is:

$$C(S, E) = A_1 S^{m_1} = 1 \times S = S \tag{10.25}$$

10.2.3 Perpetual European options

We can easily derive expressions for perpetual European options by using the Black–Scholes formulae given in Section 9.3.3. It can be seen that as the option maturity, τ, tends to infinity $d_1 \longrightarrow \infty$ and $d_2 \longrightarrow -\infty$. This means that for perpetual options we should use $N_1(d_1) \sim 1$ and $N_1(d_2) \sim 0$ in the Black–Scholes formulae. Therefore when $q > 0$, we have $c(S, E) \sim 0$ and $p(S, E) \sim 0$. Also when $q = 0$ we have $c(S, E) \sim S$ and $p(S, E) \sim 0$.

The value of a European call (when $q = 0$) is therefore:

$$c(S, E) = C(S, E) = S \tag{10.26}$$

which means that, when there are no dividends, the perpetual American call and the perpetual European call options have the same value; the current asset price S.

10.2.4 Perpetual European down and out call

Here we find the value of a perpetual down and out European call barrier option, see Merton (1973).

Let the exercise price be E and the barrier be at B where $B < E$.

Since the Black–Scholes partial differential equation governs the price of the option we can, as before, look for solutions of the form:

$$c(S, E)_{do} = A_1 S^{m_1} + A_2 S^{m_2} \tag{10.27}$$

subject to the boundary conditions: (i) $c_{do}(B, E) = 0$ and (ii) $c(\infty, E)_{do} = S$, see the previous section.

From (i) we have:

$$c_{do}(B, E) = A_1 B^{m_1} + A_2 B^{m_2} = 0, \quad \text{so} \quad A_1 = -A_2 B^{m_2 - m_1}$$

Therefore

$$c_{do}(S, E) = -A_2 B^{m_2 - m_1} S^{m_1} + A_2 S^{m_2}$$

From (ii), as $S \to \infty$:

$$c_{do}(S, E) = -A_2 B^{m_2 - m_1} S^{m_1} + A_2 S^{m_2} = S$$

However, since $m_2 < 0$, we have $A_2 S^{m_2} \to 0$, as $S \to \infty$, giving

$$c_{do}(S, E) = -A_2 B^{m_2 - m_1} S^{m_1} = S$$

So

$$A_2 = -\frac{S^{1-m_1}}{B^{m_2 - m_1}} \quad \text{and} \quad c_{do}(S, E) = \frac{S^{1-m_1} S^{m_1} B^{m_2 - m_1}}{B^{m_2 - m_1}} - \frac{S^{1-m_1} S^{m_2}}{B^{m_2 - m_1}}$$

which results in:

$$c_{do}(S, E) = S - \frac{S^{1 + m_2 - m_1}}{B^{m_2 - m_1}} \tag{10.28}$$

When there are no dividends ($q = 0$) we have already shown in Sections 10.2.1 and 10.2.2 that $m_1 = 1$ and $m_2 = -2r/\sigma^2$ so the value of a perpetual down and out call is (see Merton (1973)):

$$c_{do}(S, E) = S - \frac{S^{m_2}}{B^{m_2 - 1}} = S - B \left(\frac{S}{B} \right)^{-2r/\sigma^2} \tag{10.29}$$

10.3 APPROXIMATIONS FOR VANILLA AMERICAN OPTIONS

10.3.1 American call options with cash dividends

In this section we will consider the valuation of vanilla American call options with cash dividends, and discuss both the Roll, Geske, and Whaley method and also the Black (1975) method. We will first consider the Roll, Geske, and Whaley method.

The Roll, Geske, Whaley approximation

This method uses the work of Roll (1977), Geske (1979), and Whaley (1981). Let S be the current (time t) price of an asset which pays a single cash dividend D_1 at time t_1. At the *ex-dividend* date, t_1, there will be a decrease in the asset's value from S_{t_1} to $S_{t_1} - D_1$. Also the current asset price net of *escrowed* dividends is:

$$S_D = S - D_1 \exp(-r(t_1 - t)) \tag{10.30}$$

where r is the riskless interest rate.

Now consider an American call option, with strike price E and expiry time T, which is taken out on this asset. At t_1 there will be a given ex-dividend asset price, S^*, above which the option will be exercised early. This value can be found by solving the following equation:

$$c(S^*, E, \tau_1) = S^* + D_1 - E \tag{10.31}$$

where $c(S^*, E, \tau_1)$ is the Black–Scholes value of a European call option with strike price E and maturity $\tau_1 = T - t_1$, on an asset with current value S^* at time t_1. If just prior to the ex-dividend date $S_{t_1} > S^*$, then the American option will be exercised and realize a cash payoff of $S_{t_1} + D_1 - E$. On the other hand if $S_{t_1} \leq S^*$ then the option is worth more unexercised and it will be held until option maturity at time T.

We can rewrite Equation 10.31 so that S^* is the root of the following equation:

$$K(S^*) = c(S^*, E, \tau_1) - S^* - D_1 + E = 0 \tag{10.32}$$

where $K(S^*)$ denotes the function in the single variable S^*.

A well-known technique for solving Equation 10.32 is Newton's method, which in this case takes the form:

$$S^*_{i+1} = S^*_i - \frac{K(S^*_i)}{K'(S_i)^*} \tag{10.33}$$

where S^*_i is the ith approximation to S^*, and S^*_{i+1} is the improved $(i+1)$th approximation. If we now consider the terms in Equation 10.33 we have that

$$K(S^*_i) = c(S^*_i, E, \tau_1) - S^*_i - D_1 + E$$

and

$$K'(S^*_i) = \frac{\partial K(S^*_i)}{\partial S^*_i} = \frac{\partial c(S^*_i, E, \tau_1)}{\partial S^*_i} - 1$$

Also from Equation C.14 in Appendix C.3

$$\frac{\partial c(S^*_i, E, \tau_1)}{\partial S^*_i} = N(d_1(S^*_i))$$

We note that here the *continuous* dividend yield, $q = 0$.
So

$$K'(S^*_i) = \frac{\partial K(S^*_i)}{\partial S^*_i} = N(d_1(S^*_i)) - 1, \quad \text{where} \quad d_1 = \frac{\log(S^*_i / E) + (r + \sigma^2/2)(\tau_1)}{\sigma \sqrt{T - t_1}}$$

Substituting these results into Equation 10.33 gives:

$$S_{i+1}^* = S_i^* - \frac{\{c(S_i^*, E, \tau_1) - (S_i^* + D_1 - E)\}}{N(d_1(S_i^*)) - 1}$$

On rearrangement this yields

$$S_{i+1}^* = \frac{S_i^* N_1(d_1(S_i^*)) - c(S_i^*, E, \tau_1) + D_1 - E}{N_1(d_1(S_i^*)) - 1}, \quad \text{for} \quad i = 0, \ldots, \texttt{max\_iter} \quad (10.34)$$

where a convenient initial approximation is to choose $S_0^* = E$, and $\texttt{max\_iter}$ is the maximum number of iterations that are to be used.

We will now quote the Roll, Geske, and Whaley formula for the current value of an American call which pays a *single* cash dividend D_1 at time t_1, it is:

$$C(S, E, \tau) = S_D \left\{ N_1(b_1) + N_2(a_1, -b_1, \sqrt{(t_1 - t)/\tau}) \right\} + D_1 \exp(-r(t_1 - t)) N_1(b_2)$$

$$- E \exp(-r\tau) \left\{ N_1(b_2) \exp(r(\tau_1)) + N_2(a_2, -b_2, -\sqrt{(t_1 - t)/\tau}) \right\} \quad (10.35)$$

where S_D is given by Equation 10.30, E is the exercise price, T is the option expiry date, t represents the current time, τ is the option maturity, $N_1(a)$ is the univariate cumulative normal density function with upper integral limit a, and $N_2(a, b, \rho)$ is the bivariate cumulative normal density function with upper integral limits a and b and correlation coefficient ρ. The other symbols used in Equation 10.35 are defined as

$$a_1 = \frac{\log(S/E) + (r + \sigma^2/2)\tau}{\sigma\sqrt{\tau}}, \quad a_2 = a_1 - \sigma\sqrt{\tau}$$

$$b_2 = \frac{\log(S/S^*) + (r + \sigma^2/2)(t_1 - t)}{\sigma\sqrt{(t_1 - t)}}, \quad b_2 = b_1 - \sigma\sqrt{(t_1 - t)}$$

and S is the current (time t) asset price, S^* is found using Equation 10.34, r is the riskless interest rate, σ is the asset's volatility, $\tau = T - t$ and $\tau_1 = T - t_1$.

To compute the value of an American call option which pays n cash dividends $D_i, i = 1, \ldots, n$ at times $t_i, i = 1, \ldots, n$, we can use the fact that optimal exercise normally only ever occurs at the final ex-dividend date t_n, see for example Hull (1997). Under these circumstances Equation 10.35 can still be shown to value the American call but now $t - 1$ should be set to t_n, D_1 should be set to D_n, and S_D is given by:

$$S_D = S - \sum_{i=1}^{n} D_i \exp(-r(t_i - t)) \quad (10.36)$$

A program to compute the Roll, Geske, and Whaley approximation for an American call option with multiple cash dividends is given in Code excerpt 10.1. Here the NAG C library functions s15abc and g01hac are used to calculate the values of $N_1(a)$ and $N_2(a, b, \rho)$ respectively. Code excerpt 10.3 was used to compute the values presented in Table 10.1. These compare the Roll, Geske, and Whaley approximation with the Black approximation, which we will now briefly discuss.

Table 10.1   A comparison of the computed values for American call options with dividends, using the Roll, Geske, and Whaley approximation, and the Black approximation. The parameters used were: $E = 100.0$, $r = 0.04$, $\sigma = 0.2$, $\tau = 2.0$ and there is one cash dividend of value 5.0 at time $t = 1.0$. The current stock price, S, is varied from 80.0 to 120.0. The results are in agreement with those given in Table 1 of Whaley (1981)

Stock price	Critical price, S^*	RGW approximation	Black approximation
80.0	123.582	3.212	3.208
85.0	123.582	4.818	4.808
90.0	123.582	6.839	6.820
95.0	123.582	9.276	9.239
100.0	123.582	12.111	12.048
105.0	123.582	15.316	15.215
110.0	123.582	18.851	18.703
115.0	123.582	22.676	22.470
120.0	123.582	26.748	26.476

```
void RGW_approx(double *opt_value, double *critical_value, Integer n_divs, double dividends[],
                double Divs_T[], double S0, double X, double sigma, double T, double r, Integer *iflag)
{
/* Input parameters:
   = = = = = =
   n_divs          - the number of dividends
   dividends[]     - the dividends: dividends[0] contains the first dividend, dividend[1] the second etc.
   Divs_T[]        - the times at which the dividends are paid: Divs_T[0] is the time at which the first
                     dividend is paid Divs_T[1] is the time at which the second dividend is paid, etc.
   S0              - the current value of the underlying asset
   X               - the strike price
   sigma           - the volatility
   T               - the time to maturity
   r               - the interest rate

   Output parameters:
   = = = = = =
   opt_value       - the value of the option
   critical_value  - the critical value
   iflag           - an error indicator
*/
   double A_1,A_2,S_star,a1,a2,nt1,t1,S;
   double b1,b2,d1,alpha,h,div,beta,temp,temp1,temp2,temp3;
   double pdf,b,eur_val,fac,tol,loc_q,err,zero=0.0;
   Boolean iterate;
   Integer i,iflagx,putx;
   static NagError nagerr;

   loc_q = 0.0;
   temp = 0.0;
   for (i=0; i < n_divs; ++i) { /Check the Divs_T array */
     if ((Divs_T[i] <= temp) || (Divs_T[i] > T) || (Divs_T[i] <= zero)) {
       *flag = 2;
       return;
     }
     temp = Divs_T[i];
   }
   /* calculate the present value of the dividends (excluding the final one) */
   temp = 0.0;
   for (i=0; i < n_divs-1; ++i) {
     temp = fac + dividends[i] * exp(-r*Divs_T[i]);
   }
   t1 = Divs_T[n_divs-1];
   /* decrease the stock price by the present value of all dividends */
   div = dividends[n_divs-1];
   S = S0-temp-div*exp(-r*t1);
   iterate = TRUE;
   tol = 0.000001;
   S_star = X;
   while (iterate) { /* calculate S_star, iteratively */
     /* calculate the Black-Scholes value of a European call */
```

```
       d1 = (log(S_star/X) + (r+(sigma*sigma/2.0))*(T−t1))/(sigma*sqrt(T−t1));
       putx = 0;
       loc_q = 0.0;
       black_scholes(&eur_val,NULL,S_star,X,sigma, T−t1,r,loc_q, putx,&iflag);
       S_star = (S_star*s15abc(d1)−eur_val+div−X)/(s15abc (d1)−1.0);
       err = FABS(eur_val − (S_star + div− X))/X;
       if (err < tol) iterate = FALSE;
    }
    a1 = (log(S/X) + (r+(sigma*sigma/2.0))*T)/(sigma*sqrt(T));
    a2 = a1 − sigma*sqrt(T);
    b1 = (log(S/S_star) + (r+(sigma*sigma/2.0))*t1)/(sigma*sqrt (t1));
    b2 = b1 − sigma*sqrt(t1);
    nt1 = sqrt(t1/T);
    temp1 = S*(s15abc(b1)+g01hac(a1,−b1,−nt1,&nagerr));
    temp2 = −X*exp(−r*T)*g01hac(a2,−b2,−nt1,&nagerr)−(X−div)* exp(−r*t1)*s15abc(b2);
    *opt_value = temp1+temp2;
    *critical_value = S_star;
}
```

Code excerpt 10.1   Function to compute the Roll, Geske, and Whaley approximation for the value of an American call option with discrete dividends

We will now consider the Black approximation.

Black's approximation

The Black (1975) approximation for an American call with cash dividends is simpler than the Roll, Geske, and Whaley method we have just described. For an American call option which expires at time T, with n discrete cash dividends D_i, $i = 1, \ldots, n$, at times t_i, $i = 1, \ldots, n$, it involves calculating the prices of European options that mature at times T, and t_n, and then setting the option price to the greater of these two values, see for example Hull (1997).

The Black approximation, C_{BL}, can be expressed more concisely in terms of our previously defined notation as:

$$C_{BL}(S, E, \tau) = \max(v_1, v_2)$$

where v_1 and v_2 are the following European calls

$$v_1 = c(S_D, E, \tau) \quad \text{and} \quad v_2 = c(S_D^+, E, \tau_1), \qquad \tau = T - t \quad \tau_1 = T - t_n$$

and

$$S_D = S - \sum_{i=1}^{n} D_i \quad \text{and} \quad S_D^+ = S - \sum_{i=1}^{n-1} D_i$$

Code excerpt 10.2 below computes the Black approximation.

```
void black_approx(double *value, Integer n_divs, double dividends[], double Divs_T[],
     double S0, double X, double sigma, double T, double r, Integer put, Integer *ifail)
{

/* Input parameters:
   ═ ═ ═ ═ ═ ═ ═
   n_divs          − the number of dividends
   dividends[]     − the dividends, dividends[0] contains the first dividend, dividend[1] the second etc.
   Divs_T[]        − the times at which the dividends are paid, Divs_T[0] is the time at which the first
                     dividend is paid Divs_T[1] is the time at which the second dividend is paid, etc.
   S0              − the current value of the underlying asset
```

```
X                     - the strike price
sigma                 - the volatility
T                     - the time to maturity
r                     - the interest rate
put                   - if put is 0 then a call option, otherwise a put option


Output parameters:
= = = = = =
value                 - the value of the option, iflag - an error indicator
*/
  double zero = 0.0;
  double beta, temp, temp1, temp2, temp3;
  double tn, val_T, val_tn, tol, loc_q, err, fac;
  Integer i, ifailx;

  loc_q = 0.0;
  temp = 0.0;
  for (i=0; i < n_divs; ++i) {
    if (Divs_T[i] <= temp ) printf ("Error in Divs_T array, elements not increasing \n");
    if (Divs_T[i] > T) printf ("Error in Divs_T array element has a value greater than T \n");
    if (Divs_T[i] <= zero) printf ("Error in Divs_T array element <= zero \n");
    temp = Divs_T[i];
  }
  /* calculate the present value of the dividends */
  fac = 0.0;
  for (i=0; i < n_divs; ++i) {
    fac = fac + dividends[i] * exp(-r*Divs_T[i]);
  }
  temp = S0 - fac;
  /* calculate the value of the option on expiry */
  black_scholes(&val_T, NULL, temp, X, sigma, T, r, loc_q, put, &ifailx);

  /* calculate the value of the option on last dividend date */
  tn = Divs_T[n_divs-1];
  temp = temp + dividends[n_divs-1]*exp(-r*tn);
  nag_opt_bs(&val_tn, NULL, temp, X, sigma, tn, r, loc_q, putx, &ifailx);
  *value = MAX(val_tn, val_T);
}
```

Code excerpt 10.2   Function to compute the value of the Black approximation for the value of an American call option with discrete dividends

Code excerpt 10.3 below uses the same values as in Whaley (1981) and compares the Roll, Geske, and Whaley approximation with that of Black; the results are presented in Table 10.1.

```
double q, r, temp, loc_r;
Integer i, m, m2, m_acc;
double S0, E, T, sigma, t1, delta, value, ad_value, put_value;
Integer is_american, ifail, put;
double bin_greeks[5], greeks[5], bin_value, bs_value;
double opt_value, critical_value, E1, E2, crit1, crit2;
double black_value;
double Divs_T[3], dividends[3];
Integer n_divs, put;

  E = 100.0;
  r = 0.04;
  sigma = 0.2;
  T = 2.0;
  t1 = 1.0;
  put = 0;

/* check using the same parameters as in Whaley (1981) */
  Divs_T[0] = 1.0;
  dividends[0] = 5.0;
  n_divs = 1;
  printf ("\nPrice S  RGW Approximation    Black Approximation \n\n");
  for (i=0; i < 9; ++i) {
    put = 0;
    S0 = 80.0+(double)i*5.0;
```

```
opt_RGW_approx(&opt_value,&critical_value, n_divs, dividends,Divs_T,S0,E,sigma,T,r,&ifail);
printf("%8.4f ",S0);
printf("%12.3f %12.3f ",opt_value,critical_value);
opt_black_approx(&black_value,n_divs,dividends, Divs_T, S0,E,sigma,T,r,put,&ifail);
printf("%12.3f (%8.4e) ",black_value);
}
```

Code excerpt 10.3 Simple test program to compare the results of function `opt_RGW_approx` with function `opt_black_approx`, the parameters used are the same as in Whaley (1981)

We will now consider a more general technique for pricing both American puts and calls.

10.3.2 The MacMillan, Barone-Adesi, and Whaley method

Here we consider a method of pricing American options which relies on an approximation that reduces a transformed Black–Scholes equation into a second order ordinary differential equation, see Barone-Adesi and Whaley (1987) and MacMillan (1986). It thus provides an alternative way of evaluating American options that can be used instead of computationally intensive techniques such as finite-difference methods. Although the method prices American options it is really based on the value of an American option *relative* to the corresponding European option value (which can readily be computed using the Black–Scholes pricing formula).

Since an American option gives more choice its value is always at least that of its European counterpart. This early exercise premium ($\nu(S, E, \tau) \geq 0$) is now defined more precisely for American puts and calls. If at current time t the asset price is S, then the early exercise premium for an American call which expires at time T, and therefore has maturity $\tau = T - t$, is:

$$\nu_c(S, E, \tau) = C(S, E, \tau) - c(S, E, \tau) \geq 0 \tag{10.37}$$

where $C(S, E, \tau)$ denotes the value of the American call and $c(S, E, \tau)$ denotes the value of the corresponding European call. The early exercise premium of an American put option, $\nu_p(S, E, \tau)$, is similarly defined as:

$$\nu_p(S, E, \tau) = P(S, E, \tau) - p(S, E, \tau) \geq 0 \tag{10.38}$$

where $P(S, E, \tau)$ is the value of the American put, and $p(S, E, \tau)$ is the value of the corresponding European put. The key insight provided by the MacMillan, Barone-Adesi, and Whaley method is that since both the American and European option values satisfy the Black–Scholes partial differential equation so does the early exercise premium, $\nu(S, E, \tau)$; see Section 9.3.1. This means that we can write:

$$\frac{\partial \nu}{\partial t} + (r - q)S \frac{\partial \nu}{\partial S} + \frac{\sigma^2 S^2}{2} \frac{\partial^2 \nu}{\partial S^2} = r\nu \tag{10.39}$$

where as usual S is the asset price, r the continuously compounded interest rate, q the continuously compounded dividend, σ the volatility, and time t increases from the current time to the expiry time T.

We will now introduce the variable $h(\tau) = 1 - \exp(-r\tau)$ and use the factorization $v(S, E, \tau) = h(\tau)g(S, E, h)$. From standard calculus we obtain:

$$\frac{\partial v}{\partial t} = g\frac{\partial h}{\partial t} + h\frac{\partial g}{\partial t} = rg(h-1) + h\frac{\partial g}{\partial h}\frac{\partial h}{\partial t} = rg(h-1) + hr(h-1)\frac{\partial g}{\partial h}$$

and also

$$\frac{\partial v}{\partial S} = h\frac{\partial g}{\partial S} \quad \text{and} \quad \frac{\partial^2 v}{\partial S^2} = h\frac{\partial^2 g}{\partial S^2}$$

Substituting these results into Equation 10.39 yields the following transformed Black–Scholes equation:

$$\frac{S^2\sigma^2 h}{2}\frac{\partial^2 g}{\partial S^2} + (r-q)Sh\frac{\partial g}{\partial S} + rg(h-1) + rh(h-1)\frac{\partial g}{\partial h} = rgh \tag{10.40}$$

which can be further simplified to give:

$$S^2\sigma^2\frac{\partial^2 g}{\partial S^2} + \frac{2(r-q)S}{\sigma^2}\frac{\partial g}{\partial S} - \frac{2rg}{h\sigma^2} - \frac{2r(1-h)}{\sigma^2}\frac{\partial g}{\partial h} = rgh \tag{10.41}$$

or

$$S^2\frac{\partial^2 g}{\partial S^2} + \beta S\frac{\partial g}{\partial S} - \frac{\alpha}{h}g - (1-h)\alpha\frac{\partial g}{\partial h} = 0 \tag{10.42}$$

where $\alpha = 2r/\sigma^2$ and $\beta = (2(r-q))/\sigma^2$.

We now consider the last term of Equation 10.42 and note that when τ is large, $1 - h(\tau) \sim 0$. Also when $\tau \to 0$ the option is close to maturity, and the value of both the European and American options converge; which means that $v(S, E, \tau) \sim 0$ and $\partial g/\partial h \sim 0$. It can thus be seen that the last term is generally quite small and, the MacMillan, Barone-Adesi and Whaley approximation assumes that it can be ignored. This results in the following equation:

$$S^2\frac{\partial^2 g}{\partial S^2} + \beta S\frac{\partial g}{\partial S} - \frac{\alpha}{h}g = 0 \tag{10.43}$$

which is a second order differential equation with two linearly independent solutions of the form aS^γ. They can be found by substituting $g(S, E, h) = aS^\gamma$ into Equation 10.43 as follows:

$$\frac{\partial g}{\partial S} = \gamma S^{\gamma-1} \quad \frac{\partial^2 g}{\partial S^2} = a\gamma(\gamma-1)S^{\gamma-2} = a\gamma^2 S^{\gamma-2} - a\gamma S^{\gamma-2}$$

so

$$S^2\frac{\partial^2 g}{\partial S^2} = a\gamma^2 S^\gamma - a\gamma S^\gamma = \gamma^2 g - \gamma g$$

and

$$\beta S\frac{\partial g}{\partial S} = \beta Sa\gamma S^{\gamma-1} = \beta\gamma S^\gamma = \beta\gamma g$$

When the above results are substituted in Equation 10.43 we obtain the quadratic equation:

$$\gamma^2 g - \gamma g + \beta \gamma g - \alpha/h = g(\gamma^2 - \gamma + (\beta - 1)\gamma - \alpha/h) = 0$$

or

$$\gamma^2 - \gamma + (\beta - 1)\gamma - \alpha/h = 0 \tag{10.44}$$

which has the two solutions

$$\gamma_1 = \frac{1}{2}\left\{-(\beta - 1) - \sqrt{(\beta - 1)^2 + 4(\alpha/h)}\right\} \tag{10.45}$$

and

$$\gamma_2 = \frac{1}{2}\left\{-(\beta - 1) + \sqrt{(\beta - 1)^2 + 4(\alpha/h)}\right\} \tag{10.46}$$

where we note that since $\alpha/h > 0$, we have $\gamma_1 < 0$ and $\gamma_2 > 0$.

The general solution to Equation 10.43 is thus:

$$g(S, E, h) = a_1 S^{\gamma_1} + a_2 S^{\gamma_2} \tag{10.47}$$

We will now derive the appropriate solutions pertaining to American call options and American put options.

American call options

Here we use the fact that both the value and the early exercise premium $(v_c(S, E, \tau) = h g_c(S, E, h))$ of an American call tend to zero as the asset price $S \to 0$. This means that as $S \to 0$, $g_c(S, E, h) \to 0$.

However, since $\gamma_1 < 0$, the only way this can be achieved in Equation 10.47 is if $a_1 = 0$. So $g_c(S, E, h) = a_2 S^{\gamma_2}$, and the value of an American call is:

$$C(S, E, \tau) = c(S, E, \tau) + h a_2 S^{\gamma_2} \tag{10.48}$$

An expression for a_2 can be found by considering the critical asset price (point on the early exercise boundary), S^*, above which the American option will be exercised. For $S < S^*$, the value of the American call is governed by Equation 10.48, and when $S > S^*$ we have $C(S, E, \tau) = S - E$.

Now, since the value of the American option is continuous, at the critical asset value S^* the following equation applies:

$$S^* - E = c(S^*, E, \tau) + h a_2 S^{*\gamma_2} \tag{10.49}$$

Furthermore, since the gradient of the American option value is also continuous, at S^* we have:

$$\frac{\partial(S^* - E)}{\partial S^*} = \frac{\partial}{\partial S^*}\{c(S^*, E, \tau) + h a_2 S^{*\gamma_2}\} \tag{10.50}$$

which gives:

$$1 = \exp(-q\tau)N_1(d_1(S^*)) + \gamma_2 ha_2 S^{*(\gamma_2-1)} \tag{10.51}$$

where we have used the value of the hedge parameter Δ_c, see Section 9.3.3, for a European call

$$\Delta_c = \frac{\partial c(S^*, E, \tau)}{\partial S^*} = \exp(-q\tau)N_1(d_1(S^*))$$

Equation 10.51 can therefore be written as:

$$ha_2 S^{*\gamma_2} = \frac{S^*}{\gamma_2}\{1 - \exp(-q\tau)N_1(d_1(S^*))\} \tag{10.52}$$

When the left hand side of the above equation is substituted into Equation 10.49 we obtain the following equation for S^*:

$$S^* - E = c(S^*, E, \tau) + \frac{S^*}{\gamma_2}\{1 - \exp(-q\tau)N_1(d_1(S^*))\} \tag{10.53}$$

This equation can be solved for S^* using standard iterative methods (see the section on the numerical solution of critical asset values). Once S^* has been found Equation 10.52 gives:

$$ha_2 = A_2 S^{*-\gamma_2} \quad \text{where} \quad A_2 = \frac{S^*}{\gamma_2}\{1 - \exp(-q\tau)N_1(d_1(S^*))\}$$

From Equation 10.48 the value of an American call is thus of the form:

MacMillan, Barone-Adesi, and Whaley method: American call option

$$C(S, E, \tau) = c(S, E, \tau) + A_2\left(\frac{S}{S^*}\right)^{\gamma_2} \quad \text{when } S < S^* \tag{10.54}$$

$$C(S, E, \tau) = S - E \quad \text{when } S \geq S^* \tag{10.55}$$

American put options

For an American put option we proceed in a similar manner to that for the American call. We now use fact that both the value and early exercise premium, $v_p(S, E, \tau) = hg_p(S, E, h)$, of an American put tend to zero as the asset price $S \to \infty$. So $g_p(S, E, h) \to 0$ as $S \to \infty$. Since $\gamma_2 > 0$ the only way this can be achieved by Equation 10.47 is if $a_2 = 0$. This gives $g_p(S, E, h) = a_1 S^{\gamma_1}$ and the value of an American put is:

$$P(S, E, \tau) = p(S, E, \tau) + ha_1 S^{\gamma_1} \tag{10.56}$$

An expression for a_1 can be found by considering the critical asset price, S^{**}, below which the American option will be exercised. For $S > S^{**}$ the value of the American put is given by Equation 10.56, and for $S < S^{**}$ we have $P(S, E, \tau) = E - S$.

Continuity of the American option value at the critical asset price gives:

$$E - S^{**} = p(S^{**}, E, \tau) + ha_1 S^{**\gamma_1} \tag{10.57}$$

and continuity of the option value's gradient at the critical asset price yields:

$$\frac{\partial(E - S^{**})}{\partial S^{**}} = \frac{\partial}{\partial S^{**}} \{p(S^{**}, E, \tau) + ha_1 S^{**\gamma_1}\} \tag{10.58}$$

which can be simplified to:

$$-1 = -N_1(-d_1(S^{**})) \exp(-q\tau) + \gamma_1 a_1 S^{**(\gamma_1-1)} \tag{10.59}$$

where we have used the value of hedge parameter Δ_p for a European put (see section on the greeks):

$$\Delta_p = \frac{\partial p(S^{**}, E, \tau)}{\partial S^{**}} = \{N_1(d_1(S^{**})) - 1\} \exp(-q\tau) = -N_1(-d_1(S^{**})) \exp(-q\tau)$$

Equation 10.59 can therefore be written as:

$$ha_1 S^{**\gamma_1} = -\frac{S^{**}}{\gamma_1} \{1 - N_1(-d_1(S^{**})) \exp(-q\tau)\} \tag{10.60}$$

When the left hand side of the above equation is substituted into Equation 10.57 we obtain the following equation for S^{**}:

$$E - S^{**} = p(S^{**}, E, \tau) + \{1 - \exp(-q\tau)N[-d_1(S^{**})]\} \frac{S^{**}}{\gamma_1} \tag{10.61}$$

which can be solved iteratively to yield S^{**} (see the section on the numerical solution of critical asset values). Once S^{**} has been found Equation 10.60 gives:

$$ha_1 = A_1 S^{**-\gamma_1} \quad \text{where} \quad A_1 = -\left(\frac{S^{**}}{\gamma_1}\right)\{1 - \exp(-q\tau)N_1(-d_1(S^{**}))\}$$

We note here that $A_1 > 0$ since, $\gamma_1 < 0$, $S^{**} > 0$ and $N_1(-d_1(S^{**})) \exp(-q\tau) < 1$. From Equation 10.56 the value of an American put is thus:

MacMillan, Barone-Adesi, and Whaley method: American put option

$$P(S, E, \tau) = p(S, E, \tau) + A_1 \left(\frac{S}{S^{**}}\right)^{\gamma_2} \quad \text{when } S > S^{**} \tag{10.62}$$

$$P(S, E, \tau) = E - S \quad \text{when } S \le S^{**} \tag{10.63}$$

Numerical solution of critical asset values

We now provide details on how to iteratively solve for the critical asset price in Equations 10.53 and 10.61.

American call options

For American call options we need to solve Equation 10.53, which is:

$$S^* - E = c(S^*, E, \tau) + \frac{S^*}{\gamma_2} \{1 - \exp(-q\tau)N_1(d_1(S^*))\}$$

We denote the ith approximation to the critical asset value S^* by S_i^*, and represent the left hand side of the equation by:

$$LHS(S_i^*, E, \tau) = S_i^* - E$$

and the right hand side of the equation by:

$$RHS(S_i^*, E, \tau) = c(S_i^*, E, \tau) + \frac{S_i^*}{\gamma_2}\{1 - \exp(-q\tau)N_1(d_1(S_i^*))\}$$

If we let $K(S_i^*, E, \tau) = RHS(S_i^*, E, \tau) - LHS(S_i^*, E, \tau)$ then we want to find the value of S_i^* which (to a specified tolerance) gives $K(S_i^*, E, \tau) \sim 0$. This can be achieved with Newton's root finding method, in which a better approximation, S_{i+1}^*, can be found using:

$$S_{i+1}^* = S_i^* - \frac{K(S_i^*, E, \tau)}{K'(S_i^*, E, \tau)} \tag{10.64}$$

where

$$K'(S_i^*, E, \tau) = \frac{\partial}{\partial S_i^*}\{RHS(S_i^*, E, \tau) - LHS(S_i^*, E, \tau)\}$$

$$= \frac{\partial}{\partial S_i^*}\{RHS(S_i^*, E, \tau)\} - \frac{\partial}{\partial S_i^*}\{LHS(S_i^*, E, \tau)\}$$

$$= b_i - 1$$

Here we have used $b_i = (\partial/\partial S_i^*)\{RHS(S_i^*, E, \tau)\}$, and the expression for b_i is given by Equation 10.66, which is derived at the end of this section.

Substituting for $K(S_i^*, E, \tau)$ and $K'(S_i^*, E, \tau)$ into Equation 10.64 we therefore obtain:

$$S_{i+1}^* = S_i^* - \frac{(RHS(S_i^*, E, \tau) - LHS(S_i^*, E, \tau))}{(b_i - 1)}$$

$$= S_i^* - \frac{(RHS(S_i^*, E, \tau) - (S_i^* - E))}{(b_i - 1)}$$

$$= \frac{b_i S_i^* - RHS(S_i^*, E, \tau) - E}{(b_i - 1)}$$

The final iterative algorithm for the American call is therefore:

$$S_{i+1}^* = \frac{E + RHS(S_i^*, E, \tau) - b_i S_i^*}{(1 - b_i)} \tag{10.65}$$

where we can use $S_0^* = E$ for the initial estimate of the critical value, see computer Code excerpt 10.4.

The expression for b_i in an American call

Here we derive an expression for the term b_i which is used in Equation 10.65.

$$b_i = \frac{\partial c(S_i^*, E, \tau)}{\partial S_i^*} + \frac{1}{\gamma_2}\{1 - \exp(-q\tau)N_1(d_1(S_i^*))\} - \frac{S_i^*}{\gamma_2}\frac{\partial N_1(d_1(S_i^*))}{\partial d_1(S_i^*)}\frac{\partial d_1(S_i^*)}{\partial S_i^*}$$

We will now quote the following results which are derived in Appendix C:
Equation C.3:

$$\frac{\partial N_1(d_1(S_i^*))}{\partial d_1(S_i^*)} = n(d_1(S_i^*))$$

Equation C.6:

$$\frac{\partial d_1(S_i^*)}{\partial S_i^*} = \frac{1}{S_i^* \sigma \sqrt{\tau}}$$

Equation C.14:

$$\Delta_c = \frac{\partial c(S_i^*, E, \tau)}{\partial S_i^*} = \exp(-q\tau)N_1(d_1(S_i^*))$$

Substituting these results into the above expression we obtain:

$$b_i = \exp(-q\tau)N_1(d_1(S_i^*)) + \frac{1}{\gamma_2} - \frac{\exp(-q\tau)N_1(d_1(S_i^*))}{\gamma_2} - \frac{\exp(-q\tau)n(d_1(S_i^*))}{\gamma_2 \sigma \sqrt{\tau}}$$

which can be rearranged to yield:

$$b_i = \exp(-q\tau)N_1(d_1(S_i^*))\left\{1 - \frac{1}{\gamma_2}\right\} + \frac{1}{\gamma_2}\left\{1 - \frac{\exp(-q\tau)n(d_1(S_i^*))}{\sigma \sqrt{\tau}}\right\} \qquad (10.66)$$

American put options

For American put options we need to solve Equation 10.61 which is:

$$E - S_i^{**} = p(S_i^{**}, E, \tau) - \frac{S_i^{**}}{\gamma_1}\{1 - N_1(-d_1(S_i^{**}))\exp(-q\tau)\}$$

If we let S_i^{**} denote the ith approximation to the critical asset value S^{**}, then we can represent the left hand side of the equation by:

$$LHS(S_i^{**}, E, \tau) = E - S_i^{**}$$

and the right hand side of the equation by:

$$RHS(S_i^{**}, E, \tau) = p(S_i^{**}, \tau) - \frac{S_i^{**}}{\gamma_1}\{1 - N_1(-d_1(S_i^{**}))\exp(-q\tau)\}$$

$$= p(S_i^{**}, E, \tau) - \frac{S_i^{**}}{\gamma_1}\{1 - [1 - N_1(d_1(S_i^{**}))]\exp(-q\tau)\}$$

$$= p(S_i^{**}, E, \tau) - \frac{S_i^{**}}{\gamma_1}\{1 - \exp(-q\tau) + N_1(d_1(S_i^{**}))\exp(-q\tau)\}$$

We then denote $K(S_i^{**}, E, \tau) = RHS(S_i^{**}, E, \tau) - LHS(S_i^{**}, E, \tau)$, and using Newton's method we obtain:

$$S_{i+1}^{**} = S_i^{**} - \frac{K(S_i^{**}, E, \tau)}{K'(S_i^{**}, E, \tau)} \tag{10.67}$$

where as before:

$$K'(S_i^{**}, E, \tau) = \frac{\partial}{\partial S_i^{**}} \{RHS(S_i^{**}, E, \tau) - LHS(S_i^{**}, E, \tau)\}$$

So $K'(S_i^{**}, E, \tau) = 1 + b_i$, where $b_i = (\partial(RHS(S_i^{**}, E, \tau))/\partial S_i^{**})$, and the expression for b_i is given by Equation 10.69, which is derived at the end of this section. Equation 10.67 can therefore be written as:

$$S_{i+1}^{**} = S_i^{**} - \frac{(RHS(S_i^{**}, E, \tau) - LHS(S_i^{**}, E, \tau))}{1 + b_i}$$

$$= \frac{S_i^{**}(1 + b_i) - RHS(S_i^{**}, E, \tau) + E - S_i^{**}}{1 + b_i}$$

The final iterative algorithm for the American put is therefore:

$$S_i^{**} = \frac{E - RHS(S_i^{**}, E, \tau) + b_i S_i^{**}}{1 + b_i} \tag{10.68}$$

where we can use $S_0^{**} = E$ for the initial estimate of the critical asset value, see computer Code excerpt 10.4.

The expression for b_i in an American put

Here we derive an expression for the term b_i which is used in Equation 10.67. Since

$$b_i = \frac{\partial}{\partial S_i^{**}} \left\{ p(S_i^{**}, E, \tau) - \frac{S_i^{**}}{\gamma_1} (1 - \exp(-q\tau) + N_1(d_1(S_i^{**})) \exp(-q\tau)) \right\}$$

we have

$$b_i = \frac{\partial p(S_i^{**}, E, \tau)}{\partial S_i^{**}} - \frac{1}{\gamma_1} \{1 - \exp(-q\tau)\} - \frac{1}{\gamma_1} \exp(-q\tau) N_1(d_1(S_i^{**}))$$

$$- \frac{S_i^{**} \exp(-q\tau)}{\gamma_1} \frac{\partial N_1(d_1(S_i^{**}))}{\partial d_1(S_i^{**})} \frac{\partial d_1(S_i^{**})}{\partial S_i^{**}}$$

We will now quote the following results which are derived in Appendix C: Equation C.3:

$$\frac{\partial N_1(d_1(S_i^{**}))}{\partial d_1(S_i^{**})} = n(d_1(S_i^{**}))$$

Equation C.6:

$$\frac{\partial d_1(S_i^{**})}{\partial S_i^{**}} = \frac{1}{S_i^{**}\sigma\sqrt{\tau}}$$

Equation C.16:

$$\Delta_p = \frac{\partial p(S_i^{**}, E, \tau)}{\partial S_i^{**}} = \exp(-q\tau)\{N_1(d_1(S_i^{**})) - 1\}$$

Substituting these results into the above expression we therefore obtain:

$$b_i = \exp(-q\tau)\{N_1(d_1(S_i^{**})) - 1\} - \frac{1}{\gamma_1}\{1 - \exp(-q\tau) + N_1(d_1(S_i^{**}))\exp(-q\tau)\}$$

$$- \frac{S_i^{**}\exp(-q\tau)}{\gamma_1}\frac{\partial N_1(d_1(S_i^{**}))}{\partial d_1(S_i^{**})}\frac{\partial d_1(S_i^{**})}{\partial S_i^{**}}$$

$$= \exp(-q\tau)\{N_1(d_1(S_i^{**})) - 1\} - \frac{1}{\gamma_1}\{1 - \exp(-q\tau) + N_1(d_1(S_i^{**}))\exp(-q\tau)\}$$

$$- \frac{S_i^{**}\exp(-q\tau)n(d_1(S_i^{**}))}{\gamma_1\sigma\sqrt{\tau}}$$

which can be rearranged to yield:

$$b_i = \exp(-q\tau)N_1(d_1(S_i^{**}))\left\{1 - \frac{1}{\gamma_1}\right\}$$

$$+ \frac{1}{\gamma_1}\left\{\exp(-q\tau) - 1 - \frac{\exp(-q\tau)n(d_1(S_i^{**}))}{\sigma\sqrt{\tau}}\right\} - \exp(-q\tau) \tag{10.69}$$

The computer code to implement the MacMillan, Barone-Adesi, and Whaley method is provided below.

```
void MBW_approx(double *opt_value, double *critical_value, double S0, double X,
    double sigma, double T, double r, double q, Integer put, Integer *iflag)
{
/* Input parameters:
   = = = = = =
   S0              - the current value of the underlying asset
   X               - the strike price
   sigma           - the volatility
   T               - the time to maturity
   r               - the interest rate
   q               - the continuous dividend yield
   put             - if put is 0 then a call option, otherwise a put option

   Output parameters:
   = = = = = = =
   opt_value       - the value of the option
   critical_value  - the critical value
   iflag           - an error indicator
*/
   double A_1,A_2,S_star,gamma_2,gamma_1;
   double d1,alpha,h,beta,temp,temp1;
   double pdf,pi,b,rhs,eur_val,tol,err;
   Boolean iterate;
   Integer iflagx,putx;
```

```
pi = X01AAC;
beta = 2.0 * (r - q) / (sigma * sigma);
alpha = 2.0 * r / (sigma * sigma);
h = 1.0 - exp( -r*T);
temp = beta - 1.0;
iterate = TRUE;
tol = 0.000001;
if (!put){/* An American call */
  gamma_2 = (-temp + sqrt((temp*temp) + (4.0*alpha/h)));
  gamma_2 = gamma_2 / 2.0;
  S_star = X;
  while (iterate){/* calculate S_star, iteratively */
    d1 = log(S_star/X) + (r-q+(sigma*sigma/2.0))*T;
    d1 = d1/(sigma*sqrt(T));
    pdf = (1.0/sqrt(2.0*pi))*exp(-d1*d1/2.0);
    temp = exp (-q*T)*s15abc(d1)*(1.0 - (1.0/gamma_2));
    temp1 = (1.0 - ((exp(-q*T)*pdf)/(sigma*sqrt(T))))/gamma_2;
    b = temp + temp1;
    /* calculate the Black-Scholes value of a European call */
    putx = 0;
    black_scholes(&eur_val,NULL,S_star,X,sigma, T,r,q,putx,&iflagx);
    rhs = eur_val+(1.0-exp (-q*T)*s15abc(d1)) *S_star/gamma_2;
    S_star = (X + rhs - b*S_star)/(1.0-b);
    err = FABS((S_star - X) - rhs)/X;
    if (err < tol) iterate = FALSE;
  }
  A_2 = (S_star/gamma_2)*(1.0 - exp(-q*T)*s15abc(d1));
  if (S0 < S_star) {
    temp1 = S0/S_star;
    black_scholes(&temp,NULL,S0,X,sigma,T,r,q,putx, &iflagx);
    *opt_value = temp + A_2 * pow(temp1,gamma_2);
  }
  else {
    *opt_value = S0 - X;
  }
}
else {/* An American put */
  gamma_1 = (-temp - sqrt((temp*temp) + (4.0*alpha/h)));
  gamma_1 = gamma_1 / 2.0;
  S_star = X;
  while (iterate){/* calculate S_star, iteratively */
    d1 = log(S_star/X) + (r-q+(sigma*sigma/2.0))*T;
    d1 = d1/(sigma*sqrt(T));
    pdf = (1.0/sqrt(2.0*pi))*exp(-d1*d1/2.0);
    temp = exp(-q*T)*(s15abc(d1)*(1.0-(1.0/gamma_1))-1.0);
    temp1 = (exp(-q*T)-1.0-((exp(-q*T)*pdf)/(sigma*sqrt(T))))/gamma_1;
    b = temp + temp1;
    /* calculate the Black-Scholes value of a European put */
    putx = 1;
    black_scholes(&eur_val,NULL,S_star,X,sigma, T,r,q,putx,&iflagx);
    rhs = eur_val-(1.0-exp(-q*T)+exp(-q*T)*s15abc(d1)) *S_star/gamma_1;
    S_star = (X - rhs + b*S_star)/(1.0+b);
    err = FABS((X - S_star) - rhs)/X;
    if (err < tol) iterate = FALSE;
  }
  A_1 =-(S_star/gamma_1)*(1.0 - exp(-q*T)*s15abc(-d1));
  if (S0 > S_star) {
    temp1 = S0/S_star;
    black_scholes(&temp,NULL,S0,X,sigma,T,r,q,putx, &iflagx);
    *opt_value = temp + A_1 * pow(temp1,gamma_1);
  }
  else {
    *opt_value = X - S0;
  }
}
*critical_value = S_star;
}
```

Code excerpt 10.4   The function MBW_approx which computes the MacMillan, Barone-Adesi, and Whaley approximation for American options

Tables 10.2 and 10.3 present the results of using the function MBW_approx to compute the values of various American options.

Table 10.2   The MacMillan, Barone-Adesi, and Whaley method for American option values computed by the routine MBW_approx. The parameters used were: $\tau = 0.5$, $E = 100.0$, $r = 0.1$, $q = 0.06$, $\sigma = 0.2$. The accurate value was calculated using a standard lattice with 2000 time steps, and the error was the MacMillan, Barone-Adesi, and Whaley estimate minus the accurate value

Stock price	Call		Put	
	Accurate value	Error	Accurate value	Error
86.0	1.2064	5.54×10^{-4}	14.0987	-3.69×10^{-2}
89.0	1.8838	1.95×10^{-4}	11.5120	-4.85×10^{-2}
92.0	2.7890	7.03×10^{-4}	9.2478	-3.58×10^{-2}
95.0	3.9427	1.16×10^{-3}	7.3031	-1.66×10^{-2}
98.0	5.3522	1.15×10^{-3}	5.6674	7.19×10^{-4}
101.0	7.0119	1.10×10^{-3}	4.3209	1.35×10^{-2}
104.0	8.9043	2.21×10^{-3}	3.2362	2.22×10^{-2}
107.0	11.0072	2.63×10^{-3}	2.3823	2.63×10^{-2}
110.0	13.2905	4.20×10^{-3}	1.7235	2.80×10^{-2}
113.0	15.7264	4.77×10^{-3}	1.2272	2.66×10^{-2}

Table 10.3   The MacMillan, Barone-Adesi, and Whaley critical asset values for the early exercise boundary of an American put computed by the routine MBW_approx. The parameters used were: $S = 101.0$, $E = 101.0$, $r = 0.1$, $q = 0.06$, and $\sigma = 0.20$

Time to expiry, τ	Critical asset value, S^{**}	Time to expiry, τ	Critical asset value, S^{**}
1.0	82.1510	0.50	85.1701
0.95	82.3751	0.45	85.6199
0.90	82.6115	0.40	86.1176
0.85	82.8618	0.35	86.6740
0.80	83.1273	0.30	87.3049
0.75	83.4098	0.25	88.0333
0.70	83.7115	0.20	88.8959
0.65	84.0349	0.15	89.9568
0.60	84.3830	0.10	91.3469
0.55	84.7598	0.05	93.4260

10.4   LATTICE METHODS FOR VANILLA OPTIONS

10.4.1   Binomial lattice

In this section we will derive equations for a binomial lattice that describes the GBM movement of asset price changes. The approach that we will adopt is based on the work of Cox, Ross, and Rubinstein (1979), and will be referred to as the CRR lattice.

From Section 8.3 Equation 8.15 we know that if the price of an asset, S_t, follows GBM then the change in value of its price over time interval Δt, has the following distribution:

$$\log\left(\frac{S_{t+\Delta t}}{S_t}\right) \sim N\left(\left(r - \frac{\sigma^2}{2}\right)\Delta t, \sigma^2 \Delta t\right)$$

If we use the notation:

$$X = \frac{S_{t+\Delta t}}{S_t}, \quad \text{and} \quad \eta = (r - \sigma^2/2)\Delta t \quad v^2 = \sigma^2 \Delta t$$

the above equation becomes:

$$\log(X) \sim N(\eta, v^2) \quad \text{or equivalently} \quad X \sim \Lambda(\eta, v^2)$$

where $\Lambda(\eta, v^2)$ is the lognormal distribution *derived* from a Gaussian distribution with mean η, and variance v^2. It is well known, see for example Evans *et al.* (2000), that the first two moments of a variable X drawn from a lognormal distribution are

Lognormal mean

$$E[X] = \exp(\eta + v^2/2) \tag{10.70}$$

substituting for η and v^2 gives

$$E[X] = \exp\left\{ \left(r - \frac{\sigma^2}{2} \right) \Delta t + \frac{\sigma^2}{2} \Delta t \right\} \tag{10.71}$$

Lognormal variance

$$Var[X] = E[(X - E[X])^2] = E[X^2] - (E[X])^2 = \exp(2\eta + v^2)\{\exp(v^2) - 1\} \tag{10.72}$$

substituting for η and v^2 gives

$$Var[X] = \exp\left\{ 2r\left(r - \frac{\sigma^2}{2} \right) \Delta t + \sigma^2 \Delta t \right\}$$

which can be simplified to yield

$$Var[X] = \exp\{2r\Delta t\}\{\exp(\sigma^2 \Delta t) - 1\} \tag{10.73}$$

Since we can assume that the expected value of X grows at the riskless interest rate, r, we can also write:

$$E[X] = \exp(r\Delta t) \tag{10.74}$$

The above results can be used to find the first two moments of the asset price distribution $S_{t+\Delta t}$, given that we know the asset price, S_t, at time instant t. To do this we will use, see Appendix F.3 for a proof, the fact that for a random variable G we have:

$$E[a + bG] = E[a] + bE[G] \quad \text{and} \quad Var[a + bG] = b^2 Var[G]$$

where a and b are constants. Applying this to the variable X gives:

$$E[X] = E\left[\frac{S_{t+\Delta t}}{S_t} \right] = \frac{1}{S_t} E[S_{t+\Delta t}] \tag{10.75}$$

and

$$Var[X] = Var\left[\frac{S_{t+\Delta t}}{S_t}\right] = \frac{1}{S_t^2} Var[S_{t+\Delta t}] \tag{10.76}$$

where we have used $a = 0$ and $b = 1/S_t$. Note that it is also easy to show that:

$$Var[S_{t+\Delta t}] = Var[\Delta S] \tag{10.77}$$

where the change in asset price over the time interval Δt is denoted by $\Delta S = S_{t+\Delta t} - S_t$. This elementary result sometimes is used without proof, see for example Hull (1997) p. 344. The proof is simple:

$$Var[S_{t+\Delta t}] = Var[S_t + \Delta S] = Var[\Delta S]$$

where again we have used

$$Var[a + bG] = b^2 Var[G]$$

this time with $a = 0$ and $b = 1$.

To find expressions for the mean and variance of $S_{t+\Delta t}$ we simply substitute Equation 10.74 into Equation 10.75 and obtain:

$$E[S_{t+\Delta t}] = S_t \exp(r\Delta t) \tag{10.78}$$

and substitute Equation 10.73 into Equation 10.76 to yield:

$$Var[S_{t+\Delta t}] = S_t^2 \exp(2r\Delta t)\{\exp(\sigma^2 \Delta t) - 1\} \tag{10.79}$$

Since we are modelling asset price movements with a binomial lattice, the asset price, S_t, at any given node is only permitted to either *jump up* or *jump down* in value over the next time step Δt. Here we will assume that the new asset price, $S_{t+\Delta t}$, is $S_t u$ for an up jump and $S_t d$ for a down jump; where u and d are constants that apply to all lattice nodes. If we further denote the probability of an up jump by p then the probability of a down jump must (by definition) be $1 - p$.

Now that we have specified the lattice parameters we will use these to match the first two moments of the lognormal distribution. This results in the following equation for the mean:

$$E[S_{t+\Delta t}] = pS_t u + (1 - p)S_t d = S_t \exp(r\Delta t) \tag{10.80}$$

The corresponding equation for the variance requires a little more work:

$$Var[S_{t+\Delta t}] = E[(S_{t+\Delta t})^2] - (E[S_{t+\Delta t}])^2 \tag{10.81}$$

Since

$$E[(S_{t+\Delta t})^2] = p(S_t u)^2 + (1 - p)(S_t d)^2 = S_t^2(pu^2 + (1-p)d^2) \tag{10.82}$$

and, from Equation 10.80, we have

$$(E[S_{t+\Delta t}])^2 = \{S_t \exp(r\Delta t)\}^2 = S_t^2 \exp(2r\Delta t) \tag{10.83}$$

We can substitute Equations 10.82 and 10.83 into Equation 10.81 to obtain

$$Var[S_t + \Delta t] = S_t^2 \exp(2r\Delta t)\{\exp(\sigma^2 \Delta t) - 1\}$$
$$= S_t^2(pu^2 + (1-p)d^2) - S_t^2 \exp(2r\Delta t)$$

We therefore have:

$$\exp(2r\Delta t)(\exp(\sigma^2 \Delta t) - 1) = pu^2 + (1-p)d^2 - \exp(2r\Delta t) \tag{10.84}$$

So, restating Equation 10.80 and simplifying Equation 10.84, we obtain the following two equations:

$$pu + (1-p)d = \exp(r\Delta t) \tag{10.85}$$
$$\exp(2r\Delta t + \sigma^2 \Delta t) = pu^2 + (1-p)d^2 \tag{10.86}$$

which we will use to solve for the three parameters u, d, and p. Since there are three unknowns and only two equations, we can impose an additional constraint to obtain a unique solution. The constraint used in the CRR binomial model is:

$$u = \frac{1}{d} \tag{10.87}$$

We now use the following notation:

$$a = \exp(r\Delta t) \quad \text{and} \quad b^2 = \exp(2r\Delta t)\{\exp(\sigma^2 \Delta t) - 1\} = a^2\{\exp(\sigma^2 \Delta t) - 1\} \tag{10.88}$$

This means that Equation 10.85 can be written as

$$a = pu + (1-p)d, \quad \text{which gives} \quad p = \frac{a - d}{u - d} \tag{10.89}$$

From Equation 10.86 we have

$$\exp(2r\Delta t + \sigma^2 \Delta t) = a^2 \exp(\sigma^2 \Delta t) = a^2 + b^2$$

and so

$$a^2 + b^2 = pu^2 + (1-p)d^2$$

Rearranging we have

$$pu^2 + (1-p)d^2 - a^2 = b^2$$
$$pu^3 + (1-p)d^2u - a^2u - b^2u = 0$$

but

$$(1-p)d^2u = (1-p)d = a - pu$$

so

$$pu^3 = (a - pu) - a^2u - b^2u = 0$$

or

$$p(u^3 - u) + a - a^2 - b^2u = 0$$

Now

$$p(u^3 - u) = u^2p(u - d) = u^2(a - d) = u^2a - u$$

which gives

$$au^2 - u + a - a^2u - b^2u = 0$$

So we obtain the following quadratic equation in u:

$$au^2 - u(1 + a^2 + b^2) + a = 0$$

A solution is:

$$u = \frac{(1 + a^2 + b^2) + \sqrt{(1 + a^2 + b^2)^2 - 4a^2}}{2a}$$

If Δt is small we can obtain a *reasonable approximation* to the solution by neglecting terms of order higher than Δt.

In these circumstances we have:

$$a^2 + b^2 + 1 = \exp(2r\Delta t) + \exp(2r\Delta t)\{\exp(\sigma^2\Delta t) - 1\} + 1$$
$$\sim 1 + 2r\Delta t + (1 + 2r\Delta t)\sigma^2\Delta t + 1 \sim 2 + 2r\Delta t + \sigma^2\Delta t$$

Therefore

$$\sqrt{(a^2 + b^2 + 1)^2 - 4a^2} \sim \sqrt{(2 + 2r\Delta t + \sigma^2\Delta t)^2 - 4(1 + 2r\Delta t)}$$
$$\sim \sqrt{4 + 8r\Delta t + 4\sigma^2 - 4 - 8r\Delta t} = \sqrt{4\sigma^2\Delta t} = 2\sigma\sqrt{\Delta t}$$

and so

$$u \sim \frac{2 + 2r\Delta t + \sigma^2\Delta t + 2\sigma\sqrt{\Delta t}}{2\exp(r\Delta t)}$$

$$u \sim \left(1 + r\Delta t + \frac{\sigma^2\Delta t}{2} + \sigma\sqrt{\Delta t}\right)(1 - r\Delta t)$$

$$u \sim 1 + r\Delta t + \frac{\sigma^2\Delta t}{2} + \sigma\sqrt{\Delta t} - r\Delta t = 1 + \sigma\sqrt{\Delta t} + \frac{\sigma^2\Delta t}{2}$$

which to order Δt gives: $u = \exp(\sigma\sqrt{\Delta t})$ $\hspace{2cm}$ (10.90)

since

$$\exp(\sigma\sqrt{\Delta t}) = 1 + \sigma\sqrt{\Delta t} + \frac{\sigma^2\Delta t}{2} + \frac{\sigma^3(\Delta t)^{3/2}}{6} + \cdots \hspace{1cm} (10.91)$$

which gives:

$$d = \frac{1}{u} = \exp(-\sigma\sqrt{\Delta t}) \hspace{3cm} (10.92)$$

It is interesting to note that when $r = 0$ we have $p \to 1/2$.

Now that we know the values of the lattice parameters u, d, and p we can use these to build a lattice with a specified number of time steps. Once this has been constructed it can be used to compute the values and Greeks for various types of financial options. These could simply be American/European vanilla options, or more exotic options that may incorporate features such as: *lockout periods, barriers,* and nonstandard payoff functions.

We will now discuss how to create a lattice which can be used to value American and European vanilla options.

If the current value of the underlying asset is S, and the duration of the option is τ and we use a lattice with n equally spaced time intervals Δt, then we have:

$$\Delta t = \frac{\tau}{n}$$

The values of the asset price at various nodes in the lattice can easily be computed. This is illustrated in Figure 10.1, for a lattice with six time steps (that is seven lattice levels).

The asset values at the labelled nodes are:

Lattice level 1: Time t

$$S_R = S$$

Lattice level 2: Time $t + \Delta t$

$$S_S = Su \quad S_T = Sd$$

Lattice level 6: Time $t + 5\Delta t$

$$S_A = Su^5 \quad S_B = Su^3 \quad S_C = Su \quad S_D = Sd \quad S_E = S \quad S_F = Sd^5$$

Lattice level 7: Time $t + 6\Delta t$

$$S_G = Su^6 \quad S_H = Su^4 \quad S_I = Su^2 \quad S_J = S \quad S_K = Sd^2 \quad S_L = Sd^4 \quad S_M = Sd^6$$

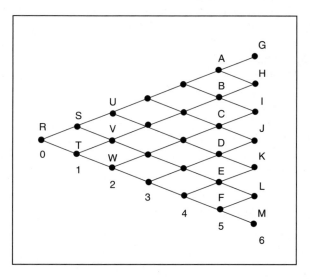

Figure 10.1   A standard binomial lattice consisting of six time steps. The root lattice node R corresponds to the current time t, the terminal nodes G to M are those at option maturity; that is time $t + \tau$, where τ is the duration of the option. The asset value at node R is S, where S is the current asset value. Asset values at other nodes are, for example, node S: Su, node T: Sd, node V: S, and node A: Su^5. Option values are computed using a backward iterative process: the option values at nodes A to F on the penultimate time step are computed from the payouts of the terminal nodes G to M, and this process continues until the root node is reached; which yields the current value of the option. Here we compute the Greeks using the following nodes: Delta uses nodes S and T, *Gamma* uses nodes U, V, and W and *Theta* uses nodes R and V

In general, at time $t + i\Delta t$, there are $i + 1$, stock prices; these are:

$$S_{i,j} = Su^j d^{i-j}, \quad j = 0, 1, \ldots, i$$

We note, that since $u = 1/d$, an up movement followed by a down movement gives the same stock price as a down movement followed by an up movement; for instance $Su^2 d = Su$. This means that the tree recombines, and the number of nodes required to represent all the different asset prices is significantly reduced.

10.4.2 Constructing and using the binomial lattice

In this section we are concerned with the practical details of how to construct, and then use, a *standard* one-dimensional binomial lattice to value American and European options. Since this lattice forms the basis for other one-dimensional and multi dimensional lattice techniques we will discuss its construction in some detail. A complete computer program for a standard binomial lattice is given in Code excerpt 10.11, and we will use this as a basis for our discussions. For easy reference we will now list the input parameters used by this computer program:

```
S0                    the current price of the underlying asset, S
X                     the strike price
sigma                 the volatility of the asset
T                     the maturity of the option in years
r                     the risk free interest rate
q                     the continuous dividend yield
put                   if put equals 1 then the option is a put option,
                      if put equals 0 then it is a call option
is_american           if is_american equals 1 then it is an American option,
                      if is_american equals 0 then it is a European option
M                     the number of time steps in the lattice
```

We will now discuss in more detail the computational issues involved in each stage of the calculation.

> **Compute the values of the constants used by the lattice**

First calculate the values of various constants that will be used.

```
dt = T/(double)M;
t1 = sigma*sqrt(dt);
u = exp(t1);
d = exp(-t1);
a = exp((r - q)*dt);
p = (a - d)/(u - d);
if ((p < zero) || (p > 1.0)) printf ("Error p out of range\n");
discount = exp(-r*dt);
p_u = discount*p;
p_d = discount*(1.0-p);
```

Code excerpt 10.5

For convenience, we have used the variables p_u and p_d to store respectively the up and down jump probabilities discounted by the interest rate r over one time step; these values will be used later on when we work backwards through the lattice to calculate the current option value.

Assign the asset values to the lattice nodes

We will now show that the number of different asset prices, $\mathcal{LS}_n$, for an n step recombining lattice is $2n + 1$.

The nodes in a recombining lattice can be considered as being composed of two kinds: those corresponding to an *even* time step, and those corresponding to an *odd* time step.

This is because the set of node asset values, $\mathcal{ET}$, for an even time step is distinct from the set of node asset values, $\mathcal{OT}$, for an odd time step. Although $\mathcal{ET} \cap \mathcal{OT} = \emptyset$, the elements of $\mathcal{ET}$ and $\mathcal{OT}$ for any consecutive pair of time steps, are related by the simple constant multiplicative factor d. Also for an even time step there is a central node corresponding to the current asset price $S0$, and the remaining nodes are symmetrically arranged about this. These features are illustrated in Figure 10.1, for a standard lattice with six time steps.

The number of distinct asset prices in a lattice is therefore the sum of the number of nodes in the last two time steps. Since the number of nodes in the ith time step, S_i, is $i + 1$ (see Figure 10.1), for an n time step lattice we have:

$$S_n = n + 1 \quad \text{and} \quad S_{n-1} = n$$

This means that the number of different asset values in an n time step lattice is:

$$\mathcal{LS}_n = S_n + S_{n-1} = 2n + 1$$

The number of nodes in an n time step lattice, $\mathcal{LN}_n$, is:

$$\mathcal{LN}_n = \sum_{i=0}^{n}(i+1) = \frac{(n+1)(n+2)}{2}$$

where we have used the fact that $\mathcal{LN}_n$ is the sum of an arithmetic progression with first term 1, increment 1 and last term $n + 1$.

One might initially think that, in order to price options, it is necessary to store the asset value of each lattice node; which would entail storing $\mathcal{LN}_n$ values. However, this is not the case. We only need to store the number of *different* asset values in the lattice; that is $\mathcal{LS}_n$ values.

Storing $\mathcal{LS}_n$ values instead of $\mathcal{LN}_n$ can result in dramatic economies of storage. For example an accurate, 1000 step lattice, has $\mathcal{LN}_n = 2001 \times 2002 \times 1/2 = 2003001$, while the corresponding value of $\mathcal{LS}_n$ is only $2 \times 1000 + 1 = 2001$.

```
s[M] = S0;
for (i = 1; i <= M; ++i) {
    s[M+i] = u*s[M+i-1];
    s[M-i] = d*s[M-i+1];
}
```

Code excerpt 10.6 A code fragment which assigns the different binomial lattice asset values to the storage array s by using the up and down jump ratios u and d defined in Section 10.4.1. The current asset value S is assigned to the central array element s[M], where M is the number of time steps in the lattice. The array elements above centre are $S[M + i] = Su^i, i = 1, \ldots, M$, and the array elements below centre are $S[M - i] = Sd^i\, i = 1, \ldots, M$

Compute the option payoff at the terminal nodes

The current value of an option is evaluated by starting at option maturity, the end of the tree and working backwards. The option values for the *terminal nodes* of the tree are just given by the payoff (at maturity) of the option; this is independent of whether the option is an American or European. For a lattice with n time steps there are $n + 1$ terminal nodes, with option values, $f_{n,j}, j = 0, \ldots, n$.

To compute the values of vanilla American and European options, with exercise price E, then we will start with the following terminal node values: for put options

$$f_{n,j} = \max(E - Su^j d^{n-j}, 0), \quad j = 0, \ldots, n$$

and for call options

$$f_{n,j} = \max(Su^j d^{n-j} - E, 0), \quad j = 0, \ldots, n$$

The computer code used to achieve this is:

```
if (((M+1)/2) == (M/2)) {/* then M is even */
   if (put)
      v[M/2] = MAX(X - s[M], zero);
   else
      v[M/2] = MAX(s[M]-X, zero);
}
P1 = 2*M;
P2 = 0;
for (i = 0; i < (M+1)/2; ++i){
   if (put){
      v[M-i] = MAX(X - s[P1], zero);
      v[i] = MAX(X - s[P2], zero);
   }
   else{
      v[M-i] = MAX(s[P1]-X, zero);
      v[i] = MAX(s[P2]-X, zero);
   }
   P1 = P1 - 2;
   P2 = P2 + 2;
}
```

Code excerpt 10.7 A code fragment that computes the payouts for puts and calls at the lattice terminal nodes. The payouts are assigned to elements of the array v and are computed using the strike price, X, and the previously computed asset values stored in array s, as before M is the number of time steps in the lattice

Iterate backwards through the lattice

The probability of moving from node (i, j) at time $i\Delta t$ to node $(i + 1, j + 1)$ at time $(i + 1)\Delta t$ is p, and the probability of moving from node (i, j) at time $i\Delta t$ to the node $(i + 1, j)$ at time $(i + 1)\Delta t$ is $1 - p$. If we assume that there is no early exercise then:

$$f_{i,j}^E = \exp(-r\Delta t)\{pf_{i+1,j+1} + (1 - p)f_{i+1,j}\}, \quad j \leq i \leq n - 1 \quad 0 \leq j \leq i \tag{10.93}$$

When early exercise, for an American option, is taken into account we have:

$$f_{i,j}^A = \max\left\{E - S_{i,j}, f_{i,j}^E\right\} \tag{10.94}$$

or for an American call option:

$$f_{i,j}^A = \max\left\{S_{i,j} - E, f_{i,j}^E\right\}, \quad j \le i \le N-1 \quad 0 \le j \le i \tag{10.95}$$

where $f_{i,j}^E$ is given by Equation 10.93.

The following code works backward through the lattice and uses the array v to store the option values.

```
P2 = 0;
for (m1 = M-1; m1 >= 2; --m1) {
  P2 = P2 + 1;
  P1 = P2;
  for (n =0; n <= m1; ++n){
    if ((v[n] == zero) && (v[n+1] == zero)){
      hold = zero;
    }
    else
      hold = p_d*v[n] + p_u*v[n+1];
    if (is_american){
      if (put)
        v[n] = MAX(hold, X-s[P1]);
      else
        v[n] = MAX(hold, s[P1]-X);
    }
    else
      v[n] = hold;
    P1 = P1 + 2;
  }
}
```

Code excerpt 10.8 Computer code that works iteratively backward through the lattice computing the option values at each time step. The array v contains the option values computed from the previous time step, and these are overwritten with option values computed for the current time step. The iteration stops at second time step, since we do not want to overwrite values in the array v which are required for calculating the Greeks in the neighbourhood of the root node

At each time step the newly calculated option values overwrite those computed by the previous time step. This process is continued until the second time step ($m1 = 2$) is reached. A different technique is then used, which doesn't overwrite the option values and thus allows the Greeks to be computed in the vicinity of the root lattice node R. In cases where we are not interested in calculating the Greeks (see for example Code excerpt 12.6) we continue working backward through the lattice until the root node R ($m1 = 0$) is reached, and the current value of the option is then given by v[0] (or its multidimensional equivalent).

The option values at all lattice nodes in time steps 0, 1, and 2 are made accessible by the following code:

```
jj = 2;
for (m1 = 2; m1 >= 1; --m1){
  ind = M-m1+1;
  for (n =0; n < m1; ++n){
    hold = p_d*v[5-jj- m1-1] + p_u*v[5-jj-m1];
    if (is_american) {
      if (put)
        v[5-jj] = MAX(hold, X-s[ind]);
      else
        v[5-jj] = MAX(hold, s[ind]-X);
    }
    else
      v[5-jj] = hold;
```

```
            --jj;
            ind = ind + 2;
        }
    }
    *value = v[5];
```

Code excerpt 10.9   Code fragment illustrating how the option values are stored for the first two time steps so that the Greeks can be computed in the vicinity of the root node R

Figure 10.2 presents the results for the valuation of an American put option.

Computing the greeks: Δ, Γ, and Θ

We will now describe how to calculate the option's hedge statistics (Greeks).

Let the option value and asset value at lattice node k be denoted by f_k and S_k respectively. So, for instance, S_T represents the asset price at node T, and f_T is the corresponding option value at node T. Table 10.4 supplies details of the lattice node values in the vicinity of the root node R.

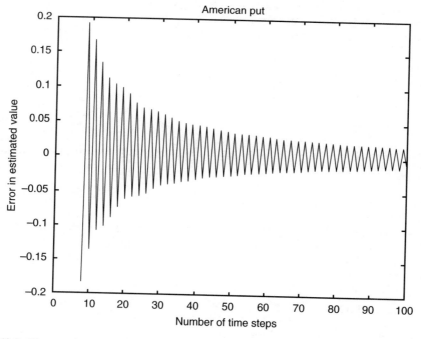

Figure 10.2   The error in the estimated value, *est_val*, of an American put using a standard binomial lattice. The parameters used were: $T = 1.0$, $S = 105.0$, $X = 105.0$, $r = 0.1$, $q = 0.02$, $\sigma = 0.3$. The very accurate value (*acc_val*) was 9.2508 and was computed using a 6000 step standard binomial lattice. The error in the estimated value was obtained as *est_val − acc_val*

Table 10.4   Lattice node values in the vicinity of the root node R

Node	Time step	Asset array element	Asset value	Option array element
R	0	s[M]	S	v[5]
S	1	s[M+1]	Su	v[4]
T	1	s[M−1]	Sd	v[3]
U	2	s[M+2]	Su^2	v[2]
V	2	s[M]	S	v[1]
W	2	s[M−2]	Sd^2	v[0]

The computation of each Greek is now considered.

Delta

The definition of Δ is the rate of change of the option value with asset price; all other parameters remaining fixed. Thus

$$\Delta = \frac{\partial f}{\partial S} = \frac{\Delta f}{\Delta S}$$

where Δf is the change option value corresponding to the change in the asset price ΔS. Ideally we would like to evaluate this partial derivative at the root node R (m1 = 0), however we can't because we need at least two lattice nodes to compute a value. The best we can do is to evaluate the derivative at the first time step (m1 = 1) as follows:

$$\Delta = \frac{f_S - f_T}{S_S - S_T} = \frac{v[4] - v[3]}{s[M+1] - s[M-1]}$$

Gamma

The definition of Γ is the rate of change of Δ with asset price; all other parameters remaining fixed. Thus

$$\Gamma = \frac{\partial^2 f}{\partial S^2} = \frac{\partial \Delta}{\partial S}$$

In order to evaluate Γ we require at least two values of Δ. The nearest this can be achieved to the root node R is at time step 2, where we have:

$$\Gamma = \frac{\Delta_{UV}^* - \Delta_{VW}^*}{S_{UV}^* - S_{VW}^*}$$

with the midpoints

$$S_{UV}^* = \frac{1}{2}\{S_U + S_V\}$$

and the values of Δ at the midpoints S_{UV}^* and S_{VW}^* denoted by Δ_{UV}^* and Δ_{VW}^* respectively. Since

$$\Delta^*_{UV} = \frac{f_U - f_V}{S_U - S_V}, \quad \Delta^*_{VW} = \frac{f_V - f_W}{S_V - S_W}$$

and

$$S^*_{UV} - S^*_{VW} = \frac{1}{2}\{S_U - S_W\}$$

we have

$$\Delta^*_{UV} = \frac{v[2] - v[1]}{s[M + 2] - s[M]}, \quad \Delta^*_{VW} = \frac{v[1] - v[0]}{s[M] - s[M - 2]}$$

The value of Γ can therefore be approximated as:

$$\Gamma = \frac{2\{\Delta^*_{UV} - \Delta^*_{VW}\}}{s[M + 2] - s[M - 2]}$$

Theta

The definition of Θ is the rate of change of option value with time; all other parameters remaining fixed. Thus

$$\Theta = \frac{\partial f}{\partial t} = \frac{\Delta f}{\Delta t}$$

The nearest to the root node R that can be computed is over the time interval from time step 0 to time step 2. We then obtain the following approximation:

$$\Theta = \frac{f_V - f_R}{2\Delta t} = \frac{v[1] - v[5]}{2\Delta t}$$

The Code excerpt 10.10 computes the Δ, Γ, and Θ by using the approximations we have just discussed.

Vega

The definition of $\mathcal{V}$ is the rate of change of the option value with volatility.

$$\mathcal{V} = \frac{\partial f}{\partial \sigma}$$

In a standard binomial lattice $\mathcal{V}$ cannot be computed directly. A simple approach is to use two binomial lattices as follows

$$\mathcal{V} = \frac{f_{\sigma + \Delta\sigma} - f_\sigma}{\Delta\sigma}$$

where $f_{\sigma + \Delta\sigma}$ is the option value computed using a binomial lattice with volatility $\sigma + \Delta\sigma$ and f_σ is the option value computed using another binomial lattice with a volatility of σ; all other lattice parameters remain constant.

```
if(greeks){
/* assign the value of delta (obtained from ml = 1) */
  greeks[1] = (v[4]-v[3])/(s[M+1]-s[M-1]);
  /* assign the value of gamma (use the values at time step ml = 2) */
```

```
dv1 = v[2] − v[1];
ds1 = s[M+2] − s[M];
dv2 = v[1] − v[0];
ds2 = s[M] − s[M−2];
h = 0.5*(s[M+2] − s[M−2]);
greeks[0] = ((dv1/ds1) − (dv2/ds2))/h;
/* assign the value of theta */
greeks[2] = (v[1]−*value)/(2.0*dt); /* can also write: greeks[2] = (v[1]−v[5])/(2.0*dt); */
}
```

Code excerpt 10.10   A code fragment that computes the values of the Greeks (*Delta*, *Gamma*, and *Theta*)
in the vicinity of the root lattice node R

```
void standard_lattice(double *value, double greeks[], double S0, double X, double sigma, double T, double r,
    double q, Integer put, Integer is_american, Integer M, Integer *iflag)
{
/* Input parameters:
   = = = = = =
   S0              − the current price of the underlying asset
   X               − the strike price
   sigma           − the volatility
   T               − the time to maturity
   r               − the interest rate
   q               − the continuous dividend yield
   put             − if put is 0 then a call option, otherwise a put option
   is_american     − if is_american is 0 then a European option, otherwise an American option
   M               − the number of time steps

   Output parameters:
   = = = = = =
   value           − the value of the option,
   greeks[]        − the hedge statistics output as follows: greeks[0] is gamma, greeks[1] is delta,
                     greeks[2] is theta,
   iflag           − an error indicator.
*/

    /* Allocate the arrays s[2*M+1], and v[M+1] */

    dt = T/(double)M;
    t1 = sigma*sqrt(dt);
    u = exp(t1);
    d = exp(−t1);
    a = exp((r−q)*dt);
    p = (a − d)/(u − d);
    if ((p < zero) || (p > 1.0)) printf ("Error p out of range\n");
    discount = exp(−r*dt);
    p_u = discount*p;
    p_d = discount*(1.0−p);


    /* assign the 2*M+1 asset values */
    s[M] = S0;
    for (i = 1; i <= M; ++i){
      s[M+i] = u*s[M+i−1];
      s[M−i] = d*s[M−i+1];
    }
    /* Find out if the number of time steps, M, is odd or even */
    if (((M+1)/2) == (M/2)){/* then M is even */
      if (put)
        v[M/2] = MAX(X − s[M], zero);
      else
        v[M/2] = MAX(s[M]−X, zero);
    }
    /* Calculate the option values at maturity */
    P1 = 2*M;
    P2 = 0;
    for (i = 0; i < (M+1)/2; ++i) {
      if (put){
        v[M−i] = MAX(X − s[P1], zero);
        v[i] = MAX(X − s[P2], zero);
      }
      else {
        v[M−i] = MAX(s[P1]−X, zero);
        v[i] = MAX(s[P2]−X, zero);
      }
```

```
      P1 = P1 - 2;
      P2 = P2 + 2;
    }
/* now work backwards through the lattice to calculate the current option value */
    P2 = 0;
    for (m1 = M-1; m1 >=2; --m1){
      P2 = P2 + 1;
      P1 = P2;
      for (n =0; n <=m1; ++n){
        if ((v[n] == zero) && (v[n+1] == zero)) {
          hold = zero;
        }
        else
          hold = p_d*v[n] + p_u*v[n+1];
        if (is_american) {
          if (put)
            v[n] = MAX(hold, X-s[P1]);
          else
            v[n] = MAX(hold, s[P1]-X);
        }
        else
          v[n] = hold;
        P1 = P1 + 2;
      }
    }
/* The values v[0], v[1] & v[2] correspond to the nodes for m1 = 2, v[3] & v[4] correspond to the nodes for m1 = 1
   and the option value (*value) is the node for m1 = 0, v[5]. For a given time step v[0] corresponds to the
   lowest asset price, v[1] to the next lowest etc.. */

    jj = 2;
    for (m1 = 2; m1 >= 1; --m1) {
      ind = M-m1+1;
      for (n =0; n < m1; ++n) {
        hold = p_d*v[5-jj-m1-1] + p_u*v[5-jj-m1];
        if (is_american) {
          if (put)
            v[5-jj] = MAX(hold, X-s[ind]);
          else
            v[5-jj] = MAX(hold, s[ind]-X);
        }
        else
          v[5-jj] = hold;
        --jj;
        ind = ind + 2;
      }
    }
    *value = v[5];
    if(greeks){
      /* assign the value of delta (obtained from m1 = 1) */
      greeks[1] = (v[4]-v[3])/(s[M+1]-s[M-1]);
      /* assign the value of gamma (use the values at time step m1 = 2) */
      dv1 = v[2] - v[1];
      ds1 = s[M+2] - s[M];
      dv2 = v[1] - v[0];
      ds2 = s[M] - s[M-2];
      h = 0.5*(s[M+2] - s[M-2]);
      greeks[0] = ((dv1/ds1) - (dv2/ds2))/h;
      /* assign the value of theta */
      greeks[2] = (v[1]-*value)/(2.0*dt); /* can also write:y greeks[2] = (v[1]-v[5])/(2.0*dt); */
    }
```

Code excerpt 10.11 Function to compute the value of an option using a standard binomial lattice

The implied volatility of American options can be computed using the method outlined for European options in Section 9.3.4; however in this case the option value and Greeks are computed using a binomial lattice.

10.4.3 Binomial lattice with a control variate

The control variate technique can be used to enhance the accuracy that a standard binomial lattice gives for the value of an American vanilla option. It involves using the same standard binomial lattice to value of both an American option and also the equivalent European option. The Black–Scholes formula is then used to compute the accurate value of the European option. If we assume that the error in pricing the European option is the same as that for the American option we can achieve an improved estimate for the value of the American option.

When applied to the valuation of an American put option this can be expressed as follows:

European pricing error,

$$\Delta_E = p^{BS}(S, \ E, \ \tau) - p^L(S, \ E, \ \tau)$$

American pricing error,

$$\Delta_A = P^*(S, \ E, \ \tau) - P^L(S, \ E, \ \tau)$$

where as usual S is the current value of the asset, E is the strike price, and τ is the maturity of the option. Also $p^{BS}(S, E, \tau)$ is the Black–Scholes value of the European put option, $p^L(S, E, \tau)$ is the binomial lattice estimate of the European put option, $P^*(S, E, \tau)$ is the (*unknown*) accurate value of the American put option and $P^L(S, E, \tau)$ is the binomial lattice estimate of the American put option.

Letting $\Delta_E = \Delta_A$ we then have

$$p^{BS}(S, \ E, \ \tau) - p^L(S, \ E, \ \tau) = P^*(S, \ E, \ \tau) - P^L(S, \ E, \ \tau)$$

which on rearrangement yields:

$$P^*(S, \ E, \ \tau) = p^{BS}(S, \ E, \ \tau) - p^L(S, \ E, \ \tau) + P^L(S, \ E, \ \tau)$$

We thus use $P^*(S, E, \tau)$ as the improved, control variate estimate, for the value of American put option. Of course exactly the same approach can be used to obtain an improved estimate for the value of an American call.

Code excerpt 10.12 shows the use of the control variate technique in a standard binomial lattice to provide improved estimates for both the value and the hedge statistics of an American option.

```
/* Set up the arrays as in the standard lattice */
    .   .   .
for (i = 0; i < (M+1)/2; ++i) { /* Calculate the option values at maturity */
  if (put){
    a_v[M-i] = MAX(X - s[P1], zero);
    a_v[i] = MAX(X - s[P2], zero);
  }
  else {
    a_v[M-i] = MAX(s[P1]-X, zero);
    a_v[i] = MAX(s[P2]-X, zero);
  }
  e_v[i] = a_v[i];
  e_v[M-i] = a_v[M-i];
  P1 = P1 - 2;
  P2 = P2 + 2;
}
/* now work backwards through the lattice to calculate the current option value */
P2 = 0;
for (m1 = M-1; m1 >= 2; --m1) {
  P2 = P2 + 1;
  P1 = P2;
  for (n =0; n <= m1; ++n){
    if ((a_v[n] == zero) && (a_v[n+1] == zero))
```

```
        hold = zero;
      else
        hold = p_d*a_v[n] + p_u*a_v[n+1];
      if (put)
        a_v[n] = MAX(hold, X-s[P1]);
      else
        a_v[n] = MAX(hold, s[P1]-X);
      if ((e_v[n] == zero) && (e_v[n+1] == zero))
        e_v[n] = zero;
      else
        e_v[n] = p_d*e_v[n] + p_u*e_v[n+1];
      P1 = P1 + 2;
    }
  }
/* The American values are stored in the array a_v, and the European values in the array e_v. The array
   indexing is the same as for the standard lattice */

jj = 2;
for (ml = 2; ml >= 1; --ml) {
  ind = M-ml+1;
  for (n =0; n < ml; ++n) {
    hold = p_d*a_v[5-jj-ml-1] + p_u*a_v[5-jj-ml];
    if (put)
      a_v[5-jj] = MAX(hold, X-s[ind]);
    else
      a_v[5-jj] = MAX(hold, s[ind]-X);
    e_v[5-jj] = p_d*e_v[5-jj-ml-1] + p_u*e_v[5-jj-ml];
    --jj;
    ind = ind + 2;
  }
}
/* v1 = American binomial approximation, v2 = European Binomial approximation, temp = exact (European)
   Black-Scholes value */
    black_scholes(&temp, bs_greeks, S0, X, sigma, T, r, q, put, &iflagx);
  *value = (a_v[5] - e_v[5]) + temp; /* return the control variate approximation */
if(greeks) {
  /* assign the value of delta (obtained from ml = 1) */
  a_delta = (a_v[4]-a_v[3])/(s[M+1]-s[M-1]);
  e_delta = (e_v[4]-e_v[3])/(s[M+1]-s[M-1]);
  greeks[1] = a_delta - e_delta + bs_greeks[1];
  /* assign the value of gamma (use the values at time step ml = 2) */
  dv1 = a_v[2] - a_v[1];
  ds1 = s[M+2] - s[M];
  dv2 = a_v[1] - a_v[0];
  ds2 = s[M] - s[M-2];
  h = 0.5*(s[M+2] - s[M-2]);
  a_gamma = ((dv1/ds1) - (dv2/ds2))/h;
  dv1 = e_v[2] - e_v[1];
  dv2 = e_v[1] - e_v[0];
  e_gamma = ((dv1/ds1) - (dv2/ds2))/h;
  greeks[0] = (a_gamma - e_gamma) + bs_greeks[0];
  /* assign the value of theta */
  a_theta = (a_v[1]-a_v[5])/(2.0*dt);
  e_theta = (e_v[1]-e_v[5])/(2.0*dt);
  greeks[2] = (a_theta - e_theta) + bs_greeks[2];
}
```

Code excerpt 10.12   Function to compute the value and hedge statistics of an American option using a
binomial lattice with a control variate

Finally we should mention that the control variate technique does not just apply to
American vanilla options. The method is quite general and can be used to obtain improved estimates for any integral (or exotic option) so long as an accurate (closed form)
solution of a *similar* integral is known. One common use of the control variate method is
to improve the accuracy of Monte Carlo estimates, see Clewlow and Strickland (1999).

10.4.4   The binomial lattice with BBS and BBSR

Here we consider the binomial Black–Scholes (BBS) method and also the binomial
Black–Scholes method with Richardson extrapolation (BBSR), see Broadie and

DeTemple (1996). As with the control variate method discussed in the previous section, both of these techniques can be used in conjunction with a standard binomial lattice to improve the computed results.

We will first discuss the BBS method.

The BBS Method

The BBS method is identical to the standard binomial lattice except that in the last time step (that is just before option maturity) the Black–Scholes formula is used to calculate the option values at maturity. For an *n* time step binomial lattice this involves evaluating the Black–Scholes formula at each of the *n* nodes in the penultimate time step, see Figure 10.1. In Code excerpt 10.13 we define the function `bs_lattice` which incorporates the BBS method into a standard binomial lattice. The reader will have noticed that `bbs_lattice` is *rather lax* concerning the amount of storage that is required, see Section 10.4.2. It uses an array of size $\mathcal{LN}_n$ rather than $\mathcal{LS}_n$ to store the lattice asset prices; the modification to use an array of size $\mathcal{LS}_n$ is left as an exercise.

```
void bbs_lattice(double *value, double greeks[], double S0, double X, double sigma, double T, double r,
      double q, Integer put, Integer M, Integer *iflag)
{
/* Input parameters:
   = = = = = = =
   S0                  - the current price of the underlying asset
   X                   - the strike price
   sigma               - the volatility
   T                   - the time to maturity
   r                   - the interest rate
   q                   - the continuous dividend yield
   put                 - if put is 0 then a call option, otherwise a put option
   M                   - the number of time steps

   Output parameters:
   = = = = = =
   value               - the value of the option, greeks[] - the hedge statistics output as follows: greeks[0] is
                         gamma, greeks[1] is delta, greeks[2] is theta,
   iflag               - an error indicator.
*/
      .   .   .
   /* allocate the arrays s[((M+2)*(M+1))/2], and v[M+1] */

   dt = T/(double)M;
   t1 = sigma*sqrt(dt);
   u = exp(t1);
   d = exp(-t1);
   a = exp((r-q)*dt);
   p = (a - d)/(u - d);
   if ((p < zero) || (p > 1.0)) return; /* Invalid probability */
   discount = exp(-r*dt);
   p_u = p*discount;
   p_d = (1.0-p)*discount;
   jj = 0;
   s[0] = S0;
   /* The "higher" the value of jj, at a given time instant,
      the lower the value of the asset price */
   for (ml = 1; ml <= M-1; ++ml){/* Calculate asset values up to (M-1)th time step */
      for (n = ml; n >= 1; --n){
         ++jj;
         s[jj] = u*s[jj-ml];
      }
      ++jj;
      s[jj] = d*s[jj-ml-1];
   }
```

```
for (n = 0; n <= M-1; ++n){/* Use Black-Scholes for the final step */
  black_scholes(&temp, NULL, s[jj], X, sigma, dt, r, q, put, &iflagx);
  v[n] = temp;
  --jj;
}
  for (m1 = M-1; m1 >= 3; --m1){/* work backwards through the lattice */
    for (n =0; n < m1; ++n){
      if ((v[n] == zero) && (v[n+1] == zero)){
        hold = zero;
      }
      else
        hold = p_d*v[n] + p_u*v[n+1];
      if (is_american){
        if (put)
          v[n] = MAX(hold, X-s[jj]);
        else
          v[n] = MAX(hold, s[jj]-X);
      }
      else
        v[n] = hold;
      --jj;
    }
  }
/* The values v[0], v[1] & v[2] correspond to the nodes for m1 = 2, v1 & v2 correspond to the nodes for m1 = 1
   and the option value (*value) is the node for m1 = 0. For a given time step v[0] corresponds to the lowest
   asset price, v[1] to the next lowest etc.. */

hold = p_d*v[0] + p_u*v[1];
if (is_american){
  if (put)
    v1 = MAX(hold, X-s[jj]);
  else
    v1 = MAX(hold, s[jj]-X);
}
else
  v1 = hold;
--jj;
hold = p_d*v[1] + p_u*v[2];
if (is_american){
  if (put)
    v2 = MAX(hold, X-s[jj]);
  else
    v2 = MAX(hold, s[jj]-X);
}
else
  v2 = hold;
--jj;
hold = p_d*v1 + p_u*v2;
if (is_american){
  if (put)
    *value = MAX(hold, X-s[0]);
  else
    *value = MAX(hold, s[0]-X);
}
else
  *value = hold;
if(greeks){
  /* assign the value of delta (obtained from m1 = 1) */
  greeks[1] = (v2-v1)/(s[1]-s[2]);
  /* assign the value of gamma (use the values at time step m1 = 2) */
  dv1 = v[2] - v[1];
  ds1 = s[3] - s[4];
  dv2 = v[1] - v[0];
  ds2 = s[4] - s[5];
  h   = 0.5*(s[3] - s[5]);
  greeks[0] = ((dv1/ds1) - (dv2/ds2))/h;
  /* assign the value of theta */
  greeks[2] = (v[1]-*value)/(2.0*dt);
}
}
```

Code excerpt 10.13   The function `bbs_lattice` which incorporates the BBS method into a standard binomial lattice. The Black–Scholes formula is evaluated by using the function `black_scholes`, given in Section 9.3.3

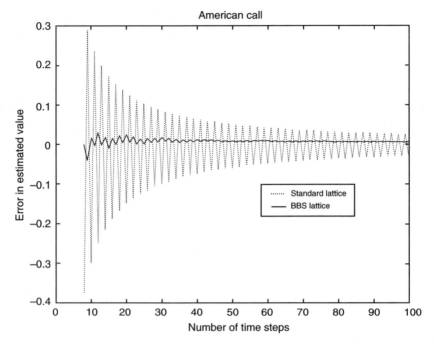

Figure 10.3   The error in the estimated value, *est_val*, of an American call using both a standard binomial
lattice and BBS binomial lattice. The parameters used were: $T = 1.0$, $S = 105.0$, $E = 105.0$, $r = 0.1$,
$q = 0.02$, $\sigma = 0.3$. The very accurate value (*acc_val*) was 16.1697, and was computed using a 6000 step
standard binomial lattice. The error in the estimated value was obtained as *est_val − acc_val*

The benefits of using the **BBS** approach to price an American call are illustrated in
Figure 10.3. Here we compare the results obtained using the function `bbs_lattice`
with those computed by the function `standard_lattice`, the standard binomial
lattice of Code excerpt 10.11. It can be clearly seen that **BBS** method is significantly
more accurate than the standard binomial lattice approach, in which option pricing
error exhibits pronounced oscillations.

The BBSR Method

The BBSR method applies two point Richardson extrapolation to the computed BBS
values, for more information concerning Richardson extrapolation see Marchuk and
Shaidurov (1983). In this method the option price estimates from two BBS lattice,
with differing number of time steps, are combined to form an improved estimate.

Here we use the following BBSR scheme to compute the value of an American
call option

$$C_{BBSR}(S,\ E,\ \tau,\ 2n) = \frac{4}{3} C_{BBS}(S,\ E,\ \tau,\ 2n) - \frac{1}{3} C_{BBS}(S,\ E,\ \tau,\ n) \qquad (10.96)$$

where S is the current asset value, E is the strike price, τ is the option maturity,
$C_{BBS}(S,\ E,\ \tau,\ n)$ is the value of the call option computed using a BBS lattice with

n time steps, $C_{BBS}(S, E, \tau, 2n)$ is the value of the call option computed using a BBS lattice with $2n$ time steps and $C_{BBSR}(S, E, \tau, 2n)$ is the BBSR estimate. We compute the value of an American put using

$$P_{BBSR}(S, E, \tau, 2n) = \frac{4}{3} P_{BBS}(S, E, \tau, 2n) - \frac{1}{3} P_{BBS}(S, E, \tau, n) \tag{10.97}$$

Figure 10.4 displays the computed BBSR results for an American call option with $S = 105.0$, $\tau = 1.0$, $E = 105.0$, $q = 0.02$, and $\sigma = 0.3$.

In Tables 10.5 and 10.6 the errors in computing both an American put and an American call option are presented; the methods used are the standard binomial lattice, the BBS lattice and the BBSR lattice. It can be seen that the BBSR lattice gives the most accurate results. This is not surprising since, from Equations 10.96 and 10.97 we see that when we use either an n time step standard binomial lattice or an n time step BBS lattice the corresponding BBSR estimate is obtained using both an n time step BBS lattice and also a $2n$ time step BBS lattice. One way of checking whether Richardson extrapolation is providing increased accuracy is to compare the results for a $2n$ time step BBS lattice with those for an n time step BBSR lattice. Inspection of the results shows that Richardson extrapolation has in fact led to an improvement. For example in Table 10.5 the error for a 160 time step BBS lattice is

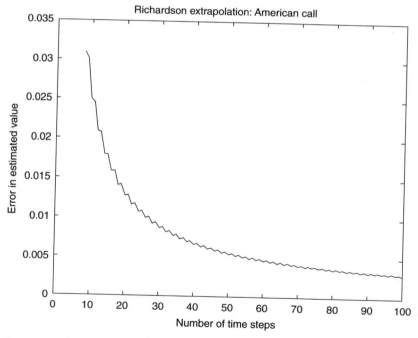

Figure 10.4   The error in the estimated value, *est_val*, of an American call, using a BBSR binomial lattice. The parameters used were: $T = 1.0$, $S = 105.0$, $E = 105.0$, $r = 0.1$, $q = 0.02$, $\sigma = 0.3$. The very accurate value (*acc_val*) was 16.1697, and was computed using a 6000 step standard binomial lattice. The error in the estimated value was obtained as *est_val − acc_val*

Table 10.5   The pricing errors for an American call option computed by a standard binomial lattice, a BBS lattice and also a BBSR lattice. The pricing error is defined as *estimated value − accurate value*, where the accurate value, 16.1697, was obtained by using a 6000 step standard binomial lattice. The option parameters used were: $T = 1.0$, $S = 105.0$, $E = 105.0$, $r = 0.1$, $q = 0.02$, and $\sigma = 0.3$

n steps	Standard lattice	BBS lattice	BBSR lattice
20	−1.5075e-001	3.6187e-002	1.2754e-002
30	−1.0057e-001	2.4526e-002	8.6771e-003
40	−7.5382e-002	1.8612e-002	6.6361e-003
50	−6.0244e-002	1.5036e-002	5.4109e-003
60	−5.0141e-002	1.2639e-002	4.5939e-003
70	−4.2919e-002	1.0922e-002	4.0103e-003
80	−3.7499e-002	9.6302e-003	3.5725e-003
90	−3.3282e-002	8.6236e-003	3.2320e-003
100	−2.9908e-002	7.8171e-003	2.9596e-003
110	−2.7146e-002	7.1565e-003	2.7367e-003
120	−2.4844e-002	6.6053e-003	2.5509e-003
130	−2.2896e-002	6.1385e-003	2.3938e-003
140	−2.1226e-002	5.7382e-003	2.2590e-003
150	−1.9778e-002	5.3909e-003	2.1423e-003
160	−1.8511e-002	5.0869e-003	2.0401e-003
170	−1.7393e-002	4.8186e-003	1.9500e-003
180	−1.6399e-002	4.5799e-003	1.8698e-003
190	−1.5510e-002	4.3663e-003	1.7981e-003
200	−1.4710e-002	4.1740e-003	1.7336e-003

Table 10.6   The pricing errors for an American put option computed by a standard binomial lattice, a BBS lattice and also a BBSR lattice. The pricing error is defined as *estimated value − accurate value*, where the accurate value, 9.2508, was obtained by using a 6000 step standard binomial lattice. The option parameters used were: $T = 1.0$, $S = 105.0$, $E = 105.0$, $r = 0.1$, $q = 0.02$, and $\sigma = 0.3$

n steps	Standard lattice	BBS lattice	BBSR lattice
20	−6.1971e-002	2.3917e-002	7.6191e-003
30	−4.1648e-002	1.6800e-002	6.0465e-003
40	−3.2264e-002	1.1694e-002	4.6165e-003
50	−2.6538e-002	8.4790e-003	4.2654e-003
60	−2.1069e-002	8.7348e-003	3.2946e-003
70	−1.8298e-002	7.2743e-003	2.9633e-003
80	−1.5885e-002	6.3858e-003	2.6088e-003
90	−1.3977e-002	5.9417e-003	2.2099e-003
100	−1.2612e-002	5.3188e-003	2.1793e-003
110	−1.1338e-002	4.9652e-003	2.0992e-003
120	−1.0239e-002	4.6547e-003	1.8723e-003
130	−9.5208e-003	4.1505e-003	1.8808e-003
140	−8.6142e-003	4.0411e-003	1.7505e-003
150	−8.2382e-003	3.6020e-003	1.7341e-003
160	−7.5811e-003	3.5531e-003	1.6411e-003
170	−7.1097e-003	3.3726e-003	1.5507e-003
180	−6.7887e-003	3.1428e-003	1.5478e-003
190	−6.3033e-003	3.1345e-003	1.4134e-003
200	−6.0276e-003	2.9642e-003	1.3973e-003

5.0869 × 10^{-3}, while that for an 80 time step BBSR lattice is 3.5725 × 10^3; in Table 10.6 the error for an 80 time step BBS lattice is 6.3858 × 10^{-3} and that for a 40 time step BBSR lattice is 3.5725 × 10^{-3}.

10.5   IMPLIED LATTICE METHODS

It is well known that market option prices are not consistent with theoretical prices derived from the Black–Scholes formula. This has led traders to quote option prices in terms of a volatility, σ_{imp}, which makes the Black–Scholes formula value equal to the observed market price. Here we refer to σ_{imp} as the implied volatility, to distinguish it from the theoretical constant volatility σ; essentially σ_{imp} is another way of quoting option prices. Empirical studies have found that:

- For vanilla options of a given maturity the value of σ_{imp} decreases with the level of the strike price, this asymmetry is termed *volatility skew*.
- For vanilla options of a given strike price the value of σ_{imp} increases with maturity, this variation is called the *volatility term structure*.

Here we follow Derman and Kani (1994) and refer to both the volatility skew and the volatility term structure as the *volatility smile*. The precise shape and magnitude of the volatility smile is dependent on the nature of the option being considered. We are thus led to consider more sophisticated option pricing methods which capture the observed deviations from these Black–Scholes formula.

Instead of assuming, as in Section 8.3, that the underlying asset price S_t follows GBM with constant drift and volatility, we will now consider the more general GBM process:

$$\frac{dS_t}{S_t} = \mu(t)dt + \sigma(S_t, \ t)dZ \tag{10.98}$$

where t is the current time, $\mu(t)$ is the time dependent risk neutral drift and $\sigma(S_t, t)$ is an unknown volatility function which depends on both the stock price and time. If we make use of Ito's lemma, and write $S_{t+\Delta t}$ for the asset price at time $t + \Delta t$, Equation 10.84 can be expressed in discretized form as:

$$\log\left(\frac{S_{t+\Delta t}}{S_t}\right) = \{\mu(t) - \sigma^2(S_t, \ t)/2\}\Delta t + \sigma(S_t, \ t)dZ \tag{10.99}$$

or equivalently

$$\log\left(\frac{S_{t+\Delta t}}{S_t}\right) \sim N(\{\mu(t) - \sigma^2(S_t, \ t)/2\}\Delta t, \ \sigma^2(S_t, \ t)\Delta t) \tag{10.100}$$

In this section we will show how the volatility function $\sigma(S_t, t)$ can be evaluated by ensuring that the option prices calculated using this model agree with those of the smile.

The *implied* binomial lattice constructed using this extended model will no longer be a regular lattice (as is the case for the simple Black–Scholes model) but will have a distorted shape *similar* to that shown in Figure 10.5 below.

It can be seen that the lattice levels are equispaced in time and are Δt apart. Lattice level 1, time t_1, corresponds to the root node (1, 1) and is the current time, at which

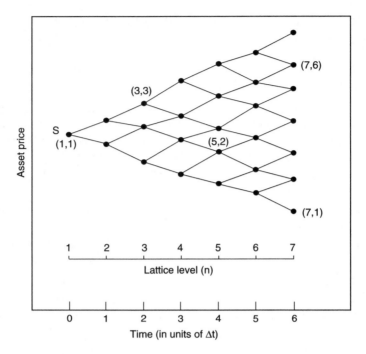

Figure 10.5   An implied binomial lattice which incorporates the volatility smile observed in traded put and call options. The *i*th node at the *n*th lattice level is denoted by (n, i). The current value (at time *t*) of the underlying asset is *S*, and this is the asset value assigned to the root lattice node $(1, 1)$. The asset values at the other lattice nodes depend on the technique used to construct the implied lattice

we want to find the value of the option. Time t_n, associated with lattice level n, is given by:

$$t_n = t_1 + (n - 1)\Delta t = t + (n - 1)\Delta t$$

so t_n is $(n - 1)\Delta t$ in the future relative to the current time t.

Construction of the implied lattice requires option prices for the complete range of strikes and maturities; these values can be obtained via interpolation from known option prices that are traded on the stock market.

Once the implied lattice has been created it can be used to price a range of European and American options.

Here we will describe the implied lattice technique developed by Derman and Kani (1994), and then consider the subsequent refinements proposed by Barle and Cakici (1995) and Chriss (1997). Of necessity our description of these techniques will be brief, and will mainly consist of explanatory detail and mathematical proofs that are not given in the original papers. For more information the reader should consult the original papers which are available (by kind permission of **RISK** Magazine) on the CD ROM which accompanies this book.

Before discussing the details of implied binomial lattices we will first consider the local volatility associated with a particular lattice node.

Local volatility

An expression for the stock volatility at the binomial lattice node (n, i) will now be derived. At time instant t_n the stock value at this node is denoted by s_i. After time Δt, time instant t_{n+1}, the stock price either has jumped up to S_u, at lattice node $(n + 1, i + 1)$, or jumped down to S_d, at lattice node $(n + 1, i)$. Applying Equation 10.100 to node (n, i) by setting $t = t_n$ and $S_t = s_i$ then gives

$$v \sim N\left(\{\mu(t_n) - \sigma^2(s_i, t_n)/2\}\Delta t, \ \sigma^2(s_i, t_n)\Delta t\right) \tag{10.101}$$

where the variate v can only take the two values $v_1 = \log(S_u/s_i)$, and $v_2 = \log(S_d/s_i)$.

We will let p_i denote the probability of taking the value $v1$, corresponding to an up jump. The probability of v having the value $v2$, corresponding to a down jump, is thus $1 - p_i$.

The quantity $\sigma(s_i, t_n)$ will be referred to as the local volatility, σ_{loc}, associated with the lattice node (n, i), and using Equation 10.101 we can write

$$Var(v) = \sigma_{loc}^2 \Delta t \tag{10.102}$$

An expression for σ_{loc} can then be obtained in terms of S_u, S_d and p_i, as follows. The variance of v is:

$$Var(v) = E[v^2] - (E[v])^2$$

where

$$E[v^2] = p_i\left\{\log\left(\frac{S_u}{s_i}\right)\right\}^2 + (1 - p_i)\left\{\log\left(\frac{S_d}{s_i}\right)\right\}^2$$

and

$$(E[v])^2 = \left\{p_i\log\left(\frac{S_u}{s_i}\right) + (1 - p_i)\log\left(\frac{S_d}{s_i}\right)\right\}^2$$

which means that

$$(E[v])^2 = p_i^2\left\{\log\left(\frac{S_u}{s_i}\right)\right\}^2 + (1 - p_i)^2\left\{\log\left(\frac{S_d}{s_i}\right)\right\}^2 + 2p_i(1 - p_i)\log\left(\frac{S_u}{s_i}\right)\log\left(\frac{S_d}{s_i}\right)$$

We can therefore write the variance as

$$Var(v) = p_i\left\{\log\left(\frac{S_u}{s_i}\right)\right\}^2 + (1 - p_i)\left\{\log\left(\frac{S_d}{s_i}\right)\right\}^2 - p_i^2\left\{\log\left(\frac{S_u}{s_i}\right)\right\}^2$$

$$- (1 - p_i)^2\left\{\log\left(\frac{S_d}{s_i}\right)\right\}^2 - 2p_i(1 - p_i)\log\left(\frac{S_u}{s_i}\right)\log\left(\frac{S_d}{s_i}\right)$$

which simplifies to

$$Var(v) = p_i(1 - p_i)\left[\left\{\log\left(\frac{S_u}{S_i}\right)\right\}^2 + \left\{\log\left(\frac{S_d}{S_i}\right)\right\}^2 - 2\log\left(\frac{S_u}{S_i}\right)\log\left(\frac{S_d}{S_i}\right)\right] \quad (10.103)$$

However

$$\log\left(\frac{S_u}{S_i}\right) - \log\left(\frac{S_d}{S_i}\right) = \log\left(\frac{S_u}{S_d}\right)$$

and

$$\left\{\log\left(\frac{S_u}{S_i}\right) - \log\left(\frac{S_d}{S_i}\right)\right\}^2 = \left\{\log\left(\frac{S_u}{S_i}\right)\right\}^2 + \left\{\log\left(\frac{S_d}{S_i}\right)\right\}^2 - 2\log\left(\frac{S_u}{S_i}\right)\log\left(\frac{S_d}{S_i}\right)$$

Substituting this into Equation 10.103 we obtain:

$$Var(v) = p_i(1 - p_i)\left\{\log\left(\frac{S_u}{S_d}\right)\right\}^2 \quad (10.104)$$

Therefore combining Equations 10.102 and 10.104 we have

$$\sigma_{loc}^2 \Delta t = p_i(1 - p_i)\left\{\log\left(\frac{S_u}{S_d}\right)\right\}^2$$

and so the local volatility is given by:

Binomial lattice: local volatility

$$\sigma_{loc} = \log\left(\frac{S_u}{S_d}\right)\sqrt{\frac{p_i(1 - p_i)}{\Delta t}} \quad (10.105)$$

In an implied lattice the transition probabilities, p_i, and the ratios S_u/S_d are (in general) different for each lattice node. This generates a volatility surface in which the local volatility σ_{loc} varies throughout the lattice. By contrast the CRR binomial lattice of Section 10.4.1 has the same value of σ_{loc} for all its lattice nodes. The reason for this that p_i and Δt are constants, and the up and down jumps are

$$S_u = s_i u \quad \text{and} \quad S_d = s_i d, \quad \text{where} \quad u = \frac{1}{d}$$

This means that

$$\frac{S_u}{S_d} = u^2$$

and the (constant) local volatility is

$$\sigma_{loc} = \log(u^2)\sqrt{\frac{p(1 - p)}{\Delta t}}$$

> **CRR binomial lattice: local volatility**
>
> $$\sigma_{loc} = 2\log(u)\sqrt{\frac{p(1-p)}{\Delta t}}$$
>
> (10.106)
>
> where we have denoted the (constant) CRR up jump probability by p.

10.5.1 Derman–Kani implied lattice

We now consider the paper by Derman–Kani (1994), henceforth referred to as DK, which describes an implied binomial lattice based on the market values of European put and call options.

The implied lattice (see Figure 10.5) consists of uniformly spaced levels Δt apart, and is built using forward iteration. To explain this technique we will assume that the first n lattice levels have been constructed and that they match the observed volatility smile for all strike prices and maturities out to time t_n. The task is to determine the $n + 1$ nodes at the $(n + 1)$th lattice level from the previously calculated n nodes at the nth lattice level.

For convenience we will now give the notation used in the formulae for constructing the lattice nodes in the $(n + 1)th$ lattice level from the known lattice node values in the nth lattice level.

r The known riskless interest rate for lattice level $(n + 1)$.

s_i The known stock price at node (n, i); that is at the ith node on lattice level n. We also note that s_i is the strike price for options expiring at lattice level $n + 1$.

F_i The known forward price at lattice level $n + 1$ of the known price s_i at lattice level n.

S_i The unknown stock price at node $(n + 1, i)$.

λ_i The known Arrow-Debreu price at node (n, i).

p_i The unknown risk-neutral up jump transition probability from node (n, i) to node $(n + 1, i + 1)$.

Here the ith node at level n has known stock price s_i, and is denoted by (n, i). The probability that the stock price s_i increases to S_{i+1} in lattice level $n + 1$ is denoted by p_i, whereas the probability that the stock price decreases to S_i in level $n + 1$ is given by $1 - p_i$.

The forward price, F_i, of s_i at lattice level $n + 1$ is simply given by the risk neutral expected value of s_i one time step later. That is $F_i = s_i \exp(r\Delta t)$, or in terms of the up and down jump probabilities p_i and $(1 - p_i)$ respectively we have:

$$F_i = p_i S_{i+1} + (1 - p_i)S_i, \quad \text{for } i = 1, \ldots, n \tag{10.107}$$

where as before S_{i+1} is the stock value at lattice level $n + 1$ following an up jump and S_i is the stock value at lattice level $n + 1$ following a down jump.

The Arrow-Debreu price, λ_i, at each lattice node (n, i) is defined as: *the probability of reaching node (n, i) from the root lattice node $(1, 1)$ discounted by the risk neutral interest rate between time t_1 and time t_n.*

The Arrow-Debreu price of a lattice node is thus the value of a security that pays $1 if the stock price reaches that node and zero otherwise. The value of λ_i corresponding to node (n, i) is computed as the sum, over all paths from the root node $(1, 1)$ to node (n, i), of the product of the riskless-discounted transition probabilities of nodes along each path from $(1, 1)$ to (n, i). We provide more detail concerning the computation of λ_i in the example calculation at the end of this section, and consider the following two methods:

1. Direct calculation of the Arrow-Debreu prices in lattice level $n + 1$ by using all paths from the root lattice node $(1, 1)$.
2. Iterative calculation of the Arrow-Debreu prices in lattice level $n + 1$ from the known Arrow-Debreu prices in lattice level n.

It is shown that direct calculation of the Arrow-Debreu prices becomes substantially more complicated as the number of lattice level increases. This is because the number of possible paths from the root node $(1, 1)$ to any given lattice node $(n + 1, i)$ increases dramatically with n. The iterative approach is thus the most practical method for computing Arrow-Debreu prices in lattices containing more than just a few lattice levels.

Let $C(K, t_{n+1})$ and $P(K, t_{n+1})$ be the current, time t, respective prices of European call and European put options with strike K and maturity corresponding to lattice level $n + 1$; the values $C(K, t_{n+1})$ and $P(K, t_{n+1})$ can be obtained via interpolation from the known market prices. An expression for $C(K, t_{n+1})$, can also be computed by using the binomial node values at lattice level n, and this method yields the following equation:

$$C(K, t_{n+1}) = \exp(-r\Delta t) \sum_{j=1}^{n} \lambda_j \{ p_j \max(S_{j+1} - K, 0)$$
$$+ (1 - p_j) \max (S_j - K, 0) \} \tag{10.108}$$

where $\max (S_j - K, 0)$ is the payout for the call at the jth lattice node on lattice level $n + 1$ and $\max (S_{j+1} - K, 0)$ is the payout for the call at the $(j + 1)$th lattice node on lattice level $n + 1$.

When the strike K equals s_i the above equation becomes

$$\exp(r\Delta t)C(s_i, t_{n+1}) = \sum_{j=1}^{n} \lambda_j \{ p_j \max(S_{j+1} - s_i, 0)$$
$$+ (1 - p_j) \max(S_j - s_i, 0) \} \tag{10.109}$$

Since the terms that contribute to the value of the call option, $C(s_i, t_{n+1})$, are those with positive payouts we only need consider j indices in the range i to n, and the ith term of the summation on the right hand side of Equation 10.109 is:

$$\lambda_i \{ p_i \max(S_{i+1} - s_i, 0) + (1 - p_i) \max(S_i - s_i, 0) \} = \lambda_i p_i (S_{i+1} - s_i) \tag{10.110}$$

where we have used (see DK Figure 4) the following: $S_{i+1} > s_i$ (S_{i+1} is the up jump stock value from lattice level n to lattice level $n + 1$) whereas $S_i < s_i$ (S_i is the down jump stock value from lattice level n to lattice level $n + 1$).

This means that we can rewrite Equation 10.109 as:

$$\exp(r\Delta t)C(s_i,\ t_{n+1}) = \lambda_i p_i (S_{i+1} - s_i) + \sum_{j=i+1}^{n} \lambda_j \{p_j(S_{j+1} - s_i)$$

$$+ (1 - p_j)(S_j - s_i)\} \tag{10.111}$$

If we subtract the constant term s_i from both sides of Equation 10.107 we obtain:

$$F_j - s_i = p_j (S_{j+1} - s_i) + (1 - p_j)(S_j - s_i),\ j = 1,\ \ldots,\ n \tag{10.112}$$

where we used $s_i = p_j s_i + (1 - p_j)s_i$. Substituting Equation 10.112 into Equation 10.111 gives:

$$\exp(r\Delta t)C(s_i,\ t_{n+1}) = \lambda_i p_i (S_{i+1} - s_i) + \bar{\Sigma} \tag{10.113}$$

where $\bar{\Sigma} = \sum_{j=i+1}^{n} \lambda_j(F_j - s_i)$. The first term in Equation 10.113 depends on the unknown values of the transition probability p_i and stock price S_{i+1}. The last term $\bar{\Sigma}$ involves a summation over the known forward prices F_j and known stock prices s_i on lattice level n. Since both F_j and $C(s_i, t_{n+1})$ are known, Equations 10.107 and 10.113 can be solved to give the following expressions for S_{i+1} and p_i, in terms of S_i:

$$p_i = \frac{F_i - S_i}{S_{i+1} - S_i} \tag{10.114}$$

and

$$S_{i+1} = \frac{S_i\{C(s_i,\ t_{n+1})\exp(r\Delta t) - \bar{\Sigma}\} - \lambda_i s_i(F_i - S_i)}{\{C(s_i,\ t_{n+1})\exp(r\Delta t) - \bar{\Sigma}\} - \lambda_i(F_i - S_i)} \tag{10.115}$$

We will now derive these two results.

Proof of Equation 10.114 (DK equation 7)
From Equation 10.107 we have:

$$F_i = p_i S_{i+1} + (1 - p_i)S_i$$

which gives:

$$F_i = p_i(S_{i+1} - S_i) + S_i \quad \text{and} \quad p_i = \frac{F_i - S_i}{S_{i+1} - S_i} \qquad QED$$

Proof of Equation 10.115 (DK equation 6)
If we substitute the value of p_i from Equation 10.115 into Equation 10.113 we obtain:

$$C(s_i,\ t_{n+1})\exp(r\Delta t) = \frac{\lambda_i(F_i - S_i)(S_{i+1} - s_i)}{S_{i+1} - S_i} + \bar{\Sigma}$$

Multiplying both sides by $S_{i+1} - S_i$ yields:

$$\exp(r\Delta t)C(s_i,\ t_{n+1})\{S_{i+1} - S_i\} = -\lambda_i F_i s_i - \lambda_i S_i S_{i+1} + \lambda_i F_i S_{i+1} + \lambda_i S_i + S_{i+1}\bar{\Sigma} - S_i\bar{\Sigma}$$

so

$$S_{i+1}\{C(s_i,\ t_{n+1})\exp(r\Delta t) + \lambda_i S_i - \lambda_i F_i - \bar{\Sigma}\}$$
$$= S_i C(s_i,\ t_{n+1})\exp(r\Delta t) - \lambda_i s_i(F_i - S_i) - S_i\bar{\Sigma}$$

or

$$S_{i+1}\{C(s_i,\ t_{n+1})\exp(r\Delta t) - \bar{\Sigma} - \lambda_i(F_i - S_i)\}$$
$$= S_i\{C(s_i,\ t_{n+1})\exp(r\Delta t) - \bar{\Sigma}\} - \lambda_i s_i(F_i - S_i)$$

and finally gives the following expression for S_{i+1}:

$$S_{i+1} = \frac{S_i\{C(s_i,\ t_{n+1})\exp(r\Delta t) - \bar{\Sigma}\} - \lambda_i s_i(F_i - S_i)}{\{C(s_i,\ t_{n+1})\exp(r\Delta t) - \bar{\Sigma}\} - \lambda_i(F_i - S_i)} \qquad QED$$

If we know S_i at one initial node then Equations 10.114 and 10.115 can be used to find iteratively the values of S_{i+1} and p_i for all $n/2 + 1$ nodes above the centre of the lattice on the $(n + 1)$th lattice level.

If $n + 1$ is odd then the initial value used for S_i is the stock value associated with the central lattice node, that is $S_i = S$. On the other hand if $n + 1$ is even then we use the CRR lattice centering condition (see Section 10.4.1). Let S_{i+1} denote the $(n + 1)$th level stock value for the node just above the centre of the lattice, and S_i denote the $(n + 1)$th level stock value just below the centre of the lattice. For a CRR $(u = 1/d)$ lattice these values are related to the central node stock value, S, at lattice level n by:

$$S_{i+1} = Su \quad \text{and} \quad S_i = Sd = \frac{S}{u}$$

and therefore

$$S_{i+1}S_i = S^2 \qquad\qquad (10.116)$$

Substituting Equation 10.116 into Equation 10.114 gives the following formula for the stock value at the node just above the centre of the lattice when $n + 1$ is even:

$$S_{i+1} = \frac{S(\Psi + \lambda_i S)}{\lambda_i F_i - \Psi}, \quad \text{for} \quad i = \left(\frac{n+1}{2}\right) \qquad (10.117)$$

where $\Psi = C(S,\ t_{n+1})\exp(r\Delta t) - \bar{\Sigma}$.

When $n + 1$ is even, Equation 10.117 can thus be used in conjunction with Equations 10.114 and 10.115 to iteratively compute the node values S_{i+1} and probabilities p_i for the $(n + 1)/2$ nodes above the lattice centre.

Proof of Equation 10.117 (DK equation 8)

From Equation 10.114 we have that the probability p_i is given by:

$$p_i = \frac{F_i - S_i}{S_{i+1} - S_i} = \frac{(F_i - S_i)S_{i+1}}{(S_{i+1} - S_i)S_{i+1}}$$

since, in Equation 10.116, $S_i S_{i+1} = S^2$ we obtain:

$$p_i = \frac{F_i S_{i+1} - S^2}{S_{i+1}^2 - S^2} = \frac{F_i S_{i+1} - S^2}{(S_{i+1} - S)(S_{i+1} + S)}$$

However from Equation 10.113

$$\exp(r\Delta t)C(s_i, t_{n+1}) = \lambda_i p_i(S_{i+1} - s_i) + \bar{\Sigma}$$

so

$$\Psi = \lambda_i p_i(S_{i+1} - s_i) \qquad (10.118)$$

When $s_i = S$ we therefore have:

$$\Psi = \lambda_i p_i(S_{i+1} - S) = \frac{\lambda_i(F_i S_{i+1} - S^2)(S_{i+1} - S)}{(S_{i+1} - S)(S_{i+1} + S)} = \frac{\lambda_i(F_i S_{i+1} - S^2)}{S_{i+1} + S}$$

which gives:

$$\Psi S_{i+1} + \Psi S = \lambda_i F_i S_{i+1} - \lambda_i S^2$$
$$S_{i+1}(\Psi - \lambda_i F_i) = -S(\Psi + \lambda_i S)$$

and finally:

$$S_{i+1} = \frac{S(\Psi + \lambda_i S)}{\lambda_i F_i - \Psi} \qquad QED$$

Similar formulae can be derived, using interpolated put prices, which enable the stock values and probabilities for nodes below the lattice centre to be computed. The formula to determine a lower node's stock value from an upper node's stock value is:

$$S_i = \frac{S_{i+1}\{P(s_i, t_{n+1})\exp(r\Delta t) - \Sigma^*\} - \lambda_i s_i(F_i - S_{i+1})}{\{P(s_i, t_{n+1})\exp(r\Delta t) - \Sigma^*\} - \lambda_i(F_i - S_{i+1})} \qquad (10.119)$$

where $P(s_i, t_{n+1})$ is the interpolated price of a put with strike s_i and expiry time t_{n+1} and

$$\Sigma^* = \sum_{j=1}^{i-1} \lambda_j(s_i - F_j)$$

denotes the sum over all nodes below the node with stock price s_i at which the put was struck.

When building the lattice the computed transition probabilities, p_i, for each lattice node must obey the constraint $0 \leq p_i \leq 1$. The upper limit $p_i \leq 1$ is equivalent to requiring that the up-node stock price S_{i+1} at the next level does not fall below the forward price F_i. This result comes from Equation 10.114

$$p_i = \frac{F_i - S_i}{S_{i+1} - S_i}$$

where it can easily be seen that if $F_i > S_{i+1}$ then $p_i > 1$. Similarly the lower limit $p_i \geq 0$ can be shown to be equivalent to requiring that the down-node stock price S_i is above the forward price F_i. From Equation 10.114 we now have:

$$p_{i+1} = \frac{F_{i+1} - S_{i+1}}{S_{i+2} - S_{i+1}}$$

and so if $S_{i+1} > F_{i+1}$ then $p_{i+1} < 0$. We thus have:

(10.120)

$$F_i < S_{i+1} < F_{i+1}$$

which is illustrated in Figure 10.6.

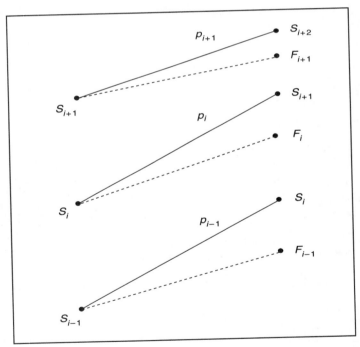

Figure 10.6 An implied lattice showing the position of the stock prices in relation to the forward prices, between the nth and $(n+1)$th lattice levels. The stock prices in lattice level n are denoted by s_{i+1}, s_i, and s_{i-1}, while those in lattice level $n+1$ are represented by S_{i+2}, S_{i+1}, and S_i. The transition probabilities between lattice level n and lattice level $n+1$ are p_{i+1}, p_i, and p_{i-1}, and the forward prices are F_{i+1}, F_i, and F_{i-1}. If the computed stock value is S_{i+1} then, in order to obtain valid transition probabilities, it must satisfy the constraint $F_i < S_{i+1} < F_{i+1}$

Bad probabilities

Figure 10.6 shows the relative positions of the computed stock values, S_i, at lattice level $n + 1$, and the forward prices F_i computed from the stock values, s_i, at lattice level n. If a computed stock value, S_{i+1}, violates the constraints imposed by Equation 10.120 then it is necessary to choose an alternative value for which the transition probability p_i is in the permitted range $0 < p_i < 1$. DK advocates choosing S_{i+1} so that the logarithmic spacing between adjacent lattice nodes is the same as that in the previous lattice level; that is:

$$\frac{S_{i+1}}{S_i} = \frac{s_i}{s_{i-1}}$$

This means replacing the value of S_{i+1} computed using Equation 10.115 with

$$S_{i+1} = S_i \left(\frac{s_i}{s_{i-1}} \right) \tag{10.121}$$

If this method still fails to produce a valid p_i then Chriss (1997) suggests the following more drastic measure in which

$$S_{i+1} = F_i + \epsilon \tag{10.122}$$

where ϵ is a very small number (say 10^{-6}). It can be seen from Equation 10.114 that the transition probability p_i will then be a very small positive number.

When we remove bad probabilities in this manner the impact on the implied lattice will depend on both the Arrow-Debreu price of the node and its payout. Nodes near the top and bottom of the lattice will have small Arrow-Debreu prices because few paths lead to them, and thus removing bad probabilities from these nodes will have little impact on the lattice. When building an implied lattice it is a good idea to count how many bad nodes have been encountered; this will give some idea of the expected quality of the implied lattice that has been constructed. A more quantitative method of assessing the expected performance of an implied lattice is by checking how well it prices the put and call options that were originally used to create it.

Example calculation

Here we provide more details concerning the example calculation given in the paper by Derman and Kani (1994). The implied lattice for this example is shown in Figures 10.7 and 10.8. It is assumed that the current stock value is 100.00, the dividend is zero, and the annually compounded riskless interest rate is 3 per cent a year for all option maturities. Since we have assumed a constant riskless interest of 3 per cent the forward price F_i for any node is 1.03 times the node's stock price, s_i.

Computation of the Arrow-Debreu prices

We have already mentioned that the Arrow-Debreu price for node (n, i) is computed as the sum, over all paths from the root node $(1, 1)$ to node (n, i), of the product of the riskless-discounted transition probabilities of nodes along each path from $(1, 1)$

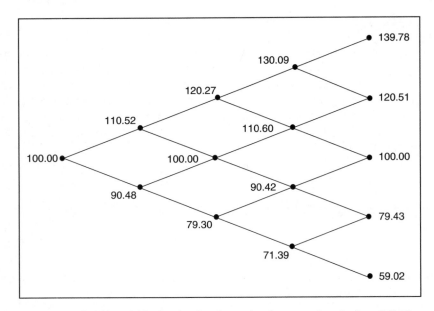

Figure 10.7   Implied binomial lattice showing the stock values at each node; from DK Figure 6

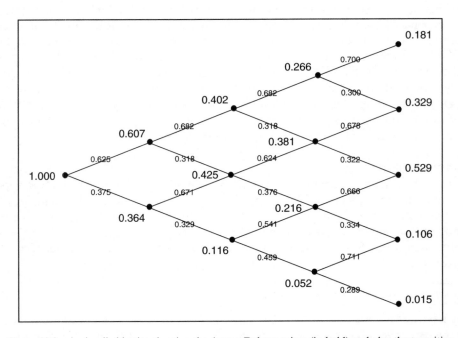

Figure 10.8   An implied lattice showing the Arrow-Debreu prices (in bold) and also the transition probabilities between nodes (in a smaller font); from DK Figure 6.

to (n, i). Here we provide more detail and show how the Arrow-Debreu prices can be computed for the first four lattice levels.

Level 1: Node $(1, 1)$ $\lambda_1 = 1.0$.
Level 2: Node $(2, 2)$: There is only one route from node $(1, 1)$ to node $(2, 2)$ and path probability is 0.625. Discounting the path probability by the riskless rate of 3 per cent gives the Arrow-Debreu price:

$$\lambda_2 = \frac{0.625}{1.03} = 0.6068$$

Node $(2, 1)$: As for node $(2, 2)$ there is only one route from node $(1, 1)$ and the path probability is $1 - 0.625 = 0.375$. Discounting by the riskless rate gives the Arrow-Debreu price:

$$\lambda_1 = \frac{0.375}{1.03} = 0.3641$$

Level 3: Node $(3, 3)$: There is only one route from node $(1, 1)$ to node $(3, 3)$ and the path probability is $0.625 \times 0.682 = 0.42625$. Discounting by the riskless rate of 3 per cent over two time steps yields the Arrow-Debreu price:

$$\lambda_3 = \frac{0.42625}{1.03 \times 1.03} = 0.40178$$

Node $(3, 2)$: There are two ways of going from node $(1, 1)$ to node $(3, 2)$. The first way, route (a) includes the nodes $(1, 1)$, $(2, 2)$, and $(3, 2)$; it has a path probability of $0.625 \times 0.318 = 0.19875$. The contribution of route (a) to λ_2, denoted as λ_2^a, is therefore $\lambda_2^a = 0.19875/(1.03 \times 1.03) = 0.18734$. The second way, route (b) includes the nodes $(1, 1)$, $(2, 1)$, and $(3, 2)$; it has a path probability of $0.375 \times 0.671 = 0.2516$. The contribution of route (b) to λ_2, denoted as λ_2^b, is thus $\lambda_2^b = 0.2516/(1.03 \times 1.03) = 0.23718$.
    The Arrow-Debreu price, λ_2, is therefore:

$$\lambda_2 = \lambda_2^a + \lambda_2^b = 0.18734 + 0.23718 = 0.4245$$

Node $(3, 1)$: There is only one route from node $(1, 1)$ to node $(3, 1)$, and the path probability is $0.375 \times 0.329 = 0.12337$. Discounting by the riskless rate of 3 per cent gives an Arrow-Debreu price:

$$\lambda_1 = \frac{0.12337}{1.03 \times 1.03} = 0.11629$$

Level 4: Node $(4, 4)$: There is only one route from node $(1, 1)$ to node $(4, 4)$, and the path probability is $0.625 \times 0.682 \times 0.682 = 0.29070$. Discounting by the riskless rate of 3 per cent over three time steps gives an Arrow-Debreu price:

$$\lambda_4 = \frac{0.26768}{1.03 \times 1.03 \times 1.03} = 0.2660$$

Node $(4, 3)$: There are three ways of going from node $(1, 1)$ to node $(4, 2)$. The first way, route (a) includes the nodes $(1, 1)$, $(2, 2)$, $(3, 3)$, and $(4, 3)$. The second way, route (b) includes the nodes $(1, 1)$, $(2, 2)$, $(3, 2)$, and $(4, 3)$. Finally the third way, route (c) includes the nodes $(1, 1)$, $(2, 1)$, $(3, 2)$, and $(4, 2)$.

The path probability for route (a) is $0.625 \times 0.682 \times 0.316 = 0.1347$, and thus yields an Arrow-Debreu price $\lambda_3^a = 0.1347/(1.03 \times 1.03 \times 1.03) = 0.1233$. The path probability for route (b) is $0.375 \times 0.671 \times 0.624 = 0.12402$, and gives an Arrow-Debreu price of $\lambda_3^b = 0.12402/(1.03 \times 1.03 \times 1.03) = 0.1135$.

Finally the path probability for route (c) is $0.375 \times 0.671 \times 0.624 = 0.157014$, and $\lambda_3^c = 0.157014/(1.03 \times 1.03 \times 1.03) = 0.1437$. The Arrow-Debreu price, λ_3, is therefore:

$$\lambda_3 = \lambda_3^a + \lambda_3^b + \lambda_3^c = 0.1233 + 0.1135 + 0.1437 = 0.3805$$

Node (4, 2): There are three ways of going from node (1, 1) to node (3, 2). The first way, route (a) includes the nodes (1, 1), (2, 2), (3, 2), and (4, 2). The second way, route (b) includes the nodes (1, 1), (2, 1), (3, 2), and (4, 2). Lastly the third way, route (c) includes the nodes (1, 1), (2, 1), (3, 1), and (4, 3).

The path probability for route (a) is $0.625 \times 0.318 \times 0.376 = 0.07473$, and yields $\lambda_2^a = 0.07473/(1.03 \times 1.03 \times 1.03) = 0.06838$. The path probability for route (b) is $0.375 \times 0.671 \times 0.376 = 0.09461$, and yields $\lambda_2^b = 0.09461/(1.03 \times 1.03 \times 1.03) = 0.0865824$.

Finally the probability for route (c) is $0.375 \times 0.329 \times 0.541 = 0.06674$, and yields $\lambda_2^c = 0.06674/(1.03 \times 1.03 \times 1.03) = 0.06108$. The Arrow-Debreu price, λ_2, is therefore:

$$\lambda_2 = \lambda_2^a + \lambda_2^b + \lambda_2^c = 0.06838 + 0.0865824 + 0.06108 = 0.21604$$

Node (4, 1): There is only one route from node (1, 1) to node (4, 1), and the path probability is $0.375 \times 0.329 \times 0.459 = 0.05663$. This gives an Arrow-Debreu price:

$$\lambda_1 = \frac{0.05663}{1.03 \times 1.03 \times 1.03} = 0.0518$$

An alternative and simpler method of obtaining the Arrow-Debreu prices for the nodes in a particular lattice level is to use forward iteration. Here we can use the fact that the Arrow-Debreu prices for the nodes in a particular level are related, in the *usual* binomial fashion, to the values in the previous level and the set of transition probabilities between levels. Since the Arrow-Debreu price for root node (1, 1) is (by definition) 1, and we know how to compute the transition probabilities between levels, all the Arrow-Debreu prices in the $(n + 1)$th lattice level can be computed from those in the nth lattice level.

We will now illustrate this, by showing how to compute the Arrow-Debreu prices in lattice level 4, λ_i, $i = 1, \ldots, 4$, from the previously computed Arrow-Debreu prices λ_i^*, $i = 1, \ldots, 3$, in level 3.

$$\lambda_4 = \frac{p_3 \times \lambda_3^*}{1+r} = \frac{0.682 \times 0.402}{1.03} = 0.266$$

$$\lambda_3 = \frac{\{(1 - p_3) \times \lambda_3^* + p_2 \lambda_2^*\}}{1+r} = \frac{\{0.402 \times 0.318 + 0.425 \times 0.624\}}{1.03} = 0.381$$

$$\lambda_2 = \frac{\{(1-p_2) \times \lambda_2^* + p_1 \lambda_1^*\}}{1+r} = \frac{\{0.425 \times 0.376 + 0.116 \times 0.541\}}{1.03} = 0.216$$

$$\lambda_1 = \frac{\{1-p_1\}\lambda_1^*}{1+r} = \frac{0.459 \times 0.116}{1.03} = 0.052$$

As a means of checking the computed Arrow-Debreu prices we can use the fact that, at any lattice level, the sum of the Arrow-Debreu prices *inflated* at the riskless interest rate to the root node is 1. That is for *n*th lattice level we have:

$$(1+r)^{n-1} \sum_{i=1}^{n} \lambda_i = 1 \tag{10.123}$$

where r is the (constant) riskless interest rate. If we take into account finite computational precision then Equation 10.123 becomes:

$$ABS\left\{\left((1+r)^{n-1} \sum_{i=1}^{n} \lambda_i\right) - 1\right\} \leq \mathbf{tol} \tag{10.124}$$

where $ABS\{X\}$ denotes the absolute value of X, and **tol** is a small number which reflects the computational accuracy. For nodes on level 4 we have:

$$ABS\left\{(1.03)^3(0.266 + 0.381 + 0.216 + 0.052) - 1\right\} \sim 1.5 \times 10^{-4}$$

10.5.2 Barle–Cakici implied lattice

Here we briefly describe modifications proposed by Barle and Cakici (1995), henceforth denoted BC, to the algorithm used by Derman and Kani for constructing the implied lattice. These improvements reduce the occurrence of bad transition probabilities and thus lead to better quality lattices.

| First modification |

The first modification proposed by BC is to use F_i (the forward of s_i) for the strike price, K, in Equation 10.109 instead of s_i. Under these circumstances Equation 10.115 (DK equation 7) becomes:

$$S_{i+1} = \frac{S_i\{C(F_i,\ t_{n+1})\exp(r\Delta t) - \bar{\Sigma}^{BC}\} - \lambda_i F_i(F_i - S_i)}{\{C(F_i,\ t_{n+1})\exp(r\Delta t) - \bar{\Sigma}^{BC}\} - \lambda_i(F_i - S_i)} \tag{10.125}$$

where

$$\bar{\Sigma}^{BC} = \sum_{j=i+1}^{n} \lambda_j(F_j - F_i)$$

Second modification

The second modification is to allow the central spine of the implied lattice to follow the values dictated by the prevailing interest rate. If the $(n+1)$th lattice level is odd this involves setting the central node to $S \exp (r - q)t_{n+1}$, where q is the continuous dividend yield, and the other symbols have already been defined in the previous section on the DK lattice. If the $(n+1)$th lattice level is even then the two central nodes now no longer satisfy Equation 10.116 but

$$S_i S_{i+1} = F_i^2 \tag{10.126}$$

where $i = (n + 1)/2$.

The asset price at the lower central node S_i is then given by:

$$S_i = \frac{F_i(\lambda_i F_i - \Psi^{BC})}{\lambda_i F_i + \Psi^{BC}} \tag{10.127}$$

whereas that at the upper central node S_{i+1} is:

$$S_{i+1} = \frac{F_i(\Psi^{BC} + \lambda_i F_i)}{\lambda_i F_i - \Psi^{BC}} \tag{10.128}$$

where $\Psi^{BC} = C(F_i, t_{n+1}) \exp (r\Delta t) - \bar{\Sigma}^{BC}$.

Proof of Equation 10.127 (BC equation 9) and Equation 10.128
From Equation 10.114 we have that the transition probability, p_i is:

$$p_i = \frac{F_i - S_i}{S_{i+1} - S_i}$$

multiplying above and below by S_{i+1} then gives:

$$p_i = \frac{(F_i - S_i)S_{i+1}}{(S_{i+1} - S_i)S_{i+1}}$$

However since we are centering at the forward price, from Equation 10.126, we have $S_i S_{i+1} = F_i^2$, and so

$$p_i = \frac{F_i S_{i+1} - F_i^2}{S_{i+1}^2 - F_i^2} = \frac{F_i S_{i+1} - F_i^2}{(S_{i+1} - F_i)(S_{i+1} + F_i)} \tag{10.129}$$

However from Equation 10.118 we have

$$\Psi^{BC} = \lambda_i p_i (S_{i+1} - F_i) \tag{10.130}$$

If we substitute the value of p_i from Equation 10.129 into Equation 10.130 we have

$$\Psi^{BC} = \lambda_i p_i (S_{i+1} - F_i) = \frac{\lambda_i (F_i S_{i+1} - F_i^2)(S_{i+1} - F_i)}{(S_{i+1} - F_i)(S_{i+1} + F_i)} = \frac{\lambda_i (F_i S_{i+1} - F_i^2)}{S_{i+1} + F_i}$$

Rearranging we obtain:

$$\Psi^{BC} S_{i+1} + \Psi^{BC} F_i = \lambda_i F_i S_{i+1} - \lambda_i F_i^2$$

$$S_{i+1}(\Psi^{BC} - \lambda_i F_i) = -F_i(\Psi^{BC} + \lambda_i F_i)$$

which gives

$$S_{i+1} = \frac{F_i(\Psi^{BC} + \lambda_i F_i)}{\lambda_i F_i - \Psi^{BC}} \qquad QED$$

To prove Equation 10.127 we simply substitute $S_{i+1} S_i = F_i^2$ into Equation 10.128 and obtain:

$$S_i = \frac{F_i^2}{S_{i+1}} = \frac{F_i^2(\lambda_i F_i - \Psi^{BC})}{F_i(\Psi^{BC} + \lambda_i F_i)}$$

So

$$S_i = \frac{F_i(\lambda F_i - \Psi^{BC})}{\lambda_i F_i + \Psi^{BC}} \qquad QED$$

Bad probabilities

If bad transition probabilities occur then this can rectified by setting S_{i+1} to any value between F_i and F_{i+1}. In these circumstances Barle and Cakici suggest setting S_{i+1} to the average of F_i and F_{i+1}.

10.5.3 Chriss implied lattice

Here we will briefly mention an implied lattice, devised by Chriss (1996), which can be built using the market values of both European and American options. This is in contrast to the algorithm of Derman–Kani which requires the market values of European options. We will not describe how to deal with American options; the reader can refer to the original paper which is available on the CD ROM. The first part of the paper, is concerned with European options and follows on from our previous discussions concerning the Derman–Kani and Barle–Cakici implied lattices.

As supplementary information we will now show how to derive equation (3) in the original paper, that is:

$$u = \frac{\nu^{PUT} + K}{K \exp(-r\Delta t) - \nu^{PUT}} \tag{10.131}$$

the notation used here is the same as that in Chriss (1996).

Proof of Equation 10.131 (Chriss equation 3)
The transition probability of an up jump from $S_{i-1,j}$ to $S_{i,j+1}$ is denoted by p_j, and
that of the corresponding down jump transition probability $1 - p_j$ by q. The forward
for $S_{i-1,j}$ is denoted by F_j and, since $S_{i-1,j} = K$, we have:

$$F_j = S_{i-1,\,j} \exp(r\Delta t) = K \exp(r\Delta t) \tag{10.132}$$

The up jump transition probability, see Equation 10.114, is

$$p_j = \frac{F_j - S_{i,j}}{S_{i,j+1} - S_{i,j}}$$

which results in a down jump probability of

$$1 - p_j = q = 1 - \frac{F_j - S_{i,j}}{S_{i,j+1} - S_{i,j}} = \frac{S_{i,j+1} - F_j}{S_{i,j+1} - S_{i,j}}$$

Multiplying top and bottom by $S_{i,j}$ we obtain

$$q = \frac{S_{i,j+1} - F_j}{S_{i,j+1} - S_{i,j}} = \frac{(S_{i,j+1} - F_j)S_{i,j}}{(S_{i,j+1} - S_{i,j})S_{i,j}} = \frac{S_{i,j+1}S_{i,j} - F_jS_{i,j}}{S_{i,j+1}S_{i,j} - S_{i,j}^2}$$

We choose to centre at the spot $S_{i,\,j+1}S_{i,\,j} = K^2$ and we have

$$q = \frac{S_{i,j+1}S_{i,j} - F_jS_{i,j}}{K^2 - S_{i,j}^2} = \frac{S_{i,j+1}S_{i,j} - F_jS_{i,j}}{(K - S_{i,j})(K + S_{i,j})} = \frac{K^2 - F_jS_{i,j}}{(K - S_{i,j})(K + S_{i,j})} \tag{10.133}$$

From the derivation of equation (1), on the first page of the original paper by
Chriss, we have:

$$v_{i-1,j}^{PUT} = q(K - S_{i,j})\exp(-r\Delta t) \tag{10.134}$$

We now use Equation 10.133 to substitute for q in Equation 10.134. This gives

$$v_{i-1,j}^{PUT} = q(K - S_{i,j})\exp(-r\Delta t) = \frac{\exp(-r\Delta t)(K^2 - F_jS_{i,j})}{K + S_{i,j}}$$

using $F_j = K \exp(r\Delta t)$ from Equation 10.132 results in

$$v_{i-1,j}^{PUT} = \frac{K(K\exp(-r\Delta t) - S_{i,j})}{K + S_{i,j}} \tag{10.135}$$

and multiplying both sides of Equation 10.135 by $K + S_{i,j}$ we obtain

$$v_{i-1,j}^{PUT}K + v_{i-1,j}^{PUT}S_{i,j} = K^2 \exp(-r\Delta t) - KS_{i,j} \tag{10.136}$$

Since we centre at the spot we have:

$$S_{i,j}S_{i,j+1} = K^2$$

so

$$S_{i,j+1} = Ku = \frac{K^2}{S_{i,j}}, \quad \text{which gives:} \quad u = \frac{K}{S_{i,j}} \tag{10.137}$$

Finally, from Equation 10.136, we have

$$K^2 \exp(-r\Delta T) - Kv_{i-1,j}^{PUT} = \left(v_{i-1,j}^{PUT} + K \right) S_{i,j}$$

so

$$\frac{1}{S_{i,j}} = \frac{v_{i-1,j}^{PUT} + K}{K^2 \exp(-r\Delta t) - Kv_{i-1,j}^{PUT}}$$

This results in

$$\frac{K}{S_{i,j}} = u = \frac{\left(v_{i-1,j}^{PUT} + K \right) K}{K^2 \exp(-r\Delta t) - Kv_{i-1,j}^{PUT}}$$

or

$$u = \frac{v_{i-1,j}^{PUT} + K}{K \exp(-r\Delta t) - v_{i-1,j}^{PUT}} \quad QED$$

More information concerning the Chriss implied lattice, and other types of implied lattices, can be found in Chriss (1997).

10.6   GRID METHODS FOR VANILLA OPTIONS

10.6.1   Introduction

In Section 10.4 we discussed the use of binomial lattice methods for valuing both European and American options. The lattice methods we described have the advantage that they are fairly easy to implement and can value simple options, such as vanilla puts and calls, *reasonably* accurately. The use of up and down jump probabilities at the lattice nodes is also an appealing feature, since they are directly related to the stochastic process which is being modelled. However, lattice techniques have the following drawbacks:

- They require small time steps to ensure numerical stability.
- There is little control over where the lattice nodes are located. This can lead to very poor accuracy when valuing certain types of options; for example those with barriers at particular asset prices.

One method of avoiding these limitations is through the use of finite-difference grids. Although this approach no longer has the probabilistic interpretation of the binomial lattice it has the following advantages:

- Fewer time steps are required to ensure numerical stability, see Appendix L for a discussion of stability.
- There is complete control over the placement of grid lines, and their associated grid nodes.

10.6.2   Uniform grids

The Black–Scholes equation for the value of an option, f is given by:

$$\frac{\partial f}{\partial t} + (r-q)S\frac{\partial f}{\partial S} + \frac{1}{2}\sigma^2 S^2 \frac{\partial^2 f}{\partial S^2} = rf \qquad (10.138)$$

We want to solve this equation over the duration of the option, that is from the current time t to the maturity of the option at time $t + \tau$. To do this we will use a grid in which the asset price S takes n_s uniformly spaced values, $S_j = j\Delta S$, $j = 0, \ldots, n_{s-1}$, where ΔS is the spacing between grid points. If S_{max} is the maximum asset value we want to represent then the grid spacing, ΔS^*, can be simply calculated as:

$$\Delta S^* = \frac{S_{max}}{(n_s - 1)} \qquad (10.139)$$

However, since we would like to solve the option values and Greeks at the current asset price S_0 we would also like an asset grid line to coincide with the current asset price, see Andersen and Brotherton-Ratcliffe (1998). This avoids the use of interpolation which is necessary when the asset value does not correspond to a grid line. The method by which we achieve this is outlined in Code excerpt 10.12. Here the user supplies the function `opt_gfd` with values for S_{max} and $n_s - 1$ from which ΔS^* is computed using Equation 10.139. We then find the integer, n_1, that is just below (or equal to) the value $S_0/\Delta S^*$, and use this to obtain a new grid spacing $\Delta S = S_0/n_1$. This leads to the new asset price discretization $S_j = j\Delta S j = 0, \ldots, n_{s-1}$, where we have now ensured that $S_{n_1} = S_0$.

The user also supplies the function `opt_gfd` with the number of time intervals for the grid. When there are n_t time intervals the grid has $n_t + 1$ uniformly spaced time instants, $t_i = i\Delta t$, $i = 0, \ldots, n_t$, and the time step is simply:

$$\Delta t = \frac{\tau}{n_t} \qquad (10.140)$$

As with the binomial lattice methods of Sections 10.4 and 10.5 we will solve the equation backwards in time from maturity (at time $t + \tau$) to the present (time t). So as we solve the equation the time index will start at $i = n_t$ (time $t + \tau$) and decrease to $i = 0$ (current time t).

Here we discuss the grid method of solving the Black–Scholes equation in terms of:

- The finite-difference approximation.
- The boundary conditions.

- Computation of the option values at a given time instant.
- Backwards iteration and early exercise.

Each of these aspects will now be considered in turn.

The finite-difference approximation

The option value corresponding to the grid node at which $t_i = i\Delta t$ and $S_j = j\Delta S$ will be denoted by $f_{i,j}$. We will approximate the partial derivative of $f_{i,j}$ w.r.t. time simply as:

$$\frac{\partial f}{\partial t} = \frac{f_{i+1,j} - f_{i,j}}{\Delta t} \tag{10.141}$$

For the other terms in Equation 10.138 we will use the weighted, Θ_m, method. This technique involves selecting an appropriate choice for Θ_m in the range $0 \le \Theta_m \le 1$ so that the *contribution* from node (i, j) is a weighted sum involving the values at nodes (i, j) and $(i + 1, j)$. For instance the term $rf|_{i,j}$ in Equation 10.138 is approximated as:

$$rf|_{i,j} = r\{\Theta_m f_{i+1,j} + (1 - \Theta_m)f_{i,j}\} \tag{10.142}$$

and the term $\partial f/\partial S|_{i,j}$ in Equation 10.138 is approximated as:

$$\left.\frac{\partial f}{\partial S}\right|_{i,j} = \left\{\Theta_m \left.\frac{\partial f}{\partial S}\right|_{i+1,j} + (1 - \Theta_m)\left.\frac{\partial f}{\partial S}\right|_{i,j}\right\} \tag{10.143}$$

Using this method we thus obtain, at node (i, j), the following discretized version of Equation 10.138:

$$\frac{f_{i+1,j} - f_{i,j}}{\Delta t} + (r - q)S_j\left\{\Theta_m f'_{i+1,j} + \Theta_m^* f'_{i,j}\right\}$$

$$+ \frac{1}{2}\sigma^2 S_j^2\left\{\Theta_m f''_{i+1,j} + \Theta_m^* f''_{i,j}\right\} = r\{\Theta_m f_{i+1,j} + \Theta_m^* f_{i,j}\} \tag{10.144}$$

where for compactness we have written $\Theta_m^* = 1 - \Theta_m$, and denote the partial derivatives w.r.t. S at node (i,j) as: $f'_{i,j} = \partial f/\partial S|_{i,j}$ and $f''_{i,j} = \partial^2 f/\partial S^2|_{i,j}$.

Finite-difference approximations for these derivatives can be obtained by considering a Taylor expansion about the point $f_{i,j}$. We proceed as follows:

$$f_{i,j+1} = f_{i,j} + f'_{i,j}\Delta S + \frac{1}{2}f''_{i,j}(\Delta S)^2 \tag{10.145}$$

$$f_{i,j-1} = f_{i,j} - f'_{i,j}\Delta S + \frac{1}{2}f''_{i,j}(\Delta S)^2 \tag{10.146}$$

Subtracting Equations 10.145 and 10.146 we obtain:

$$f_{i,j+1} - f_{i,j-1} = 2f'_{i,j}\Delta S$$

and so

$$f'_{i,j} = \frac{f_{i,j+1} - f_{i,j-1}}{2\Delta S} \tag{10.147}$$

Adding Equations 10.145 and 10.146 we obtain:

$$f_{i,j+1} + f_{i,j-1} = 2f_{i,j} + f''_{i,j}\Delta S^2$$

which gives:

$$f''_{i,j} = \frac{f_{i,j+1} - 2f_{i,j} + f_{i,j-1}}{\Delta S^2} \tag{10.148}$$

The complete finite-difference approximation to the Black–Scholes equation can then be found by substituting the approximations for the first and second partial derivatives, given in Equations 10.147 and 10.148, into Equation 10.144. We thus obtain:

$$r\Delta t\{\Theta_m f_{i+1,j} + \Theta_m^* f_{i,j}\} = f_{i+1,j} - f_{i,j} + \frac{(r-q)j\Delta t A_1}{2} + \frac{\sigma^2 j^2 \Delta t A_2}{2} \tag{10.149}$$

where we have used the fact that $S_j = j\Delta S$, and for compactness have defined the terms:

$$A_1 = \Theta_m f_{i+1,j+1} - \Theta_m f_{i+1,j-1} + \Theta_m^* f_{i,j+1} - \Theta_m^* f_{i,j-1}$$

and

$$A_2 = \Theta_m f_{i+1,j+1} + \Theta_m f_{i+1,j-1} - 2\Theta_m f_{i+1,j} + \Theta_m^* f_{i,j+1} + \Theta_m^* f_{i,j-1} - 2\Theta_m^* f_{i,j}$$

Collecting like terms in $f_{i,j}$, $f_{i+1,j}$, etc. results in:

$$B_1 f_{i,j-1} + B_2 f_{i,j} + B_3 f_{i,j+1} + C_1 f_{i+1,j-1} + C_2 f_{i+1,j} + C_3 f_{i+1,j+1} = 0 \tag{10.150}$$

where

$$B_1 = \frac{-\Theta_m^*(r-q)j\Delta t}{2} + \frac{\Theta_m^* \sigma^2 j^2 \Delta t}{2}$$

$$B_2 = -1 - r\Delta t\Theta_m^* - \Theta_m^* \sigma^2 j^2 \Delta t$$

$$B_3 = \frac{\Theta_m^*(r-q)j\Delta t}{2} + \frac{\Theta_m^* \sigma^2 j^2 \Delta t}{2}$$

$$C_1 = \frac{\Theta_m \sigma^2 j^2 \Delta t}{2} - \frac{\Theta_m(r-q)j\Delta t}{2}$$

$$C_2 = 1 - r\Delta t\Theta_m - \Theta_m \sigma^2 j^2 \Delta t$$

$$C_3 = \frac{\Theta_m(r-q)j\Delta t}{2} + \frac{\Theta_m \sigma^2 j^2 \Delta t}{2}$$

Since we are solving the equation backwards in time we want to determine the option values at time index i from the known option values ($f_{i+1,j+1}$, $f_{i+1,j}$ and

$f_{i+1,j-1}$) at time index $i+1$. This can be achieved by rearranging Equation 10.150 as follows:

Finite-difference scheme for a uniform grid

$$a_j f_{i,j-1} + b_j f_{i,j} + c_j f_{i,j+1} = R_{i+1,j} \tag{10.151}$$

where the right hand side, $R_{i+1,j}$, is:

$$R_{i+1,j} = \bar{a}_j f_{i+1,j-1} + \bar{b}_j f_{i+1,j} + \bar{c}_j f_{i+1,j+1} \tag{10.152}$$

The six coefficients are:

$$a_j = (1 - \Theta_m)\frac{\Delta t}{2}\{(r-q)j - \sigma^2 j^2\} \tag{10.153}$$

$$b_j = 1 + (1 - \Theta_m)\Delta t\{r + \sigma^2 j^2\} \tag{10.154}$$

$$c_j = -(1 - \Theta_m)\frac{\Delta t}{2}\{(r-q)j + \sigma^2 j^2\} \tag{10.155}$$

$$\bar{a}_j = -\Theta_m \frac{\Delta t}{2}\{(r-q)j - \sigma^2 j^2\} \tag{10.156}$$

$$\bar{b}_j = 1 - \Theta_m \Delta t\{r + \sigma^2 j^2\} \tag{10.157}$$

$$\bar{c}_j = \Theta_m \frac{\Delta t}{2}\{(r-q)j + \sigma^2 j^2\} \tag{10.158}$$

For each value of j Equation 10.151 gives us a relationship between three option values, $f_{i+1,j-1}, f_{i+1,j}, f_{i+1,j+1}$ at time index $i+1$, and three option values $f_{i,j-1}, f_{i,j}, f_{i,j+1}$ at time index i.

This situation is shown in Figure 10.9 where we have labelled the grid nodes that contribute to the option value $f_{5,5}$ at grid node E. These are the known option values node A: $f_{6,6}$, node B: $f_{6,5}$ and node C: $f_{6,4}$ and the unknown option values, node D: $f_{5,6}$, node E: $f_{5,5}$ and node F: $f_{5,4}$.

Before we solve Equation 10.151 we will briefly consider its characteristics for different values of the weight parameter Θ_m.

When $\Theta_m = 1$ the values of the coefficients in Equation 10.151 are $a_j = c_j = 0$ and $b_j = 1$. This means that Equation 10.151 reduces to:

$$f_{i,j} = \bar{a}_j f_{i+1,j-1} + \bar{b}_j f_{i+1,j} + \bar{c}_j f_{i+1,j+1}$$

This is termed the *explicit method*, and it can be seen that the unknown option value $f_{i,j}$, at the grid node (i,j) is just a weighted sum of the (known) option values $f_{i+1,j-1}, f_{i+1,j}, f_{i+1,j+1}$. This is the simplest situation to deal with and actually corresponds to a trinomial lattice. However, it has poor numerical properties and usually requires a very small step size to obtain accurate results, see Smith (1985).

When $\Theta_m \neq 1$, the unknown option value $f_{i,j}$ depends not only on the known option values $f_{i+1,j-1}, f_{i+1,j}, f_{i+1,j+1}$ (as in the explicit method above), but also on the

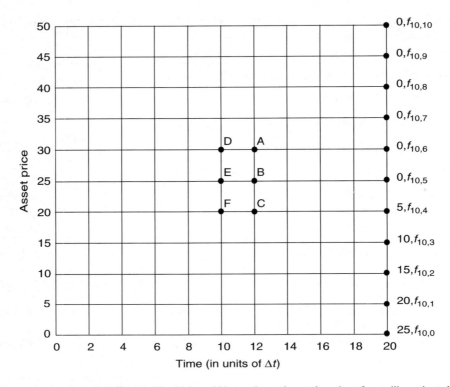

Figure 10.9   An example uniform grid, which could be used to estimate the value of a vanilla option which matures in two years time. The grid parameters are: $n_s = n_t = 10$, $\Delta t = 0.2$, $\Delta S = 5$, and $S_{max} = 50$. The option parameters are $E = 25$, $S_o = 20$, and $\tau = 2.0$. As usual we denote the grid node option values by $f_{i,j}$, where i is the time index and j is the asset index. The option values of the grid nodes at maturity for a vanilla put are thus labelled as *val*, $f_{10,j}$, $j = 0, \ldots, 10$, where *val* is the value of the option at the node; these are shown on the right hand grid boundary. Since $E = 25$ only those nodes with $j < 5$ have nonzero option values

neighbouring *unknown* option values $f_{i,j-1}$ and $f_{i,j+1}$. It is now necessary to solve a set of simultaneous in order to compute the value $f_{i,j}$. This is therefore called an *implicit method*, see Smith (1985).

The implicit method $\Theta_m = 0$ is also called the *fully implicit method*, since now the unknown value $f_{i,j}$ only depends on the neighbouring values $f_{i,j-1}$, $f_{i,j+1}$ and its *previous* value, $f_{i+1,j}$, at time step $i + 1$. This can be shown by substituting $\Theta_m = 0$ in Equations 10.153 to 10.158. We then obtain $\bar{a}_j = \bar{c}_j = 0$ and $\bar{b}_j = 1$, which means that Equation 10.151 reduces to:

$$a_j f_{i,j-1} + b_j f_{i,j} + c_j f_{i,j+1} = f_{i+1,j}$$

The implicit method $\Theta_m = 0.5$, is also termed the *Crank–Nicolson method*. This method, first used by Crank and Nicolson in 1946, see Crank and Nicolson (1947), computes $f_{i,j}$ by giving equal weight to the contributions from time step $i + 1$ and time step i. Substituting $\Theta_m = 0.5$ in Equations 10.153 to 10.149 we obtain the following Crank–Nicolson coefficients:

$$a_j = -\bar{a}_j = \frac{\Delta t}{4}\left\{(r-q)j - \sigma^2 j^2\right\}$$

$$b_j = 1 + \frac{\Delta t}{2}\left\{r + \sigma^2 j^2\right\}$$

$$\bar{b}_j = 1 - \frac{\Delta t}{2}\left\{r + \sigma^2 j^2\right\}$$

$$c_j = -\bar{c}_j = -\frac{\Delta t}{4}\left\{(r-q)j + \sigma^2 j^2\right\}$$

We notice that since we are solving backwards in time, but index time in the forward direction, our values of Θ_m corresponding to implicit and explicit are different from those normally used. For example in Smith (1985) $\Theta_m = 0$ is the explicit method and $\Theta_m = 1$ is the implicit method; the Crank–Nicolson method is still $\Theta_m = 0.5$.

The boundary conditions

In order to solve Equation 10.151 at time instant $i\Delta t$ we need to obtain the option values at the upper asset boundary, the lower asset boundary and the *initial* values that are specified at option maturity.

Here we calculate the boundary values by using the time independent payoff, p_j, at the jth asset index within the grid. If E is the strike price then vanilla call options have payoffs

$$p_j = \max(j\Delta S - E,\ 0),\ j = 0,\dots,n_{s-1}$$

and vanilla put options have payoffs

$$p_j = \max(E - j\Delta S,\ 0),\ j = 0,\dots,n_{s-1}$$

Upper asset boundary values. At the upper boundary $j = n_s - 1$, and $(n_s - 1)\Delta S = S_{\max}$; where we note that for the grid to be useful we require $S_{\max} > E$. Here we assume that $S_{\max} > E$ and so for call options

$$p_{n_{s-1}} = S_{\max} - E$$

and for put options

$$p_{n_{s-1}} = 0$$

The option value at the upper boundary, denoted by f_{BU}, is set to $p_{n_{s-1}}$, and we have $f_{i,n_{s-1}} = f_{BU},\ i = 0,\dots,n_t$.

Lower asset boundary values. At the lower boundary $j = 0$, and the value of $j\Delta S$ is zero. So for call options

$$p_0 = 0$$

and for put options

$$p_0 = E$$

The option value at the lower boundary, denoted by f_{BL}, is set to p_0, and we have $f_{i,0} = f_{BL}$, $i = 0, \ldots, n_t$.

Boundary values at option maturity. At option maturity ($i = n_t$) the initial option (boundary) values are the previously mentioned payouts. If E is the strike price then for vanilla call options

$$f_{n_t,j} = \max(j\Delta S - E,\, 0), \quad j = 0, \ldots, n_{s-1}$$

and for vanilla put options

$$f_{n_t,j} = \max(E - j\Delta S,\, 0), \quad j = 0, \ldots, n_{s-1}$$

This is illustrated in Figure 10.9 for a vanilla put option with current asset value $S_0 = 20$, strike, $E = 25$ and maturity $\tau = 2$. The grid asset price spacing is $\Delta S = 5$, and the time increment is $\Delta t = 0.2$. At option maturity, corresponding to time index $i = 10$, the value of the put option is zero for all asset indices $j \geq 5$.

| Computation of the option values at a given time instant |

Having found the option boundary values we are now in a position to solve Equation 10.151 at time instant $t_i = i\Delta t$.

First we note that since $f_{i,0} = f_{BL}$ and $f_{i,n_{s-1}} = f_{BU}$, Equation 10.151 only needs to be solved for values of the asset index j in the range $j = 1$ to $j = n_{s-2}$. We now deal with the following situations:

- *CASE 1*: $j = 1$, the asset grid line just above the lower boundary.
- *CASE 2*: $j = n_{s-2}$, the asset grid line just below the upper boundary.
- *CASE 3*: all other asset grid lines not included in *CASE 1* or *CASE 2*.

and consider the form that Equation 10.151 takes under each condition.

CASE 1: $j = 1$

Substituting $j = 1$, into Equation 10.151 we obtain:

$$a_1 f_{i,0} + b_1 f_{i,1} + c_1 f_{i,2} = \bar{a}_1 f_{i+1,0} + \bar{b}_1 f_{i+1,1} + \bar{c}_1 f_{i+1,2}$$

Now, since $f_{i,0} = f_{BL}$, this becomes:

$$b_1 f_{i,1} + c_1 f_{i,2} = (\bar{a}_1 - a_1) f_{BL} + \bar{b}_1 f_{i+1,1} + \bar{c}_1 f_{i+1,2}$$

or equivalently:

$$b_1 f_{i,1} + c_1 f_{i,2} = R_{i+1,1} \tag{10.159}$$

where

$$R_{i+1,1} = (\bar{a}_1 - a_1) f_{BL} + \bar{b}_1 f_{i+1,1} + \bar{c}_1 f_{i+1,2} \tag{10.160}$$

CASE 2: $j = n_{s-2}$

Substituting $j = n_{s-1}$ into Equation 10.151 we obtain:

$$a_{n_{s-2}}f_{i,n_{s-3}} + b_{n_{s-2}}f_{i,n_{s-2}} + c_{n_{s-2}}f_{i,n_{s-1}} = \bar{a}_{n_{s-2}}f_{i+1,n_{s-3}} + \bar{b}_{n_{s-2}}f_{i+1,n_{s-2}} + \bar{c}_{n_{s-2}}f_{i+1,n_{s-1}}$$

Since $f_{i,n_{s-1}} = f_{BU}$ this gives:

$$a_{n_{s-2}}f_{i,n_{s-3}} + b_{n_{s-2}}f_{i,n_{s-2}} = \bar{a}_{n_{s-2}}f_{i+1,n_{s-3}} + \bar{b}_{n_{s-2}}f_{i+1,n_{s-2}} + (\bar{c}_{n_{s-2}} - c_{n_{s-2}})f_{BU}$$

or equivalently:

$$a_{n_{s-2}}f_{i,n_{s-3}} + b_{n_{s-2}}f_{i,n_{s-2}} = R_{i+1,n_{s-2}} \tag{10.161}$$

where

$$R_{i+1,n_{s-2}} = \bar{a}_{n_{s-2}}f_{i+1,n_{s-3}} + \bar{b}_{n_{s-2}}f_{i+1,n_{s-2}} + (\bar{c}_{n_{s-2}} - c_{n_{s-2}})f_{BU} \tag{10.162}$$

CASE 3

In this case the boundary values do not enter into the expressions, and we simply restate Equation 10.151 as:

$$a_j f_{i,j-1} + b_j f_{i,j} + c_j f_{i,j+1} = R_{i+1,j}, \quad j = 3, \ldots, n_{s-3} \tag{10.163}$$

where as before the right hand side, $R_{i+1,j}$, is:

$$R_{i+1,j} = \bar{a}_j f_{i+1,j-1} + \bar{b}_j f_{i+1,j} + \bar{c}_j f_{i+1,j+1} \tag{10.164}$$

We can now gather all the information in Equations 10.159 to 10.164 and represent it by the following tridiagonal system:

$$\begin{pmatrix} b_1 & c_1 & 0 & 0 & 0 & 0 \\ a_2 & b_2 & c_2 & 0 & 0 & 0 \\ 0 & 0 & . & . & 0 & 0 \\ 0 & 0 & 0 & . & . & 0 \\ 0 & 0 & 0 & a_{n_s-3} & b_{n_s-3} & c_{n_s-3} \\ 0 & 0 & 0 & 0 & a_{n_s-2} & b_{n_s-2} \end{pmatrix} \begin{pmatrix} f_{i,1} \\ f_{i,2} \\ . \\ . \\ f_{i,n_s-3} \\ f_{i,n_s-2} \end{pmatrix} = \begin{pmatrix} R_{i+1,1} \\ R_{i+1,2} \\ . \\ . \\ R_{i+1,n_s-3} \\ R_{i+1,n_s-2} \end{pmatrix} \tag{10.165}$$

In matrix notation Equation 10.165 can be written as:

$$Ax = R \tag{10.166}$$

where A is the $n_{s-2} \times n_{s-2}$ tridiagonal matrix containing the known coefficients $a_j, j = 2, \ldots, n_{s-2}$, $b_j, j = 1, \ldots, n_{s-2}$, and $c_j, j = 1, \ldots, n_{s-3}$. The vector R denotes the known right hand side, $R_{i+1,j}, j = 1, \ldots, n_{s-2}$, and the vector x contains the unknown option values that we wish to compute, $f_{i,j}, j = 1, \ldots, n_{s-2}$.

It is well known that, if matrix A is non-singular, Equation 10.166 can be solved using an LU decomposition. Here we factorize the $n \times n$ matrix A as:

$$A = LU$$

where L is an $n \times n$ lower triangular matrix with 1s on the diagonal and U is an $n \times n$ upper triangular matrix. We illustrate the LU decomposition for a full 4×4 matrix below:

$$\begin{pmatrix} a_{1,1} & a_{1,2} & a_{1,3} & a_{1,4} \\ a_{2,1} & a_{2,2} & a_{2,3} & a_{2,4} \\ a_{3,1} & a_{3,2} & a_{3,3} & a_{3,4} \\ a_{4,1} & a_{4,2} & a_{4,3} & a_{4,4} \end{pmatrix} = \begin{pmatrix} 1 & 0 & 0 & 0 \\ l_{2,1} & 1 & 0 & 0 \\ l_{3,1} & l_{3,2} & 1 & 0 \\ l_{4,1} & l_{4,2} & l_{4,3} & 1 \end{pmatrix} \begin{pmatrix} u_{1,1} & u_{1,2} & u_{1,3} & u_{1,4} \\ 0 & u_{2,2} & u_{2,3} & u_{2,4} \\ 0 & 0 & u_{3,3} & u_{3,4} \\ 0 & 0 & 0 & u_{4,4} \end{pmatrix} \quad (10.167)$$

If A is a tridiagonal matrix then the LU decomposition takes the simpler form:

$$\begin{pmatrix} a_{1,1} & a_{1,2} & 0 & 0 \\ a_{2,1} & a_{2,2} & a_{2,3} & 0 \\ 0 & a_{3,2} & a_{3,3} & a_{3,4} \\ 0 & 0 & a_{4,3} & a_{4,4} \end{pmatrix} = \begin{pmatrix} 1 & 0 & 0 & 0 \\ l_{2,1} & 1 & 0 & 0 \\ 0 & l_{3,2} & 1 & 0 \\ 0 & 0 & l_{4,3} & 1 \end{pmatrix} \begin{pmatrix} u_{1,1} & u_{1,2} & 0 & 0 \\ 0 & u_{2,2} & u_{2,3} & 0 \\ 0 & 0 & u_{3,3} & u_{3,4} \\ 0 & 0 & 0 & u_{4,4} \end{pmatrix} \quad (10.168)$$

where it can be seen that now both L and U are bidiagonal.

Once the LU decomposition of A has been found it is possible to solve for x in Equation 10.166 by using a two stage method (see for example Golub and Van Loan (1989)). Here forward elimination is used to solve $Ly = \mathcal{R}$, and then back-substitution is applied to $Ux = y$. We can thus write the procedure as:

$$Ax = (LU)x = L(Ux) = Ly = \mathcal{R}$$

We will now provide code excerpts which show how to solve the $n_{s-2} \times n_{s-2}$ tridiagonal system represented by Equation 10.166. These excerpts are in fact contained within the larger Code excerpt 10.18, which displays the complete C code for the option pricing function `opt_gfd`. If the reader requires more detail concerning the precise code used for option pricing then this code should be consulted. (It should be noted that in Code excerpt 10.18, time is indexed using j and asset price using index i. We have modified the indices for the smaller code excerpts given below so that, as might be expected, time is indexed using i, and asset price using j. The author apologizes for any inconvenience this may cause.) Here, for brevity, we will assume that all the required arrays have already been allocated and loaded with the relevant information.

First we need to compute the LU decomposition of the tridiagonal matrix A. The code to achieve this is given in Code excerpt 10.14 below. Here we use the following three arrays to store the elements of the tridiagonal matrix A: array **b** contains the diagonal elements, array **c** contains the upper diagonal elements, and array **a** holds the lower diagonal elements.

```
u[1] = b[1];
if (u[1] ==0.0) printf ("ERROR in array u \n");
for(j=2; j<=ns-2; ++j) {
  u[j] = b[j] - a[j]*c[j-1]/u[j-1];
  if (u[j] ==0.0) printf ("ERROR in array u \n");
}
```

Code excerpt 10.14 Computer code which calculates the diagonal elements of the matrix U, in an LU decomposition of a tridiagonal matrix, A. The elements of matrix A are stored in the following arrays: array **b** contains the diagonal elements, array **c** contains the upper diagonal elements, and array **a** holds the lower diagonal elements. The diagonal elements of U are stored in the array **u** for later use, in Code excerpts 10.15 and 10.16

It should be noted we do not explicitly compute the elements of the matrix L. This is because all the diagonal elements of L are known to be 1, and the sub-diagonal elements of L can be computed from the diagonal elements of U by using `l[j]=a[j]/u[j-1]`. Also we do not need to compute the upper diagonal elements of U since they are known to be the same as the upper diagonal elements of the original matrix A, and are contained in the array **c**, see for example Hager (1988).

Having computed the LU decomposition we can now solve the lower triangular system $Ly = \mathcal{R}$ using forward elimination, this is shown in Code excerpt 10.15.

```
work[1] = rhs[1];
for(j=2; j<=ns-2; ++j) {
  work[j] = rhs[j] - a[j]*work[j-1]/u[j-1];
}
```

Code excerpt 10.15   Computer code which uses forward elimination to solve the lower triangular system $Ly = \mathcal{R}$, where y is stored in the array `work`

In Code excerpt 10.15 we make use of the following two arrays: the array **rhs** which is used to store the elements of the right hand side $\mathcal{R}$, and the array **work** which is both used as workspace and to store the computed solution vector y. As previously mentioned the sub-diagonal elements of L are given by `l[j] = a[j]/u[j-1]`. This means that in Code excerpt 10.15, the line:

```
work[j] = rhs[j] - a[j]* work[j-1]/u[j-1];
```

is in fact be equivalent to:

```
work[j] = rhs[j]-l[j]* work[j-1];
```

where `l[j]`, `j=2,...`, `ns-2` contains the sub-diagonal elements of L, if we had (needlessly) decided to allocate space for an extra array called `l`.

We are now in a position to solve the triangular system $Ux = y$ by using back-substitution. The code to achieve this is given in Code excerpt 10.16. Here the array **work** contains the previously computed values of y, the diagonal elements of U are contained in the array **u**, and (as previously mentioned) the upper diagonal elements of U are stored in the array **a**.

```
opt_vals[ns-2] = work[ns-2]/u[ns-2];
for(j = ns-2; j >=1; --j)
  opt_vals[j] = (work[j] - c[j]opt_vals[j+1])/u[j];
```

Code excerpt 10.16   Computer code which uses back-substitution to solve the upper triangular system $Ux = y$. At time instant $t_i = i\Delta t$, the elements of x are the calculated option values $f_{i,j}$, $i = 1, \ldots, n_{s-2}$

In Code excerpt 10.16 the array `opt_vals` contains the solution vector x. As its name suggests the contents of the array `opt_vals` are in fact the computed option values, $f_{i,j}, j = 1, \ldots, n_{s-2}$, in Equation 10.6.2 and represent the solution of the

Black–Scholes partial differential equation at time instant $t_i = i\Delta t$; based on the previously computed option values $f_{i+1,j}, j = 1, \ldots, n_{s-2}$.

Backwards iteration and early exercise

The Black–Scholes equation can be solved over the time interval t to $t + \tau$ by iteratively solving Equation 10.6.2. We iterate backwards in time by solving Equation 10.6.2 at the ith time step and then using the computed values to solve Equation 10.6.2 for the $(i-1)$th time step. The option values at current time t are obtained when time index $i = 0$ is reached. It can be seen that the grid method yields n_{s-2} option values, $f_{0,j}, j = 1, \ldots, n_{s-2}$, which correspond to the current asset prices

$$S_0^j = j\Delta S, \quad j = 1, \ldots, n_{s-2}$$

As previously mentioned the asset price S_0 coincides with grid index $j = n_1$. Therefore $S_0 = S_0^{n_1}$, and the option value for the current asset price S_0 is given by f_{0,n_1}.

This is in contrast to the lattice methods discussed in Section 10.4 which yield a single option value corresponding to the root node.

The option values obtained using the grid methods we have just described are for vanilla European options. However, vanilla European options can be more accurately valued by using the Black–Scholes option pricing formula discussed in Section 9.3.3. The importance of finite-difference grids is that, by slightly modifying our backward iterative method, we can take into account the possibility of *early exercise*, and thus price American options.

This can be achieved by using Code excerpt 10.17 to modify the option prices contained in the array `opt_vals` as follows:

```
if (put) { /* a put */
  for(j=1; j<=ns-2; ++j)
    opt_vals[j] = MAX(opt_vals[j], E-s[j]);
  }
else { /* a call */
  for(j=1; j<=ns-2; ++j)
    opt_vals[j] = MAX(opt_vals[j], s[j]-E);
  }
```

Code excerpt 10.17 Computer code which modifies the computed option values contained in array `opt_vals` to include the possibility of *early exercise*; this is required if we are to determine the value of American options. Here s[j] contains the asset value at asset index j, `opt_vals[j]` contains the option value (computed by Code excerpt 10.16) at asset index j, and E is the strike price

Now we know how to solve the Black–Scholes equation; it is possible to include, without much difficulty, more *exotic features* such as lock out periods, barriers, rebates, etc.

The routine `opt_gfd` solves the Black–Scholes equation using a uniform grid. The asset price is set to one of the grid lines, which means that interpolation is not required.

```
void opt_gfd(double theta_m, double asset_price, double sigma, double r, double T, double strike,
  Integer is_american, Integer put, double *option_value, double greeks[], double q, Integer pns,
  Integer nt, double smax, Integer *iflag)
```

```
{
/* Input parameters:
   = = = = = =
   theta_m          - the value of theta used for the finite difference method,
   asset_price      - the current price of the underlying asset,
   sigma            - the volatility,
   r                - the interest rate,
   T                - the time to maturity,
   strike           - the strike price,
   is_american      - if is_american is 0 then a European option, otherwise an American option,
   put              - if put is 0 then a call option, otherwise a put option,
   q                - the continuous dividend yield,
   pns              - the maximum asset index on the grid, corresponding to the upper boundary,
   nt               - the number of time intervals,
   smax             - the maximum asset price.
   Output parameters:
   option_value     - the value of the option,
   greeks[]         - the hedge statistics output as follows: greeks[0] is gamma, greeks[1] is delta, and
                      greeks[2] is theta,
   iflag            - an error indicator.
*/
    double *a, *b, *c, *al, *bl, *cl, *opt_vals, *vals, *rhs, *s, *work, *u;
    double ds, dt;
    Integer i, j;
    double tmp, t2, time_2mat;
    Integer n1, n2, ind=0;
    double sig2, temp[4];

    if (asset_price >= smax) printf ("ERROR asset price >=smax");
    n1 = floor((asset_price/smax)*(double)pns);
    n2 = pns - n1;
    ds = asset_price/(double)n1;
    dt = T/(double)nt; /* time interval size */
    ns = n1+n2+1;
/* Note: Now nps = ns-1. Since we define asset grid lines 0...ns-1, this is the maximum grid line;
   corresponding to the upper boundary. The lower boundary is at the asset grid line 0, and we solve for
   option values between the asset grid line 1 and the asset grid line ns-2 */

/* Allocate (all size ns+1) the arrays: a, b, c, al, bl, cl, opt_vals, vals, rhs, s, work and u */

    s[0] = 0.0;
    s[n1] = asset_price;
    for(i=1; i<=n1-1; ++i ) /* set prices below asset_price */
        s[i] = (double)i * ds;
    for(i=1; i<= n2+1; ++i ) /* set prices above asset_price */
        s[n1+i] = asset_price + (double)i * ds;

/* Set up the RHS and LHS coefficients a[], b[] and c[] are the LHS coefficients for the unknown option
   values (time step j) al[], bl[] and cl[] are the values of the RHS coefficients for the known option
   prices (time step j+1).
   Note: al, bl and cl are used to form the RHS vector rhs[] of the tridiagonal system. */
    sig2 = sigma*sigma;
    t2 = dt/2.0;
    tmp = 1.0-theta_m; /* 1 - theta (for theta method) */
    for( i=1; i<=ns-2; ++i) {/* Assign elements of the (ns-2)*(ns-2) tridiagonal matrix */
        a[i] = -i*(i*sig2-(r-q))*t2*tmp;
        al[i] = i*(i*sig2-(r-q))*t2*theta_m;;
        c[i] = -i*(i*sig2+(r-q))*t2*tmp;
        cl[i] = i*(i*sig2+(r-q))*t2*theta_m;;
        b[i] = 1.0+r*dt*tmp+(i*i*sig2)*dt*tmp;
        bl[i] = 1.0-(i*i*sig2+r)*dt*theta_m;
    }
/* Perform LU decomposition of the tridiagonal matrix with:
   diagonal elements contained in the array b[], upper diagonal elements contained in the array c[]
   and lower diagonal elements in the array a[]. Store the elements of U but not those of L
   (they will be computed from U)
   Matrix U: The diagonal elements of U are stored in the array u[] and the upper diagonal elements of U
   are just c[].
   Matrix L: For the lower triangular matrix L, the diagonal elements are 1 and the lower diagonal elements
   are l[i] = a[i]/u[i-1], where u[] is the upper diagonal of U. */

    u[1] = b[1];
    if (u[1] ==0.0) printf ("ERROR in array u \n");
    for(i=2; i <=ns-2; ++i){
        u[i] = b[i] - a[i]*c[i-1]/u[i-1];
        if (u[i] ==0.0) printf ("ERROR in array u \n");
    }
```

```
/* Set option values at maturity. Note : opt_vals[0] and opt_vals [ns-1] are the lower and upper
   (put/call) option price boundary values. */
     if (!put){/* a call */
       for( i=0; i<ns; ++i )
         opt_vals[i] = MAX(s[i] - strike, 0.0 );
     }
     else {/* a put */
       for( i=0; i<ns; ++i)
         opt_vals[i] = MAX(strike - s[i], 0.0);
     }
/* From the option values at maturity (t = nt*dt) calculate values at earlier times (nt-1)*dt etc.. */
     for( j=nt-1; j>=-2; --j) {/* Go two steps past current time (0) so that can evaluate theta */
       time_2mat = T-j*dt;
       for(i=2; i<=ns-3; ++i) /* set up the rhs of equation for Crank-Nicolson method */
         rhs[i] = a1[i]*opt_vals[i-1] + b1[i]*opt_vals[i] +c1[i] *opt_vals[i+1];

/* Incorporate the boundary conditions at the upper/lower asset value boundaries */
       rhs[1] = (a1[1] - a[1])*opt_vals[0]+ b1[1]*opt_vals[1]+ c1[1]*opt_vals[2];
       rhs[ns-2] =a1[ns-2]*opt_vals[ns-3]+b1[ns-2]*opt_vals[ns-2]+(c1[ns-2] -c[ns-2])*opt_vals[ns-1];

/* Solve the lower triangular system Ly = b, where y is stored in array work[].
   Compute the elements of L from those of U, l[i] = a[i]/u [i-1]. */
       work[1] = rhs[1];
       for( i=2; i<=ns-2; ++i ) {
         work[i] = rhs[i] - a[i]*work[i-1]/u[i-1];
       }
/* Solve the upper (ns-2)*(ns-2) triangular system Ux = y (where x = opt_vals) */
       opt_vals[ns-2] = work[ns-2]/u[ns-2];
       for( i = ns-2; i >= 1; --i )
         opt_vals[i] = (work[i] - c[i]*opt_vals[i+1])/u[i];
       if (is_american) {/* take into account early exercise for american options */
         if (put) {/* a put */
           for(i=1; i<=ns-2; ++i)
             opt_vals[i] = MAX(opt_vals[i], strike-s[i]);
         }
         else {/* a call */
           for(i=1; i<=ns-2; ++i)
             opt_vals[i] = MAX(opt_vals[i], s[i] -strike);
         }
       }
       if (j==0) {
         for (i=0; i < ns; ++i)
           vals[i] = opt_vals[i];
       }
       if ((j==1)||(j==2)||(j==-1)||(j==-2)) {/* Store option values so that can compute theta */
         temp[ind] = opt_vals[n1];
         ++ind;
       }
     }
   if (greeks) {
/* Compute gamma (4th order accuracy) */
     greeks[0] = (-vals[n1+2]+16.0 *vals[n1+1]- 30.0*vals[n1]+
       16.0*vals[n1-1]-vals[n1-2])/(12.0* ds*ds);
/* Compute delta (4th order accuracy) */
     greeks[1] = (-vals[n1+2]+8.0*vals[n1+1]- 8.0*vals [n1-1]+ vals[n1-2])/(12.0*ds);
/* Compute theta (4th order accuracy) */
     greeks[2] = (-temp[0]+8.0*temp[1]-8.0*temp[2]+temp [3])/(12.0*dt);
/* Note: could also compute theta as greeks[2] = (-temp[0]+4.0* temp[1]-3.0*vals[n1])/
     (2.0*dt); */
   }
     *option_value = vals[n1]; /* Return option value */
 }
```

Code excerpt 10.18   Function to compute the value of a vanilla option using a uniform grid

10.6.3   Nonuniform grids

In the previous section we showed how to solve the Black–Scholes equation using a uniform grid. Although this approach will provide satisfactory solutions to many option pricing problems, there are situations in which it is important to be able to place grid lines at locations which do not correspond to those available in a uniform grid. Increasing the density of grid lines in regions of interest can lead to improved accuracy in both the estimated option values and also the estimates of the hedge statistics (the Greeks).

Here we provide an example which illustrates the benefits of using nonuniform grids in the evaluation of down and out call barrier options. Later on in Section 10.6.6 we give a further example which shows the use of nonuniform grids to evaluate double barrier options.

The purpose of this section is to show how to discretize the Black–Scholes equation using a nonuniform grid, and to derive an expression, see Equation 10.176, that is equivalent to Equation 10.151. Although the tridiagonal system of equations we have to solve in this section will be different from that in Section 10.6.2, the solution method is exactly the same. This means that once we have derived Equation 10.151 all the other information which we require to evaluate both European and American options is available in Section 10.6.2 under the headings:

- The boundary conditions.
- Computation of the option values at a given time instant.
- Backwards iteration and early exercise.

We will now consider the finite-difference approximation for a nonuniform grid, and then show how to value the down and out call barrier option.

The finite-difference approximation

Here we consider how to discretize the Black–Scholes equation using a nonuniform grid, in which both the asset price interval ΔS and the time step Δt are not constant but can vary throughout the grid.

Allowing for a nonconstant time step is quite simple. The time step occurs in both the first derivative of $f_{i,j}$, see Equation 10.141, and in the finite-difference equations, see Equations 10.153 to 10.157, as the constant Δt. To incorporate a varying time step, Δt_i, $i = 0, n_t$, thus only requires setting $\Delta t = \Delta t_i$, at the ith time step and then continue with the solution method outlined in Section 10.6.2.

The incorporation of nonconstant asset price intervals requires more work. This is because the finite-difference approximations to the first and second derivatives $f'_{i,j}$ and $f''_{i,j}$, in Equations 10.147 and 10.148, are based on a Taylor expansion about the point $f_{i,j}$.

We will now derive expressions for these derivatives. If we let $\Delta X_j^- = S_j - S_{j-1}$ and $\Delta X_j^+ = S_{j+1} - S_j$ and then using a Taylor expansion about the $f_{i+1,j}$ we have

$$f_{i+1,j+1} = f_{i+1,j} + f'_{i+1,j}\Delta X_j^+ + \frac{1}{2}f''_{i+1,j}\left(\Delta X_j^+\right)^2 \tag{10.169}$$

and also

$$f_{i+1,j-1} = f_{i+1,j} - f'_{i+1,j}\Delta X_j^- + \frac{1}{2}f''_{i+1,j}\left(\Delta X_j^-\right)^2 \tag{10.170}$$

Multiplying Equation 10.169 by ΔX_j^- and adding it to ΔX_j^+ times, Equation 10.170 gives

$$\Delta X_j^+ f_{i+1,j-1} + \Delta X_j^- f_{i+1,j+1} = \Delta X_j^- f_{i+1,j} + \Delta X_j^+ f_{i+1,j}$$
$$+ \frac{1}{2} f_{i+1,j}'' \left\{ (\Delta X_j^+)^2 \Delta X_j^- + (\Delta X_j^-)^2 \Delta X_j^+ \right\}$$

Therefore

$$\frac{1}{2} f_{i+1,j}'' = \frac{\Delta X_j^+ f_{i+1,j-1} + \Delta X_j^- f_{i+1,j+1} - \Delta X_j^- f_{i+1,j} - \Delta X_j^+ f_{i+1,j}}{(\Delta X_j^+)^2 \Delta X_j^- + (\Delta X_j^-)^2 \Delta X_j^+}$$

So

$$f_{i+1,j}'' = \frac{2\left\{ \Delta X_j^+ f_{i+1,j-1} + \Delta X_j^- f_{i+1,j+1} - f_{i+1,j}(\Delta X_j^- + \Delta X_j^+) \right\}}{(\Delta X_j^+)^2 \Delta X_j^- + (\Delta X_j^-)^2 \Delta X_j^+} \qquad (10.171)$$

To calculate $f_{i+1,j}'$ we rearrange Equation 10.170 to obtain

$$-f_{i+1,j}' \Delta X_j^- = f_{i+1,j-1} - f_{i+1,j} - \frac{1}{2} f_{i+1,j}''(\Delta X_j^-)^2$$

and

$$f_{i+1,j}' = \frac{f_{i+1,j} - f_{i+1,j-1}}{\Delta X_j^-} + \frac{1}{2} f_{i+1,j}'' \Delta X_j^- \qquad (10.172)$$

If we now substitute for $f_{i+1,j}''$, from Equation 10.171, into Equation 10.172 we have

$$f_{i+1,j}' = \frac{f_{i+1,j} - f_{i+1,j-1}}{\Delta X_j^-} + \frac{\left\{ \Delta X_j^+ f_{i+1,j-1} - (\Delta X_j^- + \Delta X_j^+) f_{i+1,j} + \Delta X_j^- f_{i+1,j+1} \right\} \Delta X_j^-}{(\Delta X_j^+)^2 \Delta X_j^- + (\Delta X_j^-)^2 \Delta X_j^+}$$

which simplifies to give

$$f_{i+1,j}' = \frac{(\Delta X_j^+)^2 (f_{i+1,j} - f_{i+1,j-1}) - (\Delta X_j^-)^2 f_{i+1,j} + (\Delta X_j^-)^2 f_{i+1,j+1}}{(\Delta X_j^+)^2 \Delta X_j^- + (\Delta X_j^-)^2 \Delta X_j^+}$$

so that we finally have

$$f_{i+1,j}' = \frac{(\Delta X_j^-)^2 f_{i+1,j+1} + ((\Delta X_j^+)^2 - (\Delta X_j^-)^2) f_{i+1,j} - (\Delta X_j^+)^2 f_{i+1,j-1}}{(\Delta X_j^+)^2 \Delta X_j^- + (\Delta X_j^-)^2 \Delta X_j^+} \qquad (10.173)$$

As in Section 10.6.2, we can now substitute the expressions for $f'_{i+1,j}$ and $f''_{i+1,j}$ given in Equations 10.173 and 10.171, into the Equation 10.144; the discretized Black–Scholes equation. If we let $D = (\Delta X_j^+)^2 \Delta X_j^- + (\Delta X_j^-)^2 \Delta X_j^+$ we then obtain

$$r\Delta t(\Theta_m f_{i+1,j} + \Theta_m^* f_{i,j}) = f_{i+1,j} - f_{i,j} + \frac{(r-q)S_j \Delta t A_1}{D} + \frac{\sigma^2 S_j^2 \Delta t A_2}{D} \tag{10.174}$$

where $\Theta_m^* = 1 - \Theta_m$, and

$$A_1 = \Theta_m \left[f_{i+1,j+1}(\Delta X_j^-)^2 - f_{i+1,j-1}(\Delta X_j^+)^2 - f_{i+1,j}\{(\Delta X_j^-)^2 - (\Delta X_j^+)^2\} \right]$$
$$+ \Theta_m^* \left[f_{i,j+1}(\Delta X_j^-)^2 - f_{i,j-1}(\Delta X_j^+)^2 - f_{i,j}\{(\Delta X_j^-)^2 - (\Delta X_j^+)^2\} \right]$$

and

$$A_2 = \Theta_m \left[f_{i+1,j+1}\Delta X_j^- + f_{i+1,j-1}\Delta X_j^+ - f_{i+1,j}\{\Delta X_j^- + \Delta X_j^+\} \right]$$
$$+ \Theta_m^* \left[f_{i,j+1}\Delta X_j^- + f_{i,j-1}\Delta X_j^+ - f_{i,j}\{\Delta X_j^- + \Delta X_j^+\} \right]$$

Collecting like terms we obtain:

$$B_1 f_{i,j-1} + B_2 f_{i,j} + B_3 f_{i,j+1} + C_1 f_{i+1,j-1} + C_2 f_{i+1,j} + C_3 f_{i+1,j+1} = 0 \tag{10.175}$$

where

$$B_1 = \frac{-\Theta_m^*(r-q)S_j \Delta t(\Delta X_j^+)^2}{D} + \frac{(1-\theta)\sigma^2 S_j^2 \Delta t \Delta X_j^+}{D}$$

$$B_2 = -1 - r\Delta t \Theta_m^* - \frac{\Theta_m^* \sigma^2 S_j^2 \Delta t(\Delta X_j^- + \Delta X_j^+)}{D} - \frac{\Theta_m^*(r-q)S_j \Delta t\{(\Delta X_j^-)^2 - (\Delta X_j^+)^2\}}{D}$$

$$B_3 = \frac{\Theta_m^*(r-q)S_j \Delta t(\Delta X_j^-)^2}{D} + \frac{\Theta_m^* \sigma^2 S_j^2 \Delta t \Delta X_j^-}{D}$$

$$C_1 = \frac{\Theta_m \sigma^2 S_j^2 \Delta t \Delta X_j^+}{D} - \frac{\Theta_m(r-q)S_j \Delta t(\Delta X_j^+)^2}{D}$$

$$C_2 = 1 - r\Delta t \Theta_m - \frac{\Theta_m(r-q)S_j \Delta t\{(\Delta X_j^-)^2 - (\Delta X_j^+)^2\}}{D} - \frac{\Theta_m \sigma^2 S_j^2 \Delta t\{\Delta X_j^- + \Delta X_j^+\}}{D}$$

$$C_3 = \frac{\Theta_m(r-q)S_j \Delta t(\Delta X_j^-)^2}{D} + \frac{\Theta_m \sigma^2 S_j^2 \Delta t \Delta X_j^-}{D}$$

Since we are solving the Black–Scholes equation backwards in time we will rearrange Equation 10.175 as:

Finite-difference scheme for a nonuniform grid

$$a_j f_{i,j-1} + b_j f_{i,j} + c_j = R_{i+1,j} \tag{10.176}$$

where the right hand side $R_{i+1,j}$ is:

$$R_{i+1,j} = \bar{a}_j f_{i+1,j-1} + \bar{b}_j f_{i+1,j} + \bar{c}_j f_{i+1,j+1} \tag{10.177}$$

and the coefficients are

$$a_j = \Theta_m^* \Delta t \left\{ \frac{(r-q)S_j(\Delta X_j^+)^2}{D} - \frac{\sigma^2 S_j^2 \Delta X_j^+}{D} \right\} \tag{10.178}$$

$$b_j = 1 + \Delta t \Theta_m^* \left\{ r + \frac{\sigma^2 S_j^2 (\Delta X_j^- + \Delta X_j^+)}{D} \right.$$

$$\left. + \frac{(r-q)S_j \left\{ (\Delta X_j^-)^2 - (\Delta X_j^+)^2 \right\}}{D} \right\} \tag{10.179}$$

$$c_j = \Theta_m^* \Delta t \left\{ \frac{-(r-q)S_j(\Delta X_j^-)^2}{D} - \frac{\sigma^2 S_j^2 \Delta X_j^-}{D} \right\} \tag{10.180}$$

$$\bar{a}_j = \Theta_m \Delta t \left\{ \frac{\sigma^2 S_j^2 \Delta X_j^+}{D} - \frac{(r-q)S_j(\Delta X_j^+)^2}{D} \right\} \tag{10.181}$$

$$\bar{b}_j = 1 - \Theta_m r \Delta t$$

$$- \Theta_m \Delta t \left\{ \frac{(r-q)S_j \left\{ (\Delta X_j^-)^2 - (\Delta X_j^+)^2 \right\}}{D} + \frac{\sigma^2 S_j^2 \left\{ \Delta X_j^- + \Delta X_j^+ \right\}}{D} \right\} \tag{10.182}$$

$$\bar{c}_j = \Theta_m \Delta t \left\{ \frac{(r-q)S_j(\Delta X_j^-)^2}{D} + \frac{\sigma^2 S_j^2 \Delta X_j^-}{D} \right\} \tag{10.183}$$

Here Equation 10.176, as is the case for Equation 10.151 in Section 10.6.2, provides the relationship between the three option values $f_{i+1,j-1}, f_{i+1,j}, f_{i+1,j+1}$ at time index $i+1$, and the three option values $f_{i,j-1}, f_{i,j}, f_{i,j+1}$ at time index i. It can also be seen that Equation 10.176 is the nonuniform grid equivalent of Equation 10.151 given in Section 10.6.2. We will now show that Equations 10.176 and 10.151 are identical when a uniform grid is used, that is $\Delta X_j^+ = \Delta X_j^-$. We proceed as follows:

Let

$$\Delta X_j^+ = \Delta X_j^- = \Delta S, \quad \text{and} \quad S_j = j \Delta S$$

so

$$D = (\Delta X_j^+)^2 \Delta X_j^- + (\Delta X_j^-)^2 \Delta X_j^+ = 2(\Delta S)^3$$

$$\frac{(\Delta X_j^+)^2}{D} = \frac{(\Delta X_j^-)^2}{D} = \frac{(\Delta S)^2}{2(\Delta S)^3} = \frac{1}{2\Delta S}$$

$$\frac{\Delta X_j^+}{D} = \frac{\Delta X_j^-}{D} = \frac{1}{2\Delta S^2}$$

$$\frac{(\Delta X_j^+)^2 - (\Delta X_j^-)^2}{D} = 0$$

If we substitute the above values into Equations 10.178 to 10.183 we obtain the following expressions for the coefficients in Equation 10.176.

$$a_j = (1 - \Theta_m)\Delta t\left\{\frac{(r-q)S_j}{2\Delta S} - \frac{\sigma^2 S_j^2}{2\Delta S^2}\right\} = (1 - \Theta_m)\frac{\Delta t}{2}\{(r-q)j - \sigma^2 j^2\}$$

$$b_j = 1 + \Delta t(1 - \Theta_m)\left\{r + \frac{\sigma^2 S_j^2}{\Delta S^2}\right\} = 1 + (1 - \Theta_m)\Delta t\{r + \sigma^2 j^2\}$$

$$c_j = (1 - \Theta_m)\Delta t\left\{\frac{-(r-q)S_j}{2\Delta S} - \frac{\sigma^2 S_j^2}{2\Delta S^2}\right\} = -(1 - \Theta_m)\frac{\Delta t}{2}\{(r-q)j + \sigma^2 j^2\}$$

$$\bar{a}_j = \Theta_m\Delta t\left\{\frac{\sigma^2 S_j^2}{2\Delta S^2} - \frac{(r-q)S_j}{2\Delta S}\right\} = -\Theta_m\frac{\Delta t}{2}\{(r-q)j - \sigma^2 j^2\}$$

$$\bar{b}_j = 1 - \Theta_m r\Delta t - \frac{\Theta_m \sigma^2 S_j^2 \Delta t}{\Delta S^2} = 1 - \Theta_m\Delta t\{r + \sigma^2 j^2\}$$

$$\bar{c}_j = \Theta_m\Delta t\left\{\frac{(r-q)S_j}{2\Delta S} + \frac{\sigma^2 S_j^2}{\Delta S^2}\right\} = -\Theta_m\frac{\Delta t}{2}\{(r-q)j + \sigma^2 j^2\}$$

It can be seen that these coefficients are identical to those given in Section 10.6.2, Equations 10.153 to 10.158.

We now provide examples of using nonuniform grids to evaluate European down and out call options.

| Valuation of a down and out call option |

Here the improved accuracy that can be achieved by using nonuniform grids instead of uniform grids is illustrated in Figures 10.11 and 10.12. The uniform grids are constructed using the method outlined in Section 10.6.2 and Code excerpt 10.18. That is an asset grid line is set to coincide with the current asset price S_0, and the other grid lines are positioned above and below S_0 with a uniform spacing of ΔS. The disadvantage of this approach is that there will be an unspecified pricing error that depends on the distance, d_s, of the barrier level, B, to the the nearest asset grid line. Futhermore, as the number of asset points, n_s, increases the magnitude of d_s will oscillate within the range 0 to $\Delta S/2$.

When $d_s \sim 0$ the grid will be accurate, but when $|d_s| \sim \Delta S/2$ there will be a large pricing error. This gives rise to the oscillating pricing errors shown in Figures 10.11 and 10.12.

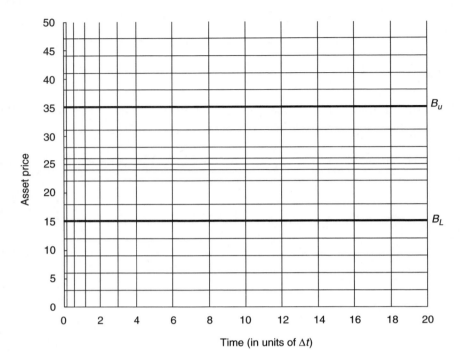

Figure 10.10   A nonuniform grid in which the grid spacing is reduced near current time t, and also in the neighbourhood of the asset price 25; this can lead to greater accuracy in the computed option values and the associated *Greeks*. Grid lines are also placed at asset prices of B_U and B_L, this enables the accurate evaluation of options which have barriers at these asset prices

The nonuniform grids are constructed using the techniques mentioned earlier in this section, and also Code excerpt 10.19. We now, irrespective of n_s, arrange for one asset grid line to coincide with the current asset value, S_0, and another asset grid line to coincide with B, the barrier asset price. In Figure 10.10 this corresponds to setting B_L to B and not using B_U.

It can be seen in Figures 10.11 and 10.12 that in this case the pricing error is very much less, and also doesn't exhibit the pronounced oscillations that are produced by a uniform grid. In Code excerpt 10.19 below, we give the computer program which was used to obtain the nonuniform grid values for the down and out call options presented in Figures 10.11 and 10.12. Although this program only deals with European options it can easily be altered, using the same techniques as in Code excerpt 10.18, to deal with American style options; this is left as an exercise for the reader.

```
void barrier_downout (double barrier_level, double theta_m, double asset_price, double sigma, double r,
    double T, double strike, Integer put, double *option_value, double greeks[], double q, Integer ns,
    Integer nt, double smax, Integer *ifail)
{
  /* ns - the number of asset intervals
     nt - the number of time intervals
  */
    double *a, *b, *c, *a1, *b1, *c1, *opt_vals, *vals, *rhs, *s, *work, *u;
```

```
double ds, time_step;
Integer i, j, barrier_index;
double tmp, t2, time_2mat, zero = 0.0;
Integer n1, n2, ind=0, ns1;
double sig2, temp[4], ds_plus, ds_minus, temp1, temp2, temp3;
double D;
   n1 = floor((asset_price/smax)*(double)ns);
   if (n1 < 3){
     printf ("increase the number of asset points \n");
   }
   n2 = ns - n1;
   ds = asset_price/(double)n1;
   time_step = T/(double)nt; /* time interval size */
   ns1 = n1+n2+2; /* number of nodes - including extra grid line*/
   /* allocate the required arrays (all of size ns1+1): a, b, c, a1, b1, c1, opt_vals, vals, rhs, s, work, u */
     . . .
   /* set prices below asset_price */
   s[0] = zero;
   s[n1] = asset_price;
   for(i=1; i < n1; ++i )
     s[i] = (double)i * ds;
   /* set prices above asset_price */
   for(i=1; i<= n2+2; ++i ){
     s[n1+i] = asset_price + (double)i * ds;
   }
/* find out the index corresponding to barrier_level */
   barrier_index = 0;
   while(barrier_level > s[barrier_index]){
     ++barrier_index;
   }
```

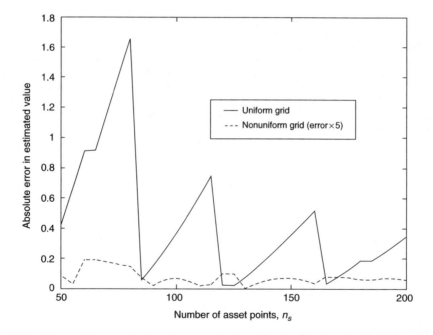

Figure 10.11   The absolute error in the estimated values for a European down and out call barrier option ($B < E$) as the number of asset grid points, n_s, is varied. Here we show a comparison of the results obtained using both uniform and nonuniform grids; logarithmic transformations were not employed. The algorithm for the uniform grid is described in Section 10.6.2, and that for the nonuniform grid is outlined in Section 10.6.3. The Crank–Nicolson method ($\Theta_m = 0.5$) was used and the other parameters were $E = 50.0$, $B = 47.5$, $S_0 = 55.0$, $S_{max} = 300.0$, $T = 0.5$, $\sigma = 0.2$, $r = \log(1.1)$, $q = 0.0$, $n_t = 100$. The correct option value was 7.6512 which was obtained using the analytic formulae given in Section 9.4 and Code excerpt 9.6

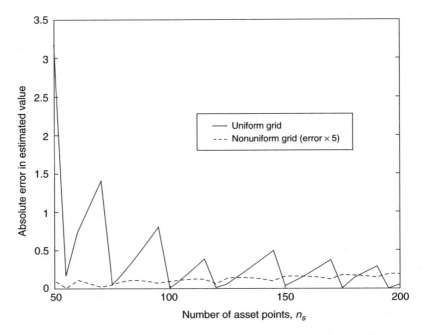

Figure 10.12   The absolute error in the estimated values for a European down and out call barrier option $(E < B)$ as the number of asset grid points, n_s, is varied. Here we show a comparison of the results obtained using both uniform and nonuniform grids; logarithmic transformations are not employed. The algorithm for the uniform grid is described in Section 10.6.2 and that for the nonuniform grid is outlined in Section 10.6.3. The Crank–Nicolson method $(\Theta_m = 0.5)$ was used and the other parameters were $E = 50.0$, $B = 52.5$, $S_0 = 65.0$, $S_{\max} = 300.0$, $T = 0.5$, $\sigma = 0.2$, $r = \log{(1.1)}$, $q = 0.0$, $n_t = 100$. The correct option value was 17.0386 which was obtained using the analytic formulae given in Section 9.4 and Code excerpt 9.6

```
if (barrier_level != s[barrier_index]){/* decrement barrier index */
    --barrier_index;
}
if (s[barrier_index] != barrier_level){/* then barrier does not correspond to an existing grid line so
                                        create another one*/
    for (i=1; i < ns1-barrier_index; ++i){
        s[barrier_index+1+i] = s[barrier_index] + (double)i*d s;
    }
    ++barrier_index;
    s[barrier_index] = barrier_level;
    if (n1>barrier_index){
        ++n1;
    }
}
/* set up the RHS and LHS coefficients a[], b[] and c[] are the LHS coefficients for the unknown option
    values (time step j) a1[], b1[] and c1[] are the values of the RHS coefficients for the known option
    prices (time step j+1).
    Note: a1, b1 and c1 are used to form the RHS vector rhs[] of the tridiagonal system. */
sig2 = sigma*sigma;
t2 = time_step/2.0;
tmp = 1.0-theta_m; /* 1 - theta (for theta method) */
/* assign elements of the (ns1-2)*(ns1-2) tridiagonal matrix */
for( i=1; i<=ns1-2; ++i){
    ds_plus = s[i+1]-s[i];
    ds_minus = s[i] - s[i-1];
    D = ((ds_plus*ds_plus*ds_minus) + (ds_minus*ds_minus*ds_ plus));
    temp1 = tmp*time_step/D;
```

```
            a1[i] = -(temp1*((r-q)*s[i]*ds_plus*ds_plus) - temp1* ds_plus*(s[i]*s[i]*sig2));
            temp1 = (ds_minus*ds_minus)/D;
            temp2 = ds_minus/D;
            c[i] = -time_step*tmp*(temp1*s[i]*(r-q)+(sig2*s[i]* s[i]*temp2));
            c1[i] = time_step*theta_m*(temp1*s[i]*(r-q)+(sig2*s[i] *s[i]*temp2));
            temp1 = ((ds_minus*ds_minus) - (ds_plus*ds_plus))/D;
            temp2 = (ds_minus+ds_plus)/D;
            b[i] = 1.0+time_step *tmp*(r+((r-q)*s[i]*temp1)+ (s[i]* s[i]*sig2)*temp2);
            b1[i] = 1.0-time_step *theta_m*(r+((r-q)*s[i]*temp1)+ (s[i]*s[i]*sig2)*temp2);
         }
    /* Perform LU decomposition of the tridiagonal matrix with: diagonal elements contained in the array b[],
       upper diagonal elements contained in the array c[] and lower diagonal elements in the array a[].
       Store the elements of U but not those of L (they will be computed from U)
       Matrix U: The diagonal elements of U are stored in the array u[] and the upper diagonal elements of U are
       just c[].
       Matrix L: For the lower triangular matrix L, the diagonal elements are 1 and the lower diagonal elements
       are l[i] = a[i]/u[i-1], where u[] is the upper diagonal of U. */
    u[1] = b[1];
    if (u[1] == zero) printf ("error in array u \n");
    for( i=2; i <=ns1-2; ++i){
        u[i] = b[i] - a[i]*c[i-1]/u[i-1];
        if (u[i] == zero) printf ("error in array u \n");
    }
/* Set option values at maturity. Note : opt_vals[0] amd opt_vals[ns1-1] are the lower and upper (put/call)
   option price boundary values. */
    if (!put){/* a call */
        for( i=0; i<ns1; ++i )
          opt_vals[i] = MAX(s[i]-strike, zero );
        /* now modify option values to include the barrier */
        for( i=0; i <= barrier_index; ++i )
          opt_vals[i] = zero;
    }

    else{/* a put */
        for( i=0; i<ns1; ++i )
          opt_vals[i] = MAX(strike - s[i], zero );
    }
    /* From the option values at maturity, t = nt*time_step, compute
       the values at times (nt-1)*time_step to 0 (current time) */
    for( j=nt-1; j>=-2; --j){/* go two steps past current time so that can evaluate theta */
        time_2mat = T-j*time_step;
        /* set up the rhs of equation for the Theta method */
        for(i=2; i<=ns1-3; ++i)
          rhs[i] = a1[i]*opt_vals[i- 1]+b1[i]*opt_vals[i]+c1[i]* opt_vals[i+1];
        /* incorporate the boundary conditions1 at the upper/lower asset value boundaries */
        rhs[1] = (a1[1]-a[1])*opt_vals[0]+ b1[1]*opt_vals[1]+c1[1]*opt_vals[2];
        rhs[ns1-2] = a1[ns1-2]*opt_vals[ns1-3]+ b1[ns1-2]*opt_vals[ns1-2]+
              (c1[ns1-2]-c[ns1-2])*opt_vals[ns1-1];
        /* Solve the lower triangular system Ly = b, where y is stored in array work[].
           Compute the elements of L from those of U, l[i] = a[i]/u[i-1]. */
        work[1] = rhs[1];
        for( i=2; i<=ns1-2; ++i ){
            work[i] = rhs[i] - a[i]*work[i-1]/u[i-1];
        }
        /* Solve the upper (ns1-2)*(ns1-2) triangular system Ux = y (where x = opt_vals) */
        opt_vals[ns1-2] = work[ns1-2]/u[ns1-2];
        for( i = ns1-2; i >= 1; --i )
          opt_vals[i] = (work[i] - c[i]*opt_vals[i+1])/u[i];
        if (j==0){
            for (i=0; i < ns1; ++i)
              vals[i] = opt_vals[i];
        }
        /* store option values so that can compute theta */
        if ((j==1)||(j==2)||(j==-1)||(j==-2)){
            temp[ind] = opt_vals[n1];
            ++ind;
        }
        /* now modify for barrier */
        for( i=0; i <= barrier_index; ++i )
          opt_vals[i] = zero;
    }
    if (greeks){/* assume an irregular grid */
        ds_minus = s[n1]-s[n1-1];
        ds_plus = s[n1+1]-s[n1];
        D = (ds_minus*ds_minus*ds_plus) + (ds_plus*ds_plus*ds_minus);
        temp1 = ds_minus*ds_minus;
```

```
  temp2 = ds_plus*ds_plus;
  temp3 = temp1-temp2;
/* GAMMA */
  greeks[0] = (ds_minus*vals[n1+1] +ds_plus*vals[n1-1] - vals [n1]*(ds_plus+ds_minus))/(0.5*D);
/* DELTA */
  greeks[1] = (temp1*vals[n1+1] - temp2*vals[n1-1] - vals[n1]*temp3)/D;
/* THETA */
  greeks[2] = (-temp[0]+8.0*temp[1]- 8.0*temp[2]+temp[3])/(12.0*time_step);
/* could also compute theta like this:
  greeks[2] = (-temp[0]+4.0*temp[1]-3.0*vals[n1])/(2.0* time_step); */
}
*option_value = vals[n1]; /* Return option value */
/* deallocate the arrays that were previously allocated */
  . . .
}
```

Code excerpt 10.19   Function to compute the value of a European down and out barrier option using a nonuniform grid

10.6.4   The log transformation and uniform grids

Up to this point we have been dealing with the standard Black–Scholes equation, which is

$$\frac{\partial f}{\partial t} + (r-q)S\frac{\partial f}{\partial S} + \frac{\sigma^2 S^2}{2}\frac{\partial^2 f}{\partial S^2} = rf \tag{10.184}$$

However, if we introduce the change of variable $Z = \log S$, we obtain the following equation:

$$\frac{\partial f}{\partial t} + b\frac{\partial f}{\partial Z} + \frac{\sigma^2}{2}\frac{\partial^2 f}{\partial Z^2} = rf \tag{10.185}$$

where $b = r - q - (\sigma^2/2)$. This has beneficial numerical properties since it does not contain the original Black–Scholes terms in S and S^2.

Derivation of Equation 10.185
We will now derive an expression for the logarithmic Black–Scholes equation, and show that it agrees with Equation 10.185.

Since $Z = \log S$ we have $\partial Z/\partial S = 1/S$. This gives:

$$\frac{\partial f}{\partial S} = \frac{\partial f}{\partial Z}\frac{\partial Z}{\partial S} = \frac{1}{S}\frac{\partial f}{\partial Z}$$

and

$$\frac{\partial^2 f}{\partial S^2} = \frac{\partial}{\partial S}\left(\frac{\partial f}{\partial S}\right) = \frac{1}{S^2}\frac{\partial f}{\partial Z} + \frac{1}{S}\frac{\partial}{\partial S}\left(\frac{\partial f}{\partial Z}\right) = -\frac{1}{S^2}\frac{\partial f}{\partial Z} + \frac{1}{S}\frac{\partial Z}{\partial S}\frac{\partial}{\partial Z}\left(\frac{\partial f}{\partial Z}\right)$$

$$\frac{\partial^2 f}{\partial S^2} = -\frac{1}{S^2}\frac{\partial f}{\partial Z} + \frac{1}{S^2}\frac{\partial^2 f}{\partial Z^2}$$

Substituting the above values into Equation 10.184

$$\frac{\partial f}{\partial t} + \frac{(r-q)S}{S}\frac{\partial f}{\partial Z} - \frac{\sigma^2 S^2}{2S^2}\frac{\partial f}{\partial Z} + \frac{\sigma^2 S^2}{2S^2}\frac{\partial^2 f}{\partial Z^2} = rf$$

and setting $b = r - q - \sigma^2/2$ we obtain:

$$\frac{\partial f}{\partial t} + b\frac{\partial f}{\partial Z} + \frac{\sigma^2}{2}\frac{\partial^2 f}{\partial Z^2} = rf \qquad QED \qquad (10.186)$$

We will now consider the finite-difference discretization of Equation 10.185.

The finite-difference method

Application of the finite difference method to the log transformed Black–Scholes equation is very similar to that already outlined in Sections 10.6.2 and 10.6.3.
Use of the Θ_m method on Equation 10.185 results in:

$$\frac{f_{i+1,j} - f_{i,j}}{\Delta t} + b\left\{\Theta_m f'_{i+1,j} + \Theta^*_m f'_{i,j}\right\}$$

$$+ \frac{1}{2}\sigma^2\left\{\Theta_m f''_{i+1,j} + \Theta^*_m f''_{i,j}\right\} = r\left\{\Theta_m f_{i+1,j} + \Theta^*_m f_{i,j}\right\}$$

where $\Theta^*_m = 1 - \Theta_m$. Applying a uniform discretization at node (i, j) we obtain:

$$f_{i+1,j} - f_{i,j} + \frac{b\Delta t \mathcal{A}_1}{2\Delta Z} + \frac{\sigma^2 \Delta t \mathcal{A}_2}{2\Delta Z^2} = r\Delta t\left\{\Theta_m f_{i+1,j} + \Theta^*_m f_{i,j}\right\} \qquad (10.187)$$

where

$$\mathcal{A}_1 = \Theta_m\left\{f_{i+1,j+1} - f_{i+1,j-1}\right\} + \Theta^*_m\left\{f_{i,j+1} - f_{i,j-1}\right\}$$

$$\mathcal{A}_2 = \Theta_m\left\{f_{i+1,j+1} - 2f_{i+1,j} + f_{i+1,j-1}\right\} + \Theta^*_m\left\{f_{i,j+1} - 2f_{i,j} + f_{i,j-1}\right\}$$

Collecting like terms obtain:

$$\mathcal{B}_1 f_{i,j-1} + \mathcal{B}_2 f_{i,j} + \mathcal{B}_3 f_{i,j+1} + \mathcal{C}_1 f_{i+1,j-1} + \mathcal{C}_2 f_{i+1,j} + \mathcal{C}_3 f_{i+1,j+1} = 0$$

where

$$\mathcal{B}_1 = \frac{-\Theta^*_m b\Delta t}{2\Delta Z} + \frac{\Theta^*_m \sigma^2 \Delta t}{2\Delta Z^2}$$

$$\mathcal{B}_2 = -1 - r\Delta t\Theta^*_m - \frac{\Theta^*_m \sigma^2 \Delta t}{\Delta Z^2}$$

$$\mathcal{B}_3 = \frac{\Theta^*_m b\Delta t}{2\Delta Z} + \frac{\Theta^*_m \sigma^2 \Delta t}{2\Delta Z^2}$$

$$\mathcal{C}_1 = \frac{\Theta_m \sigma^2 \Delta t}{2\Delta Z^2} - \frac{\Theta_m b\Delta t}{2\Delta Z}$$

$$\mathcal{C}_2 = 1 - r\Delta t\Theta_m - \frac{\Theta_m \sigma^2 \Delta t}{\Delta Z^2}$$

$$\mathcal{C}_3 = \frac{\Theta_m b\Delta t}{2\Delta Z} + \frac{\Theta_m \sigma^2 \Delta t}{2\Delta Z^2}$$

If we rearrange we have the following equation:

Finite-difference scheme for a uniform grid and log transformation

$$a_j f_{i,j-1} + b_j f_{i,j} + c_j = \bar{a}_j f_{i+1,j-1} + \bar{b}_j f_{i+1,j} + \bar{c}_j f_{i+1,j+1} \qquad (10.188)$$

where:

$$a_j = \frac{(1 - \Theta_m)\Delta t}{2\Delta Z^2} \{b\Delta Z - \sigma^2\} \qquad (10.189)$$

$$b_j = 1 + (1 - \Theta_m)\Delta t \left\{ r + \frac{\sigma^2}{\Delta Z^2} \right\} \qquad (10.190)$$

$$c_j = -\frac{(1 - \Theta_m)\Delta t}{2\Delta Z^2} \{b\Delta Z + \sigma^2\} \qquad (10.191)$$

$$\bar{a}_j = -\frac{\Theta_m \Delta t}{2\Delta Z^2} \{b\Delta Z - \sigma^2\} \qquad (10.192)$$

$$\bar{b}_j = 1 - \Theta_m \Delta t \left\{ r + \frac{\sigma^2}{\Delta Z^2} \right\} \qquad (10.193)$$

$$\bar{c}_j = \frac{\Theta_m \Delta t}{2\Delta Z^2} \{b\Delta Z + \sigma^2\} \qquad (10.194)$$

It can be seen that, unlike in Section 10.6.2, the coefficients in Equations 10.188 to 10.194 are independent of the asset price index j.

When $\Theta_m = 0.5$ (the Crank–Nicolson method) we have the following coefficients:

$$a_j = -\bar{a}_j = \frac{\Delta t}{4\Delta Z^2} \{b\Delta Z - \sigma^2\}$$

$$b_j = 1 + \frac{\Delta t}{2} \left\{ r + \frac{\sigma^2}{\Delta Z^2} \right\}$$

$$c_j = -\bar{c}_j = -\frac{\Delta t}{4\Delta Z^2} \{b\Delta Z + \sigma^2\}$$

$$\bar{b}_j = 1 - \frac{\Delta t}{2} \left\{ r + \frac{\sigma^2}{\Delta Z^2} \right\}$$

The method of using the finite-difference grid to compute option prices is identical to that already outlined in Section 10.6.2, which solves the standard (nonlogarithmic) Black–Scholes equation. Table 10.7 compares the results obtained with and without a logarithmic transformation. It is shown in Appendix L.2 that the implicit method, $\Theta_m = 0$, is unconditionally stable.

10.6.5   The log transformation and nonuniform grids

In the previous section we considered the use of a uniform grid to discretize the logarithmically transformed Black–Scholes equation.

$$\frac{\partial f}{\partial t} + b\frac{\partial f}{\partial Z} + \frac{\sigma^2}{2}\frac{\partial^2 f}{\partial Z^2} = rf \qquad (10.195)$$

Table 10.7 Valuation results and pricing errors for a vanilla American put option using a uniform grid with and without a logarithmic transformation; the implicit method and Crank–Nicolson method are used. The accurate values (obtained using a logarithmic transformed grid with $\Theta_m = 0.0$, $n_s = 1000$ and $n_t = 1000$) are presented in the column labelled 'Value'. The absolute pricing errors (*ABS*) (*accurate value – estimated value*) are presented in the column labelled BS were obtained using a standard uniform grid (as outlined in Section 10.6.2), and those in the column labelled Log BS use a uniform grid and logarithmic transformation as explained in this section. The maturity of the option was varied from 0.1 to 1.5 years, the other parameters were: $S = 9.0$, $X = 9.7$, $r = 0.1$, $q = 0.0$, $\sigma = 0.30$, $S_{\max} = 100.0$, $n_s = 50$, and $n_t = 50$

| Time | Value | $\Theta_m = 0.0$ | | $\Theta_m = 0.5$ | |
		BS	Log BS	BS	Log BS
0.1	0.7598	1.5142×10^{-2}	7.7803×10^{-3}	1.5077×10^{-2}	7.6165×10^{-3}
0.2	0.8334	4.6192×10^{-2}	1.2924×10^{-2}	4.5935×10^{-2}	1.1892×10^{-2}
0.3	0.8920	6.4526×10^{-2}	1.4125×10^{-2}	6.3969×10^{-2}	1.2426×10^{-2}
0.4	0.9401	7.4973×10^{-2}	1.6559×10^{-2}	7.4030×10^{-2}	1.4483×10^{-2}
0.5	0.9810	8.0546×10^{-2}	1.8471×10^{-2}	7.9155×10^{-2}	1.5842×10^{-2}
0.6	1.0164	8.3022×10^{-2}	1.9125×10^{-2}	8.1141×10^{-2}	1.5845×10^{-2}
0.7	1.0477	8.3496×10^{-2}	1.8959×10^{-2}	8.1098×10^{-2}	1.5029×10^{-2}
0.8	1.0755	8.2672×10^{-2}	1.8408×10^{-2}	7.9743×10^{-2}	1.3894×10^{-2}
0.9	1.1006	8.1012×10^{-2}	1.7756×10^{-2}	7.7547×10^{-2}	1.2736×10^{-2}
1.0	1.1234	7.8827×10^{-2}	1.7138×10^{-2}	7.4829×10^{-2}	1.1695×10^{-2}
1.1	1.1442	7.6332×10^{-2}	1.6643×10^{-2}	7.1807×10^{-2}	1.0855×10^{-2}
1.2	1.1633	7.3671×10^{-2}	1.6290×10^{-2}	6.8631×10^{-2}	1.0217×10^{-2}
1.3	1.1810	7.0946×10^{-2}	1.6092×10^{-2}	6.5404×10^{-2}	9.7921×10^{-3}
1.4	1.1973	6.8227×10^{-2}	1.6042×10^{-2}	6.2196×10^{-2}	9.5649×10^{-3}
1.5	1.2126	6.5559×10^{-2}	1.6128×10^{-2}	5.90565×10^{-2}	9.5098×10^{-3}

where

$$b = r - q - \frac{\sigma^2}{2} \quad \text{and} \quad Z = \log S$$

Here we will generalize these results and use a nonuniform grid to solve Equation 10.195.

Our description will be very brief since most of the details have already been discussed in previous sections. Here we are only concerned with the finite-difference approximation and derive the equations that need to be solved at each time step. Later, in Section 10.6.6, we will apply our results to solving a European double knockout barrier option.

The finite-difference approximation

At the grid node (i, j) we have

$$\Delta Z_j^- = Z_j - Z_{j-1} \quad \text{and} \quad \Delta Z_j^+ = Z_j + 1 - Z_j$$

Following Section 10.6.3 the first and second derivatives of f w.r.t. Z are

$$f_{i+1,j}'' = \frac{2 \left\{ \Delta Z_j^+ f_{i+1,j-1} + \Delta Z_j^- f_{i+1,j+1} - \Delta Z_j^- f_{i+1,j} - \Delta Z_j^+ f_{i+1,j} \right\}}{(\Delta Z_j^+)^2 \Delta Z_j^- + (\Delta Z_j^-)^2 \Delta Z_j^+}$$

and

$$f'_{i+1,j} = \frac{(\Delta Z_j^-)^2 f_{i+1,j+1} + ((\Delta Z^+)^2 - (\Delta Z_j^-)^2)f_{i+1,j} - (\Delta Z_j^+)^2 f_{i+1,j-1}}{(\Delta Z_j^+)^2 \Delta Z_j^- + (\Delta Z_j^-)^2 \Delta Z^+}$$

Then discretizing Equation 10.195 in the *usual manner* we obtain

$$\frac{f_{i+1,j} - f_{i,j}}{\Delta t} + b\left\{\Theta_m f'_{i+1,j} + \Theta_m^* f'_{i,j}\right\} + \frac{\sigma^2}{2}\left\{\Theta_m f''_{i+1,j} + \Theta_m^* f''_{i,j}\right\}$$

$$= r\left\{\Theta_m f_{i+1,j} + \Theta_m^* f_{i,j}\right\}$$

where $\Theta_m^* = 1 - \Theta_m$. Letting $D = (\Delta Z_j^+)^2 \Delta Z_j^- + (\Delta Z_j^-)^2 \Delta Z_j^+$ we obtain

$$r\Delta t(\Theta_m f_{i+1,j} + \Theta_m^* f_{i,j}) = f_{i+1,j} - f_{i,j} + \frac{b\Delta t \mathcal{A}_1}{D} + \frac{\sigma^2 \Delta t \mathcal{A}_2}{D} \tag{10.196}$$

where

$$\mathcal{A}_1 = \Theta_m\left[f_{i+1,j+1}(\Delta Z_j^-)^2 - f_{i+1,j-1}(\Delta Z_j^+)^2 - f_{i+1,j}\{(\Delta Z_j^-)^2 - (\Delta Z_j^+)^2\}\right]$$

$$+ \Theta_m^*\left[f_{i,j+1}(\Delta Z_j^-)^2 - f_{i,j-1}(\Delta Z_j^+)^2 - f_{i,j}\{(\Delta Z_j^-)^2 - (\Delta Z_j^+)^2\}\right]$$

$$\mathcal{A}_2 = \Theta_m\left[f_{i+1,j+1}\Delta Z_j^- + f_{i+1,j-1}\Delta Z_j^+ - f_{i+1,j}\{\Delta Z_j^- + \Delta Z_j^+\}\right]$$

$$+ \Theta_m^*\left[f_{i,j+1}\Delta Z_j^- + f_{i,j-1}\Delta Z_j^+ - f_{i,j}\{\Delta Z_j^- + \Delta Z_j^+\}\right]$$

Collecting like terms obtain:

$$\mathcal{B}_1 f_{i,j-1} + \mathcal{B}_2 f_{i,j} + \mathcal{B}_3 f_{i,j+1} + \mathcal{C}_1 f_{i+1,j-1} + \mathcal{C}_2 f_{i+1,j} + \mathcal{C}_3 f_{i+1,j+1} = 0$$

where

$$\mathcal{B}_1 = \frac{-\Theta_m^* b\Delta t(\Delta Z_j^+)^2}{D} + \frac{\Theta_m^* \sigma^2 \Delta t \Delta Z_j^+}{D}$$

$$\mathcal{B}_2 = -1 - r\Delta t\Theta_m^* - \frac{\Theta_m^* \sigma^2 \Delta t(\Delta Z_j^- + \Delta Z_j^+)}{D} - \frac{\Theta_m^* b\Delta t\{(\Delta Z_j^-)^2 - (\Delta Z_j^+)^2\}}{D}$$

$$\mathcal{B}_3 = \frac{\Theta_m^* b\Delta t(\Delta Z_j^-)^2}{D} + \frac{\Theta_m^* \sigma^2 \Delta t \Delta Z^-}{D}$$

$$\mathcal{C}_1 = \frac{\Theta_m \sigma^2 \Delta t \Delta Z_j^+}{D} - \frac{\Theta_m b\Delta t(\Delta Z_j^+)^2}{D}$$

$$\mathcal{C}_2 = 1 - r\Delta t\Theta_m - \frac{\Theta_m b\Delta t\{(\Delta Z_j^-)^2 - (\Delta Z_j^+)^2\}}{D} - \frac{\Theta_m \sigma^2 \Delta t\{\Delta Z_j^- + \Delta Z_j^+\}}{D}$$

$$\mathcal{C}_3 = \frac{\Theta_m b\Delta t(\Delta Z_j^-)^2}{D} + \frac{\Theta_m \sigma^2 \Delta t \Delta Z_j^-}{D}$$

If we rearrange we have the following equation:

Finite-difference scheme for a nonuniform grid and log transformation

$$a_j f_{i,j-1} + b_j f_{i,j} + c_j = \bar{a}_j f_{i+1,j-1} + \bar{b}_j f_{i+1,j} + \bar{c}_j f_{i+1,j+1} \tag{10.197}$$

where:

$$a_j = (1 - \Theta_m)\Delta t \left\{ \frac{b(\Delta Z_j^+)^2}{D} - \frac{\sigma^2 \Delta Z_j^+}{D} \right\} \tag{10.198}$$

$$b_j = 1 + \Delta t(1 - \Theta_m)\left\{ r - \frac{\sigma^2(\Delta Z_j^- + \Delta Z_j^+)}{D} \right.$$

$$\left. - \frac{b\{(\Delta Z_j^-)^2 - (\Delta Z_j^+)^2\}}{D} \right\} \tag{10.199}$$

$$c_j = (1 - \Theta_m)\Delta t \left\{ \frac{-b(\Delta Z_j^-)^2}{D} - \frac{\sigma^2 \Delta Z_j^-}{D} \right\} \tag{10.200}$$

$$\bar{a}_j = \Theta_m \Delta t \left\{ \frac{\sigma^2 \Delta Z_j^+}{D} - \frac{b(\Delta Z_j^+)^2}{D} \right\} \tag{10.201}$$

$$\bar{b}_j = 1 - \Theta_m r \Delta t - \Theta_m \Delta t \left\{ \frac{b\{(\Delta Z_j^-)^2 - (\Delta Z_j^+)^2\}}{D} \right.$$

$$\left. + \frac{\sigma^2\{\Delta Z_j^- + \Delta Z_j^+\}}{D} \right\} \tag{10.202}$$

$$\bar{c}_j = \Theta_m \Delta t \left\{ \frac{b(\Delta Z_j^-)^2}{D} + \frac{\sigma^2 \Delta Z_j^-}{D} \right\} \tag{10.203}$$

The incorporation of boundary conditions and the solution of Equation 10.197 is similar in manner to that already discussed in Section 10.6.2. If further details are required Code excerpt 10.19, which uses a nonuniform grid to solve the log transformed Black–Scholes equation, can be consulted.

When a uniform grid is used $\Delta Z_j^+ = \Delta Z_j^- = \Delta Z$ and therefore

$$D = (\Delta Z_j^+)^2 \Delta Z_j^- + (\Delta Z_j^-)^2 \Delta Z_j^+ = 2(\Delta Z)^3$$

$$\frac{(\Delta Z_j^+)^2}{D} = \frac{(\Delta Z_j^-)^2}{D} = \frac{(\Delta Z)^2}{2(\Delta Z)^3} = \frac{1}{2\Delta Z}$$

$$\frac{\Delta Z_j^+}{D} = \frac{\Delta Z_j^-}{D} = \frac{1}{2\Delta Z^2} \quad \text{and} \quad \frac{(\Delta Z_j^+)^2 - (\Delta Z_j^-)^2}{D} = 0$$

In these circumstances

$$a_j = \frac{(1 - \Theta_m)\Delta t}{2\Delta Z^2} \{b\Delta Z - \sigma^2\}$$

$$b_j = 1 + \Delta t(1 - \Theta_m)\left\{r - \frac{\sigma^2}{\Delta Z^2}\right\}$$

$$c_j = (1 - \Theta_m)\Delta t\left\{\frac{-b}{2\Delta Z} - \frac{\sigma^2}{2\Delta Z^2}\right\}$$

$$\bar{a}_j = -\frac{\Theta_m\Delta t}{2\Delta Z^2}\{b\Delta Z - \sigma^2\}$$

$$\bar{b}_j = 1 - \Theta_m\Delta t\left\{r + \frac{\sigma^2}{\Delta Z^2}\right\}$$

$$\bar{c}_j = \frac{\Theta_m\Delta t}{2\Delta Z^2}\{b\Delta Z + \sigma^2\}$$

which are the same as Equations 10.188 to 10.194 in Section 10.6.4.

10.6.6 The double knockout call option

The purpose of this section is to provide an example which illustrates the benefits to be gained from using both the log transformed Black–Scholes equation and also a nonuniform grid.

The problem we will consider is the European double knockout call option with strike price E, and expiry date T. This is a barrier option with both an upper barrier at B_U and a lower barrier at B_L. If, during the life of the option, the asset price either goes above the upper barrier or below the lower barrier then the option becomes worthless. If, on the other hand, the asset price stays between the barriers then the option has value $\max(S_T - E, 0)$, where S_T is the asset price at time T.

This problem has been previously investigated by Boyle and Tian (1998), henceforth referred to as BT, who used an explicit finite-difference method based on a modified trinomial lattice. The method we use here is based on the finite-difference equations given in Section 10.6.5, and all the results in Tables 10.8 to 10.12 were obtained by using the function dko_call which is provided in Code excerpt 10.19.

```
void dko_call(double lower_barrier, double upper_barrier, double theta_m,
    double S0, double sigma_array[], double sigma_times[], Integer n_sigma, double r,
    double opt_mat, double X, double *option_value, double greeks[], double q,
    Integer ns_below_S0, Integer ns_above_S0, Integer nt, Integer *iflag)
{
/* Input parameters:
   == == == == ==
    lower_barrier     - the asset price corresponding to the lower barrier,
    upper_barrier     - the asset price corresponding to the upper barrier,
    theta_m           - the value of theta used for the finite difference method,
    S0                - the current price of the underlying asset,
    sigma_array[]     - an array containing values of the volatility: sigma_array[0] is the first value of
                        the volatility, sigma_array[1] is the second value of the volatility, etc...,
    sigma_times[]     - an array containing the times for different volatilities: sigma_times[0] is the time
                        corresponding to the first volatility, sigma_times[1] is the time corresponding to the
                        second volatility, etc...,
    n_sigma           - the number of elements in sigma_array[], and sigma_times [],
    r                 - the interest rate,
    opt_mat           - the time to maturity,
    X                 - the strike price,
    q                 - the continuous dividend yield,
    ns_below_S0       - the number of asset intervals below the current price S0,
    ns_above_S0       - the number of asset intervals above the current price S0,
    nt                - the number of time intervals.

   Output parameters:
   == == == == ==
    option_value      - the value of the option,
    greeks[]          - the hedge statistics output as follows: greeks[0] is gamma, greeks[1] is delta,
                        and greeks[2] is theta,
    iflag             - an error indicator.
*/
    double *a, *b, *c, *vals, *a1, *b1, *c1, *opt_vals, *rhs, *z, *delta, *gamma, *work, *u;
    double dt, dz, dz1, dz2, zmax, zmin;
    Integer i, j;
    double tmp, t2, t4, dt2;
    Integer ind=0, n1, n2, ns1;
    double ds, log_asset, sig2, alpha, v2, b_fac, temp[4];
    double zero = 0.0;
    Integer barrier_index, ind2;
    double dz_shift, time_step, log_barrier_level1, log_barrier_level2;
    double temp1, temp2, ds_plus, ds_minus, bb, D;
    double curr_time;

    if (S0 >= upper_barrier) printf ("ERROR current asset price is greater than upper_barrier \n");
    if (lower_barrier >= S0) printf("ERROR lower barrier is greater than current asset price \n");
    if (S0 <= zero) printf ("ERROR asset price is not > 0 \n");
    if (upper_barrier <= lower_barrier) printf ("ERROR upper_barrier must be > lower_barrier \n");
    log_asset = log(S0);
    log_barrier_level1 = log(lower_barrier);
    log_barrier_level2 = log(upper_barrier);
    dz1 = (log_asset-log_barrier_level1)/(double)ns_below_S0;
    n1 = ns_below_S0;
/* Include 5 extra points above the asset price so that don't get discontinuity in grid spacing
   which may adversely affect the computation of the greeks */
    n2 = ns_above_S0 + 5;
    dz_shift = dz1*5.0; /* shift caused by extra 5 grid points */
    dz2 = (log_barrier_level2-log_asset- dz_shift)/(double) ns_above_S0;
    dt = opt_mat/(double)nt; /* time interval size */
    time_step = dt;
    --n2;
    ns1 = n1 +n2 + 2;
/* Set up the RHS and LHS coefficients a[], b[] and c[] are the LHS coefficients for the unknown option values
   (time step j) a1[], b1[] and c1[] are the values of the RHS coefficients for the known option prices (time
   step j+1). Note: a1, b1 and c1 are used to form the RHS vector rhs[] of the tridiagonal system. */

/* Allocate the required arrays (all of size (ns1+2): a, b, c, a1, b1, c1, opt_vals, vals, rhs, z, delta,
   gamma, work, u */

/* Set up the RHS and LHS coefficients a[], b[] and c[] are the LHS coefficients for the unknown option values
   (time step j) a1[], b1[] and c1[] are the values of the RHS coefficients for the known option prices (time
   step j + 1). Note: a1, b1 and c1 are used to form the RHS vector rhs[] of the tridiagonal system. */
/* Set grid line asset values, set one grid spacing to align with the asset price, then won't have to
   interpolate to get the option value */
    z[n1] = log_asset;
    for (i=1; i <=n1; ++i) /* This should be the fine mesh */
        z[n1 - i] = log_asset - (double)i*dz1;
```

```
      for (i=1; i<=5; ++i) /* Include 5 extra fine mesh points here */
        z[nl+i] = log_asset + (double)i*dz1;
      for (i=6; i <=n2+2; ++i){/* The coarse mesh */
        j=i-5;
        z[nl+i] =z[nl+5] + (double)j*dz2;
      }
/* Set option values at maturity (for a call). Note : opt_vals[0] and opt_vals[ns1-1] are the lower and upper
   (put/call) option price boundary values. */
      for( i=1; i<ns1; ++i ){
        opt_vals[i] = MAX(exp(z[i])-X, zero);
      }
      opt_vals[0] = zero;
      opt_vals[ns1-1] = zero;
      tmp = 1.0-theta_m; /* 1 - theta (for theta method) */
      curr_time = -1.0;
      ind2 = n_sigma - 1;
      for( j=nt-1; j>=-2; --j){/* Iterate from maturity to current time */
        if ((ind2 >= 0) && (curr_time <= sigma_times[ind2])){
          sig2 = sigma_array[ind2]*sigma_array[ind2];
          t2 = time_step/2.0;
          bb = r - q - (sig2/2.0);
          --ind2;
          for( i=1; i<=ns1-2; ++i){/* Assign elements of the (ns1-2)*(ns1-2) tridiagonal matrix */
            ds_plus = z[i+1]-z[i];
            ds_minus = z[i] - z[i-1];
            D = ((ds_plus*ds_plus*ds_minus) + (ds_minus *ds_minus *ds_plus));
            temp1 = tmp*time_step/D;
            a[i] = temp1*(bb*ds_plus*ds_plus)-temp1 *ds_plus *(sig2 );
            temp1 = theta_m*time_step/D;
            a1[i] = temp1*ds_plus*(sig2)-temp1*(bb*ds_plus *ds_plus);
            temp1 = (ds_minus*ds_minus)/D;
            temp2 = ds_minus/D;
            c[i] = -time_step*tmp*(temp1*bb+(sig2*temp2));
            c1[i] = time_step*theta_m*(temp1*bb+(sig2*temp2));
            temp1 = ((ds_minus*ds_minus) - (ds_plus*ds_plus))/D;
            temp2 = (ds_minus+ds_plus)/D;
            b[i] =1.0+time_step*tmp*(r+(bb*temp1)+(sig2) *temp2);
            b1[i] =1.0- time_step*theta_m*(r+(bb*temp1)+ (sig2)*temp2);
          }
          u[1] = b[1];
          if (u[1] == zero) printf ("ERROR in array u \n");
          for( i=2; i <=ns1-2; ++i){
            u[i] = b[i] - a[i]*c[i-1]/u[i-1];
            if (u[i] == zero) printf ("ERROR in array u \n");
          }
        }
        curr_time = j*dt;
/* Set up the rhs of equation for the theta method */
        for(i=2; i<=ns1-3; ++i)
          rhs[i] = a1[i]*opt_vals[i-1]+b1[i]*opt_vals[i]+ c1[i]*opt_vals[i+1];
/* Incorporate the boundary conditions1 at the upper/lower asset value boundaries */
        rhs[1] = (a1[1]-a[1])*opt_vals[0]+ b1[1]*opt_vals[1]+ c1[1]*opt_vals[2];
        rhs[ns1-2] = a1[ns1-2]*opt_vals[ns1-3]+b1[ns1-2] *opt_vals[ns1-2]+
          (c1[ns1-2]-c[ns1-2])*opt_vals[ns1-1];
/* Solve the lower triangular system Ly = b, where y is stored in array work[]. Compute the elements of L from
   those of U, l[i] = a[i]/u[i-1]. */
        work[1] = rhs[1];
        for(i=2; i<=ns1-2; ++i){
          work[i] = rhs[i] - a[i]*work[i-1]/u[i-1];
        }
/* Solve the upper (ns1-2)*(ns1-2) triangular system Ux = y (where x = vold) */
        opt_vals[ns1-2] = work[ns1-2]/u[ns1-2];
        for(i = ns1-2; i >= 1; --i)
          opt_vals[i] = (work[i] - c[i]*opt_vals[i+1])/u[i];
        if (j==0){
          for (i=0; i < ns1; ++i)
            vals[i] = opt_vals[i];
        }
/* Store option values so that can compute theta */
        if ((j==1)||(j==2)||(j==-1)||(j==-2)){
          temp[ind] = opt_vals[nl];
          ++ind;
        }
      }
      if (greeks){
/* Compute gamma and delta (4th order accuracy) */
```

```
        greeks [1] = (-vals [n1+2]+8.0*vals [n1+1]- 8.0*vals [n1-1]+ vals [n1-2])/(12.0*dz1);
/* Compute gamma (4th order accuracy) - use chain rule to obtain derivative wrt S */
        greeks [0] = (-vals [n1+2]+16.0*vals [n1+1]- 30.0*vals [n1]+16.0*vals [n1-1]-vals [n1-2])/
            (12.0*dz1*dz1);
        greeks [0] = greeks [0]-greeks [1];
        greeks [0] = greeks [0]/(S0*S0);
        greeks [1] = greeks [1]/S0;
/* Compute theta (4th order accuracy) */
        greeks [2]=(-temp [0]+8.0*temp [1]-8.0*temp [2]+temp [3])/ (12.0*dt);
        /* could also compute theta as: greeks [2] = (- temp [0]+4.0* temp [1]- 3.0*vals [n1])/(2.0*dt); */
    }
    *option_value = vals [n1];
}
```

Code excerpt 10.19 Function to compute the value and Greeks of a European double knock out call option using a nonuniform grid and a logarithmic transformation

Inspection of the results shows that that the finite-difference grid method has both greater accuracy and faster convergence than the method proposed by BT. The key to the accuracy achieved by dko_call is a combination of:

- The logarithmic transformation of the Black–Scholes equation.
- The ability to place a grid line at both the upper barrier B_U, and also at the lower boundary B_L.
- The use of a weighted Θ_m finite-difference scheme, $0 \le \Theta_m \le 1$, instead of the numerically unstable explicit finite-difference method used by a trinomial lattice; which in *our notation* (see Section 10.6.2) is equivalent to $\Theta_m = 1$.

Table 10.8 Estimated value of a European double knock out call option. The values in column two were computed by the function dko_call, and those in column three are the results reported in Table 2 of Boyle and Tian (1998). The model parameters were: current asset price $S = 95.0$, exercise price $E = 100.0$, volatility $\sigma = 0.25$, maturity $\tau = 1.0$, interest rate $r = 0.1$, dividend yield $q = 0.0$. The upper barrier level is set at 140.0 and the lower barrier is set at 90.0. The other parameters used by the function dko_call were: nt $= n$, ns_below_S0 $= n/2$, ns_above_S0 $= n/2$, and $\Theta_m = 0.5$ (i.e. the Crank–Nicolson method)

Time steps (n)	Estimated value	Boyle and Tian (1998)
50	1.4569	1.4238
100	1.4578	1.4437
200	1.4583	1.4495
300	1.4583	1.4524
400	1.4584	1.4542
500	1.4584	1.4553
600	1.4584	1.4557
700	1.4584	1.4559
800	1.4584	1.4563
900	1.4584	1.4565
1000	1.4584	1.4566
2000	1.4584	1.4576
3000	1.4584	1.4578
4000	1.4584	1.4580
5000	1.4584	1.4581

Table 10.9   The estimated values of European down and out call options calculated
by the function dko_call. The fixed model parameters were: exercise price $E = 100.0$, volatility
$\sigma = 0.25$, maturity $\tau = 1.0$, interest rate $r = 0.1$, dividend yield $q = 0.0$ and the lower barrier is set at 90.0.
The other parameters used by the function dko_call were: nt $= n$, ns_below_S0 $= n/2$,
ns_above_S0 $= n/2$, upper_barrier $= 1000.0$, lower_barrier $= 90.0$, and $\Theta_m = 0.5$
(i.e. the Crank–Nicolson method)

Time steps	Stock price					
	92	91	90.5	90.4	90.3	90.2
50	2.5652	1.3046	0.6588	0.5282	0.3971	0.2653
100	2.5221	1.2816	0.6466	0.5182	0.3894	0.2601
200	2.5104	1.2758	0.6435	0.5157	0.3875	0.2588
300	2.5080	1.2747	0.6429	0.5152	0.3871	0.2585
400	2.5072	1.2743	0.6427	0.5150	0.3869	0.2584
500	2.5069	1.2742	0.6426	0.5149	0.3869	0.2584
600	2.5067	1.2741	0.6425	0.5149	0.3868	0.2583
700	2.5066	1.2740	0.6425	0.5149	0.3868	0.2583
800	2.5065	1.2740	0.6424	0.5148	0.3868	0.2583
900	2.5065	1.2739	0.6424	0.5148	0.3868	0.2583
1000	2.5064	1.2739	0.6424	0.5148	0.3868	0.2583
2000	2.5063	1.2738	0.6424	0.5148	0.3868	0.2583
Closed form	2.5063	1.2738	0.6424	0.5148	0.3868	0.2583

Table 10.10   The estimated values of European down and out call options as calculated
by the function dko_call. The fixed parameters used were: exercise price $E = 100.0$ volatility
$\sigma = 0.25$, maturity $\tau = 1.0$, interest rate $r = 0.1$, dividend yield $q = 0.0$, and the lower barrier is set
at 90.0. The other parameters used by the function dko_call were: nt $= n$, ns_below_S0 $= n/2$,
ns_above_S0 $= n/2$, upper_barrier $= 1000.0$, lower_barrier $= 90.0$, and $\Theta_m = 0.0$ (i.e. the
implicit method)

Time steps	Stock price					
	92	91	90.5	90.4	90.3	90.2
50	2.5572	1.3005	0.6567	0.5266	0.3958	0.2645
100	2.5181	1.2796	0.6455	0.5174	0.3888	0.2597
200	2.5084	1.2748	0.6429	0.5153	0.3872	0.2586
300	2.5067	1.2741	0.6425	0.5149	0.3869	0.2584
400	2.5062	1.2738	0.6424	0.5148	0.3868	0.2583
500	2.5061	1.2738	0.6424	0.5148	0.3868	0.2583
600	2.5061	1.2737	0.6423	0.5148	0.3867	0.2583
700	2.5060	1.2737	0.6423	0.5147	0.3867	0.2583
800	2.5060	1.2747	0.6423	0.5147	0.3867	0.2583
900	2.5060	1.2737	0.6423	0.5147	0.3867	0.2583
1000	2.5060	1.2737	0.6423	0.5147	0.3867	0.2583
2000	2.5061	1.2737	0.6423	0.5147	0.3867	0.2583
Closed form	2.5063	1.2738	0.6424	0.5148	0.3868	0.2583

Table 10.11 The estimated values of European double knock out call options computed by the function dko_call. In columns 2 and 3 the values given in Boyle and Tian (1998), Table 5, are shown for comparison. The fixed model parameters were: exercise price $E = 100.0$, volatility $\sigma = 0.25$, dividend yield $q = 0.0$, maturity $\tau = 1.0$, interest rate $r = 0.1$, the lower barrier is set at 90.0 and the upper barrier is set at 140.0. The other parameters used by the function dko_call were: nt $= n$, ns_below_S0 $= n/2$, ns_above_S0 $= n/2$, and $\Theta_m = 0.5$ (i.e. the Crank–Nicolson method)

	Stock price					
Time steps	92	91	90.5	90.4	90.3	90.2
50	0.6251 (0.6184)	0.3189 (0.3177)	0.1610	0.1290	0.0969	0.0647
100	0.6260 (0.6212)	0.3194 (0.3184)	0.1613	0.1292	0.0971	0.0649
200	0.6263 (0.6228)	0.3196 (0.3186)	0.1613	0.1293	0.0972	0.0649
300	0.6263 (0.6236)	0.3196 (0.3187)	0.1613	0.1293	0.0972	0.0649
400	0.6263 (0.6242)	0.3196 (0.3189)	0.1613	0.1293	0.0972	0.0649
500	0.6263 (0.6252)	0.3196 (0.3190)	0.1613	0.1293	0.0972	0.0649
600	0.6263 (0.6253)	0.3196 (0.3191)	0.1613	0.1293	0.0972	0.0649
700	0.6263 (0.6253)	0.3196 (0.3191)	0.1613	0.1293	0.0972	0.0649
800	0.6263 (0.6255)	0.3196 (0.3192)	0.1613	0.1293	0.0972	0.0649
900	0.6263 (0.6256)	0.3196 (0.3192)	0.1613	0.1293	0.0972	0.0649
1000	0.6263 (0.6255)	0.3196 (0.3192)	0.1613	0.1293	0.0972	0.0649
2000	0.6263 (0.6260)	0.3196 (0.3195)	0.1613	0.1293	0.0972	0.0649

Table 10.12 The estimated Greeks for European double knock out call options computed by the function dko_call. The fixed model parameters: the exercise price $E = 100.0$, volatility $\sigma = 0.25$, dividend yield $q = 0.0$, maturity $\tau = 1.0$, interest rate $r = 0.1$, the lower barrier is set at 90.0 and the upper barrier is set at 140.0. The other parameters used by the function dko_call were: nt $= 200$, ns_below_S0 $= 100$, ns_above_S0 $= 100$, and $\Theta_m = 0.5$ (i.e. the Crank–Nicolson method). The results for $\Theta_m = 0.0$ (i.e. the implicit method) are shown in brackets; see Table 6, Boyle and Tian (1998)

Asset price	Gamma	Delta	Theta
95.0	−0.0165 (−0.0166)	0.2536 (0.2551)	2.3982 (2.3928)
92.0	−0.0141 (−0.0141)	0.2998 (0.3016)	1.0268 (1.0242)
91.0	−0.0129 (−0.0130)	0.3133 (0.3151)	0.5237 (0.5224)
90.5	−0.0123 (−0.0123)	0.3196 (0.3215)	0.2643 (0.2636)
90.4	−0.0121 (−0.0122)	0.3208 (0.3227)	0.2119 (0.2113)
90.3	−0.0120 (−0.0121)	0.3221 (0.3239)	0.1592 (0.1588)
90.2	−0.0119 (−0.0119)	0.3233 (0.3251)	0.1063 (0.1060)

It should be mentioned that the function dko_call could, without much difficulty, be modified to deal with:

- American double knockout call options
- European double knockout put options
- American double knockout put options,

and also a range of other variations which may include lockout periods, rebates, etc. In particular, options with time varying barrier levels can be dealt with by using grid lines to locate the barrier position at each time instant.

10.7   PRICING AMERICAN OPTIONS USING A STOCHASTIC LATTICE

In this section, we consider the use of Monte Carlo simulation and stochastic lattices to price American options. Information on the use of Monte Carlo simulation to value both single asset and multiasset European options is provided in Sections 11.1 and 12.3. The main difficulty in using simulation to value American options is the need to incorporate optimal early exercise policies. The standard simulation algorithms for valuing European contracts are *forward in time*. That is each price path, which contributes to the value of the option, is generated by stepping forward from current time, t, to option maturity, $t + \tau$, where τ is the duration of the option. For instance if there are n equispaced time steps of size Δt, and only one underlying asset then we use the asset values S_i, $i = 0, \ldots, n$, where S_i corresponds to the asset value at the ith time instant, t_i, and $t_0 = t$. Here S_{i+1} is generated from the previous asset value S_i as follows:

$$\frac{S_{i+1}}{S_i} = dS_i, \quad \text{for} \quad i = 0, \ldots, n-1 \tag{10.204}$$

where dS_i is a random variate taken from a *given* distribution. When S_i follows **GBM** we have from Equation 12.5 that:

$$\frac{S_{i+1}}{S_i} = \exp\{(r - \sigma_i^2/2)\Delta t + \sigma_i dX_i\}, \quad i = 0, \ldots, n-1 \tag{10.205}$$

where $dX_i \sim N(0, \Delta t)$ and the usual definitions are used for σ_i and r.

For European exotic options (such as time dependent barrier options) the value of a particular price path will depend on the asset values S_i, $i = 0, \ldots, n$. This is not true of European vanilla options whose value only depends on S_n, the underlying asset price at option maturity. The Monte Carlo approximation to the value of a European option is thus:

$$f = \frac{\sum_{j=1}^{nsim} p_j(n_j)}{nsim}$$

where *nsim* is the number of simulations used, n_j is the number of time steps associated with the jth price path, and $p_j(n_j)$ is the value of the jth price path. In the case of European vanilla options we can use $n_j = 1$, $j = 1, \ldots, nsim$; the accuracy obviously improves with increasing *nsim*.

The valuation of American style options, which include the possibility of early exercise, is more complicated. In Section 10.4, we described the use of binomial lattices to price American options when the underlying asset price process is GBM. Dynamic programming was used and the option prices were computed by working backwards in time through the lattice. The application of Monte Carlo methods for pricing American options is described in Fu *et al.* (2001), Tilley (1993), Barraquand and Martineau (1995) and also Boyle *et al.* (1997). Here we will outline the stochastic lattice approach discussed in Broadie and Glasserman (1997), where both a high estimator and a low estimator of the American option value are calculated. Since both of these biased estimators converge (with increasing number of simulations and lattice nodes) to the true option value we will only consider how to compute the high estimator, θ_H. We summarize the approach as follows:

- Set the parameters
- Generate the lattice asset prices
- Compute the lattice option prices
- Compute the Monte Carlo estimate.

We will now consider each of these steps in more detail.

Set the parameters

First we set the simulation parameters, that is: *nsim* is the number of lattice simulations, *b* is the number of branches per lattice node and *d* is the number of time instants in the lattice. Note: This definition of *d* here is different from that used in the original paper by Broadie and Glasserman (1997) where *d* is defined as the number of time steps in the lattice.

Generate the lattice asset prices

Next we generate the asset prices for the *p*th stochastic lattice. This is done forwards in time by using a modified version of Equation 10.205. Since the lattice is nonrecombining at the *i*th lattice time instant there are b^i nodes/asset prices. This contrasts with the binomial lattice of Section 10.4 where the asset prices at a given time step are arranged in ascending order, that is S_i^j increases with increasing *j*. We will denote the *j*th value at the *i*th time step by S_i^j. For example in Figure 10.13, where $b = 3$ and $d = 3$, we have for the first time step

$$S_1^1 = 115, \quad S_1^2 = 60, \quad \text{and} \quad S_1^3 = 114$$

and for the second time step

$$S_2^1 = 116, \quad S_2^2 = 90, \quad S_2^3 = 149, \dots, \quad S_2^7 = 102, \quad S_2^8 = 88, \quad S_2^9 = 80$$

The *k*th asset price at the *i*th time step, S_i^k then generates the following asset prices at the $(i + 1)$th time step:

$$\frac{S_{i+1}^{(k-1)b+j}}{S_i^k} = dS^j, \quad j = 1, \dots, b, \quad k = 1, \dots, b^i$$

where dS^j is, as before, a random variate from a *given* distribution. When S_i follows GBM we therefore have:

$$\frac{S_{i+1}^{(k-1)b+j}}{S_i^k} = \exp\{(r - \sigma_i^2/2)\Delta t + \sigma_i dX_i\}, \quad j = 1, \dots, b, \quad k = 1, \dots, b^i$$

Compute the lattice option prices

The method used to compute the option values is *similar* to that used by the binomial lattice. The main difference is that there are now *b* branches per node

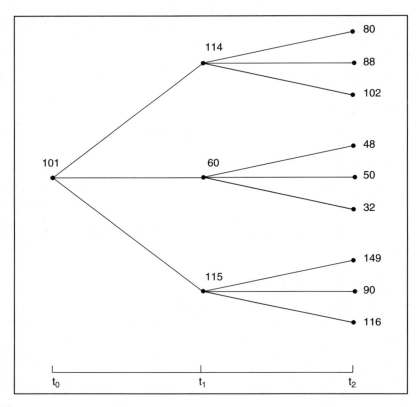

Figure 10.13   An example showing the asset prices generated for a stochastic lattice with three branches per node and two time steps, that is $b = 3$ and $d = 3$. The current asset value, 101, is at time t_0, and the asset values at option maturity are at time t_2

instead of two. The option values are computed by starting at the lattice terminal nodes and then iterating backwards. Here we denote the kth option value at the ith time step by f_i^k.

The option values at the terminal nodes, time instant t_{d-1}, are computed in the usual manner. For a put we have:

$$f_{d-1}^k = \max(E - S_{d-1}^k, 0), \quad k = 1, \ldots, b^{d-1}$$

where E is the exercise price.

The option values at the $(i-1)$th time step are computed from those at the ith time step as follows:

$$f_{i-1}^k = \max(g_{i-1}^k, h_{i-1}^k)$$

where

$$h_{i-1}^k = \frac{\exp(-r\Delta t)}{b} \sum_{j=1}^{b} f_i^{(k-1)b+j}$$

and

$$g_{i-1}^k = \max(E - S_{i-1}^k, 0)$$

The option value for the *p*th stochastic lattice is therefore:

$$\theta_H^p = f_0^1 = \frac{\exp(-r\Delta t)}{b} \sum_{j=1}^{b} f_1^j$$

Figure 10.14 shows the option values for an American call with strike price $E = 100$ and interest rate $r = 0$, when the lattice asset prices in Figure 10.13 are been used. To make things as clear as possible we will show how the value of each node is computed.

Terminal nodes

The option values at the terminal nodes are:

$$f_2^1 = \max(116 - 100, 0) = 16,$$
$$f_2^2 = \max(90 - 100, 0) = 0,$$
$$f_2^3 = \max(149 - 100, 0) = 49$$

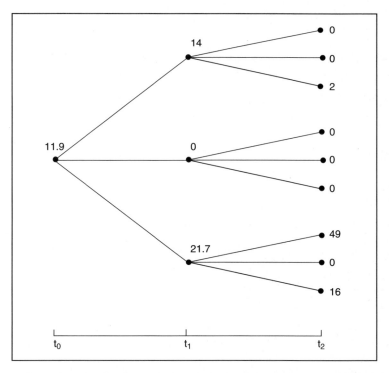

Figure 10.14 The option prices for the $b = 3$, $d = 3$ lattice in Figure 10.13 corresponding to an American put with strike $E = 100$ and interest rate $r = 0$. The option values at the lattice nodes are computed backwards in time from the payoffs at maturity, t_2 to the current time t_0; the value of the option is 11.9

$$f_2^4 = \max(32 - 100, 0) = 0,$$
$$f_2^5 = \max(50 - 100, 0) = 0,$$
$$f_2^6 = \max(48 - 100, 0) = 0$$
$$f_2^7 = \max(102 - 100, 0) = 2,$$
$$f_2^8 = \max(88 - 100, 0) = 0,$$
$$f_2^9 = \max(80 - 100, 0) = 0$$

Time step 1

Here we have:

$$g_1^1 = \max(115 - 100, 0) = 15, \quad g_1^2 = \max(60 - 100, 0) = 0,$$
$$g_1^3 = \max(114 - 100, 0) = 14$$

Since $r = 0$ we have $\exp(-r\Delta t) = 1$ which gives:

$$h_1^1 = \frac{1}{3}\{f_2^1 + f_2^2 + f_2^3\} = \frac{1}{3}\{16 + 0 + 49\} = 21.7$$

$$h_1^2 = \frac{1}{3}\{f_2^4 + f_2^5 + f_2^6\} = \frac{1}{3}\{0 + 0 + 0\} = 0$$

$$h_1^3 = \frac{1}{3}\{f_2^7 + f_2^8 + f_2^9\} = \frac{1}{3}\{2 + 0 + 0\} = 0.66$$

The option values are then computed as follows:

$$f_1^1 = \max(h_1^1, g_1^1) = \max(21.7, 15) = 21.7$$
$$f_1^2 = \max(h_1^2, g_1^2) = \max(0, 0) = 0$$
$$f_1^3 = \max(h_1^3, g_1^3) = \max(0.66, 14.0) = 14.0$$

Time step 0

Here

$$g_0^1 = \max(101 - 100, \ 0) = 1, \quad \text{and}$$

$$h_0^1 = \frac{1}{3}\{f_1^1 + f_1^2 + f_1^3\} = \frac{1}{3}\{21.7 + 0 + 0.66\} = 11.9$$

The final value of the option for this particular lattice is therefore:

$$f_1^1 = \max(h_0^1, g_0^1) = \max(11.9, \ 1) = 11.9$$

| Compute the Monte Carlo estimate |

The Monte Carlo estimate, θ_H, is computed as the average of θ_H^p, $p = 1, \ldots, nsim$, where *nsim* is the number of simulations.

$$\theta_H = \frac{\sum\limits_{i=1}^{nsim} \theta_H^i}{nsim}$$

Below, in Code excerpt 10.20, we provide a computer program which prices single asset American put and call options using a stochastic lattice. The method used by the program is the *depth first* procedure outlined in Broadie and Glasserman (1997), which has the advantage that the memory requirements are only of order $b \times d$; as before b is the number of branches per node and d is the number of time intervals.

Here it is assumed the underlying asset following GBM and the NAG function g05ddc(M, S) is used to generate a normal distribution with mean M and standard deviation S. We can therefore check the acuracy of the simulation with that obtained by a closed form solution which assumes a lognormal asset distribution, in this case the formula in Geske and Johnson (1984).

However, the real power of this method is when the underlying asset follows a more realistic process which is nonGaussian and time varying. The only modification to the code is to replace the call to g05ddc with that of another probability distribution and supply the time varying parameters to it.

```c
#include <nag.h>
#include <stdio.h>
#include <nag_stdlib.h>
#include <math.h>
#include <nagg05.h>
// Stochastic lattice for computing the value of American and European options via Monte Carlo simulation.
// Here we assume that the asset prices have a lognormal distribution, and so generate
// normal variates; this assumption can easily be removed.
void__cdecl main()
{
  long i, j, jj, is_put, is_american, w[200], num_simulations, b, d, seed;
  double T, time_step, sqrt_time_step, opt_value, pay_off, log_fac, asset_price;
  double temp, opt_val, hold, sum_opt_val, disc;
  double tot_opt_vals, X, drift_term, std_term, S0, q, r, sigma, zero =0.0;
  double v[200][60], opt_v[200][60];

  printf("Stochastic lattice for pricing European and American options \n");
  is_put =1;        // If is_put == 0 then a call option, otherwise a put option
  T =1.0;           // The time to maturity of the option
  is_american =1;   // If is_american == 0 then an European option, otherwise an American option
  sigma =0.2;       // The volatility of the underlying asset
  X =110.0;         // The strike price
  S0 =100.0;        // The current price of the underlying assset
  r =0.1;           // The risk free interest rate
  q =0.05;          // The continuous dividend yield
  d =4;             // The number of time steps, the number time intervals = d - 1
  b =50;            // The number of branches per node in the lattice
  time_step = T/(double)(d-1); // time step = T/(number of time intervals)
  sqrt_time_step = sqrt(time_step);
  disc = exp(-r*time_step); // The discount factor between time steps
  std_term = sigma*sqrt(time_step); // The standard deviation of each normal variate generated
  drift_term = (r - q - sigma*sigma*0.5)*time_step; // The mean value of each normal variate generated
  seed =111; // The seed for the random number generator
  g05cbc(seed);
  tot_opt_vals = zero;
  num_simulations =100;
  for (jj =1; jj <= num_simulations; ++jj) {
    v[1][1] = S0;
    w[1] = 1;
    asset_price = S0;
    for (j =2; j <= d; ++j){
      w[j] = 1;
      log_fac = g05ddc(drift_term, std_term); // A normal variate:mean==drift_term, standard
                                              // deviation==std_term
      asset_price = asset_price*exp(log_fac); // Compute the new asset price: assuming a lognormal
                                              // distribution
      v[1][j] = asset_price;
    }
    j = d;
```

```
while (j > 0) {
   if ((j == d) && (w[j] < b)) { // CASE 1::Terminal node, set asset prices for b branches, and option values
                                 // for b-1 branches
      if (is_put) {
         pay_off = MAX (X - v[w[j]][j], zero);
      }
      else {
         pay_off = MAX (v[w[j]][j]-X, zero);
      }
      opt_v[w[j]][j] = pay_off;
      asset_price = v[w[j-1]][j-1];
      log_fac = g05ddc(drift_term, std_term);
      v[w[j]+1][j] = asset_price*exp(log_fac);
      w[j] = w[j] +1;
   }
   else if ((j == d) && (w[j] == b)) { // CASE 2::Terminal node, set option value for last branch
      if (is_put) {
         pay_off = MAX (X - v[w[j]][j], zero);
      }
      else {
         pay_off = MAX (v[w[j]][j]-X, zero);
      }
      opt_v[w[j]][j] = pay_off;
      w[j] = 0;
      j = j -1;
   }
   else if ((j < d) && (w[j] < b)) { // CASE 3::Internal node,
                                     // calculate option value for node (parent wrt to cases 1 & 2)
      sum_opt_val = zero; // Also generate a new terminal node and set asset values.
      for (i =1; i <= b; ++i) {
         sum_opt_val += opt_v[i][j+1];
      }
      temp = sum_opt_val/(double)b;
      hold = temp*disc;
      if (is_american) { // An American option
         if (is_put) {
            pay_off = MAX(X-v[w[j]][j], zero); // pay off for a put option
         }
         else {
            pay_off = MAX(v[w[j]][j]-X, zero); // pay off for a call option
         }
         opt_val = MAX(pay_off, hold);
      }
      else { // A European option
         opt_val = hold;
      }
      opt_v[w[j]][j] = opt_val;
      if (j > 1) {
         asset_price = v[w[j-1]][j-1];
         log_fac = g05ddc(drift_term, std_term);
         v[w[j]+1][j] = asset_price*exp(log_fac);
         w[j]=w[j] +1;
         for (i = j +1; i <= d; ++i) { // Generate a new terminal node
            log_fac = g05ddc(drift_term, std_term);
            asset_price = asset_price*exp(log_fac);
            v[1][i] = asset_price;
            w[i] =1;
         }
         j = d;
      }
      else {
         j = 0;
      }
   }
   else if ((j < d) && (w[j] == b)) { // CASE 4::Internal node, calculate the option value for the last branch
      sum_opt_val = zero;
      for (i =1; i <= b; ++i) {
         sum_opt_val += opt_v[i][j+1];
      }
      temp = sum_opt_val/(double)b;
      hold = temp*disc;
      if (is_american) { // An American option
         if (is_put) {
            pay_off = MAX(X - v[w[j]][j], zero); // pay off for a put option
         }
         else {
```

```
        pay_off = MAX(v[w[j]][j]-X, zero); // pay off for a call option
      }
      opt_val = MAX(pay_off, hold);
    }
    else { // A European option
      opt_val = hold;
    }
    opt_v[w[j]][j] = opt_val;
    w[j] = 0;
    j = j - 1;
  }
 }
 tot_opt_vals = tot_opt_vals + opt_v[1][1]; // Sum the option values for each simulation
}
opt_value = tot_opt_vals/(double)num_simulations; // Compute the average option value
printf ("The estimated option value = %12.4f\n", opt_value);
}
```

Code excerpt 10.20   A computer program which uses a stochastic lattice to value American
and European options

In Table 10.13 below we present computed values of an American put option
with maturity τ, that can only be exercised at the following four times:
t, $t + \tau/3$, $t + 2\tau/3$, and $t + \tau$, where t is the current time.

The column labelled MC_{50}^{100} presents the results obtained using 100 simulations
of a stochastic lattice with 50 branches per node, and the column labelled MC_{250}^{1}
presents the values computed using a single stochastic lattice with 250 branches
per node. These values demonstrate that one high accuracy stochastic lattice can
give better results than using the average of 100 lower accuracy lattices. In the
last two columns we present the computed binomial lattice values for the American
put and also the corresponding European put. The binomial lattice had 6000

Table 10.13   American put options values, computed using the stochastic lattice given in Code excerpt
10.20, with four the exercise times t, $t + \tau/3$, $t + 2\tau/3$, and $t + \tau$. The option parameters used were:
$r = 0.1$, $q = 0.05$, $\tau = 1.0$, $\sigma = 0.2$, $S = 100.0$ and E, the strike price, is varied from 70 to 130. The column
labelled MC_{50}^{100} refers to the results obtained using $d = 4$, $b = 50$, *num_simulations* $= 100$, and the column
labelled MC_{250}^{1} refers to the results obtained using $d = 4$, $b = 50$, *num_ simulations* $= 1$. The *true* values
are those given in Broadie and Glasserman (1997), and were computed with the formula in Geske and
Johnson (1984). The absolute error, *ABS(stochastic_lattice_value − true_value)*, is given in brackets.
The last two columns are the computed results using an accurate (6000 time step) binomial lattice; the
column labelled BL_A contains the American put option values, and the column labelled BL_E contains
the European put option values. It can be seen that in all cases the American put option has a
significant early exercise premium

E	MC_{50}^{100}	MC_{250}^{1}	True	BL_A	BL_E
70	0.118 (0.003)	0.123 (0.002)	0.121	0.126	0.120
80	0.663 (0.007)	0.672 (0.002)	0.670	0.696	0.654
90	2.317 (0.014)	2.307 (0.004)	2.303	2.389	2.198
100	5.830 (0.099)	5.720 (0.011)	5.731	5.928	5.301
110	11.564 (0.223)	11.361 (0.020)	11.341	11.770	10.155
120	20.205 (0.205)	20.000 (0.000)	20.000	20.052	16.547
130	30.054 (0.054)	30.000 (0.000)	30.000	30.000	24.065

time steps and it was possible to exercise the option at every time step. It can be seen that the computed binomial option values for the American put are higher than the *true* values, which only permit the option to be exercised at four distinct times. This is in agreement with the extra flexibility present in the binomial lattice. Inspection of the computed European put and American put binomial option values also reveals that the American put option has a significant early exercise premium.

Chapter 11

Monte Carlo simulation

11.1 INTRODUCTION

Monte Carlo simulation and random number generation are techniques that are widely used in financial engineering as a means of assessing the level of exposure to risk. Typical applications include the pricing of financial derivatives and scenario generation in portfolio management. In fact many of the financial applications that use Monte Carlo simulation involve the evaluation of various stochastic integrals which are related to the probabilities of particular events occurring.

For instance in Section 9.1 we gave the value of a European call option as:

$$c(S, E, \tau) = \exp\{-r\tau\} \int_{-\infty}^{\infty} p(S_T) \max(E - S_T, 0) dS_T$$

and that of a put as:

$$p(S, E, \tau) = \exp\{-r\tau\} \int_{-\infty}^{\infty} p(S_T) \max(E - S_T, 0) dS_T$$

where E is the strike price, T is the expiry date, t is the current time, $\tau = T - t$, r is the riskless interest rate and $p(S_T)$ is the probability that the asset will have market value S_T at maturity.

In many cases however, the assumptions of constant volatility and a lognormal distribution for S_T are quite restrictive. Real financial applications may require a variety of extensions to the standard Black–Scholes model. Common requirements are for: nonlognormal distributions, time varying volatilities, caps, floors, barriers, etc. In these circumstances it is often the case that there is no closed form solution to the problem. Monte Carlo simulation can then provide a very useful means of evaluating the required integrals.

When we evaluate the integral of a function, $f(x)$, in the dimensional unit cube, I^S, by the Monte Carlo method we are in fact calculating the average of the function at a set of randomly sampled points. This means that each point adds linearly to the accumulated sum that will become the integral and also linearly to the accumulated sum of squares that will become the variance of the integral.

When there are N sample points the integral is:

$$\nu = \frac{1}{N} \sum_{i=1}^{N} f(x^i) \tag{11.1}$$

where ν is used to denote the approximation to the integral and $x^1, x^2, \ldots, x^N$ are the N, s-dimensional, sample points. If a pseudorandom number generator is used the points x^i will be (*should be*) independently and identically distributed. From standard statistical results we can then estimate the expected error of the integral as shown below.

If we set $\chi^i = f(x^i)$ then since x^i is independently and identically distributed χ^i is also independently and identically distributed. The mean of χ^i is ν and we will denote the variance as $Var(\chi^i) = \Delta^2$. It is a well-known statistical property that the variance of ν is given by $Var(\nu) = N^{-1}\Delta^2$, see Appendix F.1 for further details. We can therefore conclude that the estimated integral ν has a standard error of $N^{-1/2}\Delta$. This means that the estimated error of the integral will decrease at the rate of $N^{-1/2}$.

It is possible to achieve faster convergence than this if the sample points are chosen to lie on a Cartesian grid. If we sample each grid point exactly once then the Monte Carlo method effectively becomes a deterministic quadrature scheme, whose fractional error decreases at the rate of N^{-1} or faster. The trouble with the grid approach is that it is necessary to decide in advance how fine it should be, and all the grid points need to be used. It is therefore not possible to sample until some convergence criterion has been met.

Quasirandom number sequences seek to bridge the gap between the flexibility of pseudorandom number generators and the advantages of a regular grid. They are designed to have a high level of uniformity in multidimensional space, but unlike pseudorandom numbers they are not statistically independent.

11.2   PSEUDORANDOM AND QUASIRANDOM SEQUENCES

Here we consider the generation of multidimensional pseudorandom and quasirandom sequences to approximate the multidimensional uniform distribution over the interval $[0, 1]$, that is the distribution $U(0, 1)$.

Quasirandom numbers are also called low discrepancy sequences. The discrepancy of a sequence is a measure of its uniformity and is defined below.

Given a set of points $x^1, x^2, \ldots, x^N \in I^S$ and a subset $G \subset I^S$, define the counting function $S_N(G)$ as the number of points $x^i \in G$. For each $x = (x_1, x_2, \ldots, x_s) \in I^S$, let G_x be the rectangular s-dimensional region $G_x = [0, x_1) \times [0, x_2) \times \cdots \times [0, x_s)$, with volume $x_1, x_2, \ldots, x_n$. Then the discrepancy of the points $x^1, x^2, \ldots, x^N$ is given by:

$$D_N^*(x^1, x^2, \ldots, x^N) = sup_{x \in I^S} |S_N(G_x) - Nx_1x_2, \ldots, x_s|$$

The discrepancy is therefore computed by comparing the actual number of sample points in a given volume of multidimensional space with the number of sample points that should be there assuming a uniform distribution.

It can be shown that the discrepancy of the first terms of quasirandom sequence has the form:

$$D_N^*(x^1, x^2, \ldots, x^N) \le C_S(\log N)^S + O((\log N)^{S-1})$$

for all $N \ge 2$.

The principal aim in the construction of low-discrepancy sequences is thus to find sequences in which the constant is as small as possible. Various sequences have been constructed to achieve this goal. Here we consider the following quasirandom sequences proposed by Niederreiter (1992), Sobol (1967), and Faure (1982).

The results of using various random number generators are shown below. Figures 11.1 to 11.3 illustrate the visual uniformity of the sequences. They were created by generating one thousand, sixteen dimensional $U(0, 1)$, sample points, and then plotting the 4th dimension component of each point against its 5th dimension component.

In Figure 11.1, it can be seen that the pseudorandom sequence exhibits clustering of points, and there are regions with no points at all.

Visual inspection of Figures 11.2 and 11.3 show that both the Sobol and Niederreiter quasirandom sequences appear to cover the area more uniformly.

It is interesting to note that the Sobol sequence appears to be a structured lattice which still has some gaps. The Niederreiter sequence on the other hand appears to be more irregular and covers the area better. However, we cannot automatically conclude from this that the Niederreiter sequence is the best. This is because we have not considered all the other possible pairs of dimensions.

Perhaps the easiest way to evaluate the random number sequences is to use them to calculate an integral.

In Figure 11.4 Monte Carlo results are presented for the calculation of the six-dimensional integral:

$$I = \int_0^1 \int_0^1 \int_0^1 \int_0^1 \int_0^1 \int_0^1 \prod_{i=1}^{6} \cos(ix_i)\,dx_1\,dx_2\,dx_3\,dx_4\,dx_5\,dx_6$$

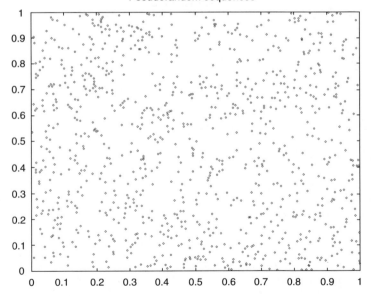

Pseudorandom sequences

Figure 11.1 The scatter diagram formed by one thousand points from a sixteen dimensional $U(0, 1)$ pseudorandom sequence. For each point the 4th dimension component is plotted against the 5th dimension component

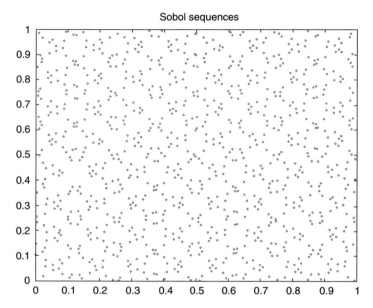

Figure 11.2 The scatter diagram formed by one thousand points from a sixteen dimensional $U(0, 1)$ Sobol sequence. For each point the 4th dimension component is plotted against the 5th dimension component

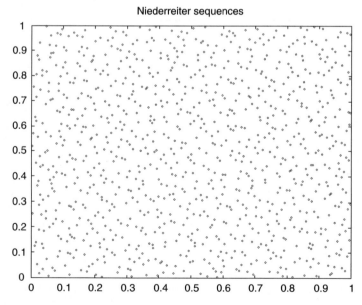

Figure 11.3 The scatter diagram formed by one thousand points from a sixteen dimensional $U(0, 1)$ Niederreiter sequence. For each point the 4th dimension component is plotted against the 5th dimension component

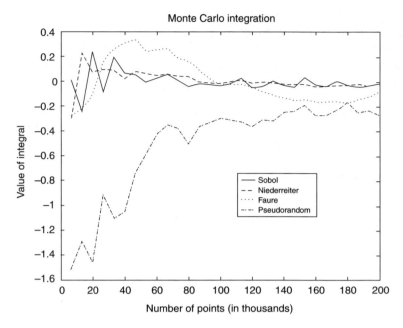

Figure 11.4 Monte Carlo integration using random numbers

The exact value of this integral is:

$$I = \prod_{i=1}^{6} \sin(i)$$

which for $i = 6$, gives $I = -0.0219$.

It can be seen that the pseudorandom sequence gives the worst performance. But as the number of points increases its approximation to the integral improves. Of the quasirandom sequences it can be seen that the Faure sequence has the worst performance, whilst both the Sobol and Neiderreiter sequences give rapid convergence to the solution.

Finance literature contains many references to the benefits of using quasirandom numbers for computing important financial integrals. For instance Brotherton-Ratcliffe (1994) discusses the use of Sobol sequences for the valuation of geometric mean stock options, and provides results which show that the root mean squared pricing error obtained using quasirandom numbers is considerably less than that computed with pseudorandom numbers. Another financial application of quasirandom numbers is the efficient pricing mortgage backed securities, Caflisch *et al.* (1997). Here Brownian bridge techniques are employed to reduce the effective dimension of the problem and thus provide greater pricing accuracy than if pseudorandom numbers were used.

11.2.1 Portfolio allocation

In this example quasirandom numbers are applied to a Markowitz style portfolio allocation problem, see Markowitz (1989, 1994). It should be mentioned that many portfolio problems can be solved very efficiently using Newton (gradient based) numerical optimization software to minimize a given object function subject to certain constraints. However, this approach fails if the gradient of the objective function is discontinuous; this is not the case when (quasi) random numbers are used.

We will start with an initial portfolio and use quasirandom numbers to plot out the feasible region in which portfolios must lie in order to satisfy the portfolio constraints and transaction costs. The asset vector X specifies the amount of each asset in a given portfolio, and the initial portfolio allocation is denoted by the asset vector X^I. In particular we would like to be able to identify efficient portfolios, that is those which for a given portfolio return minimize the portfolio risk. The problem of determining efficient portfolios can be expressed as follows:

$$\text{minimize } V = X^T C X \tag{11.2}$$

subject to the following constraints:

$$\sum_{i=1}^{n} X_i = 1, \quad L_i < X_i < U_i, \quad i = 1, \ldots, n \tag{11.3}$$

and

$$E = \mu X - \sum_{i=1}^{n} \phi_i ABS(X_i^I - X_i) \tag{11.4}$$

where E is the expected portfolio return, V is the portfolio risk, μ is the vector of expected asset returns, C is the covariance matrix of the assets, X is an asset vector which specifies the amount of each asset $ABS(X)$ is the absolute value of X, and L_i, U_i are the respective lower and upper bounds on the ith asset.

The transaction costs, ϕ_i, that are used in equation are $\phi_i = \phi_s$ when $X_i^I > X_i$, and $\phi_i = \phi_b$ when $X_i^I < X_i$, where ϕ_s is the cost of selling shares and ϕ_b is the cost of buying shares.

Here we consider a twenty asset portfolio, $n = 20$, with either no transaction costs or $\phi_b = 0.07$ and $\phi_s = 0.04$. The initial asset vector X^I is such that there are equal amounts of each asset, that is

$$X_i^I = \frac{1}{20}, \quad i = 1, \ldots, 20$$

```
Private Sub Command2_Click()

    Dim quasi(50), fcall, method1, n As Variant
    Dim i, j, k, X, Y, num As Long
    Dim XI(100), XP(100), V, E As Double
    Dim Ret(100), C(50, 50) As Double
    Dim sum As Double
    Dim buy_cost, sell_cost As Double
    Dim count, maxcount As Long
    Dim max_holding(50), min_holding(50) As Double

    Picture1.Cls
    Picture1.DrawWidth = 4
    n = 20
    For i = 0 To n - 1   ' set up the expected asset returns
        Ret(i) = 0.008 * CDbl(i)
    Next i
```

```
      Ret(n - 1) = 0.06
      For i = 0 To n - 1   ' set up the initial portfolio
        XI(i) = 1# / CDbl(n)
      Next i
      For i = 0 To n - 1   ' set up the covariance matrix
        For j = 0 To n - 1
          C(i, j) = 0.01 * CDbl(i + j)
          If (i = j) Then
            C(i, j) = CDbl(i) * 0.6
          End If
        Next j
      Next i
      C(6, 4) = -0.4
      C(4, 6) = C(6, 4)
      C(18, 10) = -0.8
      C(10, 18) = C(18, 10)
      fcall = 1
      method1 = 3   ' Use Sobol sequences
      COMP11.generate fcall, n, method1, quasi(0)
      MsgBox "Starting quasi-random generation"
      fcall = 0

      buy_cost = 0#    ' set the transaction costs
      sell_cost = 0#
      'buy_cost = 0.07
      'sell_cost = 0.04

      For i = 0 To n - 1   ' set the maximum and minimum constraints
        max_holding(i) = 0.1
        min_holding(i) = 0.005
      Next i
      max_holding(0) = 0.4
      max_holding(1) = 0.4
      max_holding(2) = 0.1
      max_holding(18) = 0.7
      max_holding(19) = 0.8

      count = 0
      maxcount = 500000
      Do While (count < maxcount)
        COMP11.generate fcall, n, method1, quasi(0)
        sum = 0#
        For j = 0 To n - 2
          XP(j) = quasi(j) * (max_holding(j) - min_holding(j)) + min_holding(j)
          sum = sum + XP(j)
        Next j
        If (sum <= 1) Then
          XP(n - 1) = 1# - sum
          E = 0#
          For j = 0 To n - 1
            E = E + Ret(j) * XP(j)
          Next j
          For j = 0 To n - 1 ' transaction costs
            If (XP(j) > XI(j)) Then
              E = E - buy_cost * (XP(j) - XI(j))
            End If
            If (XP(j) < XI(j)) Then
              E = E - sell_cost * (XI(j) - XP(j))
            End If
          Next j
          V = 0#
          For j = 0 To n - 1
            For k = 0 To n - 1
              V = V + C(j, k) * XP(j) * XP(k)
            Next k
          Next j
          Y = 5000 - E * 4000 * 8
          X = V * 3000
          Picture1.PSet (X, Y), RGB(0, 0, 255)
        End If
        count = count + 1
      Loop
End Sub
```

Code excerpt 11.1   Visual Basic code which uses a twenty-dimensional quasirandom Sobol sequence to plot the feasible region of a constrained portfolio consisting of twenty assets, and possible transaction costs

The basic method is very simple, and full details can be found in Code excerpt 11.1. We generate a quasirandom asset vector X, and then check that its elements satisfy the constraints given in Equation 11.3. If they do not then we reject the asset vector X and generate another one. If the asset vector X does satisfy the constraints in Equation 11.3 we use Equation 11.2 to calculate the portfolio risk, V, and Equation 11.4 to calculate the portfolio return, E. The point E, V is then plotted on the diagram. This process is repeated a specified number of times.

In Code excerpt 11.1 we generate 500,000 vectors Q from a $U(0, 1)$ twenty-dimensional quasirandom Sobol sequence, and the elements of each vector satisfy $0 \le Q_i \le 1$, for $i = 1, \ldots, 20$. In order to ensure that not too many vectors get rejected we generate the portfolio allocation vector by using the following transformation:

$$X_i = Q_i(U_i - L_i) + L_i, \quad i = 1, \ldots, 20$$

where L_i and U_i have already been mentioned in Equation 11.3.

The resulting return/risk plots for the portfolios are shown in Figures 11.5 and 11.6. In both cases the efficient frontier is clearly visible and, as expected, the return in Figure 11.5 without transaction costs is higher than in Figure 11.6 where transaction costs are included. Furthermore, by examining the components of the asset vectors X, on the efficient boundary we can find the optimal (minimum risk) portfolio composition for a given portfolio return.

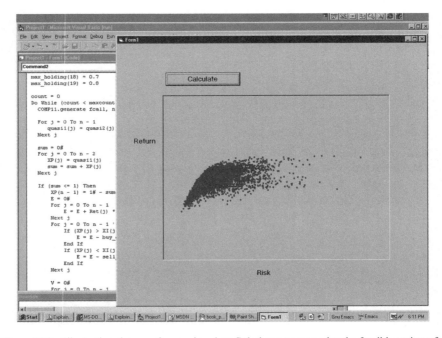

Figure 11.5   Illustrating the use of a quasirandom Sobol sequence to plot the feasible region of a constrained portfolio containing twenty assets, with the transaction costs set to zero. The plot was generated by the Visual Basic Code excerpt 11.1

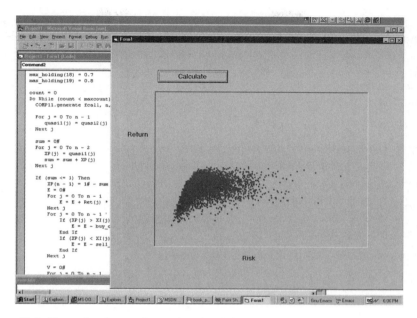

Figure 11.6 Illustrating the use of a quasirandom Sobol sequence to plot the feasible region of a constrained portfolio containing twenty assets, with transaction costs for buy and sell set to 0.07 and 0.04 respectively. The plot was generated by the Visual Basic Code excerpt 11.1

11.3 GENERATION OF MULTIVARIATE DISTRIBUTIONS: INDEPENDENT VARIATES

In this section we show how to generate independent variates from multivariate distributions; that is the variates have zero correlation.

11.3.1 Normal distribution

The most fundamental distribution is the univariate standard normal distibution, $N(0, 1)$, with zero mean and unit variance. In the case of p independent variates this takes the form of a p variate independent normal distribution $N(0, I_p)$ with zero mean and $p \times p$ unit covariance matrix I_p.

First we will quote a result concerning multivariate probability density functions, see Press *et al.* (1992). If $x_1, x_2, \ldots$ are random variates with a joint probability density function $p(x_1, x_2, \ldots)$, and if there are an equal number of y variates $y_1, y_2, \ldots$ that are functions of the x's, then the joint probability density function of the y variates, $p(y_1, y_2, \ldots)$ is given by the following expression:

$$p(y_1, y_2, \ldots)dy_1 dy_2, \ldots = p(x_1, x_2, \ldots)\mathcal{J}_{x,y}dy_1 dy_1 \tag{11.5}$$

where $\mathcal{J}_{x,y}$ is the Jacobian determinant of the x's with respect to the y's.

An important application of this result is the Box Muller transformation, see Box and Muller (1958), in which a p variate independent normal distribution $N(0, I_p)$ is generated from a p variate uniform distribution $U(0, 1)$.

The method works as follows: Consider two independently distributed $N(0, 1)$ variables x and y, and use the polar transformation to obtain:

$$x = r\cos\theta, \quad y = r\sin\theta, \quad \text{and} \quad r^2 = x^2 + y^2 \tag{11.6}$$

From Equation 11.5 the joint probability density functions $f(r, \theta)$ and $f(x, y)$ obey the equation

$$f(r, \theta)\, dr\, d\theta = f(x, y)\mathcal{J}_{xy,r\theta}\, dr\, d\theta$$

where the Jacobian is

$$\mathcal{J}_{xy,r\theta} = \begin{vmatrix} \cos\theta & \sin\theta \\ -r\sin\theta & r\cos\theta \end{vmatrix} = r$$

We therefore have

$$f(r, \theta) = rf(x, y) \tag{11.7}$$

Furthermore since x and y are independent $N(0, 1)$

$$f(x, y) = f(x)\, f(y), \quad \text{where} \quad f(x) = \frac{e^{-x^2/2}}{\sqrt{2\pi}} \quad \text{and} \quad f(y) = \frac{e^{-y^2/2}}{\sqrt{2\pi}}$$

Therefore:

$$f(r, \theta) = rf(x)f(y) = r\frac{e^{-x^2/2}}{\sqrt{2\pi}}\frac{e^{-y^2/2}}{\sqrt{2\pi}}$$

which gives

$$f(r, \theta) = \frac{r}{2\pi}e^{(-x^2+y^2)/2} = \frac{1}{2\pi}re^{-r^2/2} = f(\theta)f(r) \tag{11.8}$$

where $f(\theta) = 1/2\pi$, $f(r) = re^{-r^2/2}$ are independent probability density functions.

The corresponding cumulative probability distribution functions $F(\theta)$ and $F(r)$ can be found by evaluating the following integrals:

$$F(\theta) = \frac{1}{2\pi}\int_0^\theta d\theta = \frac{\theta}{2\pi}$$

and

$$F(r) = \int_0^r re^{-r^2/2}dr = \left[-e^{-r^2/2}\right]_0^r = 1 - e^{-r^2/2}$$

We can now use the result, see for example Evans *et al.* (2000), that any variate x with a probability density function $f(x)$, has a cumulative distribution function $F(x) = \int_{-\infty}^x f(x)dx$, which is $F(x) \sim U(0, 1)$, where $U(0, 1)$ is the uniform distribution between 0 and 1.

The variables $V_1' = F(r) = 1 - e^{-r^2/2}$ and $V_2' = F(\theta) = \theta/2\pi$ are therefore uniformly distributed on the interval $(0, 1)$.

For convenience we will define the, $U(0, 1)$, variables

$$V_1 = 1 - V_1' = e^{-r^2/2} \quad \text{and} \quad V_2 = V_2'$$

So we have:

$$V_1 = e^{-r^2/2}, \quad V_2 = \frac{\theta}{2\pi}$$

Therefore

$$\log V_1 = -r^2/2, \quad r = (-2\log V_1)^{1/2}, \quad \text{and} \quad \theta = 2\pi V_2$$

Substituting these results into Equation 11.6 gives

$$x = (-2\log V_1)^{1/2}\cos 2\pi V_2, \quad y = (-2\log V_1)^{1/2}\sin 2\pi V_2 \tag{11.9}$$

where x and y are $N(0,1)$.

The Box Muller method is contained in Equation 11.9, which shows that the $N(0, 1)$ variates are generated in pairs from the uniform distribution $U(0, 1)$ variates V_1 and V_2.

Since the $N(0, 1)$ variates are created two at a time, if we want to generate a normal distribution with an odd number of dimensions, n_{odd}, it is necessary to generate $n_{odd} + 1$ dimensions and discard one of the dimensions.

It is easy to modify Equation 11.9 so that we can specify the means (μ_1 and μ_2) and variances (σ_1^2 and σ_2^2) of the generated variates x and y; this is accomplished as follows:

The Box–Muller method

$$x = \sigma_1(-2\log V_1)^{1/2}\cos 2\pi V_2 + \mu_1, \quad y = \sigma_2(-2\log V_1)^{1/2}\sin 2\pi V_2 + \mu_2 \tag{11.10}$$

where the distributions of x and y are:

$$x \sim N(\mu_1, \sigma_1^2) \quad \text{and} \quad y \sim N(\mu_2, \sigma_2^2)$$

V_1 and V_2 are independent variates from the uniform distribution $U(0,1)$.

Code excerpt 11.2 illustrates how to generate quasirandom normal variates with given means and standard deviations.

```
long Quasi_Normal_Independent (long fcall, long seq, double xmean[], double std[], long idim, double quasi[])
{
/* Input parameters:
   = = = = =
   fcall      - if fcall ==1 then it is an initialisation call, if fcall ==0 then a continuation call
   seq        - if seq ==0 then a Faure sequence, if seq ==1 then a Niederreiter sequence,
                if seq ==2 then a Sobol sequence
   xmean[]    - the means of the independent normal variates
   std[]      - the standard deviations of the independent normal variates
   idim       - the number of independent normal variates, idim must be less than 40


   Output parameters:
   = = = = = =
   quasi[]    - the elements quasi[0], .. quasi[idim−1] contain the independent normal variates
*/

long ierr, i, j;
double twopi, v1, v2, pi;
```

```
long ind1, ind2;
#define QUASI(I) quasi[(I)-1]
#define STD(I) std[(I)-1]
#define XMEAN(I) xmean[(I)-1]

  if ((idim / 2) * 2 != idim) {
    printf(''Error on entry, idim is not an even number: idim = 1d \n'', idim);
    return 1;
  }else if (idim > 40) {
    printf(''On entry, idim > 40: idim = 1d\n'', idim);
    return 1;
  }
  for (i = 1; i <= idim; ++i) {
    if (STD(i) <= 0.0) {
      printf("On entry, the standard deviation is not greater than zero: STD(%ld) = %12.4f\n", i, STD(i));
      return 1;
    }
  }
  pi = 4.0*atan(1.0);
  if (fcall) {/* first call for initialisation */
    if (seq == 0) {
      Generate_Faure_Sequence(fcall, idim, &QUASI(1));
    }
    else if (seq == 1) {
      Generate_Niederreiter_Sequence(fcall, idim, &QUASI(1));
    }
    else if (seq == 2) {
      Generate_Sobol_Sequence(fcall, idim, &QUASI(1));
    }
  }else{/* a continuation call */
    if (seq == 0) {
      Generate_Faure_Sequence(fcall, idim, &QUASI(1));
    }
    else if (seq == 1) {
      Generate_Niederreiter_Sequence(fcall, idim, &QUASI(1));
    }
    else if (seq == 2) {
      Generate_Sobol_Sequence(fcall, idim, &QUASI(1));
    }
    for (i = 1; i <= idim/2; ++i) {/* generate the normal variates */
      ind1 = i * 2 - 1;
      ind2 = i * 2;
      twopi = pi * 2.0;
      v1 = sqrt(log(QUASI(ind1)) * -2.0);
      v2 = twopi * QUASI(ind2);
      QUASI(ind1) = XMEAN(ind1) + STD(ind1) * v1 * cos(v2);
      QUASI(ind2) = XMEAN(ind2) + STD(ind2) * v1 * sin(v2);
    }
  }
  return 0 ;
}
```

Code excerpt 11.2   Generating quasirandom normal variates using the Box–Muller transformation

11.3.2 Lognormal distribution

The lognormal distribution can be generated from the normal distribution discussed in the previous section by means of a simple transformation. Here we denote a lognormal distribution with mean $\bar{m}$ and variance s^2 by $\Lambda(\bar{m}, s^2)$, and if a variate $\ell \sim \Lambda(\bar{m}, s^2)$, then $\log(\ell) \sim N(\mu, \sigma^2)$, where values for μ and σ^2 are given below.

The lognormal density function, see Aitchison and Brown (1966), is:

$$f(x) = \frac{1}{x\sigma(2\pi)^{1/2}} \times \exp\left(\frac{-(\log x - \mu)^2}{2\sigma^2}\right) \tag{11.11}$$

If $z_i, i = 1, \ldots, p$ are independent normal variates $N(\mu_i, \sigma_i^2), i = 1, \ldots, p$ then lognormal variates $\ell_i, i = 1, \ldots, p$ can be generated using the transformation:

$$\ell_i = \exp(z_i), \quad i = 1, \ldots, p \tag{11.12}$$

where the mean of the ith lognormal variate is

$$\bar{m}_i = \exp\left(\mu_i + \frac{\sigma_i^2}{2}\right) \tag{11.13}$$

and the variance is

$$s_i^2 = \exp(2\mu_i + \sigma_i^2)(\exp(\sigma_i^2) - 1) \tag{11.14}$$

The ratio of variance to the mean squared is therefore

$$\frac{s_i^2}{\bar{m}_i^2} = \exp(\sigma_i^2) - 1 \tag{11.15}$$

or equivalently

$$\sigma_i^2 = \log\left(1 + \frac{s_i^2}{\bar{m}_i^2}\right) \tag{11.16}$$

A lognormal distribution consisting of p independent variates with means $\bar{m}_i, i = 1, \ldots, p$ and variances $s_i^2, i = 1, \ldots, p$ can thus be generated using the following procedure.

First generate the p independent normal variates

$$z_i \sim N(\mu_i, \sigma_i^2), \quad i = 1, \ldots, p$$

where

$$\mu_i = \log(\bar{m}_i) - \frac{\sigma_i^2}{2} \tag{11.17}$$

and

$$\sigma_i^2 = \log\left(1 + \frac{s_i^2}{\bar{m}_i^2}\right) \tag{11.18}$$

Then create the independent lognormal variates using

$$\ell_i = \exp(z_i), \quad i = 1, \ldots, p$$

11.3.3 Student's t distribution

If $S_t(\mu, \nu)$ represents the Student's t distribution with mean μ and number of degrees of freedom ν, then variates $X \sim S_t(0, \nu)$ can be generated as follows:

$$X \sim \frac{Z}{\sqrt{Y/\nu}} \tag{11.19}$$

where $Z \sim N(0, 1)$, and $Y \sim \chi_\nu^2$. The variance of X is:

$$E[X^2] = \frac{\nu}{\nu - 2}$$

Variates X' from a Student's t distribution having ν degrees of freedom with mean μ and variance s can be generated by modifying Equation 11.19 as follows:

$$X' \sim \mu + \frac{s^{1/2}}{\sqrt{\nu/(\nu - 2)}} \frac{Z}{\sqrt{Y/\nu}} \tag{11.20}$$

The probability density function, $f(x)$, for X' is:

$$f(x) = \frac{\Gamma((\nu + 1)/2)(\nu - 2)^{-1/2}s^{-1/2}}{\pi^{1/2}\Gamma(\nu/2)} \left[1 + \frac{(x - \mu)^2}{s(\nu - 2)}\right]^{-(\nu+1)/2} \tag{11.21}$$

where $\nu > 2$.

11.4 GENERATION OF MULTIVARIATE DISTRIBUTIONS: CORRELATED VARIATES

In this section we will show how to generate multivariate distributions with known mean and covariance matrix. We will see later that variates from these distributions are important in Monte Carlo option pricing methods.

Multivariate generalization of univariate distributions, see for example Mardia *et al.* (1988).

11.4.1 Normal distribution

Here we consider how to generate a p variate normal distribution with a given mean and covariance matrix.

We will denote the vector containing the variates of the ith observation from a p variate zero mean normal distribution by Z_i; that is we write a sample of n observations as

$$Z_i \sim N(0, C), \quad i = 1, \ldots, n \tag{11.22}$$

where C is the $p \times p$ covariance matrix.

Further $Z_{i,k}$ is used to denote the kth element of Z_i, which contains the value of the kth variate for the ith observation.

From a computational point of view we can then consider a sample of n observations to be represented by the $n \times p$ matrix Z. The ith row of Z contains the values for ith observation, and the kth column of the ith row, $Z_{i,k}$, contains the value of the kth variate for the ith observation.

Also, since the distribution has zero mean, the sample covariance matrix is given by $C = ZZ^T$. To generate variates with covariance matrix C we can use the fact that, if the matrix C is positive definite, a Cholesky factorisation exists in which:

$$C = AA^T \tag{11.23}$$

where A is lower triangular.

We can therefore generate p variates which have a covariance matrix C as follows. First generate, by (for example) using the Box Muller method described in Section 11.3.1, the independent normal variates:

$$X \sim N(0, I_p)$$

where the vector X contains the p variates, I_p is the unit matrix, and $XX^T = I_p$. Then, using the Cholseky factorisation of Equation 11.23, form

$$Y = AX \tag{11.24}$$

where Y is a p element vector.

Now since $YY^T = AX(AX)^T = A(XX^T)A^T = AA^T = C$, we have that

$$Y \sim N(0, C)$$

Variates that have nonzero means $\mu_k, k = 1, \ldots, p$ can be obtained by simply modifying Equation 11.24 to:

$$Y' = AX + \mu \tag{11.25}$$

where Y' is a p variate vector that is distributed as $N(\mu, C)$, and the p elements of vector μ contain the means of the variates $Y'_k, k = 1, \ldots, p$.

The problem with this approach is that if the matrix C is not positive definite (this could be caused by highly correlated variates or by rounding errors, etc.) then it is not possible to compute the Cholesky decomposition.

An alternative method is to use the spectral decomposition of the covariance matrix C,

$$C = V\Sigma V^T$$

where Σ is a $p \times p$ diagonal matrix of eigenvalues λ_i, $i = 1, \ldots, p$ and the columns of the $p \times p$ matrix V are the corresponding eigenvectors.

We can therefore write

$$C = V\Sigma^{1/2}\Sigma^{T/2}V^T = AA^T$$

where $A = V\Sigma^{1/2}$, and $\Sigma^{1/2} = \sqrt{\lambda_i}$, is the square root of the ith eigenvalue.

Equation 11.24 is then:

$$Y = V\Sigma^{1/2}X \tag{11.26}$$

and Equation 11.25 is

$$Y' = V\Sigma^{1/2}X + \mu \tag{11.27}$$

If the matrix C is not positive definite then some (say $p - r$) of the eigenvalues will be negative. We can construct an approximation to the covariance matrix $C_r \sim C$ using only the r positive eigenvalues as follows:

$$C_r = V_r\Sigma_r V_r^T = V_r\Sigma_r^{1/2}\Sigma_r^{T/2}V_r^T$$

where C_r is a $p \times p$ matrix, V_r is a $p \times r$ matrix and Σ_r is a $r \times r$ matrix.

Under these circumstances the p element vectors Y and Y' are generated using the following modified versions of Equations 11.26 and 11.27

$$Y = V_r \Sigma_r^{1/2} X_r \quad \text{and} \quad Y' = V_r \Sigma_r^{1/2} X_r + \mu \qquad (11.28)$$

where the r element vector X_r is just a subset of the p element vector X. A function to generate correlated normal and lognormal variates is given in Code excerpt 11.3.

```
long Quasirandom_Normal_LogNormal_Correlated(long fcall, long seq, long lnorm, double means[], long n,
    double c[], long tdc, double tol, long *irank, double x[], double work[],long lwk){

/* Input parameters:
   ================
    fcall      -   if fcall ==1 then it is an initialisation call, if fcall ==0 then a continuation call
    seq        -   if seq ==0 then a Faure sequence, if seq ==1 then a Niederreiter sequence,
                   if seq ==2 then a Sobol sequence
    lnorm      -   if lnorm ==1 then it is a lognormal distribution, if lnorm ==0 then a normal distribution
    n          -   the number of variates, n must be less than 40
    c[]        -   a matrix which contains the required covariance matrix, C
    tdc        -   the second dimension of the matrix C
    tol        -   the tolerance used for calculating the rank of the covariance matrix C
    means[]    -   the means of the independent normal variates
    std[]      -   the standard deviations of the independent normal variates
    lwk        -   the size of the work array, work

   Output parameters:
   ================
    rank       -   the computed rank of the covariance matrix C
    x[]        -   the elements x[0], .. x[n−1] contain the variates


   Input/Output parameters:
   ================
    work       -   a work array
*/
    double zero =0.0, one =1.0, two =2.0;
    long n1, i, j, k, kk;
    double mtol, alpha;
    long ptrc, ptre, ptrv, ptrw, ptrw0, ptrw1;

#define C(I,J) c[((I)−1) * tdc + ((J)−1)]
#define MEANS(I) means[(I)−1]
#define X(I) x[(I)−1]
#define WORK(I) work[(I)−1]

    if (lwk < (2+3*n +2*n*n +3)){
        printf ("Error lwk is too small \n");
        return 1;
    }
    ptre =2;
    ptrv =n+2;
    ptrw =n*n +n +2;
/* add extra 1 to allow for odd values of n */
    ptrw0 = ptrw +1 + n;
    ptrw1 = ptrw0 +1 + n;
    ptrc = ptrw1 +n +1;
    n1 = n;
    if (((n/2)*2) != n) {/* test for odd n */
        n1 =n +1;
    }
    if (fcall){/* first call for initialisation */
        if (lnorm){/* lognormal distribution */
            for (i =1; i <=n; ++i){/* Load the modified covariance matrix into WORK */
                for (j =1; j <= n; ++j){
                    WORK(ptrc+(i−1)*n+j−1) = log(one + C(i,j)/(MEANS(i)*MEANS(j)));
                }
            }
        }
        else{/* normal distribution */
            for (i = 1; i <=n; ++i){/* Load the covariance matrix into WORK */
                for (j =1; j <= n; ++j){
                    WORK(ptrc+(i−1)*n+j −1) = C(i,j);
                }
```

```
          }
        }
        /* calculate the eigenvalues and eigenvector of the matrix that has been loaded into WORK */
        calc_eigvals_eigvecs (n,&WORK(ptrc),n,&WORK(ptre), &WORK(ptrv),n); /* The code uses NAG routine f02abc */
        *irank =0;
/*      printf ("The eigenvalues are \ n");
        for (j=n; j >=1; --j){
          printf (''%12.5f \n'', WORK(ptre+j-1));
        }
*/
        for (j=n; j >=1; --j){/* use the eigenvalues to calculate the rank of the matrix */
          if (WORK(ptre+j-1) < tol) goto L24;
          *irank = *irank +1;
        }
        printf ("*irank = %ld \n",*irank);
    L24:
        mtol = -tol;
        if (WORK(ptre) < mtol){
          printf ("Warning there is an eigenvalue less than %12.4f \n",mtol);
        }
        for (j=1; j <= *irank; ++j){
          kk =1;
          for (k=1; k <=n; ++k){
            if(WORK(ptrv+(k-1)*n+(j-1)) != zero) goto L28;
            kk = kk +1;
          }
    L28:
        /* ensure that all eigenvectors have the same sign on different machines */
          alpha = sqrt(WORK(ptre+j-1));
          if (WORK(ptrv+(kk-1)*n+(j-1)) < zero) alpha = -sqrt(WORK(ptre+j-1));
          for (i =1; i <= n; ++i){
            WORK(ptrv+(j-1)+(i-1)*n)= WORK(ptrv+(j-1)+(i-1)*n)*alpha;
          }
        }
/*      printf ("The eigenvectors are \n");
        for (j=1; j <= *irank; ++j){
          for (i =1; i <= n; ++i){
            printf ("%10.5f ", WORK(ptrv+(j-1)+(i-1)*n));
          }
          printf ("\n");
        }
*/
        for (i =1; i <=n; ++i){/* store a vector of ones and zeros for generating the quasi-random numbers */
          WORK(ptrw0+i-1) = zero;
          WORK(ptrw1+i-1) = one;
        }
        for (i = n; i <= n1; ++ i){
          WORK(ptrw0+i-1) = zero;
          WORK(ptrw1+i-1) = one;
        }
      }/* end of first call section */

    /* generate a vector of n1 random variables from a standard normal distribution, zero mean and unit variance */
      Quasi_Normal_Independent(fcall, seq, &WORK(ptrw0), &WORK(ptrw1), n1, &WORK(ptrw));

/* printf ("The quasi random numbers are:\n");
    for (i =1; i <= n; ++i){
      printf ("%12.4f \n", WORK(ptrw+(i-1)));
    }
*/
    /* Now generate variates with the specified mean and variance */
      if (lnorm){/* a lognormal distribution */
        for (i =1; i <= n; ++i){
          X(i) = log(MEANS(i)) - WORK(ptrc+(i-1)*n+i-1)/two;
          for (k =1; k <= *irank; ++k){
            X(i)=X(i)+WORK(ptrv+(k-1)+(i-1)*n)* WORK(ptrw+k-1);
          }
        }
        for (i =1; i <= n; ++i){
          X(i) = exp(X(i));
        }
      }
      else{/* a normal distribution */
        for (i =1; i <=n; ++i){
          X(i) = MEANS(i);
          for (k =1; k <= * irank; ++k){
            X(i)=X(i)+WORK(ptrv+(k-1)+(i-1)*n)* WORK(ptrw+k-1);
```

```
      }
    }
  }
/*    printf ("The generated variates are:\n");
      for (i =1; i <= n; ++i){
        printf (" %12.4f \n", X(i));
      }
*/
      return 0;
    }
```

Code excerpt 11.3   The functions Quasirandom_Normal_LogNormal Correlated which generates
correlated quasirandom normal variates and correlated quasirandom lognormal variates

In order to visualize the effect of the covariance matrix we will display the results
of using function Quasirandom_Normal_LogNormal_ Correlated to generate the following variates:

- A vector of three normal independent variates with covariance matrix:

$$C_1 = \begin{pmatrix} 1.0 & 0.0 & 0.0 \\ 0.0 & 1.0 & 0.0 \\ 0.0 & 0.0 & 1.0 \end{pmatrix}$$

- A vector of three normal variates in which the elements of the covariance matrix
  are all positive; the covariance matrix is:

$$C_2 = \begin{pmatrix} 1.0 & 0.8 & 0.8 \\ 0.8 & 1.0 & 0.8 \\ 0.8 & 0.8 & 1.0 \end{pmatrix}$$

- A vector of three normal variates in which two elements of the covariance matrix
  are negative; the covariance matrix is:

$$C_3 = \begin{pmatrix} 1.0 & -0.7 & 0.2 \\ -0.7 & 1.0 & 0.2 \\ 0.2 & 0.2 & 1.0 \end{pmatrix}$$

In all cases the mean vector is given by:

$$\mu = \begin{pmatrix} 2.0 \\ 2.0 \\ 2.0 \end{pmatrix}$$

The results are displayed in Figures 11.7 to 11.9.

11.4.2 Lognormal distribution

The multivariate lognormal distribution is important because it is the asset returns
distribution assumed by the Black–Scholes equation. We will denote a p variate
vector L which has a lognormal distribution with p element mean vector $\bar{m}$ and
$p \times p$ covariance matrix S as:

$$L \sim \Lambda(\bar{m}, S)$$

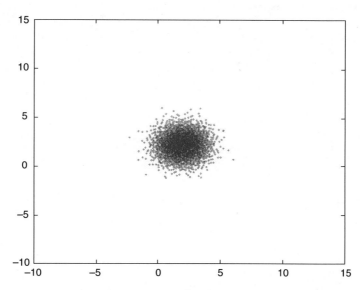

Figure 11.7   Scatter diagram for a sample of 3000 observations ($Z_i, i = 1, \ldots, 3000$) generated from a multivariate normal distribution consisting of three variates with covariance matrix C_1 and mean μ. Here we plot the values of the first variate against the values of the second variate. If we use the notation of Equation 11.22, then the (x, y) co-ordinates for the points are $x_i = Z_{i,1}, i = 1, \ldots, 3000$ and $y_i = Z_{i,2}, i = 1, \ldots, 3000$

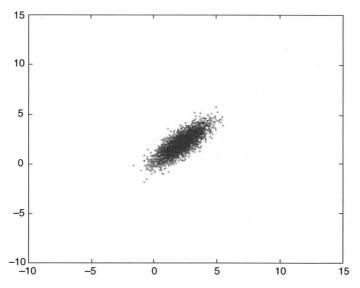

Figure 11.8   Scatter diagram for a sample of 3000 observations ($Z_i, i = 1, \ldots, 3000$) generated from a multivariate normal distribution consisting of three variates with covariance matrix C_2 and mean μ. Here we plot the values of the first variate against the values of the second variate. If we use the notation of Equation 11.22, then the (x, y) co-ordinates for the points are $x_i = Z_{i,1}, i = 1, \ldots, 3000$ and $y_i = Z_{i,2}, i = 1, \ldots, 3000$

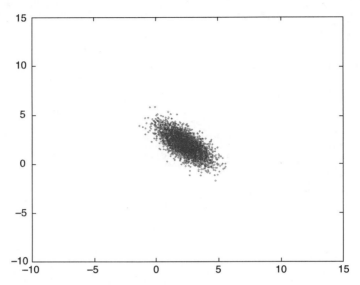

Figure 11.9   Scatter diagram for a sample of 3000 observations $(Z_i, i = 1, \ldots, 3000)$ generated from a multivariate normal distribution consisting of three variates with covariance matrix C_3 and mean μ. Here we plot the values of the first variate against the values of the second variate. If we use the notation of Equation 11.22, then the (x, y) co-ordinates for the points are $x_i = Z_{i,1}, i = 1, \ldots, 3000$ and $y_i = Z_{i,2}, i = 1, \ldots, 3000$

This means that:

$$\log(L) \sim N(\mu, \Sigma)$$

where μ is a p element vector and Σ is a $p \times p$ matrix. It can be shown that

$$\Sigma_{i,j} = \log\left(1 + \frac{S_{i,j}}{\bar{m}_i \bar{m}_j}\right) \tag{11.29}$$

and

$$\mu_i = \log(\bar{m}_i) - \frac{\Sigma_{i,i}}{2}, \quad i = 1, \ldots, p, \quad \text{and} \quad j = 1, \ldots, p \tag{11.30}$$

For the case of independent variates we then have:

$$\mu_i = \log(\bar{m}_i) - \frac{\sigma_i^2}{2}, \quad i = 1, \ldots, p$$

and

$$\Sigma_{i,i} = \sigma_i^2 = \log\left(1 + \frac{s_i^2}{\bar{m}_i^2}\right), \quad i = 1, \ldots, p, \quad \text{and} \quad \text{for } i \neq j, \quad \Sigma_{i,j} = 0$$

which are just Equations 11.17 and 11.18 given in Section 11.3.2.

Code excerpt 11.4 shows how to generate a multivariate lognormal distribution with a given mean $\bar{m}$ and covariance matrix S. More complete information can be found in the function `Quasirandom_Normal_LogNormal_Correlated` which is provided in Code excerpt 11.3.

```
double sig[40][40], s[40][40]; /* limit of 40 */
double means[40], x[40], lx[40], tmp;
      .   .   .
#define S(I,J) s[(I)-1][(J)-1]
#define SIG(I,J) sig[(I)-1][(J)-1]
#define MEANS(i) means[(I)-1] /* the means of the lognormal distribution */
#define X(I) x[(I)-1] /* normal variates */
#define LX(I) lx[(I)-1] /* lognormal variates */
      .   .   .
/* obtain the Gaussian covariance matrix SIG, that corresponds to the lognormal
   covariance matrix S. */

   for (i=1; i<=m; ++i) {
     for (j=1; j<=m; ++j) {
       tmp = MEANS(i) * MEANS(j);
       SIG(i,j) = log( 1 + (S(i,j)/tmp));
     }
   }
      .   .   .
/* Generate multivariate Gaussian variates X(i), i=1, . . . ,m, with zero mean
   and covariance matrix SIG, using section .. */
      .   .   .
/* Generate normal variates with the correct mean */
   for (i=1; i<=m; ++i) {
     X(i) = X(i) + log(MEANS(i)) - SIG(i,i)/2;
   }
/* Now exponentiate to create lognormal lognormal variates with mean
   XMEAN, and covariance matrix S */
   for (i=1; i<=m; ++i) {
     LX(i) = exp(X(i));
   }
```

Code excerpt 11.4 Illustrating how to generate variates from a lognormal distribution with a given mean an covariance matrix

11.4.3 Student's *t* distribution

See Dickey (1967), Anderson (1984), and also Glasserman *et al.* (2000). Here we show how to generate observations from a multivariate Student's *t* distribution.

The probability density function, $f(x)$, for the p variate multivariate Student's t distribution with covariance matrix C is:

$$f(x) = \frac{\Gamma((m+\nu)/2)(\nu-2)^{-1/2}|C|^{-1/2}\nu^{1/2}}{(\nu\pi)^{m/2}\Gamma(\nu/2)}\left[1 + \frac{x^T C^{-1} x}{(\nu-2)}\right]^{-(m+\nu)/2} \tag{11.31}$$

where C represents the determinant of C, and $\nu > 2$.

Let Λ be a matrix with spectral decomposition $\Lambda = V\Sigma V^T$ and T^* be a vector of p independent Student's t variates, each with ν degrees of freedom. Then the vector $T_o = V\Sigma^{1/2}T^*$ has a multivariate Student's t distribution with zero mean and a covariance matrix of $C = \nu/(\nu-2)\Lambda$. So if we want to generate a p variate vector

T from a multivariate Student's t distribution with mean vector μ and covariance matrix C we do the following:
Create a scaled covariance matrix

$$B = C\frac{(\nu - 2)}{\nu}$$

Perform the spectral decomposition

$$B = V\Sigma V^T$$

Then use the results of Section 11.3.3 to obtain a p variate vector T^* of independent Student's t variates and generate the required vector as

$$T = \mu + V\Sigma^{1/2}T^* \tag{11.32}$$

A multivariate sample of n observations will be denoted by $T_i, i = 1, \ldots, n$, and the value of the kth variate for the ith observation will be denoted by $T_{i,k}$.

Of course, as in Section 11.4.1, we can if required choose to use only r eigenvalues and eigenvectors. In these circumstances the Equation 11.32 becomes:

$$T = \mu + V_r\Sigma_r^{1/2}T_r^* \tag{11.33}$$

where V_r is a $p \times r$ matrix, $\Sigma_r^{1/2}$ is an $r \times r$ diagonal matrix and the r element vector T_r^* is just a subset of vector T^*.

```
SUBROUTINE STDENT(FCALL,IGEN,ISEED,RWSAV, MEANS,DF,N,C,LDC,TOL,IRANK, X,WORK,LWK,IFLAG)

    IMPLICIT NONE
    INTEGER N1,I,J,K,KK,N,LDC,IFLAG,LWK,IRANK
    DOUBLE PRECISION ZERO, ONE, TWO
    PARAMETER (ZERO = 0.0D0, ONE = 1.0D0, TWO = 2.0D0)
    LOGICAL FCALL
    DOUBLE PRECISION MEANS(N), RWSAV(9)
    DOUBLE PRECISION WORK(LWK)
    DOUBLE PRECISION TOL,C(N,N),X(N)
    DOUBLE PRECISION MTOL,ALPHA,RND,DF,FAC
    INTEGER PTRC,PTRE,PTRV,PTRW,PTRW0,PTRW1
    INTEGER IFLAGX, ISEED(4), IGEN
    DOUBLE PRECISION G05HKW
    EXTERNAL F02ABZ, G05YBF, G05HKW
    INTRINSIC SQRT, EXP, LOG


    IF (LWK.LT.(2+3*N+2*N*N+3)) THEN
        PRINT*,'ERROR: LWK IS TOO SMALL'
    END IF
    PTRE = 2
    PTRV = N+2
    PTRW = N*N + N +2
*   ADD EXTRA 1 TO ALLOW FOR ODD VALUES OF N
    PTRW0 = PTRW +1+N
    PTRW1 = PTRW0 +1+N
    PTRC = PTRW1 + N +1
    N1 = N
*   TEST FOR ODD N
    IF (((N/2)*2).NE.N) THEN
        N1 = N +1
    END IF

    IF (FCALL) THEN
        RWSAV(1) =   1.0D0
        RWSAV(2) = -1.0D0
```

```
            RWSAV(3) =   0.0D0
            RWSAV(4) =   0.0D0
            RWSAV(5) =   0.0D0
            RWSAV(6) =   0.0D0
            RWSAV(7) =   0.0D0
            RWSAV(8) =   0.0D0
            RWSAV(9) =   0.0D0
            FAC =   (DF - TWO)/DF
* SCALE THE COVARIANCE MATRIX BY FAC TO PRODUCE THE EQUIVALENT SIGMA MATRIX
          DO 10 I = 1, N
            DO 11 J = 1, N
               WORK(PTRC+(I-1)*N+J-1) = C(I,J)*FAC
11         CONTINUE
10        CONTINUE
          CALL F02ABZ(WORK(PTRC),N,N,WORK(PTRE),WORK(PTRV), N,WORK(PTRW),IFLAGX)
*          PRINT*,'THE EIGENVALUES ARE:'
*          DO 3323 J = N, 1, -1
*             PRINT*, J, WORK(PTRE+J-1)
* 3323 CONTINUE
          IRANK = 0
          DO 23 J = N, 1, -1
            IF(WORK(PTRE + J - 1).LT.TOL) GOTO 24
            IRANK = IRANK + 1
23        CONTINUE
24        CONTINUE


*          PRINT*,'POINT A THE EIGENVECTORS:'
*          DO 627 J = 1, IRANK
*             WRITE(*,'(10F10.5)') (WORK(PTRV+((J-1)*N)+I-1),I=1,N)
* 627    CONTINUE


          MTOL =-TOL
          IF (WORK(PTRE).LT.MTOL) THEN
            PRINT*,'WARNING THERE IS AN EIGENVALUE LESS THAN ',MTOL
          END IF
          DO 25 J = 1, IRANK
            KK = 1
            DO 27 K = 1, N
            IF(WORK(PTRV + K- 1+(J-1)*N).NE.ZERO) GOTO 28
               KK = KK + 1
27        CONTINUE
28        CONTINUE
* ENSURE THAT ALL EIGENVECTORS HAVE THE SAME SIGN ON DIFFERENT MACHINES
          ALPHA = SQRT(WORK(PTRE + J-1))
          IF (WORK(PTRV + KK-1+(J-1)*N).LT.ZERO)
*        ALPHA = - SQRT (WORK (PTRE +J-1))
          DO 29 I = 1, N
            WORK (PTRV+((J-1)*N)+I-1)=WORK (PTRV +((J-1)*N+I-1)) *ALPHA
29        CONTINUE
25        CONTINUE
*          PRINT*,'THE EIGENVECTORS:'
*          DO 625 J = 1, IRANK
*             WRITE(*,'(10F10.5)') (WORK(PTRV+((J-1)*N)+I-1),I=1,N)
*625    CONTINUE
        END IF
* GENERATE A VECTOR OF N1 INDEPENDENT RANDOM VARIABLES FROM A STUDENT'S T DISTRIBUTION AND STORE THEN IN
* VECTOR WORK(PTRW)
          IFLAGX = 0
          DO 222 I = 0, N1 - 1
          WORK(PTRW + I) = G05HKW(DF,IGEN, ISEED,RWSAV, IFLAGX)
*             PRINT*,'WORKPTRW+ I) = ',WORK(PTRW+ I)
222      CONTINUE
          IFLAG = IFLAGX
          DO 133 I = 1, N
            X(I) = MEANS(I)
            DO 134 K = 1, IRANK
            X(I)=X(I)+WORK(PTRV+((K-1)*N)+I-1) *WORK(PTRW+K-1)
134         CONTINUE
133     CONTINUE
        END
```

Code excerpt 11.5 The Fortran 77 function STDENT which generates correlated variates from a Student's *t* distribution

In order to visualize the effects of both the covariance matrix and the number of degrees of freedom, ν, we display results from using the function STDENT to generate the following variates:

- Three Student's t variates with covariance matrices C_1, C_2, C_3, mean μ and $\nu = 25.5$.
- Three Student's t variates with covariance matrices C_1, C_2, C_3, mean μ and $\nu = 4.5$.

The values of μ, C_1, C_2, and C_3 are those previously defined in Section 12.4.1.

The results are displayed in Figures 11.10 to 11.13. It can be seen that when $\nu = 25.5$ the distribution of points is very similar to that for the normal distribution; for example compare Figure 11.7 with Figure 11.3. However, for $\nu = 4.5$, the Student's t variates have more points in the tail of the distribution than the corresponding normal variates. This has applications in finance where asset return distributions have been found to exhibit such effects.

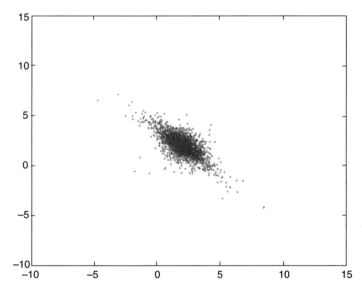

Figure 11.10   Scatter diagram for a sample of 3000 observations ($T_i, i = 1, \ldots, 3000$) generated from a multivariate Student's t distribution consisting of three variates with covariance matrix C_3, number of degrees of freedom $\nu = 4.5$ and mean μ, see Section 11.4.1. Here we plot the values of the first variate against the values of the second variate. The (x, y) co-ordinates for the points are therefore
$$x_i = T_{i,1}, \, i = 1, \ldots, 3000 \text{ and } y_i = T_{i,2}, \, i = 1, \ldots, 3000$$

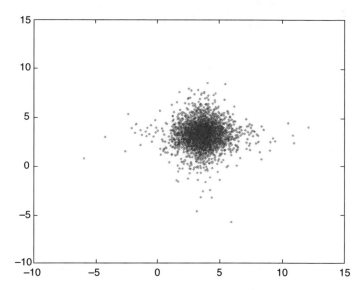

Figure 11.11 Scatter diagram for a sample of 3000 observations $(T_i, i = 1, \ldots, 3000)$ generated from a multivariate Student's t distribution consisting of three variates with covariance matrix C_1, number of degrees of freedom $\nu = 4.5$ and mean μ. Here we plot the values of the first variate against the values of the second variate. The (x, y) co-ordinates for the points are therefore $x_i = T_{i,1}$, $i = 1, \ldots, 3000$ and
$$y_i = T_{i,2}, \ i = 1, \ldots, 3000$$

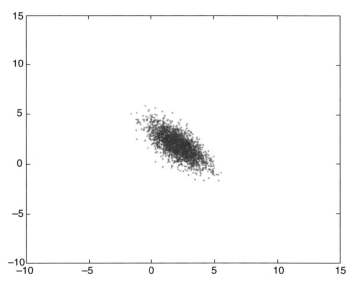

Figure 11.12 Scatter diagram for a sample of 3000 observations $(T_i, i = 1, \ldots, 3000)$ generated from a multivariate Student's t distribution consisting of three variates with covariance matrix C_3, number of degrees of freedom $\nu = 25.5$ and mean μ, see Section 11.4.1. Here we plot the values of the first variate against the values of the second variate. The (x, y) co-ordinates for the points are therefore
$$x_i = T_{i,1}, \ i = 1, \ldots, 3000 \text{ and } y_i = T_{i,2}, \ i = 1, \ldots, 3000$$

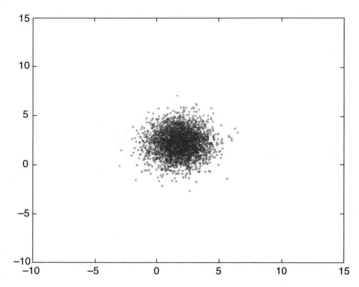

Figure 11.13   Scatter diagram for a sample of 3000 observations ($T_i, i = 1, \ldots, 3000$) generated from a multivariate Student's t distribution consisting of three variates with covariance matrix C_1, number of degrees of freedom $\nu = 25.5$ and mean μ, see Section 11.4.1. Here we plot the values of the first variate against the values of the second variate. The (x, y) co-ordinates for the points are therefore
$$x_i = T_{i,1}, i = 1, \ldots, 3000 \text{ and } y_i = T_{i,2}, i = 1, \ldots, 3000$$

Chapter 12

Multiasset European and American options

12.1 INTRODUCTION

In this section we consider the valuation of multiasset, *basket*, options within the Black–Scholes pricing framework. Here we will show how to price options on the maximum and minimum value of the assets in a basket using:

- Analytic methods
- Monte Carlo methods
- Multidimensional lattices.

Analytic methods can be useful for pricing multiasset European options which have a known *closed form* solution. They are particularly appropriate for low dimensional European options, when the closed form expressions are not too difficult to evaluate.

Monte Carlo methods have the advantage that they can easily compute the value of multiasset European options, but have difficultly including the possibility of early exercise; this is required for American style options.

On the other hand multidimensional lattice techniques allow American options to be evaluated with ease. However lattices become increasingly difficult to program as the number of dimensions increases, and the constraint of computer storage limit their use to problems involving (about) four or less assets.

12.2 THE MULTIASSET BLACK–SCHOLES EQUATION

In Section 8.3 we showed that when the price, S, of a single asset follows GBM the change in price, dS, over a time interval, dt, is given by:

$$dS = rSdt + \sigma SdX$$

where r is the risk free interest rate, σ is the volatility of asset S, and dX is drawn from a normal distribution with mean zero and variance dt.

We also proved, see Equation 8.14 of Section 8.3, using Ito's lemma that the process followed by $Y = \log(S)$ is:

$$dY = (r - \sigma^2/2)dt + \sigma dX$$

where dY is the change in the value of $\log(S)$ over the time interval dt. Later on, in Section 9.3.1, we derived the (Black–Scholes) partial differential equation that is satisfied by the value, V, of an option written on a single underlying asset follows GBM; this equation is:

$$\frac{\partial V}{\partial t} + \frac{\sigma^2 S^2}{2}\frac{\partial^2 V}{\partial S^2} + rS\frac{\partial V}{\partial S} - rV = 0$$

The above results for a single asset can be generalized to deal with multiasset options. For m assets we have the following processes:

$$dY_i = (r - \sigma_i^2/2)dt + \sigma_i dX_i, \quad i = 1,\ldots,m \tag{12.1}$$

where the subscript i refers to the value associated with the ith asset. We can also write the above equation in vector form by introducing the m element vector dY which is normally distributed as:

$$dY \sim N(\mu, C) \tag{12.2}$$

where μ is the mean vector and C is the covariance matrix. The elements of the covariance matrix are:

$$C_{ii} = \sigma_i^2 dt, \quad i = 1,\ldots,m,$$
$$C_{ij} = \sigma_i \sigma_j \rho_{ij}\, dt, \quad i \neq j, i = 1,\ldots,m,\ j = 1,\ldots,m \tag{12.3}$$

where ρ_{ij} is the correlation coefficient between assets i and j. The elements of the mean vector μ are:

$$\mu_i = r - \sigma_i^2/2, \quad i = 1,\ldots,m \tag{12.4}$$

The value V of an option written on n assets satisifies the following partial differential equation:

$$\frac{\partial V}{\partial t} + \frac{1}{2}\sum_{i=1}^{m}\sum_{j=1}^{m}\sigma_i\sigma_j\rho_{ij}S_iS_j\frac{\partial^2 V}{\partial S_i \partial S_j} + r\sum_{i=1}^{m}S_i\frac{\partial V}{\partial S_i} - rV = 0$$

For a European call on the maximum of m assets the payoff $\mathcal{P}_c^{MAX}$ at maturity (time τ) is given by $\mathcal{P}_c^{MAX} = \max(\max(S_1^\tau, S_2^\tau, \ldots, S_m^\tau) - E, 0)$, where $S_i^\tau, i = 1,\ldots,m$ denotes the value of the ith asset at maturity, and E represents the strike price. Similarly a European put option on the minimum of m assets has a payoff, $\mathcal{P}_p^{MIN}$, at time τ, given by $\mathcal{P}_p^{MIN} = \max(E - \min(S_1^\tau, S_2^\tau, \ldots, S_m^\tau), 0)$.

12.3   MULTIDIMENSIONAL MONTE CARLO METHODS

We have already mentioned that Monte Carlo simulation can easily price European multiasset options (also sometimes referred to as basket options or rainbow options) involving a large number of assets (say 20 or more).

In addition Monte Carlo simulation can also include the following features into a option without much difficulty:

- NonGaussian distribution of stock returns; distributions with *heavy tails* are usually of interest because they more accurately represent what is observed in the financial markets.
- Options with path dependency (such as barrier options, etc.); these are known as *exotic options*.
- Complex time dependency (e.g. ARMA, GARCH, or Levy processes) of model parameters such as interest rates, asset prices, etc.

The main drawbacks with Monte Carlo simulation are:

- It is difficult to compute the value of American style options.
- It is difficult (or impossible) to achieve the same accuracy that can be obtained using finite-difference methods.

In a different section of this book we will show how Monte Carlo simulation can be used to price American options by using a hybrid *Monte Carlo lattice* approach originally developed by Boyle *et al.* (1997).

In Chapter 11 we showed that when pseudorandom numbers are used the standard errors of integrals computed via Monte Carlo simulation decrease at the rate $N^{1/2}$, where N is the number of simulations. This means that it can require hundreds of thousands of simulations just to achieve an accuracy of 10^{-1} or 10^{-2} in the estimated option price. It is because of this that various Monte Carlo variance reduction techniques are used to increase the accuracy of the computed integral.

In this section we show how to price a three asset basket option using Monte Carlo simulation; the accuracy of the results obtained with quasirandom numbers and pseudorandom numbers is compared.

The options we consider are European put and call options on the maximum and minimum of three assets. All the options have a maturity of one year, and the other model parameters used are given in Tables 12.1 and 12.2.

In Code excerpt 12.1 most of the work is done by the routine `Quasirandom_Normal_LogNormal_Correlated`, which was described in Section 11.4.1. This generates a vector of multivariate quasirandom numbers with a particular covariance matrix. In the program the values of the assets at current time, t are $S_1 = S_2 = S_3 = 100$. To compute the asset prices when the option matures, at $T = 1$, we make use of Equation 12.1.

Another way of writing Equation 12.1 is

$$dY_i = \log(S_{i,t+dt}) - \log(S_{i,t}) = \left(r - \sigma_i^2/2\right)dt + \sigma_i dX_i, \quad i = 1, \ldots, m$$

where we have used the notation $S_{i,t}$ to denote the value of the ith asset at current time t, and $S_{i,t+dt}$ to denote the value of the asset at the future time $t + dt$. Simple rearrangement of the above equation gives:

$$\log\left(\frac{S_{i,t+dt}}{S_{i,t}}\right) = \left(r - \sigma_i^2/2\right)dt + \sigma_i dX_i, \quad i = 1, \ldots, m$$

Table 12.1   The computed values and absolute errors, in brackets, for European options on the maximum of three assets. Monte Carlo simulation was used with both quasirandom (Sobol) sequences and pseudorandom sequences. The number of paths used varied from 500 to 3000. The parameters were: $E = 100.0$, $S_1 = S_2 = S_3 = 100.0$, $r = 0.1$, $\tau = 1.0$, $\sigma_1 = \sigma_2 = \sigma_3 = 0.2$, $\rho_{12} = \rho_{13} = \rho_{23} = 0.5$, $q_1 = q_2 = q_3 = 0.0$. The accurate values were 0.936 for a put and 22.672 for a call, see Table 12.7 of Section 12.6 and Table 2 of Boyle, Evnine, and Gibbs (1989)

	Put		Call	
nsim	Quasi	Pseudo	Quasi	Pseudo
500	0.890 (4.5948×10^{-2})	1.1044 (1.6839×10^{-1})	22.629 (4.3231×10^{-2})	22.4089 (2.6312×10^{-1})
1000	0.924 (1.1534×10^{-2})	1.0193 (8.3297×10^{-2})	22.683 (1.1306×10^{-2})	22.3520 (3.1998×10^{-1})
1500	0.919 (1.6807×10^{-2})	0.8957 (4.0344×10^{-2})	22.670 (2.2954×10^{-3})	22.6346 (3.7430×10^{-2})
2000	0.932 (4.3221×10^{-3})	0.8995 (3.6488×10^{-2})	22.685 (1.3299×10^{-2})	22.7675 (9.5491×10^{-2})
2500	0.932 (3.5698×10^{-3})	0.8886 (4.7352×10^{-2})	22.670 (1.6619×10^{-3})	22.9326 (2.6058×10^{-1})
3000	0.937 (1.1376×10^{-3})	0.9025 (3.3548×10^{-2})	22.679 (7.2766×10^{-3})	22.8050 (1.3301×10^{-1})

Table 12.2   The computed values and absolute errors, in brackets, for European options on the minimum of three assets. Monte Carlo simulation was used with both quasirandom (Sobol) sequences and pseudorandom sequences. The number of paths used varied from 500 to 3000. The parameters were: $E = 100.0$, $S_1 = S_2 = S_3 = 100.0$, $r = 0.1$, $\tau = 1.0$, $\sigma_1 = \sigma_2 = \sigma_3 = 0.2$, $\rho_{12} = \rho_{13} = \rho_{23} = 0.5$, $q_1 = q_2 = q_3 = 0.0$. The *accurate* values were 7.403 for a put and 5.249 for a call, see Table 12.8 of Section 12.6 and Table 2 of Boyle, Evnine, and Gibbs (1989)

	Put		Call	
nsim	Quasi	Pseudo	Quasi	Pseudo
500	7.365 (3.8122×10^{-2})	7.6760 (2.7298×10^{-1})	5.312 (6.3431×10^{-2})	5.3086 (5.9591×10^{-2})
1000	7.425 (2.1554×10^{-2})	7.7607 (3.5772×10^{-1})	5.293 (4.3958×10^{-2})	5.4376 (1.8857×10^{-1})
1500	7.408 (5.1232×10^{-3})	7.5654 (1.6240×10^{-1})	5.253 (4.0761×10^{-3})	5.4121 (1.6307×10^{-1})
2000	7.399 (3.6364×10^{-3})	7.4820 (7.8995×10^{-2})	5.266 (1.7236×10^{-2})	5.4029 (1.5390×10^{-1})
2500	7.407 (4.1463×10^{-3})	7.3592 (4.3754×10^{-2})	5.267 (1.7707×10^{-2})	5.4690 (2.2005×10^{-1})
3000	7.400 (2.7166×10^{-3})	7.3997 (3.3236×10^{-3})	5.245 (3.5024×10^{-3})	5.4331 (1.8407×10^{-1})

Taking exponentials of both sides we obtain:

$$\frac{S_{i,t+dt}}{S_{i,t}} = \exp\{(r - \sigma_i^2/2)dt + \sigma_i dX_i\}, \quad i = 1,\ldots,m$$

which is equivalent to:

$$S_{i,t+dt} = S_{i,t} \exp\{(r - \sigma_i^2/2)dt + \sigma_i dX_i\} \tag{12.5}$$

```
.. Header files etc ..
/* Monte Carlo simulation: 3 dimensional Black-Scholes, The results are compared with those of Boyle
   et al.,1989 George Levy: 2003
*/
__cdecl main()
{
  long i,seed, skip, m, lwk, irank, num_simulations;
  double sqrt_T, zero =0.0,half=0.5, r, opt_val;
```

```
double T, the_max, the_min, E, ST1, ST2, ST3, S1, S2, S3;
double disc, sumit_max_put, sumit_max_call, sumit _min_put, sumit_min_call;
double *rvec = (double *)0, rho_12, rho_13, rho_23;
double *c3, *z, *means, tol, *work, tmp1, tmp2, sigma1, sigma2, sigma3;
long lnorm, seq, fcall;
#define MEANS(I) means[(I)-1]
#define WORK(I) work[(I)-1]
#define Z(I) z[(I)-1]
#define C3(I,J) c3[((I)-1) * 3+((J)-1)]
    m=3; // the number of assets
    lwk=100000;
    c3 = (double*)malloc((size_t)(sizeof(double)*3*3));
    means = (double *)malloc((size_t)(sizeof(double)*3));
    z = (double *)malloc((size_t)(sizeof(double)*3));
    work=(double*)malloc((size_t)(sizeof(double)*lwk));
    if ((!means) || (!z) || (!work)) {
      printf("Allocation error \n");
    }
    T=1.0;                     // the maturity of the options
    r=0.1;                     // the riskless interest rate
    sqrt_T = sqrt(T);
    disc = exp(-r*T);
    tol =1.0e-8;
    skip =1000;
    sigma1=0.2;                // the volatility of asset 1
    sigma2=0.2;                // the volatility of asset 2
    sigma3=0.2;                // the volatility of asset 3
    S1=100.0;                  // the current price of asset 1
    S2=100.0;                  // the cuurent price of asset 2
    S3=100.0;                  // the current price of asset 3
    E=100.0;                   // the strike price
    rho_12=0.5;                // the correlation coefficient between asset 1 and asset 2
    rho_13=0.5;                // the correlation coefficient between asset 1 and asset 3
    rho_23=0.5;                // the correlation coefficient between asset 2 and asset 3
    C3(1,1) = sigma1*sigma1*T;  // set the elements of the covariance matrix
    C3(2,2) = sigma2*sigma2*T;
    C3(3,3) = sigma3*sigma3*T;
    C3(1,2) = sigma1*sigma2*T*rho_12;
    C3(2,3) = sigma2*sigma3*T*rho_23;
    C3(1,3) = sigma1*sigma3*T*rho_13;
    C3(2,1) = C3(1,2);
    C3(3,1) = C3(1,3);
    C3(3,2) = C3(2,3);
    MEANS(1) = (r - sigma1*sigma1*half)*T;
    MEANS(2) = (r - sigma2*sigma2*half)*T;
    MEANS(3) = (r - sigma3*sigma3*half)*T;
    printf ("THREE ASSET OPTIONS USING QUASIRANDOM NUMBERS \n");
    fcall =1;                  // initialisation call
    seq =2;                    // use Sobol sequences
    lnorm =0;                  // generate a normal distribution
    Quasirandom_Normal_LogNormal_Correlated(fcall, seq, lnorm, &MEANS(1), m, &C3(1,1), m, tol, &irank,
        &Z(1), &WORK(1), lwk);
    fcall =0;                  // continuation call
    sumit_max_put = zero;
    sumit_max_call = zero;
    sumit_min_put = zero;
    sumit_min_call = zero;
    num_simulations =3000; // the number of simulations to use
    for (i=1; i <= num_simulations ; ++i) {
      Quasirandom_Normal_LogNormal_Correlated(fcall, seq, lnorm,&MEANS(1), m,&C3(1,1), m, tol, & irank, &Z(1),
          &WORK(1), lwk);
      ST1 = S1*exp(Z(1));      // the price of asset 1 at option maturity
      ST2 = S2*exp(Z(2));      // the price of asset 2 at option maturity
      ST3 = S3*exp(Z(3));      // the price of asset 3 at option maturity
    // options on the maximum
      tmp2 = MAX(ST1, ST2);
      the_max = MAX(tmp2, ST3);
      tmp1 = the_max-E;
      opt_val = MAX(tmp1, zero);
      sumit_max_call += opt_val*disc;
      tmp1 = E-the_max;
      opt_val = MAX(tmp1, zero);
      sumit_max_put += opt_val*disc;
    // options on the minimum
      tmp2 = MIN(ST1, ST2);
      the_min = MIN(tmp2, ST3);
```

```
    tmp1 = the_min-E;
    opt_val = MAX(tmp1, zero);
    sumit_min_call += opt_val*disc;
    tmp1 = E-the_min;
    opt_val = MAX(tmp1, zero);
    sumit_min_put += opt_val*disc;
  }
  opt_val = sumit_max_put/(double)num_simulations;
  printf("MAX:PUT= %12.4f <%8.4e> (0.936)\n",opt_val, FABS(opt_val-0.936));
  opt_val = sumit_max_call/(double)num_simulations;
  printf("MAX:CALL=%12.4f<%8.4e>(22.672) \n",opt_val, FABS(opt_val-22.672));
  opt_val = sumit_min_put/(double)num_simulations;
  printf("MIN:PUT=%12.4f<%8.4e>(7.403)\n",opt_val, FABS(opt_val-7.403));
  opt_val = sumit_min_call/(double)num_simulations;
  printf("MIN:CALL=%12.4f<%8.4e>(5.249) \n",opt_val, FABS(opt_val-5.249));
}
```

Code excerpt 12.1   A Monte Carlo simulation computer program, using quasirandom numbers, for estimating the value of European put and call options on the maximum and minimum of three underlying assets. The results are presented in Tables 12.1 and 12.2

```
.. Initialisation of model parameters etc the same as for  quasirandom code ..
printf ("PSEUDORANDOM NUMBERS \n");
INIT_FAIL(flag);
seed = 111;    // set the seed for the pseudorandom numbers
g05cbc(seed);
g05eac(&MEANS(1),m,&C3(1,1),m,tol,&rvec,&flag);
sumit_max_put = zero;
sumit_max_call = zero;
sumit_min_put = zero;
sumit_min_call = zero;
for (i =1; i <= num_simulations ; ++i) {
    g05ezc(&Z(1),rvec);
    ST1 = S1*exp(Z(1));
    ST2 = S2*exp(Z(2));
    ST3 = S3*exp(Z(3));
// options on the maximum
    tmp2 = MAX(ST1,ST2);
    the_max = MAX(tmp2,ST3);
    tmp1 = the_max-E;
    opt_val = MAX(tmp1, zero);
    sumit_max_call += opt_val*disc;
    tmp1 = E-the_max;
    opt_val = MAX(tmp1, zero);
    sumit_max_put += opt_val*disc;
// options on the minimum
    tmp2 = MIN(ST1,ST2);
    the_min = MIN(tmp2,ST3);
    tmp1 = the_min-E;
    opt_val = MAX(tmp1, zero);
    sumit_min_call += opt_val*disc;
    tmp1 = E-the_min;
    opt_val = MAX(tmp1, zero);
    sumit_min_put += opt_val*disc;
}
opt_val = sumit_max_put/(double)num_simulations;
printf ("PSEUDORANDOM OPTION MAX PUT = %12.4f <%8.4e> (0.936)\n",opt_val,FABS(opt_val-0.936));
opt_val = sumit_max_call/(double)num_simulations;
printf ("PSEUDORANDOM OPTION MAX CALL = %12.4f <%8.4e> (22.672 ) \n",opt_val,FABS(opt_val-22.672));
opt_val = sumit_min_put/(double)num_simulations;
printf ("PSEUDORANDOM OPTION MIN PUT = %12.4f <%8.4e> (7.403) \n",opt_val,FABS(opt_val-7.403));
opt_val = sumit_min_call/(double)num_simulations;
printf ("PSEUDORANDOM OPTION MIN CALL = %12.4f <%8.4e> (5.249) \n",opt_val,FABS(opt_val-5.249));
}
```

Code excerpt 12.2   A Monte Carlo simulation computer program, using pseudorandom numbers, for estimating the value of European put and call options on the maximum and minimum of three underlying assets. It can be seen that, apart from code concerned with calling the random number generator, the program is identical to that given in Code excerpt 12.1 above. The results are presented in Tables 12.1 and 12.2

12.4 MULTIDIMENSIONAL LATTICE METHODS

Finite-difference lattices can be used to value options on up to about four assets before they require impossibly large amounts of computer memory. The main advantage of finite-difference method is that they are able to easily cater for American style early exercise facilities within the option. This is not true of Monte Carlo methods. They can easily model complex European options, but have difficulty modelling American style options.

In this section we use the approach of Kamrad and Ritchken (1991), and Boyle, Evnine and Gibbs (1989), which we will call the BEGKR method), to price multiasset options. We first derive expressions for the jump size and jump probabilities for a single asset, and show that these are equivalent to those of the Cox, Ross, and Rubinstein binomial lattice (CRR lattice) discussed in Section 10.4.1. We will then give a expression for the jump sizes and jump probabilities of a general multiasset option.

Finally there will be a brief discussion of two lattice techniques, namely *truncated lattices* and *recursive lattices*, that the author has found useful in computing multi-asset option values.

To derive the BEGKR equations for one asset we first assume that the asset follows a lognormal processes with drift $\mu = r - \sigma^2/2$, where r is the riskless interest rate and σ is the instantaneous volatility.

Therefore if S_t is the price of the asset at time t, and $S_{t+\Delta t}$ is the price at time instant $t+\Delta t$, we then have the following equations:

$$\log(S_{t+\Delta t}) = \log(S_t) + \epsilon_t, \quad \epsilon_t \sim N(\mu\Delta t, \sigma^2\Delta t)$$

or equivalently

$$\log\left(\frac{S_{t+\Delta t}}{S_t}\right) \sim N(\mu\Delta t, \sigma^2\Delta t)$$

where ϵ_t represents a random variable and as usual $N(\mu\Delta t, \sigma^2\Delta t)$ denotes a Gaussian with mean $\mu\Delta t$ and variance $\sigma^2\Delta t$.

We will now consider how to construct a binomial lattice by only allowing ϵ_t to jump up or down by an amount $\nu = \sigma\sqrt{\Delta t}$ at each lattice node. This means that:

For an up jump

$$\log\left(\frac{S_{t+\Delta t}}{S_t}\right) = \sigma\sqrt{\Delta t}, \quad \text{or} \quad S_{t+\Delta t} = S_t \exp(\sigma\sqrt{\Delta t}) \tag{12.6}$$

For a down jump

$$\log\left(\frac{S_{t+\Delta t}}{S_t}\right) = -\sigma\sqrt{\Delta t}, \quad \text{or} \quad S_{t+\Delta t} = S_t \exp(-\sigma\sqrt{\Delta t}) \tag{12.7}$$

The reader will notice that these expressions are the same as those for the nodes of the CCR lattice described in Section 10.4.1. That is: for an up jump $S_{t+\Delta t} = S_t u$, for a down jump $S_{t+\Delta t} = S_t d$, and $u = 1/d = \exp(\sigma\sqrt{\Delta t})$.

The probability of undergoing either an up or down jump occurring can be found by matching the mean and variance of ϵ_t.

From the mean:

$$E[\epsilon_t] = \nu(p_u - p_d) = \mu \Delta t \tag{12.8}$$

and from the variance:

$$Var[\epsilon_t] = \nu^2(p_u + p_d) = \sigma^2 \Delta t \tag{12.9}$$

Eliminating p_d from Equations 12.8 and 12.9 gives

$$\nu \mu \Delta t + \sigma^2 \Delta t = 2\nu^2 p_u$$

and so

$$p_u = \frac{1}{2} \left\{ \frac{\sigma^2 \Delta t}{\nu^2} + \frac{\mu \Delta t}{\nu} \right\}$$

which on substituting $\nu = \sigma \sqrt{\Delta t}$ yields

$$p_u = \frac{1}{2} \left\{ 1 + \frac{\mu \sqrt{\Delta t}}{\sigma} \right\} \tag{12.10}$$

$$p_d = 1 - p_u = \frac{1}{2} \left\{ 1 - \frac{\mu \sqrt{\Delta t}}{\sigma} \right\} \tag{12.11}$$

We shall now show that, to first order, the jump probabilities in Equations 12.10 and 12.11 are the same as those for the CRR lattice.

For the CRR lattice (Section 10.4.1, Equation 10.89) we have:

$$p_u = \frac{\exp(r\Delta t) - d}{u - d}$$

expanding $\exp(r\Delta t)$, u and d to order Δt we obtain

$$\exp(r\Delta t) \sim 1 + r\Delta t$$

$$u = \exp(\sigma \sqrt{\Delta t}) \sim 1 + \sigma \sqrt{\Delta t} + \frac{\sigma^2}{2} \Delta t$$

$$d = \exp(\sigma \sqrt{\Delta t}) \sim 1 - \sigma \sqrt{\Delta t} + \frac{\sigma^2}{2} \Delta t$$

so $\exp(r\Delta t) - d \sim r\Delta t + \sigma \sqrt{\Delta t} - \dfrac{\sigma^2 \Delta t}{2}$

and $u - d \sim 2\sigma \sqrt{\Delta t}$

So

$$p_u = \frac{\exp(r\Delta t) - d}{u - d} \sim \frac{r\Delta t + \sigma - \sigma^2/2\Delta t}{2\sigma \sqrt{\Delta t}}$$

which simplifies to

$$p_u = \frac{1}{2}\left\{1 + \frac{\mu\sqrt{\Delta t}}{\sigma}\right\}$$

and therefore

$$p_d = 1 - p_u = \frac{1}{2}\left\{1 - \frac{\mu\sqrt{\Delta t}}{\sigma}\right\}$$

which are the expressions for p_u and p_d given in Equations 12.10 and 12.11 respectively. So we have shown that, to first order in Δt, both the size of the jump and the probability of the jump are the same as the CRR binomial lattice.

The attractive feature of the BEGKR binomial lattice model is that it can easily be generalized to describe a model consisting of k assets. Here we will merely quote the results in Kamrad and Ritchken (1991). As before, it is assumed that the asset prices follow a multivariate lognormal distribution. Let $\mu_i = r - \sigma_i^2/2$, and σ_i be the instantaneous mean and variance respectively ($i = 1, 2, \ldots, k$) and let ρ_{ij} be the correlation between assets i and j. There are now 2^k different jumps from each lattice node over the time interval Δt, and

---

The jump probabilities for a k-asset binomial lattice: Kamrad and Ritchken (1991)

The 2^k jump probabilities, $p_m, m = 1, \ldots, 2^k$, for each lattice node are:

$$p_m = \frac{1}{2^k}\left\{1 + \sqrt{\Delta t}\sum_{i=1}^{k} x_{im}\left(\frac{\mu_i}{\sigma_i}\right) + \sum_{i=1}^{k-1}\sum_{j=i+1}^{k}(x_{ij}^m \rho_{ij})\right\},$$

$$m = 1, 2, \ldots, 2^k, \quad k \geq 2 \tag{12.12}$$

where $x_{im} = 1$ if asset i has an up jump in state m, and $x_{im} = -1$ if asset i has a down jump in state m. In addition $x_{ij}^m = 1$ if assets i and j have jumps in the same direction in state m, and $x_{ij}^m = -1$ if assets i and j have jumps in the opposite direction in state m.

12.4.1   Truncated lattices

The truncated lattice makes use of the fact that not all of the lattice will contribute *significantly* to the value of the option. This can be seen by merely considering the probability of undergoing *n jumps in a given direction*. It can be seen from Equation 12.12 that, for a k asset lattice, each of the 2^k jumps from an individual lattice node has a probability $p \sim 1/2^k$. The probability of undergoing n jumps in a given direction is p^n, and since $p < 1$, it follows that $p^n \sim 0$ for large n. This means that the probability of attaining the very high or very low asset values which occur in the *wings* of the lattice is extremely small. This approach is similar to that used in the Hull and White interest rate model, see Hull and White (1994).

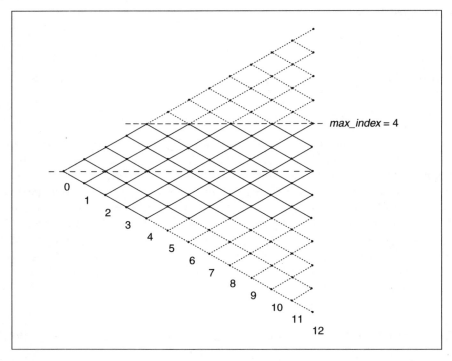

Figure 12.1   Diagram illustrating a one-dimensional truncated binomial lattice in which *max_index* = 4. This means that there are only nine different asset values in the lattice: the current asset price, four above the current asset value and four below the current asset value

12.4.2   Recursive lattices

The recursive lattice used here is a multiasset extension of the BBS binomial lattice described in Section 10.4.4, where the analytic Black–Scholes formula was used to compute the option values of the last lattice step. If we want to use exactly the same technique then we would need to use some complicated expression involving multi-dimensional cumulative normal distribution functions, see Section 12.5 where these are given for two asset options. One way round this problem is to approximate the analytic solution by using a higher accuracy lattice to compute the last step. This can be achieved by a recursive call to the original lattice as shown in the code excerpt below (the complete code for a two-dimensional recursive lattice is given in Appendix D.2).

```
void RECURSIVE_2D_binomial(double *value, double S1, double S2, double X,
   double sigma1, double sigma2, double rho, double T, double r, double q1, double q2,
   Integer put, Integer M, Integer opt_type, Integer is_american, Integer recc, Integer *iflag)
{
   .  .  .
   if (recc ==0) { /* called without recursion, assign terminal nodes as for a standard two dimensional
                lattice */
   .  .  .
   }
```

```
else { /* called with recursive last step */
  P1 = 1;
  for (i = 0; i <= M−1; ++i) {
    P2 = 1;
    for (j = 0; j <= M−1; ++j) {
      loc_T = dt;
      loc_M = 10;
      loc_recc = 0;
      loc_iflag = 0;
      loc_is_american = is_american;
      recursive_2D_binomial(&hold, s1[P1], s2[P2], X, sigma1, sigma2, rho,
          loc_T, r, q1, q2, put, loc_M, opt_type, loc_is_american, loc_recc, &loc_iflag);
      if (is_american) { /* An american option so use
                       hold, s1[P1], and s2[P2] to calculate the option value */
        .  .  .
      }
      else {
        V(i,j) = hold;
      }
      P2 = P2 + 2;
    }
    P1 = P1 + 2;
  }
}
for (m1 = M−1−recc; m1 >= 0; −−m1) { /* work backwards through the lattice to calculate the option value */
  P1 = M−m1;
  /* Identical code to the equivalent loop of the standard 2 dimensional binomial lattice
     see code excerpt 3.11 */
  .  .  .
}
*value = V(0,0);
}
```

Code excerpt 12.3   Code excerpt showing the recursive calculation for the last time step, using a ten step lattice over the time interval *dt*

In Sections 12.5 and 12.6 we present results showing the benefits of using a recursive lattice for options on the maximum or minimum of two and three assets.

12.5   TWO ASSET OPTIONS

Here we consider options based on the underlying prices of two assets, S_1 and S_2. We give analytic formulae to value European options based on the maximum and minimum of two assets and also show how two-dimensional binomial lattices can be constructed to value American style options.

12.5.1   European options

We begin by presenting results from Stulz (1982) and Johnson (1987) concerning the value of European call option on the maximum and minimum of two assets.

| Call options on the maximum and minumum of two assets |

Let the value of a European call option on the minimum of two assets, S_1 and S_2, with strike price E, maturity τ and correlation coefficient ρ, be denoted by c_{min}. The value of the corresponding call option on the maximum of these assets will be represented by c_{max}.

Then, following Stulz (1982) and Johnson (1987), we have:

$$c_{max} = S_1 N_2(d_1(S_1, E, \sigma_1^2), d_1'(S_1, S_2, \sigma_*^2), \rho_1) + S_2 N_2(d_1(S_2, E, \sigma_2^2), d_1'(S_2, S_1, \sigma_*^2), \rho_2)$$
$$- E \exp(-r\tau)\{1 - N_2(-d_2(S_1, E, \sigma_1^2), -d_2(S_2, E, \sigma_2^2), \rho)\} \qquad (12.13)$$

and

$$c_{min} = S_1 N_2(d_1(S_1, E, \sigma_1^2), -d_1'(S_1, S_2, \sigma_*^2), -\rho_1)$$
$$+ S_2 N_2(d_1(S_2, E, \sigma_2^2), -d_1'(S_2, S_1, \sigma_*^2), -\rho_2)$$
$$- E \exp(-r\tau) N_2(d_2(S_1, E, \sigma_1^2), d_2(S_2, E, \sigma_2^2), \rho) \qquad (12.14)$$

where $N_2(a_1, b_1, c_1)$ is the bivariate cumulative normal with ..., this can for instance be computed using the NAG routine g01hac. The other symbols are defined as follows:

$$\sigma_*^2 = \sigma_1^2 - 2\rho\sigma_1\sigma_2 + \sigma_2^2$$

$$d_1(S_i, E, \sigma_i^2) = \frac{\log(S_i/E) + (r + \sigma_i^2/2)\tau}{\sigma_i\sqrt{\tau}}, \quad i = 1, 2$$

$$d_2(S_i, E, \sigma_i^2) = \frac{\log(S_i/E) + (r - \sigma_i^2/2)\tau}{\sigma_i\sqrt{\tau}}, \quad i = 1, 2$$

$$d_1'(S_i, S_j, \sigma_*^2) = \frac{\log(S_i/S_j) + (\sigma_*^2/2)\tau}{\sigma_*\sqrt{\tau}}, \quad \text{for} \quad i = 1, j = 2, \text{ or } i = 2, j = 1$$

and

$$\rho_1 = \frac{\sigma_1 - \rho\sigma_2}{\sigma_*}, \quad \rho_2 = \frac{\sigma_2 - \rho\sigma_1}{\sigma_*}$$

It can also be shown that:

$$c_{max}(S_1, S_2, E, \tau) + c_{min}(S_1, S_2, E, \tau) = c(S_1, E, \tau) + c(S_2, E, \tau) \qquad (12.15)$$

where $c(S, E, \tau)$ is the value of a vanilla European call. We will now derive expression for the value of the corresponding European put options.

Put options on the minimum of two assets

It will now be shown that the price of a European put option on the minimum of two assets, $p_{min}(S_1, S_2, E, \tau)$ is:

$$p_{min}(S_1, S_2, E, \tau) = E \exp(-r\tau) - c_{min}(S_1, S_2, 0, \tau) + c_{min}(S_1, S_2, E, \tau) \qquad (12.16)$$

where the meaning of the symbols has been previously defined. This result can be proved by considering the following two investments:

Portfolio A

Purchase one put option on the minimum of S_1 and S_2 with exercise price E.

Portfolio B

Purchase one discount bond which pays E at maturity. Write (that is sell) one option on the minimum of S_1 and S_2 with an exercise price of zero. Purchase one option on the minimum of S_1 and S_2 with exercise price E.

We now consider the values of these portfolios at option maturity, time τ.

If min $(S_1, S_2) \geq E$

Portfolio A: Pays zero
Portfolio B: Pays $E - \min(S_1, S_2) + \min(S_1, S_2) - E = 0$

If min $(S_1, S_2) = S_1 < E$

Portfolio A: Pays $E - S_1$
Portfolio B: Pays $E - S_1 + 0 = E - S_1$

If min $(S_1, S_2) = S_2 < E$

Portfolio A: Pays $E - S_2$
Portfolio B: Pays $E - S_2 + 0 = E - S_2$

We have therefore shown that, under all possible circumstances, Portfolio A has the same value as Portfolio B. This means that Equation 12.16 is true.

Put options on the maximum of two assets

It will now be shown that the price of a European put option on the maximum of two assets, $p_{max}(S_1, S_2, E, \tau)$ is:

$$p_{max}(S_1, S_2, E, \tau) = E \exp(-r\tau) - c_{max}(S_1, S_2, 0, \tau) + c_{max}(S_1, S_2, E, \tau) \qquad (12.17)$$

where, as before, the meaning of the symbols has been previously defined. This result can be proved by considering the following two investments:

Portfolio A:

Purchase one put option on the maximum of S_1 and S_2 with exercise price E.

Portfolio B:

Purchase one discount bond which pays E at maturity. Write (that is sell) one option on the maximum of S_1 and S_2 with an exercise price of zero. Purchase one option on the maximum of S_1 and S_2 with exercise price E.

As before we now consider the values of these portfolios at option maturity, time τ.

If max $(S_1, S_2) \geq E$

Portfolio A: Pays zero
Portfolio B: Pays $E - \max(S_1, S_2) + \max(S_1, S_2) - E = 0$

If max $(S_1, S_2) = S_2 < E$

Portfolio A: Pays $E - S_1$
Portfolio B: Pays $E - S_1 + 0 = E - S_1$

If max $(S_1, S_2) = S_2 < E$

Portfolio A: Pays $E - S_2$
Portfolio B: Pays $E - S_2 + 0 = E - S_2$

It therefore follows that, under all possible circumstances, Portfolio A has the same value as Portfolio B, and this means that Equation 12.17 is true.

```
void rainbow_bs_2d(double *opt_value, double S1, double S2, double X, double sigma1,
    double sigma2, double rho, double opt_mat, double r, Integer is_max, Integer *iflag)
{
/* Input parameters:
   ================
  S1            - the current price of the underlying asset 1,
  S2            - the current price of the underlying asset 2,
  X             - the strike price,
  sigma1        - the volatility of asset 1,
  sigma2        - the volatility of asset 2,
  rho           - the correlation coefficient between asset 1 and asset 2,
  opt_mat       - the time to maturity,
  r             - the interest rate,
  is_max        - if is_max is 1 then the option is a call on the maximum of two assets, otherwise the option is a
                  call on the minimum of two assets.

   Output parameters:
   ================
  opt_value     - the value of the option,
  iflag         - an error indicator.
*/
double one=1.0,two=2.0,zero=0.0;
double eps,d1,d2_1,d2_2,temp,temp1,temp2,pi,np;
double rho_112, rho_212, d1_prime;
double sigma, term1, term2, term3;
static NagError nagerr;

  eps = X02AJC;
  if(X < eps) printf ("ERROR the strike price is too small\n") ;
  if (sigma1 < eps) printf ("ERROR the volatility (sigma1) is too small \n");
  if (sigma2 < eps) printf ("ERROR the volatility (sigma2) is too small \n");
  if (opt_mat < eps) printf ("ERROR the time to maturity (opt_mat) is too small \n");
  sigma = sqrt((sigma1*sigma1 + sigma2*sigma2) - two* sigma1*sigma2*rho);

  if (is_max == 1) { /* then the maximum of two assets */
    /* calculate term1 */
    temp = log(S1/X);
    d1 = temp+(r+(sigma1*sigma1/two))*opt_mat;
    d1 = d1/(sigma1*sqrt(opt_mat));
    temp = log(S1/S2);
    d1_prime = temp+(sigma*sigma/two)*opt_mat;
    d1_prime = d1_prime/(sigma*sqrt(opt_mat));
    rho_112 = (sigma1 - rho*sigma2) / sigma;
    term1 = g01hac(d1,d1_prime,rho_112,&nagerr);
    term1 = term1*S1;
    /* calculate term2 */
    temp = log(S2/X);
    d1 = temp+(r+(sigma2*sigma2/two))*opt_mat;
    d1 = d1/(sigma2*sqrt(opt_mat));
    temp = log(S2/S1);
```

```
        d1_prime = temp+(sigma*sigma/two)*opt_mat;
        d1_prime = d1_prime/(sigma*sqrt(opt_mat));
        rho_212 = (sigma2 - rho*sigma1) / sigma;
        term2=S2*g01hac(d1,d1_prime,-rho_212,&nagerr);
        /* calculate term3 */
        temp = log(S1/X);
        d2_1 = temp+(r-(sigma1*sigma1/two))*opt_mat;
        d2_1 = d2_1/(sigma1*sqrt(opt_mat));
        temp = log(S2/X);
        d2_2 = temp+(r-(sigma2*sigma2/two))*opt_mat;
        d2_2 = d2_2/(sigma2*sqrt(opt_mat));
        term3 = -g01hac(-d2_1,-d2_2,rho,&nagerr);
        *opt_value= term1+term2-X*exp(-r*opt_mat)*term3;
    }
    else { /* the minimum of two assets */
        /* calculate term1 */
        temp = log(S1/X);
        d1 = temp+(r+(sigma1*sigma1/two))*opt_mat;
        d1 = d1/(sigma1*sqrt(opt_mat));
        temp = log(S1/S2);
        d1_prime = temp+(sigma*sigma/two)*opt_mat;
        d1_prime = d1_prime/(sigma*sqrt(opt_mat));
        rho_112 = (sigma1 - rho*sigma2) / sigma;
        term1 = g01hac(d1,-d1_prime,-rho_112,&nagerr);
        term1 = term1*S1;
        /* calculate term2 */
        temp = log(S2/X);
        d1 = temp+(r+(sigma2*sigma2/two))*opt_mat;
        d1 = d1/(sigma2*sqrt(opt_mat));
        temp = log(S2/S1);
        d1_prime = temp+(sigma*sigma/two)*opt_mat;
        d1_prime = d1_prime/(sigma*sqrt(opt_mat));
        rho_212 = (sigma2 - rho*sigma1) / sigma;
        term2=S2*g01hac(d1,-d1_prime,-rho_212,&nagerr);
        /* calculate term3 */
        temp = log(S1/X);
        d2_1 = temp+(r-(sigma1*sigma1/two))*opt_mat;
        d2_1 = d2_1/(sigma1*sqrt(opt_mat));
        temp = log(S2/X);
        d2_2 = temp+(r-(sigma2*sigma2/two))*opt_mat;
        d2_2 = d2_2/(sigma2*sqrt(opt_mat));
        term3 = g01hac(d2_1,d2_2,rho,&nagerr);
        *opt_value= term1+term2-X*exp(-r*opt_mat)*term3;
    }
    return;
```

Code excerpt 12.4 Function to calculate the value of a European call on the maximum or minimum of two assets using the analytic result of Johnson (1987) and Stulz (1982)

```
void opt_rainbow_bs_2d(double *opt_value, double S1, double S2, double X, double sigma1,
    double sigma2, double rho, double opt_mat, double r, Integer is_max, Integer putcall, Integer *flag)
{
/* Input parameters:
   = = = = = =

    S1          - the current price of the underlying asset 1,
    S2          - the current price of the underlying asset 2,
    X           - the strike price,
    sigma1      - the volatility of asset 1,
    sigma2      - the volatility of asset 2,
    rho         - the correlation coefficient between asset 1 and asset 2,
    opt_mat     - the time to maturity,
    r           - the interest rate,
    is_max      - if is_max is 1 then the option is on the maximum of two assets, otherwise the option is on
                  the minimum of two assets,
    putcall     - if putcall is 0 then the option is a call, otherwise the option is a put.


   Output parameters:
   = = = = = =

    opt_value   - the value of the option,
    iflag       - an error indicator.
*/

    double temp1;
    double temp2;
```

```
double fac;
double a_zero =1.0e- 6; /* approximate zero number to prevent overflow in rainbow_bs_2d */
if (putcall) { /* a put option */
  fac = X*exp(-r*opt_mat);
  rainbow_bs_2d(&temp1, S1, S2, a_zero, sigma1, sigma2, rho, opt_mat, r, is_max, flag);
  rainbow_bs_2d(&temp2, S1, S2, X, sigma1, sigma2, rho, opt_mat, r, is_max, flag);
  *opt_value = fac - temp1 + temp2;
}else { /* a call option */
  rainbow_bs_2d(opt_value, S1, S2, X, sigma1, sigma2, rho, opt_mat, r, is_max, flag);
  }
}
```

Code excerpt 12.5 Function to calculate the value of a European put or call on the maximum or minimum of two assets using the analytic result of Johnson (1987) and Stulz (1982)

Option prices computed, using a two-dimensional binomial lattice and also the analytic formula of Johnson and Stulz, are presented in Tables 12.3 and 12.4.

Table 12.3 The computed values and absolute errors for European put and call options on the maximum of two assets. The results were obtained using a binomial lattice and the analytic formula (Johnson, 1987; Stulz, 1982). The time to maturity of the option is varied from 0.1 to 0.8 years. The parameters are: $E = 44.0$, $S_1 = 40.0$, $S_2 = 50.0$, $r = 0.1$, $\sigma_1 = 0.2$, $\sigma_2 = 0.2$, $q_1 = q_2 = 0.0$, $\rho = 0.5$, $n\_steps = 50$

	Call			Put		
Time	Analytic	Lattice	Error	Analytic	Lattice	Error
0.1	6.45320	6.45245	7.4972×10^{-4}	0.01524	0.01451	7.3344×10^{-4}
0.2	6.96192	6.95953	2.3845×10^{-3}	0.08252	0.08001	2.5106×10^{-3}
0.3	7.49587	7.49376	2.1084×10^{-3}	0.15787	0.15580	2.0675×10^{-3}
0.4	8.03710	8.04022	3.1260×10^{-3}	0.22362	0.22680	3.1768×10^{-3}
0.5	8.57808	8.57916	1.0757×10^{-3}	0.27762	0.27683	7.8867×10^{-4}
0.6	9.11529	9.10809	7.2006×10^{-3}	0.32115	0.31872	2.4328×10^{-3}
0.7	9.64700	9.64838	1.3826×10^{-3}	0.35598	0.35714	1.1548×10^{-3}
0.8	10.17238	10.17663	4.2571×10^{-3}	0.38372	0.38711	3.3891×10^{-3}

Table 12.4 The computed values and absolute errors for European put and call options on the minimum of two assets. The results were obtained using a binomial lattice and the analytic formula (Johnson, 1987; Stulz, 1982). The time to maturity of the option is varied from 0.1 to 0.8 years. The parameters are: $E = 44.0$, $S_1 = 40.0$, $S_2 = 50.0$, $r = 0.1$, $\sigma_1 = 0.2$, $\sigma_2 = 0.2$, $q_1 = q_2 = 0.0$, $\rho = 0.5$, $n\_steps = 50$

	Call			Put		
Time	Analytic	Lattice	Error	Analytic	Lattice	Error
0.1	0.10810	0.10753	5.7048×10^{-4}	3.67044	3.66993	5.0955×10^{-4}
0.2	0.40862	0.40781	8.1047×10^{-4}	3.54551	3.54514	3.6961×10^{-4}
0.3	0.74162	0.73418	7.4339×10^{-3}	3.47882	3.47206	6.7642×10^{-3}
0.4	1.06989	1.07299	3.1076×10^{-3}	3.43283	3.43715	4.3214×10^{-3}
0.5	1.38675	1.38909	2.3414×10^{-3}	3.39540	3.40159	6.1826×10^{-3}
0.6	1.69203	1.69025	1.7757×10^{-3}	3.36145	3.35775	3.6964×10^{-3}
0.7	1.98691	1.96939	1.7520×10^{-2}	3.32859	3.31517	1.3417×10^{-2}
0.8	2.27276	2.26274	1.0018×10^{-2}	3.29566	3.29157	4.0885×10^{-3}

12.5.2 American options

We assume that the prices of assets 1 and 2 follow a lognormal process with drift terms of $\mu_1 = r - \sigma_1^2/2$, and $\mu_2 = r - \sigma_2^2/2$ respectively. As before r is the riskless interest rate and σ_1 and σ_2 are the instantaneous volatilities of assets 1 and 2.

If we let $S_{1,t}$ and $S_{2,t}$ denote the respective prices of assets 1 and 2 at time t, then we can write:

$$\log(S_{1,t+\Delta t}) = \log(S_{1,t}) + \epsilon_{1,t} \tag{12.18}$$

and

$$\log(S_{2,t+\Delta t}) = \log(S_{2,t}) + \epsilon_{2,t} \tag{12.19}$$

where $\epsilon_{1,t}$ is a random normal variable with mean $\mu_1\Delta t$ and variance $\sigma_1^2\Delta t$, and $\epsilon_{2,t}$ is a random normal variable with mean $\mu_2\Delta t$ and variance $\sigma_2^2\Delta t$.

In the binomial lattice model, over the time interval Δt, the variate $\log(S_{1,t})$ is only allowed to jump up or down by an amount $\nu_1 = \sigma_1\sqrt{\Delta t}$, and similarly the variate $\log(S_{2,t})$ is only permitted to jump up and down by the amount $\nu_2 = \sigma_2\sqrt{\Delta t}$. We will denote the probability of both $\log(S_{1,t})$ and $\log(S_{2,t})$ having an up jump over time interval Δt by p_{uu}, and the probability of $\log(S_{1,t})$ having an up jump and $\log(S_{2,t})$ having a down jump by p_{ud}, etc.

The mean values in Equations 12.18 and 12.19 then give

$$E[\epsilon_{1,t}] = \nu_1(p_{uu} + p_{ud} - p_{dd} - p_{du}) = \mu_1\Delta t \tag{12.20}$$

$$E[\epsilon_{2,t}] = \nu_2(p_{uu} + p_{ud} - p_{dd} - p_{du}) = \mu_2\Delta t \tag{12.21}$$

and the variance/covariance terms yields

$$Var[\epsilon_{1,t}] = \nu_1^2(p_{uu} + p_{ud} + p_{dd} + p_{du}) = \sigma_1^2\Delta t \tag{12.22}$$

$$Var[\epsilon_{2,t}] = \nu_2^2(p_{uu} + p_{ud} + p_{dd} + p_{du}) = \sigma_2^2\Delta t \tag{12.23}$$

$$E[\epsilon_{1,t}\epsilon_{2,t}] = \nu_1\nu_2(p_{uu} - p_{ud} + p_{dd} - p_{du}) = \rho\sigma_1\sigma_2\Delta t \tag{12.24}$$

where ρ is the correlation coefficient between $\epsilon_{1,t}$ and $\epsilon_{2,t}$.

We therefore obtain:

$$p_{uu} + p_{ud} - p_{dd} + p_{du} = \frac{\mu_1\sqrt{\Delta t}}{\sigma_1}$$

$$p_{uu} - p_{ud} - p_{dd} + p_{du} = \frac{\mu_2\sqrt{\Delta t}}{\sigma_2}$$

$$p_{uu} + p_{ud} + p_{dd} + p_{du} = 1$$

$$p_{uu} - p_{ud} + p_{dd} - p_{du} = \rho$$

These lead to the following jump probabilities:

$$p_{uu} = \frac{1}{4}\left\{1 + \sqrt{\Delta t}\left(\frac{\mu_1}{\sigma_1} + \frac{\mu_2}{\sigma_2}\right) + \rho\right\}$$

$$p_{ud} = \frac{1}{4}\left\{1 + \sqrt{\Delta t}\left(\frac{\mu_1}{\sigma_1} - \frac{\mu_2}{\sigma_2}\right) - \rho\right\}$$

$$p_{dd} = \frac{1}{4}\left\{1 + \sqrt{\Delta t}\left(-\frac{\mu_1}{\sigma_1} - \frac{\mu_2}{\sigma_2}\right) + \rho\right\}$$

$$p_{du} = \frac{1}{4}\left\{1 + \sqrt{\Delta t}\left(-\frac{\mu_1}{\sigma_1} + \frac{\mu_2}{\sigma_2}\right) - \rho\right\}$$

In Code excerpt 12.6, we provide the computer code for a standard binomial lattice which prices options on the maximum and minimum of two assets.

The parameter M is the number of time steps used, and the lattice is constructed under the assumption that M is even.

```
void standard_2D_binomial(double *value, double S1, double S2, double X, double sigma1, double sigma2,
    double rho, double T, double r, double q1, double q2, Integer put, Integer M, Integer opt_type, Integer
    is_american, Integer *iflag)
{
/* Input parameters:
   == == == == ==
   S1           - the current price of the underlying asset 1
   S2           - the current price of the underlying asset 2
   X            - the strike price
   sigma1       - the volatility of asset 1
   sigma2       - the volatility of asset 2
   rho          - the correlation coefficient between asset 1 and asset 2
   T            - the time to maturity
   r            - the interest rate
   q1           - the continuous dividend yield for asset 1
   q2           - the continuous dividend yield for asset 2
   put          - if put is 0 then a call option, otherwise a put option
   M            - the number of time steps, the zeroth time step is the root node of the lattice
   opt_type     - if opt_type is 0 then an option on the maximum of two asset otherwise an option
                  on the minimum of two assets
   is_american - if is_american is 0 then a European option, otherwise an American option


   Output parameters:
   == == == == == ==
   value        - the value of the option,
   iflag        - an error indicator.
*/
   double discount,t1,dt,d1,d2,u1,u2;
   Integer i,j,m1,n,iflagx,jj,ind;
   double zero=0.0,hold;
   double temp,ds1,ds2,dv1,dv2,h,tmp;
   double *s1, *s2, *v;
   double p[4];
   Integer P1,P2,tdv;
   double sqrt_dt, t, mu1, mu2, jp1, jp2;
   double one = 1.0, half = 0.5, quarter = 0.25;
   Integer v1;

   if (!((M+1)/2 == M/2)) {
     printf ("ERROR THE NUMBER OF TIME STEPS IS NOT EVEN \n");
     return;
   }
     tdv = M+1;
```

```
#define V(I,J) v[(I) * tdv + (J)]
#define UU 0
#define UD 1
#define DD 2
#define DU 3
  dt = T/(double)M;
  sqrt_dt = sqrt(dt);
  jp1 = sigma1*sqrt_dt;
  jp2 = sigma2*sqrt_dt;
  mu1 = r - q1 - sigma1*sigma1*half;
  mu2 = r - q2 - sigma2*sigma2*half;
  u1 = exp(jp1); /* assign the jump sizes */
  u2 = exp(jp2);
  d1 = exp(-jp1);
  d2 = exp(-jp2);
  p[UU] = quarter*(one + sqrt_dt * ((mu1/sigma1) + (mu2/sigma2)) + rho); /* set up the jump probabilities */
  p[UD] = quarter*(one + sqrt_dt * ((mu1/sigma1) - (mu2/sigma2)) - rho);
  p[DD] = quarter*(one + sqrt_dt * (-(mu1/sigma1) - (mu2/sigma2)) + rho);
  p[DU] = quarter*(one + sqrt_dt * (-(mu1/sigma1) + (mu2/sigma2)) - rho);
  for (i = 0; i < 4; ++i) {
    if ((p[i] < zero) || (p[i] > 1.0)) printf ("ERROR p out of range\n");
  }
  discount = exp(-r*dt);
  for (i = 0; i < 4; ++i) {
    p[i] = p[i]*discount;
  }
/* Allocate the arrays v[(M+1)*(M+1)], s1[2*M+1] and s2[2*M+1] */

  s1[M] = S1; /* assign the 2*M+1 asset values for s1 */
  for (i = 1; i <= M; ++i) {
    s1[M+i] = u1*s1[M+i-1];
    s1[M-i] = d1*s1[M-i+1];
  }
  s2[M] = S2; /* assign the 2*M+1 asset values for s2 */
  for (i = 1; i <= M; ++i) {
    s2[M+i] = u2*s2[M+i-1];
    s2[M-i] = d2*s2[M-i+1];
  }
  P1 = 0;
  for (i = 0; i <= M; ++i) { /* Calculate the option values at maturity */
    P2 = 0;
    for (j = 0; j <= M; ++j) {
      if (opt_type == 0) { /* Maximum of two assets */
        if (put) {
          V(i,j) = MAX(X - MAX(s1[P1],s2[P2]),zero);
        }
        else {
          V(i,j) = MAX(MAX(s1[P1],s2[P2])-X,zero);
        }
      }
      else {
        if (put) { /* Minimum of two assets */
          V(i,j) = MAX(X-MIN(s1[P1],s2[P2]), zero);
        }
        else {
          V(i,j) = MAX(MIN(s1[P1],s2[P2])-X,zero);
        }
      }
      P2 = P2 + 2;
    }
    P1 = P1 + 2;
  }
for (m1 = M-1; m1 >= 0; --m1) { /* work backwards through the lattice to calculate option value */
  P1 = M-m1;
  for (i = 0; i <= m1; ++i) {
    P2 = M-m1;
    for (j = 0; j <= m1; ++j) {
      hold = p[UD]*V(i+1,j) + p[UU]*V(i+1,j+1) + p[DU]*V(i,j+1) + p[DD]*V(i,j);
      if (is_american) { /* An American option */
        if (opt_type == 0) { /* Maximum of two assets */
          if (put)
            V(i,j) = MAX(hold, X-MAX(s1[P1],s2[P2]));
          else
            V(i,j) = MAX(hold,MAX(s1[P1], s2[P2])-X);
        }
        else { /* Minimum of two assets */
```

```
    if (put)
        V(i,j)= MAX(hold,X-MIN(s1[P1], s2[P2]));
    else
        V(i,j)= MAX(hold,MIN(s1[P1],s2[P2])-X);
    }
    }
    else {
        V(i,j) = hold;
    }
    P2 = P2 +2;
    }
    P1 = P1+2;
    }
}
*value = V(0,0);
}
```

Code excerpt 12.6   Function to calculate the value of a European put or call on the maximum or minimum of two assets using a standard binomial lattice

The computer code for a truncated two-dimensional binomial lattice is given in Appendix D.1.

Table 12.5   The computed values and absolute errors for an American put option on the maximum of two assets. A truncated binomial lattice was used and we show how the accuracy depends on the value of max_index. The parameters are: $E = 100.0$, $S_1 = S_2 = 100.0$, $r = 0.2$, $\tau = 1.0$, $\sigma_1 = \sigma_2 = 0.2$, $\rho = 0.5$, $q_1 = q_2 = 0.0$. The first column gives the value of max_index, the second column the computational time in milliseconds, the third column the computed value of the option, and the last column the absolute error. The *accurate* value took 280 ms to compute and was obtained using a standard lattice with n_steps $= 200$

max_index	Time (ms)	Value	Error
22	10.0	1.8478	6.3912×10^3
26	20.0	1.8525	1.7179×10^{-3}
40	30.0	1.8542	1.277×10^{-5}
48	40.0	1.8542	5.0338×10^{-7}
52	50.0	1.8542	8.6936×10^{-8}
58	60.0	1.8542	5.1993×10^{-9}

Table 12.6   The computed values and absolute errors for an American put option on the minimum of two assets. A truncated binomial lattice was used and we show how the accuracy depends on the value of max_index. The parameters are: $E = 100.0$, $S_1 = S_2 = 100.0$, $r = 0.2$, $\tau = 1.0$, $\sigma_1 = \sigma_2 = 0.2$, $\rho = 0.5$, $q_1 = q_2 = 0.0$. The first column gives the value of max_index, the second column the computational time in milliseconds, the third column the computed value of the option, and the last column the absolute error. The *accurate* value took 311 ms to compute and was obtained using a standard lattice with n_steps $= 200$

max_index	Time (ms)	Value	Error
26	10.0	4.7008	3.8500×10^{-2}
32	20.0	4.7301	9.2094×10^{-3}
40	30.0	4.7383	1.0258×10^{-3}
44	40.0	4.7390	2.9951×10^{-4}
48	50.0	4.7392	7.9631×10^{-5}
52	60.0	4.7393	1.9230×10^{-5}

12.6   THREE ASSET OPTIONS

For three assets we have the following jump probabilities:

$$p_{uuu} = \frac{1}{8}\left\{1 + \sqrt{\Delta t}\left(\frac{\mu_1}{\sigma_1} + \frac{\mu_2}{\sigma_2} + \frac{\mu_3}{\sigma_3}\right) + \rho_{12} + \rho_{13} + \rho_{23}\right\}$$

$$p_{uud} = \frac{1}{8}\left\{1 + \sqrt{\Delta t}\left(\frac{\mu_1}{\sigma_1} + \frac{\mu_2}{\sigma_2} - \frac{\mu_3}{\sigma_3}\right) + \rho_{12} - \rho_{13} - \rho_{23}\right\}$$

$$p_{udu} = \frac{1}{8}\left\{1 + \sqrt{\Delta t}\left(\frac{\mu_1}{\sigma_1} - \frac{\mu_2}{\sigma_2} + \frac{\mu_3}{\sigma_3}\right) - \rho_{12} + \rho_{13} - \rho_{23}\right\}$$

$$p_{udd} = \frac{1}{8}\left\{1 + \sqrt{\Delta t}\left(\frac{\mu_1}{\sigma_1} - \frac{\mu_2}{\sigma_2} - \frac{\mu_3}{\sigma_3}\right) - \rho_{12} - \rho_{13} + \rho_{23}\right\}$$

$$p_{duu} = \frac{1}{8}\left\{1 + \sqrt{\Delta t}\left(-\frac{\mu_1}{\sigma_1} + \frac{\mu_2}{\sigma_2} + \frac{\mu_3}{\sigma_3}\right) - \rho_{12} - \rho_{13} + \rho_{23}\right\}$$

$$p_{dud} = \frac{1}{8}\left\{1 + \sqrt{\Delta t}\left(-\frac{\mu_1}{\sigma_1} + \frac{\mu_2}{\sigma_2} + \frac{\mu_3}{\sigma_3}\right) - \rho_{12} + \rho_{13} - \rho_{23}\right\}$$

$$p_{ddu} = \frac{1}{8}\left\{1 + \sqrt{\Delta t}\left(-\frac{\mu_1}{\sigma_1} - \frac{\mu_2}{\sigma_2} + \frac{\mu_3}{\sigma_3}\right) + \rho_{12} - \rho_{13} - \rho_{23}\right\}$$

$$p_{ddd} = \frac{1}{8}\left\{1 + \sqrt{\Delta t}\left(-\frac{\mu_1}{\sigma_1} - \frac{\mu_2}{\sigma_2} - \frac{\mu_3}{\sigma_3}\right) + \rho_{12} + \rho_{13} + \rho_{23}\right\}$$

The computer code for a standard three-dimensional lattice is given in Code excerpt 12.7 below. Code for truncated and recursive lattices is supplied on the CD ROM.

```
void standard_3D_binomial (double *value, double S1, double S2, double S3, double X, double sigma1,
    double sigma2, double sigma3, double rho_12, double rho_13, double rho_23, double T, double r,
    Integer put, Integer M, Integer opt_type, Integer is_american, Integer *iflag)
{

/* Input parameters:
   == == == == ==
   S1              - the current price of the underlying asset 1
   S2              - the current price of the underlying asset 2
   S3              - the current price of the underlying asset 3
   X               - the strike price
   sigma1          - the volatility of asset 1
   sigma2          - the volatility of asset 2
   sigma3          - the volatility of asset 3
   rho_12          - the correlation coefficient between asset 1 and asset 2
   rho_13          - the correlation coefficient between asset 1 and asset 3
   rho_23          - the correlation coefficient between asset 2 and asset 3
   T               - the time to maturity
   r               - the interest rate
```

```
put          - if put is 0 then a call option, otherwise a put option
M            - the number of time steps, the zeroth time step is the root node of the lattice
opt_type     - if opt_type is 0 then an option on the maximum of two asset otherwise an option on the minimum
               of two assets
is_american  - if is_american is 0 then a European option, otherwise an American option.


Output parameters:
==================
value        - the value of the option,
iflag        - an error indicator.
*/
  double discount, t1, dt, d1, d2, d3, u1, u2, u3;
  Integer i, j, k, m1, n, iflagx, jj, ind;
  double zero=0.0, hold;
  double temp, ds1, ds2, dv1, dv2, h, tmp, tmp1, tmp2;
  double *s1, *s2, *s3, *v;
  double p[9];
  Integer P1, P2, P3, tdv, tdv2;
  double sqrt_dt, t, mu1, mu2, mu3, jp1, jp2, jp3;
  double one =1.0, half =0.5, eighth =0.125;
  Integer v1;

  if (!((M+1)/2 == M/2)) {
    printf ("ERROR THE NUMBER OF TIME STEPS IS NOT EVEN \n");
    return;
  }
  tdv = M+1;
  tdv2 = tdv*tdv;
#define V(I, J, K) v[(I) * tdv2 + (J)*tdv + (K)]
#define UUU  0
#define UUD  1
#define UDU  2
#define UDD  3
#define DUU  4
#define DUD  5
#define DDU  6
#define DDD  7
  dt = T/(double)M;
  sqrt_dt = sqrt(dt);
  jp1 = sigma1*sqrt_dt;
  jp2 = sigma2*sqrt_dt;
  jp3 = sigma3*sqrt_dt;
  mu1 = r - sigma1*sigma1*half;
  mu2 = r - sigma2*sigma2*half;
  mu3 = r - sigma3*sigma3*half;
  u1 = exp(jp1); /* assign the jump sizes */
  u2 = exp(jp2);
  u3 = exp(jp3);
  d1 = exp(-jp1);
  d2 = exp(-jp2);
  d3 = exp(-jp3);
/* set up the jump probabilities */
  p[UUU] = eighth*(one + sqrt_dt * ((mu1/sigma1) + (mu2/sigma2) + (mu3/sigma3)) + rho_12 + rho_13 + rho_23);
  p[UUD] = eighth*(one + sqrt_dt * ((mu1/sigma1) + (mu2/sigma2) - (mu3/sigma3)) + rho_12 - rho_13 - rho_23);
  p[UDU] = eighth*(one + sqrt_dt * ((mu1/sigma1) - (mu2/sigma2) + (mu3/sigma3)) - rho_12 + rho_13 - rho_23);
  p[UDD] = eighth*(one + sqrt_dt * ((mu1/sigma1) - (mu2/sigma2) - (mu3/sigma3)) - rho_12 - rho_13 + rho_23);
  p[DUU] = eighth*(one + sqrt_dt * (-(mu1/sigma1) + (mu2/sigma2) + (mu3/sigma3)) - rho_12 - rho_13 +
         rho_23);
  p[DUD] = eighth*(one + sqrt_dt * (-(mu1/sigma1) + (mu2/sigma2) - (mu3/sigma3)) - rho_12 + rho_13 -
         rho_23);
  p[DDU] = eighth*(one + sqrt_dt * (-(mu1/sigma1) - (mu2/sigma2) + (mu3/sigma3)) + rho_12 - rho_13 -
         rho_23);
  p[DDD] = eighth*(one + sqrt_dt * (-(mu1/sigma1) - (mu2/sigma2) - (mu3/sigma3)) + rho_12 + rho_13 +
         rho_23);
  for (i =0; i <8; ++i) {
    if ((p[i] < zero) || (p[i] >1.0)) printf ("ERROR p[%1d] = %12.4f out of range\n", i, p[i]);
  }
  discount = exp(-r*dt);
  for (i =0; i <8; ++i) {
    p[i] = p[i]*discount;
  }
/* Allocate the arrays v[(M+1)*(M+1)*(M+1)], s1[2*M+1], s2[2*M+1], and s3[2*M+1] */

  s1[M] = S1;
  for (i =1; i <= M; ++i) { /* assign the 2*M+1 asset values for s1 */
```

```
    s1[M+i] = u1*s1[M+i-1];
    s1[M-i] = d1*s1[M-i+1];
}
s2[M] = S2;
for (i=1; i <= M; ++i) { /* assign the 2*M+1 asset values for s2 */
    s2[M+i] = u2*s2[M+i-1];
    s2[M-i] = d2*s2[M-i+1];
}
s3[M] = S3;
for (i=1; i <= M; ++i) { /* assign the 2*M+1 asset values for s2 */
    s3[M+i] = u3*s3[M+i-1];
    s3[M-i] = d3*s3[M-i+1];
}
/* Calculate the option values at maturity */
P1=0;
for (i = 0; i <= M; ++i) {
    P2=0;
    for (j =0; j <= M; ++j) {
        P3=0;
        for (k =0; k <= M; ++k) {
            if (put) { /* put */
                if (opt_type ==0) { /* Maximum of 3 assets */
                    tmp = MAX(s1[P1], s2[P2]);
                    V(i, j, k) = MAX(X - MAX(tmp, s3[P3]), zero);
                }
                else if (opt_type ==1) { /* Minimum of 3 assets */
                    tmp = MIN(s1[P1], s2[P2]);
                    V(i, j, k) = MAX(X - MIN(tmp, s3[P3]), zero);
                }
            }
            else { /* call */
                ** Insert call option code using the supplied put option code as a template **
            }
            P3=P3+2;
        }
        P2=P2+2;
    }
    P1=P1+2;
}
for (m1 = M-1; m1 >=0; --m1) { /* work backwards through the lattice to calculate the option value */
    P1 = M-m1;
    for (i = 0; i <= m1; ++i) {
        P2 = M-m1;
        for (j =0; j <= m1; ++j) {
            P3 = M-m1;
            for (k =0; k <= m1; ++k) {
                hold = p[UUU] *V(i+1, j+1, k+1) + p[UUD] *V(i+1, j+1, k) + p[UDU] *V(i+1, j, k+1) +
                    p[UDD] *V(i+1, j, k)+ p[DUU] *V(i, j+1, k+1) + p[DUD] *V(i, j+1, k) +
                    p[DDU] *V(i, j, k+1) + p[DDD] *V(i, j, k);
                if (is_american) {
                    if (put) {
                        if (opt_type ==0) { /* Maximum of 3 assets */
                            tmp = MAX(s1[P1], s2[P2]);
                            tmp1 = MAX(tmp, s3[P3]);
                            tmp2 = MAX(X-tmp1, hold);
                            V(i, j, k) = MAX(tmp2, zero);
                        }
                        else if (opt_type ==1) { /* Minimum of 3 assets */
                            tmp = MIN(s1[P1], s2[P2]);
                            tmp1 = MIN(tmp, s3[P3]);
                            tmp2 = MAX(X-tmp1, hold);
                            V(i, j, k) = MAX(tmp2, zero);
                        }
                    }
                    else { /* call option */
                        ** Insert call option code using the supplied put option code as a template **
                    }
                }
                else { /* European option */
                    V(i, j, k) = hold;
                }
                P3=P3+2;
            }
            P2=P2+2;
        }
```

```
    P1 = P1 + 2;
  }
 }
 *value = V(0, 0, 0);
}
```

Code excerpt 12.7   Standard three-dimensional binomial lattice

The results of pricing three asset options, in which $\rho_{13} = \rho_{23} = 0.5$, are given in Tables 12.7 to 12.9; standard, truncated, and recursive lattices are used.

Table 12.7   The computed values and absolute errors for European options on the maximum of three assets. A binomial lattice was used and we show how the accuracy of the results depends on the number of time steps. The parameters are: $E = 100.0$, $S_1 = S_2 = S_3 = 100.0$, $r = 0.1$, $\tau = 1.0$, $\sigma_1 = \sigma_2 = \sigma_3 = 0.2$, $\rho_{12} = \rho_{13} = \rho_{23} = 0.5$, $q_1 = q_2 = q_3 = 0.0$. The *accurate* values are 0.936 for a put and 22.672 for a call, see Table 2 Boyle, Evnine, and Gibbs (1989)

	Put		Call	
n steps	Standard lattice	Recursive lattice	Standard lattice	Recursive lattice
10	0.9112 (2.485×10^{-2})	0.9617 (2.574×10^{-2})	21.8601 (8.119×10^{-1})	22.2488 (4.232×10^{-1})
20	0.9192 (1.678×10^{-2})	0.9463 (1.030×10^{-2})	22.2807 (3.913×10^{-1})	22.4640 (2.080×10^{-1})
30	0.9232 (1.276×10^{-2})	0.9416 (5.640×10^{-3})	22.4137 (2.583×10^{-1})	22.5339 (1.381×10^{-1})
40	0.9254 (1.056×10^{-2})	0.9394 (3.370×10^{-3})	22.4792 (1.928×10^{-1})	22.5686 (1.034×10^{-1})
50	0.9268 (9.180×10^{-3})	0.9380 (2.025×10^{-3})	22.5182 (1.538×10^{-1})	22.5894 (8.259×10^{-2})
60	0.9278 (8.236×10^{-3})	0.9371 (1.135×10^{-3})	22.5441 (1.279×10^{-1})	22.6033 (6.875×10^{-2})

Table 12.8   The computed values and absolute errors for European options on the minimum of three assets. A binomial lattice was used and we show how the accuracy of the results depends on the number of time steps. The parameters are: $E = 100.0$, $S_1 = S_2 = S_3 = 100.0$, $r = 0.1$, $\tau = 1.0$, $\sigma_1 = \sigma_2 = \sigma_3 = 0.2$, $\rho_{12} = \rho_{13} = \rho_{23} = 0.5$, $q_1 = q_2 = q_3 = 0.0$. The *accurate* values are 7.403 for a put and 5.249 for a call, see Table 2 Boyle, Evnine, and Gibbs (1989)

	Put		Call	
n steps	Standard lattice	Recursive lattice	Standard lattice	Recursive lattice
10	7.0759 (3.271×10^{-1})	7.3658 (3.723×10^{-2})	5.2072 (4.176×10^{-2})	5.2359 (1.312×10^{-2})
20	7.2402 (1.628×10^{-1})	7.3865 (1.653×10^{-2})	5.2263 (2.269×10^{-2})	5.2406 (8.414×10^{-3})
30	7.2953 (1.077×10^{-1})	7.3931 (9.926×10^{-2})	5.2334 (1.560×10^{-2})	5.2429 (6.060×10^{-2})
40	7.3229 (8.015×10^{-2})	7.3963 (6.676×10^{-3})	5.2371 (1.192×10^{-2})	5.2443 (4.749×10^{-3})
50	7.3394 (6.357×10^{-2})	7.3983 (4.741×10^{-3})	5.2393 (9.665×10^{-2})	5.2451 (3.922×10^{-3})
60	7.3505 (5.251×10^{-2})	7.3995 (3.459×10^{-3})	5.2409 (8.143×10^{-3})	5.2456 (3.353×10^{-3})

Table 12.9 The computed values and absolute errors for a European put option on the maximum of three assets. A truncated binomial lattice was used and we show how the accuracy depends on the value of max_index. The parameters are: $E = 100.0$, $S_1 = S_2 = S_3 = 100.0$, $r = 0.1$, $\tau = 1.0$, $\sigma_1 = \sigma_2 = \sigma_3 = 0.2$, $\rho_{12} = \rho_{13} = \rho_{23} = 0.5$, $q_1 = q_2 = q_3 = 0.0$. The first column gives the value of max_index, the second column the computational time in milliseconds and the third column the computed value of the option and also the absolute error in brackets. The *accurate* value is 0.9290 (took 1633 ms to compute) and was obtained using a standard lattice with n_steps = 80

max_index	Time (ms)	Value (error)
14	20	0.3464 (5.8254 $\times 10^{-1}$)
16	30	0.4976 (4.3142 $\times 10^{-1}$)
18	50	0.6344 (2.9458 $\times 10^{-1}$)
20	60	0.7432 (1.8581 $\times 10^{-1}$)
22	81	0.8204 (1.0858 $\times 10^{-1}$)
24	100	0.8700 (5.8935 $\times 10^{-2}$)
26	121	0.8992 (2.9782 $\times 10^{-2}$)
28	140	0.9149 (1.4036 $\times 10^{-2}$)
30	181	0.9228 (6.1763 $\times 10^{-3}$)
32	220	0.9264 (2.5393 $\times 10^{-3}$)
34	270	0.9280 (9.7559 $\times 10^{-4}$)
36	320	0.9286 (3.5018 $\times 10^{-4}$)
38	391	0.9289 (1.1735 $\times 10^{-4}$)
40	441	0.9289 (3.6673 $\times 10^{-5}$)
42	521	0.9290 (1.0672 $\times 10^{-5}$)

The result of pricing three asset options, in which $\rho_{12} = \rho_{13} = -0.5$, and $\rho_{23} = 0.5$, are given in Tables 12.10 to 12.12.

Table 12.10 The computed values and absolute errors for European options on the maximum of three assets. A binomial lattice was used and we show how the accuracy depends on the number of time steps. The parameters are: $E = 100.0$, $S_1 = S_2 = S_3 = 100.0$, $r = 0.1$, $\tau = 1.0$, $\sigma_1 = \sigma_2 = \sigma_3 = 0.2$, $\rho_{12} = -0.5$, $\rho_{13} = -0.5$, $\rho_{23} = 0.5$, $q_1 = q_2 = q_3 = 0.0$. The *accurate* values are 0.0526 for a put and 27.8271 for a call, and were computed using Monte Carlo simulation with 10^7 paths

	Put		Call	
n steps	Standard lattice	Recursive lattice	Standard lattice	Recursive lattice
10	0.0122 (4.041 $\times 10^{-2}$)	0.0273 (2.531 $\times 10^{-2}$)	27.3180 (5.091 $\times 10^{-1}$)	27.5666 (2.605 $\times 10^{-1}$)
20	0.0295 (2.314 $\times 10^{-2}$)	0.0396 (1.301 $\times 10^{-2}$)	27.5743 (2.528 $\times 10^{-1}$)	27.6963 (1.308 $\times 10^{-1}$)
30	0.0366 (1.600 $\times 10^{-2}$)	0.0438 (8.770 $\times 10^{-3}$)	27.6589 (1.682 $\times 10^{-1}$)	27.7396 (8.745 $\times 10^{-2}$)
40	0.0404 (1.221 $\times 10^{-2}$)	0.0460 (6.618 $\times 10^{-3}$)	27.7010 (1.261 $\times 10^{-1}$)	27.7614 (6.568 $\times 10^{-2}$)
50	0.0427 (9.868 $\times 10^{-3}$)	0.0473 (5.316 $\times 10^{-3}$)	27.7263 (1.008 $\times 10^{-1}$)	27.7745 (5.258 $\times 10^{-2}$)
60	0.0443 (8.280 $\times 10^{-3}$)	0.0482 (4.444 $\times 10^{-3}$)	27.7431 (8.396 $\times 10^{-2}$)	27.7833 (4.383 $\times 10^{-2}$)

Table 12.11   The computed values and absolute errors for European options on the minimum of three assets. A binomial lattice was used and we show how the accuracy depends on the number of time steps. The parameters are: $E = 100.0$, $S_1 = S_2 = S_3 = 100.0$, $r = 0.1$, $\tau = 1.0$, $\sigma_1 = \sigma_2 = \sigma_3 = 0.2$, $\rho_{12} = -0.5$, $\rho_{13} = -0.5$, $\rho_{23} = 0.5$, $q_1 = q_2 = q_3 = 0.0$. The *accurate* values are 9.2776 for a put and 1.5847 for a call, and were computed using Monte Carlo simulation with 10^7 paths

	Put		Call	
n steps	Standard lattice	Recursive lattice	Standard lattice	Recursive lattice
10	8.9646 (3.130 $\times 10^{-1}$)	9.2791 (1.457 $\times 10^{-3}$)	1.4047 (1.800 $\times 10^{-1}$)	1.5446 (4.007 $\times 10^{-2}$)
20	9.1231 (1.545 $\times 10^{-1}$)	9.2796 (1.979 $\times 10^{-3}$)	1.4963 (8.836 $\times 10^{-2}$)	1.5634 (2.125 $\times 10^{-2}$)
30	9.1749 (1.027 $\times 10^{-1}$)	9.2792 (1.594 $\times 10^{-3}$)	1.5261 (5.857 $\times 10^{-2}$)	1.5703 (1.440 $\times 10^{-2}$)
40	9.2007 (7.694 $\times 10^{-2}$)	9.2789 (1.299 $\times 10^{-3}$)	1.5409 (4.381 $\times 10^{-2}$)	1.5738 (1.089 $\times 10^{-2}$)
50	9.2161 (6.151 $\times 10^{-2}$)	9.2787 (1.088 $\times 10^{-3}$)	1.5497 (3.499 $\times 10^{-2}$)	1.5759 (8.752 $\times 10^{-3}$)
60	9.2264 (5.123 $\times 10^{-2}$)	9.2785 (9.336 $\times 10^{-4}$)	1.5556 (2.913 $\times 10^{-2}$)	1.5774 (7.317 $\times 10^{-3}$)

Table 12.12   The computed values and absolute errors for a European put option on the maximum of three assets. A truncated binomial lattice was used and we show how the accuracy depends on the value of max_index. The parameters are: $E = 100.0$, $S_1 = S_2 = S_3 = 100.0$, $r = 0.1$, $\tau = 1.0$, $\sigma_1 = \sigma_2 = \sigma_3 = 0.2$, $\rho_{12} = -0.5$, $\rho_{13} = -0.5$, $\rho_{23} = 0.5$, $q_1 = 0.0$, $q_2 = 0.0$, $q_3 = 0.0$. The first column gives the value of max_index, the second column the computational time in milliseconds and the third column the computed value of the option and also the absolute error in brackets. The *accurate* value is 0.0463 (took 1632 ms to compute) and was obtained using a standard lattice with n_steps = 80

max_index	Time (ms)	Value (error)
14	20	0.0328 (1.3545 $\times 10^{-2}$)
16	30	0.0397 (6.6100 $\times 10^{-3}$)
18	41	0.0434 (2.8917 $\times 10^{-3}$)
20	60	0.0452 (1.1577 $\times 10^{-3}$)
22	70	0.0459 (4.2916 $\times 10^{-4}$)
24	100	0.0462 (1.4810 $\times 10^{-4}$)
26	120	0.0463 (4.7659 $\times 10^{-5}$)
28	150	0.0463 (1.4299 $\times 10^{-5}$)

12.7   FOUR ASSET OPTIONS

The jump probabilities for a binomial lattice which computes options on four assets is given in Appendix D.3, and computer code is available on the CD ROM. The results of using a four-dimensional binomial lattice to price options are presented in Tables 12.13 and 12.14.

Table 12.13   The computed values and absolute errors for European options on the maximum of four assets. A binomial lattice was used and we show how the accuracy depends on the number of time steps. The parameters are: $E = 100.0$, $S_1 = S_2 = S_3 = S_4 = 100.0$, $r = 0.1$, $\tau = 1.0$, $\sigma_1 = \sigma_2 = \sigma_3 = \sigma_4 = 0.2$, $\rho_{12} = 0.5$, $\rho_{13} = 0.5$, $\rho_{23} = 0.5$, $q_1 = q_2 = q_3 = q_4 = 0.0$. The *accurate* values are 0.6309 for a put and 25.2363 for a call, and were computed using Monte Carlo simulation with 10^7 paths

	Put		Call	
n steps	Estimated value	Error	Estimated value	Error
4	0.6548	2.386×10^{-2}	22.1403	3.096
8	0.6268	4.129×10^{-3}	23.8640	1.372
12	0.6246	6.275×10^{-3}	24.3630	8.733×10^{-1}
16	0.6251	5.836×10^{-3}	24.5934	6.429×10^{-1}
20	0.6257	5.167×10^{-3}	24.7270	5.093×10^{-1}
24	0.6263	4.570×10^{-3}	24.8144	4.219×10^{-1}
28	0.6268	4.074×10^{-3}	24.8762	3.601×10^{-1}
32	0.6272	3.665×10^{-3}	24.9222	3.141×10^{-1}

Table 12.14   The computed values and absolute errors for European options on the minimum of four assets. A binomial lattice was used and we show how the accuracy depends on the number of time steps. The parameters are: $E = 100.0$, $S_1 = S_2 = S_3 = S_4 = 100.0$, $r = 0.1$, $\tau = 1.0$, $\sigma_1 = \sigma_2 = \sigma_3 = \sigma_4 = 0.2$, $\rho_{12} = 0.5$, $\rho_{13} = 0.5$, $\rho_{23} = 0.5$, $q_1 = q_2 = q_3 = q_4 = 0.0$. The *accurate* values are 8.5394 for a put and 4.0662 for a call, and were computed using Monte Carlo simulation with 10^7 paths

	Put		Call	
n steps	Estimated value	Error	Estimated value	Error
4	7.8274	7.120×10^{-1}	3.5676	4.986×10^{-1}
8	8.1571	3.823×10^{-1}	3.8528	2.134×10^{-1}
12	8.2794	2.600×10^{-1}	3.9300	1.362×10^{-1}
16	8.3429	1.965×10^{-1}	3.9659	1.003×10^{-1}
20	8.3815	1.579×10^{-1}	3.9868	7.944×10^{-2}
24	8.4075	1.319×10^{-1}	4.0004	6.577×10^{-2}
28	8.4262	1.132×10^{-1}	4.0101	5.612×10^{-2}
32	8.4402	9.920×10^{-2}	4.0173	4.894×10^{-2}

Chapter 13

Dealing with missing data

13.1   INTRODUCTION

So far in all our discussions we have assumed that there are no missing values in the financial data that is used to estimate the asset volatility. In practice this is rarely the case. Reasons for this include: the variation in trading times of the stock exchanges across the world, technical problems with storing/retrieving the data, and disruptive social/economic events in various countries.

Some very simplistic approaches to dealing with missing data include:

- Replacing the missing value by the preceding (known) value.
- Excluding all the data collected at a given time if it contains at least one missing value.

The last method could result in a large amount of very useful information being ignored. For example, just because no data is available from one country's stock exchange does not mean the data collected from all the other financial markets is not useful.

Accurately replacing missing data is of great importance if good estimates of the volatility and covariance of assets are to be obtained, and used as input parameters to the option pricing and portfolio models that are discussed here.

Here we will consider data with values *missing at random*, that is when the probability of a missing variate value is not related to the values of other variates. The data is assumed to consist of n observations (rows) and p variates (columns), and takes the form of a n by p matrix. We will let the p element vector X_i denote the ith observation and the row vector $\bar{X}$ denote the mean variate values. The kth element of X_i, $X_{i,k}$, represents the value of the kth variate for the ith observation, and the kth element of $\bar{X}, \bar{X}_k$ represents the mean value of the kth variate. If there are no missing values then we calculate the $p \times p$ covariance matrix as follows:

$$C_{jk} = \frac{1}{n} \sum_{i=1}^{n} (X_{i,j} - \bar{X}_i)(X_{i,k} - \bar{X}_k)$$

or in more compact notation:

$$C = \frac{1}{n} \sum_{i=1}^{n} (X_i - \bar{X})(X_i - \bar{X})^T$$

where

$$\bar{X} = \sum_{i=1}^{p} X_i$$

However, when the data contains missing values it is not possible to calculate the covariance matrix in this manner.

In this section two methods of filling in missing data are considered, they are:

- Iterative multivariate regression, which we call *MREG*.
- The *EM* algorithm.

We will now describe both of these approaches in more detail.

13.2 ITERATIVE MULTIPLE LINEAR REGRESSION, *MREG*

This method fills in missing values by performing multiple linear regression on the columns of the data matrix; see Beale and Little (1975), Orchard and Woodbury (1972), and Little and Rubin (1987). We will denote the n element column vector containing the observations of the kth variate by y^k.

The procedure is as follows:

Step 1

Replace any missing values in column vectors y^k, $k = 1, \ldots, p$ by the corresponding mean value. That is if the kth column vector y^k contains n_m missing values then these are replaced by $\bar{y}^k$, which is calculated as

$$\bar{y}^k = \frac{1}{(n - n_m)} \sum_{i=1}^{n} X_{i,k}$$

where $X_{i,k}$ is taken to be zero if it is missing.

Step 2

Starting with the first column as the dependent variable perform a multiple linear regression for each variable on the remaining $p - 1$ independent variables. After each regression update the missing values in the dependent variable with those values obtained from the regression.

This works as follows: with the first column as the dependent variable the n element regression vector $\hat{y}^1$ can be written as:

$$\hat{y}^1 = C + \beta_2 y^2 + \beta_3 y^3 + \cdots + \beta_p y^p$$

where C is a vector of size n with all elements C_i, $i = 1, \ldots, n = c$, and the scalars β_i, $i = 2, \ldots, p$ are the regression coefficients.

Here we assume that the data has been centred about the origin and use

$$\hat{y}^1 = \beta_2 y^2 + \beta_3 y^3 + \cdots + \beta_p y^p$$

We denote the *i*th element of $\hat{y}^1$ by $\hat{y}_i^1$, and if the *i*th element of y^1 is a missing value, which is the data element $X_{i,1}$, we update using:

$$X_{i,1} = \hat{y}_i^1$$

Similarly when the *k*th column is the dependent variable we have:

$$\hat{y}^k = \beta Y$$

where Y is a $(p-1) \times n$ matrix which contains all the column vectors y^j, $j = 1, \ldots, p$, except y^k, and the $(p-1)$ element vector β contains the regression coefficients. If the *i*th element of y^k, denoted by y_i^k, is a missing value, then we update the data using:

$$X_{i,k} = \hat{y}_i^k$$

Step 3

We now compute the current mean values of each variable. The mean value of the *k*th variable is computed as:

$$\bar{y}^k = \frac{1}{n} \sum_{i=1}^{n} X_{i,k}$$

If the difference between the current mean values and the previous mean values is greater than a specified tolerance we repeat step 2. If step 2 has been repeated more than a specified number of times we stop. The function *MREG*, which implements this method, is given in Code excerpt 13.1 below.

```
void MREG (double x[], long num, long m, double tol, long max_cycle, long *iflag)
{
/* Input parameters:
   = = = = = = =
   x[]          - if put is 0 then a call option, otherwise a put option
   num          - the number of time steps, the zeroth time step is the root node of the lattice
   m            - the number of time steps, the zeroth time step is the root node of the lattice
   tol          - if opt_type is 0 then an option on the maximum of two asset otherwise an option on the minimum
                  of two assets
   max_cycle    - if is_american is 0 then a European option, otherwise an American option.

   Output parameters:
   = = = = = = = =
   x[]          - the value of the option,
   iflag        - an error indicator.
*/

/* The missing data in the matrix X is overwritten by the estimated values */
   double rss;
   long row_ptr, col_ptr, i, jj, ip, rank, j, k;
   double df, zero = 0.0;
   Boolean svd;
   Nag_IncludeMean mean;
   double loc_tol, tmp, sum, *b;
   double *nmeans, *means, *cov, *h, *p, *q, *res, *se, *com_ar, *y;
   double *wtptr = (double *)0;
   long *sx, dep_var, tdq, count;
   NagError loc_fail;
   Boolean terminate;
   long num_missing, *missing_row, *missing_column;
```

```
#define Y(I) y[(I)-1]
#define MISSING_ROW(I) missing_row[(I)-1]
#define MISSING_COLUMN(I) missing_column[(I)-1]
#define SX(I) sx[(I)-1]
#define MEANS(I) means[(I)-1]
#define NMEANS(I) nmeans[(I)-1]
#define X(I,J) x[((I)-1) * m + ((J)-1)]
#define WX(I,J) wx[((I)-1) * m + ((J)-1)]
#define RES(I) res[(I)-1]
#define B(I) b[(I)-1]

  mean = 286; /* There is no constant term in the regression, it will pass through the origin */
  ip = m - 1;
  tdq = ip + 1;

/* Allocate arrays: cov(ip*(ip+1)/2), b(ip), se(ip), res(num), sx(ip), h(num), y(num), q(num*tdq),
   p((2*ip)+(ip*ip)),com_ar (5*(ip-1)+ip*ip), means(m), nmeans(m) */
/* Initial processing of the missing data set all missing values to the variable means */
  *iflag = 0;
  num_missing = 0;
  for (j = 1; j <=m; ++j) {
    sum = zero;
    for (i = 1; i <= num; ++i) {
      if(X(i,j) != -999.0) {
        sum = sum + X(i,j);
      }
      else {
        ++num_missing;
      }
    }
    MEANS(j) = sum/(double)(num - num_missing);
  }
/* Allocate arrays: missing_row(num_missing+1), missing_ column(num_missing+1) */
/* Set the indices for the missing data Note: Here (as opposed to the EM) we use column order
   addressing - since the algorithm is column based. */
  num_missing = 0;
  for (j = 1; j <=m; ++j) {
    for (i = 1; i <= num; ++i) {
      if (X(i,j) == -999.0) {
        ++num_missing;
        MISSING_ROW(num_missing) = i;
        MISSING_COLUMN(num_missing) = j;
      }
    }
  }
  dep_var = 1;
  count = 0;
  terminate = FALSE;
  loc_tol = 1.0e-8;
  while ((!terminate)&&(count <= max_cycle)) { /* outer cycle loop */
    /* replace missing variable values with their means */
    col_ptr = 1;
    row_ptr = 1;
    for (j = 1; j <= m; ++j) {
      for (i = 1; i <= num; ++i) {
        while ((col_ptr <= num_missing) && (MISSING_COLUMN (col_ptr) == j)) {
          i = MISSING_ROW(row_ptr);
          X(i,j) = MEANS(j);
          ++row_ptr;
          ++col_ptr;
        }
      }
      /* if (col_ptr > num_missing) printf ("col_ptr > num_ missing /n"); */
    }
    col_ptr = 1;
    row_ptr = 1;
    for (jj = 1; jj <= m; ++jj) { /* loop over all the variables selecting one as the dependent */
                                  /* variable for a multiple regression on the others */
      for (j=1; j <=m; ++j) {
        SX(j) = 1;
      }
      SX(dep_var) = 0;
      for (i=1; i <= num; ++i) { /* load the dependent variable into the vector y */
        Y(i) = X(i,dep_var);
      }
      g02dac(mean, num, &X(1,1), m, m, &SX(1), ip, &Y(1), wtptr, &rss, &df, &B(1),se, cov, &RES(1), h, q, tdq,
        &svd, &rank, p, loc_tol, com_ar, &loc_fail);
```

```
/* load the estimated values back into the data matrix WX */
for (i=1; i <= num; ++i) {
  if ((MISSING_COLUMN(col_ptr) == dep_var) && (MISSING_ ROW(row_ptr) == i)) {
    k = MISSING_ROW(row_ptr);
    ++row_ptr;
    ++col_ptr;
    X(k,dep_var) = Y(i) - RES(i);
  }
}
if (loc_fail.code != NE_NOERROR) printf ("ERROR in routine \n");
sum = zero;
for (i =1; i <= num; ++i) { /* calculate the new means */
  sum = sum + X(i,dep_var);
}
NMEANS(dep_var) = sum/(double)num;
dep_var = dep_var +1;
if (dep_var > m) dep_var =1;
}
/* now check for the termination criterion */
terminate = TRUE;
for (j =1; j <= m; ++j) {
  tmp = FABS(MEANS(j)-NMEANS(j));
  if (tmp > tol) {
    terminate = FALSE;
  }
}
for (j =1; j <= m; ++j) {
  MEANS(j) = NMEANS(j);
}
if (terminate) printf ("Stop iterating /n");
count = count +1;
  }
}
```

Code excerpt 13.1   Function *MREG*, which uses iterative multiple linear regression to fill in missing values

13.3   THE *EM* ALGORITHM

The *EM* algorithm is an iterative method and involves both an *Estimation step (or E-step)* and a *Prediction step*, also known as a *Maximum likelihood step (or M-step)*, see Dempster *et al.* (1977) and Little and Rubin (1987).

Here we assume that the incomplete $n \times p$ data matrix has been generated by a p variate normal distribution and we would like to estimate the mean and covariance matrix of this distribution. Code excerpt 13.2 provides an implementation of the *EM* algorithm which uses a one-pass updating technique for both the mean and covariance matrix, see West (1979) and Chan *et al.* (1982).

The steps are explained below.

The estimation step

Here we estimate the sample mean $\tilde{X}$ (also denoted μ), and sample covariance matrix $\tilde{\Sigma}$ using the current sample data values. The estimates, of the mean, sum of squares about the mean, and the covariance matrix, based on the first i observations are denoted by $\bar{X}_{[i]}$, $S^2_{[i]}$ and $P_{[i]}$ respectively.

The updating equations, see Appendix F.5, for these quantities are, for the mean

$$\bar{X}_{[i]} = \bar{X}_{[i-1]} + \frac{1}{i} \left(X_i - \bar{X}_{[i-1]} \right) \qquad (13.1)$$

the sum of squares about the mean is updated as

$$S^2_{[i]} = S^2_{[i-1]} + \left(\frac{i-1}{i}\right)(X_i - \bar{X}_{[i-1]})(X_i - \bar{X}_{[i-1]}) \tag{13.2}$$

and the sum of cross products about the mean is updated as

$$P_{[i]} = P_{[i-1]} + \left(\frac{i-1}{i}\right)(X_i - \bar{X}_{[i-1]})(Y_i - \bar{Y}_{[i-1]}) \tag{13.3}$$

The estimated covariance matrix $\tilde{\Sigma}$, based on the first i observations, is then obtained using

$$\tilde{\Sigma} = \frac{P_{[i]}}{i-1} \tag{13.4}$$

The prediction step

For each vector X_j with missing values let $x_j^{(1)}$ denote the missing components and $x_j^{(2)}$ denote those components which are known. Thus we have: $X_j = [x_j^{(1)}, x_j^{(2)}]$ and $\mu = [\mu_j^{(1)}, \mu_j^{(2)}]$. Given the estimates $\tilde{\mu}$ and $\tilde{\Sigma}$ from the E-step we use the mean of the conditional normal distribution of $x^{(1)}$, given $x^{(2)}$, to predict the missing values. That is:

$$\tilde{x}_j^{(1)} = E(x_j^{(1)}|x_j^{(2)}; \tilde{\mu}, \tilde{\Sigma}) = \tilde{\mu}^{(1)} + \tilde{\Sigma}_{12}\tilde{\Sigma}_{22}^{-1}(x_j^{(2)} - \tilde{\mu}^{(2)}) \tag{13.5}$$

In Equation 13.5 we have used the result, see Appendix E, that if:

$$X_j \sim N(\mu, \Sigma)$$

with $\mu = \mu^{(1)}/\mu^{(2)}$ and $\Sigma = (\Sigma_{11}|\Sigma_{12})/(\Sigma_{21}|\Sigma_{22})$, and $|\Sigma_{22}| > 0$ then:

$$x_j^{(1)} \sim N(\mu', \Sigma')$$

where

$$\mu' = \mu^{(1)} + \Sigma_{12}\Sigma_{22}^{-1}(x^{(2)} - \mu^{(2)})$$

and

$$\Sigma' = \Sigma_{11} - \Sigma_{12}\Sigma_{22}^{-1}\Sigma_{21}$$

It can thus be seen that the covariance matrix does not depend on the value of the conditioning variable, $x^{(2)}$.

```
void EM(double x[], long num, long m, double tol, long max_cycle, long *iflag)
{
  long l_count, i, j, k, l, p, q;
  double zero =0.0;
  double fac, loc_tol, tmp, tmp1, tmp2, sum;
  double *wx, *nmeans, *means, *xmeans, *sigma, *nsigma, *sigma_kk, *sigma_uu, *sigma_ku;
  double *work_mat, *xsigma, *work_vec;
```

```
long row_ptr, col_ptr, ii, num_missing, id;
double d1;
long *missing_index, *known_index, n_missing, n_known, count, ind, *missing_row, *missing_column;
NagError loc_fail;
Boolean terminate;

/* define for easy referencing of vectors and matrices */
#define MISSING_INDEX(I) missing_index[(I)-1]
#define MISSING_ROW(I) missing_row[(I)-1]
  .  .  .
#define SIGMA_UU(I,J) sigma_uu[((I)-1) * m + ((J)-1)]

/* Allocate arrays: sigma(m*m), nsigma(m*m), sigma_kk(m*m), sigma_uu(m*m), means(m), nmeans(m),
   work_mat(m*m), work_vec(m), missing_index(m), known_index(m) */
/* initial processing of the missing data set all missing values to the variable means */
num_missing = 0;
for (j = 1; j <= m; ++j) {
  sum = zero;
  count = 0;
  for (i = 1; i <= num; ++i) {
    if (X(i,j) != -999.0) {
      sum = sum + X(i,j);
      ++count;
    }
    else {
      ++num_missing;
    }
  }
  MEANS(j) = sum/(double)count; /* calculate the overall means */
}
/* Allocate arrays: missing_row(num_missing+1), missing_column (num_missing+1) */
/* Set the indices for the missing values */
num_missing = 0;
for (i = 1; i <= num; ++i) {
  for (j = 1; j <= m; ++j) {
    if (X(i,j) == -999.0) {
      ++num_missing;
      MISSING_ROW(num_missing) = i;
      MISSING_COLUMN(num_missing) = j;
      X(i,j) = MEANS(j);
    }
    else {
      X(i,j) = X(i,j);
    }
  }
}
/* Initialise data matrix */
row_ptr = 1;
col_ptr = 1;
for (i = 1; i <= num; ++i) { /* Set missing values to the appropriate variate mean */
  while ((row_ptr <= num_missing) && (MISSING_ROW(row_ptr) == i)) {
    j = MISSING_COLUMN(col_ptr);
    X(i,j) = MEANS(j);
    ++row_ptr;
    ++col_ptr;
  }
}
for (i = 1; i <= m; ++i) {
  for (j = 1; j <= m; ++j) {
    SIGMA(i,j) = zero;
  }
}
for (i = 1; i <= m; ++i) { /* Estimate the initial matrix SIGMA */
  for (j = 1; j <= m; ++j) {
    tmp1 = zero;
    for (k = 1; k <= num; ++k) {
      SIGMA(i,j) = SIGMA(i,j) + (X(k,i) - MEANS(i)) * (X(k,j) - MEANS(j));
    }
    SIGMA(i,j) = (SIGMA(i,j)/(double)(num));
  }
}
count = 0;
terminate = FALSE;
loc_tol = 1.0e-8;
while ((!terminate) && (count <= max_cycle)) { /* Outer cycle loop */
  for (j = 1; j <= m; ++j) { /* initialize NMEANS */
```

```
      NMEANS(j) = zero;
   }
/* Initialize NSIGMA, it will be used to provide an estimate for a new value of SIGMA,
   based on West's updating method */
for (i = 1; i <=m; ++i){
   for (j = 1; j <=m; ++j){
     NSIGMA(i,j) = zero;
   }
}
row_ptr = 1;
col_ptr = 1;
for (ii = 1; ii <= num; ++ii) { /* Loop over all observations */
   n_missing = 0;
   n_known = 0;
   while ((row_ptr <= num_missing) && (MISSING_ROW(row_ptr) == ii)){
     j = MISSING_COLUMN(col_ptr);
     ++row_ptr;
     ++col_ptr;
     ++n_missing;
     MISSING_INDEX(n_missing) = j;
   }
   k = 1;
   for (j = 1; j <=m; ++j){
     if ((k <=n_missing) && (MISSING_INDEX(k) == j)){
       ++k;
     }
     else {
       ++n_known;
       KNOWN_INDEX(n_known) = j;
     }
   }
   if (n_missing > 0) { /* Are there missing values? */

     if (n_missing == m) { /* deal with the special case in which all the observation is missing */
       for (i = 1; i <= m; ++i){
         X(ii,i) = MEANS(i);
       }
     }
     else { /* Form the partial covariance matrices SIGMA_UU, SIGMA_KK and SIGMA_KU */
       for (i = 1; i <= n_missing; ++i) { /* SIGMA_UU */
         p = MISSING_INDEX(i);
         for (j = 1; j <= n_missing; ++j){
           q = MISSING_INDEX(j);
           SIGMA_UU(i,j) = SIGMA(p,q);
         }
       }
       for (i = 1; i <= n_known; ++i) { /* SIGMA_KK */
         p = KNOWN_INDEX(i);
         for (j = 1; j <= n_known; ++j){
           q = KNOWN_INDEX(j);
           SIGMA_KK(i,j) = SIGMA(p,q);
         }
       }
       for (i = 1; i <= n_known; ++i) { /* SIGMA_KU */
         p= KNOWN_INDEX(i);
         for (j = 1; j <= n_missing; ++j){
           q= MISSING_INDEX(j);
           SIGMA_KU(i,j) = SIGMA(p,q);
         }
       }
       /* Obtain INVERSE(SIGMA_KK) * SIGMA_KU by solving SIGMA _KK * X = SIGMA_KU */
       /* Can use cholseky factorisation since SIGMA_KK is positive definite */
       f03aec (n_known, &SIGMA_KK(1,1), m, &WORK_VEC(1), &d1, &id, &loc_fail);
       if (loc_fail.code != NE_NOERROR){
         printf ("Cholesky factorisation error /n");
         return;
       }
       else { /* solve the equation */
         f04agc(n_known, n_missing, &SIGMA_KK(1,1), m, &WORK_VEC(1),
               &SIGMA_KU(1,1), m, &WORK_MAT(1,1), m, &loc_fail);
       }
       /* Predict the mean values of the missing data in the current observation */
       /* These values are stored in the array WORK_VEC */
       for (i = 1; i <= n_missing; ++i){
         WORK_VEC(i) = zero;
         sum = zero;
```

```
      for (k = 1; k <= n_known; ++k){
        p = KNOWN_INDEX(k);
        sum = sum + WORK_MAT(k,i) * (X(ii,p) - MEANS(p));
      }
      q = MISSING_INDEX(i);
      WORK_VEC(i) = MEANS(q) + sum;
      X(ii,q) = WORK_VEC(i); /* store the new estimates */
    }
  }/* end of else clause */
}/* end of n_missing > 0 clause */
/* Use West's (1979) algorithm to update the means and predicted the covariance terms corresponding
    to the cross product X_U * X_K^T in NSIGMA (Use West's (1979) algorithm) */
fac = (double)(ii - 1)/(double)ii;
fac = fac/(double)num;
for (i = 1; i <= n_missing; ++i){
  p = MISSING_INDEX(i);
  for (j = 1; j <= n_missing; ++j){
    q = MISSING_INDEX(j);
    NSIGMA(p,q) = NSIGMA(p,q) + (X(ii,p) - NMEANS(p)) * (X (ii,q) - NMEANS(q))*fac;
  }
}
for (i = 1; i <= n_missing; ++i){
  p = MISSING_INDEX(i);
  for (j = 1; j <= n_known; ++j){
    q = KNOWN_INDEX(j);
    NSIGMA(p,q) = NSIGMA(p,q) + (X(ii,p) - NMEANS(p)) * (X (ii,q) - NMEANS(q))*fac;
  }
}
for (i = 1; i <= n_missing; ++i){
  p = MISSING_INDEX(i);
  for (j = 1; j <= n_known; ++j){
    q = KNOWN_INDEX(j);
    NSIGMA(q,p) = NSIGMA(p,q);
  }
}
/* Now update the covariance matrix using the known values, using West's (1979) algorithm. */
for (i = 1; i <= n_known; ++i){
  p = KNOWN_INDEX(i);
  for (j = 1; j <= n_known; ++j){
    q = KNOWN_INDEX(j);
    NSIGMA(p,q) = NSIGMA(p,q) +(X(ii,p) - NMEANS(p)) * (X (ii,q) - NMEANS(q))*fac;
  }
}
for (j = 1; j <= n_missing; ++j){
  l = MISSING_INDEX(j);
  NMEANS(l) = NMEANS(l) + ((X(ii,l) - NMEANS(l))/ (double )ii);
}
for (j = 1; j <= n_known; ++j){
  l = KNOWN_INDEX(j);
  NMEANS(l) = NMEANS(l) + ((X(ii,l) - NMEANS(l))/ (double)ii);
}
}/* end of the observation loop (ii) */

/* Now check for the termination criterion */
terminate = TRUE;
for (j = 1; j <= m; ++j){
  tmp = FABS(MEANS(j) - NMEANS(j));
  if (tmp > tol){
    terminate = FALSE;
  }
}
/* get ready for the next iteration through the data */
for (j = 1; j <= m; ++j){
  MEANS(j) = NMEANS(j);
}
for (i = 1; i <= m; ++i){
  for (j = 1; j <= m; ++j){
    SIGMA(i,j) = NSIGMA(i,j);
  }
}
if (terminate) printf ("will terminate /n");
count = count + 1;
}  /* count loop */
}
```

Code excerpt 13.2   Function which uses the *EM* algorithm to fill in missing values

To test the accuracy of the missing data algorithms we generate sample data with known mean μ^s and known covariance matrix C^s. We then remove, at random, a given percentage of the data, and try to reconstruct the original data using either the *EM* algorithm or function *MREG*, which uses iterative multiple linear regression. If $\bar{C}^s$ is the sample covariance matrix of the reconstructed data then the quality of this estimate can be quantified using the following distance:

$$D^* = \left\{ \sum_{i=1}^{p} \sum_{j=1}^{p} (C_{ij}^s - \bar{C}_{i,j}^s)^2 \right\}^{1/2} \tag{13.6}$$

or in more compact notation:

$$D^* = ||C^s - \bar{C}^s|| \tag{13.7}$$

The sample data was generated from a normal distribution with mean μ and covariance matrix C given by:

$$C_{ij} = \frac{i \times j}{10}, \quad i = 1, \ldots, p, \text{ for } i \neq j \tag{13.8}$$

$$C_{ii} = 1.1i, \quad i = 1, \ldots, p \tag{13.9}$$

and let the variate means be defined by:

$$\mu_i = 2i, \quad i = 1, \ldots, p \tag{13.10}$$

Inspection of the results in Tables 13.1 to 13.3 shows that the time taken by the *EM* algorithm increases as the amount of missing data is raised from 5 per cent to 25 per cent; this is in contrast to the time taken by *MREG* which is almost

Table 13.1   Five per cent of the data is missing at random. A comparison of the accuracy of the estimated covariance matrix computed using the *EM* algorithm, given in Code excerpt 13.2, algorithm and the function *MREG*, given in Code excerpt 13.1. The n observations were generated from a multivariate normal distribution $N(\mu, C)$, with μ and C obtained from Equations 13.8 to 13.10, with $p = 8$. The computational time is measured in milliseconds and the quality of estimation, D^*, is defined by Equation 13.6

	MREG		*EM*	
n	Time (ms)	Distance, D^*	Time (ms)	Distance, D^*
100	80	0.6528	30	0.6980
400	100	0.6293	60	0.7306
5000	2523	0.6193	540	0.6404
10000	5448	0.6299	1031	0.6642
100000	5561	0.6394	9674	0.6990
300000	165157	0.6396	26758	0.7048

Table 13.2   Ten per cent of the data is missing at random. A comparison of the accuracy of the estimated covariance matrix computed using the *EM* algorithm, given in Code excerpt 13.2, and the function *MREG*, given in Code excerpt 13.1. The *n* observations were generated from a multivariate normal distribution $N(\mu, C)$, with μ and C obtained from Equations 13.8 to 13.10, with $p = 8$. The computational time is measured in milliseconds and the quality of estimation, D^*, is defined by Equation 13.6

	MREG		*EM*	
n	Time (ms)	Distance, D^*	Time (ms)	Distance, D^*
100	50	1.8500	50	1.7981
400	80	0.9742	100	1.1453
5000	2503	1.0006	871	1.0819
10000	5377	1.0120	1422	1.0814
100000	56141	1.0184	12969	1.0901
300000	164887	1.0165	38885	1.0906

Table 13.3   Twenty per cent of the data is missing at random. A comparison of the accuracy of the estimated covariance matrix computed using the *EM* algorithm, given in Code excerpt 13.2, and the function *MREG*, given in Code excerpt 13.1. The *n* observations were generated from a multivariate normal distribution $N(\mu, C)$, with μ and C obtained from Equations 13.8 to 13.10, with $p = 8$. The computational time is measured in milliseconds and the quality of estimation, D^*, is defined by Equation 13.6

	MREG		*EM*	
n	Time (ms)	Distance, D^*	Time (ms)	Distance, D^*
100	30	2.3360	50	2.6281
400	80	1.7587	120	1.6857
5000	2924	1.7648	1191	1.6113
10000	6329	1.7600	2233	1.5871
100000	65454	1.734	18407	1.5729
300000	195611	1.7587	48369	1.5703

independent of the amount of missing data. It can be seen that, for less than 400 observations, the performance of *MREG* is similar to that of the *EM* algorithm. However, as the number of observations is increased the speed of *MREG* decreases dramatically; although the accuracy of achieved is still similar to that obtained by the *EM* algorithm.

Part III

Financial Econometrics

Chapter 14

Introduction

Here we are concerned with modelling financial *returns*, see Section 14.1, which are generated from share prices, stock market indices, or currency exchange rates.

Here we describe the financial returns data using regression-based models of the form:

$$y_i = X_i^T \beta + \epsilon_i, \quad i = 1, \ldots, n \tag{14.1}$$

where n is the length of the time series, y_i is the ith return, X_i is a vector of size k, β is a vector of k regression coefficients and ϵ_i are the residuals. The variance σ_i^2 of the ith residual is thus given by $\sigma_i^2 = E[\epsilon_i^2]$. In finance literature the term *volatility* depends on context, and refers either to the variance σ_i^2 or the standard deviation σ_i. Equation 14.1 looks deceptively simple and it hides the fact that we are really interested in determining the characteristics of ϵ_i so that we can model the volatility.

Empirical studies suggest that financial returns have the following characteristics:

(i) Large returns occur more frequently than expected for a Gaussian distribution. This means that the *unconditional* probability distribution for ϵ_i has fatter tails (and therefore a larger unconditional kurtosis) than that of a Gaussian distribution.

(ii) The variance (volatility) of the returns exhibit clustering. There are periods of high volatility separated by regions of low volatility.

(iii) When *bad news* occurs it is often followed by high volatility. That is negative stock market returns are usually followed by high volatility. For exchange rate returns data it is not clear what constitutes bad news, since a large fall in the exchange rate may be good or bad depending on your point of view.

(iv) In stock market data large negative returns (corresponding to bad news) occur more frequently than large positive returns. This means that the unconditional probability distribution of ϵ_i is asymmetric about zero, and the probabilities on the negative side of the distribution are higher than the probabilities on the positive side. This asymmetry can be measured in terms of *skewness*. We thus state that stock market data has been found to exhibit negative skewness. Again there is no reason why exchange rate returns should have any particular sign associated with the skewness.

In this part of the book we show how points (i) to (iv) can be modelled by using symmetric and assymmetric **GARCH** models with the conditional probability distribution of the residuals, ϵ_i, having a Gaussian distribution with time varying conditional variance h_i. The standardized residuals $\mathcal{Z}_i = \epsilon_i/\sqrt{h_i}$ should then be distributed as *NID*(0, 1), and so have a kurtosis of 3. However, it has also been found that the standardized residuals are non-Gaussian and so other conditional probability distributions for the residuals such as the Student's *t* distribution and the Generalized Error distribution are also considered.

Estimates of return volatility are used to assess the level of risk associated with many financial products. Accurate measures and reliable forecasts of volatility are crucial for option pricing techniques as well as trading and hedging strategies that arise in portfolio allocation problems.

We assume minimal prior knowledge of statistics and aim to provide mathematical details and proofs that may be taken for granted or omitted from more advanced econometric literature. This is especially the case for the information provided concerning the properties of various statistical distributions. Here the expected values of the distribution are derived from first principles using integration, rather than the more usual approach of either quoting standard results or using moment generating functions. Here we concentrate on standard linear and nonlinear univariate GARCH processes. However, information is also provided concerning other models such as component GARCH, stochastic volatility models and Levy processes. The testing of GARCH software is covered and comprehensive information is supplied concerning the calculation of the first and second order derivatives of the log likelihood function.

Before embarking on a detailed study of time series methods and applications to forecast the volatility of financial assets we will quote from a recent article by Granger (2002). There reference is made to a survey of 40 papers which compare the forecasting ability of techniques such as: historical and implied volatility (see Part II Section 9.3.4), stochastic volatility (SV), and GARCH. It is stated that:

1. Five papers find that GARCH beats HISTORICAL.
2. Five papers find that HISTORICAL beats GARCH.
3. Only three papers consider SV forecasts; one finds SV better than GARCH, one finds GARCH better than SV, and a third paper finds SV better that GARCH for stocks but the reverse for currencies.
4. Thirteen papers compare IMPLIED with HISTORICAL, with twelve preferring IMPLIED.
5. Fourteen papers compare IMPLIED with GARCH; all but one find that IMPLIED provides better forecasts. One paper also finds that IMPLIED performs better than SV.

Granger concludes that:

Overall, IMPLIED seems to be the superior technique with GARCH and HISTORICAL roughly equal second. The result is not really surprising as the IMPLIED forecasts are based on a wider information set than the alternatives, not just depending on the past returns but also on using option prices. On the other hand, suitable options may not always be available and so *these forecasts cannot be used on many occasions*.

14.1 ASSET RETURNS

The return can be defined in several different ways.

If we let P_t denote the price (or index) at time t, and for simplicity assume a series of n values $P_t, t = 1, \ldots, n$ in which the sampling period is the unit time interval, then the *Simple net return*, $\mathcal{R}_t$, between instant $t-1$ and instant t, is:

$$SR_t = \frac{P_t - P_{t-1}}{P_{t-1}} = \frac{P_t}{P_{t-1}} - 1 \tag{14.2}$$

the *Gross return*, R_t, is defined as:

$$R_t = \frac{P_t}{P_{t-1}} \tag{14.3}$$

The gross return compounded over k periods takes the form:

$$R_t(k) = \frac{P_{t+k}}{P_{t-1}} = \left(\frac{P_t}{P_{t-1}}\right)\left(\frac{P_{t+1}}{P_t}\right)\left(\frac{P_{t+2}}{P_{t+1}}\right) \cdots \left(\frac{P_{t+k-1}}{P_{t+k-2}}\right)\left(\frac{P_{t+k}}{P_{t+k-1}}\right)$$

An alternative approach is to use the continuously compounded returns (or logarithmic returns). This is defined using:

$$r_t = \log\left(\frac{P_t}{P_{t-1}}\right) = \log(P_t) - \log(P_{t-1}) \tag{14.4}$$

where log denotes the natural logarithm.

The return compounded over k periods is:

$$r_t(k) = \log(P_{t+k}) - \log(P_{t-1})$$
$$= \log(P_{t+k}) - \log(P_{t+k-1}) + \log(P_{t+k-1}) - \cdots + \log(P_t) - \log(P_{t-1})$$
$$r_t(k) = r_t + r_{t+1} + \cdots + r_{t+k-1} + r_{t+k} \tag{14.5}$$

Thus unlike multiperiod gross compounding which is a multiplicative process, multiperiod continuous compounding is additive.

We also note that:

$$\log(x) = (x - 1) - \frac{1}{2}(x - 1)^2 \cdots \quad \text{for } 2 \geq x > 0$$

and therefore $\log(x) \sim x$ when $x \sim 1$.

Since $(P_t)/(P_{t-1}) \sim 1$, Equations 14.2 and 14.4 give: $r_t \sim \mathcal{R}_t$. This means that the simple net return is virtually the same as the logarithmic return. It may also be convenient to create a scaled return series using:

$$r_t = \phi\{\log(P_t) - \log(P_{t-1})\} \tag{14.6}$$

where ϕ is the scale factor. When $\phi = 100$ the series gives the percentage logarithm returns.

If dividend payments, D_t, are included then Equation 14.4 takes the form:

$$r_t = \log\left(\frac{P_t + D_t}{P_t}\right) \tag{14.7}$$

This can be re-expressed using the following steps:

$$r_t = \log(P_t) - \log(P_{t-1}) + \log(P_t + D_t) - \log(P_t)$$

$$r_t = \log(P_t) - \log(P_{t-1}) + \log\left(1 + \frac{D_t}{P_t}\right)$$

$$r_t = p_t - p_{t-1} + \log(1 + \exp(d_t - p_t)) \tag{14.8}$$

where $p_t = \log(P_t)$ and $d_t = \log(D_t)$. Equation 14.7 is a nonlinear function of the logarithm of the dividend to price ratio, $\lambda_t = \log(D_t/P_t)$. If we linearize about the mean value of λ_t, $\bar{\lambda}$, we then obtain:

$$r_t = k + \rho\, p_t + (1 - \rho)\, d_t - p_{t-1} \tag{14.9}$$

where

$$\rho = \frac{1}{1 + \exp(\bar{\lambda})} \quad \text{and} \quad k = -\log(\rho) - (1 - \rho)\left\{\log\left(\frac{1}{\rho} - 1\right)\right\}$$

It can be seen that the returns r_t are computed using a weighted sum of the logarithm of stock price and the logarithm of the dividend. Empirical studies, see Campbell *et al.* (1997), have found that ρ is about 0.96, which means that nearly all of the contribution to the value of returns is from the stock price.

Proof of Equation 14.9

Since $\lambda_t = d_t - p_t$ we have from Equation 14.8 that:

$$r_t = p_t - p_{t-1} + f(\lambda_t) \tag{14.10}$$

where $f(\lambda_t) = \log(1 + \exp(\lambda_t))$.

Using a Taylor expansion about the mean value $\bar{\lambda}$ we have:

$$f(\lambda_t) = f(\bar{\lambda}) + f'(\bar{\lambda})(\lambda_t - \bar{\lambda}) \tag{14.11}$$

Now from elementary calculus we have:

$$f'(\bar{\lambda}) = \frac{\exp(\bar{\lambda})}{1 + \exp(\bar{\lambda})}$$

Substituting into Equation 14.11 we obtain:

$$f(\lambda_t) = f(\bar{\lambda}) + \frac{\exp(\bar{\lambda})}{1 + \exp(\bar{\lambda})}(\lambda_t - \bar{\lambda}) \tag{14.12}$$

letting $\rho = \dfrac{1}{1 + \exp(\bar{\lambda})}$ we have:

$$\log(1 + \exp(\bar{\lambda})) = -\log(\rho), \quad \exp(\bar{\lambda}) = \left(\frac{1}{\rho} - 1\right) \text{ and } \bar{\lambda} = \log\left(\frac{1}{\rho} - 1\right)$$

Therefore Equation 14.11 gives:

$$f(\lambda_t) = -\log(\rho) + \left(\frac{1}{\rho} - 1\right)\rho(\lambda_t - \bar{\lambda})$$

$$f(\lambda_t) = -\log(\rho) + (1 - \rho)\lambda_t - (1 - \rho)\bar{\lambda}$$

Substituting into Equation 14.10 we have:

$$r_t = p_t - p_{t-1} - \log(\rho) + (1 - \rho)\lambda_t - (1 - \rho)\bar{\lambda}$$

subsituting for $\bar{\lambda}$

$$r_t = -\log(\rho) - (1 - \rho)\left\{\log\left(\frac{1}{\rho} - 1\right)\right\} - p_{t-1} + (1 - \rho)d_t + \rho p_t$$

which gives

$$r_t = k + \rho\, p_t + (1 - \rho)d_t - p_{t-1} \qquad QED$$

where

$$k = -\log(\rho) - (1 - \rho)\left\{\log\left(\frac{1}{\rho} - 1\right)\right\}$$

Empirical studies have shown that in many instances the logarithm of dividend to price ratio, D_t/P_t, can be taken as a constant, and in these circumstances we have $\lambda_t = \lambda, t = 1, \ldots, n$; where λ is a constant.

14.2 NONSYNCHRONOUS TRADING

The nonsynchronous trading effect arises when data is assumed to be recorded at certain times when in fact it is collected at other times. As an example the daily closing security prices, which give the last transaction price for each security on the previous day, do not occur at the same time each day. By referring to these values as *daily* closing prices we incorrectly assume that they occur at equally spaced 24 hour time intervals. As another example consider two stocks A and B, whose prices are independent but stock A trades less frequently than B. If stock market news arrives near the close of trade it is more likely to be reflected in the closing price of stock B than that of stock A; this is because stock A may not trade after the arrival of the information. The fact that stock A will respond to the new information after a significant time lag can induce spurious correlations between the daily returns of stocks A and B, if these are based on daily closing prices. This lagged response can also induce negative autocorrelations in the daily returns of A. This is because when A is not trading its observed return is zero, and when it does trade its returns revert to the cumulated mean return.

Lo and MacKinlay (1990) have developed a nonsynchronous trading model which captures these effects. It is assumed that a security has in each time period t an unobserved or virtual continuously compounded return r_t. These virtual returns represent the changes in the *true* underlying value of the security; they reflect changes in value caused by both company information and general stock market information.

We suppose that at each time period there is the probability γ that the security does not trade; the probability that the security trades is then $(1 - \gamma)$. The observed return, r_t^o, depends on whether the security trades or not. If the security does not trade in period t then $r_t^o = \log(P_t/P_{t-1}) = \log(1) = 0$. If on the other hand the security trades in period t, its observed return is taken as the sum of the virtual returns in period t and all previous consecutive periods in which the security did not trade.

For example consider a sequence of six consecutive time periods in which the security trades in periods 1, 2, and 6, but does not trade in periods 3, 4, and 5. The nontrading model implies that the observed return in period 2 is the virtual return, $r_2^o = r_2$, the observed return in periods 3, 4, and 5 are zero, $r_3^o = r_4^o = r_5^o = 0$, and the observed return in period 6 is the sum of the virtual returns from periods 3 to 6, $r_6^o = r_3 + r_4 + r_5 + r_6$. Here the impact of news is captured in the virtual returns process and the lag caused by nontrading is modelled in the observed returns process r_t^o. We will now define the variable k_t which is the number of past consecutive periods, at time t, for which the asset has not been traded. The mean and variance of k_t are related to the nontrading probability, γ, in the following manner:

$$E[k_t] = \frac{\gamma}{1-\gamma}, \quad \text{Var}[k_t] = \frac{\gamma}{(1-\gamma)^2} \tag{14.13}$$

Proof of Equation 14.13
First we will prove the equation for the mean.

$$E[k_t] = 0(1-\gamma) + (1-\gamma)\gamma + 2(1-\gamma)\gamma^2 + 3(1-\gamma)\gamma^3 + 4(1-\gamma)\gamma^4 + \cdots$$

$$E[k_t] = (1-\gamma)(\gamma + 2\gamma^2 + 3\gamma^3 + 4\gamma^4 + 5\gamma^5 + \cdots) \tag{14.14}$$

$$= \gamma + 2\gamma^2 + 3\gamma^3 + 4\gamma^4 + 5\gamma^5 - \gamma^2 - 2\gamma^3 - 3\gamma^4 - 4\gamma^5 - \cdots$$

$$E[k_t] = \gamma + \gamma^2 + \gamma^3 + \gamma^4 + \gamma^5 + \cdots \tag{14.15}$$

This is a Geometric Progression with first term γ and common ratio γ, therefore:

$$E[k_t] = \sum_{j=1}^{\infty} \gamma^j = \frac{\gamma}{1-\gamma} \quad QED$$

Now we consider the equation for the variance of k_t.

$$\text{Var}[k_t] = E[k_t^2] - (E[k_t])^2 \tag{14.16}$$

$$E[k_t^2] = 0(1-\gamma) + (1-\gamma)\gamma + 4(1-\gamma)\gamma^2 + 9(1-\gamma)\gamma^3 + 16(1-\gamma)\gamma^4$$
$$\quad + 25(1-\gamma)\gamma^5 + \cdots$$
$$= (1-\gamma)\{\gamma + 4\gamma^2 + 9\gamma^3 + 16\gamma^4 + 25\gamma^5 + \cdots\}$$
$$= \gamma + 4\gamma^2 + 9\gamma^3 + 16\gamma^4 + 25\gamma^5 + \cdots - \gamma^2 - 4\gamma^3 - 9\gamma^4 - 16\gamma^5 - \cdots$$
$$E[k_t^2] = \gamma + 3\gamma^2 + 5\gamma^3 + 7\gamma^4 + 9\gamma^5 + \cdots$$

Now from Equation 14.15 we have

$$(E[k_t])^2 = (\gamma + \gamma^2 + \gamma^3 + \gamma^4 + \gamma^5 + \cdots)^2 = \gamma^2 + 2\gamma^3 + 3\gamma^4 + 4\gamma^5 + \cdots$$

So substituting into Equation 14.16

$$\text{Var}[k_t] = \gamma + 3\gamma^2 + 5\gamma^3 + 7\gamma^4 + 9\gamma^5 + \cdots - \gamma^2 - 2\gamma^3 - 3\gamma^4 - 4\gamma^5 - \cdots$$
$$\text{Var}[k_t] = \gamma + 2\gamma^2 + 3\gamma^3 + 4\gamma^4 + 5\gamma^5 + \cdots \tag{14.17}$$

From Equations 14.14 and 14.13 we have:

$$E[k_t] = \frac{\gamma}{1-\gamma} = (1-\gamma)(\gamma + 2\gamma^2 + 3\gamma^3 + 4\gamma^5 + \cdots) \tag{14.18}$$

which means that Equation 14.17 can be written as:

$$Var[k_t] = \frac{\gamma}{(1-\gamma)^2} \qquad QED$$

Substituting into Equation 14.13 we find that if $\gamma = 0.75$ then the average number of consecutive periods of nontrading is three. If the asset trades on every period then $\gamma = 0$ and both the mean and variance of k_t are zero.

Lo and MacKinlay (1990) consider a virtual returns process of the form:

$$r_t = \mu + \epsilon_t \tag{14.19}$$

where μ is a constant drift term, ϵ_t is zero mean IID noise. In this case:

$$E[r_t^o] = \mu \qquad Var[r_t^o] \; y = \sigma^2 + \frac{2\gamma}{1-\gamma}\mu^2 \tag{14.20}$$

and

$$Corr[r_t^o \; r_{t+n}^o] = \frac{-\mu^2\gamma^n}{\sigma^2 + g\mu^2}, \quad n > 0 \tag{14.21}$$

where $\sigma^2 = Var[r_t]$ and $g = 2\gamma/(1-\gamma)$.

We thus conclude that nontrading does not affect the mean of the observed returns. However, if the expected return of the security is nonzero, then nontrading increases the observed variance of the security returns, and also induces negative serial correlation in the returns.

14.3 BID-ASK SPREAD

The presence of the bid-ask spread means that instead of one price for each asset there are now three: the bid price, the ask price and the actual transaction price which need not be either the bid or ask price. To account for the impact of the bid-ask spread Roll (1984) proposed the following model:

$$P_t = P_t^* + I_t \frac{s}{2} \tag{14.22}$$

where P_t is the observed asset price at time t, P_t^* is the *true* asset price, s is the bid-ask spread, and the IID indicator variable I_t which takes the value $+1$ with probability 0.5 (to signify a buyer initiated bid) and the value -1 with probability 0.5 to indicate a seller initiated ask.

The assumption that P_t^* is the *true* value of the security implies that $E[I_t] = 0$, and hence $Pr(I_t = 1) = Pr(I_t = -1) = 0.5$.

If the true security value, P_t^*, does not change with time then the process for the price observed changes is:

$$\Delta P_t = (I_t - I_{t-1})\frac{s}{2} \tag{14.23}$$

which means that:

$$Var[\Delta P_t] = \frac{s^2}{2} \tag{14.24}$$

$$Cov[\Delta P_{t-1}, \Delta P_t] = \frac{-s^2}{4} \tag{14.25}$$

$$Cov[\Delta P_{t-k}, \Delta P_t] = 0, \quad k > 1 \tag{14.26}$$

$$Corr[\Delta P_{t-1}, \Delta P_t] = -\frac{1}{2} \tag{14.27}$$

It can be seen that despite the fact that the true value is fixed ΔP_t has volatility and also negative correlation. This is caused by the bid-ask bounce. The reason for this is as follows: If P_t^* is fixed than the observed price can only take on two values, the bid price and the ask price. If the current price is the ask then the price change between the current price and the previous price must either be zero or s, and the price change between the next price and the current price must either be zero or $-s$; which induces negative covariance. The same is true if the current price is the bid price.

If P_t^* changes with time, and its increments are serially uncorrelated and independent of I_t, then Equation 14.25 still applies. However, Equation 14.27 is no longer true, and the correlation is now given by:

$$Corr[\Delta P_{t-1}, \Delta P_t] = -\frac{s^2/4}{s^2/2 + \sigma_p^2} \tag{14.28}$$

where σ_p^2 is the variance of ΔP_t^*.

The bid-ask spread s can be estimated from the covariance of the price changes using:

$$s = 2\sqrt{-Cov[\Delta P_{t-1}\Delta P_t]} \tag{14.29}$$

Estimating the bid-ask spread in this manner may seem rather strange when it is already available from market data. However, the quoted value can differ from the *effective* value, and in many cases transactions occur at prices within the bid-ask spread. This is because discounts may be given to certain customers, and also, if updating is not frequent enough, the quoted values for s may not be the actual values used.

Roll's model assumes that the value for s is a given constant, and is independent of the value of P_t^*. For a more sophisticated model of the bid-ask spread see Glosten and Milgrom (1985).

14.4   MODELS OF VOLATILITY

In this section we provide a brief overview of two methods that are commonly used to model volatility in finance: stochastic volatility processes and Levy processes. Here we give a short definition of each process. Section 14.5 gives more information on stochastic autoregressive processes and Section 14.6 provides more information on the generalized hyperbolic Levy process.

14.4.1   Stochastic volatility models

A continuous standard Brownian process X can be discretized as:

$$X_t = \mu t + \sigma \epsilon_t, \quad \epsilon_t \sim NID(0, 1) \tag{14.30}$$

where X_t is the value of the Brownian variate at time t, $X_0 = 0$, μ is the constant drift, and σ is the constant volatility.

The stochastic volatility model, see Ghysels *et al.* (1996) and Taylor (1994), which permits a time varying volatility, generalizes Equation 14.30 to:

$$X_t = \mu + \sigma_t \epsilon_t, \quad \epsilon_t \sim NID(0, 1) \tag{14.31}$$

where the time dependent volatility, σ_t, is termed the *stochastic volatility*. We will assume that the process σ_t has no *causal* relationship with the process ϵ_t. Thus it is assumed that the process ϵ_t is not *caused* by the process σ_t, and also that the process ϵ_t does not *cause* the process σ_t.

We will now consider the following two σ_t processes.

1. σ_t is an independent stochastic process

Here we take σ_t to be a stochastic process that is independent of the information set ψ_{t-1}.

An example is the stochastic random autoregressive (ARV) model, which is discussed in Section 14.5.

The general form of an ARV(1) model is:

$$X_t = \mu + \sigma_{t-1} \epsilon_t \tag{14.32}$$

and

$$\log(\sigma_t) = \alpha + \phi \log(\sigma_{t-1}) + \eta_t \tag{14.33}$$

where μ, α and ϕ are constants. The variates ϵ_t and η_t are from an IID bivariate normal distribution with correlation coefficient ρ.

2. σ_t is a deterministic function of the information set ψ_{t-1}

In this case σ_t is a deterministic function of previous process values, contained in the information set ψ_{t-1}.

An example is the generalized autoregressive conditional heteroskeolostic GARCH(p,q) process which is defined as follows:

$$X_t = \mu + \sigma_t \epsilon_t, \quad \epsilon_t \sim NID(0, 1)$$

or equivalently

$$X_t = \mu + \epsilon_t, \quad \epsilon_t \sim NID(0, \sigma_t^2)$$

and

$$\sigma_t^2 = \alpha_0 + \sum_{j=1}^{q} \alpha_j \epsilon_{t-j}^2 + \sum_{j=1}^{p} \beta_j h_{t-j}, \quad t=1,\ldots,n, \quad \epsilon_t|\psi_{t-1} \sim NID(0,\sigma_t^2) \tag{14.34}$$

It can be seen from Equation 14.34 that σ_t^2 is a weighted sum of the previous values of ϵ_t and h_t.

More information on GARCH models can be found in Chapter 15 and the following sections.

14.4.2   Levy processes

In constrast to Brownian motion and stochastic volatility models which describe continuous process, a Levy process X_t consists of discontinuous jumps.

If the first moment is finite then the Levy process can be represented as:

$$X_t = Z_t + \mu t + \sigma \epsilon_t, \quad \epsilon_t \sim NID(0,1) \tag{14.35}$$

where σ is the volatility, μ is a continuous drift term and Z_t is a discontinuous Martingale process, see Part II Section 8.2, independent of ϵ_t.

When the term Z_t in Equation 14.35 is set to zero we obtain the equation for continuous Brownian motion; that is:

$$X_t = \mu t + \sigma \epsilon_t, \quad \epsilon_t \sim NID(0,1) \tag{14.36}$$

We now give a more formal definition of a Levy process. The process X is a Levy process if:

1. X has increments that are independent of the past:

   This means that $X_t - X_s$ is independent of $\mathcal{F}_s, 0 \le s < t < \infty$, where $\mathcal{F}_s$ denotes the history up to time $t = s$.

2. X has stationary increments:

   That is $X_t - X_s$ has the same distribution as $X_{t-s}, 0 \le s < t < \infty$.

3. X is continuous in probability:

   So $X_t \to X_s$ as $t \to s$.

   In Section 14.6 we consider the use of generalized hyperbolic Levy motion to model asset returns.

14.5   STOCHASTIC AUTOREGRESSIVE VOLATILITY, ARV

A popular form of ARV(1) model, see Taylor (1994), is:

$$\log(P_t) = \log(P_{t-1}) + \mu + \sigma_{t-1}\epsilon_t \tag{14.37}$$

and

$$\log(\sigma_t) = \alpha + \phi\{\log(\sigma_{t-1}) - \alpha\} + \theta\eta_t \tag{14.38}$$

where μ, α, ϕ, and θ are constants. The pairs (ϵ_t, η_t) are IID bivariate normal and the standard normal variates ϵ_t and η_t have correlation coefficient ρ. The logarithm of the volatility follows a stationary AR(1) process when $-1 < \phi < 1$.

Since the volatility appears as σ_{t-1} in Equation 14.37 the process is termed a lagged ARV(1) model. Another specification, see Taylor (1986), is:

$$\log(P_t) = \log(P_{t-1}) + \mu + \sigma_t \sum_t \tag{14.39}$$

in which case Equations 14.38 and 14.39 define a *contemporaneous* ARV(1) model.

The stationary ARV(1) has five parameters that need to be estimated: $\mu, \alpha, \phi, \theta$, and ρ. Estimation of the parameter ϕ is of particular interest because it provides information concerning the persistence of the volatility shocks. Various techniques have been used to estimate this parameter, including:

- Moment-matching methods, Taylor (1986).
- The generalized method of moments, Duffie and Singleton (1989) and Melino and Turnbill (1990).
- ARMA techniques, Chesney and Scott (1989) and Scott (1991).
- Maximum-likelihood techniques, Harvey *et al.* (1994).

These studies have shown that the value of ϕ is greater than 0.95; which means that volatility shocks have a high level of persistence.

14.6 GENERALIZED HYPERBOLIC LEVY MOTION

Barndorff-Nielsen (1977) introduced the generalized hyperbolic (*GH*) distribution and used it to model the grain size distributions of wind blown sand. It can be shown, see Barndorff-Nielsen and Halgreen (1977), that the generalized hyperbolic distribution generates a (discontinuous) Levy process with increments of length 1.

The generalized hyperbolic distribution

The one dimensional density function of the generalized hyperbolic (*GH*) distribution is:

$$GH(x) = \mathcal{A} \times (\delta^2 + (x - \mu)^2)^{(\lambda - 1/2)/2}$$
$$\times K_{\lambda - 1/2}\left(\alpha\sqrt{\delta^2 + (x - \mu)^2}\right) \exp\left(\beta(x - \mu)\right) \tag{14.40}$$

where $\alpha > 0$, $0 \geq |\beta| < \alpha$, $\delta > 0$ and

$$\mathcal{A} = \frac{(\alpha^2 - \beta^2)^{\lambda/2}}{\sqrt{2\pi}\alpha^{\lambda - 1/2}\delta^\lambda K_\lambda\left(\delta\sqrt{\alpha^2 - \beta^2}\right)}$$

and K_λ is a modified Bessel function of the third kind with index ν. The integral representation of K_ν is:

$$K_\nu(x) = \frac{1}{2} \int_0^\infty y^{\nu-1} \exp\left(-\frac{1}{2}x(y + y^{-1})\right) dy$$

For $\lambda = n + 1/2, n = 0, 2, \ldots$, the Bessel function K_λ is:

$$K_{n+1}(x) = \frac{\pi}{2} x^{-1/2} \exp(-x) \left(1 + \sum_{i=1}^n \frac{(n+i)!}{(n-i)!i!}(2x)^{-i}\right)$$

Since $K_\lambda(x) = K_{-\lambda}(x)$, and $K_{1/2}(x) = K_{-1/2}(x) = \sqrt{\pi/2}x^{-1/2}\exp(-x)$; which is used below to simplify the expressions for the cases $\lambda = 1$, and $\lambda = -1/2$.

From Equation 14.40 it can easily be shown that the generalized hyperbolic log-likelihood, for n independent observations, $X_i, i = 1, \ldots, n$ is:

$$L = \log(A) + \left(\frac{\lambda}{2} - \frac{1}{4}\right) \sum_{i=1}^n \log\left(\delta^2 + (X_i - \mu)^2\right)$$

$$+ \sum_{i=1}^n \left\{\log\left(K_{\lambda-1/2}\left(\alpha\sqrt{\delta^2 + (X_i - \mu)^2}\right) + \beta(X_i - \mu)\right)\right\} \tag{14.41}$$

The five parameters in the *GH* density $\alpha, \beta, \delta, \mu$, and λ allow much more flexibility in modelling financial data than the Gaussian distribution which only has two parameters μ and σ. Estimates for the parameter values can be obtained by using numerical optimization software to maximize the log-likehood function for a particular set of data values.

The parameter α controls the shape, β the skewness, δ the scaling (similar to σ in the normal distribution), μ the location and λ the heaviness of the tails. The normal distribution is obtained as a limiting case of the generalized hyperbolic distribution for $\delta \to \infty$ and $\delta/\alpha \to \sigma^2$.

The mean of *GH* is:

$$E[X] = \mu + \frac{\beta\delta}{\sqrt{\alpha^2 - \beta^2}} \frac{K_{\lambda+1}(\zeta)}{K_\lambda(\zeta)} \tag{14.42}$$

the variance of *GH* is:

$$Var[X] = \delta^2 \left(\frac{K_{\lambda+1}(\zeta)}{\zeta K_\lambda(\zeta)} + \frac{\beta^2}{\alpha^2 - \beta^2} \left\{\frac{K_{\lambda+2}(\zeta)}{K_\lambda(\zeta)} - \left(\frac{K_{\lambda+1}(\zeta)}{K_\lambda(\zeta)}\right)^2\right\}\right) \tag{14.43}$$

where $\zeta = \delta\sqrt{\alpha^2 - \beta^2}$. The variance term (in large brackets) multiplied by δ^2 is independent of μ and δ.

When the *GH* distribution is centred ($\mu = 0$) and symmetric ($\beta = 0$) then $\zeta = \delta\alpha$, and the mean and variance are simply:

$$E[X] = 0 \text{ and } Var[X] = \frac{\delta}{\alpha} \tag{14.44}$$

We will now consider two cases of special interest, namely when $\lambda = 1$ and when $\lambda = 1/2$.

The hyperbolic distribution

This is the special case when $\lambda = 1$. In these circumstances the generalized hyperbolic distribution (GH) simplifies to the hyperbolic distribution (H) which has density:

$$H(x) = \frac{\sqrt{\alpha^2 - \beta^2}}{2\delta\alpha K_1\left(\delta\sqrt{\alpha^2 - \beta^2}\right)} \exp\left(-\alpha\sqrt{\delta^2 + (x - \mu)^2} + \beta(x - \mu)\right) \qquad (14.45)$$

where $0 \geq \delta$, and $|\beta| < \alpha$.

The normal inverse Gaussian

This is the special case when $\lambda = -1/2$.

In these circumstances the generalized hyperbolic distribution (GH) simplifies to the normal inverse Gaussian distribution (NIG), see Barndorff-Nielsen (1998), which has the density:

$$NIG(x) = \frac{\alpha\delta}{\pi}\exp\left(\delta\sqrt{\alpha^2 - \beta^2} + \beta(x - \mu)\right) \frac{K_1\left(\alpha\sqrt{\delta^2 + (x - \mu)^2}\right)}{\sqrt{\delta^2 + (x - \mu)^2}} \qquad (14.46)$$

where $0 \geq \delta$, and $0 \geq |\beta| \geq \alpha$.

When the skewness parameter β is zero and also the mean value μ is zero, we have the symmetric centred NIG distribution, NIG_{sc}, which has the density:

$$NIG_{sc}(x) = \frac{\alpha\delta}{\pi}\exp(\delta\alpha) \frac{K_1(\alpha\sqrt{\delta^2 + x^2})}{\sqrt{\delta^2 + x^2}} \qquad (14.47)$$

An alternative parameterization of Equation 14.47, see Forsberg and Bollerslev (2002), is:

$$NIG_{sc}(x) = \frac{\alpha^{*1/2}}{\pi\sigma^*}\exp(\alpha^*)q\left(\frac{x}{\sigma^*\alpha^{*1/2}}\right)^{-1} K_1\left(\alpha^* q\left(\frac{x}{\sigma^*\alpha^{*1/2}}\right)\right) \qquad (14.48)$$

where $q(x) = 1/(1 + x^2)$, $\alpha^* = \alpha\delta$, and $\sigma^* = \delta^{1/2}/\alpha^{1/2}$.

We can show this as follows. Substituting for α^* and σ^* into Equation 14.48 we obtain:

$$NIG_{sc}(x) = \frac{\alpha^{1/2}\delta^{1/2}\alpha^{1/2}}{\pi\delta^{1/2}}\exp(\alpha\delta)q\left(\frac{x}{\delta}\right)^{-1} K_1\left(\alpha\delta q\left(\frac{x}{\delta}\right)\right)$$

where we have made use of the fact that $\sigma^*\alpha^{*1/2} = \delta$. Simplifying further we have:

$$NIG_{sc}(x) = \frac{\alpha}{\pi}\exp(\alpha\delta) \frac{1}{\sqrt{1 + x^2/\delta^2}} K_1\left(\alpha\delta\sqrt{1 + x^2/\delta^2}\right)$$

and finally:

$$NIG_{sc}(x) = \frac{y\delta\alpha}{\pi}\exp(\delta\alpha)\frac{K_1\left(\alpha\sqrt{\delta^2 + x^2}\right)}{\sqrt{\delta^2 + x^2}} \qquad QED$$

14.6.1   Modelling asset returns

The empirical distributions of financial returns data show that, compared to the normal distribution, there is: more mass near the origin, less in the flanks and considerably more in the tails. This means that tiny price movements occur with higher frequency, small- and medium-sized movements with lower frequency and big price changes are much more frequent than that predicted by a Gaussian distribution. The generalized hyperbolic distribution allows for an almost perfect statistical match to these empirical distributions, see Prause (1999), Raible (2000), and Eberlein (2001).

If there are n stock prices and they are modelled as:

$$P_i = P_{i-1}\exp(X_i), \quad i = 1,\ldots,n$$

where $X_{i\geq 0}$ is generalized hyperbolic Levy motion, then

$$\log(P_i) - \log(P_{i-1}) = X_i, \quad i = 1,\ldots,n$$

and the five parameters defining the generalized hyperbolic distribution can be estimated by maximizing Equation 14.41; the log-likelihood function.

| GARCH–NIG model |

Although the generalized hyperbolic distribution can adequately capture the fat tailed unconditional distribution of the returns, it does not take into account volatility clustering. In order to take these effects into account, Forsberg and Bollerslev (2002) proposed the following GARCH–*NIG* model.

$$\epsilon_t|\psi_{t-1} \sim NIG_{sc}(\sigma_t^{*2}, \alpha^*) \tag{14.49}$$

$$\sigma_t^{*2} = \alpha_o + \alpha_1\epsilon_{t-1}^2 + \beta_1\sigma_{t-1}^{*\,2} \tag{14.50}$$

where we have written the distribution corresponding to the probability density function $NIG_{sc}(x)$ as $NIG_{sc}(\sigma_t^{*2}, \alpha^*)$ to show the dependence on the parameters σ_t^{*2} and α^*. Equations 14.49 and 14.50 describe a GARCH(1,1) model, see Section 15.2, and the parameters $\alpha_0, \alpha_1, \beta_1$, and α^* can be estimated using maximum likelihood techniques, see Chapter 18.

Chapter 15

GARCH models

In this chapter we discuss the properties of linear GARCH models, in terms of the more fundamental AR and ARMA processes; further details can be found in the Box and Jenkins (1976), Hamilton (1994), and Engle (1995).

15.1 BOX JENKINS MODELS

This approach concerns the modelling of n observations $y_i, i = 1, \ldots, n$ in the presence of white noise $\nu_i, i = 1, \ldots, n$. The aim is to explain any observation y_i in terms of the current noise ν_i and also a weighted linear sum of previous (lagged) observations and noise.

An autoregressive time series model of order p obeys the following equation:

$$y_i = c + \sum_{j=1}^{p} \phi_j y_{i-j} + \nu_i, \quad \text{for } i = 1, \ldots, n \tag{15.1}$$

where the $\phi_j, j = 1, \ldots, p$ are termed the autoregressive coefficients and ν_i is white noise satisfying:

$$E[\nu_i] = 0, \quad E[\nu_i \nu_j] = 0, \quad i \neq j, \quad E[\nu_i^2] = \sigma_0^2 \tag{15.2}$$

Such a process is also denoted as AR(p) and it can be shown that y_i is covariance stationary provided the roots, z^j, of the polynomial,

$$P(z) = 1 - \phi_1 z - \phi_2 z^2 - \cdots - \phi_p z^p = 0 \tag{15.3}$$

all have modulus greater than 1, that is $|z^j| > 1$, for $j = 1, \ldots, p$

If the AR(p) process is covariance stationary then $E[y_i] = \mu$, for all i, where μ is the unconditional mean of the sequence. Taking expectations of Equation 15.1 and using our previous results concerning $E[y_i]$ and $E[\nu_i]$, we have:

$$E[y_i] = c + \sum_{j=1}^{p} \phi_j E[y_{i-j}] + E[\nu_i] \tag{15.4}$$

$$\mu = c + \mu \sum_{j=1}^{p} \phi_j \tag{15.5}$$

We thus have:

The unconditional mean of an AR(p) process is:

$$\mu = c \left\{ 1 - \sum_{j=1}^{p} \phi_j \right\}^{-1}$$

(15.6)

An autoregressive process can be generalized into a autoregressive moving average process by the inclusion of extra lagged terms as follows:

$$y_i = c + \sum_{j=1}^{p} \phi_j y_{i-j} + \sum_{j=1}^{q} \theta_j \nu_{i-j} + \nu_i, \quad \text{for } i = 1, \dots, n$$

(15.7)

where all terms have the same meaning as before and θ_j, $j = 1$, q are called the moving average coefficients.

Such a process is also denoted as ARMA(p,q) and it can be shown that the conditions for y_i to be covariance stationary are the same as those for an AR(p) process. That is the extra q moving average coefficients do not affect the conditions for the process to be covariance stationary. Taking expectations of Equation 15.7, and using our previous results concerning $E[y_i]$ and $E[\nu_i]$, we have:

$$E[y_i] = c + \sum_{j=1}^{p} \phi_j E[y_{i-j}] + \sum_{j=1}^{q} \theta_j E[\nu_{i-j}] + E[\nu_i]$$

$$\mu = c + \mu \sum_{j=1}^{p} \phi_j$$

(15.8)

So

The unconditional mean of an ARMA(p,q) process is:

$$\mu = c \left\{ 1 - \sum_{j=1}^{p} \phi_j \right\}^{-1}$$

(15.9)

which is the same as for an AR(p) process.

$E[y_i]$ denotes the unconditional expectation of y_i and $E[y_i|\psi_{i-1}]$, denotes the expectation of y_i conditional on all relevant information up to instant $i - 1$. Since neither of these expectations is time-dependent the above process is said to be both unconditionally and conditionally *homoskedastic*.

15.2 GAUSSIAN LINEAR GARCH

GARCH relaxes this constraint and allows the conditional variance of y_i to vary with time. For example when $p = 0$ and $c = 0$ in Equation 15.1 we now have:

$$y_i = \epsilon_i, \quad i = 1, \ldots, n$$

where $E(\epsilon_i^2) = h_i$ and h_i is the time-dependent conditional variance. However the unconditional variance of ϵ_i is still constant,

$$E[\epsilon_i^2] = E[E(\epsilon_i^2|\psi_{i-1})] = E[h_i] = \sigma_0^2$$

In a similar manner to the Box Jenkins approach described above in Section 15.1, we can define an autoregressive conditional heteroskedastic process of order q, ARCH(q), process, with Gaussian residuals as follows:

$$h_i = \alpha_0 + \sum_{j=1}^{q} \alpha_j \epsilon_{i-j}^2, \quad i = 1, \ldots, n \quad \epsilon_i|\psi_{i-1} \sim NID(0, h_i) \tag{15.10}$$

This can then be generalized to a GARCH(p,q) process in the same way that an ARMA(p,q) is a generalization of an AR(q) process.

In the same way that an ARMA(p,q) is a generalization of an AR(q) process, we can define a generalized autoregressive conditional heteroskedastic of order (p, q), GARCH(p,q) as follows:

Linear GARCH(p,q)

$$h_i = \alpha_0 + \sum_{j=1}^{q} \alpha_j \epsilon_{i-j}^2 + \sum_{j=1}^{p} \beta_j h_{i-j}, \quad i = 1, \ldots, n \quad \epsilon_i|\psi_{i-1} \sim NID(0, h_i) \tag{15.11}$$

The relationship between GARCH and ARMA processes can be illustrated as follows:

$$h_i = \alpha_0 + \sum_{j=1}^{q} \alpha_j \epsilon_{i-j}^2 + \sum_{j=1}^{p} \beta_j h_{i-j}, \quad i = 1, \ldots, n \tag{15.12}$$

If ϵ_i^2 is added to both sides, and the zero term $\sum_{j=1}^{p} \beta_j \epsilon_{i-j}^2 - \sum_{j=1}^{p} \beta_j \epsilon_{i-j}^2$ is added to the right hand side we have:

$$h_i + \epsilon_i^2 = \alpha_0 + \sum_{j=1}^{q} \alpha_j \epsilon_{i-j}^2 + \sum_{j=1}^{p} \beta_j \epsilon_{i-j}^2 + \epsilon_i^2 - \sum_{j=1}^{p} \beta_j (\epsilon_{i-j}^2 - h_{i-j})$$

So

$$\epsilon_i^2 = \alpha_0 + \sum_{j=1}^{\kappa} (\alpha_j + \beta_j) \epsilon_{i-j}^2 + \epsilon_i^2 - h_i - \sum_{j=1}^{p} \beta_j (\epsilon_{i-j}^2 - h_{i-j}) \tag{15.13}$$

where $\kappa = \max(p, q)$ and we have $\alpha_i = 0$, for $i > q$, and $\beta_i = 0$, for $i > p$.

We notice that h_i is the forecast for ϵ_i^2 based on its own lagged values. The term $v_i = \epsilon_i^2 - h_i$ is the forecast error associated with this forecast, and is therefore a white noise process. Substituting for v_i in Equation 15.13 we then have:

$$\epsilon_i^2 = \alpha_0 + \sum_{j=1}^{\kappa}(\alpha_j + \beta_j)\epsilon_{i-j}^2 - \sum_{j=1}^{p}\beta_j v_{i-j} + v_i \tag{15.14}$$

Comparing this with the above equation for an ARMA(p,q) process we see that the sequence ϵ_i^2 is an ARMA(κ,p) process with κ autoregressive coefficients $(\alpha_j + \beta_j)$, $j = 1, \ldots, \kappa$, and p moving average coefficients β_j, $j = 1, \ldots, p$. So if the residuals ϵ_i are described by a GARCH(p,q) process then ϵ_i^2 are described by an ARMA(κ,p) process, where $\kappa = \max$ (p,q).

From standard results for ARMA processes, ϵ_i^2 is covariance stationary provided v_i has finite variance and the roots, z^j, of the polynomial

$$P(z) = 1 - (\beta_1 + \alpha_1)z - (\beta_2 + \alpha_2)z^2 - \cdots - (\beta_\kappa + \alpha_\kappa)z^\kappa = 0 \tag{15.15}$$

all have modulus greater than 1, that is $|z^j| > 1$, for $j = 1, \ldots, \kappa$, Box and Jenkins (1976), and Levi (1942).

If we impose the nonnegativity requirement $\alpha_0 > 0$ and $\alpha_j \geq 0, \beta_j \geq 0$, for $j = 1, \ldots, \kappa$ then we will now show that the condition for ϵ_i^2 to be covariance stationary is:

Condition for GARCH to be covariance stationary:

$$(\beta_1 + \alpha_1) + (\beta_2 + \alpha_2) + \cdots + (\beta_\kappa + \alpha_\kappa) < 1 \tag{15.16}$$

or more concisely

$$\sum_{j=1}^{\kappa}(\beta_j + \alpha_j) < 1$$

which means that $|z^j| > 1$, for $j = 1, \ldots, \kappa$.

The proof is as follows:

1. *Show that if $\sum_{j=1}^{\kappa}(\beta_j + \alpha_j) \geq 1$ then ϵ_i^2 can't be stationary*

If $\sum_{j=1}^{\kappa}(\beta_j + \alpha_j) \geq 1$ then because $\alpha_j \geq 0, \beta_j \geq 0$, $P(1) = 1 - \sum_{j=1}^{\kappa}(\beta_j + \alpha_j) < 0$, and $P(0) = 1 > 0$. Since the polynomial has changed sign between 0 and 1 this means that there is a root in this interval. So under these circumstances we must have at least one root z_j with $|z^j| < 0$, which means that the process is not covariance stationary.

2. *Show that if* $\sum_{j=1}^{\kappa}(\beta_j + \alpha_j) < 1$ *then* ϵ_i^2 *must be stationary*

If $\sum_{j=1}^{\kappa}(\beta_j + \alpha_j) < 0$ and there is a root of $P(z)$, z^i, with $|z^i| < 1$, then we have

$P(z^i) = 1 - \sum_{j=1}^{\kappa}(\beta_j + \alpha_j)z^j = 0$ that is: $1 = |\sum_{j=1}^{\kappa}(\beta_j + \alpha_j)z^j|$

But since $\alpha_j \geq 0, \beta_j \geq 0$ and $z^j \leq |z^j|$ we have:

$1 = |\sum_{j=1}^{\kappa}(\beta_j + \alpha_j)z^j| \leq \sum_{j=1}^{\kappa}(\beta_j + \alpha_j)|z^j| \leq \sum_{j=1}^{\kappa}(\beta_j + \alpha_j) < 1$ which is inconsistent.

So if $\sum_{j=1}^{\kappa}(\beta_j + \alpha_j) < 1$ then we must have $|z^j| > 1$, for $j = 1, \ldots, \kappa$ QED

We will now assume that ϵ_i^2 is covariance stationary and calculate its unconditional variance by taking expectations in Equation 15.14 as follows:

$$E[\epsilon_i^2] = \alpha_0 + \sum_{j=1}^{\kappa}(\alpha_j + \beta_j)E[\epsilon_{i-j}^2] - \sum_{j=1}^{p}\beta_j E[\nu_{i-j}] + E[\nu_i] \qquad (15.17)$$

But since ϵ_i^2 is covariance stationary and ν_i is white noise we have:

$$E[\epsilon_i^2] = E[\epsilon_{i-j}^2] \quad \text{and} \quad E[\nu_i] = E[\nu_{i-j}] = 0$$

Therefore:

$$E[\epsilon_i^2] = \alpha_0 + \sum_{j=1}^{\kappa}(\alpha_j + \beta_j)E[\epsilon_i^2] \qquad (15.18)$$

and

GARCH unconditional variance:

$$\sigma_0^2 = E[\epsilon_i^2] = \alpha_0\left\{1 - \sum_{j=1}^{\kappa}(\alpha_j + \beta_j)\right\}^{-1} \qquad (15.19)$$

15.2.1   The unconditional kurtosis of the residuals

In Equation 15.11 the conditional distribution of the residuals, ϵ_i, was:

$\epsilon_i|\psi_{i-1} \sim NID(0, h_i)$

For convenience we will now rewrite this as:

$\epsilon_i = \sqrt{h_i}\mathcal{Z}_i, \quad \text{where} \quad \mathcal{Z}_i \sim NID(0, 1)$

Therefore $\epsilon_i^4 = h_i^2 \mathcal{Z}_i^4$. Using the fact that h_i and $\mathcal{Z}_i$ are independent of each other we have $E[\epsilon_i^4] = E[h_i^2 \mathcal{Z}_i^4] = E[h_i^2]E[\mathcal{Z}_i^4]$.

Jensen's inequality (see Goldberger (1997) and Appendix F.6), states that for a random variate X, $E[X^2] \geq E[X]^2$, since the function X^2 is convex.

Using this result we have:

$E[h_i^2] \geq E[h_i]^2$, which gives $E[h_i^2]E[\mathcal{Z}_i^4] \geq E[h_i]^2 E[\mathcal{Z}_i^4]$

Using $E[h_i] = E[\epsilon_i^2]$ results in $E[\epsilon_i^4] = E[h_i^2]E[\mathcal{Z}_i^4] \geq E[\epsilon_i^2]^2 E[\mathcal{Z}_i^4]$.
Therefore the unconditional kurtosis is:

$$\aleph = \frac{E[\epsilon_i^4]}{E[\epsilon_i^2]^2} \geq E[\mathcal{Z}_i^4]$$

But since $\mathcal{Z}_i$ comes from a standardized Gaussian distribution it has variance $E[\mathcal{Z}_i^2] = 1$, and a kurtosis of 3, see Chapter 17. This means that:

$$\frac{E[\mathcal{Z}_i^4]}{E[\mathcal{Z}_i^2]^2} = E[\mathcal{Z}_i^4] = 3, \quad \text{so} \quad \aleph = \frac{E[\epsilon_i^4]}{E[\epsilon_i^2]^2} \geq 3$$

This shows that although the residuals have a Gaussian conditional distribution their unconditional distribution is *leptokurtic* and therefore non-Gaussian.

In fact we can use Jensen's inequality in a similar manner to show that for any arbitrary conditional distribution $\mathcal{R}(0, h_i)$ the unconditional kurtosis of ϵ_i will be higher than the kurtosis of $\mathcal{R}(0, h_i)$.

We will now derive the value of the unconditional kurtosis of an ARCH(1) process.

Kurtosis for an ARCH(1) process

For an ARCH(1) process we have:

$$\epsilon_i = \{\alpha_0 + \alpha_1 \epsilon_{i-1}^2\}^{1/2} \mathcal{Z}_i, \quad \mathcal{Z}_i \sim NID(0, 1)$$

Therefore

$$E[\epsilon_i^4] = E[(\alpha_0 + \alpha_1 \epsilon_{i-1}^2)^2 \mathcal{Z}_i^4] = E[(\alpha_0 + \alpha_1 \epsilon_{i-1}^2)^2]E[\mathcal{Z}_i^4]$$

But

$$E[(\alpha_0 + \alpha_1 \epsilon_{i-1}^2)^2 = E[\alpha_0^2 + \alpha_1^2 \epsilon_{i-1}^4 + 2\alpha_0\alpha_1 \epsilon_{i-1}^2]$$
$$= \alpha_0^2 + \alpha_1^2 E[\epsilon_{i-1}^4] + 2\alpha_0\alpha_1 E[\epsilon_{i-1}^2]$$

But since $E[\epsilon_{i-1}^4] = E[\epsilon_i^4]$ and $E[\epsilon_{i-1}^2] = E[\epsilon_i^2]$ we have:

$$E[\epsilon_i^4] = 3(\alpha_0^2 + \alpha_1^2 E[\epsilon_i^4] + 2\alpha_0\alpha_1 E[\epsilon_i^2]) = 3\alpha_0^2 + 3\alpha_1^2 E[\epsilon_i^4] + 6\alpha_0\alpha_1 E[\epsilon_i^2]$$

using $E[\epsilon_i^2] = (\alpha_0)/(1 - \alpha_1)$ we have:

$$E[\epsilon_i^4](1 - 3\alpha_1^2) = 3\left(\alpha_0^2 + \frac{2\alpha_0^2\alpha_1}{1 - \alpha_1}\right) = \frac{3\alpha_0^2}{(1 - 3\alpha_1^2)}\left(\frac{1 + \alpha_1}{1 - \alpha_1}\right)$$

which gives:

$$\aleph = \frac{E[\epsilon_i^4]}{E[\epsilon_i^2]^2} = \frac{3\alpha_0^2}{(1 - 3\alpha_1^2)} \left(\frac{1 + \alpha_1}{1 - \alpha_1}\right) \frac{(1 - \alpha_1^2)^2}{\alpha_0^2}$$

So the kurtosis is:

$$\aleph = 3\frac{(1 + \alpha_1)(1 - \alpha_1)}{1 - 3\alpha_1^2} = 3\frac{(1 - \alpha_1^2)}{1 - 3\alpha_1^2}$$

For finite values of $E[\epsilon_i^2]$ and $E[\epsilon_i^4]$, we require $\alpha_1 < 1$ and $3\alpha_1 < 1$ respectively. Since $1 - \alpha_1^2 > 1 - 3\alpha_1^2$ we have $\aleph > 3$, which means that the ARCH model has heavier tails than a Gaussian distribution.

| Kurtosis for a GARCH(1,1) process |

To derive the unconditional kurtosis of a GARCH(1,1) is quite complicated, so we simply present the following results, see Bollerslev (1986):
   For GARCH(1,1) we have:

$$E(\epsilon_i^4) = \left[\frac{3\alpha_0^2(1 + (\alpha_1 + \beta_1))}{(1 - (\alpha_1 - \beta_1))(1 - \beta_1^2 - 2\alpha_1\beta_1 - 3\alpha_1^2)}\right]$$

and from Equation 15.19 the conditional variance is:

$$E[\epsilon_i^2] = \frac{\alpha_0}{1 - (\alpha_1 + \beta_1)}$$

Therefore the unconditional kurtosis of a GARCH(1,1) process is:

$$\aleph = \left[\frac{3\alpha_0^2(1 + (\alpha_1 + \beta_1))}{(1 - (\alpha_1 - \beta_1))(1 - \beta_1^2 - 2\alpha_1\beta_1 - 3\alpha_1^2)}\right]\left[\frac{(1 - (\alpha_1 + \beta_1))^2}{\alpha_0^2}\right]$$

$$= 3 + \frac{6\alpha_1^2}{(1 - \beta_1^2 - 2\alpha_1\beta_1 - 3\alpha_1^2)}$$

For a finite value of $E[\epsilon_i^4]$, we require $3\alpha_1^2 + 2\alpha_1\beta_1 + \beta_1^2 < 1$. When this constraint is satisfied $\aleph > 3$.

15.2.2 Forecasting and mean-reversion in a GARCH(1,1) process

Here we derive an expression for the T step ahead volatility forecast of a GARCH(1,1) process. Given the information set ψ_{i-1} the expected volatility $E[h_i|\psi_{i-1}]$, at instant i as:

$$E[h_i|\psi_{i-1}] = \alpha_0 + \alpha_1\epsilon_{i-1}^2 + \beta_1 h_{i-1}$$

and at instant $i + 1$, $E[h_{i+1}|\psi_{i-1}]$ is thus:

$$E[h_{i+1}|\psi_{i-1}] = \alpha_0 + \alpha_1 E[\epsilon_i^2] + \beta_1 E[h_i|\psi_{i-1}]$$

Now since $E[\epsilon_i^2|\psi_{i-1}] = E[h_i|\psi_{i-1}]$ we have:

$$E[h_{i+1}|\psi_{i-1}] = \alpha_0 + (\alpha_1 + \beta_1)E[h_i|\psi_{i-1}] \tag{15.20}$$

Proceeding in a simliar manner we have:

$$E[h_{i+2}|\psi_{i-1}] = \alpha_0 + \alpha_1 E[\epsilon_{i+1}^2|\psi_{i-1}] + \beta_1 E[h_{i+1}|\psi_{i-1}]$$
$$E[h_{i+2}|\psi_{i-1}] = \alpha_0 + (\alpha_1 + \beta_1)E[h_{i+1}|\psi_{i-1}]$$
$$E[h_{i+2}|\psi_{i-i}] = \alpha_0 + (\alpha_1 + \beta_1)\{\alpha_0 + (\alpha_1 + \beta_1)E[h_i|\psi_{i-1}]\}$$
$$E[h_{i+2}|\psi_{i-1}] = \alpha_0 + \alpha_0(\alpha_1 + \beta_1) + (\alpha_1 + \beta_1)^2 E[h_i|\psi_{i-1}] \tag{15.21}$$

$$E[h_{i+3}|\psi_{i-1}] = \alpha_0 + \alpha_1 E[\epsilon_{i+2}^2|\psi_{i-1}] + \beta_1 E[h_{i+2}|\psi_{i-1}]$$
$$E[h_{i+3}|\psi_{i-1}] = \alpha_0 + (\alpha_1 + \beta_1)E[h_{i+2}|\psi_{i-1}]$$
$$E[h_{i+3}|\psi_{i-1}] = \alpha_0 + (\alpha_1 + \beta_1)\{\alpha_0 + \alpha_0(\alpha_1 + \beta_1) + (\alpha_1 + \beta_1)^2 E[h_i|\psi_{i-1}]\}$$
$$E[h_{i+3}|\psi_{i-1}] = \alpha_0 + \alpha_0(\alpha_1 + \beta_1) + \alpha_0(\alpha_1 + \beta_1)^2 + (\alpha_1 + \beta_1)^3 E[h_i|\psi_{i-1}] \tag{15.22}$$

So we have:

$$E[h_{i+T}|\psi_{i-1}] = \alpha_0 + \alpha_0(\alpha_1 + \beta_1) + \alpha_0(\alpha_1 + \beta_1)^2 + \cdots + (\alpha_1 + \beta_1)^{T-1}$$
$$+ (\alpha_1 + \beta_1)^T E[h_i|\psi_{i-1}] \tag{15.23}$$

Equation 15.23 is the sum of T terms of a Geometric Progression with first term α_0 and common factor $(\alpha_1 + \beta_1)$, and there is also an additional term $(\alpha_1 + \beta_1)^T E[h_i|\psi_{i-1}]$. So

---

GARCH(1,1) forecast:

$$E[h_{i+T}|\psi_{i-1}] = \alpha_0 \frac{\left\{1 - (\alpha_1 + \beta_1)^T\right\}}{1 - (\alpha_1 + \beta_1)} + (\alpha_1 + \beta_1)^T E[h_i|\psi_{i-1}] \tag{15.24}$$

Since $\alpha_1 + \beta_1 < 1$ for a stationary sequence, as $T \to \infty$ we have

$$E[h_{i+T}|\psi_{i-1}] = \frac{\alpha_0}{1 - (\alpha_1 + \beta_1)} \tag{15.25}$$

This is just the unconditional variance of the GARCH sequence. It can thus be seen from Equations 15.24 and 15.25 that the GARCH volatility forecast is mean reverting, and that the smaller the value of $\alpha_1 + \beta_1$ the faster is the reversion speed.

15.3 THE IGARCH MODEL

It has been found that the use of a GARCH(1,1) model on financial data often results in $\beta_1 > 0.7$ and $\alpha_1 \approx 1 - \beta_1$. This has motivated the *integrated* GARCH(p,q), also termed IGARCH(p,q), in which $\alpha_1 + \beta_1 = 1$, see Engle and Bollerslev (1986).

From Equation 15.19 it can be seen that the unconditional variance of the sequence, $E(\epsilon_i^2)$, is infinite, and from Equation 15.26 that the sequence is not covariance-stationary. However, Nelson (1990) shows that:

$$h_i = \alpha_0 \left(\sum_{j=1}^{i-1} \prod_{k=1}^{j} (\alpha_1 \zeta_{i-k} + \beta_1) \right) + \prod_{j=1}^{i} (\alpha_1 \zeta_{i-j} + \beta_1) h_0$$

where $\zeta_k = \epsilon_k^2 / h_k$, and that the sequence is strictly stationary if $E[\log(\alpha_1 \zeta_{i-j} + \beta_1)] < 0$. When this condition is satisfied the effect of the initial value h_0 disappears asymptotically.

15.3.1 Exponentially weighted moving average: EWMA

The exponentially weighted moving average (EWMA) method is a special case of the IGARCH(1,1) model:

$$h_i = \alpha_0 + \alpha_1 \epsilon_{i-1}^2 + (1 - \alpha_1) h_{i-1}, \quad i = 1, \ldots, n$$

In the case of EWMA we take $\alpha_0 = 0$ and obtain the scheme:

$$h_i = \lambda \epsilon_{i-1}^2 + (1 - \lambda) h_{i-1}, \quad i = 1, \ldots, n \tag{15.26}$$

where the parameter λ is known as the *weight*, or *decay factor*. It can be seen that the value of h_i is the weighted average of ϵ_{i-1}^2 and h_{i-1}.

Risk metrics, J. P. Morgan (1996) advocate this method of modelling volatility, and selected $\lambda = 0.97$ as the optimal value to use.

15.4 THE GARCH-M MODEL

Finance theory suggests that, on average, an asset with a higher risk should have a higher return.

Engle *et al.* (1987) proposed the ARCH-M model to capture this effect. A simple GARCH-M model is:

$$y_i = \delta h_i + \epsilon_i \tag{15.27}$$

$$\epsilon_i | \psi_{i-1} = N(0, h_i) \tag{15.28}$$

$$h_i = \alpha_0 + \sum_{j=1}^{q} \alpha_j \epsilon_{i-j}^2 + \sum_{j=1}^{p} \beta_j h_{i-j}, \quad i = 1, \ldots, n \tag{15.29}$$

Here y_i is the mean asset return at time i, and h_i the variance of ϵ_i, is a measure of the associated risk. It can be seen that the extra term δh_i leads to increased returns for higher values of h_i.

15.5 REGRESSION-GARCH AND AR-GARCH

Up to now we have used GARCH models with variables defined as $y_i = \epsilon_i$.

We will now include linear regression into the GARCH model.

A regression-GARCH(p,q) sequence containing n terms with Gaussian shocks, ϵ_i, takes the following form:

$$y_i = b_0 + X_i^T b + \epsilon_i, \quad \epsilon_i | \psi_{i-1} \sim NID(0, h_i) \tag{15.30}$$

$$h_i = \alpha_0 + \sum_{j=1}^{q} \alpha_j \epsilon_{i-j}^2 + \sum_{j=1}^{p} \beta_j h_{i-j}, \quad i = 1, \ldots, n \tag{15.31}$$

This process is described by $q + 1$ coefficients α_j, $j = 0, \ldots, q$, p coefficients β_j, $j = 1, \ldots, p$, mean b_0, k linear regression coefficients b_j, $j = 1, \ldots, k$, endogenous/exogenous variables y_i and X_i respectively, shocks ϵ_i, h_i the conditional variance, and the set of all information up to time i, ψ_i. The conditional probability distribution of ϵ_i is denoted by $P(0, h_i)$, a distribution with zero mean and time-varying variance h_i.

Here X_i denotes the k element row vector of exogenous variables at time i, and b refers to the k element column vector or regression coefficients. We also use X_i^T to indicate the column vector formed by the transpose of X_i, and the k individual elements of X_i are denoted by X_i^j, $j = 1, \ldots, k$.

It should be noted that the n term regression-GARCH(p,q) model above can easily be used to model an n–m term AR(m)–GARCH(p,q) sequence defined as follows:

$$y_i = c + \sum_{j=1}^{p} \phi_j y_{i-j} + \epsilon_i, \quad i = m+1, \ldots, n \tag{15.32}$$

$$h_i = \alpha_0 + \sum_{j=1}^{q} \alpha_j \epsilon_{i-j}^2 + \sum_{j=1}^{p} \beta_j h_{i-j}, \quad i = m+1, \ldots, n \tag{15.33}$$

where the terms y_i, $i = 1, \ldots, m$ are used as the pre-observed values for the AR(m)–GARCH(p,q) sequence.

If we let $k = m$ then the mean term b_0 is identified as c and the k time-dependent exogenous variables are replaced by the lagged values of y_i. That is the row vector $X_i = (y_{i-1}, y_{i-2}, \ldots, y_{i-m})$.

Chapter 16

Nonlinear GARCH

The standard GARCH model assumes that both positive and negative shocks of equal magnitude have an identical effect on future volatility. However, empirical studies on stock returns have shown that they are characterized by increased volatility following negative shocks (bad news). This *leverage* effect was first recognized by Black (1976), who reasoned that it is connected with the way in which firms are financed. When the value of a firm's stock decreases the debt-to-equity ratio increases, which leads to an increase in the volatility of the returns on equity. The leverage effect suggests that positive and negative shocks have an *asymmetric* impact on the conditional volatility of subsequent observations. It has been found that the returns for different asset classes display different leverage characteristics. The returns for equities and equity indices have negative leverage (negative shocks increase subsequent volatility). By contrast the returns for commodities and commodity futures exhibit both positive and negative leverage effects, McKenzie *et al.* (2001). Finally exchange rate returns, where the concept of good/bad news is less well defined, have no leverage effects at all. This is because a return series of currency X in terms of currency Y can be inverted (negative shocks now transformed into positive shocks) to yield a return series of currency Y in terms of currency X.

Since linear GARCH models cannot capture these effects various nonlinear GARCH extensions have been proposed. These models include: Exponential GARCH (EGARCH) (Nelson, 1991), Asymmetric GARCH (AGARCH) (Engle and Ng, 1993), GJR–GARCH (Glosten *et al.*, 1993), Markov-Switching GARCH (MSW-GARCH) (Dueker, 1997), and Asymmetric Nonlinear Smooth Transition GARCH (ANST-GARCH) (Anderson *et al.*, 1999). Hentschel (1995) provides a more comprehensive overview of nonlinear GARCH models.

Empirical studies have also found that both the conditional and unconditional distributions of financial returns exhibit leptokurtosis (have fatter tails than a normal distribution). A popular choice, Bollerslev (1987), Engle and Gonzalez-Rivera (1991), is to assume that, instead of a Gaussian distribution, the errors ϵ_i have a Student's t distribution with ν degrees of freedom.

Here we consider asymmetric effects in AGARCH-I, AGARCH-II, and GJR–GARCH sequences, which can be modelled by the inclusion of an extra asymmetry parameter, γ. The mathematical definition of these processes is as follows:

AGARCH-I

$$h_i = \alpha_0 + \sum_{j=1}^{q} \alpha_j(\epsilon_{i-j} + \gamma)^2 + \sum_{j=1}^{p} \beta_j h_{i-j}, \quad i = 1, \ldots, n \qquad (16.1)$$

AGARCH-II

$$h_i = \alpha_0 + \sum_{j=1}^{q} \alpha_j(|\epsilon_{i-j}| + \gamma\epsilon_{i-j})^2 + \sum_{j=1}^{p} \beta_j h_{i-j}, \quad i = 1, \ldots, n \qquad (16.2)$$

GJR–GARCH

$$h_i = \alpha_0 + \sum_{j=1}^{q} (\alpha_j + \gamma S_{i-j})\epsilon_{i-j}^2 + \sum_{j=1}^{p} \beta_j h_{i-j}, \quad i = 1, \ldots, n \qquad (16.3)$$

where $S_i = 1$, if $\epsilon_i < 0$ and $S_i = 0$, if $\epsilon_i \geq 0$.

EGARCH

$$\log(h_i) = \alpha_0 + \sum_{j=1}^{q} \alpha_j \mathcal{Z}_{i-j} + \sum_{j=1}^{q} \phi_i(|\mathcal{Z}_{i-j}| - E[|\mathcal{Z}_{i-j}|])$$

$$+ \sum_{j=1}^{p} \beta_j \log(h_{i-j}), \quad i = 1, \ldots, n \qquad (16.4)$$

where $\mathcal{Z}_i = \epsilon_i / \sqrt{h_i}$ and $E[|\mathcal{Z}_{i-j}|]$ denotes the expected value of $|\mathcal{Z}_{i-j}|$.

In AGARCH-I the asymmetric effects are modelled via the extra parameter. For example, in the standard GARCH(1,1) model when h_{i-1} is fixed $h_i = h(\epsilon_{i-1})$ is a parabola with a minimum at $\epsilon_{i-1} = 0$. The introduction of the additional parameter γ shifts the parabola horizontally so that the minimum occurs at $\epsilon_{i-1} = -\gamma$. The conditional variance following negative shocks can therefore be enhanced by choosing $\gamma < 0$, so that $h(-\epsilon_{i-1}) > h(\epsilon_{i-1})$ for $\epsilon_{i-1} > 0$.

In an AGARCH-II model the inclusion of γ can also result in an enhancement of h_i following a negative shock ϵ_{i-1}. For a GARCH(1,1) model $h(-\epsilon_{i-1}) > h(\epsilon_{i-1})$ for $\epsilon > 0$ and $\gamma < 0$.

Similarly in the GJR–GARCH(1,1) model the value of h_i is increased above the symmetric case when $\epsilon_{i-1} < 0$ and $\gamma > 0$.

For EGARCH, asymmetric response arises from the term $\sum_{j=1}^{q} \alpha_j \mathcal{Z}_{i-j}$. In an EGARCH(1,1), if $\alpha_1 < 0$ then a negative shock ϵ_{i-1} increases the value of h_i, that is $\log\{h(-\mathcal{Z}_{i-1})\} > \log\{h(\mathcal{Z}_{i-1})\}$.

16.1 AGARCH-I

From Equation 16.1 the AGARCH-I process is defined as:

$$h_i = \alpha_0 + \sum_{j=1}^{q} \alpha_j(\epsilon_{i-j} + \gamma)^2 + \sum_{j=1}^{p} \beta_j h_{i-j}, \quad i = 1, \ldots, n$$

Since $(\epsilon_{i-j} + \gamma)^2 = \epsilon_{i-j}^2 + 2\gamma\epsilon_{i-j} + \gamma^2$ we have

$$h_i = \alpha_0 + \sum_{j=1}^{q} \alpha_j \epsilon_{i-j}^2 + \sum_{j=1}^{p} \beta_j h_{i-j} + 2\gamma \sum_{j=1}^{q} \epsilon_{i-j} + \sum_{j=1}^{q} \alpha_j \gamma^2$$

Following the same procedure as in Section 16.2 we have

$$\epsilon_i^2 = \alpha_0 + \sum_{j=1}^{\kappa} (\alpha_j + \beta_j)\epsilon_{i-j}^2 - \sum_{j=1}^{p} \beta_j \nu_{i-j} + \nu_i + 2\gamma \sum_{j=1}^{q} \epsilon_{i-j} + \sum_{j=1}^{q} \alpha_j \gamma^2$$

where $\kappa = \max(p,q)$ and we have $\alpha_i = 0$, for $i > q$ and $\beta_i = 0$, for $i > p$. Taking expectations gives:

$$E[\epsilon_i^2] = \alpha_0 + \sum_{j=1}^{\kappa} (\alpha_j + \beta_j)E[\epsilon_{i-j}^2] - \sum_{j=1}^{p} \beta_j E[\nu_{i-j}] + E[\nu_i]$$

$$+ 2\gamma \sum_{j=1}^{q} E[\epsilon_{i-j}] + \sum_{j=1}^{q} \alpha_j \gamma^2 \tag{16.5}$$

Now since $E[\nu_i] = 0$ and $E[\epsilon_i] = 0$ we have:

$$E[\epsilon_i^2] = \alpha_0 + \sum_{j=1}^{\kappa} (\alpha_j + \beta_j)E[\epsilon_{i-j}^2] + \sum_{j=1}^{q} \alpha_j \gamma^2$$

This is an AR(κ) process and the condition for ϵ_i^2 to be covariance stationary is:

$$\sum_{j=1}^{\kappa} (\alpha_j + \beta_j) < 1 \tag{16.6}$$

which is the same condition as for the standard linear GARCH(p,q) process.

Assuming that ϵ_i^2 is covariance stationary we have $\sigma_0^2 = E[\epsilon_i^2] = E[\epsilon_{i-j}^2]$ and so

$$E[\epsilon_i^2] = \alpha_0 + \gamma^2 \sum_{j=1}^{q} \alpha_j + \sum_{j=1}^{\kappa} (\alpha_j + \beta_j)E[\epsilon_i^2]$$

which results in

AGARCH-I unconditional variance

$$\sigma_0^2 = E[\epsilon_i^2] = \frac{(\alpha_0 + \gamma^2 \sum_{j=1}^q \alpha_j)}{(1 - \sum_{j=1}^\kappa (\alpha_j + \beta_j))} \tag{16.7}$$

16.1.1 Kurtosis

We will now calculate the kurtosis for an AGARCH-I(0,1) process:

$$\epsilon_i = \left\{ \alpha_0 + \alpha_1 (\epsilon_{i-1} + \gamma)^2 \right\}^{1/2} \mathcal{Z}_i, \quad \mathcal{Z}_i \sim NID(0,1)$$

Therefore

$$E[\epsilon_i^4] = E[(\alpha_0 + \alpha_1 (\epsilon_{i-1} + \gamma)^2)^2 \mathcal{Z}_i^4] = E[(\alpha_0 + \alpha_1 (\epsilon_{i-1} + \gamma)^2)^2] E[\mathcal{Z}_i^4]$$

We will assume that process is covariance stationary and use the fact that the expectation of odd powers of ϵ_i is zero and that $E[\mathcal{Z}_i^4] = 3$.

$$E[\epsilon_i^4] = 3 \left(\alpha_0^2 + 2\alpha_0\alpha_1\gamma^2 + \alpha_1^2\gamma^4 + 2\alpha_1\alpha_0 E[\epsilon_i^2] + 6\alpha_1^2\gamma^2 E[\epsilon_i^2] + \alpha_1^2 E[\epsilon_i^4] \right)$$

which gives

$$E[\epsilon_i^4](1 - 3\alpha_1^2) = 3 \left\{ (\alpha_0 + \alpha_1\gamma^2)^2 + E[\epsilon_i^2](6\alpha_1^2\gamma^2 + 2\alpha_1\alpha_0) \right\}$$

substituting for $E[\epsilon_i^2]$ we have:

$$E[\epsilon_i^4](1 - 3\alpha_1^2) = 3(\alpha_0 + \alpha_1\gamma^2) \left\{ (\alpha_0 + \alpha_1\gamma^2) + \frac{(6\alpha_1^2\gamma^2 + 2\alpha_1\alpha_0)}{(1 - \alpha_1)} \right\}$$

$$= \frac{3(\alpha_0 + \alpha_1\gamma^2)}{(1 - \alpha_1)} \left\{ (\alpha_0 + \alpha_1\gamma^2)(1 - \alpha_1) + (6\alpha_1^2\gamma^2 + 2\alpha_1\alpha_0) \right\}$$

But

$$(\alpha_0 + \alpha_1\gamma^2)(1 - \alpha_1) + (6\alpha_1^2\gamma^2 + 2\alpha_1\alpha_0) = (\alpha_0 + \alpha_1\gamma^2)(1 + \alpha_1) + 4\alpha_1^2\gamma^2$$

Therefore

$$E[\epsilon_i^4] = \frac{3(\alpha_0 + \alpha_1\gamma^2)}{(1 - 3\alpha_1^2)(1 - \alpha_1)} \left\{ (\alpha_0 + \alpha_1\gamma^2)(1 + \alpha_1) + 4\alpha_1^2\gamma^2 \right\}$$

So the kurtosis is:

$$\aleph = \frac{E[\epsilon_i^4]}{(E[\epsilon_i^2])^2} = \frac{3(1 - \alpha_1^2 + \mathcal{F})}{1 - 3\alpha_1^2}, \quad \text{where} \quad \mathcal{F} = \frac{4\alpha_1^2\gamma^2(1 - \alpha_1)}{\alpha_0 + \alpha_1\gamma^2} \tag{16.8}$$

It is therefore evident that when $\gamma = 0$ we have $\mathcal{F} = 0$, and the kurtosis is the same as for the linear ARCH(1). However, for any non-zero value of γ the kurtosis will be greater than that for the standard ARCH(1). Furthermore, since $\mathcal{F}$ increases monotonically with the absolute value of γ, the unconditional kurtosis increases with γ.

16.1.2 Skewness

We assume the non-negativity constraints $\alpha_0 > 0$ and $\alpha_1 > 0$.

$$\epsilon_i = \left\{ \alpha_0 + \alpha_1 (\epsilon_{i-1} + \gamma)^2 \right\}^{1/2} \mathcal{Z}_i, \quad \mathcal{Z}_i \sim \mathcal{R}(0, 1)$$

where $\mathcal{Z}_i$ is an arbitrary symmetric distribution.
Therefore:

$$E[\epsilon_i^3] = E\left[\left\{ \alpha_0 + \alpha_1 (\epsilon_{i-1} + \gamma)^2 \right\}^{3/2} \mathcal{Z}_i^3 \right], \quad \mathcal{Z}_i \sim \mathcal{R}(0, 1)$$

By decomposing this expectation into the part with $\epsilon_i \geq 0$, and the part with $\epsilon_i < 0$, we have:

$$E[\epsilon_i^3] = E\left[\left\{ \alpha_0 + \alpha_1 (|\epsilon_{i-1}| - \gamma)^2 \right\}^{3/2} \right] E[\mathcal{Z}_i^{3+}] + E\left[\left\{ \alpha_0 + \alpha_1 (|\epsilon_{i-1}| + \gamma)^2 \right\}^{3/2} \right] E[\mathcal{Z}_i^{3-}]$$

where because $\mathcal{R}(0, 1)$ is symmetric we have $E[\mathcal{Z}_i^3] = 0 = E[\mathcal{Z}_i^{3+}] + E[\mathcal{Z}_i^{3-}]$.
This means that:

$$E[\epsilon_i^3] = \left\{ E\left[\left\{ \alpha_0 + \alpha_1 (|\epsilon_{i-1}| - \gamma)^2 \right\}^{3/2} \right] - E\left[\left\{ \alpha_0 + \alpha_1 (|\epsilon_{i-1}| + \gamma)^2 \right\}^{3/2} \right] \right\} E[\mathcal{Z}_i^{3+}]$$

Since $E[\epsilon_i^2] > 0$, the skewness is:

$$S = \frac{E[\epsilon_i^3]}{E[\epsilon_i^2]^{3/2}} \tag{16.9}$$

It can be seen that the skewness is zero for $\gamma = 0$, and becomes increasingly negative as the value of γ is raised.

16.1.3 Forecasting and mean-reversion in an AGARCH-I(1,1) process

Here we derive an expression for the T step ahead volatility forecast of an AGARCH-I(1,1) process. Given the information set ψ_{i-1} we can forecast the expected volatility $E[h_i|\psi_{i-1}]$ at time instant i as:

$$E[h_i|\psi_{i-1}] = \alpha_0 + \alpha_1 (\epsilon_{i-1} + \gamma)^2 + \beta_1 h_{i-1}$$

and at instant $i + 1$, $E[h_{i+1}|\psi_{i-1}]$ is:

$$E[h_{i+1}|\psi_{i-1}] = \alpha_0 + \alpha_1 E[\epsilon_i^2|\psi_{i-1}] + \beta_1 E[h_i|\psi_{i-1}] + \alpha_1 \gamma^2 + 2\gamma E[\epsilon_i|\psi_{i-1}]$$

Now since $E[\epsilon_i|\psi_{i-1}] = 0$, and $E[\epsilon_i^2|\psi_{i-1}] = E[h_i|\psi_{i-1}]$ we have:

$$E[h_{i+1}|\psi_{i-1}] = \alpha_0 + \alpha_1 \gamma^2 + (\alpha_1 + \beta_1) E[h_i|\psi_{i-1}] \tag{16.10}$$

Proceeding in a similiar manner we have:

$$E[h_{i+2}|\psi_{i-1}] = \alpha_0 + \alpha_1 E[\epsilon_{i+1}^2|\psi_{i-1}] + \beta_1 E[h_{i+1}|\psi_{i-1}] + \alpha_1\gamma^2 + 2\gamma E[\epsilon_{i+1}|\psi_{i-1}]$$

$$E[h_{i+2}|\psi_{i-1}] = \alpha_0 + \alpha_1\gamma^2 + (\alpha_1 + \beta_1)E[h_{i+1}|\psi_{i-1}]$$

$$E[h_{i+2}|\psi_{i-1}] = \alpha_0 + \alpha_1\gamma^2 + (\alpha_1 + \beta_1)\{\alpha_0 + \alpha_1\gamma^2 + (\alpha_1 + \beta_1)E[h_i|\psi_{i-1}]\}$$

$$E[h_{i+2}|\psi_{i-1}] = (\alpha_0 + \alpha_1\gamma^2)\{1 + (\alpha_1 + \beta_1)\} + (\alpha_1 + \beta_1)^2 E[h_i|\psi_{i-1}] \qquad (16.11)$$

$$E[h_{i+3}|\psi_{i-1}] = \alpha_0 + \alpha_1 E[\epsilon_{i+2}^2|\psi_{i-1}] + \beta_1 E[h_{i+2}|\psi_{i-1}] + \alpha_1\gamma^2 + 2\gamma E[\epsilon_{i+2}|\psi_{i-1}]$$

$$E[h_{i+3}|\psi_{i-1}] = \alpha_0 + \alpha_1\gamma^2 + (\alpha_1 + \beta_1)E[h_{i+2}|\psi_{i-1}]$$

$$E[h_{i+3}|\psi_{i-1}] = \alpha_0 + \alpha_1\gamma^2 + (\alpha_1 + \beta_1)$$
$$\times \left\{(\alpha_0 + \alpha_1\gamma^2)(1 + (\alpha_1 + \beta_1) + (\alpha_1 + \beta_1)^2 E[h_i|\psi_{i-1}]\right\}$$

$$E[h_{i+3}|\psi_{i-1}] = (\alpha_0 + \alpha_1\gamma^2)\left\{1 + (\alpha_1 + \beta_1) + (\alpha_1 + \beta_1)^2\right\}$$
$$+ (\alpha_1 + \beta_1)^3 E[h_i|\psi_{i-1}] \qquad (16.12)$$

So in general we have:

$$E[h_{i+T}|\psi_{i-1}] = (\alpha_0 + \alpha_1\gamma^2)\left\{1 + (\alpha_1 + \beta_1) + \cdots + (\alpha_1 + \beta_1)^{T-1}\right\}$$
$$+ (\alpha_1 + \beta_1)^T E[h_i|\psi_{i-1}] \qquad (16.13)$$

Equation 16.13 is the sum of T terms of a Geometric Progression with first term $\alpha_0 + \alpha_1\gamma^2$ and common factor $(\alpha_1 + \beta_1)$, and also additional term $(\alpha_1 + \beta_1)^T E[h_i|_{i-1}]$. So

---

AGARCH-I(1,1) forecast:

$$E[h_{i+T}|\psi_i] = \frac{\left\{\alpha_0 + \alpha_1\gamma^2 - (\alpha_1 + \beta_1)^T\right\}}{1 - (\alpha_1 + \beta_1)} + (\alpha_1 + \beta_1)^T E[h_i|\psi_{i-1}] \qquad (16.14)$$

Since $\alpha_1 + \beta_1 < 1$ for a stationary process, as $T \to \infty$ we have

$$E[h_{i+T}|\psi_{i-1}] = \frac{\alpha_0 + \alpha_1\gamma^2}{1 - (\alpha_1 + \beta_1)} \qquad (16.15)$$

which is just the unconditional variance of the GARCH sequence. It can be seen from Equations 16.13 and 16.15 that the volatility forecast is mean reverting, and that the smaller the value of $\alpha_1 + \beta_1$ the faster is the reversion speed.

16.2   AGARCH-II

The AGARCH-II process is defined by:

$$h_i = \alpha_0 + \sum_{j=1}^{q}\alpha_j(|\epsilon_{i-j}| + \gamma\epsilon_{i-j})^2 + \sum_{j=1}^{p}\beta_j h_{i-j}, \quad i = 1, \ldots, n$$

Following the same procedure as in Section 15.2 we have

$$\epsilon_i^2 = \alpha_0 + \sum_{j=1}^{\kappa}(\alpha_j + \beta_j + \gamma^2\Delta_j)\epsilon_{i-j}^2 - \sum_{j=1}^{p}\beta_j\nu_{i-j} + \nu_i + 2\gamma\sum_{j=1}^{q}\alpha_j|\epsilon_{i-j}|\epsilon_{i-j}$$

where $\kappa = \max(p,q)$ and we have $\Delta_j = \alpha_j = 0$, for $j > q$, $\beta_j = 0$, for $j > p$, and $\Delta_j = 1$ for $j \leq q$. Taking expectations gives:

$$E[\epsilon_i^2] = \alpha_0 + \sum_{j=1}^{\kappa}(\alpha_j + \beta_j + \gamma^2\Delta_j)E[\epsilon_{i-j}^2]$$

since $E[\nu_i] = 0$ and $E[|\epsilon_i|\epsilon_i] = 0$.

This is an AR(κ) process, and the condition for ϵ_i^2 to be covariance stationary is :

$$\sum_{j=1}^{\kappa}(\alpha_j + \beta_j + \gamma^2\Delta_j) < 1 \tag{16.16}$$

Assuming that ϵ_i^2 is covariance stationary we have $\sigma_0^2 = E[\epsilon_i^2] = E[\epsilon_{i-j}^2]$ and so

$$E[\epsilon_i^2] = \alpha_0 + \sum_{j=1}^{\kappa}(\alpha_j + \beta_j + \gamma^2\Delta_j)E[\epsilon_i^2]$$

which results in

AGARCH-II unconditional variance

$$\sigma_0^2 = E[\epsilon_i^2] = \frac{\alpha_0}{(1 - \sum_{j=1}^{\kappa}(\alpha_j + \beta_j + \gamma^2\Delta_j))} \tag{16.17}$$

16.3   GJR–GARCH

The GJR–GARCH(p,q) process is defined as:

$$h_i = \alpha_0 + \sum_{j=1}^{q}(\alpha_j + \gamma S_{i-j})\epsilon_{i-j}^2 + \sum_{j=1}^{p}\beta_j h_{i-j}, \quad i = 1,\ldots,n$$

where $S_i = 1$, if $\epsilon_i < 0$ and $S_i = 0$, if $\epsilon_i \geq 0$.

Following the same procedure as in Section 15.2 we have

$$\epsilon_i^2 = \alpha_0 + \sum_{j=1}^{\kappa}(\alpha_j + \beta_j + \gamma S_{i-j}\Delta_j)\epsilon_{i-j}^2 - \sum_{j=1}^{p}\beta_j\nu_{i-j} + \nu_i$$

where $\kappa = \max(p,q)$ and we have $\Delta_j = \alpha_j = 0$, for $j > q$, $\beta_j = 0$, for $j > p$, and $\Delta_j = 1$ for $j \leq q$. Taking expectations gives:

$$E[\epsilon_i^2] = \alpha_0 + \sum_{j=1}^{\kappa}(\alpha_j + \beta_j + E[S_{i-j}]\gamma\Delta_j)E[\epsilon_{i-j}^2]$$

$$E[\epsilon_i^2] = \alpha_0 + \sum_{j=1}^{\kappa}(\alpha_j + \beta_j + \frac{\gamma}{2}\Delta_j)E[\epsilon_{i-j}^2]$$

Since the probability distribution for ϵ_i is symmetric about zero we have the probability for $\epsilon_i < 0$ is $1/2$ and $E[S_i] = 1/2$.

This is an AR(κ) process, and the condition for ϵ_i^2 to be covariance stationary is :

$$\sum_{j=1}^{\kappa}(\alpha_j + \beta_j + \frac{\gamma}{2}\Delta_j) < 1 \tag{16.18}$$

Assuming that ϵ_i^2 is covariance stationary we have $\sigma_0^2 = E[\epsilon_i^2] = E[\epsilon_{i-j}^2]$ and so

$$E[\epsilon_i^2] = \alpha_0 + \sum_{j=1}^{\kappa}(\alpha_j + \beta_j + \frac{\gamma}{2}\Delta_j)E[\epsilon_i^2]$$

We therefore have

GJR–GARCH unconditional variance

$$\sigma_0^2 = E[\epsilon_i^2] = \alpha_0\left\{1 - \sum_{j=1}^{\kappa}(\alpha_j + \beta_j + \frac{\gamma}{2}\Delta_j)\right\}^{-1} \tag{16.19}$$

Chapter 17

GARCH conditional probability distributions

Here we give some useful results concerning various conditional probability distributions that are commonly used in GARCH models. For each distribution we give the following information:

- The probability density function, $f(\epsilon_i)$.
- The quantity $\mathcal{L}_i(\theta)$, which is *minus* the log likelihood (see Chapter 18). Here θ is the vector of GARCH model parameters, and the subscript i indicates the contribution from the i term in the sequence. The sample log likelihood for the complete n term GARCH sequence is $\mathcal{L}(\theta) = -\Sigma_{i=1}^{n}\mathcal{L}_i(\theta)$. In this section we assume that vector θ contains the model parameters for a non-linear regression-GARCH(p,q) process in which the residuals, ϵ_i, are described by a single asymmetry parameter, γ, and a given conditional probability density function. Thus the parameter vector θ given here is correct for AGARCH-I, AGARCH-II, and GJR–GARCH processes, but would require extra elements for an EGARCH process. More information concerning the use of $\mathcal{L}_i(\theta)$ in parameter estimation can be found in Chapter 18.
- The value of $E[|\epsilon_i|]$, which is used in the EGARCH model.
- The value of the kurtosis, which indicates how thick the tails of the distribution are.

17.1   GAUSSIAN DISTRIBUTION

17.1.1   The probability density function

The probability density function for Gaussian shocks, ϵ_i, with zero mean and variance h_i is:

Gaussian probability density function

$$f(\epsilon_i) = \frac{1}{\sqrt{2\pi h_i}} \exp\left(-\frac{\epsilon_i^2}{2h_i}\right) \qquad (17.1)$$

17.1.2   The kurtosis

The kurtosis for a Gaussian distribution is 3. This can be proved as follows:

$$E[\epsilon_i^2] = \frac{1}{\sqrt{2\pi h_i}} \int_{-\infty}^{\infty} \epsilon_i^2 \exp\left(-\frac{\epsilon_i^2}{2h_i}\right) d\epsilon_i = \frac{2}{\sqrt{2\pi h_i}} \int_0^{\infty} \epsilon_i^2 \exp\left(-\frac{\epsilon_i^2}{2h_i}\right) d\epsilon_i$$

Using the standard integral results in Appendix K, and the substitution $a = 1/2h_i$ we have:

$$E[\epsilon_i^2] = \frac{4h_i}{4\sqrt{2\pi h_i}}\sqrt{2\pi h_i} = h_i$$

Similarly

$$E[\epsilon_i^4] = \frac{1}{\sqrt{2\pi h_i}}\int_{-\infty}^{\infty}\epsilon_i^4\exp\left(-\frac{\epsilon_i^2}{2h_i}\right)d\epsilon_i = \frac{2}{\sqrt{2\pi h_i}}\int_0^{\infty}\epsilon_i^4\exp\left(-\frac{\epsilon_i^2}{2h_i}\right)d\epsilon_i$$

$$E[\epsilon_i^4] = \frac{2}{\sqrt{2\pi h_i}}\frac{12h_i^2}{8}\sqrt{2\pi h_i} = 3h_i^2$$

Therefore

Gaussian kurtosis

$$\aleph = \frac{E[\epsilon_i^4]}{(E[\epsilon_i^2])^2} = \frac{3h_i^2}{h_i^2} = 3 \qquad (17.2)$$

17.1.3 The log likelihood

If we take the logarithm of the probability density function in Section 17.1.1 we obtain the following expression for the log likelihood:

$$\mathcal{L}_i(\theta) = \frac{1}{2}\log(2\pi) + \frac{1}{2}\log(h_i) + \frac{1}{2}\frac{\epsilon_i^2}{h_i} \qquad (17.3)$$

or ignoring the constant term:

Gaussian log likelihood

$$\mathcal{L}_i(\theta) = \frac{1}{2}\log(h_i) + \frac{1}{2}\frac{\epsilon_i^2}{h_i} \qquad (17.4)$$

where $\theta = (w^T, b_0, b^T)$, $w^T = (\alpha_0, \alpha_1, \ldots, \alpha_q, \beta_1, \ldots, \beta_p, \gamma)$ and $b^T = (b_1, \ldots, b_k)$.

17.1.4 Calculation of $E[|\epsilon_i|]$

$$E[|\epsilon_i|] = \frac{1}{\sqrt{2\pi h_i}}\int_{-\infty}^{\infty}|\epsilon_i|\exp\left(-\frac{\epsilon_i^2}{2h_i}\right)d\epsilon_i$$

$$= \frac{2}{\sqrt{2\pi h_i}}\int_0^{\infty}\epsilon_i\exp\left(-\frac{\epsilon_i^2}{2h_i}\right)d\epsilon_i$$

Using the standard integral results given in Appendix K, and on the substitution of $y = \epsilon_i/\sqrt{2h_i}$ we have:

$$E[|\epsilon_i|] = \frac{2h_i}{\sqrt{2\pi h_i}}\frac{1}{2} = \sqrt{\frac{2h_i}{\pi}} \qquad (17.5)$$

17.2 STUDENT'S t DISTRIBUTION

17.2.1 The probability density function

The probability density function for shocks ϵ_i following a Student's t distribution with ν degrees of freedom, zero mean, and variance h_i is (DeGroot, 1970):

Student's t distribution probability density function

$$f(\epsilon_i) = \frac{\Gamma((\nu + 1)/2)(\nu - 2)^{-1/2}h_i^{-1/2}}{\pi^{1/2}\Gamma(\nu/2)}\left[1 + \frac{\epsilon_i^2}{h_i(\nu - 2)}\right]^{-(\nu+1)/2}, \qquad \text{where } \nu > 2$$

$$(17.6)$$

17.2.2 The kurtosis

The kurtosis is (see Appendix J):

Student's t distribution kurtosis

$$\aleph = \frac{3(\nu - 2)}{(\nu - 4)}, \qquad \text{where } \nu > 4 \qquad (17.7)$$

For convenience we now tabulate the kurtosis, $\aleph$, for different values of ν:

ν	$\aleph$
4.2	33.000
5.0	9.000
10.0	4.000
20.0	3.375
50.0	3.1304
100.0	3.0625

It can be seen that $\aleph$ is always greater than the kurtosis for a Gaussian distribution. However, for values of ν below about 5 the tails are very thick compared to a Gaussian distribution, while when ν is above about 20.0 they are almost identical to a Gaussian distribution.

17.2.3 The log likelihood

The log likelihood is obtained by taking the logarithm of the probability density function given in Section 17.2.1, and is:

$$\mathcal{L}_i(\theta) = -\log(\Gamma((\nu+1)/2)) + \log(\Gamma(\nu/2)) + \frac{1}{2}\log(\pi) + \frac{1}{2}\log(\nu-2))$$

$$+ \frac{1}{2}\log(h_i) + \frac{\nu+1}{2}\log\left(1 + \frac{\epsilon_i^2}{(\nu-2)h_i}\right) \tag{17.8}$$

or ignoring the constant term:

Student's *t* distribution log likelihood

$$\mathcal{L}_i(\theta) = -\log(\Gamma((\nu+1)/2)) + \log(\Gamma(\nu/2)) + \frac{1}{2}\log(\nu-2))$$

$$+ \frac{1}{2}\log(h_i) + \frac{\nu+1}{2}\log\left(1 + \frac{\epsilon_i^2}{(\nu-2)h_i}\right) \tag{17.9}$$

where $\theta = (\omega^T, \nu, b_0, b^T)$, $\omega^T = (\alpha_0, \alpha_1, \ldots, \alpha_q, \beta_1, \ldots, \beta_p, \gamma)$, and $b^T = (b_1, \ldots, b_k)$.

17.2.4 Calculation of $E[|\epsilon_i|]$

As previously stated the Student's *t* distribution density function is:

$$f(\epsilon_i) = \mathcal{K}\left[1 + \frac{\epsilon_i^2}{h_i(\nu-2)}\right]^{-(\nu+1)/2}$$

where

$$\mathcal{K} = \frac{\Gamma((\nu+1)/2)(\nu-2)^{-1/2}h_i^{-1/2}}{\pi^{1/2}\Gamma(\nu/2)}$$

we have:

$$E[|\epsilon_i|] = \mathcal{K}\int_{-\infty}^{\infty}\left(1 + \frac{\epsilon_i^2}{h_i(\nu-2)}\right)^{-(\nu+1)/2}|\epsilon_i|d\epsilon_i$$

$$= 2\mathcal{K}\int_0^{\infty}\frac{\epsilon_i d\epsilon_i}{(1 + \epsilon_i^2/(h_i(\nu-2)))^{(\nu+1)/2}}$$

$$= 2\mathcal{K}(h_i(\nu-2))^{(\nu+1)/2}\int_0^{\infty}\frac{\epsilon_i d\epsilon_i}{(h_i(\nu-2) + \epsilon_i^2)^{(\nu+1)/2}}$$

Using the value of the integral $\int_0^\infty (\epsilon_i^a d\epsilon_i)/((m + \epsilon_i^b)^c)$ in Appendix K, with $a = 1, b = 2, c = (\nu + 1)/2$ and $m = (\nu - 2)h_i$ we have:

$$\frac{m^{(a+1-bc)/b}}{b} = \frac{(h_i(\nu - 2))^{(1-\nu)/2}}{2}, \; \Gamma\left(\frac{a+1}{b}\right) = \Gamma(1) = 1, \; \Gamma\left(c - \frac{a+1}{b}\right)$$

$$= \Gamma\left(\frac{\nu - 1}{2}\right), \; \Gamma(c) = \Gamma\left(\frac{\nu + 1}{2}\right)$$

This gives:

$$E[|\epsilon_i|] = 2\mathcal{K}(h_i(\nu - 2))^{(\nu+1)/2} \frac{(h_i(\nu - 2))^{(1-\nu)/2}}{2} \frac{\Gamma((\nu - 1)/2)}{\Gamma((\nu + 1)/2)}$$

Substituting for $\mathcal{K}$ and cancelling similar terms we obtain:

$$E[|\epsilon_i|] = \frac{((\nu - 2)h_i)^{1/2}\Gamma((\nu - 1)/2)}{\pi^{1/2}\Gamma(\nu/2)}$$

Using $((\nu - 1)/2)\Gamma((\nu - 1)/2) = \Gamma((\nu - 1)/2 + 1) = \Gamma((\nu + 1)/2)$ we obtain

$$E[|\epsilon_i|] = \frac{2((\nu - 2)h_i)^{1/2}\Gamma((\nu + 1)/2)}{\pi^{1/2}\Gamma(\nu/2)(\nu - 1)} \tag{17.10}$$

Note: This corrects an error in the literature (Taylor, 1994) which, for $h_i = 1$, gives the expression as:

$$E[|\epsilon_i|] = \frac{2((\nu - 2))^{1/2}\Gamma((\nu/2 + 1))}{\pi^{1/2}\Gamma(\nu/2)(\nu - 1)}$$

17.3 GENERAL ERROR DISTRIBUTION

This distribution is also known as: the exponential power distribution, the error distribution and the generalized error distribution. The distribution is symmetric about the mean, and the kurtosis can be varied by the altering the value of the distribution's shape parameter.

17.3.1 The probability density function

The general error distribution function, see for example Nelson (1991), is:

General error distribution probability density function

$$f(\epsilon_i) = \frac{a}{\lambda \, 2^{(1+1/a)}\Gamma(1/a)} \exp\left(-\frac{1}{2}\left|\frac{\epsilon_i}{\lambda}\right|^a\right) \tag{17.11}$$

where λ is the scale factor, a is the exponent (or shape parameter), and the distribution has zero mean.

Sometimes this equation is written in the form:

$$f(\epsilon_i) = \frac{1}{\lambda 2^{(1+1/a)}\Gamma(1+1/a)} \exp\left(-\frac{1}{2}\left|\frac{\epsilon_i}{\lambda}\right|^a\right) \tag{17.12}$$

where we have used $1/a\ \Gamma(1/a) = \Gamma(1+1/a)$.

Another form, see for example Good (1979) and Tadikamalla (1980), is:

$$f(\epsilon_i) = \frac{1}{2\ \Gamma(1+1/a)} \exp(-|\epsilon_i|^a) \tag{17.13}$$

This is just Equation 17.11 with a scale factor $\lambda = 1/2^{1/a}$.

If the variance of the distribution is h_i then we have (see Appendix I.1):

$$\lambda = \left(\frac{2^{-2/a}\Gamma\ (1/a)\ h_i}{\Gamma(3/a)}\right)^{1/2} \tag{17.14}$$

17.3.2   The kurtosis

The kurtosis of the distribution (see Appendix I.2) is:

General error distribution kurtosis

$$\aleph = \frac{\Gamma(5/a)\Gamma(1/a)}{\Gamma(3/a)\Gamma(3/a)} \tag{17.15}$$

We will now illustrate how the kurtosis of the distribution changes with the shape parameter, *a*.

When $a = 1$, then $f(\epsilon_i)$ becomes the Laplace distribution (double-sided exponential distribution), since:

$$f(\epsilon_i) = \frac{1}{2\mu}\exp\left(-\left|\frac{\epsilon_i}{\mu}\right|\right)$$

where $\mu = 2\lambda$ is the width of the distribution, and $\lambda = \left\{\frac{\Gamma(1)h_i}{4\Gamma(3)}\right\}^{1/2} = \frac{1}{2}\sqrt{\frac{h_i}{6}}$.

The kurtosis of a Laplace distribution is 6. This can be verified by using $\Gamma(n) = (n-1)!$, and substituting $a = 1$ into Equation 17.15:

$$\aleph = \frac{\Gamma(5)\ \Gamma(1)}{\Gamma(3)\ \Gamma(3)} = \frac{4 \times 3 \times 2 \times 1}{2 \times 2} = 6$$

When $a = 2$, then $f(\epsilon_i)$ simplifies to the Gaussian distribution: $\lambda = \{(2^{-1}\Gamma(1/2)h_i)/(\Gamma(3/2))\}^{1/2} = \sqrt{h_i}$, using $\Gamma(3/2) = (1/2)\Gamma(1/2)$ and since $\Gamma(1/2) = \sqrt{\pi}$ we have:

$$f(\epsilon_i) = \frac{2h_i^{-1/2}}{2^{3/2}\Gamma(1/2)}\exp\left(-\frac{\epsilon_i^2}{2h_i}\right) = \frac{1}{\sqrt{2\pi h_i}}\exp\left(-\frac{\epsilon_i^2}{2h_i}\right)$$

The kurtosis of a Gaussian distribution is 3. This can easily be verified by using $\Gamma(3/2) = \sqrt{\pi}/2, \Gamma(5/2) = 3\sqrt{\pi}/4$, and substituting $a = 2$ into Equation 17.15:

$$\aleph = \frac{\Gamma(5/2)\ \Gamma(1/2)}{\Gamma(3/2)\ \Gamma(3/2)} = \frac{3/4\sqrt{\pi}\ \sqrt{\pi}}{1/2\sqrt{\pi}\ 1/2\ \sqrt{\pi}} = 3$$

When $a \longrightarrow \infty$, then we have (Nelson, 1991 and Appendix I.3):

$$f(\epsilon_i) \longrightarrow \mathcal{U}(-(3h_i)^{1/2}, (3h_i)^{1/2})$$

where $\mathcal{U}(a, b)$ is a uniform distribution with lower and upper limits a and b respectively, and a kurtosis of 9/5.

In summary then, when $a < 2$, the distribution is *leptokurtic* (has tails that are thicker than those for a Gaussian), and when $a > 2$ the distribution is *platykurtic* (has tails that are thinner than those for a Gaussian).

17.3.3 The log likelihood

The log likelihood is obtained by taking the logarithm of the probability density function given in Section 17.3.1, and is:

$$\mathcal{L}_i(\theta) = -\log(a) + \log(\lambda) + (1 + 1/a)\log(2) + \log(\Gamma(1/a)) + \frac{1}{2}\left|\frac{\epsilon_i}{\lambda}\right|^a$$

or ignoring the constant term, $\log(2)$, we have:

General error distribution log likelihood

$$\mathcal{L}_i(\theta) = -\log(a) + \log(\lambda) + \frac{1}{a}\log(2) + \log(\Gamma(1/a)) + \frac{1}{2}\left|\frac{\epsilon_i}{\lambda}\right|^a \qquad (17.16)$$

where $\theta = (w^T, a, \lambda, b_0, b^T)$, $w^T = (\alpha_0, \alpha_1, \ldots, \alpha_q, \beta_1, \ldots, \beta_p, \gamma)$, and $b^T = (b_1, \ldots, b_k)$.

17.3.4 Calculation of $E[|\epsilon_i|]$

$$E[|\epsilon_i|] = \mathcal{K}\int_{-\infty}^{\infty}|\epsilon_i|\exp\left(-\frac{1}{2}\left|\frac{\epsilon_i}{\lambda}\right|^a\right)d\epsilon_i = 2\mathcal{K}\int_0^{\infty}\epsilon_i\exp\left(-\frac{1}{2}\left(\frac{\epsilon_i}{\lambda}\right)^a\right)d\epsilon_i$$

Using the standard integral results in Appendix K with $n = 1$, $p = a$, and $b = (1/2)(1/\lambda)^a$ gives:

$$E[|\epsilon_i|] = \frac{2\mathcal{K}}{a}\Gamma\left(\frac{2}{a}\right)\left\{\frac{1}{2}\left(\frac{1}{\lambda}\right)^a\right\}^{-2/a}$$

After some simplification this yields:

$$E[|\epsilon_i|] = \frac{2\lambda^2 \mathcal{K}}{a} \Gamma\left(\frac{2}{a}\right)\left(\frac{1}{2}\right)^{-2/a}$$

and substituting for $\mathcal{K}$ we then have:

$$E[|\epsilon_i|] = \frac{\Gamma(2/a)\lambda 2^{1/a}}{\Gamma(1/a)} \qquad\qquad (17.17)$$

Chapter 18

Maximum likelihood parameter estimation

In this chapter we will discuss how the model parameter vector θ for a GARCH sequence can be estimated. For a standard linear GARCH(p,q) with regression terms we have $\theta = (\omega^T, b^T)$, where $\omega^T = (\alpha_0, \alpha_1, \ldots, \alpha_q,\ \beta_1, \ldots, \beta_p)$ and $b^T = (b_1, \ldots, b_k)$.

18.1 THE CONDITIONAL LOG LIKELIHOOD

Assume we have a standard linear GARCH(p,q) sequence of length n, in which the observations $y_i, i = 1, \ldots, n$ are given by:

$$y_i = b_0 + X_i^T b + \epsilon_i, \quad \epsilon_i | \psi_{i-1} \sim \mathcal{R}(0, h_i) \tag{18.1}$$

$$h_i = \alpha_0 + \sum_{j=1}^{q} \alpha_j \epsilon_{i-j}^2 + \sum_{j=1}^{p} \beta_j h_{i-j}, \quad i = 1, \ldots, n \tag{18.2}$$

The residuals, ϵ_i, are independently distributed according to the arbitrary probability distribution $\mathcal{R}(0, h_i)$, which has zero mean and time-dependent variance h_i.

The notation ψ_{i-1} has been used to denote information content up to and including time instant $i - 1$, that will affect the conditional distribution of ϵ_i. In this case ψ_{i-1} represents the information that affects the variance h_i of $\mathcal{R}(0, h_i)$. The syntax $\epsilon_i | \psi_{i-1}$ is used to indicate that the PDF of the residual ϵ_i is conditional on ψ_{i-1}. For the GARCH models considered here it is only the variance h_i of the PDF for ϵ_i that is affected by the information ψ_{i-1}. Also, since ϵ_i is independently distributed to ϵ_{i-1} we have that $E(\epsilon_i^2 | \psi_{i-1}) = 0$ and $E(\epsilon_i^2 | \psi_{i-1} \epsilon_{i-1}^2 | \psi_{i-2}) = E(\epsilon_i^2 | \psi_{i-1})\ E(\epsilon_{i-1}^2 | \psi_{i-2})$.

The joint density distribution for a sample of independently distributed variables can be obtained by taking the product of the individual probability densities.

This means that the joint probability density distribution of the first two residuals in a GARCH sequence is:

$$f(\epsilon_2, \epsilon_1; \theta) = f(\epsilon_2 | \psi_1; \theta) f(\epsilon_1 | \psi_0; \theta)$$

where we have used the notation $f(\epsilon_2 | \psi_1; \theta)$ to indicate that the distribution of ϵ_2 is conditional on ψ_1 and depends on the parameter vector θ.

Similarly the joint probability density distribution of the first three residuals in a GARCH sequence is:

$$f(\epsilon_3, \epsilon_2, \epsilon_1; \theta) = f(\epsilon_3 | \psi_2; \theta) f(\epsilon_2 | \psi_1; \theta) f(\epsilon_1 | \psi_0; \theta)$$

Continuing this process for all the residuals in the sequence yields the sample joint probability density function, $F(\theta)$, for the residuals of the complete series:

$$F(\theta) = f(\epsilon_n, \ldots, \epsilon_1; \theta) = \prod_{i=1}^{n} f(\epsilon_i | \psi_{i-1}; \theta)$$

Taking natural logarithms we obtain:

$$\log(F(\theta)) = \sum_{i=1}^{n} \log(f(\epsilon_i | \psi_{i-1}; \theta)) \tag{18.3}$$

If Equation 18.2 is conditioned using known pre-observed values $\epsilon_i, \epsilon_i^2, h_i, i \leq 0$, (see Section 20.1 for more details) then we can use the parameter vector θ to iteratively evaluate the time dependent variance $h_1, \ldots, h_n$ and also determine the information content $\psi_1, \ldots, \psi_{n-1}$. This means that we can substitute $\epsilon_i = y_i - b_0 - X_i^T b$ into the PDF for $\mathcal{R}(0, h_i)$ and thus obtain the probabilities $f(\epsilon_i | \psi_{i-1}; \theta)$.

We can then evaluate the sample log likelihood, $\mathcal{L}(\theta)$, using:

$$-\log(F(\theta)) = \mathcal{L}(\theta) = \sum_{i=1}^{n} \mathcal{L}_i(\theta)$$

where $\mathcal{L}_i(\theta) = -\log(f(\epsilon_i | \psi_{i-1}; \theta))$, see Chapter 17.

The maximum likelihood estimator, $\hat{\theta}$, for the parameter vector θ is that which *minimises* $\mathcal{L}(\theta)$ (see Section 18.2) and is the solution to the likelihood equations:

$$\frac{\partial \mathcal{L}(\theta)}{\partial \theta} = 0$$

At the *minimum* the Hessian $\partial^2 \mathcal{L}(\theta)/\partial\theta\partial\theta^T$ is a positive definite matrix. However, care needs to be exercised since this does not guarantee that a *global* minimum rather than a *local* minimum has been reached.

18.2 THE COVARIANCE MATRIX OF THE PARAMETER ESTIMATES

In this section we will show how the covariance matrix of the maximum likelihood parameter estimates are related to the Hessian of the log likelihood function. For convenience we have adopted the $\mathcal{D}$ operator convention:

$$\mathcal{D}\mathcal{L}(\theta) = \frac{\partial \mathcal{L}(\theta)}{\partial \theta} \quad \text{and} \quad \mathcal{D}^2 \mathcal{L}(\theta) = \frac{\partial^2 \mathcal{L}(\theta)}{\partial \theta^2}$$

We will assume that the log likelihood is *locally well behaved* about its minimum and also that the minimum is *far enough away* from any boundaries that have been imposed during the optimization process. If θ_0 is the *true* value for the model parameter vector θ and $\hat{\theta}$ is the maximum likelihood estimator for θ then we can use a Taylor expansion for the value of the log likelihood about the true value as follows:

$$\mathcal{L}(\hat{\theta}) \approx \mathcal{L}(\theta_0) + (\hat{\theta} - \theta_0)\mathcal{D}\mathcal{L}(\theta_0) + \frac{(\hat{\theta} - \theta_0)^2}{2} \mathcal{D}^2 \mathcal{L}(\theta_0)$$

Where $D\mathcal{L}(\theta_0)$ is the gradient evaluated at θ_0 and $D^2\mathcal{L}(\theta_0)$ is the Hessian evaluated at θ_0. We can also expand the gradient $D\mathcal{L}(\theta)$ about the true value θ_0 as:

$$D\mathcal{L}(\hat{\theta}) \approx D\mathcal{L}(\theta_0) + (\hat{\theta} - \theta_0)D^2\mathcal{L}(\theta_0)$$

However, at a minimum (which is a solution of the likelihood equations in Section 18.1) we must have $D\mathcal{L}(\hat{\theta}) = 0$. This gives:

$$(\hat{\theta} - \theta_0)D^2\mathcal{L}(\theta_0) = -D\mathcal{L}(\theta_0)$$

and the estimation error of $(\hat{\theta} - \theta_0)$ is:

$$(\hat{\theta} - \theta_0) \approx -\frac{D\mathcal{L}(\theta_0)}{D^2\mathcal{L}(\theta_0)} \tag{18.4}$$

We will now assume that θ is a scalar and show how the variance of $(\hat{\theta} - \theta_0)$ is related to $D^2\mathcal{L}(\theta_0)$.

For a sample of n observations we must, by definition, have:

$$\int_{-\infty}^{\infty} \cdots \int_{-\infty}^{\infty} F d\epsilon_1, \ldots, d\epsilon_n = 1$$

where for convenience the sample joint probability density function $F(\theta)$ from Section 18.1 has been denoted by F.

Differentiating w.r.t θ we have:

$$\frac{\partial}{\partial \theta} \int_{-\infty}^{\infty} \cdots \int_{-\infty}^{\infty} F d\epsilon_1, \ldots, d\epsilon_n = \int_{-\infty}^{\infty} \cdots \int_{-\infty}^{\infty} \frac{\partial F}{\partial \theta} d\epsilon_1, \ldots, d\epsilon_n = 0$$

Now since $(\partial \log(F))/(\partial \theta) = (\partial \log(F)/(\partial F))(\partial F/\partial \theta) = (1/F)(\partial F/\partial \theta)$ we have:

$$\int_{-\infty}^{\infty} \cdots \int_{-\infty}^{\infty} \left(\frac{1}{F}\frac{\partial F}{\partial \theta}\right) F d\epsilon_1, \ldots, d\epsilon_n = \int_{-\infty}^{\infty} \cdots \int_{-\infty}^{\infty} \left(\frac{\partial \log(F)}{\partial \theta}\right) F d\epsilon_1, \ldots, d\epsilon_n$$

so $\quad E\left[\dfrac{\partial \log(F)}{\partial \theta}\right] = \displaystyle\int_{-\infty}^{\infty} \cdots \int_{-\infty}^{\infty} \left(\frac{\partial \log(F)}{\partial \theta}\right) F d\epsilon_1, \ldots, d\epsilon_n = 0$

Differentiating again w.r.t θ we have:

$$\frac{\partial}{\partial \theta} \int_{-\infty}^{\infty} \cdots \int_{-\infty}^{\infty} \left(\frac{1}{F}\frac{\partial F}{\partial \theta}\right) F d\epsilon_1, \ldots, d\epsilon_n = \int_{-\infty}^{\infty} \cdots \int_{-\infty}^{\infty} \left\{ F \frac{\partial}{\partial \theta}\left(\frac{1}{F}\frac{\partial F}{\partial \theta}\right) \right.$$
$$\left. + \left(\frac{1}{F}\frac{\partial F}{\partial \theta}\right)\frac{\partial F}{\partial \theta} \right\} d\epsilon_1, \ldots, d\epsilon_n = 0$$

But $(\partial^2 \log(F))/\partial \theta = (\partial/\partial \theta)((1/F)(\partial F/\partial \theta))$ so we have:

$$\int_{-\infty}^{\infty} \cdots \int_{-\infty}^{\infty} \left\{ \frac{\partial^2 \log(F)}{\partial \theta^2} + \left(\frac{1}{F}\frac{\partial F}{\partial \theta}\right)^2 \right\} F d\epsilon_1, \ldots, d\epsilon_n = 0$$

which gives

$$\int_{-\infty}^{\infty} \cdots \int_{-\infty}^{\infty} \left\{ \frac{\partial^2 \log(F)}{\partial \theta^2} + \left(\frac{\partial \log(F)}{\partial \theta}\right)^2 \right\} F d\epsilon_1, \ldots, d\epsilon_n = 0$$

So we have:

$$\int_{-\infty}^{\infty} \cdots \int_{-\infty}^{\infty} \left(\frac{\partial \log(F)}{\partial \theta} \right)^2 F d\epsilon_1, \ldots, d\epsilon_n = -\int_{-\infty}^{\infty} \cdots \int_{-\infty}^{\infty} \left(\frac{\partial^2 \log(F)}{\partial \theta^2} \right) F d\epsilon_1, \ldots, d\epsilon_n$$

which using Equation 18.3 gives:

$$E \left[\sum_{i=1}^{n} \left\{ \frac{\partial \log(f(\epsilon_i | \psi_{i-1}; \theta))}{\partial \theta} \right\}^2 \right] = -E \left[\sum_{i=1}^{n} \frac{\partial^2 \log(f(\epsilon_i | \psi_{i-1}; \theta))}{\partial \theta^2} \right] = \mathcal{F}_\theta$$

This can be restated as:

$$\frac{1}{n} \left\{ \frac{\partial \mathcal{L}(\theta)}{\partial \theta} \right\}^2 = \frac{1}{n} \frac{\partial^2 \mathcal{L}(\theta)}{\partial \theta^2} = \mathcal{F}_\theta \quad \text{or equivalently:} \quad \mathcal{D}^2 \mathcal{L}(\theta) = n \mathcal{F}_\theta \qquad (18.5)$$

where $\mathcal{F}_\theta$ is the *average* variance of the independent random variables

$$\frac{\partial \log(f(\epsilon_i | \psi_{i-1}; \theta))}{\partial \theta}, \quad i = 1, \ldots, n$$

If we denote the variance of the ith variable by σ_i^2 and the sum of these variables by σ_n^2 then:

$$\sigma_n^2 = \left\{ \frac{\log(f(\epsilon_i | \psi_{i-1}; \theta))}{\partial \theta} \right\}^2 \quad \text{and} \quad \sigma_n^2 = \sum_{i=1}^{n} \sigma_i^2 = n \mathcal{F}_\theta$$

For convenience we will also use:

$$S_n = \sum_{i=1}^{n} \frac{\log(f(\epsilon_i | \psi_{i-1}; \theta))}{\partial \theta} = -\mathcal{D} \mathcal{L}(\theta)$$

Now the generalized central limit theorem (Feller, 1971) states that as $n \longrightarrow \infty$ the variable S_n / σ_n becomes distributed as $N(0, 1)$. So at $\theta = \theta_0$ we have:

$$\eta = -\frac{\mathcal{D} \mathcal{L}(\theta_0)}{(n \mathcal{F}_{\theta_0})^{1/2}} \qquad (18.6)$$

where $\eta \sim N(0, 1)$

However, from Equations 18.4 and 18.5, we have:

$$\hat{\theta} - \theta_0 = -\frac{\mathcal{D} \mathcal{L}(\theta_0)}{\mathcal{D}^2 \mathcal{L}(\theta_0)} = -\frac{\mathcal{D} \mathcal{L}(\theta_0)}{n \mathcal{F}_{\theta_0}} \qquad (18.7)$$

So using Equation 18.6 to substitute for $\mathcal{D} \mathcal{L}(\theta_0)$ in Equation 18.7 we obtain:

$$\hat{\theta} - \theta_0 = \frac{\eta}{(n \mathcal{F}_{\theta_0})^{1/2}} \qquad (18.8)$$

This means that: $\eta' \sim N(0, n^{-1} \mathcal{F}_{\theta_0}^{-1})$

where $\eta' = \hat{\theta} - \theta_0$. The maximum likelihood estimate $\hat{\theta}$ is therefore distributed about the true value θ_0 as:

$$\hat{\theta} = N(\theta_0, n^{-1}\mathcal{F}_{\theta_0}^{-1}) \tag{18.9}$$

The value $\mathcal{F}_{\theta_0}$ was called by Fisher (1925) the *information* about θ_0, see Silvey (1975), and Cox and Hinkley (1979). The justification for this is simply that when there is more Fisher information the variance of the estimate $\hat{\theta}$ will be lower and therefore the maximum likelihood estimate will improve.

We have just considered the estimation of a single parameter θ and thus $\mathcal{F}_{\theta_0}$ is a scalar. In the more general case θ is a vector of N_p model parameters and the $N_p \times N_p$ matrix $\mathcal{F}_{\theta_0}$ is termed the Fisher *information matrix*. Under these circumstances Equation 18.5 then becomes:

$$E\left[\frac{\partial \mathcal{L}(\theta)}{\partial \theta}\frac{\partial \mathcal{L}(\theta)}{\partial \theta^T}\right] = E\left[\frac{\partial^2 \mathcal{L}(\theta)}{\partial \theta \partial \theta^T}\right] = \mathcal{F}_\theta \tag{18.10}$$

and in Equation 18.9 $n^{-1}\mathcal{F}_{\theta_0}^{-1}$ is the inverse of an $N_p \times N_p$ matrix which yields the covariance matrix, $\mathcal{C}$, of the estimated parameter vector θ.

At first sight the preceding discussion seems to have provided us with a very useful result. There is however a major problem. We don't know the true parameter vector θ_0, and so we can't evaluate $\mathcal{F}_{\theta_0}$. Indeed if we did know the value of θ_0 it would be *rather* pointless computing $\hat{\theta}$.

The only way forward is to use some kind of approximation to $\mathcal{F}_{\theta_0}$. The most obvious is to evaluate $\mathcal{F}_\theta$ at $\theta = \hat{\theta}$, and then use $\mathcal{F}_{\theta_0} \approx \mathcal{F}_{\hat{\theta}}$.

We can now rewrite Equation 18.9 in the following *usable* form:

$$\hat{\theta} = N(\theta_0, n^{-1}\mathcal{F}_{\hat{\theta}}^{-1}), \quad \text{where} \quad n^{-1}\mathcal{F}_{\hat{\theta}}^{-1} \quad \text{is} \quad \left[\frac{\partial^2 \mathcal{L}(\theta)}{\partial \theta \partial \theta^T}\right]_{\theta = \hat{\theta}}^{-1} \tag{18.11}$$

In the next section we will discuss numerical optimization and show how $\mathcal{F}_{\hat{\theta}}^{-1}$ occurs naturally in the equations that are used to maximize the log likelihood.

18.2.1 The standard errors and significance

The variance of each estimated parameter is contained in the corresponding diagonal element of the covariance matrix $\mathcal{C}$. So for a model with N_p parameters the standard errors of the estimated parameters are:

$$\sigma_i = \sqrt{\mathcal{C}_{i,i}}, \quad i = 1, \ldots, N_p$$

where $\mathcal{C}_{i,i}$ is used to denote the ith diagonal element of the covariance matrix. The standardized parameter estimate, t statistic, of the estimated value is given by the estimated value divided by the estimated standard error. So for the ith estimated parameter we have a t statistic of $t_i = \hat{\theta}_i/\sigma_i$.

We can use the value of t_i to provide evidence against the *null hypothesis*, H_0, that the actual parameter value is zero. That is H_0 assumes that the distribution of the ith standardized parameter estimate is $N(0, 1)$.

To illustrate how t_i can be used we will now use the following data for a standard-ized Gaussian distribution:

$$Pr(t_i \geq 0.52) = 0.3, \qquad Pr(t_i \geq 1.64) = 0.05$$
$$Pr(t_i \geq 1.96) = 0.025, \quad Pr(t_i \geq 2.57) = 0.005$$

where $Pr(t_i \geq X)$ is the probability that the value of t_i will be greater or equal to X.

For instance if the estimated value of t_i is 2.57 then, the probability of obtaining this value or greater from H_0 is only 0.5 per cent. Under these conditions we should reject the null hypothesis, and the estimated parameter value θ_i is then said to be significant at the 0.5 per cent level.

If however the estimated value of t_i is only 0.52 then, the probability of obtaining this value or greater from H_0 is 30 per cent (which is quite high). We therefore cannot reject the null hypothesis that the value of θ_i is zero. The estimated value of θ_i is then said to be not significant.

18.3   NUMERICAL OPTIMIZATION

The GARCH model parameters θ can be estimated by using numerical optimization to maximize the conditional log likelihood, or equivalently the value of θ which *minimizes minus* the log likelihood. From now on we will denote *minus* the log likelihood by $\mathcal{L}(\theta)$, and for simplicity refer to this quantity as the *log likelihood*, see Section 18.1.

Most optimization procedures use gradient information (either analytic or numeric) in order to iterate to a global maximum (or minimum).

In most gradient algorithms the kth iteration used to *minimize* $\mathcal{L}(\theta)$ takes the form:

$$\hat{\theta}^k = \hat{\theta}^{k-1} - \lambda H^{-1} \mathcal{DL}(\hat{\theta}^{k-1}) \tag{18.12}$$

where $\hat{\theta}^{k-1}$ is the estimate of the parameter vector obtained after $k-1$ iterations, H is some approximation to the Hessian computed at $\hat{\theta}^{k-1}$, which determines the direction of the kth step, λ is a scalar which specifies the step size in the given direction and $\mathcal{DL}(\hat{\theta}^{k-1})$ the gradient is computed at $\hat{\theta}^{k-1}$.

Some commonly used approximations to H are as follows:

- The actual Hessian $\partial^2 \mathcal{L}(\theta)/\partial\theta\partial\theta^T$.
- The conditional expectation of the Hessian.
- A positive definite matrix that is an approximation to the Hessian.
- The outer product $(\partial \mathcal{L}(\theta)/\partial\theta)(\partial \mathcal{L}(\theta)/\partial\theta^T)$.

When the Hessian is approximated by the outer product the method is known as the BHHH algorithm, see Berndt *et al.* (1974).

We note that when $\lambda = 1$ and H is the actual Hessian $\partial^2 \mathcal{L}(\theta)/\partial\theta\partial\theta^T$ then the optimization algorithm is called *Newton–Raphson* or simply *Newton*.

In maximum likelihood estimation it is often convenient to approximate the Hessian by $n \, \mathcal{F}_\theta$, where $\mathcal{F}_\theta$ is the Fisher information matrix. When this is done we have the *method of scoring*, and Equation 18.12 then becomes:

$$\hat{\theta}^k = \hat{\theta}^{k-1} - \lambda n^{-1} \mathcal{F}_{\hat{\theta}}^{-1} \mathcal{DL}(\hat{\theta}^{k-1}) \tag{18.13}$$

This technique is likely to have a lower convergence rate than a straightforward Newton method because the information matrix is only an approximation to the Hessian. However, in may instances the information matrix has a simple form and is much easier to compute than the complete Hessian. Also the information matrix will always be positive definite and so its inverse can be computed, this is not necessarily the case for the actual Hessian.

Quasi-Newton methods do not require the Hessian to be explicitly evaluated (Gill *et al.*, 1981; Murtagh and Saunders, 1983). The iterative scheme is of the form of Equation 18.12 and the matrix H must be a positive definite. At each iteration H is updated in such a way as to yield a series of positive definite matrices which eventually converge to the inverse of the Hessian. The initial H matrix can be any positive definite matrix, and a common choice is the identity matrix.

In Chapter 21 results are presented which show the relative advantages/disadvantages of using numeric/analytic gradients during maximum likelihood optimization. These results are from GARCH software which used a general purpose quasi-Newton nonlinear optimization routine. First derivatives could be supplied either in analytic form or computed numerically by finite-difference techniques. The optimization process relied on a Hessian which was always computed internally by the nonlinear optimizer. However, it was possible to retrieve the Hessian at the solution point $\hat{\theta}$, and thus use it as an approximation to the Fisher information matrix. GARCH stationary conditions could be ensured by imposing the linear constraint $\sum_{j=1}^{q} \alpha_j + \sum_{j=1}^{p} \beta_j < 1$ during the numerical optimization.

In Chapter 21 the following approximations to the Fisher information matrix were used:

- The second-derivative estimate, based on the *actual value of the Hessian* at the solution point $\hat{\theta}$, that is $(\partial^2 \mathcal{L}(\theta))/(\partial\theta\partial\theta_{\theta=\hat{\theta}}^T)$. This is calculated numerically using finite differences.
- The second-derivative estimate, based on the *conditional expectation of the Hessian* at the solution point $\hat{\theta}$, that is $E((\partial^2 \mathcal{L}(\theta))/(\partial\theta\partial\theta^T))_{\theta=\hat{\theta}}$.

The difficulty of modelling a GARCH(p,q) sequence depends on both p and q and also on how much volatility memory there is in the process. Higher values of the parameters $\beta_j, j = 1, \ldots, p$, give rise to more volatility memory and are therefore harder to model accurately. Increasing the number of model parameters will also make the model more difficult to model simply because there are more variables to numerically optimize. This suggests the following order of difficulty ARCH(1), ARCH(2), ARCH(3), GARCH(1,1), GARCH(1,2), GARCH(2,2), etc.

In Chapter 19 information is given on how to compute the analytic gradients for a regression GJR–GARCH(p,q) sequence. Chapter 20 elaborates on the information in Chapter 19, and provides complete pseudocode that enables the reader to write computer programs to calculate both the conditional log likelihood and its gradients.

18.4   SCALING THE DATA

Numerical optimization procedures can have difficulty in minimizing a function in which the magnitudes of the individual variables differ by a large factor (say 10^6 or greater). This can occur in GARCH(p,q) processes where the parameters α_i, $i = 1, \ldots, p$, β_i, $i = 1, \ldots, q$ are usually in the range 0.1 to 1, but the parameter α_0 can be very small. In these circumstances scaling the observations, y_i, $i = 1, \ldots, n$, by λ will result in a time series in which α_0 is multiplied by the factor λ^2. For instance if α_0 is 10^{-6} in the original sequence, then scaling the data by 100 gives a new series with $\alpha_0 = 10^{-2}$.

Here we will consider data scaling for both linear and nonlinear GARCH models, and show how the model parameters for the scaled data are related to those of the original data.

18.4.1   Scaling a linear GARCH process

Here we consider the effect of scaling the GARCH process:

$$y_i = X_i^T b + b_0 + \epsilon_i, \quad \epsilon_i | \psi_{i-1} \sim \mathcal{R}(0, h_i)$$

$$h_i = \alpha_0 + \sum_{j=1}^q \alpha_j \epsilon_{i-j}^2 + \sum_{j=1}^p \beta_j h_{i-j}, \quad i = 1, \ldots, n$$

If the observations y_i are scaled by the factor λ then we have the new GARCH process:

$$Y_i = X_i^T B + B_0 + E_i, \quad E_i | \psi_{i-1} \sim \mathcal{R}(0, H_i)$$

$$H_i = L_0 + \sum_{j=1}^q \alpha_j E_{i-j}^2 + \sum_{j=1}^p \beta_j H_{i-j}, \quad i = 1, \ldots, n$$

where $Y_i = \lambda y_i$, $L_0 = \lambda^2 \alpha_0$, $B = \lambda b$, $B_0 = \lambda b_0$, $E_i = \lambda \epsilon_i$, and $H_i = \lambda^2 h_i$.

The GARCH model parameter vector, θ, of the scaled process is:

$$\theta = (L_0, \alpha_i, i = 1, \ldots, q, \ \beta_i, i = 1, \ldots, p, B, B_0)$$

18.4.2   Scaling an AGARCH-I process

Referring to the AGARCH-I process specification in Chapter 16, and proceeding in a similar manner to Section 18.3.1, we have:

$$Y_i = X_i^T B + B_0 + E_i, \quad E_i | \psi_{i-1} \sim \mathcal{R}(0, H_i)$$

$$H_i = L_0 + \sum_{j=1}^q \alpha_j (E_{i-j} + G)^2 + \sum_{j=1}^p \beta_j H_{i-j}, \quad i = 1, \ldots, n$$

where λ is the scale factor and $Y_i = \lambda y_i$, $H_i = \lambda^2 h_i$, $L_0 = \lambda^2 \alpha_0$, $E_i = \lambda_i \epsilon_i$, $G = \lambda \gamma$, $B = \lambda b$, and $B_0 = \lambda b_0$.

The GARCH model parameter vector, θ, of the scaled process is then:

$$\theta = (L_0, \alpha_i, i = 1, \ldots, q, \beta_i, i = 1, \ldots, p, G, B, B_0)$$

18.4.3 Scaling an AGARCH-II process

Referring to the AGARCH-II process specification in Chapter 16, and proceeding in a similar manner to Section 18.3.1, we have:

$$Y_i = X_i^T B + B_0 + E_i, \quad E_i|\psi_{i-1} \sim \mathcal{R}(0, H_i)$$

$$H_i = \alpha_0 + \sum_{j=1}^{q} \alpha_j (|E_{i-j}| + \gamma E_{i-j})^2 + \sum_{j=1}^{p} \beta_j H_{i-j}, \quad i = 1, .., n$$

where λ is the scale factor, and $L_0 = \lambda^2 \alpha_0, H_i = \lambda^2 h_i, E_i = \lambda_i \epsilon_i, B = \lambda b,$ and $B_0 = \lambda b_0$.

The GARCH model parameter vector, θ, of the scaled process is then:

$$L_0, \alpha_i, i = 1, \ldots, q, \beta_i, i = 1, \ldots, p, \gamma, B \text{ and } B_0$$

18.4.4 Scaling a GJR–GARCH process

Referring to the GJR–GARCH process specification in Chapter 16, and proceeding in a similar manner to Section 18.3.1, we have:

$$Y_i = X_i^T B + B_0 + E_i, \quad E_i|\psi_{i-1} \sim \mathcal{R}(0, H_i)$$

$$H_i = L_0 + \sum_{j=1}^{q} (\alpha_j + \gamma S_{i-j}) E_{i-j}^2 + \sum_{j=1}^{p} \beta_j H_{i-j}, \quad i = 1, \ldots, n$$

where λ is the scale factor and $S_i = 1$, if $E_i < 0$, and $S_i = 0$, if $E_i \geq 0$. The scaled parameters are now: $L_0 = \lambda^2 \alpha_0, H_i = \lambda^2 h_i, E_i = \lambda_i \epsilon_i, B = \lambda b,$ and $B_0 = \lambda b_0$.

The GARCH model parameter vector, θ, of the scaled process is then: $L_0, \alpha_i, i = 1, \ldots, q, \beta_i, i = 1, \ldots, p, \gamma, B$ and B_0.

Chapter 19

Analytic derivatives of the log likelihood

In this chapter we show how to calculate analytic expressions for the first and second order partial derivatives of the log likelihood function. As previously mentioned in Section 18.3 these partial derivatives are used by Newton type numerical optimizers to *minimize* the log likelihood and thus obtain an estimate for the GARCH model parameter vector, θ. The analytic second derivative is used to as an approximation to the Fisher information matrix, and as a means of calculating the standard errors.

Information on how to compute the analytic derivatives of a standard regression-GARCH(p,q) process with Gaussian residuals is available in the literature, Fiorentini *et al.* (1996).

In Section 19.1 we show how to compute the first derivatives of a regression-GARCH(p,q) process which has either Gaussian distributed residuals or Student's t distributed residuals.

In Section 19.2 we show how to compute the conditional expectation of the Hessian for a regression-GARCH(p,q) process with Gaussian distributed residuals. This is used as an approximation for the Fisher information matrix.

The results of this section will be used in Chapter 20 to derive computational algorithms which compute the derivatives of a regression-GJR–GARCH model. The results are also used in Appendix H to compute the derivatives of a regression-AGARCH-I model.

19.1   THE FIRST DERIVATIVES

19.1.1   Gaussian distribution

Here we obtain expressions for the partial derivatives of the Gaussian log likelihood, Equation 17.4.

Partial derivatives w.r.t. the parameter vector ω:

$$\frac{\partial \mathcal{L}_i(\theta)}{\partial \omega} = \frac{1}{2} \frac{\partial(\log h_i)}{\partial h_i} \frac{\partial h_i}{\partial \omega} + \frac{\epsilon_i^2}{2} \frac{\partial(1/h_i)}{\partial h_i} \frac{\partial h_i}{\partial \omega}$$

$$\frac{\partial \mathcal{L}_i(\theta)}{\partial \omega} = \frac{1}{2h_i} \frac{\partial h_i}{\partial \omega} - \frac{\epsilon_i^2}{2h_i^2} \frac{\partial h_i}{\partial \omega} \tag{19.1}$$

Partial derivative w.r.t. the parameter b_0:

$$\frac{\partial \mathcal{L}_i(\theta)}{\partial b_0} = \frac{1}{2} \frac{\partial \log(h_i)}{\partial b_0} + \frac{1}{2} \frac{\partial \epsilon_i^2}{\partial b_0} \frac{1}{h_i} + \frac{\epsilon_i^2}{2} \frac{\partial(1/h_i)}{\partial h_i} \frac{\partial h_i}{\partial b_0}$$

$$= \frac{1}{2h_i} \frac{\partial h_i}{\partial b_0} + \frac{1}{2h_i} \frac{\partial \epsilon_i^2}{\partial b_0} - \frac{\epsilon_i^2}{2h_i^2} \frac{\partial h_i}{\partial b_0} \qquad (19.2)$$

But since $\epsilon_i = y_i - X_i^T b - b_0$ we obtain:

$$\frac{\partial \epsilon_i^2}{\partial b_0} = 2\epsilon_i \frac{\partial \epsilon_i}{\partial b_0} = 2\epsilon_i \frac{\partial(y_i - X_i^T b - b_0)}{\partial b_0} = -2\epsilon_i$$

$$\frac{\partial \mathcal{L}_i(\theta)}{\partial b_0} = \frac{1}{2h_i} \frac{\partial h_i}{\partial b_0} - \frac{\epsilon_i}{h_i} - \frac{\epsilon_i^2}{2h_i^2} \frac{\partial h_i}{\partial b_0}$$

$$\frac{\partial \mathcal{L}_i(\theta)}{\partial b_0} = -\frac{\epsilon_i}{h_i} - \frac{1}{2h_i} \frac{\partial h_i}{\partial b_0} \left(\frac{\epsilon_i^2}{h_i^2} - 1 \right) \qquad (19.3)$$

Similarly we obtain the partial derivative w.r.t. the parameter vector b:

$$\frac{\partial \mathcal{L}_i(\theta)}{\partial b} = \frac{1}{2} \frac{\partial \log(h_i)}{\partial b} + \frac{1}{2} \frac{\partial \epsilon_i^2}{\partial b} \frac{1}{h_i} + \frac{\epsilon_i^2}{2} \frac{\partial(1/h_i)}{\partial h_i} \frac{\partial h_i}{\partial b}$$

$$= \frac{1}{2h_i} \frac{\partial h_i}{\partial b} + \frac{1}{2h_i} \frac{\partial \epsilon_i^2}{\partial b} - \frac{\epsilon_i^2}{2h_i^2} \frac{\partial h_i}{\partial b} \qquad (19.4)$$

Since

$$\frac{\partial \epsilon_i^2}{\partial b} = 2\epsilon_i \frac{\partial \epsilon_i}{\partial b} = 2\epsilon_i \frac{\partial(y_i - X_i^T b - b_0)}{\partial b} = -2\epsilon_i X_i$$

$$\frac{\partial \mathcal{L}_i(\theta)}{\partial b} = \frac{1}{2h_i} \frac{\partial h_i}{\partial b} - \frac{\epsilon_i X_i}{h_i} - \frac{\epsilon_i^2}{2h_i^2} \frac{\partial h_i}{\partial b}$$

$$\frac{\partial \mathcal{L}_i(\theta)}{\partial b} = -\frac{\epsilon_i X_i}{h_i} - \frac{1}{2h_i} \frac{\partial h_i}{\partial b} \left(\frac{\epsilon_i^2}{h_i^2} - 1 \right) \qquad (19.5)$$

In summary we have:

Gaussian log likelihood partial derivatives

$$\frac{\partial \mathcal{L}(\theta)}{\partial \omega} = -\sum_{i=1}^{n} \left[\frac{1}{2h_i} \frac{\partial h_i}{\partial \omega} \left(\frac{\epsilon_i^2}{h_i} - 1 \right) \right] \qquad (19.6)$$

$$\frac{\partial \mathcal{L}(\theta)}{\partial b_0} = -\sum_{i=1}^{n} \left[\frac{\epsilon_i}{h_i} + \frac{1}{2h_i} \frac{\partial h_i}{\partial b_0} \left(\frac{\epsilon_i^2}{h_i} - 1 \right) \right] \qquad (19.7)$$

$$\frac{\partial \mathcal{L}(\theta)}{\partial b} = -\sum_{i=1}^{n} \left[\frac{\epsilon_i X_i}{h_i} + \frac{1}{2h_i} \frac{\partial h_i}{\partial b} \left(\frac{\epsilon_i^2}{h_i} - 1 \right) \right] \qquad (19.8)$$

19.1.2   Student's *t* distribution

Here we obtain expressions for the partial derivatives of the log likelihood when the series shocks have a Student's *t* distribution. Using Equation 17.8 we have:

Partial derivatives w.r.t. the parameter vector ω:

$$\frac{\partial \mathcal{L}_i(\theta)}{\partial \omega} = \frac{1}{2h_i}\frac{\partial h_i}{\partial \omega} + \frac{(\nu+1)}{2}\frac{\partial \log\left(1 + \epsilon_i^2/((\nu-2)h_i)\right)}{\partial\left(1 + \epsilon_i^2/((\nu-2)h_i)\right)}\frac{\partial\left(1 + \epsilon_i^2/((\nu-2)h_i)\right)}{\partial \omega}$$

$$= \frac{1}{2h_i}\frac{\partial h_i}{\partial \omega} + \frac{\nu+1}{2(1 + \epsilon_i^2/((\nu-2)h_i))}\frac{\partial\left(\epsilon_i^2/(h_i(\nu-2))\right)}{\partial \omega}$$

$$= \frac{1}{2h_i}\frac{\partial h_i}{\partial \omega} - \frac{\nu+1}{2(1 + \epsilon_i^2/((\nu-2)h_i))}\frac{\epsilon_i^2}{h_i^2(\nu-2)}\frac{\partial h_i}{\partial \omega}$$

$$= \frac{1}{2h_i}\frac{\partial h_i}{\partial \omega} - \frac{(\nu+1)\epsilon_i^2}{2h_i^2((\nu-2) + \epsilon_i^2/h_i)}\frac{\partial h_i}{\partial \omega}$$

$$\frac{\partial \mathcal{L}_i(\theta)}{\partial \omega} = \frac{1}{2h_i}\frac{\partial h_i}{\partial \omega} - \frac{\epsilon_i^2}{2h_i^2}\frac{\partial h_i}{\partial \omega}\mathcal{G}, \quad \text{where} \quad \mathcal{G} = \frac{(\nu+1)}{(\nu-2) + (\epsilon_i^2/h_i)} \tag{19.9}$$

Similarly we obtain the partial derivative w.r.t. the mean term, b_0:

$$\frac{\partial \mathcal{L}_i(\theta)}{\partial b_0} = -\frac{\epsilon_i}{h_i}\mathcal{G} + \frac{1}{2h_i}\left(1 - \mathcal{G}\frac{\epsilon_i^2}{h_i}\right)\frac{\partial h_i}{\partial b_0} \tag{19.10}$$

Partial derivatives w.r.t. the parameter vector *b*:

$$\frac{\partial \mathcal{L}_i(\theta)}{\partial b} = \frac{1}{2}\frac{\partial(\log h_i)}{\partial h_i}\frac{\partial h_i}{\partial b} + \frac{(\nu+1)}{2(1 + \epsilon_i^2/((\nu-2)h_i))}\frac{\partial\left(1 + \epsilon_i^2/((\nu-1)h_i)\right)}{\partial b}$$

$$= \frac{1}{2h_i}\frac{\partial h_i}{\partial b} + \frac{\nu+1}{2h_i(\nu-2)}\left(\frac{1}{1 + \epsilon_i^2/((\nu-2)h_i)}\right)\frac{\partial\epsilon_i^2}{\partial b}$$

$$+ \frac{(\nu+1)\epsilon_i^2}{2(\nu-2)}\left(\frac{1}{(1 + \epsilon_i^2/((\nu-2)h_i))}\right)\frac{\partial(1/h_i)}{\partial b} \tag{19.11}$$

Since $\partial(1/h_i)/\partial b = -(1/h_i^2)(\partial h_i/\partial b)$ we obtain:

$$\frac{\partial \mathcal{L}_i(\theta)}{\partial b} = \frac{1}{2h_i}\frac{\partial h_i}{\partial b} - \frac{(\nu+1)\epsilon_i^2}{2h_i^2(\nu-2)}\left(\frac{1}{1 + \epsilon_i^2/((\nu-2)h_i)}\right)\frac{\partial h_i}{\partial b}$$

$$- \frac{2\epsilon_i X_i(\nu+1)}{2h_i(\nu-2)}\left(\frac{1}{1 + \epsilon_i^2/((\nu-2)h_i)}\right)$$

$$= -\frac{\epsilon_i X_i(\nu+1)}{(\nu-2)h_i}\left(\frac{1}{1 + \epsilon_i^2/((\nu-2)h_i)}\right)$$

$$+ \frac{1}{2h_i}\left(1 - \frac{\epsilon_i^2(\nu+1)}{h_i(\nu-2)}\left(\frac{1}{1 + \epsilon_i^2/((\nu-2)h_i)}\right)\right)$$

$$\frac{\partial \mathcal{L}_i(\theta)}{\partial b} = -\frac{\epsilon_i X_i}{h_i}\mathcal{G} + \frac{1}{2h_i}\left(1 - \mathcal{G}\frac{\epsilon_i^2}{h_i}\right)\frac{\partial h_i}{\partial b} \tag{19.12}$$

Partial derivative w.r.t. the number of degrees of freedom, ν:
Since $(\partial(\log\Gamma(x)))/\partial x = \psi(x)$ we have the following, Abramowitz and Stegun (1968):

$$\frac{\partial(\log\Gamma((\nu+1)/2))}{\partial\nu} = \frac{1}{2}\psi\left(\frac{\nu+1}{2}\right) \quad \text{and} \quad \frac{\partial(\log\Gamma(\nu/2))}{\partial\nu} = \frac{1}{2}\psi\left(\frac{\nu}{2}\right)$$

Using this we obtain:

$$\frac{\partial\mathcal{L}_i(\theta)}{\partial\nu} = -\frac{1}{2}\psi\left(\frac{\nu+1}{2}\right) + \frac{1}{2}\psi(\nu/2) + \frac{1}{2(\nu-2)} + \frac{1}{2}\log\left(1 + \frac{\epsilon_i^2}{(\nu-2)h_i}\right)$$

$$-\frac{\nu+1}{2(1 + \epsilon_i^2/((\nu-2)h_i))} \frac{\epsilon_i^2}{h_i(\nu-2)^2}$$

$$\frac{\partial\mathcal{L}_i(\theta)}{\partial\nu} = -\frac{1}{2}\psi\left(\frac{\nu+1}{2}\right) + \frac{1}{2}\psi\left(\frac{\nu}{2}\right) + \frac{1}{2(\nu-2)}$$

$$+\frac{1}{2}\log\left(1 + \frac{\epsilon_i^2}{(\nu-2)h_i}\right) - \frac{\epsilon_i^2}{2(\nu-2)h_i}\mathcal{G} \tag{19.13}$$

In summary we have:

Student's *t* distribution log likelihood partial derivatives

$$\frac{\partial\mathcal{L}(\theta)}{\partial w} = -\sum_{i=1}^{n}\left[\frac{1}{2h_i}\frac{\partial h_i}{\partial w}\left(\frac{\epsilon_i^2}{h_i}\mathcal{G} - 1\right)\right] \tag{19.14}$$

$$\frac{\partial\mathcal{L}(\theta)}{\partial\nu} = -\sum_{i=1}^{n}\left[\mathcal{K} - \frac{1}{2}\log\left(1 + \frac{\epsilon_i^2}{(\nu-2)h_i}\right) + \frac{\epsilon_i^2}{2(\nu-2)h_i}\mathcal{G}\right] \tag{19.15}$$

$$\frac{\partial\mathcal{L}(\theta)}{\partial b_0} = -\sum_{i=1}^{n}\left[\frac{\epsilon_i}{h_i}\mathcal{G} + \frac{1}{2h_i}\frac{\partial h_i}{\partial b_0}\left(\frac{\epsilon_i^2}{h_i}\mathcal{G} - 1\right)\right] \tag{19.16}$$

$$\frac{\partial\mathcal{L}(\theta)}{\partial b} = -\sum_{i=1}^{n}\left[\frac{\epsilon_i X_i}{h_i}\mathcal{G} + \frac{1}{2h_i}\frac{\partial h_i}{\partial b}\left(\frac{\epsilon_i^2}{h_i}\mathcal{G} - 1\right)\right] \tag{19.17}$$

where $\mathcal{G} = \left(\dfrac{(\nu+1)}{(\nu-2) + \epsilon_i^2/h_i}\right)$ and $\mathcal{K} = \dfrac{1}{2}\psi\left(\dfrac{\nu+1}{2}\right) - \dfrac{1}{2}\psi\left(\dfrac{\nu}{2}\right) - \dfrac{1}{2(\nu-2)}$

19.2 THE SECOND DERIVATIVES

As previously mentioned the Hessian of the log likelihood can be used as an approximation to the Fisher information matrix. Here we will assume that the conditional PDF of the residuals is Gaussian and calculate the conditional expectation of the Hessian. We will use the result (Engle, 1982) that the off-diagonal block elements of this matrix are zero, and will only compute the diagonal block elements.

We will denote the standardized residuals $\epsilon_i/\sqrt{h_i}$ by $\mathcal{Z}_i$. So we have $\mathcal{Z}_i|\psi_{i-1} \sim NID(0, 1)$. Further we will use following results:

$$E(\mathcal{Z}_i|\psi_{i-1}) = 0, E(\mathcal{Z}_i^2|\psi_{i-1}) = 1, \text{ and } E(\mathcal{Z}_i^2|\psi_{i-1} - 1) = 0 \tag{19.18}$$

We note, ϵ_j and ϵ_k, $k \neq j$ are independent, and since in a GARCH(p,q) process h_i only depends on past values of the residuals, $\epsilon_i, i = 1, \ldots, q$, we have that h_i and $\mathcal{Z}_i$ are independent.

Using this gives:

$$E\left(\frac{\mathcal{Z}_i^2}{h_i^2}\right) = E(\mathcal{Z}_i^2)E\left(\frac{1}{h_i^2}\right) = \frac{1}{h_i^2} \tag{19.19}$$

Calculation of the diagonal block $\partial^2 \mathcal{L}_i(\theta)/\partial\omega\partial\omega^T$

Recalling from Section 19.1 that the first derivative is:

$$\frac{\partial \mathcal{L}_i(\theta)}{\partial\omega} = -\frac{1}{2h_i}\frac{\partial h_i}{\partial\omega}\left\{\frac{\epsilon_i^2}{h_i} - 1\right\}$$

Taking second derivatives w.r.t. ω we have:

$$\frac{\partial^2 \mathcal{L}_i(\theta)}{\partial\omega\partial\omega^T} = -\left\{\frac{\epsilon_i^2}{h_i} - 1\right\}\frac{\partial}{\partial\omega^T}\left\{\frac{1}{2h_i}\frac{\partial h_i}{\partial\omega}\right\} - \frac{1}{2h_i}\frac{\partial h_i}{\partial\omega}\frac{\partial}{\partial\omega^T}\left\{\frac{\epsilon_i^2}{h_i} - 1\right\}$$

$$= -\left\{\frac{\epsilon_i^2}{h_i} - 1\right\}\frac{\partial}{\partial\omega^T}\left\{\frac{1}{2h_i}\frac{\partial h_i}{\partial\omega}\right\} - \frac{\epsilon_i^2}{2h_i}\frac{\partial h_i}{\partial\omega}\frac{\partial(1/h_i)}{\partial h_i}\frac{\partial h_i}{\partial\omega^T}$$

$$= -\left\{\frac{\epsilon_i^2}{h_i} - 1\right\}\frac{\partial}{\partial\omega^T}\left\{\frac{1}{2h_i}\frac{\partial h_i}{\partial\omega}\right\} + \frac{\epsilon_i^2}{2h_i^3}\frac{\partial h_i}{\partial\omega}\frac{\partial h_i}{\partial\omega^T}$$

which expressed using standardized residuals is:

$$\frac{\partial^2 \mathcal{L}_i(\theta)}{\partial\omega\partial\omega^T} = -\{\mathcal{Z}_i^2 - 1\}\frac{\partial}{\partial\omega^T}\left\{\frac{1}{2h_i}\frac{\partial h_i}{\partial\omega}\right\} + \frac{\mathcal{Z}_i^2}{2h_i^2}\frac{\partial h_i}{\partial\omega}\frac{\partial h_i}{\partial\omega^T}$$

Therefore the conditional expectation of the block at time instant i is:

$$E\left(\frac{\partial^2 \mathcal{L}_i(\theta)}{\partial\omega\partial\omega^T}\right) = E\left(-\{\mathcal{Z}_i^2 - 1\}\frac{\partial}{\partial\omega^T}\left\{\frac{1}{2h_i}\frac{\partial h_i}{\partial\omega}\right\} + \frac{E(\mathcal{Z}_i^2)}{2h_i^2}\frac{\partial h_i}{\partial\omega}\frac{\partial h_i}{\partial\omega^T}\right)$$

$$E\left(\frac{\partial^2 \mathcal{L}_i(\theta)}{\partial\omega\partial\omega^T}\right) = -E(\{\mathcal{Z}_i^2 - 1\})\frac{\partial}{\partial\omega^T}\left\{\frac{1}{2h_i}\frac{\partial h_i}{\partial\omega}\right\} + \frac{1}{2h_i^2}\frac{\partial h_i}{\partial\omega}\frac{\partial h_i}{\partial\omega^T}$$

which gives

$$E\left(\frac{\partial^2 \mathcal{L}_i(\theta)}{\partial \omega \partial \omega^T}\right) = \frac{1}{2h_i^2} \frac{\partial h_i}{\partial \omega} \frac{\partial h_i}{\partial \omega^T}$$

The sample diagonal block is therefore:

$$E\left(\frac{\partial^2 \mathcal{L}(\theta)}{\partial \omega \partial \omega^T}\right) = \sum_{i=1}^n \frac{1}{2h_i^2} \frac{\partial h_i}{\partial \omega} \frac{\partial h_i}{\partial \omega^T} \qquad (19.20)$$

Calculation of the diagonal block $\partial^2 \mathcal{L}_i(\theta)/\partial b \partial b^T$

Recalling from Section 19.1 that the first derivative is:

$$\frac{\partial \mathcal{L}_i(\theta)}{\partial b} = -\frac{\epsilon_i X_i}{h_i} + \frac{1}{2h_i} \frac{\partial h_i}{\partial b} \left\{ \frac{\epsilon_i^2}{h_i} - 1 \right\}$$

Taking second derivatives w.r.t. to b we have:

$$\frac{\partial^2 \mathcal{L}_i(\theta)}{\partial b \partial b^T} = -\frac{X_i}{h_i} \frac{\partial \epsilon_i}{\partial b^T} - \epsilon_i X_i \frac{\partial(1/h_i)}{\partial h_i} \frac{\partial h_i}{\partial b^T} - \frac{1}{2} \frac{\partial(1/h_i)}{\partial h_i} \frac{\partial h_i}{\partial b^T} \frac{\partial h_i}{\partial b} \left\{ \frac{\epsilon_i^2}{h_i} - 1 \right\}$$

$$- \frac{1}{2h_i} \frac{\partial h_i}{\partial b} \frac{\partial}{\partial b^T} \left\{ \frac{\epsilon_i^2}{h_i} - 1 \right\}$$

But since $\epsilon_i = y_i - X_i^T b - b_0$

$$\frac{\partial \epsilon_i}{\partial b^T} = \frac{\partial(y_i - X_i^T b - b_0)}{\partial b^T} = X_i^T \quad \text{and} \quad \frac{\partial \epsilon_i^2}{\partial b^T} = -2\epsilon_i X_i$$

We have:

$$\frac{\partial^2 \mathcal{L}_i(\theta)}{\partial b \partial b^T} = \frac{X_i X_i^T}{h_i} + \frac{\epsilon_i X_i}{h_i^2} \frac{\partial h_i}{\partial b^T} - \frac{1}{2} \frac{\partial(1/h_i)}{\partial h_i} \frac{\partial h_i}{\partial b^T} \frac{\partial h_i}{\partial b} \left\{ \frac{\epsilon_i^2}{h_i} - 1 \right\} + \frac{\epsilon_i X_i}{h_i^2} \frac{\partial h_i}{\partial b^T} + \frac{\epsilon_i^2}{2h_i^3} \frac{\partial h_i}{\partial b} \frac{\partial h_i}{\partial b^T}$$

Therefore using standardized residuals and taking conditional expectations of the block at time instant i we have:

$$\left(\frac{\partial^2 \mathcal{L}_i(\theta)}{\partial b \partial b^T}\right) = \frac{X_i X_i^T}{h_i} + \frac{E(\epsilon_i) X_i}{h_i^2} \frac{\partial h_i}{\partial b^T} - \frac{1}{2} \frac{\partial(1/h_i)}{\partial h_i} \frac{\partial h_i}{\partial b^T} \frac{\partial h_i}{\partial b} E(\{\mathcal{Z}_i^2 - 1\})$$

$$+ \frac{E(\epsilon_i) X_i}{h_i^2} \frac{\partial h_i}{\partial b^T} + \frac{E(\mathcal{Z}_i^2)}{2h_i^2} \frac{\partial h_i}{\partial b} \frac{\partial h_i}{\partial b^T}$$

which gives:

$$E\left(\frac{\partial^2 \mathcal{L}_i(\theta)}{\partial b \partial b^T}\right) = \frac{X_i X_i^T}{h_i} + \frac{1}{2h_i^2} \frac{\partial h_i}{\partial b} \frac{\partial h_i}{\partial b^T}$$

The sample diagonal block is therefore:

$$E\left(\frac{\partial^2 \mathcal{L}(\theta)}{\partial b \partial b^T}\right) = \sum_{i=1}^{n}\left(\frac{X_i X_i^T}{h_i} + \frac{1}{2h_i^2}\frac{\partial h_i}{\partial b}\frac{\partial h_i}{\partial b^T}\right) \tag{19.21}$$

Calculation of the diagonal block $\partial^2 \mathcal{L}_i(\theta)/\partial b_0 \partial b_0^T$

Recalling from Section 19.1 that the first derivative is:

$$\frac{\partial \mathcal{L}_i(\theta)}{\partial b_0} = -\frac{\epsilon_i}{h_i} + \frac{1}{2h_i}\frac{\partial h_i}{\partial b_0}\left\{\frac{\epsilon_i^2}{h_i} - 1\right\}$$

Taking second derivatives w.r.t. to b_0 we have:

$$\frac{\partial^2 \mathcal{L}_i(\theta)}{\partial b_0 \partial b_0^T} = -\frac{1}{h_i}\frac{\partial \epsilon_i}{\partial b_0^T} - \epsilon_i\frac{\partial(1/h_i)}{\partial h_i}\frac{\partial h_i}{\partial b_0^T} - \frac{1}{2}\frac{\partial(1/h_i)}{\partial h_i}\frac{\partial h_i}{\partial b_0^T}\frac{\partial h_i}{\partial b_0}\left\{\frac{\epsilon_i^2}{h_i} - 1\right\}$$

$$- \frac{1}{2h_i}\frac{\partial h_i}{\partial b_0}\frac{\partial}{\partial b_0^T}\left\{\frac{\epsilon_i^2}{h_i} - 1\right\}$$

But since $\epsilon_i = y_i - X_i^T b - b_0$

$$\frac{\partial \epsilon_i}{\partial b_0^T} = \frac{\partial(y_i - X_i^T b - b_0)}{\partial b_0^T} = -\frac{\partial b_0}{\partial b_0} = -1 \quad\text{and}\quad \frac{\partial \epsilon_i^2}{\partial b^T} = -2\epsilon_i$$

We have:

$$\frac{\partial^2 \mathcal{L}_i(\theta)}{\partial b_0 \partial b_0^T} = \frac{1}{h_i} + \frac{\epsilon_i}{h_i^2}\frac{\partial h_i}{\partial b_0^T} - \frac{1}{2}\frac{\partial(1/h_i)}{\partial h_i}\frac{\partial h_i}{\partial b_0^T}\frac{\partial h_i}{\partial b_0}\left\{\frac{\epsilon_i^2}{h_i} - 1\right\} + \frac{\epsilon_i}{h_i^2}\frac{\partial h_i}{\partial b_0^T} + \frac{\epsilon_i^2}{2h_i^3}\frac{\partial h_i}{\partial b_0}\frac{\partial h_i}{\partial b_0^T}$$

Therefore using standardized residuals and taking conditional expectations of the block at time instant i we have:

$$E\left(\frac{\partial^2 \mathcal{L}_i(\theta)}{\partial b_0 \partial b_0^T}\right) = \frac{1}{h_i} + \frac{E(\epsilon_i)}{h_i^2}\frac{\partial h_i}{\partial b_0^T} - \frac{1}{2}\frac{\partial(1/h_i)}{\partial h_i}\frac{\partial h_i}{\partial b_0^T}\frac{\partial h_i}{\partial b_0}E(\{\mathcal{Z}_i^2 - 1\})$$

$$+ \frac{E(\epsilon_i)}{h_i^2}\frac{\partial h_i}{\partial b_0^T} + \frac{E(\mathcal{Z}_i^2)}{2h_i^2}\frac{\partial h_i}{\partial b_0}\frac{\partial h_i}{\partial b_0^T}$$

which gives:

$$E\left(\frac{\partial^2 \mathcal{L}_i(\theta)}{\partial b_0 \partial b_0^T}\right) = \frac{1}{h_i} + \frac{1}{2h_i^2}\frac{\partial h_i}{\partial b_0}\frac{\partial h_i}{\partial b_0^T}$$

The sample diagonal block is therefore:

$$E\left(\frac{\partial^2 \mathcal{L}(\theta)}{\partial b_0 \partial b_0^T}\right) = \sum_{i=1}^{n}\left(\frac{1}{h_i} + \frac{1}{2h_i^2}\frac{\partial h_i}{\partial b_0}\frac{\partial h_i}{\partial b_0^T}\right) \tag{19.22}$$

In summary we obtain:

The blocks of the Fisher information matrix

$$E\left(\frac{\partial^2 \mathcal{L}(\theta)}{\partial \omega \partial \omega^T}\right) = \sum_{i=1}^{n} \frac{1}{2h_i^2} \frac{\partial h_i}{\partial \omega} \frac{\partial h_i}{\partial \omega^T} \tag{19.23}$$

$$E\left(\frac{\partial^2 \mathcal{L}(\theta)}{\partial b_0 \partial b_0^T}\right) = \sum_{i=1}^{n} \left(\frac{1}{h_i} + \frac{1}{2h_i^2} \frac{\partial h_i}{\partial b_0} \frac{\partial h_i}{\partial b_0^T}\right) \tag{19.24}$$

$$E\left(\frac{\partial^2 \mathcal{L}(\theta)}{\partial b \partial b^T}\right) = \sum_{i=1}^{n} \left(\frac{X_i X_i^T}{h_i} + \frac{1}{2h_i^2} \frac{\partial h_i}{\partial b} \frac{\partial h_i}{\partial b^T}\right) \tag{19.25}$$

It can be seen that these diagonal blocks of the information matrix involve the *outer product* of the following first derivative vectors $\sum_{i=1}^{n} \partial h_i / \partial \omega$, $\sum_{i=1}^{n} \partial h_i / \partial b$, and also the square of the scalar derivative $\sum_{i=1}^{n} \partial h_i / \partial b_0$. Once these terms have been computed it is easy to calculatethe information matrix. Chapter 20 provides details on how this can be accomplished.

Chapter 20

GJR–GARCH algorithms

We will now use the information in Chapter 19 to show how the partial derivatives of the log likelihood can be computed. Practical details concerning initial estimates and pre-observed values are discussed. Pseudocode is also provided to facilitate computer implementations of the regression-GJR–GARCH model.

The notation used in this section is as follows:

num   the number of terms in the GARCH sequence, num is synonymous with the mathematical symbol n.

mn   indicates whether the mean term b_0 is included in the model. If mn==1 then b_0 is included, otherwise it is not.

nreg   the number of regression terms in the model, nreg is synonymous with the mathematical symbol k.

npar   the number of heteroskedastic parameters in a *standard symmetric* Gaussian GARCH model, that is $1 + p + q$.

$\hat{b}$ the initial estimate for b, the k element vector of regression coefficients.

$\hat{b}_0$ the initial estimate for b_0, the mean term.

$\hat{\theta}_k$ the kth element of the regression-GARCH parameter vector θ. The order of the elements is the same as given in Chapter 17. That is:
$\theta_1 = \alpha_0$, $\theta_{k+1} = \alpha_k$, $k = 1, \ldots, q$, $\theta_{1+q+k} = \beta_k$, $k = 1, \ldots, p$, $\theta_{npar+1} = \gamma$, etc.

$\mathcal{H}(i - k)$ a function which has the value 1 when $i > k$ and zero otherwise.

N_p the total number of parameters to estimate. In the Gaussian regression-GJR–GARCH $N_p = 2 + p + q + mn + nreg$, and in the Student's t distribution $N_p = 3 + p + q + mn + nreg$.

All other symbols have been previously defined in Chapters 14 and 15.

20.1 INITIAL ESTIMATES AND PRE-OBSERVED VALUES

In this section we consider how to estimate the initial values that are required for computing both the log likelihood and its partial derivatives.

The initial estimates of the regression coefficients, $\hat{b}_i$, $i = 1 - mn, \ldots, k$, can be obtained using linear regression.

If mn is 1 then the residuals are calculated as:

$$\epsilon_i = y_i - X_i \hat{b} - \hat{b}_0, \quad i = 1, \ldots, n \tag{20.1}$$

otherwise they are:

$$\epsilon_i = y_i - X_i \hat{b}, \quad i = 1, \ldots, n \tag{20.2}$$

In all GARCH processes the conditional variance h_i satisifies a recursive equation. For instance the basic linear GARCH model has:

$$h_i = \alpha_0 + \sum_{j=1}^{q} \alpha_j \epsilon_{i-j}^2 + \sum_{j=1}^{p} \beta_j h_{i-j}, \quad t = 1, \ldots, n$$

This means that the conditional variance for the term h_1 is given by:

$$h_1 = \alpha_0 + \sum_{j=1}^{q} \alpha_j \epsilon_{1-j}^2 + \sum_{j=1}^{p} \beta_j h_{1-j}$$

which relies on the terms $\epsilon_0^2, \epsilon_{-1}^2, \ldots, \epsilon_{1-j}^2$, and $h_0, h_{-1}, \ldots, h_{1-j}$, that refer to times before the sequence started. We will call this terms *pre-observed values*. There are various methods of providing estimates for these values.

One simple approach is to model an alternative time series which starts at the data point $i = \max(p, q)$ and has the reduced length $n - \max(p, q)$. The first $\max(p, q)$ terms are then used to calculate the pre-observed values.

The pre-observed values of ϵ_i can now use the actual values, and ϵ_i^2 can be used as an estimate for h_i.

However, this method is not entirely satisfactory as we are not modelling the true data and also the single value ϵ_i^2 is unlikely to be a good estimate of the conditional variance h_i.

Here we use a different technique. The initial value for the variance, σ_0^2, is taken as the average value of ϵ_i^2 using the first τ terms of the sequence:

$$\sigma_0^2 = \frac{1}{\tau} \sum_{i=1}^{\tau} \epsilon_i^2 \tag{20.3}$$

The optimal value of τ to use will depend on the nature of the data. If the sequence has high initial volatility then τ should be short enough to capture this. For sequences with less initial variation the estimate σ_0^2 will benefit from an increased value of τ.

Here we used, the compromise value $\tau = N_p$. This value is used in Equation 20.3 to calculate the pre-observed conditional variance and residuals squared, i.e.:

$$\epsilon_i^2 = h_i = \sigma_0^2, \quad i \leq 0$$

The pre-observed values for the residuals, ϵ_i, are taken as:

$$\epsilon_i = E[\epsilon_j] = 0, \quad \text{where } i \leq 0 \quad \text{and} \quad j = 1, \ldots, n$$

Since $\partial h_i / \partial \theta_k$ is calculated recursively from previous terms such as $\Sigma_{j=1}^p \beta_j (\partial h_{i-j} / \partial \theta_k)$ and $\Sigma_{j=1}^q \alpha_j (\partial \epsilon_{i-j}^2)/(\partial \theta_k)$ we can make use of the fact that $\partial \epsilon_i^2 / \partial \theta_k = \partial h_i / \partial \theta_k = 0$, $k = 1, \ldots, N_p, i \leq 0$, i.e.:

$$\frac{\partial \epsilon_i^2}{\partial \omega} = \frac{\partial \epsilon_i^2}{\partial b_0} = \frac{\partial \epsilon_i^2}{\partial b} = 0, \quad i \leq 0 \tag{20.4}$$

and

$$\frac{\partial h_i}{\partial \omega} = \frac{\partial h_i}{\partial b_0} = \frac{\partial h_i}{\partial b} = 0, \quad i \leq 0 \tag{20.5}$$

Note: Although this is correct for a Gaussian distribution it is not strictly true for a Student's t distribution, since the derivative term $\partial h_i / \partial v$ does not depend on its previous value.

Using the above results, for $i \leq q$ we now have:

$$\sum_{j=1}^q \alpha_j \frac{\partial \epsilon_{i-j}^2}{\partial \theta_k} = \sum_{j=1}^{i-1} \alpha_j \frac{\partial \epsilon_{i-j}^2}{\partial \theta_k} \tag{20.6}$$

and

$$\sum_{j=1}^p \beta_j \frac{\partial h_{i-j}}{\partial \theta_k} = \sum_{j=1}^p \beta_j \frac{\partial h_{i-j}}{\partial \theta_k} \mathcal{H}(i-j) \tag{20.7}$$

Further details are provided in the pseudocode provided in the following section.

20.2　GAUSSIAN DISTRIBUTION

20.2.1　The log likelihood

Deal with the first q terms of the sequence:

$$\gamma = \hat{\gamma}$$

$$\mathcal{L}(\theta) = 0$$

```
For i = 1 To num
```

　　If (mn == 1) $\epsilon_i = y_i - X_i^T \hat{b}$

　　If (mn == 0) $\epsilon_i = y_i - \hat{b}_0 - X_i^T \hat{b}$

```
Next i
For i = 1 To q
```

$$h_i = \alpha_0 + \sum_{j=1}^{i-1} (\alpha_j + \gamma S_{i-j}) \epsilon_{i-j}^2 + \sum_{j=i}^q \alpha_j \sigma_0^2 + \sum_{k=1}^p h_{i-k} \beta_k$$

Store the current value of h_i and keep all the previous values of h_i.

$$\mathcal{L}(\theta) = \mathcal{L}(\theta) + \frac{1}{2} \left(\log(h_i) + \frac{\epsilon_i^2}{h_i} \right)$$

```
Next i
```

Deal with the remaining terms of the sequence:

```
For i = q +1 To num
```

$$h_i = \alpha_0 + \sum_{j=1}^{q} (\alpha_j + \gamma S_{i-j})\epsilon_{i-j}^2 + \sum_{k=1}^{p} h_{i-k}\beta_k$$

Store the current value of h_i and keep N_p previous values of h_i.

$$\mathcal{L}(\theta) = \mathcal{L}(\theta) + \frac{1}{2}\left(\log(h_i) + \frac{\epsilon_i^2}{h_i} \right)$$

```
Next i
```

20.2.2 The first derivatives of the log likelihood

Algorithm for the first q terms of the sequence:

$$\frac{\partial \mathcal{L}(\theta)}{\partial \theta_k} = 0, \quad k = 1, \ldots, N_p$$

```
For i =1 to q
```

$$\frac{\partial h_i}{\partial \alpha_0} = 1 + \sum_{k=1}^{p} \beta_k \frac{\partial h_{i-k}}{\partial \alpha_0}$$

```
   For j =1 to i −1
```

$$\frac{\partial h_i}{\partial \alpha_j} = \epsilon_{i-j}^2$$

```
   Next j
   For j = i to q
```

$$\frac{\partial h_i}{\partial \alpha_j} = \sigma_0^2$$

```
   Next j
   For j =1 to q
```

$$\frac{\partial h_i}{\partial \alpha_j} = \frac{\partial h_i}{\partial \alpha_j} + \sum_{k=1}^{p} \beta_k \frac{\partial h_{i-k}}{\partial \alpha_j}$$

```
   Next j
   For j =1 to p
```

$$\frac{\partial h_i}{\partial \beta_j} = h_{i-j} + \sum_{k=1}^{p} \beta_j \frac{\partial h_{i-k}}{\partial \beta_k}$$

```
   Next j
```

$$\frac{\partial h_i}{\partial \gamma} = \sum_{j=1}^{i-1} \epsilon_{i-j}^2 + \sum_{k=1}^{p} \beta_k \frac{\partial h_{i-k}}{\partial \gamma}$$

$$h_i = \alpha_0 + \sum_{k=1}^{p} h_{i-k}\beta_k + \sum_{j=1}^{i-1}(\alpha_j + \gamma S_{i-j})\epsilon_{i-j}^2 + \sum_{j=i}^{q} \alpha_j \sigma_0^2$$

```
if (mn == 1) then
```

$$\frac{\partial h_i}{\partial b_0} = -2\sum_{k=1}^{i-1}(\alpha_k + \gamma S_{i-k})\epsilon_{i-k} + \sum_{k=1}^{p} \beta_k \frac{\partial h_{i-k}}{\partial b_0} \mathcal{H}(i-k)$$

```
end if
For j = 1 to nreg
```

$$\frac{\partial h_i}{\partial b_j} = -2\sum_{k=1}^{i-1}(\alpha_k + \gamma S_{i-k})\epsilon_{i-k} X_{i-k}^j + \sum_{k=1}^{p} \beta_k \frac{\partial h_{i-k}}{\partial b_j} \mathcal{H}(i-k)$$

```
Next j
```

Store the current values of h_i and $\partial h_i/\partial\theta$ and keep all the previous values of h_i and $\partial h_i/\partial\theta$.

```
For k = 1 to npar + 1
```

$$\frac{\partial \mathcal{L}(\theta)}{\partial \theta_k} = \frac{\partial \mathcal{L}(\theta)}{\partial \theta_k} - \frac{1}{2h_i}\left(\frac{\epsilon_i^2}{h_i} - 1\right)\frac{\partial h_i}{\partial \theta_k}$$

```
Next k
if (mn == 1) then
```

$$\frac{\partial \mathcal{L}(\theta)}{\partial b_0} = \frac{\partial \mathcal{L}(\theta)}{\partial b_0} - \frac{\epsilon_i}{h_i} - \frac{1}{2h_i}\left(\frac{\epsilon_i^2}{h_i} - 1\right)\frac{\partial h_i}{\partial b_0}$$

```
end if
For k = 1 to nreg
```

$$\frac{\partial \mathcal{L}(\theta)}{\partial b_k} = \frac{\partial \mathcal{L}(\theta)}{\partial b_k} - \frac{X_i^k \epsilon_i}{h_i} - \frac{1}{2h_i}\left(\frac{\epsilon_i^2}{h_i} - 1\right)\frac{\partial h_i}{\partial b_k}$$

```
Next k
Next i
```

Algorithm for the remaining terms of the sequence:

```
For i = q+1 to num
```

$$\frac{\partial h_i}{\partial \alpha_0} = 1 + \sum_{k=1}^{p} \beta_k \frac{\partial h_{i-k}}{\partial \alpha_0}$$

```
For j = 1 to q
```

$$\frac{\partial h_i}{\partial \alpha_j} = \epsilon_{i-j}^2$$

```
Next j
For j = 1 to q
```

$$\frac{\partial h_i}{\partial \alpha_j} = \frac{\partial h_i}{\partial \alpha_j} + \sum_{k=1}^{p} \beta_k \frac{\partial h_{i-k}}{\partial \alpha_j}$$

```
Next j
For j = 1 to p
```

$$\frac{\partial h_i}{\partial \beta_j} = h_{i-j} + \sum_{k=1}^{p} \beta_j \frac{\partial h_{i-k}}{\partial \beta_k}$$

```
Next j
```

$$\frac{\partial h_i}{\partial \gamma} = \sum_{j=1}^{q} \epsilon_{i-j}^2 + \sum_{k=1}^{p} \beta_k \frac{\partial h_{i-k}}{\partial \gamma}$$

$$h_i = \alpha_0 + \sum_{k=1}^{p} h_{i-k}\beta_k + \sum_{j=1}^{q} (\alpha_j + \gamma S_{i-j})\epsilon_{i-j}^2$$

```
if (mn == 1) then
```

$$\frac{\partial h_i}{\partial b_0} = -2\sum_{k=1}^{q} (\alpha_k + \gamma S_{i-k})\epsilon_{i-k} + \sum_{k=1}^{p} \beta_k \frac{\partial h_{i-k}}{\partial b_0} \mathcal{H}(i-k)$$

```
end if
For j = 1 to nreg
```

$$\frac{\partial h_i}{\partial b_j} = -2\sum_{k=1}^{q} (\alpha_k + \gamma S_{i-k})\epsilon_{i-k}X_{i-k}^j + \sum_{k=1}^{p} \beta_k \frac{\partial h_{i-k}}{\partial b_j} \mathcal{H}(i-k)$$

```
Next j
```

Store the current values of h_i and $\partial h_i/\partial \theta$ and keep N_p previous values of h_i and $\partial h_i/\partial \theta$.

```
For k = 1 to npar + 1
```

$$\frac{\partial \mathcal{L}(\theta)}{\partial \theta_k} = \frac{\partial \mathcal{L}(\theta)}{\partial \theta_k} - \frac{1}{2h_i}\left(\frac{\epsilon_i^2}{h_i} - 1\right)\frac{\partial h_i}{\partial \theta_k}$$

```
Next k
if (mn == 1) then
```

$$\frac{\partial \mathcal{L}(\theta)}{\partial b_0} = \frac{\partial \mathcal{L}(\theta)}{\partial b_0} - \frac{\epsilon_i}{h_i} - \frac{1}{2h_i}\left(\frac{\epsilon_i^2}{h_i} - 1\right)\frac{\partial h_i}{\partial b_0}$$

```
end if
For k = 1 to nreg
```

$$\frac{\partial \mathcal{L}(\theta)}{\partial b_k} = \frac{\partial \mathcal{L}(\theta)}{\partial b_k} - \frac{X_i^k \epsilon_i}{h_i} - \frac{1}{2h_i}\left(\frac{\epsilon_i^2}{h_i} - 1\right)\frac{\partial h_i}{\partial b_k}$$

```
Next k
Next i
```

20.3   STUDENT'S *t* DISTRIBUTION

20.3.1   The log likelihood

Deal with the first q terms of the sequence:

$$\gamma = \hat{\gamma}$$
$$\mathcal{L}(\theta) = 0$$
$$M_\nu = \log(\Gamma((\nu + 1)/2)) - \log(\Gamma(\nu/2)) - \frac{1}{2}\log(\nu - 2)$$

```
For i = 1 To num
```

$$\text{If mn == 1}\quad \epsilon_i = y_i - X_i^T \hat{b}$$
$$\text{If mn == 0}\quad \epsilon_i = y_i - \hat{b}_0 - X_i^T \hat{b}$$

```
Next i
For i = 1 To q
```

$$h_i = \alpha_0 + \sum_{j=1}^{i-1}(\alpha_j + \gamma S_{i-j})\epsilon_{i-j}^2 + \sum_{j=i}^{q}\alpha_j\sigma_0^2 + \sum_{k=1}^{p}\beta_k h_{i-k}$$

Store the current value of h_i and keep all the previous values of h_i.

$$\mathcal{L}(\theta) = \mathcal{L}(\theta) - M_\nu + \frac{1}{2}\log(h_i) + \frac{\nu + 1}{2}\log\left(1 + \frac{\epsilon_i^2}{(\nu - 2)h_i}\right)$$

```
Next i
```

Deal with the remaining terms of the sequence:

```
For i = q + 1 To num
```

$$h_i = \alpha_0 + \sum_{j=1}^{q}(\alpha_j + \gamma S_{i-j})\epsilon_{i-j}^2 + \sum_{k=1}^{p}\beta_k h_{i-k}$$

Store the current value of h_i and keep N_p previous values of h_i.

$$\mathcal{L}(\theta) = \mathcal{L}(\theta) - M_\nu + \frac{1}{2}\log(h_i) + \frac{\nu + 1}{2}\log\left(1 + \frac{\epsilon_i^2}{(\nu - 2)h_i}\right)$$

```
Next i
```

20.3.2   The first derivatives of the log likelihood

Algorithm for the first q terms of the sequence:

$$\frac{\partial \mathcal{L}(\theta)}{\partial \theta_k} = 0, \quad k = 1, \ldots, N_p$$

```
For i = 1 to q
```

Compute h_i as described in Section 20.2.1. Also calculate the derivatives $\partial h_i/\partial \theta_j$, $j = 1, \ldots, N_p$, as described for a Gaussian distribution in Section 20.1.2. Store h_i and $\partial h_i/\partial \theta_j$, $j = 1, \ldots, N_p$, and keep all the previous values of h_i and $\partial h_i/\partial \theta$.

Set $\mathcal{G} = \left(\dfrac{(\nu + 1)}{(\nu - 2) + \epsilon_i^2/h_i} \right)$

For k = 1 to npar + 1

$$\frac{\partial \mathcal{L}(\theta)}{\partial \theta_k} = \frac{\partial \mathcal{L}(\theta)}{\partial \theta_k} - \frac{1}{2h_i} \left(1 - \frac{\epsilon_i^2}{h_i} \mathcal{G} \right) \frac{\partial h_i}{\partial \theta_k}$$

Next k

$$\frac{\partial \mathcal{L}(\theta)}{\partial \nu} = \frac{\partial \mathcal{L}(\theta)}{\partial \nu} - \frac{1}{2} \psi\left(\frac{\nu + 1}{2} \right) + \frac{1}{2} \psi\left(\frac{\nu}{2} \right) + \frac{1}{2(\nu - 2)}$$

$$+ \frac{1}{2} \log\left(1 + \frac{\epsilon_i^2}{(\nu - 2)h_i} \right) - \frac{\epsilon_i^2}{2(\nu - 2)h_i} \mathcal{G}$$

if (mn == 1) then

$$\frac{\partial \mathcal{L}(\theta)}{\partial b_0} = \frac{\partial \mathcal{L}(\theta)}{\partial b_0} - \frac{\epsilon_i}{h_i} \mathcal{G} - \frac{1}{2h_i} \left(\frac{\epsilon_i^2}{h_i} \mathcal{G} - 1 \right) \frac{\partial h_i}{\partial b_0}$$

end if
For k = 1 to nreg

$$\frac{\partial \mathcal{L}(\theta)}{\partial b_k} = \frac{\partial \mathcal{L}(\theta)}{\partial b_k} - \frac{X_i^k \epsilon_i}{h_i} \mathcal{G} - \frac{1}{2h_i} \left(\frac{\epsilon_i^2}{h_i} \mathcal{G} - 1 \right) \frac{\partial h_i}{\partial b_k}$$

Next k
Next i

Algorithm for the remaining terms of the sequence:

For i = q+1 to num

Compute h_i as described in Section 20.2.1. Also calculate the derivatives $\partial h_i/\partial \theta_j$, $j = 1, \ldots, N_p$, as described for a Gaussian distribution in Section 20.1.2. Store h_i and $\partial h_i/\partial \theta_j$, $j = 1, \ldots, N_p$, and keep N_p previous values of h_i and $\partial h_i/\partial \theta$.

Set $\mathcal{G} = \left(\dfrac{(\nu + 1)}{(\nu - 2) + \epsilon_i^2/h_i} \right)$

For k = 1 to npar + 1

$$\frac{\partial \mathcal{L}(\theta)}{\partial \theta_k} = \frac{\partial \mathcal{L}(\theta)}{\partial \theta_k} - \frac{1}{2h_i} \left(1 - \frac{\epsilon_i^2}{h_i} \mathcal{G} \right) \frac{\partial h_i}{\partial \theta_k}$$

Next k

$$\frac{\partial \mathcal{L}(\theta)}{\partial \nu} = \frac{\partial \mathcal{L}(\theta)}{\partial \nu} - \frac{1}{2}\psi\left(\frac{\nu+1}{2}\right) + \frac{1}{2}\psi\left(\frac{\nu}{2}\right) + \frac{1}{2(\nu-2)}$$
$$+ \frac{1}{2}\log\left(1 + \frac{\epsilon_i^2}{(\nu-2)h_i}\right) - \frac{\epsilon_i^2}{2(\nu-2)h_i}\mathcal{G}$$

```
if (mn == 1) then
```

$$\frac{\partial \mathcal{L}(\theta)}{\partial b_0} = \frac{\partial \mathcal{L}(\theta)}{\partial b_0} - \frac{\epsilon_i}{h_i}\mathcal{G} - \frac{1}{2h_i}\left(\frac{\epsilon_i^2}{h_i}\mathcal{G} - 1\right)\frac{\partial h_i}{\partial b_0}$$

```
end if
For k = 1 to nreg
```

$$\frac{\partial \mathcal{L}(\theta)}{\partial b_k} = \frac{\partial \mathcal{L}(\theta)}{\partial b_k} - \frac{X_i^k \epsilon_i}{h_i}\mathcal{G} - \frac{1}{2h_i}\left(\frac{\epsilon_i^2}{h_i}\mathcal{G} - 1\right)\frac{\partial h_i}{\partial b_k}$$

```
   Next k
Next i
```

Chapter 21

GARCH software

In this chapter we will describe some of the expected capabilities of practical GARCH software, and also how to test whether the software performs as expected.

21.1 EXPECTED SOFTWARE CAPABILITIES

To illustrate we will consider the requirements for the regression-GJR–GARCH model discussed in Chapter 20. We will assume a GARCH modelling component is to be developed and will list some important *input* and *output* properties that should be considered in its design.

Inputs

- The conditional probability distribution to use, i.e. Gaussian distribution, Student's t distribution, etc.
- The required initial estimates for the model parameters.
- The input data, y_i, $i = 1, \ldots, n$, and X_i, $i = 1, \ldots, n$.
- The number of GARCH model parameters, α_j, $j = 0, \ldots, q$, $\beta_j = 1, \ldots, p$, regression coefficients b_j, $j = 1, \ldots, k$, and mean term b_0.
- A flag to indicate whether the GARCH stationary constraint is to be enforced.
- A flag to indicate whether the user wants to provide initial estimates for the regression coefficients b_j, $j = 1, \ldots, k$, mean term b_0, and pre-observed conditional variance σ_0^2, or let the component calculate these.

Outputs

- The estimated GARCH model parameters, $\hat{\theta}$.
- The value of the *minimized* log likelihood, $\mathcal{L}(\hat{\theta})$.
- The estimated conditional variances, h_i, $i = 1, \ldots, n$.
- The estimated residuals, ϵ_i, $i = 1, \ldots, n$.
- The standard errors associated with each estimated parameter.
- The covariance matrix of the estimated GARCH model parameters $\hat{\theta}$.

It is also useful to have information concerning the underlying numerical optimization of the log likelihood, such as the maximum number of iterations allowed for convergence, and also the tolerance used during the optimization process.

The software could also provide the scores for each estimated GARCH model parameter, $\partial\mathcal{L}(\theta)/\partial\theta_{i\ \theta=\hat{\theta}}$. In the absence of constraints all these partial derivatives, at $\mathcal{L}(\hat{\theta})$ should be nearly zero. However, when the stationary constraint is imposed, a high value for the kth score indicates that the feasible boundary for this parameter has been reached. This means that it has not been possible to optimize $\mathcal{L}(\theta)$ any further through variation of the parameter θ_k.

21.2   TESTING GARCH SOFTWARE

We will now give details concerning the implementation and testing, see Levy (2000), of regression-GJR–GARCH estimation software, developed using the algorithms outlined in Chapter 20. The log likelihood was *minimized* using a general purpose *quasi*-Newton type numerical optimizer, see Gill *et al.* (1981), and Murtagh and Saunders (1983), which employed either analytic or numeric derivatives (calculated using finite differences). The optimizer also had the capability of returning a finite-difference approximation to the Hessian at the solution point, $\hat{\theta}$, which was used as the second-derivative estimate of the Fisher information matrix, $\mathcal{F}$. All the results presented here are based on Monte Carlo simulations involving the generation and parameter estimation of 200 regression-GJR–GARCH sequences. Each sequence was created using the NAG routine G05HMF and estimated with the following optimization settings:

- The maximum number of iterations required for convergence to a solution set to 100.
- GARCH stationary condition enforced.
- The optimality tolerance set to 10^{-8}, that is, the optimimal value of the log likelihood has eight figure accuracy.

The simulation results are shown in Tables 21.1 to 21.10. The first column labelled 'Estimated Value' refers to the average parameter estimate using 200 simulations. The second column labelled 'Estimated Standard Error' refers to the average of the standard errors computed by the GARCH software. The third column labelled 'Standard Error of Estimates' refers to the actual standard error of the parameter estimates. The parameters are output in the order in which they occur in θ, i.e.:

- A Gaussian process has $\theta = (\omega^T, b_0, b^T)$.
- A Student's t distribution has $\theta = (\omega^T, \nu, b_0, b^T)$.

Here $\omega^T = (\alpha_0, \alpha_1, \ldots, \alpha_q, \beta_1, \ldots, \beta_p, \gamma)$ and $b^T = (b_1, \ldots, b_k)$.

Each table also reports the total CPU time in seconds required to estimate the model parameters for the 200 GARCH sequences. The tables labelled *Numeric Derivatives* refer to results obtained using a finite-difference approximation to both the gradient and the Hessian. Those labelled *Analytic Derivatives* refer to results obtained using the algorithms of Chapter 20 and an approximation to the Fisher information matrix based on the conditional expectation of the Hessian at the solution point, $\hat{\theta}$.

21.2.1   Gaussian distribution

In Tables 21.1 to 21.6 we present the results of Monte Carlo simulations to check the parameter estimation software for the following Gaussian regression-GJR–GARCH(1,1) process:

$$k = 2 \quad \alpha_0 = 0.01 \quad \alpha_1 = 0.1 \quad \beta_1 = 0.8$$
$$\gamma = 0.2 \quad b_0 = 1.1 \quad b_1 = -1.5 \quad b_2 = 2.5$$
$$X_i^1 = \frac{1}{100} + 0.7 \times \sin\left(\frac{i}{100}\right), \quad X_i^2 = \frac{1}{2} + \left(\frac{i}{1000}\right), \quad \text{for} \quad i = 1, \dots, n$$

where the value of β_1 was taken as *realistically high* for a financial time series.

The initial values for the regression coefficients, b_i, $i = 0, \dots, k$, and the pre-observed conditional variance σ_0^2 were estimated using OLS regression, as outlined in Section 20.1. The initial estimates for the elements of the parameter vector w were all set to 0.1.

| Numeric derivatives |

Table 21.1   Sequence length 300, CPU time = 111.1 s

Estimated value	Estimated standard error	Standard error of estimates	Correct values
0.0167	0.0155	0.0139	0.01
0.0869	0.0679	0.4217	0.10
0.7911	0.0801	0.3019	0.80
0.2075	0.0975	0.2788	0.20
1.1225	0.3737	1.1738	1.10
−1.5211	0.1910	0.6548	−1.50
2.4646	0.6003	1.4521	2.50

Table 21.2   Sequence length 1000, CPU time = 380.7 s

Estimated value	Estimated standard error	Standard error of estimates	Correct values
0.0111	0.0037	0.0038	0.01
0.0956	0.0336	0.0304	0.10
0.8001	0.0301	0.0269	0.80
0.2014	0.0531	0.0511	0.20
1.0976	0.0639	0.0623	1.10
−1.5008	0.0356	0.0361	−1.50
2.5004	0.0613	0.0585	2.50

Table 21.3   Sequence length 3000, CPU time = 1246.0 s

Estimated value	Estimated standard error	Standard error of estimates	Correct values
0.0105	0.0020	0.0020	0.01
0.1000	0.0173	0.0174	0.10
0.7982	0.0163	0.0152	0.80
0.2015	0.0290	0.0296	0.20
1.0990	0.0210	0.0240	1.10
−1.5000	0.0180	0.0190	−1.50
2.5004	0.0096	0.0180	2.50

Analytic derivatives

Table 21.4   Sequence length 300, CPU time = 141.8 s

Estimated value	Estimated standard error	Standard error of estimates	Correct values
0.0167	0.0155	0.0097	0.01
0.0870	0.0677	0.0538	0.10
0.7910	0.0799	0.0559	0.80
0.2074	0.0976	0.0899	0.20
1.1228	0.3734	0.2577	1.10
−1.5209	0.1911	0.1627	−1.50
2.4639	0.5997	0.3922	2.50

Table 21.5   Sequence length 1000, CPU time = 520.2 s

Estimated value	Estimated standard error	Standard error of estimates	Correct values
0.0111	0.0037	0.0036	0.01
0.0956	0.0336	0.0286	0.10
0.8001	0.0301	0.0260	0.80
0.2014	0.0531	0.0470	0.20
1.0976	0.0639	0.0586	1.10
−1.5008	0.0356	0.0339	−1.50
2.5004	0.0613	0.0554	2.50

Table 21.6   Sequence length 3000, CPU time = 1597.3 s

Estimated value	Estimated standard error	Standard error of estimates	Correct values
0.0105	0.0020	0.0019	0.01
0.1000	0.0173	0.0165	0.10
0.7982	0.0163	0.0147	0.80
0.2015	0.0290	0.0270	0.20
1.0990	0.0210	0.0225	1.10
−1.5000	0.0180	0.0179	−1.50
2.5004	0.0096	0.0103	2.50

It can be seen that the estimated values are in agreement with the actual values, and as expected, the standard error of the parameter estimates decreases as the GARCH sequence length increases.

It is also evident that, for small sample sizes, the use of analytic derivatives leads to significantly better estimates of the standard errors. As the sequence length is increased both the numeric and analytic results become very similar. Here the numeric approach has the advantage of being considerably faster. This is because finite-difference approximations to the derivatives can be achieved by merely evaluating the log likelihood at several points in the neighbourhood of the current estimate for the parameter vector θ. This is in contrast to analytic derivatives, which are computed recursively using all the terms in the GARCH sequence.

21.2.2 Student's t distribution

In Tables 21.7 to 21.10 we present the results of Monte Carlo simulations to check the parameter estimation software for the following Student's t regression–GJR– GARCH(1,2) process:

$$k = 2 \quad \alpha_0 = 0.08 \quad \alpha_1 = 0.05 \quad \alpha_2 = 0.1 \quad \beta_1 = 0.4$$
$$\gamma = 0.2 \quad \nu = 4.2, \quad b_0 = 1.1 \quad b_1 = -1.5 \quad b_2 = 2.5$$
$$X_i^1 = \frac{1}{100} + 0.7 \times \sin\left(\frac{i}{100}\right), \quad X_i^2 = \frac{1}{2} + \left(\frac{i}{1000}\right), \quad \text{for} \quad i = 1, \ldots, n$$

The initial values for the regression coefficients, b_i, $i = 0, \ldots, k$ and the pre-observed conditional variance σ_0^2 were estimated using OLS regression, as outlined in Section 20.1. The initial estimates for all the elements of the parameter vector ω were all set to 0.1. In addition the initial value for the number of degrees of freedom for the Student's t distribution, ν, was taken as 100.0, which effectively assumes a Gaussian distribution as the starting approximation.

Numeric derivatives

Table 21.7 Sequence length 800, CPU time $= 555.2$ s

Estimated value	Estimated standard error	Standard error of estimates	Correct values
0.0820	0.0241	0.0354	0.08
0.0921	0.0726	0.1683	0.10
0.1064	0.0716	0.1941	0.10
0.3863	0.1138	0.2033	0.40
0.2176	0.0841	0.1451	0.20
4.4595	0.8290	0.8984	4.20
1.1016	0.0581	0.0726	1.10
-1.4973	0.0311	0.0354	-1.50
2.4970	0.0619	0.0767	2.50

Table 21.8   Sequence length 3000, CPU time = 1933.2 s

Estimated value	Estimated standard error	Standard error of estimates	Correct values
0.0802	0.0124	0.0108	0.08
0.0969	0.0371	0.0328	0.10
0.1007	0.0416	0.0394	0.10
0.3974	0.0645	0.0565	0.40
0.2059	0.0441	0.0404	0.20
4.2642	0.3563	0.3307	4.20
1.0972	0.0176	0.0190	1.10
−1.4985	0.0158	0.0152	−1.50
2.5011	0.0081	0.0087	2.50

Analytic Derivatives

Table 21.9   Sequence length 800, CPU time = 770.9 s

Estimated value	Estimated standard error	Standard error of estimates	Correct values
0.0820	0.0241	0.0257	0.08
0.0922	0.0724	0.1189	0.10
0.1063	0.0716	0.1116	0.10
0.3863	0.1138	0.1376	0.40
0.2176	0.0841	0.1056	0.20
4.4596	0.8289	0.8229	4.20
1.1016	0.0581	0.0634	1.10
−1.4973	0.0311	0.0314	−1.50
2.4970	0.0619	0.0678	2.50

Table 21.10   Sequence length 3000, CPU time = 2987.6 s

Estimated value	Estimated standard error	Standard error of estimates	Correct values
0.0802	0.0124	0.0123	0.08
0.0969	0.0371	0.0390	0.10
0.1007	0.0416	0.0531	0.10
0.3974	0.0645	0.0706	0.40
0.2059	0.0441	0.0425	0.20
4.2642	0.3563	0.3287	4.20
1.0972	0.0176	0.0189	1.10
−1.4985	0.0158	0.0150	−1.50
2.5011	0.0081	0.0086	2.50

The characteristics of these tables are similar to those of Section 21.2.1. However, here nine GARCH model parameters are estimated in contrast to the seven model parameters in Section 21.2.1. It is also interesting to note the high standard error associated with the Student's t distribution parameter ν.

It has been shown that analytic derivatives provide more accurate results than numeric derivatives for short GARCH sequences. However, numeric derivatives are considerably faster. This suggests that practical GARCH software should have the ability to switch from analytic to numeric derivatives when appropriate. The precise benefits to be gained from using analytic derivatives will depend on the numerical optimization software used and the accuracy of the finite-difference approximations to the derivatives.

The results demonstrate that good GARCH model estimates can be obtained even when the initial parameter estimates are simple, see Section 22.5. This suggests the construction of easy to use software packages in which initial estimates (for ω and ν) are not required from the user.

Chapter 22

GARCH process identification

In this chapter we consider the practical aspects of GARCH modelling. We deal with the statistical tests that can be performed on the modelled data in order to identify the best GARCH process. The results of using a GJR–GARCH model on S&P 500 index data are presented. Also two GARCH windows demonstrations are discussed which illustrate the practical use of the mathematics given earlier in this chapter. Each demonstration either uses a standard linear GARCH model or an AGARCH-I model, and the conditional probability distribution of the residuals is assumed to be Gaussian. Detailed information concerning the construction of these applications is provided elsewhere in the book.

22.1 LIKELIHOOD RATIO TEST

A popular approach for testing the significance of parameters estimated using maximum likelihood techniques is the *likelihood ratio test*. It is useful in the following situation.

Suppose we have modelled data using a GARCH process N_p parameters, θ_k, $k = 1, \ldots, N_p$, and have obtained a maximized log likelihood $\mathcal{L}(\hat{\theta})$. We now want to know if by increasing the number of model parameters to $N_p + m$ we can obtain a *significantly* better model to the data. If we let the (improved) maximized log likelihood using the increased number of parameters be $\mathcal{L}(\bar{\theta})$, then we can use the result that:

$$2\left[\mathcal{L}(\bar{\theta}) - \mathcal{L}(\hat{\theta})\right] \approx \chi^2(m)$$

22.2 SIGNIFICANCE OF THE ESTIMATED PARAMETERS

As described in Section 18.2.1 the significance of an estimated parameter can be determined by the value of its t statistic. For the ith parameter estimate $\hat{\theta}_i$ the t statistic is $\hat{\theta}_i/\sigma_i$, where σ_i is the standard error.

It is common practice to reject the null hypothesis of no significance at the 0.5 per cent level, in which case estimates with t statistic values greater than 2.57 are considered significant.

22.3 THE INDEPENDENCE OF THE STANDARDIZED RESIDUALS

In Section 15.2 we showed that the GARCH(p,q) process:

$$h_i = \alpha_0 + \sum_{j=1}^{q} \alpha_j \epsilon_{i-j}^2 + \sum_{j=1}^{p} \beta_j h_{i-j}, \quad i = 1, \ldots, n, \quad \epsilon_i \sim R(0, h_i)$$

Gives rise to an ARMA(κ, p) process in ϵ_i^2 of the form:

$$\epsilon_i^2 = \alpha_0 + \sum_{j=1}^{\kappa}(\alpha_j + \beta_j)\epsilon_{i-j}^2 - \sum_{j=1}^{p}\beta_j\nu_{i-j} + \nu_i$$

where $\kappa = \max(p, q)$. If the model is correctly specified then the standardized sequence $\mathcal{Z}_i^2 = \epsilon_i^2/h_i$, $i = 1, n$ should constitute white noise. This can be checked by computing the sample autocorrelations.

The statistical independence of the elements $\mathcal{Z}_i^2$ can be checked by computing the values of the sample autocorrelations.

The kth sample autocorrelation is defined as:

$$r_k = \sum_{i=1}^{n} \mathcal{Z}_i^2 \mathcal{Z}_{i-k}^2, \quad i = k+1, \ldots, n \tag{22.1}$$

The *Box–Pierce Q – statistic* is defined as:

$$\mathcal{Q}_{stat} = \sum_{k=1}^{P} r_k \tag{22.2}$$

If the model is correctly specified then $\mathcal{Q}_{stat}$ has a χ_2^2 distribution with $P - \kappa - q$ degrees of freedom. High values of $\mathcal{Q}_{stat}$ lead to reject of the hypothesis that the standardized residuals are independently distributed.

22.4   THE DISTRIBUTION OF THE STANDARDIZED RESIDUALS

The standardized residuals $\mathcal{Z}_i = \epsilon_i/\sqrt{h_i}$, $i = 1, \ldots, n$ should have the distribution $\mathcal{R}(0, 1)$.

In the case of $\mathcal{R}(0, 1)$ being a Gaussian distribution $N(0, 1)$ we can check for non-normality in the following manner.

Remembering that the kurtosis is defined as:

$$\aleph = \frac{E[\epsilon_i^4]}{\sigma^2}$$

and that the skewness is defined as:

$$\mathcal{S} = \frac{E[\epsilon_i^3]}{\sigma^3}$$

where $E[\epsilon_i^4] = \dfrac{1}{n}\sum_{i=1}^{n}\epsilon_i^4$, $\quad E[\epsilon_i^3] = \dfrac{1}{n}\sum_{i=1}^{n}\epsilon_i^3$, $\quad$ and $\quad \sigma^2 = \dfrac{1}{n}\sum_{i=1}^{n}\epsilon_i^2$

For large samples we have:

$$\mathcal{S} \sim N(0, 6/n) \quad \text{and} \quad \aleph \sim N(3, 24/n)$$

A test statistic for non-normality of the residuals is given by:

$$N_{stat} = \frac{n}{6}\mathcal{S}^2 + \frac{n}{24}(\aleph - 3) \tag{22.3}$$

Under the null hypothesis N_{stat} has a χ_2^2 distribution, Harvey (1990). In practical terms this means that if $N_{stat} < 3$ then we can reject the alternative hypothesis of non-normality in favour of normality.

22.5   MODELLING THE S&P 500 INDEX

This section concerns the use of GJR–GARCH to model 3000 daily returns from the S&P 500 index, for the years 1960–1972; see Levy (2003) for more details.

Analytic derivatives were used in the numerical optimization, and the shocks were either from a Gaussian distribution or a Student's t distribution. Tables 22.1 and 22.2 show the maximized log likelihood, $LGF(\theta)$, and parameter estimates for GJR–GARCH(1,1), AR(1)–GJR–GARCH(1,1), and AR(2)–GJR–GARCH(1,1) models. The format of these results is $\left\{ \hat{\theta} \, (\Delta\hat{\theta}) \, [t] \right\}$, where $\hat{\theta}$ is the vector of estimated model parameters, $\Delta\hat{\theta}$ is the vector of estimated standard errors, and t is the vector of significance statistics, $t = \hat{\theta}/\Delta\hat{\theta}$. Here we consider parameters with $t > 1.96$ (i.e. 2.5 per cent probability level) as significant.

It is evident from Table 22.1 that the preferred Gaussian model for the S&P 500 index data is AR(1)–GJR–GARCH(1,1), with $\alpha_0 = 0.0196$, $\alpha_1 = 0.0716$, $\beta_1 = 0.7938$, $\gamma = 0.1851$, $c = 0.0267$, and $\phi_1 = 0.2280$.

The results for the Student's t distribution in Table 22.2 show that the log likelihood surface is very flat, and the parameters ϕ_1, and ϕ_2 are not significant at the 2.5 per cent probability level. Here the preferred model for the S&P 500 index data is GJR–GARCH(1,1), with $\alpha_0 = 0.0128$, $\alpha_1 = 0.0545$, $\beta_1 = 0.8373$, $\gamma = 0.1568$, $\nu = 8.1160$, and $c = 0.0483$.

It was found that the optimized parameter estimates did not depend strongly on the initial estimates. This observation was investigated by studying the shape of the log likelihood surface for both the Gaussian distribution AR(1)–GJR–GARCH(1,1) model, and the Student's t distribution GJR–GARCH(1,1) model. Figures 22.1 and 22.2 show the results for analytic derivatives. Here the value of $LGF(\theta)$ is plotted as each GARCH parameter is individually incremented in steps of 0.04, while all

Table 22.1   Gaussian distribution, estimated model parameters. $\hat{\theta}$ is the vector of estimated model parameters, $\Delta\hat{\theta}$ is the vector of estimated standard errors, $t = \hat{\theta}/\Delta\hat{\theta}$ is the vector of significance statistics, and $LGF(\hat{\theta})$ is the value of the maximized log likelihood at $\hat{\theta}$

Parameters	GJR–GARCH(1,1) $LGF(\hat{\theta}) = 132.716$			AR(1)–GJR–GARCH(1,1) $LGF(\hat{\theta}) = 198.32$			AR(2)–GJR–GARCH(1,1) $LGF(\hat{\theta}) = 134.23$		
θ	$\hat{\theta}$	$\Delta\hat{\theta}$	t	$\hat{\theta}$	$\Delta\hat{\theta}$	t	$\hat{\theta}$	$\Delta\hat{\theta}$	t
α_0	0.0189	(0.0028)	[6.78]	0.0196	(0.0028)	[6.83]	0.0184	(0.0027)	[6.71]
α_1	0.0680	(0.0131)	[5.19]	0.0716	(0.0132)	[5.41]	0.0663	(0.0129)	[5.12]
β_1	0.8106	(0.0162)	[50.01]	0.7938	(0.0167)	[47.35]	0.8135	(0.0160)	[50.07]
γ	0.1524	(0.0203)	[7.48]	0.1851	(0.0243)	[7.60]	0.1533	(0.0205)	[7.46]
c	0.0458	(0.0087)	[5.23]	0.0267	(0.0085)	[3.11]	0.0420	(0.0089)	[4.72]
ϕ_1				0.2280	(0.0191)	[11.94]	0.0180	(0.0201)	[0.89]
ϕ_2							0.0279	(0.0197)	[1.41]

Table 22.2 Student's t distribution, estimated model parameters. $\hat{\theta}$ is the vector of estimated model parameters, $\Delta\hat{\theta}$ is the vector of estimated standard errors, $t = \hat{\theta}/\Delta\hat{\theta}$ is the vector of significance statistics, and $LGF(\hat{\theta})$ is the value of the maximized log likelihood at $\hat{\theta}$

Parameters	GJR–GARCH(1,1) $LGF(\theta) = -2554.96$			AR(1)–GJR–GARCH(1,1) $LGF(\theta) = -2554.95$			AR(2)–GJR–GARCH(1,1) $LGF(\theta) = -2553.17$		
θ	$\hat{\theta}$	$\Delta\hat{\theta}$	t	$\hat{\theta}$	$\Delta\hat{\theta}$	t	$\hat{\theta}$	$\Delta\hat{\theta}$	t
α_0	0.0128	(0.0029)	[4.35]	0.0128	(0.0030)	[4.21]	0.0125	(0.0032)	[3.92]
α_1	0.0545	(0.0149)	[3.65]	0.0544	(0.0153)	[3.55]	0.0521	(0.0147)	[3.54]
β_1	0.8373	(0.0208)	[40.21]	0.8373	(0.0216)	[38.81]	0.8402	(0.0224)	[37.43]
γ	0.1568	(0.0236)	[6.64]	0.1570	(0.0236)	[6.65]	0.1573	(0.0705)	[2.23]
ν	8.1160	(1.0360)	[7.83]	8.1260	(1.0910)	[7.44]	8.1080	(3.0980)	[2.61]
c	0.0483	(0.0092)	[5.27]	0.0481	(0.0095)	[5.04]	0.0451	(0.0264)	[1.71]
ϕ_1				0.0021	(0.0194)	[0.11]	0.0010	(0.1001)	[0.01]
ϕ_2							0.0351	(0.1191)	[0.29]

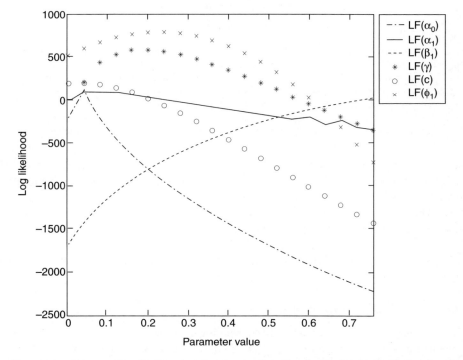

Figure 22.1 The *partial* log likelihood surface for the Gaussian AR(1)–GJR–GARCH(1,1) model presented in Table 22.1. In order to display the results on a single graph symbols have been used which incorporate various scale factors. The symbol definitions are as follows: $LF(\alpha_0) = LGF(\alpha_0|\hat{\theta})$, $LF(\alpha_1) = 0.5 \times LGF(\alpha_1|\hat{\theta})$, $LF(\beta_1) = 0.2 \times LGF(\beta_1|\hat{\theta})$, $LF(\gamma) = 3 \times LGF(\gamma|\hat{\theta})$, $LF(c) = LGF(c|\hat{\theta})$, $LF(\phi_1) = 4 \times LGF(\phi_1|\hat{\theta})$. The parameter values range from 0 to 0.76, with an increment of 0.04

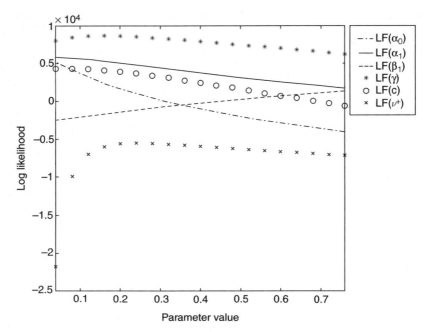

Figure 22.2   The *partial* log likelihood surface for the Student's *t* GJR–GARCH(1,1) model presented in Table 22.2. In order to display the results on a single graph symbols have been used which incorporate various scale factors and offsets. The symbol definitions are as follows:
$LF(\alpha_0) = 4 \times [4000 + LGF(\alpha_0|\hat{\theta})]$, $LF(\alpha_1) = 4 \times [4000 + LGF(\alpha_1|\hat{\theta})]$, $LF(\beta_1) = 4000 + LGF(\beta_1|\hat{\theta})$, $LF(\gamma) = 6 \times [4000 + LGF(\gamma |\hat{\theta})]$, $LF(c) = 3 \times [4000 + LGF(c|\hat{\theta})]$, $LF(\nu^+) = 100 \times [2500 + LGF(\nu|\hat{\theta})]$, where $\nu = 25\nu^+ + 2$. The parameter values range from 0.04 to 0.76, with an increment of 0.04. This gives values of ν which range from 3 to 21, and (for example) a parameter value of $\nu^+ = 0.4$ corresponds to $\nu = 12$

the other GARCH parameters are held fixed at the values which maximize the log likelihood function. For the *k*th GARCH model parameter, θ_k, we will denote this *partial* log likelihood function by $LGF(\theta_k|\hat{\theta})$. Inspection of Figures 22.1 and 22.2 shows that, to within the step tolerance, the location of the *partial* log likelihood maxima are in agreement with the parameter estimates given in Tables 22.1 and 22.2. It can also be seen that the *partial* log likelihood surface is both smooth and convex. This explains why a Newton-type numerical optimizer can converge to a *global* maximum even when poor initial estimates are supplied.

22.6   EXCEL DEMONSTRATION

This demonstration is concerned with modelling currency exchange rate returns data. It illustrates how to identify the best GARCH model to suit a particular time series, and is composed of the following components:

- Two ActiveX plot controls, to display the orginal data and also the modelled standardized residuals $\mathcal{Z}_i = \epsilon_i/\sqrt{h_i}$, $i = 1, \dots, n$.
- Microsoft TextBox controls to allow the user to select the order of the GARCH model.

- Microsoft Radio controls to allow the user to select the *type* of GARCH model.
- Microsoft Button controls to perform actions such as: *Clear*, *Calculate*, and *Show Data*.
- A Microsoft Grid control to display the modelled values and parameter estimates.

It can be seen that the user has the choice of selecting either an AGARCH-I or an AGARCH-II model, and there is also an *asymmetry option*. It should be noted that when AGARCH-I is used without asymmetry this is equivalent to the standard linear GARCH model. All the results presented here are for an AGARCH-I model either with or without asymmetry.

We found the Microsoft Grid control to be a very versatile means of showing information. In this example it was used to display the following results:

- The initial parameter estimates. Although they were all automatically set to 0.1, they could if required be edited to different values.
- The computed parameter estimates, $\hat{\theta}_k$, $k = 1, \ldots, N_p$.
- The standard errors, σ_k, $k = 1, \ldots, N_p$.
- The significance statistics for the estimated parameters, $\mathcal{T}_k = \hat{\theta}_k / \sigma_k$, $k = 1, \ldots, N_p$.
- The value of the log likelihood for the estimated parameter values, $-\mathcal{L}(\hat{\theta})$.
- The partial derivatives (also termed scores) $\partial \mathcal{L}(\theta) / \partial \theta_k$, $k = 1, \ldots, N_p$ for the estimated parameters.
- The normality test statistic N_{stat} described in Section 22.4.

The top graph in Figures 22.3 to 22.7 plots the exchange rate returns data, and is identical in each figure. It can be seen that the data clearly exhibits volatility clustering. The bottom graph in Figures 22.3 to 22.7 plots the standardized residuals $\mathcal{Z}_i = \epsilon_i / \sqrt{h_i}$, $i = 1, \ldots, n$. If the data has been modelled well then these values should have the distribution NID(0,1). This means that the closer the lower graph corresponds to white noise the better the GARCH model. Of course it may be difficult to perform this appraisal *visually*, so that is why we also report the normality test statistic. We could also look at the autocorrelation structure, but we have not done that here.

Figure 22.3 shows the results of using a simple GARCH(0,1), that is ARCH(1), on the data. The log likelihood is 4122.57 and the normality test statistic, N_{stat}, is 1499.48. This value of N_{stat} is very large, and we can clearly see clustering in the lower graph. In Figures 22.4 and 22.5 we experiment with using high order ARCH models to describe the data.

Figure 22.4 shows the results of using a GARCH(0,10). Here the log likelihood is 4337.0 and the normality test statistic, N_{stat} is 2.922. It can be seen that only the parameters α_0, α_1, α_2, and α_5 have t statistic values above 3.0. This model is certainly better than the simple GARCH(0,1) model since the log likelihood is higher and also N_{stat} is considerably lower.

Figure 22.5 shows the results of using an AGARCH-I(0,10). The inclusion of asymmetry has improved on the GARCH(0,10) model, since the log likelihood has now increased to 4353.97 and N_{stat} has reduced to 1.562. It can be seen that the parameters α_0, α_1, α_2, α_4, α_5, and the asymmetry parameter γ have t statistic values above 3.

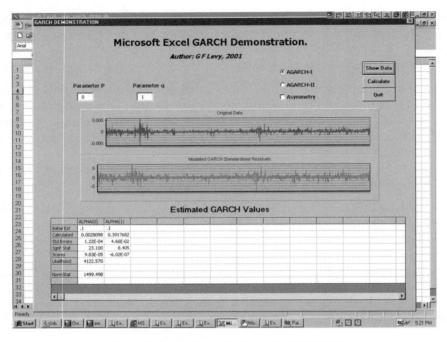

Figure 22.3   Modelling the data with GARCH(0,1)

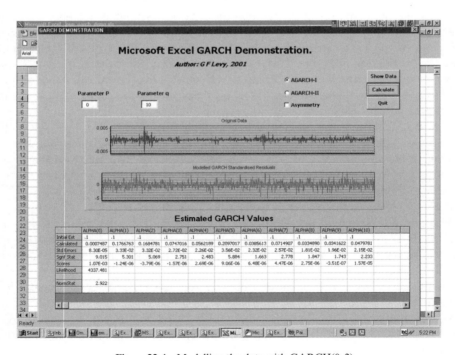

Figure 22.4   Modelling the data with GARCH(0, 2)

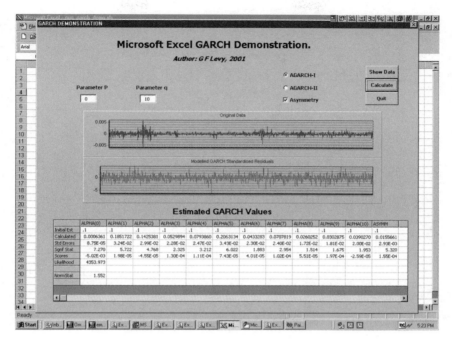

Figure 22.5 Modelling the data with GARCH(0,10)

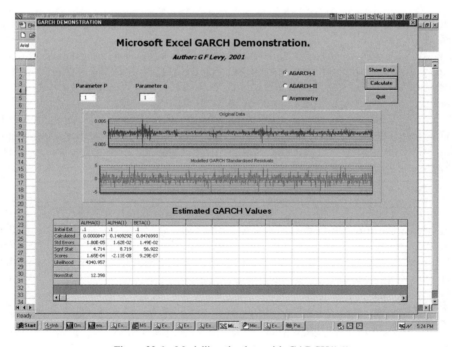

Figure 22.6 Modelling the data with GARCH(1,1)

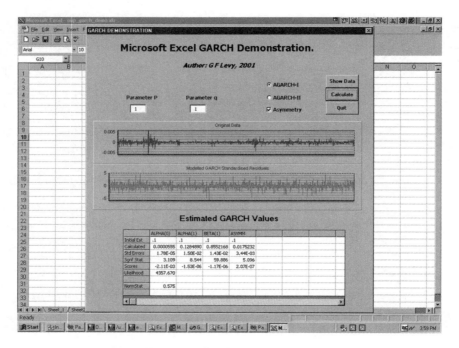

Figure 22.7   Modelling the data with AGARCH(1,1)

In Figures 22.6 and 22.7 we see if a GARCH(1,1) models will do better than the ARCH(10) models.

Figure 22.6 shows the results of using a GARCH(1,1). Here the likelihood is 4340.95 and the normality test statistic, N_{stat} is 12.39. All the parameters have t statistic values above 3, and the value β_1 is 56.922. However, these results are not as good those we obtained from the AGARCH-I(0,10) model.

Figure 22.7 shows the results of using an AGARCH-I(1,1). Here the likelihood is 4357.67 and the normality test statistic, N_{stat} is 0.575. All the parameters have t statistic values above 3, and the value β_1 is 59.886. Clearly this is the preferred model is an AGARCH-I(1,1) model with:

$$\alpha_0 = 5.55 \times 10^{-5}, \quad \alpha_1 = 0.128, \quad \beta_1 = 0.852, \quad \gamma = 0.0175$$

It is interesting to note that the asymmetry parameter γ is positive. This is because we are modelling currency exchange rate returns data and (since it is not clear that negative exchange rate returns indicate *bad* news) there is no preference in the sign of the asymmetry. However, if we were modelling stock market returns data we would expect γ to be negative.

22.7   INTERNET EXPLORER DEMONSTRATION

This demonstration illustrates how GARCH modelling could be carried out with a Web Browser on an Internet Web page.

It shows how ActiveX components on a Web page can be used to model the volatility of the share price for a particular company. This Web page contains the following ActiveX components:

- Three Microsoft ActiveX button controls
- Two ActiveX graphical controls, called Plot1 and Plot2
- The GARCH modelling ActiveX control, GARCH1.

All the data input and computation is performed by the aggregated ActiveX component GARCH1. This control was created using Visual Basic and uses textboxes to input the model parameters and company name. It also extracts company share returns from a Microsoft Access database and models this data by calling computational GARCH routines contained within a Visual C++ DLL.

Figures 22.8 to 22.10 show how this demonstration is used. Appropriate values of p, q and the company name are entered into the textboxes of GARCH1. The data corresponding to the selected company (in this case it is merely called *ASSET*) is displayed on the lower plot region by clicking the button labelled 'Show Data'. This runs the subroutine Show_Data_ Click() which calls the EXTRACT_DATA property of GARCH1 to retrieve data from the Access database and then display it using the ActiveX component Plot2. When the button labelled 'Calculate' is clicked Calculate_GARCH_Click() is run and a GARCH(p,q) process used to model the data. If the user wishes to try alternative value of *p* and *q*, then clicking the 'Clear' button deletes the previous results and the data can be remodelled.

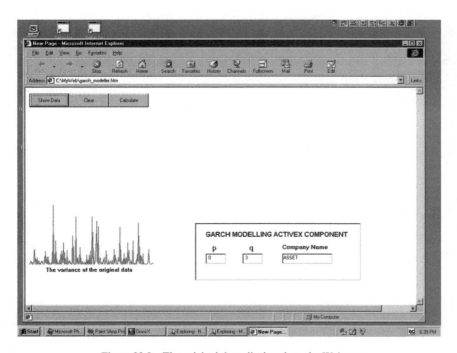

Figure 22.8 The original data displayed on the Web page

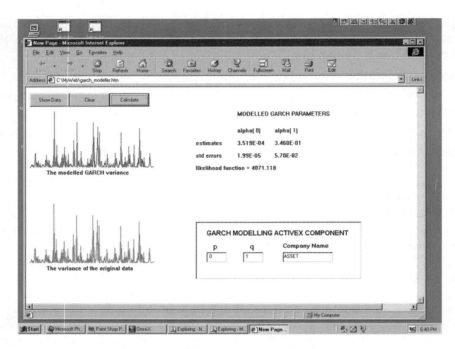

Figure 22.9 Modelling the data with ARCH(1)

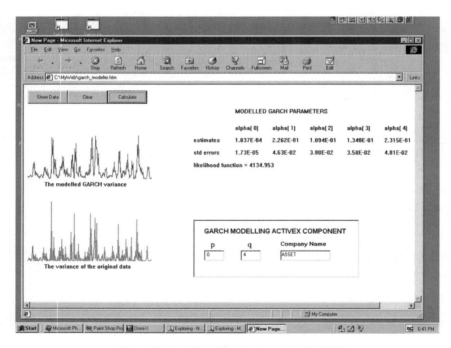

Figure 22.10 Modelling the data with ARCH(4)

Chapter 23

Multivariate time series

So far we have been concerned with modelling the volatility of single assets. However, most practical financial applications consist of portfolios containing many assets, and it is therefore necessary to model multivariate time series and their associated time varying covariance matrices.

One of the main problems connected with doing this is the number of parameters that may require estimating. For instance a typical portfolio consisting of 100 assets has a 100×100 covariance matrix which is described by 5050 terms. One way round this problem is to use principal component analysis to reduce the number of parameters which describe the multivariate process.

23.1 PRINCIPAL COMPONENT GARCH

Principal component or orthogonal GARCH provides a parsimonious way in which to model multivariate time series, see Ding (1994) and Alexander (2000).

Consider T observations of m variables and let these be represented by the $T \times m$ matrix Y, so that the ith column of Y, Y^i, contains the T observations of the ith variable. We will also denote the row vector containing the values of the m variables at instant t by Y_t. If the unconditional mean of the Y^i is μ_i then we can construct the matrix X, where the ith column of X is $X^i = Y^i - \mu_i$, and the $m \times m$ covariance matrix, C, of the data matrix Y is given by:

$$C = X^T X \tag{23.1}$$

Since the covariance matrix is symmetric and positive definite we can obtain the following spectral decomposition

$$C = W \Sigma W^T \tag{23.2}$$

where the columns of the $m \times m$ matrix W contain the eigenvectors of C and the elements of the $m \times m$ diagonal matrix Σ contain the corresponding eigenvalues, λ_i, $i = 1, \ldots, m$.

If k of the eigenvalues are much greater than the other $m - k$ eigenvalues, then a good approximation to the covariance matrix is:

$$C \approx W_k \Sigma_k W_k{}^T$$

where Σ_k is the $k \times k$ diagonal matrix containing the kth largest eigenvalues, and W_k is the $m \times k$ matrix of eigenvectors formed using the appropriate k columns of W.

The time-dependent scores, S_t^i, $t = 1, \ldots, T$, corresponding to the ith eigenvector (principal component) are calculated as:

$$S_t^i = X_t W^i, \quad t = 1, \ldots, T$$

where S_t^i is the $(T \times 1)$ score vector at time instant t corresponding to the ith eigenvalue, X_t is the the row of the $(T \times m)$ matrix X in Equation 23.1 corresponding to time t, and W^i is the corresponding $(m \times 1)$ eigenvector.

In matrix notation, if the k largest eigenvalues are used, then we obtain the following scores matrix:

$$S = XW_k \tag{23.3}$$

where S is now a $T \times k$ matrix, X is a $T \times m$ matrix, and W_k is a $m \times k$ matrix.

All the columns of S (that is the score vector corresponding to each principal component) are orthogonal, and so $S^T S$ results in the diagonal matrix Σ. This can easily be shown as follows:

$$\begin{aligned} S^T S &= (XW)^T XW \\ &= W^T (X^T X) W \\ &= W^T C W \\ &= \Sigma \end{aligned} \tag{23.4}$$

The variance of the score vector for the ith principal component is thus equal to the ith eigenvalue, λ_i. That is:

$$E[S^{i^T} S^i] = \sum_{t=1}^{T} S_t^i S_t^i = \lambda_i, \quad i = 1, \ldots, k$$

The instantaneous covariance matrix at time t, V_t, can thus be approximated as follows:

$$V_t = X_t^T X_t$$

where X_t is the row of matrix X corresponding to time t.

From Equation 23.3 we have $S = XW$ and therefore:

$$SW^T = XWW^T = X, \quad \text{since} \quad WW^T = I$$

Thus $X = SW^T$ and $X^T X = WS^T SW^T$.

Since $S^T S$ is diagonal we can write V_t as:

$$V_t = W\Omega_t W^T, \quad t = 1, \ldots, T \tag{23.5}$$

where each time dependent variance, Ω_t^i, $i = 1, \ldots, k$, in the diagonal matrix Ω_t is modelled using a *univariate* GARCH process. Note: The eigenvectors W are assumed to be time independent.

For example, suppose we want to model the time dependent covariance matrix of three exchange rate return series r_j^i, $i = 1, \ldots, 3$, $j = 1, \ldots, T$, then we would employ the steps explained below.

Construct the covariance matrix, C

The value of the element in the ith row and jth column of matrix C is:

$$C_{i,j} = \sum_{k=1}^{T} (r_k^i - \bar{r}^i)(r_k^j - \bar{r}^j), \quad i = 1, \ldots, 3, \quad j = 1, \ldots, 3$$

where $\bar{r}^i$ is the mean value of the ith return series,

---
Form the eigenvalue decomposition

From Equation 23.2 we have:

$$C = W\Sigma W^T$$

where the ith eigenvector is the column vector $W^i = (W_1^i, W_2^i, W_3^i)^T$. We will assume that $\lambda_1 \sim \lambda_2$, and $\lambda_1 \gg \lambda_3$, so $k = 2$.

Use the eigenvectors to form the scores

From Equation 23.1 the scores are given by $S = XW_k$, where $k = 2$

The scores for the first principal component are:

$$S_1^1 = X_1^1 W_1^1 + X_1^2 W_2^1 + X_1^3 W_3^1$$
$$S_2^1 = X_2^1 W_1^1 + X_2^2 W_2^1 + X_2^3 W_3^1$$
$$S_3^1 = X_3^1 W_1^1 + X_3^2 W_2^1 + X_3^3 W_3^1$$

$$\cdot \quad \cdot$$
$$\cdot \quad \cdot$$
$$\cdot \quad \cdot$$

$$S_T^1 = X_T^1 W_1^1 + X_T^2 W_2^1 + X_T^3 W_3^1$$

The scores for the second principal component are:

$$S_1^2 = X_1^2 W_1^2 + X_1^2 W_2^2 + X_1^3 W_3^2$$
$$S_2^2 = X_2^1 W_1^2 + X_2^2 W_2^2 + X_2^3 W_3^2$$
$$S_3^2 = X_3^1 W_1^2 + X_3^2 W_2^2 + X_3^3 W_3^2$$

$$\cdot \quad \cdot$$
$$\cdot \quad \cdot$$
$$\cdot \quad \cdot$$

$$S_T^2 = X_T^1 W_1^2 + X_T^2 W_2^2 + X_T^3 W_3^2$$

| Model the univariate scores using GARCH |

Use an appropriate univariate GARCH process to model the variance of the scores, $h_t^i = (S_t^i)^2 = \Omega_t^i$, $i = 1, \ldots, k$, $t = 1, \ldots, T$ for each sequence S_t^i, $t = 1, \ldots, T$, where $i \leq k$. So, using $k = 2$ and assuming a basic GARCH(p,q) process, then the two diagonal elements (Ω_t^1 and Ω_t^2) of Ω_t are modelled as follows:

The GARCH(p_1, q_1) process for the first principal component score vector is:

$$\Omega_t^1 = (S_t^1)^2 = h_t^1 = \alpha_0^1 + \sum_{j=1}^{q_1} \alpha_j^1 \epsilon_{t-j}^2 + \sum_{j=1}^{p_1} \beta_j^1 h_{t-j}, \quad t = 1, \ldots, T$$

and the GARCH(p_2, q_2) process for the second principal component score vector is:

$$\Omega_t^2 = (S_t^2)^2 = h_t^2 = \alpha_0^2 + \sum_{j=1}^{q_2} \alpha_j^2 \epsilon_{t-j}^2 + \sum_{j=1}^{p_2} \beta_j^1 h_{t-j}, \quad t = 1, \ldots, T$$

| Compute the time dependent covariance matrix |

From Equation 23.5 we use:

$$V_t = W \Omega_t W^T, \quad t = 1, \ldots, T$$

For this example it is easy to perform the matrix multiplications as follows:

$$V_t = \begin{pmatrix} V_{11} & V_{12} & V_{13} \\ V_{21} & V_{22} & V_{23} \\ V_{31} & V_{32} & V_{33} \end{pmatrix} = \begin{pmatrix} W_1^1 & W_1^2 \\ W_2^1 & W_2^2 \\ W_3^1 & W_3^2 \end{pmatrix} \begin{pmatrix} h_t^1 & 0 \\ 0 & h_t^2 \end{pmatrix} \begin{pmatrix} W_1^1 & W_2^1 & W_3^1 \\ W_1^2 & W_2^2 & W_3^2 \end{pmatrix}$$

$$= \begin{pmatrix} W_1^1 & W_1^2 \\ W_2^1 & W_2^2 \\ W_3^1 & W_3^2 \end{pmatrix} \begin{pmatrix} h_t^1 W_1^1 & h_t^1 W_2^1 & h_t^1 W_3^1 \\ h_t^2 W_1^2 & h_t^2 W_2^2 & h_t^2 W_3^2 \end{pmatrix}$$

This yields the orthogonal GARCH estimate of the time dependent covariance matrix as:

$$V_t = \begin{pmatrix} h_t^1 W_1^1 W_1^1 + h_t^2 W_1^2 W_1^2 & h_t^1 W_1^1 W_2^1 + h_t^2 W_1^2 W_2^2 & h_t^1 W_1^1 W_3^1 + h_t^2 W_1^2 W_3^2 \\ h_t^1 W_2^1 W_1^1 + h_t^2 W_2^2 W_1^2 & h_t^1 W_2^1 W_2^1 + h_t^2 W_2^2 W_2^2 & h_t^1 W_2^1 W_3^1 + h_t^2 W_2^2 W_3^2 \\ h_t^1 W_3^1 W_1^1 + h_t^2 W_3^2 W_1^2 & h_t^1 W_3^1 W_2^1 + h_t^2 W_3^2 W_2^2 & h_t^1 W_3^1 W_3^1 + h_t^2 W_3^2 W_3^2 \end{pmatrix}$$

More details concerning orthogonal GARCH models can be found in Van der Weide (2002).

APPENDICES

Appendix A

Computer code for Part I

This Appendix contains complete code for the examples referenced in the main text.

A.1   THE ODL FILE FOR THE DERIVATIVE PRICING CONTROL

The complete ODL file for the derivative pricing control used in Section 3.3 and Chapter 4 is given below.

```
// NAGDBS.odl : type library source for ActiveX Control project.
// This file will be processed by the Make Type Library (mktyplib) tool to
// produce the type library (NAGDBS.tlb) that will become a resource in
// NAGDBS.ocx.

#include <olectl.h>
#include <idispids.h>

[uuid(8B7F2A94-E828-11D2-AD08-0060087ED9F1),version(1.0),
 helpfile("NAGDBS.hlp"),
 helpstring("NAGDBS ActiveX Control module"),
 control ]
library NAGDBSLib
{
    importlib(STDOLE_TLB);
    importlib(STDTYPE_TLB);
    typedef enum
    {
    [helpstring("Call")] Call = 0,
    [helpstring("Put")] Put = 1
 }
 PUTCALLTYPE;
    typedef enum
    {
    [helpstring("European")] European = 0,
    [helpstring("American")] American = 1,
    [helpstring("Cntrl_American")] Cntrl_American = 2
 }
 EXTYPE;
    typedef enum
    {
    [helpstring("Lattice u = 1/d")] Lattice_standard = 0,
    [helpstring("Lattice p = 1/2")] Lattice_prob_half = 1,
    [helpstring("Analytic")] Analytic = 2
 }
 METHODTYPE;
    // Primary dispatch interface for CNAGDBSCtrl
    [uuid(8B7F2A95-E828-11D2-AD08-0060087ED9F1),
      helpstring("Dispatch interface for NAGDBS Control"), hidden ]
    dispinterface_DNAGDBS
    {
      properties:
        // NOTE - ClassWizard will maintain property
        // information here.
        // Use extreme caution when editing this section.
        //{{AFX_ODL_PROP(CNAGDBSCtrl)
        [id(1)] METHODTYPE method;
        [id(2)] EXTYPE extype;
        [id(3)] double sigma;
        [id(4)] long numsteps;
```

```
      [id(5)] double intrate;
      [id(6)] double dividends;
      [id(7)] double curval;
      [id(8)] double optval;
      [id(9)] double strike;
      [id(10)] PUTCALLTYPE putcall;
      [id(11)] double maturity;
      [id(DISPID_CAPTION), bindable, requestedit] BSTR Caption;
      [id(DISPID_BACKCOLOR), bindable, requestedit] OLE_COLOR BackColor;
      [id(DISPID_FORECOLOR), bindable, requestedit] OLE_COLOR ForeColor;
      //}}AFX_ODL_PROP
   methods:
      // NOTE - ClassWizard will maintain method information here.
      // Use extreme caution when editing this section.
      //{{AFX_ODL_METHOD(CNAGDBSCtrl)
      [id(12)] void Calculate();
      [id(13)] void greeks(double* greekvals);
      //}}AFX_ODL_METHOD
      [id(DISPID_ABOUTBOX)] void AboutBox();
   };
   // Event dispatch interface for CNAGDBSCtrl
   [ uuid(8B7F2A96-E828-11D2-AD08-0060087ED9F1),
     helpstring("Event interface for NAGDBS Control") ]
   dispinterface_DNAGDBSEvents
   {
      properties:
         // Event interface has no properties
      methods:
         // NOTE - ClassWizard will maintain event information here.
         // Use extreme caution when editing this section.
         //{{AFX_ODL_EVENT(CNAGDBSCtrl)
         [id(DISPID_CLICK)] void Click();
         [id(DISPID_MOUSEMOVE)] void MouseMove(short Button, short Shift,
            OLE_XPOS_PIXELS x, OLE_YPOS_PIXELS y);
         //}}AFX_ODL_EVENT
   };
   // Class information for CNAGDBSCtrl
   [ uuid(8B7F2A97-E828-11D2-AD08-0060087ED9F1),
     helpstring("NAGDBS Control"), control ]
   coclass NAGDBS
   {
      [default] dispinterface_DNAGDBS;
      [default,source] dispinterface_DNAGDBSEvents;
   };
   //{{AFX_APPEND_ODL}}
   //}}AFX_APPEND_ODL}}
};
```

Appendix B

Some more option pricing formulae

In this section we list some more derivative pricing formula; use is made of the following symbols:

$$d_1 = \frac{\log(S/E) + (r - q + \sigma^2/2)\tau}{\sigma\sqrt{\tau}} \tag{B.1}$$

$$d_2 = \frac{\log(S/E) + (r - q - \sigma^2/2)\tau}{\sigma\sqrt{\tau}} = d_1 - \sigma\sqrt{\tau} \tag{B.2}$$

B.1 BINARY OPTIONS

A binary *cash or nothing* call option pays nothing if the stock price ends up below the the strike and an amount Q if it ends up above the strike price. The value is:

$$V_c = Q\exp(-r\tau)N_1(d_2) \tag{B.3}$$

A binary *asset or nothing* call option pays nothing if the stock price ends up below the strike and the stock price itself if it ends up above the strike price. The value is:

$$V_c = S\exp(-r\tau)N_1(d_1) \tag{B.4}$$

B.2 OPTION TO EXCHANGE ONE ASSET FOR ANOTHER

$$V = S_2\exp(-q_2\tau)N_1(d-1) - S_1\exp(-q_1\tau)N_1(d_2) \tag{B.5}$$

where

$$d_1 = \frac{\log(S_2/S_1) + (q_1 - q_2 + \sigma^2/2)\tau}{\sigma\sqrt{\tau}}$$

$$d_2 = d_1 - \sigma\sqrt{\tau}$$

and

$$\sigma = \sqrt{\sigma_1^2 + \sigma_2^2 - 2\rho\sigma_1\sigma_2}$$

It is interesting to note that this formula is independent of the interest rate r.

B.3   LOOKBACK OPTIONS

The value of a European lookback call at time zero is:

$$V_c = S \exp(-q\tau)\left\{ N_1(a_1) - \frac{\sigma^2}{2(r-q)} N_1(-a_1) \right\}$$

$$- S_{\min} \exp(-r\tau)\left\{ N_1(a_2) - \frac{\sigma^2}{2(r-q)} \exp(Y_1) N_1(-a_3) \right\} \tag{B.6}$$

where

$$a_1 = \frac{\log(S/S_{\min}) + (r - q + \sigma^2/2)\tau}{\sigma\sqrt{\tau}}, \quad a_2 = a_1 - \sigma\sqrt{\tau}$$

$$a_3 = \frac{\log(S/S_{\min}) + (-r + q + \sigma^2/2)\tau}{\sigma\sqrt{\tau}}, \quad Y_1 = -\frac{\log(S/S_{\min})2(-r - q - \sigma^2/2)}{\sigma^2}$$

and $S_{\min}$ is the minimum stock price achieved to date. If the lookback option has just been originated then $S_{\min} = S$ and the valuation simplifies to:

$$V_c = S \exp(-q\tau)\{N_1(g_1) - WN_1(-g_1)\} - S \exp(-r\tau)\{N_1(g_2) - WN_1(g_2)\} \tag{B.7}$$

where

$$W = \frac{\sigma^2}{2(r-q)}, \quad g_1 = \frac{(r - q + \sigma^2/2)\tau}{\sigma\sqrt{\tau}}, \quad g_2 = g_1 - \sigma\sqrt{\tau}$$

The value of a European lookback put is:

$$V_p = S \exp(-q\tau)\left\{ -N_1(b_2) + \frac{\sigma^2}{2(r-q)} N_1(-b_2) \right\}$$

$$+ S_{\max} \exp(-r\tau)\left\{ N_1(b_1) - \frac{\sigma^2}{2(r-q)} \exp(Y_2) N_1(-b_3) \right\} \tag{B.8}$$

where

$$b_1 = \frac{\log(S_{\max}/S) + (-r + q + \sigma^2/2)\tau}{\sigma\sqrt{\tau}}, \quad b_2 = b_1 - \sigma\sqrt{\tau}$$

$$b_3 = \frac{\log(S_{\max}/S) + (r - q - \sigma^2/2)\tau}{\sigma\sqrt{\tau}}, \quad Y_2 = -\frac{\log(S_{\max}/S)2(r - q - \sigma^2/2)}{\sigma^2}$$

and $S_{\max}$ is the maximum stock price achieved to date. If the lookback option has just been originated then $S_{\max} = S$ and the valuation simplifies to:

$$V_p = S \exp(-q\tau)\{-N_1(b_2) + WN_1(-b_2)\} + S \exp(-r\tau)\{N_1(b_1) - WN_1(b_1)\} \tag{B.9}$$

where

$$W = \frac{\sigma^2}{2(r-q)}, \quad b_1 = \frac{(-r + q + \sigma^2/2)\tau}{\sigma\sqrt{\tau}}, \quad b_2 = b_1 - \sigma\sqrt{\tau}$$

Appendix C

Derivation of the Greeks for vanilla European options

C.1 INTRODUCTION

In this section we will present some useful results which will be used later on to derive expressions for the Greeks.

A fundamental result of calculus is that:

$$\frac{\partial}{\partial x} \int f(x)dx = f(x) \tag{C.1}$$

Also the indefinite integral, $\int f(x)dx$, can be expressed as a definite integral with variable upper bound as follows:

$$\int f(x)dx = \int_a^x f(x)dx + c$$

so

$$\frac{\partial}{\partial x} \int_a^x f(x)dx = f(x) \tag{C.2}$$

We can now use this result to obtain the derivative of the cumulative distribution function:

$$N_1(x) = \frac{1}{\sqrt{2\pi}} \int_{-\infty}^x \exp(-x^2/2)dx$$

which gives

$$\frac{\partial N_1(x)}{\partial x} = n(x) \tag{C.3}$$

where

$$n(x) = \frac{1}{\sqrt{2\pi}} \exp(-x^2/2)$$

We now derive various results for the parameters d_1 and d_2 which appear in the Black–Scholes equation, see Part I Section 2.3.3.

$$d_1 = \frac{\log(S/E) + (r - q + \sigma^2/2)(T - t)}{\sigma\sqrt{T - t}} \tag{C.4}$$

and

$$d_2 = \frac{\log(S/E) + (r - q - \sigma^2/2)(T - t)}{\sigma\sqrt{T - t}} = d_1 - \sigma\sqrt{(T - t)} \tag{C.5}$$

We have:

$$\frac{\partial d_2}{\partial S} = \frac{\partial d_1}{\partial S} = \frac{1}{S\sigma\sqrt{T - t}} \tag{C.6}$$

$$\frac{\partial d_2}{\partial \sigma} = \frac{\partial d_1}{\partial \sigma} - \sqrt{T - t} \tag{C.7}$$

$$\frac{\partial d_1}{\partial r} = \frac{\partial d_2}{\partial r} = \frac{\sqrt{T - t}}{\sigma} \tag{C.8}$$

$$\frac{\partial d_2}{\partial t} = \frac{\partial d_1}{\partial t} + \frac{\sigma}{2(T - t)} \tag{C.9}$$

Also:

$$n(d_2) = \frac{1}{\sqrt{2\pi}} \exp(-d_2^2/2)$$

$$= \frac{1}{\sqrt{2\pi}} \exp(-d_1^2/2) \exp\left\{\sigma d_1\sqrt{T - t} - \sigma^2(T - t)/2\right\}$$

$$= n(d_1) \exp\left\{\log(S/E) + (r - q + \sigma^2/2)(T - t) - \sigma^2(T - t)/2\right\}$$

so

$$n(d_2) = \frac{S}{E} n(d_1) \exp(r(T - t)) \exp(-q(T - t)) \tag{C.10}$$

C.2   GAMMA

Gamma is defined as the second derivative of the option value with respect to the underlying stock price. This means, see Section C.3, it is the rate of change of *Delta* with the underlying stock price.

For a European call the value of *Gamma* is:

$$\Gamma_c = \frac{\partial^2 c}{\partial S^2} = \frac{\partial \Delta_c}{\partial S} = \frac{\partial}{\partial S}\{N_1(d_1)\exp(-q(T - t))\}$$

where the value of Δ_c, is given in Section C.3. So

$$\Gamma_c = \exp(-q(T - t))\frac{\partial N_1(d_1)}{\partial S} = \exp(-q(T - t))n(d_1)\frac{\partial d_1}{\partial S}$$

Therefore:

$$\Gamma_c = \frac{n(d_1)}{S\sigma\sqrt{T - t}}\exp(-q(T - t)) \tag{C.11}$$

The value of *Gamma* for a European put can be calculated similarly:

$$\Gamma_p = \frac{\partial^2 p}{\partial S^2} = \frac{\partial \Delta_p}{\partial S} = \frac{\partial}{\partial S}\{(N_1(d_1) - 1)\exp(-q(T - t))\}$$

where we have used the value of Δ_p, derived in Section C.3. Therefore:

$$\Gamma_p = \exp(-q(T-t))\frac{\partial(N_1(d_1)-1)}{\partial S} = \exp(-q(T-t))n(d_1)\frac{\partial d_1}{\partial S}$$

So

$$\Gamma_p = \Gamma_c = \frac{n(d_1)}{S\sigma\sqrt{T-t}}\exp(-q(T-t)) \qquad (C.12)$$

So the value of *Gamma* for both a put and a call is the same.

C.3 DELTA

Delta is defined as the rate of change of option value with the underlying stock price. For a European call we have:

$$\Delta_c = \frac{\partial c}{\partial S} = \frac{\partial}{\partial S}\{S\exp(-q(T-t))N_1(d_1) - E\exp(-r(T-t))N_1(d_2)\}$$

So

$$\Delta_c = \exp(-q(T-t))\left\{N_1(d_1) + Sn(d_1)\frac{\partial d_1}{\partial S}\right\} - E\exp(-r(T-t))n(d_2)\frac{\partial d_2}{\partial S} \qquad (C.13)$$

Substituting for $n(d_2)$, and $\partial d_2/\partial S$ we obtain:

$$\Delta_c = \exp(-q(T-t))N_1(d_1) \qquad (C.14)$$

In similar manner we have for a European put:

$$\Delta_p = \frac{\partial p}{\partial S} = \frac{\partial}{\partial S}\{E\exp(-r(T-t))(1-N_1(d_2)) - S\exp(-q(T-t))(1-N_1(d_1))\}$$

So

$$\Delta_p = -E\exp(-r(T-t))n(d_2)\frac{\partial d_2}{\partial S}$$

$$- \exp(-q(T-t))\left\{(1-N_1(d_1)) + Sn(d_1)\frac{\partial d_1}{\partial S}\right\} \qquad (C.15)$$

substituting for $n(d_2)$, and $\partial d_2/\partial S$ we obtain:

$$\Delta_p = \exp(-q(T-t))\{N_1(d_1)-1\} \qquad (C.16)$$

C.4 THETA

Theta is defined as the rate of change of the option value with time. For a European call option we have:

$$\Theta_c = \frac{\partial c}{\partial t} = \frac{\partial}{\partial t}\{S\exp(-q(T-t))N_1(d_1) - E\exp(-r(T-t))N_1(d_2)\}$$

$$= q\exp(-q(T-t))SN_1(d_1) + \exp(-q(T-t))Sn(d_1)\frac{\partial d_1}{\partial t}$$

$$- rE\exp(-r(T-t))N_1(d_2) - E\exp(-r(T-t))n(d_2)\frac{\partial d_2}{\partial t}$$

substituting for $n(d_2)$ and $\partial d_2/\partial t$ we obtain:

$$\Theta_c = q\exp(-q(T-t))SN_1(d_1) - rE\exp(-r(T-t))N_1(d_2)$$
$$+ \exp(-q(T-t))Sn(d_1)\frac{\partial d_1}{\partial t} - E\exp(-r(T-t))n(d_1)$$
$$\times \frac{S}{E}\exp(r(T-t))\exp(-q(T-t))\left\{\frac{\partial d_1}{\partial t} + \frac{\sigma}{2(T-t)}\right\}$$
$$= q\exp(-q(T-t))SN_1(d_1) - rE\exp(-r(T-t))N_1(d_2) - \frac{Sn(d_1)\sigma\exp(-q(T-t))}{2\sqrt{T-t}}$$

Therefore the value of theta is:

$$\Theta_c = \exp(-q(T-t))\left\{q - SN_1(d_1)\frac{Sn(d_1)\sigma}{2\sqrt{T-t}}\right\} - rE\exp(-r(T-t))N_1(d_2) \qquad (C.17)$$

For a put we can similarly show that

$$\Theta_p = \frac{\partial p}{\partial t} = \frac{\partial}{\partial t}\{E\exp(-r(T-t))(1-N_1(d_2)) - S\exp(-q(T-t))(1-N_1(d_1))\}$$
$$\Theta_p = rE\exp(-r(T-t))(1-N_1(d_2)) - E\exp(-r(T-t))n(d_2)\frac{\partial d_2}{\partial t}$$
$$- qS\exp(-q(T-t))(1-N_1(d_1)) + S\exp(-q(T-t))n(d_1)\frac{\partial d_1}{\partial t}$$

substituting for $n(d_2)$ and $\partial d_2/\partial t$ we obtain:

$$\Theta_p = rE\exp(-r(T-t))N_1(-d_2) - qS\exp(-q(T-t))N_1(-d_1)$$
$$- E\exp(-r(T-t))\exp(r(T-t))\exp(-q(T-t))$$
$$\times n(d_1)\frac{S}{E}\left\{\frac{\partial d_1}{\partial t} + \frac{\partial \sigma}{2(T-t)}\right\} + S\exp(-q(T-t))n(d_1)\frac{\partial d_1}{\partial t}$$

So we have:

$$\Theta_p = -\exp(-q(T-t))\left\{qSN_1(-d_1) + \frac{Sn(d_1)\sigma}{2\sqrt{T-t}}\right\}$$
$$+ rE\exp(-r(T-t))N_1(-d_2) \qquad (C.18)$$

C.5   RHO

Rho is the rate of change of the option value with interest rate.
   For a call we have:

$$\rho_c = \frac{\partial c}{\partial r} = \frac{\partial}{\partial r}\{S\exp(-q(T-t))N_1(d_1) - E\exp(-r(T-t))N_1(d_2)\}$$
$$= S\exp(-q(T-t))n(d_1)\frac{\partial d_1}{\partial r} + E(T-t)N_1(d_2) - E\exp(-r(T-t))n(d_2)\frac{\partial d_2}{\partial r}$$

substituting for $n(d_2)$ and $\partial d_2/\partial r$ we obtain:

$$\rho_c = E(T-t)N_1(d_2) \qquad (C.19)$$

For a European put we have:

$$\rho_p = \frac{\partial p}{\partial r} = \frac{\partial}{\partial r}\{E\exp(-r(T-t))(1-N_1(d_2)) - S\exp(-q(T-t))(1-N_1(d_2))\}$$

$$= -E(T-t)(1-N_1(d_2)) - E\exp(-r(T-t))n(d_2)\frac{\partial d_2}{\partial r}$$

$$+ S\exp(-q(T-t))n(d_1)\frac{\partial d_1}{\partial r}$$

$$= -E(T-t)N_1(-d_2) - E\exp(-r(T-t))n(d_2)\frac{\partial d_2}{\partial r}$$

$$+ S\exp(-q(T-t))n(d_1)\frac{\partial d_1}{\partial r}$$

substituting for $n(d_2)$ and $\partial d_2/\partial r$ we obtain:

$$\rho_p = -E(T-t)N_1(-d_2) \tag{C.20}$$

C.6 VEGA

Vega is the rate of change of option value with volatility. For a call we have:

$$V_c = \frac{\partial c}{\partial \sigma}$$

$$= \frac{\partial}{\partial \sigma}\{S\exp(-q(T-t))N_1(d_1) - E\exp(-r(T-t))N_1(d_2)\}$$

$$= S\exp(-q(T-t))n(d_1)\frac{\partial d_1}{\partial \sigma} - E\exp(-r(T-t))n(d_2)\frac{\partial d_2}{\partial r} \tag{C.21}$$

substituting for $n(d_2)$ and $\partial d_2/\partial \sigma$ we obtain:

$$V_c = S\exp(-q(T-t))n(d_1)\frac{\partial d_1}{\partial \sigma} - Sn(d_1)\exp(-q(T-t))\left\{\frac{\partial d_1}{\partial \sigma} - \sqrt{T-t}\right\}$$

Therefore

$$V_c = S\exp(-q(T-t))n(d_1)\sqrt{T-t} \tag{C.22}$$

For a European put we have:

$$V_p = \frac{\partial c}{\partial \sigma}$$

$$= \frac{\partial}{\partial \sigma}\{E\exp(-r(T-t))(1-N_1(d_2)) - S\exp(-q(T-t))(1-N_1(d_1))\}$$

$$= -E\exp(-r(T-t))n(d_2)\frac{\partial d_2}{\partial \sigma} + S\exp(-q(T-t))n(d_1)\frac{\partial d_1}{\partial \sigma} \tag{C.23}$$

substituting for $n(d_2)$ and $\partial d_2/\partial \sigma$ we obtain:

$$V_p = S\exp(-q(T-t))n(d_1)\sqrt{T-t} \tag{C.24}$$

which is the same as for a call.

Appendix D

Multiasset binomial lattices

D.1 TRUNCATED TWO ASSET BINOMIAL LATTICE

```
void truncated_2D_binomial(double *value, double tol, double S1, double S2,
    double X, double sigma1, double sigma2, double rho, double T, double r, double q1,
    double q2, Integer put, Integer M, Integer opt_type, Integer is_american, Integer *iflag)
{
/* Input parameters:
   = = = = = =
   tol            — the parameter which controls when lattice truncation occurs
   S1             — the current price of the underlying asset 1
   S2             — the current price of the underlying asset 2
   X              — the strike price
   sigma1         — the volatility of asset 1
   sigma2         — the volatility of asset 2
   rho            — the correlation coefficient between asset 1 and asset 2
   T              — the time to maturity
   r              — the interest rate
   q1             — the continuous dividend yield for asset 1
   q2             — the continuous dividend yield for asset 2
   put            — if put is 0 then a call option, otherwise a put option
   M              — the number of time steps, the zeroth time step is the root node of the lattice
   opt_type       — if opt_type is 0 then an option on the maximum of two asset, otherwise an option on the
                    minimum of two assets,
   is_american    — if is_american is 0 then a European option, otherwise an American option

   Output parameters:
   = = = = = =
   value          — the value of the option,
   iflag          — an error indicator.
*/
    double discount,t1,dt,d1,d2,u1,u2;
    Integer i,j,m1,n,iflagx,jj,ind;
    double zero=0.0,hold;
    double temp,ds1,ds2,dv1,dv2,h,tmp;
    double *s1, *s2, *v;
    double p[4];
    Integer max_index, P1,P2,tdv;
    double sqrt_dt, t, mu1, mu2, jp1, jp2;
    double one = 1.0, half = 0.5, quarter = 0.25;
    Integer v1, array_size;
    Boolean odd_step;

    if (!((M+1)/2 == M/2)){
       printf (''ERROR THE NUMBER OF TIME STEPS IS NOT EVEN \n'');
       return;
    }
#define UU 0
#define UD 1
#define DD 2
#define DU 3
    dt = T/(double)M;
    sqrt_dt = sqrt(dt);
    jp1 = sigma1*sqrt_dt;
    jp2 = sigma2*sqrt_dt;
    mu1 = r - q1 - sigma1*sigma1*half;
    mu2 = r - q2 - sigma2*sigma2*half;
    u1 = exp(jp1); /* assign the jump sizes */
    u2 = exp(jp2);
```

```
        d1 = exp(-jp1);
        d2 = exp(-jp2);
        p[UU] = quarter*(one + sqrt_dt * ((mu1/sigma1) + (mu2/sigma2)) + rho); /* set up the jump probabilities */
        p[UD] = quarter*(one + sqrt_dt * ((mu1/sigma1) - (mu2/sigma2)) - rho);
        p[DD] = quarter*(one + sqrt_dt * (-(mu1/sigma1) - (mu2/sigma2)) + rho);
        p[DU] = quarter*(one + sqrt_dt * (-(mu1/sigma1) + (mu2/sigma2)) - rho);
        for (i=0; i<4; ++i){
          if ((p[i] < zero) || (p[i] > 1.0)) printf (''ERROR p out of range\n'');
        }
        temp = floor(log(tol)/log(p[UU])); /* calculate the maximum index to use */
        max_index = (Integer)temp + 1;
        if (!((max_index+1)/2 == max_index/2)){/*then max_index is odd, so make it even */
          max_index = max_index + 1;
        }
        tdv = max_index+1;
#define V(I,J) v[(I) * tdv + (J)]
        discount = exp(-r*dt);
        for (i=0; i<4; ++i){
          p[i] = p[i]*discount;
        }
/* Allocate the arrays v[(max_index+1)*(max_index+1)], s1[2*max_index+1] and s2[2*max_index+1] */

        /* assign the 2*max_index+1 asset values for s1 */
        s1[max_index] = S1;
        for (i=1; i <= max_index; ++i){
          s1[max_index+i] = u1*s1[max_index+i-1];
          s1[max_index-i] = d1*s1[max_index-i+1];
        }
        /* assign the 2*max_index+1 asset values for s2 */
        s2[max_index] = S2;
        for (i=1; i <= max_index; ++i){
          s2[max_index+i] = u2*s2[max_index+i-1];
          s2[max_index-i] = d2*s2[max_index-i+1];
        }
        P1 = 0;
        for (i=0; i <= max_index; ++i){/* Calculate the option values at maturity */
          P2 = 0;
          for (j=0; j <= max_index; ++j){
            if (opt_type == 0){/* Maximum of two assets */
              if (put){
                V(i,j) = MAX(X - MAX(s1[P1],s2[P2]),zero);
              }
              else{
                V(i,j) = MAX(MAX(s1[P1],s2[P2])-X,zero);
              }
            }
            else{/* Minimum of two assets */
              if (put){
                V(i,j) = MAX(X - MIN(s1[P1],s2[P2]),zero);
              }
              else{
                V(i,j) = MAX(MIN(s1[P1],s2[P2])-X,zero);
              }
            }
            P2 = P2 + 2;
          }
          P1 = P1 + 2;
        }
/* now work backwards through the lattice to calculate the current option value */
        odd_step = FALSE;
        for (m1 = M-1; m1 >= 0; --m1){
          odd_step = !odd_step;
          if (m1 < max_index){/* use normal lattice */
            P1 = max_index-m1;
            for (i=0; i <= m1; ++i){
              P2 = max_index-m1;
              for (j=0; j <= m1; ++j){
                hold = p[UD]*V(i+1,j) + p[UU]*V(i+1,j+1) + p[DU]*V(i,j+1) + p[DD]*V(i,j);
                if (is_american){
                  **Insert code fragment 4.1 to deal with option type: put/call, max/min **
                }
                else{
                  V(i,j) = hold;
                }
                P2 = P2 + 2;
              }
```

```
      P1 = P1 + 2;
    }
  }
  else{/* using a restricted lattice */
    if (odd_step) {/* compute the option values in reverse order */
                   /*((only to index 1) so that don't overwrite storage */
      array_size = max_index;
      P1 = 2*max_index - 1;
      for (i = array_size; i>=1; --i){
        P2 = 2*max_index - 1;
        for (j = array_size; j>=1; --j){
          hold = p[UD]*V(i,j-1) + p[UU]*V(i,j) + p[DU]*V(i-1,j) + p[DD]*V(i-1,j-1);
          if (is_american){
            **Insert code fragment 4.1 to deal with option type: put/call, max/ min**
          }
          else{
            V(i,j) = hold;
          }
          P2 = P2 - 2;
        }
        P1 = P1 - 2;
      }
    }
    else{/* even time step, grow extra nodes at the top and bottom. Compute the */
         /* option values in forward order making sure that don't overwrite storage */
      array_size = max_index + 1;
      P2 = 0;
      P1 = 0;
      for (i = 0; i <= array_size - 1; ++i){
        P2 = 0;
        for (j = 0; j <= array_size - 1; ++j){
          if ( i == 0){
            hold = p[UU]*V(1,j);
          }
          else if (j == 0){
            hold = p[UU]*V(i,1);
          }
          else if (i == array_size - 1){
            hold = p[DD]*V(array_size-1,j);
          }
          else if (j == array_size - 1){
            hold = p[DD]*V(i,array_size-1);
          }
          else{
            hold=p[UD]*V(i+1,j) + p[UU]*V(i+1,j+1) +
                 p[DU]*V(i,j+1) + p[DD]*V(i,j);
          }
          if (is_american){
            ** Insert code fragment 4.1 to deal with option type: put/call, max/min **
          }
          else{
            V(i,j) = hold;
          }
          P2 = P2 + 2;
        }
        P1 = P1 + 2;
      }
    }
  }
  tmp = V(0,0);
  *value = tmp;
}
```

Code excerpt D.1   Function that uses a truncated binomial lattice to compute options on the maximum and minimum of two assets

D.2   RECURSIVE TWO ASSET BINOMIAL LATTICE

Here, in Code excerpt D.2, we show the code for a recursive binomial lattice to price options on the maximum or minimum of two assets.

The parameter M is the number of time intervals used, and the lattice is constructed under the assumption that M is even. The parameter recc control whether or not a recursive call to the function is made.

```c
void RECURSIVE_2D_binomial( double *value, double S1, double S2, double X,
    double sigma1, double sigma2, double rho, double T, double r, double q1, double q2,
    Integer put, Integer M, Integer opt_type, Integer is_american, Integer recc, Integer *iflag)
{
/* Input parameters:
   = = = = = =
   S1               -  the current price of the underlying asset 1
   S2               -  the current price of the underlying asset 2
   X                -  the strike price
   sigma1           -  the volatility of asset 1
   sigma2           -  the volatility of asset 2
   rho              -  the correlation coefficient between asset 1 and asset 2
   T                -  the time to maturity
   r                -  the interest rate
   q1               -  the continuous dividend yield for asset 1
   q2               -  the continuous dividend yield for asset 2
   put              -  if put is 0 then a call option, otherwise a put option
   M                -  the number of time steps, the zeroth node is the root node of the lattice
   opt_type         -  if opt_type is 0 then an option on the maximum of two asset, otherwise an option on the
                       minimum of two assets
   is_american      -  if is_american is 0 then a European option, otherwise an American option
   recc             -  if recc is 0 then not a recursive call, otherwise a recursive call

   Output parameters:
   = = = = = =
   value            -  the value of the option,
   iflag            -  an error indicator.
*/
   double discount,t1,dt,d1,d2,u1,u2;
   Integer i,j,m1,n,iflagx,jj,ind;
   double zero=0.0,hold;
   double temp,ds1,ds2,dv1,dv2,h,tmp;
   double *s1, *s2, *v;
   double p[4];
   Integer P1,P2,tdv;
   double loc_T, sqrt_dt, t, mu1, mu2, jp1, jp2;
   double one = 1.0, half = 0.5, quarter = 0.25;
   Integer v1;
   Integer loc_M, loc_recc, loc_iflag;
   Integer loc_is_american;

   if (!((M+1)/2 == M/2)){
     printf (" ERROR THE NUMBER OF TIME STEPS IS NOT EVEN \n");
     return;
   }
   if (!((recc == 0) || (recc == 1))){
     printf ("ERROR IN THE VALUE OF RECC recc = %ld \n", recc);
     return;
   }
   tdv = M+1;
#define V(I,J) v[(I) * tdv + (J)]
#define UU 0
#define UD 1
#define DD 2
#define DU 3
   dt = T/(double)M;
   sqrt_dt = sqrt(dt);
   jp1 = sigma1*sqrt_dt;
   jp2 = sigma2*sqrt_dt;
   mu1 = r - q1 - sigma1*sigma1*half;
   mu2 = r - q2 - sigma2*sigma2*half;
   u1 = exp(jp1);
   u2 = exp(jp2);
   d1 = exp(-jp1);
   d2 = exp(-jp2);
   p[UU] = quarter*(one + sqrt_dt * ((mu1/sigma1) + (mu2/sigma2)) + rho);
   p[UD] = quarter*(one + sqrt_dt * ((mu1/sigma1) - (mu2/sigma2)) - rho);
   p[DD] = quarter*(one + sqrt_dt * (-(mu1/sigma1) - (mu2/sigma2)) + rho);
   p[DU] = quarter*(one + sqrt_dt * (-(mu1/sigma1) + (mu2/sigma2)) - rho);
   for (i=0; i<4; ++i){
```

```
     if ((p[i] < zero) || (p[i] > 1.0)) printf (''ERROR p out of range\n'');
   }
   discount = exp(-r*dt);
   for (i = 0; i < 4; ++i){
     p[i] = p[i]*discount;
   }
/* Allocate the arrays v[(M+1)*(M+1)], s1[2*M+1] and s2[2*M+1] */
     . .   .
     s1[M] = S1;
     for (i = 1; i <= M; ++i){/* assign the 2*M+1 asset values for s1 */
       s1[M+i] = u1*s1[M+i-1];
       s1[M-i] = d1*s1[M-i+1];
     }
     s2[M] = S2;
     for (i = 1; i <= M; ++i){/* assign the 2*M+1 asset values for s2 */
       s2[M+i] = u2*s2[M+i-1];
       s2[M-i] = d2*s2[M-i+1];
     }
     /* Calculate the option values at maturity */
     if (recc == 0){/* called without recursion */
       P1 = 0;
       for (i = 0; i <= M; ++i){
         P2 = 0;
         for (j = 0; j <= M; ++j){
           if (opt_type == 0){/* Maximum of two assets */
             if (put){
               V(i,j) = MAX(X - MAX(s1[P1],s2[P2]),zero);
             }
             else{
               V(i,j) = MAX(MAX(s1[P1],s2[P2])-X,zero);
             }
           }
           else{/* Minimum of two assets */
             if (put){
               V(i,j) = MAX(X - MIN(s1[P1],s2[P2]),zero);
             }
             else{
               V(i,j) = MAX(MIN(s1[P1],s2[P2])-X,zero);
             }
           }
           P2 = P2 + 2;
         }
         P1 = P1 + 2;
       }
     }
     else{/* called with recursive last step */
       P1 = 1;
       for (i = 0; i <= M-1; ++i){
         P2 = 1;
         for (j = 0; j <= M-1; ++j){
           loc_T = dt;
           loc_M = 10;
           loc_recc = 0;
           loc_iflag = 0;
           loc_is_american = is_american;
           recursive_2D_binomial(&hold, s1[P1], s2[P2], X, sigma1, sigma2, rho,
               loc_T, r, q1, q2, put, loc_M, opt_type, loc_is_american, loc_recc, &loc_iflag);
           if (is_american){
             if (opt_type == 0){/* Maximum of two assets */
               if (put)
                 V(i,j) = MAX(hold,X-MAX(s1[P1],s2[P2]));
               else
                 V(i,j) = MAX(hold,MAX(s1[P1],s2[P2])-X);
             }
             else{/* Minimum of two assets */
               if (put)
                 V(i,j) = MAX(hold,X-MIN(s1[P1],s2[P2]));
               else
                 V(i,j) = MAX(hold,MIN(s1[P1],s2[P2])-X);
             }
           }
           else{
             V(i,j) = hold;
           }
           P2 = P2 + 2;
         }
```

```
    P1 = P1+2;
  }
}
for (m1=M-1-recc; m1 >= 0; --m1){/* work backwards through the lattice to calculate the option value */
  P1 = M-m1;
    /* Identical code to the equivalent loop of the standard 2 dimensional binomial lattice
       see code excerpt 5.7 */
    . . .
}
*value = V(0,0);
}
```

Code excerpt D.2 Function that uses a recursive binomial lattice to compute options on the maximum and minimum of two assets

D.3 FOUR ASSET JUMP PROBABILITIES

The jump probabilities for a binomial lattice which models four assets are given below:

$$p_{uuuu} = \frac{1}{16}\left\{1 + \sqrt{\Delta t}\left(\frac{\mu_1}{\sigma_1} + \frac{\mu_2}{\sigma_2} + \frac{\mu_3}{\sigma_3} + \frac{\mu_4}{\sigma_4}\right) + \rho_{12} + \rho_{13} + \rho_{14} + \rho_{23} + \rho_{24} + \rho_{34}\right\}$$

$$p_{uuud} = \frac{1}{16}\left\{1 + \sqrt{\Delta t}\left(\frac{\mu_1}{\sigma_1} + \frac{\mu_2}{\sigma_2} + \frac{\mu_3}{\sigma_3} - \frac{\mu_4}{\sigma_4}\right) + \rho_{12} + \rho_{13} - \rho_{14} + \rho_{23} - \rho_{24} + \rho_{34}\right\}$$

$$p_{uudu} = \frac{1}{16}\left\{1 + \sqrt{\Delta t}\left(\frac{\mu_1}{\sigma_1} + \frac{\mu_2}{\sigma_2} - \frac{\mu_3}{\sigma_3} + \frac{\mu_4}{\sigma_4}\right) + \rho_{12} - \rho_{13} + \rho_{14} - \rho_{23} + \rho_{24} - \rho_{34}\right\}$$

$$p_{uudd} = \frac{1}{16}\left\{1 + \sqrt{\Delta t}\left(\frac{\mu_1}{\sigma_1} + \frac{\mu_2}{\sigma_2} - \frac{\mu_3}{\sigma_3} - \frac{\mu_4}{\sigma_4}\right) + \rho_{12} - \rho_{13} - \rho_{14} - \rho_{23} - \rho_{24} + \rho_{34}\right\}$$

$$p_{uduu} = \frac{1}{16}\left\{1 + \sqrt{\Delta t}\left(\frac{\mu_1}{\sigma_1} - \frac{\mu_2}{\sigma_2} + \frac{\mu_3}{\sigma_3} + \frac{\mu_4}{\sigma_4}\right) - \rho_{12} + \rho_{13} + \rho_{14} - \rho_{23} - \rho_{24} + \rho_{34}\right\}$$

$$p_{udud} = \frac{1}{16}\left\{1 + \sqrt{\Delta t}\left(\frac{\mu_1}{\sigma_1} - \frac{\mu_2}{\sigma_2} + \frac{\mu_3}{\sigma_3} - \frac{\mu_4}{\sigma_4}\right) - \rho_{12} + \rho_{13} - \rho_{14} - \rho_{23} + \rho_{24} - \rho_{34}\right\}$$

$$p_{uddu} = \frac{1}{16}\left\{1 + \sqrt{\Delta t}\left(\frac{\mu_1}{\sigma_1} - \frac{\mu_2}{\sigma_2} - \frac{\mu_3}{\sigma_3} + \frac{\mu_4}{\sigma_4}\right) - \rho_{12} - \rho_{13} + \rho_{14} + \rho_{23} - \rho_{24} - \rho_{34}\right\}$$

$$p_{uddd} = \frac{1}{16}\left\{1 + \sqrt{\Delta t}\left(\frac{\mu_1}{\sigma_1} - \frac{\mu_2}{\sigma_2} - \frac{\mu_3}{\sigma_3} - \frac{\mu_4}{\sigma_4}\right) - \rho_{12} - \rho_{13} - \rho_{14} + \rho_{23} + \rho_{24} + \rho_{34}\right\}$$

$$p_{duuu} = \frac{1}{16}\left\{1 + \sqrt{\Delta t}\left(-\frac{\mu_1}{\sigma_1} + \frac{\mu_2}{\sigma_2} + \frac{\mu_3}{\sigma_3} + \frac{\mu_4}{\sigma_4}\right) - \rho_{12} - \rho_{13} - \rho_{14} + \rho_{23} + \rho_{24} + \rho_{34}\right\}$$

$$p_{duud} = \frac{1}{16}\left\{1 + \sqrt{\Delta t}\left(-\frac{\mu_1}{\sigma_1} + \frac{\mu_2}{\sigma_2} + \frac{\mu_3}{\sigma_3} - \frac{\mu_4}{\sigma_4}\right) - \rho_{12} - \rho_{13} + \rho_{14} + \rho_{23} - \rho_{24} - \rho_{34}\right\}$$

$$p_{dudu} = \frac{1}{16}\left\{1 + \sqrt{\Delta t}\left(-\frac{\mu_1}{\sigma_1} + \frac{\mu_2}{\sigma_2} - \frac{\mu_3}{\sigma_3} + \frac{\mu_4}{\sigma_4}\right) - \rho_{12} + \rho_{13} - \rho_{14} - \rho_{23} + \rho_{24} - \rho_{34}\right\}$$

$$p_{dudd} = \frac{1}{16}\left\{1 + \sqrt{\Delta t}\left(-\frac{\mu_1}{\sigma_1} + \frac{\mu_2}{\sigma_2} - \frac{\mu_3}{\sigma_3} - \frac{\mu_4}{\sigma_4}\right) - \rho_{12} + \rho_{13} + \rho_{14} - \rho_{23} - \rho_{24} + \rho_{34}\right\}$$

$$p_{dduu} = \frac{1}{16}\left\{1 + \sqrt{\Delta t}\left(-\frac{\mu_1}{\sigma_1} - \frac{\mu_2}{\sigma_2} + \frac{\mu_3}{\sigma_3} + \frac{\mu_4}{\sigma_4}\right) + \rho_{12} - \rho_{13} - \rho_{14} - \rho_{23} - \rho_{24} + \rho_{34}\right\}$$

$$p_{ddud} = \frac{1}{16}\left\{1 + \sqrt{\Delta t}\left(-\frac{\mu_1}{\sigma_1} - \frac{\mu_2}{\sigma_2} + \frac{\mu_3}{\sigma_3} - \frac{\mu_4}{\sigma_4}\right) + \rho_{12} - \rho_{13} + \rho_{14} - \rho_{23} + \rho_{24} - \rho_{34}\right\}$$

$$p_{dddu} = \frac{1}{16}\left\{1 + \sqrt{\Delta t}\left(-\frac{\mu_1}{\sigma_1} - \frac{\mu_2}{\sigma_2} - \frac{\mu_3}{\sigma_3} + \frac{\mu_4}{\sigma_4}\right) + \rho_{12} + \rho_{13} - \rho_{14} + \rho_{23} - \rho_{24} - \rho_{34}\right\}$$

$$p_{dddd} = \frac{1}{16}\left\{1 + \sqrt{\Delta t}\left(-\frac{\mu_1}{\sigma_1} - \frac{\mu_2}{\sigma_2} - \frac{\mu_3}{\sigma_3} - \frac{\mu_4}{\sigma_4}\right) + \rho_{12} + \rho_{13} - \rho_{14} + \rho_{23} + \rho_{24} + \rho_{34}\right\}$$

Appendix E

Derivation of the conditional mean and covariance for a multivariate normal distribution

Let $X = [X_1/X_2]$ be distributed as $N_p(\mu, \Sigma)$ with $\mu = [\mu_1/\mu_2]$ and $\Sigma = [(\Sigma_{11}|\Sigma_{12})/(\Sigma_{21}|\Sigma_{22})]$ and $|\Sigma_{22}| > 0$.

We will prove that the conditional distribution of X_1, given that $X_2 = x_2$, is normal and has:

Mean $= \mu_1 + \Sigma_{11}\Sigma_{22}^{-1}(x_2 - \mu_2)$, and covariance $= \Sigma_{11} - \Sigma_{12}\Sigma_{22}^{-1}\Sigma_{21}$. Let the inverse of Σ be Σ^{-1}, where:

$$\Sigma^{-1} = \begin{pmatrix} \Sigma^{11} & \Sigma^{12} \\ \Sigma^{21} & \Sigma^{22} \end{pmatrix} \tag{E.1}$$

So $\Sigma^{-1}\Sigma = I_p$, where I_p represents the $p \times p$ unit matrix, and:

$$\begin{pmatrix} \Sigma^{11} & \Sigma^{12} \\ \Sigma^{21} & \Sigma^{22} \end{pmatrix} \begin{pmatrix} \Sigma_{11} & \Sigma_{12} \\ \Sigma_{21} & \Sigma_{22} \end{pmatrix} = \begin{pmatrix} I_q & 0 \\ 0 & I_{p-q} \end{pmatrix} \tag{E.2}$$

Multiplying out these matrices yields the following equations:

$$\Sigma^{11}\Sigma_{11} + \Sigma^{21}\Sigma_{21} = I_q \tag{E.3}$$

$$\Sigma^{21}\Sigma_{11} + \Sigma^{22}\Sigma_{22} = 0 \tag{E.4}$$

$$\Sigma^{11}\Sigma_{12} + \Sigma^{12}\Sigma_{22} = 0 \tag{E.5}$$

$$\Sigma^{21}\Sigma_{12} + \Sigma^{22}\Sigma_{22} = I_{p-q} \tag{E.6}$$

Multiplying Equation E.5 on the left by $(\Sigma^{11})^{-1}$ and on the right by Σ_{22}^{-1} gives:

$$(\Sigma^{11})^{-1}\Sigma^{12} = -\Sigma_{12}\Sigma_{22}^{-1} \tag{E.7}$$

Multiplying Equation E.3 on the left by $(\Sigma^{11})^{-1}$ yields

$$\Sigma_{11} + (\Sigma^{11})^{-1}\Sigma^{12}\Sigma_{21} = (\Sigma_{11})^{-1} \tag{E.8}$$

and substituting for $(\Sigma^{11})^{-1}\Sigma^{12}$ from Equation E.7 into Equation E.8 gives

$$(\Sigma_{11})^{-1} = \Sigma_{11} - \Sigma_{12}\Sigma_{22}^{-1}\Sigma_{21} \tag{E.9}$$

The joint probability density function of x is:

$$f(x) = (2\pi)^{-p/2}|\Sigma|^{-1/2}\exp\left\{-\frac{1}{2}(x - \mu)^T\Sigma^{-1}(x - \mu)\right\}$$

writing x, μ and Σ^{-1} in their partitioned form and expanding gives:

$$f(x) = (2\pi)^{-p/2}|\Sigma|^{-1/2}\exp\left[-\frac{1}{2}\left\{(x_1 - \mu_1)^T\Sigma^{11}(x_1 - \mu_1)\right.\right.$$

$$\left.\left.+2(x_1 - \mu_1)^T\Sigma^{12}(x_2 - \mu_2) + (x_2 - \mu_2)^T\Sigma^{22}(x_2 - \mu_2)\right\}\right] \quad \text{(E.10)}$$

The conditional distribution of x_1 given the value of x_2 is thus obtained by dividing this density by the marginal density of x_2, and treating x_2 as constant in the resulting expression. The only portion of the resultant that is not constant is the portion involving terms in x_1. It can easily be shown that:

$$f(x_1|x_2) \propto \exp\left[-\frac{1}{2}\left\{(x_1 - \mu_1)^T\Sigma^{11}(x_1 - \mu_1) + 2(x_1 - \mu_1)^T\Sigma^{12}(x_2 - \mu_2)\right\}\right]$$

where the constant of proportionality is obtained using $\int f(x_1|x_2)dx_1 = 1$.
If we let

$$\mathcal{G} = (x_1 - \mu_1)^T\Sigma^{11}(x_1 - \mu_1) + 2(x_1 - \mu_1)^T\Sigma^{12}(x_2 - \mu_2)$$

we then obtain:

$$\mathcal{G} = (x_1 - \mu_1)^T\Sigma^{11}(x_1 - \mu_1) + (x_1 - \mu_1)^T\Sigma^{12}(x_2 - \mu_2) + (x_2 - \mu_2)^T\Sigma^{21}(x_1 - \mu_1)$$

$$\mathcal{G} = \left\{x_1 - \mu_1 + (\Sigma^{11})^{-1}\Sigma^{12}(x_2 - \mu_2)\right\}^T\Sigma^{11}\left\{x_1 - \mu_1 + (\Sigma^{11})^{-1}\Sigma^{12}(x_2 - \mu_2)\right\}$$

$$- (x_2 - \mu_2)^T\Sigma^{21}(\Sigma^{12})^{-1}(x_2 - \mu_2) \quad \text{(E.11)}$$

where, for instance we have used, the fact that the scalar quantity

$$\left\{(x_1 - \mu_1)^T\Sigma^{12}(x_2 - \mu_2)\right\}^T = (x_2 - \mu_2)^T\Sigma^{21}(x_1 - \mu_1)$$

Since the last term in Equation E.11 only involves constants (as far as $f(x_1|x_2)$ is concerned), it follows that:

$$f(x_1|x_2) \propto \exp\left[-\frac{1}{2}\left\{x_1 - \mu_1 + (\Sigma^{11})^{-1}\Sigma^{12}(x_2 - \mu_2)\right\}^T\right.$$

$$\left.\times \Sigma^{11}\left\{x_1 - \mu_1 + (\Sigma^{11})^{-1}\Sigma^{12}(x_2 - \mu_2)\right\}\right]$$

which is the density of a multivariate normal distribution that has a mean of $\mu_1 - (\Sigma^{11})^{-1}\Sigma^{12}(x_2 - \mu_2)$, which from Equation E.7 can be expressed as $\mu_1 + \Sigma_{12}\Sigma_{22}^{-1}(x_2 - \mu_2)$. The covariance matrix is $(\Sigma^{11})^{-1}$, which from Equation E.9 can be written as $\Sigma_{11} - \Sigma_{12}\Sigma_{22}^{-1}\Sigma_{21}$.

Appendix F

Standard statistical results

F.1 THE LAW OF LARGE NUMBERS

Let $X_1, X_2, \ldots$ be a sequence of independent, identically distributed random variables (IID), each with expected value μ and variance σ^2. Define the sequence of averages

$$Y_n = \frac{X_1 + X_2 + \cdots + X_n}{n}, \quad n = 1, 2, \ldots$$

Then Y_n converges to μ as $n \to \infty$.

We will not rigorously prove this theorem but show that it is plausible. For the mean of Y_n we have:

$$E[Y_n] = \frac{1}{n}(E[X_1] + E[X_2] + + \cdots + E[X_n]) = \frac{1}{n}n\mu = \mu$$

For the variance of Y_n we have:

$$Var(Y_n) = \sum_{i=1}^{n} Var\left(\frac{X_i}{n}\right) = \sum_{i=1}^{n} \frac{\sigma^2}{n^2} = \frac{\sigma^2}{n}$$

where we have used the fact that the variance of the sum of independent random variables is the sum of their variances, see Section F.2.

So as $n \to \infty$, we have $Var(Y_n) \to 0$.

F.2 THE CENTRAL LIMIT THEOREM

This is similar to the Law of Large numbers. In this case we divide by $\sqrt{n}$ instead of n, which prevents the variance of Y_n converging to zero as $n \to \infty$.

Let $X_1, X_2, \ldots$ be a sequence of independent, identically distributed random variables (IID), each with expected value μ and variance σ^2. Define:

$$Z_n = \frac{(X_1 - \mu) + (X_2 - \mu) + \cdots + (X_n - \mu)}{\sqrt{n}}, \quad n = 1, 2, \ldots$$

so that each Z_n has expected value zero and variance

$$Var(Z_n) = \sum_{i=1}^{n} Var\left(\frac{(X_i - \mu)}{\sqrt{n}}\right) = \sum_{i=1}^{n} \frac{\sigma^2}{n} = \sigma^2$$

The central Limit Theorem states that as $n \to \infty$ the distribution of Z_n approaches that of a normal random variable (say x) with mean zero and variance σ^2. In other words the probability density function of Z_n is:

$$P(Z_n) \to \frac{1}{\sigma\sqrt{2\pi}}\exp\left(-\frac{x^2}{2\sigma^2}\right) \text{ as } n \to \infty$$

F.3   THE MEAN AND VARIANCE OF LINEAR FUNCTIONS OF RANDOM VARIABLES

Let X be a variate from a given distribution, and Z be the following linear function of this variate:

$$Z = a + bX$$

where a and b are constants. Then

$$E[Z] = E[a] + E[bX] = a + bE[X]$$

and

$$\begin{aligned} Var[Z] &= E[(Z - E[Z])^2] \\ &= E[(a + bX - a - bE[X])^2] \\ &= E[(bX - bE[X])^2] \\ &= E[b^2(X - E[X])^2] \\ &= b^2 E[(X - E[X])^2] \end{aligned}$$

Therefore the mean is $bE[X]$, and the variance is $b^2 Var[X]$.

The variance of the sum of random identical independently distributed variables (IID).

F.3.1   The sum of 2 variables

Let $Z_2 = X_1 + X_2$, where X_1 and X_2 are IID variables. Then we have:

$$\begin{aligned} Var[Z_2] &= E[((X_1 + X_2) - E[X_1 + X_2])^2] \\ &= E[((X_1 - E[X_1]) + (X_2 - E[X_2]))^2] \\ &= E[(X_1 - E[X_1])^2 + (X_2 - E[X_2])^2 + 2(X_1 - E[X_1])(X_2 - E[X_2])] \\ &= E[(X_1 - E[X_1])^2] + E[(X_2 - E[X_2])^2] \\ &= Var[X_1] + Var[X_2], \end{aligned}$$

where we have used the fact that, since the variables are independent $E[(X_1 - E[X_1])(X_2 - E[X_2])] = 0$. Therefore:

$$Var[X_1 + X_2] = Var[X_1] + Var[X_2]$$

F.3.2 The sum of 3 variables

Let $Z_3 = X_1 + X_2 + X_3$, where X_1, X_2, and X_3 are IID variables. Then we have:

$$\begin{aligned}
Var[Z_3] &= E[((X_1 + X_2 + X_3) - E[X_1 + X_2 + X_3])^2] \\
&= E[((X_1 - E[X_1]) + (X_2 - E[X_2]) + (X_3 - E[X_3]))^2] \\
&= E[(X_1 - E[X_1])^2 + (X_2 - E[X_2])^2 + (X_2 - E[X_2])^2 \\
&\quad + 2(X_1 - E[X_1])(X_2 - E[X_2]) + 2(X_1 - E[X_1])(X_3 - E[X_3]) \\
&\quad + 2(X_2 - E[X_2])(X_3 - E[X_3])] \\
&= E[(X_1 - E[X_1])^2] + E[(X_2 - E[X_2])^2] + E[(X_3 - E[X_3])^2] \\
&= Var[X_1] + Var[X_2] + Var[X_3]
\end{aligned}$$

where, as before, we have used the fact that $E[(X_i - E[X_i])\ (X_j - E[X_j])] = 0$, $i = 1, \ldots, 3, j = 1, \ldots, 3, i \neq j$. Therefore:

$$Var[X_1 + X_2 + X_3] = Var[X_1] + Var[X_2] + Var[X_3]$$

F.3.3 The sum of *n* variables

Let $Z_n = \sum_{i=1}^{n} X_i$

Then we have:

$$\begin{aligned}
Var[Z_n] &= E\left[\left\{\sum_{i=1}^{n} X_i - E[X_i]\right\}^2\right] \\
&= \sum_{i=1}^{n} E[(X_i - E[X_i])^2] + \sum_{i=1}^{n} \sum_{j=1(j\neq i)}^{n} E[(X_i - E[X_i])(X_j - E[X_j])] \\
&= \sum_{i=1}^{n} E[(X_i - E[X_i])^2] \\
&= \sum_{i=1}^{n} Var[X_i]
\end{aligned}$$

Therefore:

$$Var\left[\sum_{i=1}^{n} X_i\right] = \sum_{i=1}^{n} Var[X_i]$$

F.4 STANDARD ALGORITHMS FOR THE MEAN AND VARIANCE

In this section we provide standard results concerning the computation of the mean and variance (covariance) of the observations contained in a given data set.

The variance of X is defined as:

$$Var[X] = E[(X - E[X])^2]$$

The simplest way of computing the variance is to use a *two pass* method. We illustrate this with a simple Monte Carlo program which is designed to stop when the result has attained a given accuracy.

```
double result[1000000]  // need to provide a large array to store the results
    . . .
tol = 0.1
mean_X = 0.0
i = 1
while (variance > tol) {  // keep going until the variance is smallenough
//call a Monte Carlo function, with n parameters, which return the current estimate
   result[i] = my_monte_carlo(param_1, param_2, ..., param_n)

   mean_X = (mean_X + result[i])/i  // first pass to calculate the mean

   for (j=1, j <=i; ++i) {  // second pass to calculate the variance
      variance = (result[i] - mean_X)*(result[i] - mean_X)
   }
   variance = variance/(double)i

   i = i + 1
}
```

Although numerical stable (West, 1979) this approach requires the allocation of the very large array `result`, and also contains a *nested for loop*.

We can get round this problem by expanding the terms in the variance as follows:

$$Var[X] = E[(X - E[X])^2]$$
$$= E[X^2 + (E[X])^2 - 2XE[X]]$$
$$= E[X^2] + (E[X])^2 - 2(E[X])^2 \qquad (F.1)$$

Therefore $Var[X] = E[X^2] - (E[X])^2$. This approach leads to the so-called *textbook algorithm* which allows the variance to be computed by using only *one pass* through the data. The program for our original problem then becomes:

```
tol = 0.1
mean_X = 0.0
mean_X_squared = 0.0
i = 1.0
while (variance > tol) {// keep going until the variance is small enough
// call a Monte Carlo function, with n parameters, which return the current estimate
   result = my_monte_carlo(param_1, param_2, ..., param_n)

   // calculate the running mean
   mean_X = (mean_X + result)/i

   // calculate the running mean value of the square of the result
   mean_X_squared = (mean_X_squared + result*result)/i

   // calculate the running variance
   variance = mean_X_squared - (mean_X*mean_X)

   i = i + 1.0
}
```

Although this method doesn't require extra memory allocation and doesn't require a second pass through the data, it is numerically unstable (Chan *et al.*, 1982; West, 1979) and the algorithm given in Section F.5 should be used if accurate results are required.

The textbook algorithm can easily be extended to compute the covariance rather than the variance.

If we consider two random variates X and Y then the covariance, $COV[X, Y]$, is defined as:

$$COV[X, Y] = E[(X - E[X])(Y - E[Y])]$$

This can be expanded as follows:

$$\begin{aligned} COV[X, Y] &= E[(X - E[X])(Y - E[Y])] \\ &= E[XY] + E[X]E[Y] - YE[X] - XE[Y] \\ &= E[XY] + E[X]E[Y] - E[Y]E[X] - E[X]E[Y] \end{aligned}$$

Therefore the covariance is given by the following equation:

$$COV[X, Y] = E[XY] - E[X]E[Y] \tag{F.2}$$

F.5   THE HANSON AND WEST ALGORITHM FOR THE MEAN AND VARIANCE

Here we describe a method of computing the mean and variance (covariance) of a data set that is more numerically stable than the textbook algorithm given in Section F.4, West (1979).

We will consider an $n \times p$ data matrix of n observations on p variates. The observations are represented by the p element vector $X_i, i = 1, \ldots, n$.

Let the mean of the first $i - 1$ observations be denoted by $\bar{X}_{[i-1]} = \sum_{k=1}^{i-1} X_k / i - 1$. Then we have:

$$\bar{X}_{[i]} = \frac{\sum_{k=1}^{i} X_k}{i} = \frac{X_i}{i} + \frac{\sum_{k=1}^{i-1} X_k}{i} = \frac{X_i}{i} + \frac{i-1}{i} \frac{\sum_{k=1}^{i-1} X_k}{i-1}$$

Therefore:

$$\bar{X}_{[i]} = \frac{X_i}{i} + \frac{i-1}{i} \bar{X}_{i-1} = \bar{X}_{[i-1]} + \frac{1}{i}(X_i - \bar{X}_{[i-1]}) \tag{F.3}$$

Let $\sigma_{[i-1]}^2$ be the variance of the first $i - 1$ observations. This means that the sum of squares about the mean $S_{[i-1]}^2$, of the first $i - 1$ observations is $S_{[i-1]}^2 = (i - 1)\sigma_{[i-1]}^2$. Now from the definition of variance we have:

$$\frac{S_{[i-1]}^2}{i-1} = \sigma_{[i-1]}^2 = \left(\frac{1}{i-1} \sum_{k=1}^{i-1} X_k^2\right) - (\bar{X}_{[i-1]})^2$$

so

$$\sum_{k=1}^{i-1} X_k^2 = S_{[i-1]}^2 + (i-1)(\bar{X}_{[i-1]})^2$$

Now the inclusion of the ith observation X_i results in the new sum of squares about the mean $S_{[i]}^2$:

$$S_{[i]}^2 = \left(\sum_{k=1}^{i} X_k^2\right) - i(\bar{X}_{[i]})^2$$

$$S_{[i]}^2 = \left(\sum_{k=1}^{i-1} X_k^2\right) + X_i^2 - i(\bar{X}_{[i]})^2$$

$$S_{[i]}^2 = S_{i-1}^2 + (i-1)(\bar{X}_{[i-1]})^2 + X_i^2 - i(\bar{X}_{[i]})^2 \tag{F.4}$$

But

$$i(\bar{X}_{[i]})^2 = \frac{i}{i^2}\left(X_i + (i-1)\bar{X}_{[i-1]}\right)^2$$

$$i(\bar{X}_{[i]})^2 = \frac{1}{i}\left\{(i-1)^2(\bar{X}_{[i-1]})^2 + 2(i-1)X_i\bar{X}_{[i-1]} + X_i^2\right\} \tag{F.5}$$

So we have:

$$S_{[i]}^2 = S_{i-1}^2 + (i-1)(\bar{X}_{[i-1]})^2 + X_i^2 - \frac{(i-1)^2}{i}(\bar{X}_{[i-1]})^2 - \frac{2(i-1)}{i}X_i\bar{X}_{[i-1]} - \frac{X_i^2}{i}$$

$$= S_{i-1}^2 + (i-1)\left(1 - \frac{i-1}{i}\right)(\bar{X}_{[i-1]})^2 + \left(1 - \frac{1}{i}\right)X_i^2 - \frac{2(i-1)}{i}X_i\bar{X}_{[i-1]}$$

Therefore

$$S_{[i]}^2 = S_{i-1}^2 + \frac{(i-1)}{i}(\bar{X}_{[i-1]})^2 + \left(\frac{i-1}{i}\right)X_i^2 - \frac{2(i-1)}{i}X_i\bar{X}_{[i-1]} \tag{F.6}$$

The above equation can be written in more compact form since:

$$\left(\frac{i-1}{i}\right)\left(X_i - \bar{X}_{[i-1]}\right)\left(X_i - \bar{X}_{[i-1]}\right) = \frac{i-1}{i}X_i^2 + \frac{i-1}{i}\left(\bar{X}_{[i-1]}\right)^2 - 2\left(\frac{i-1}{i}\right)X_i\bar{X}_{[i-1]}$$

which gives the final updating equation for the sum of squares about the mean as:

$$S_{[i]}^2 = S_{i-1}^2 + \left(\frac{i-1}{i}\right)\left(X_i - \bar{X}_{[i-1]}\right)\left(X_i - \bar{X}_{[i-1]}\right) \tag{F.7}$$

This useful equation gives the sum of squares about the mean $S_{[i]}^2$, given the previous sum of squares about the mean $S_{[i-1]}^2$, the previous mean $\bar{X}_{[i-1]}$, and the new data point X_i.

The estimated variance, $Var[X]$, computed using the data X_i, $i = 1, \ldots, n$, is therefore given by:

$$Var[X] = \frac{S_{[n]}^2}{n-1}$$

The following code excerpt shows how the algorithm works in practice

```
tol = 0.1

// call a Monte Carlo function, with n parameters, which return the current estimate
   result = my_monte_carlo(param_1, param_2, ...,param_n)
```

```
mean_X = result
SS_X = 0.0
i = 2.0

while (variance > tol){// keep going until the variance is small enough
// call a Monte Carlo function, with n parameters, which return the current estimate
  result = my_monte_carlo(param_1, param_2, . . . ,param_n)

  temp = result - mean_X

  // calculate the running mean
  mean_X = mean_X + (temp/i)
  // calculate the running sum of squares about the mean, SS_X

  SS_X = SS_X + (((i-1.0)/i) * temp * temp)
  variance = SS_X/i
  i = i +1.0
}
```

The above method can easily be extended to compute the covariance of two variables X and Y. The covariance is defined as follows:

$$COV(X, Y) = \frac{1}{n-1} \sum_{i=1}^{n} (X_i - \bar{X})(Y_i - \bar{Y})$$

where

$$\bar{X} = \frac{1}{n} \sum_{i=1}^{n} X_i, \quad \bar{Y} = \frac{1}{n} \sum_{i=1}^{n} Y_i$$

X_i and Y_i denote the ith data values of X and Y respectively, and the expression $(X_i - \bar{X})(Y_i - \bar{Y})$ is termed the ith cross product about the means $\bar{X}$ and $\bar{Y}$. As before we will also let $\bar{X}_i$ and $\bar{Y}_i$ denote the *running* means of the first i observations, of the X and Y variables respectively.

The ith sum of the *cross products* about the means is updated according to the following equation:

$$P_{[i]} = P_{[i-1]} + \left(\frac{i-1}{i}\right) \left(X_i - \bar{X}_{[i-1]}\right) \left(Y_i - \bar{Y}_{[i-1]}\right) \tag{F.8}$$

where $P_{[i]}$ denotes the updated sum of the cross products about the mean, $P_{[i-1]}$ denotes the previous sum of the cross products about the mean, $\bar{X}_{[i-1]}$ is the previous mean of the variable X, $\bar{Y}_{[i-1]}$ is the previous mean of the variable Y, and the new variate values are X_i and Y_i.

The estimated covariance, $COV[X, Y]$, computed using the data $X_i, i = 1, \ldots, n$, and $Y_i, i = 1, \ldots, n$, is therefore given by:

$$COV[X, Y] = \frac{P_{[n]}}{n-1}$$

F.6 JENSEN'S INEQUALITY

This states that if the function $h(X)$ of a random variable X is convex and $E[X] = \mu$, then $E[h(X)] \geq h(\mu)$.

F.6.1   Proof

Let X be a random variable with expected value $E[X] = \mu$ and the variable Y be a nonlinear function of X, $Y = h(X)$. Then $\partial Y/\partial X = h'(X)$. If Z is the tangent to $h(X)$ at the point μ then:

$$Z = h(\mu) + h'(\mu)(X - \mu)$$

Since $h(\mu)$ and $h'(\mu)$ are constants we have that:

$$E[Z] = h(\mu) + h'(\mu)E[(X - \mu)] = h(\mu) + h'(\mu)(E[X] - \mu) = h(\mu)$$

If the function $h(X)$ is convex then $Y \geq Z$ everywhere. Then regardless of the distibution of X we have:

$$E[Y] \geq E[Z], \text{ but } E[Z] = h(\mu) \quad \text{so} \quad E[Y] \geq h(\mu)$$

Therefore for a convex function $h(X)$ we have that:

$$E[h(X)] \geq h(\mu)$$

For a concave function we obviously have:

$$E[h(X)] \leq h(\mu)$$

An example of a convex function is $h(X) = X^2$. So regardless of the distribution of X we have that $E(X^2) \geq (E[X])^2$.

An example of a concave function is $h(X) = \log(X)$. So regardless of the distribution of X we have that $E(\log(X)) \leq \log(E[X])$.

Appendix G

Derivation of barrier option integrals

G.1 THE DOWN AND OUT CALL

We will now derive the formula for the value, c_{do}, of a down and out call option which was given in Part I Section 2.4.2.

$$c_{do} = \frac{\exp(-r\tau)}{\sigma\sqrt{\tau}\sqrt{2\pi}} \int_{X=\log(E/S)}^{\infty} \{S\exp(X) - E\} f(X > B) dX \qquad (G.1)$$

where

$$f(X > B) = \frac{1}{\sigma\sqrt{\tau}\sqrt{2\pi}} \exp\left(-\frac{\{X - (r - \sigma^2/2)\tau\}^2}{2\sigma^2\tau}\right)$$

$$\times \left\{1 - \exp\left(\frac{2\log(B/S)(X - \log(B/S))}{\sigma^2\tau}\right)\right\}$$

We will represent this integral as:

$$c_{do} = I_A + I_B$$

where

$$I_A = \frac{\exp(-r\tau)}{\sigma\sqrt{\tau}\sqrt{2\pi}} \int_{X=\log(E/S)}^{\infty} \{S\exp(X) - E\} \exp\left(-\frac{\{X - (r - \sigma^2/2)\tau\}^2}{2\sigma^2\tau}\right) dX$$

and

$$I_B = -\frac{\exp(-r\tau)}{\sigma\sqrt{\tau}\sqrt{2\pi}} \int_{X=\log(E/S)}^{\infty} \{S\exp(X) - E\} \exp\left(-\frac{\{X - (r - \sigma^2/2)\tau\}^2}{2\sigma^2\tau}\right)$$

$$\times \exp\left(\frac{2\log(B/S)(X - \log(B/S))}{\sigma^2\tau}\right) dX$$

G.1.1 Evaluation of integral I_A

Now comparing I_A with Equation 2.34 in Part I Section 2.3.3 we can identify I_A as $c(S,E,\tau)$, the price of a European call. That is:

$$I_A = SN_1(d_1) - E\exp(-r\tau)N_1(d_2) \qquad (G.2)$$

where:

$$d_1 = \frac{\log(S/E) + (r + \sigma^2/2)\tau}{\sigma\sqrt{\tau}} \quad \text{and} \quad d_2 = \frac{\log(S/E) + (r - \sigma^2/2)\tau}{\sigma\sqrt{\tau}}$$

G.1.2   Evaluation of integral I_B

We will now consider the integral I_B, and let $I_B = I_C + I_D$ where:

$$I_C = -\frac{S\exp(-r\tau)}{\sigma\sqrt{\tau}\sqrt{2\pi}} \int_{X=\log(E/S)}^{\infty} \exp(X)\exp\left(-\frac{\{X - (r - \sigma^2/2)\tau\}^2}{2\sigma^2\tau}\right)$$

$$\times \exp\left(\frac{2\log(B/S)(X - \log(B/S))}{\sigma^2\tau}\right)dX$$

and

$$I_D = \frac{E\exp(-r\tau)}{\sigma\sqrt{\tau}\sqrt{2\pi}} \int_{X=\log(E/S)}^{\infty} \exp\left(-\frac{\{X - (r - \sigma^2/2)\tau\}^2}{2\sigma^2\tau}\right)$$

$$\times \exp\left(\frac{2\log(B/S)(X - \log(B/S))}{\sigma^2\tau}\right)dX$$

G.1.3   Evaluation of integral I_D

We will first consider I_D and factor the integrand as follows:

$$-\exp\left(-\frac{\{X - (r - \sigma^2/2)\tau\}^2}{2\sigma^2\tau}\right)\exp\left(\frac{2\log(B/S)(X - \log(B/S))}{\sigma^2\tau}\right)$$

$$= \exp\left(-\frac{\{X - (r - \sigma^2/2)\tau\}^2 - 4\log(B/S)(X - \log(B/S))}{2\sigma^2\tau}\right)$$

$$= \exp\left(-\frac{\{X - (r - \sigma^2/2)\tau - 2\log(B/S)\}^2}{2\sigma^2\tau}\right)\exp\left(\frac{4(r - \sigma^2/2)\tau\log(B/S)}{2\sigma^2\tau}\right) \quad \text{(G.3)}$$

This means that I_D can be expressed as:

$$I_D = \left(\frac{B}{S}\right)^{2(r-\sigma^2/2)/\sigma^2}\frac{E\exp(-r\tau)}{\sigma\sqrt{\tau}\sqrt{2\pi}}$$

$$\times \int_{X=\log(E/S)}^{\infty} \exp\left(-\frac{\{X - (r - \sigma^2/2)\tau - 2\log(B/S)\}^2}{2\sigma^2\tau}\right)dX$$

Letting $u = (X - (r - \sigma^2/2)\tau - 2\log(B/S))/\sigma\sqrt{\tau}$ we have $dX = \sigma\sqrt{(\tau)}du$ and

$$I_D = \left(\frac{B}{S}\right)^{2(r-\sigma^2/2)/\sigma^2} \frac{E \exp(-r\tau)}{\sigma\sqrt{\tau}\sqrt{2\pi}} \int_{u=k3}^{\infty} \exp\left(-\frac{u^2}{2}\right) du$$

where

$$k_3 = \frac{\log(E/S) - (r - \sigma^2/2)\tau - 2\log(B/S)}{\sigma\sqrt{\tau}} = \frac{\log(ES/B^2) - (r - \sigma^2/2)\tau}{\sigma\sqrt{\tau}}$$

So

$$I_D = \left(\frac{B}{S}\right)^{2r/\sigma^2 - 1} E \exp(-r\tau) N_1(-k_3) \tag{G.4}$$

Letting $d_3 = -k_3$ we have:

$$I_D = \left(\frac{B}{S}\right)^{2r/\sigma^2 - 1} E \exp(-r\tau) N_1(d_3), \quad \text{where} \quad d_3 = \frac{\log(B^2/SE) + (r - \sigma^2/2)\tau}{\sigma\sqrt{\tau}} \tag{G.5}$$

G.1.4 Evaluation of integral I_C

Now consider the term

$$I_C = \frac{S \exp(-r\tau)}{\sigma\sqrt{\tau}\sqrt{2\pi}} \int_{X=\log(E/S)}^{\infty} \exp(X) \exp\left(-\frac{\{X - (r - \sigma^2/2)\tau\}^2}{2\sigma^2\tau}\right)$$

$$\times \exp\left(\frac{2\log(B/S)(X - \log(B/S))}{\sigma^2\tau}\right) dX$$

Now we have:

$$\exp(X) \exp\left(-\frac{(X - (r - \sigma^2/2)\tau)^2}{2\sigma^2\tau}\right) \exp\left(\frac{2\log(B/S)(X - \log(B/S))}{\sigma^2\tau}\right)$$

$$= \exp\left(\frac{-\{(X - (r - \sigma^2/2)\tau)^2 - 2\sigma^2\tau X - 4\log(B/S)X + 4(\log(B/S))^2\}}{2\sigma^2\tau}\right)$$

$$= \exp\left(\frac{(\sigma^2\tau)^2 + 2(r - \sigma^2/2)\tau^2\sigma^2 + 4(r - \sigma^2/2)\tau\log(B/S) + 4\sigma^2\tau\log(B/S)}{2\sigma^2\tau}\right)$$

$$\times \exp\left(\frac{-\{X - (r - \sigma^2/2)\tau - \sigma^2\tau - 2\log(B/S)\}^2}{2\sigma^2\tau}\right)$$

$$= \exp(r\tau) \exp\left(\left\{\frac{2r}{\sigma^2} + 1\right\}\log(B/S)\right) \exp\left(\frac{-\{X - (r - \sigma^2/2)\tau - \sigma^2\tau - 2\log(B/S)\}^2}{2\sigma^2\tau}\right)$$

$$= \exp(r\tau) \left(\frac{B}{S}\right)^{2r/\sigma^2 + 1} \exp\left(\frac{-\{X - (r - \sigma^2/2)\tau - \sigma^2\tau - 2\log(B/S)\}^2}{2\sigma^2\tau}\right)$$

So we have:

$$I_C = -\left(\frac{B}{S}\right)^{2r/\sigma^2+1} \frac{S}{\sigma\sqrt{\tau}\sqrt{2\pi}}$$

$$\times \int_{X=\log(E/S)}^{\infty} \exp\left(-\frac{\{X - (r - \sigma^2/2)\tau - \sigma^2\tau - 2\log(B/S)\}^2}{2\sigma^2\tau}\right) dX$$

Letting $u = (X - (r - \sigma^2/2)\tau - \sigma^2\tau - 2\log(B/S))/(\sigma\sqrt{\tau})$ we have $dX = \sigma\sqrt{\tau}du$ and

$$I_C = S\left(\frac{B}{S}\right)^{2r/\sigma^2+1} N_1(-k_4) \tag{G.6}$$

where

$$k_4 = \frac{\log(E/S) - (r - \sigma^2/2)\tau - \sigma^2\tau - 2\log(B/S)}{\sigma\sqrt{\tau}} = \frac{\log(ES/B^2) - (r + \sigma^2/2)\tau}{\sigma\sqrt{\tau}}$$

which gives

$$I_C = S\left(\frac{B}{S}\right)^{2r/\sigma^2+1} N_1(-k_4)$$

or letting $d_4 = -k_4$ we have

$$I_C = -S\left(\frac{B}{S}\right)^{2r/\sigma^2+1} N_1(d_4), \quad \text{where} \quad d_4 = \frac{\log(B^2/ES) + (r + \sigma^2/2)\tau}{\sigma\sqrt{\tau}} \tag{G.7}$$

Therefore the value for the down and out call option is: $c_{do} = I_A + I_C + I_D$ which, on collecting all the terms, yields:

Value of the down and out call option

$$c_{do} = S\left(N_1(d_1) - N_1(d_4)\left(\frac{B}{S}\right)^{2r/\sigma^2+1}\right)$$

$$- E\exp(-r\tau)\left(N_1(d_2) - N_1(d_3)\left(\frac{B}{S}\right)^{2r/\sigma^2-1}\right) \tag{G.8}$$

G.2   THE UP AND OUT CALL

We will now derive the formula for the value, c_{uo}, of an up and out call option which was given in Part I Section 2.4.3.

$$c_{uo} = \frac{\exp(-r\tau)}{\sigma\sqrt{\tau}\sqrt{2\pi}} \int_{X=\log(E/S)}^{\log(B/S)} \{S\exp(X) - E\}f(X < B)dX \tag{G.9}$$

where

$$f(X < B) = \frac{1}{\sigma\sqrt{\tau}\sqrt{2\pi}} \sqrt{\frac{2}{\pi}} \exp\left(-\frac{\{X - (r - \sigma^2/2)\tau\}^2}{2\sigma^2\tau}\right)$$
$$\times \left\{1 - \exp\left(\frac{2\log(B/S)(X - \log(B/S))}{\sigma^2\tau}\right)\right\} \tag{G.10}$$

We will represent this integral as:

$$c_{uo} = I_A + I_B$$

where:

$$I_A = \frac{\exp(-r\tau)}{\sigma\sqrt{\tau}\sqrt{2\pi}} \int_{X=\log(E/S)}^{\log(B/S)} \{S\exp(X) - E\}\exp\left(-\frac{\{X - (r - \sigma^2/2)\tau\}^2}{2\sigma^2\tau}\right)dX$$

and

$$I_B = -\frac{\exp(-r\tau)}{\sigma\sqrt{\tau}\sqrt{2\pi}} \int_{X=\log(E/S)}^{\log(B/S)} \{S\exp(X) - E\}\exp\left(-\frac{\{X - (r - \sigma^2/2)\tau\}^2}{2\sigma^2\tau}\right)$$
$$\times \exp\left(\frac{2\log(B/S)(X - \log(B/S))}{\sigma^2\tau}\right)dX$$

G.2.1   Evaluation of integral I_A

Letting $I_A = I_1 + I_2$ where

$$I_1 = \frac{S\exp(-r\tau)}{\sigma\sqrt{\tau}\sqrt{2\pi}} \int_{X=\log(E/S)}^{\log(B/S)} \exp(X)\exp\left(-\frac{\{X - (r - \sigma^2/2)\tau\}^2}{2\sigma^2\tau}\right)dX$$

and

$$I_2 = \frac{-E\exp(-r\tau)}{\sigma\sqrt{\tau}\sqrt{2\pi}} \int_{X=\log(E/S)}^{\log(B/S)} \exp\left(-\frac{\{X - (r - \sigma^2/2)\tau\}^2}{2\sigma^2\tau}\right)dX$$

From our previous derivation of the Black–Scholes formula in Part I Section 2.3.3 we have:

$$I_1 = \frac{S\exp(-r\tau)}{\sigma\sqrt{\tau}\sqrt{2\pi}} \int_{u=k_1}^{k_2} \exp\left(-\frac{u^2}{2}\right)du = S\{N_1(k_2) - N_1(k_1)\}$$

where

$$k_1 = \frac{\log(E/S) - (r + \sigma^2/2)\tau}{\sigma\sqrt{\tau}} \quad \text{and} \quad k_2 = \frac{\log(B/S) - (r + \sigma^2/2)\tau}{\sqrt{\tau}}$$

$$I_2 = \frac{-E\exp(-r\tau)}{\sigma\sqrt{\tau}\sqrt{2\pi}} \int_{u=k_3}^{k_4} \exp\left(-\frac{u^2}{2}\right)du = -E\exp(-r\tau)\{N_1(k_4) - N_1(k_3)\}$$

where $k_3 = \dfrac{\log(E/S) - (r - \sigma^2/2)\tau}{\sigma\sqrt{\tau}}$ and $k_4 = \dfrac{\log(B/S) - (r - \sigma^2/2)\tau}{\sigma\sqrt{\tau}}$

Therefore

$$I_A = S\{N_1(k_2) - N_1(k_1)\} - E\exp(-r\tau)\{N_1(k_4) - N_1(k_3)\} \tag{G.11}$$

Letting $I_B = I_C + I_D$ where:

$$I_C = -\frac{S\exp(-r\tau)}{\sigma\sqrt{\tau}\sqrt{2\pi}} \int_{X=\log(E/S)}^{\log(B/S)} \exp(X)\exp\left(-\frac{\{X - (r - \sigma^2/2)\tau\}^2}{2\sigma^2\tau}\right)$$

$$\times \exp\left(\frac{2\log(B/S)(X - \log(B/S))}{\sigma^2\tau}\right)dX$$

and

$$I_D = \frac{E\exp(-r\tau)}{\sigma\sqrt{\tau}\sqrt{2\pi}} \int_{X=\log(E/S)}^{\log(B/S)} \exp\left(-\frac{\{X - (r - \sigma^2/2)\tau\}^2}{2\sigma^2\tau}\right)$$

$$\times \exp\left(\frac{2\log(B/S)(X - \log(B/S))}{\sigma^2\tau}\right)dX$$

G.2.2 Evaluation of integral I_D

In a similar manner to that in Section G.1 we have:

$$I_D = \left(\frac{B}{S}\right)^{2(r-\sigma^2/2)/\sigma^2} \frac{E\exp(-r\tau)}{\sigma\sqrt{\tau}\sqrt{2\pi}}$$

$$\times \int_{X=\log(E/S)}^{\log(B/S)} \exp\left(-\frac{\{X - (r - \sigma^2/2)\tau - 2\log(B/S)\}^2}{2\sigma^2\tau}\right)dX$$

Letting $u = \dfrac{X - (r - \sigma^2/2)\tau - 2\log(B/S)}{\sigma\sqrt{\tau}}$ gives

$$I_D = \left(\frac{B}{S}\right)^{2(r-\sigma^2/2)/\sigma^2} \frac{E\exp(-r\tau)}{\sigma\sqrt{\tau}\sqrt{2\pi}} \int_{u=k_5}^{k_6} \exp\left(-\frac{u^2}{2}\right)du \tag{G.12}$$

where

$$k_5 = \frac{\log(E/S) - (r - \sigma^2/2)\tau - 2\log(B/S)}{\sigma\sqrt{\tau}} = \frac{\log(ES/B^2) - (r - \sigma^2/2)\tau}{\sigma\sqrt{\tau}}$$

and

$$k_6 = \frac{\log(B/S) - (r - \sigma^2/2)\tau - 2\log(B/S)}{\sigma\sqrt{\tau}} = \frac{\log(S/B) - (r - \sigma^2/2)\tau}{\sigma\sqrt{\tau}}$$

Therefore:

$$I_D = \left(\frac{B}{S}\right)^{2r/\sigma^2 - 1} E\{\exp(-r\tau)N_1(k_6) - N_1(k_5)\} \tag{G.13}$$

G.2.3 Evaluation of integral I_C

Now consider the term

$$I_C = -\frac{S\exp(-r\tau)}{\sigma\sqrt{\tau}\sqrt{2\pi}} \int_{X=\log(E/S)}^{\log(B/S)} \exp(X)\exp\left(-\frac{\{X - (r - \sigma^2/2)\tau\}^2}{2\sigma^2\tau}\right)$$

$$\times \exp\left(\frac{2\log(B/S)(X - \log(B/S))}{\sigma^2\tau}\right) dX$$

In a similar manner to that in Section G.1 we have:

$$I_C = -\left(\frac{B}{S}\right)^{2r/\sigma^2 + 1} \frac{S}{\sigma\sqrt{\tau}\sqrt{2\pi}}$$

$$\times \int_{X=\log(E/S)}^{\log(B/S)} \exp\left(-\frac{\{X - (r - \sigma^2/2)\tau - \sigma^2\tau - 2\log(B/S)\}^2}{2\sigma^2\tau}\right) dX$$

Letting $u = (X - (r - \sigma^2/2)\tau - \sigma^2\tau - 2\log(B/S))/(\sigma\sqrt{\tau})$ gives

$$I_C = -S\left(\frac{B}{S}\right)^{2r/\sigma^2 + 1} \{N_1(k_8) - N_1(k_7)\} \tag{G.14}$$

where

$$k_7 = \frac{\log(E/S) - (r - \sigma^2/2)\tau - \sigma^2\tau - 2\log(B/S)}{\sigma\sqrt{\tau}} = \frac{\log(ES/B^2) - (r + \sigma^2/2)\tau}{\sigma\sqrt{\tau}}$$

$$k_8 = \frac{\log(B/S) - (r - \sigma^2/2)\tau - \sigma^2\tau - 2\log(B/S)}{\sigma\sqrt{\tau}} = \frac{\log(S/B) - (r + \sigma^2/2)\tau}{\sigma\sqrt{\tau}}$$

So we have: $c_{uo} = I_A + I_C + I_D$, which on collecting terms gives:

Value of the up and out call option

$$c_{uo} = S\left(\frac{B}{S}\right)^{2r/\sigma^2 + 1} \{N_1(k_7) - N_1(k_8)\} - \left(\frac{B}{S}\right)^{2r/\sigma^2 - 1}$$

$$\times E\{\exp(-r\tau)\ N_1(k_5) - N_1(k_6)\}$$

$$+ S\{N_1(k_2) - N_1(k_1)\} - E\exp(-r\tau)\{N_1(k_4) - N_1(2k_3)\} \tag{G.15}$$

Appendix H

Algorithms for an AGARCH-I process

Here we provide pseudocode which calculates the log likelihood and is partial derivatives for a regression-AGARCH-I process. We consider residuals which have either a Gaussian distribution or a Student's t distribution. The notation used is the same as that given in Section 20 of PART III.

H.1 GAUSSIAN DISTRIBUTION

H.1.1 The log likelihood

Deal with the first q terms of the sequence:

$$\gamma = \hat{\gamma}$$
$$\mathcal{L}(\theta) = 0$$

```
For i = 1 To num
```
$$\text{If } (\text{mn} == 1) \quad \epsilon_i = y_i - X_i^T \hat{b}$$
$$\text{If } (\text{mn} == 0) \quad \epsilon_i = y_i - \hat{b}_0 - X_i^T \hat{b}$$

```
Next i
For i = 1 To q
```

$$h_i = \alpha_0 + \sum_{j=1}^{i-1} \alpha_j (\epsilon_{i-j} + \gamma)^2 + \sum_{j=i}^{q} \alpha_j \sigma_0^2 + \sum_{k=1}^{p} h_{i-k} \beta_k$$

Store the current value of h_i and keep all the previous values of h_i.

$$\mathcal{L}(\theta) = \mathcal{L}(\theta) + \frac{1}{2}\left(\log(h_i) + \frac{\epsilon_i^2}{h_i}\right)$$

```
Next i
```

Deal with the remaining terms of the sequence:

```
For i = q + 1 To num
```

$$h_i = \alpha_0 + \sum_{j=1}^{q} \alpha_j (\epsilon_{i-j} + \gamma)^2 + \sum_{k=1}^{p} \beta_k h_{i-k}$$

Store the current value of h_i and keep N_p previous values of h_i.

$$\mathcal{L}(\theta) = \mathcal{L}(\theta) + \frac{1}{2}\left(\log(h_i) + \frac{\epsilon_i^2}{h_i}\right)$$

```
Next i
```

H.1.2   The first derivatives of the log likelihood

Algorithm for the first q terms of the sequence:

$$\frac{\partial \mathcal{L}(\theta)}{\partial \theta_k} = 0, \quad k = 1, \ldots, N_p$$

```
For i = 1 to q
```

$$\frac{\partial h_i}{\partial \alpha_0} = 1 + \sum_{k=1}^{p} \beta_k \frac{\partial h_{i-k}}{\partial \alpha_0}$$

```
    For j = 1 to i - 1
```

$$\frac{\partial h_i}{\partial \alpha_j} = (\epsilon_{i-j} + \gamma)^2$$

```
Next j
For j = i to q
```

$$\frac{\partial h_i}{\partial \alpha_j} = \sigma_0^2$$

```
Next j
For j = 1 to q
```

$$\frac{\partial h_i}{\partial \alpha_j} = \frac{\partial h_i}{\partial \alpha_j} + \sum_{k=1}^{p} \beta_k \frac{\partial h_{i-k}}{\partial \alpha_j}$$

```
Next j
For j = 1 to p
```

$$\frac{\partial h_i}{\partial \beta_j} = h_{i-j} + \sum_{k=1}^{p} \beta_j \frac{\partial h_{i-k}}{\partial \beta_k}$$

```
Next j
```

$$\frac{\partial h_i}{\partial \gamma} = \sum_{j=1}^{i-1} 2(\epsilon_{i-j} + \gamma)\alpha_j + \sum_{k=1}^{p} \beta_k \frac{\partial h_{i-k}}{\partial \gamma}$$

$$h_i = \alpha_0 + \sum_{k=1}^{p} h_{i-k}\beta_k + \sum_{j=1}^{i-1} \alpha_j(\epsilon_{i-j} + \gamma)^2 + \sum_{j=i}^{q} \alpha_j\sigma_0^2$$

```
if (mn == 1) then
```

$$\frac{\partial h_i}{\partial b_0} = -2\sum_{k=1}^{i-1}(\epsilon_{i-k} + \gamma)\alpha_k + \sum_{k=1}^{p} \beta_k \frac{\partial h_{i-k}}{\partial b_0}\mathcal{H}(i - k)$$

```
end if
For j = 1 to nreg
```

$$\frac{\partial h_i}{\partial b_j} = -2 \sum_{k=1}^{i-1} (\epsilon_{i-k} + \gamma) \alpha_k X_{i-k}^j + \sum_{k=1}^{p} \beta_k \frac{\partial h_{i-k}}{\partial b_j} \mathcal{H}(i-k)$$

```
Next j
```

Store the current values of h_i and $\partial h_i / \partial \theta$ and keep all the previous values of h_i and $\partial h_i / \partial \theta$.

```
For k = 1 to npar + 1
```

$$\frac{\partial \mathcal{L}(\theta)}{\partial \theta_k} = \frac{\partial \mathcal{L}(\theta)}{\partial \theta_k} - \frac{1}{2h_i} \left(\frac{\epsilon_i^2}{h_i} - 1 \right) \frac{\partial h_i}{\partial \theta_k}$$

```
Next k
if (mn == 1) then
```

$$\frac{\partial \mathcal{L}(\theta)}{\partial b_0} = \frac{\partial \mathcal{L}(\theta)}{\partial b_0} - \frac{\epsilon_i}{h_i} - \frac{1}{2h_i} \left(\frac{\epsilon_i^2}{h_i} - 1 \right) \frac{\partial h_i}{\partial b_0}$$

```
end if
For k = 1 to nreg
```

$$\frac{\partial \mathcal{L}(\theta)}{\partial b_k} = \frac{\partial \mathcal{L}(\theta)}{\partial b_k} - \frac{X_i^k \epsilon_i}{h_i} - \frac{1}{2h_i} \left(\frac{\epsilon_i^2}{h_i} - 1 \right) \frac{\partial h_i}{\partial b_k}$$

```
Next k
Next i
```

Algorithm for the remaining terms of the sequence:

```
For i = q + 1 to num
```

$$\frac{\partial h_i}{\partial \alpha_0} = 1 + \sum_{k=1}^{p} \beta_k \frac{\partial h_{i-k}}{\partial \alpha_0}$$

```
For j = 1 to q
```

$$\frac{\partial h_i}{\partial \alpha_j} = \sum_{k=1}^{p} \beta_k \frac{\partial h_{i-k}}{\partial \alpha_j}$$

```
Next j
For j = 1 to p
```

$$\frac{\partial h_i}{\partial \beta_j} = h_{i-j} + \sum_{k=1}^{p} \beta_j \frac{\partial h_{i-k}}{\partial \beta_k}$$

```
Next j
```

$$\frac{\partial h_i}{\partial \gamma} = \frac{\partial h_i}{\partial \gamma} + \sum_{j=1}^{q} 2(\epsilon_{i-j} + \gamma)\alpha_j + \sum_{k=1}^{p} \beta_k \frac{\partial h_{i-k}}{\partial \gamma}$$

$$h_i = \alpha_0 + \sum_{k=1}^{p} h_{i-k}\beta_k + \sum_{j=1}^{q} \alpha_j(\epsilon_{i-j} + \gamma)^2$$

```
if (mn == 1) then
```

$$\frac{\partial h_i}{\partial b_0} = -2 \sum_{k=1}^{q} (\epsilon_{i-k} + \gamma)\alpha_k + \sum_{k=1}^{p} \beta_k \frac{\partial h_{i-k}}{\partial b_0} \mathcal{H}(i-k)$$

```
end if
For j = 1 to nreg
```

$$\frac{\partial h_i}{\partial b_j} = -2 \sum_{k=1}^{q} (\epsilon_{i-k} + \gamma)\alpha_k X_{i-k}^j + \sum_{k=1}^{p} \beta_k \frac{\partial h_{i-k}}{\partial b_j} \mathcal{H}(i-k)$$

```
Next j
```

Store the current values of h_i and $\partial h_i / \partial \theta$ and keep N_p previous values of h_i and $\partial h_i / \partial \theta$.

```
For k = 1 to npar + 1
```

$$\frac{\partial \mathcal{L}(\theta)}{\partial \theta_k} = \frac{\partial \mathcal{L}(\theta)}{\partial \theta_k} - \frac{1}{2h_i}\left(\frac{\epsilon_i^2}{h_i} - 1\right)\frac{\partial h_i}{\partial \theta_k}$$

```
Next k
if (mn == 1) then
```

$$\frac{\partial \mathcal{L}(\theta)}{\partial b_0} = \frac{\partial \mathcal{L}(\theta)}{\partial b_0} - \frac{\epsilon_i}{h_i} - \frac{1}{2h_i}\left(\frac{\epsilon_i^2}{h_i} - 1\right)\frac{\partial h_i}{\partial b_0}$$

```
end if
For k = 1 to nreg
```

$$\frac{\partial \mathcal{L}(\theta)}{\partial b_k} = \frac{\partial \mathcal{L}(\theta)}{\partial b_k} - \frac{X_i^k \epsilon_i}{h_i} - \frac{1}{2h_i}\left(\frac{\epsilon_i^2}{h_i} - 1\right)\frac{\partial h_i}{\partial b_k}$$

```
Next k
Next i
```

H.2   STUDENT'S *t* DISTRIBUTION

H.2.1   The log likelihood

Deal with the first q terms of the sequence:

$$\gamma = \hat{\gamma}$$
$$\mathcal{L}(\theta) = 0$$
$$\mathcal{M}_\nu = \log(\Gamma((\nu+1)/2)) - \log(\Gamma(\nu/2)) - \frac{1}{2}\log(\nu-2)$$

```
For i = 1 To num
```

$$\text{If } (\text{mn} == 1) \quad \epsilon_i = y_i - X_i^T \hat{b}$$

$$\text{If } (\text{mn} == 0) \quad \epsilon_i = y_i - \hat{b}_0 - X_i^T \hat{b}$$

```
Next i
For i = 1 To q
```

$$h_i = \alpha_0 + \sum_{j=1}^{i-1} \alpha_j(\epsilon_{i-j} + \gamma)^2 + \sum_{j=i}^{q} \alpha_j \sigma_0^2 + \sum_{k=1}^{p} h_{i-k}\beta_k$$

Store the current value of h_i and keep all the previous values of h_i.

$$\mathcal{L}(\theta) = \mathcal{L}(\theta) - \mathcal{M}_\nu + \frac{1}{2}\log(h_i) + \frac{\nu+1}{2}\log\left(1 + \frac{\epsilon_i^2}{(\nu-2)h_i}\right)$$

```
Next i
```

Deal with the remaining terms of the sequence:

```
For i = q + 1 To num
```

$$h_i = \alpha_0 + \sum_{j=1}^{q} \alpha_j(\epsilon_{i-j} + \gamma)^2 + \sum_{k=1}^{p} \beta_k h_{i-k}$$

Store the current value of h_i and keep N_p previous values of h_i.

$$\mathcal{L}(\theta) = \mathcal{L}(\theta) - \mathcal{M}_\nu + \frac{1}{2}\log(h_i) + \frac{\nu+1}{2}\log\left(1 + \frac{\epsilon_i^2}{(\nu-2)h_i}\right)$$

```
Next i
```

H.2.2   The first derivatives of the log likelihood

Algorithm for the first q terms of the sequence:

$$\frac{\partial \mathcal{L}(\theta)}{\partial \theta_k} = 0, \quad k = 1, \ldots, N_p$$

```
For i = 1 to q
```

Compute h_i as described in Section H.2.1. Also calculate the derivatives $\partial h_i/\partial \theta_j$, $j = 1, \ldots, N_p$ as described for a Gaussian distribution in Section H.1.2. Store h_i and $\partial h_i/\partial \theta_j$, $j = 1, \ldots, N_p$, and keep all the previous values of h_i and $\partial h_i/\partial \theta$. Set

$$\mathcal{G} = \left(\frac{(\nu+1)}{(\nu-2) + (\epsilon_i^2/h_i)}\right)$$

```
For k = 1 to npar + 1
```

$$\frac{\partial \mathcal{L}(\theta)}{\partial \theta_k} = \frac{\partial \mathcal{L}(\theta)}{\partial \theta_k} - \frac{1}{2h_i}\left(1 - \frac{\epsilon_i^2}{h_i}\mathcal{G}\right)\frac{\partial h_i}{\partial \theta_k}$$

```
Next k
```

$$\frac{\partial \mathcal{L}(\theta)}{\partial \nu} = \frac{\partial \mathcal{L}(\theta)}{\partial \nu} - \frac{1}{2}\psi\left(\frac{\nu+1}{2}\right) + \frac{1}{2}\psi\left(\frac{\nu}{2}\right) + \frac{1}{2(\nu-2)}$$

$$+ \frac{1}{2}\log\left(1 + \frac{\epsilon_i^2}{(\nu-2)h_i}\right) - \frac{\epsilon_i^2}{2(\nu-2)h_i}\mathcal{G}$$

```
if (mn == 1) then
```

$$\frac{\partial \mathcal{L}(\theta)}{\partial b_0} = \frac{\partial \mathcal{L}(\theta)}{\partial b_0} - \frac{\epsilon_i}{h_i}\mathcal{G} - \frac{1}{2h_i}\left(\frac{\epsilon_i^2}{h_i}\mathcal{G} - 1\right)\frac{\partial h_i}{\partial b_0}$$

```
end if
For k = 1 to nreg
```

$$\frac{\partial \mathcal{L}(\theta)}{\partial b_k} = \frac{\partial \mathcal{L}(\theta)}{\partial b_k} - \frac{X_i^k \epsilon_i}{h_i}\mathcal{G} - \frac{1}{2h_i}\left(\frac{\epsilon_i^2}{h_i}\mathcal{G} - 1\right)\frac{\partial h_i}{\partial b_k}$$

```
Next k
Next i
```

Algorithm for the remaining terms of the sequence:

```
For i = q+1 to num
```

Compute h_i as described in Section H.2.1. Also calculate the derivatives $\partial h_i/\partial \theta_j$, $j = 1, \ldots, N_p$ as described for a Gaussian distribution in Section H.1.2. Store h_i and $\partial h_i/\partial \theta_j$, $j = 1, \ldots, N_p$, and keep N_p previous values of h_i and $\partial h_i/\partial \theta$.
Set

$$\mathcal{G} = \left(\frac{(\nu+1)}{(\nu-2) + (\epsilon_i^2/h_i)}\right)$$

```
For k = 1 to npar + 1
```

$$\frac{\partial \mathcal{L}(\theta)}{\partial \theta_k} = \frac{\partial \mathcal{L}(\theta)}{\partial \theta_k} - \frac{1}{2h_i}\left(1 - \frac{\epsilon_i^2}{h_i}\mathcal{G}\right)\frac{\partial h_i}{\partial \theta_k}$$

```
Next k
```

$$\frac{\partial \mathcal{L}(\theta)}{\partial \nu} = \frac{\partial \mathcal{L}(\theta)}{\partial \nu} - \frac{1}{2}\psi\left(\frac{\nu+1}{2}\right) + \frac{1}{2}\psi\left(\frac{\nu}{2}\right) + \frac{1}{2(\nu-2)}$$

$$+ \frac{1}{2}\log\left(1 + \frac{\epsilon_i^2}{(\nu-2)h_i}\right) - \frac{\epsilon_i^2}{2(\nu-2)h_i}\mathcal{G}$$

```
if (mn == 1) then
```

$$\frac{\partial \mathcal{L}(\theta)}{\partial b_0} = \frac{\partial \mathcal{L}(\theta)}{\partial b_0} - \frac{\epsilon_i}{h_i}\mathcal{G} - \frac{1}{2h_i}\left(\frac{\epsilon_i^2}{h_i}\mathcal{G} - 1\right)\frac{\partial h_i}{\partial b_0}$$

```
end if
For k = 1 to nreg
```

$$\frac{\partial \mathcal{L}(\theta)}{\partial b_k} = \frac{\partial \mathcal{L}(\theta)}{\partial b_k} - \frac{X_i^k \epsilon_i}{h_i}\mathcal{G} - \frac{1}{2h_i}\left(\frac{\epsilon_i^2}{h_i}\mathcal{G} - 1\right)\frac{\partial h_i}{\partial b_k}$$

```
Next k
Next i
```

Appendix I

The general error distribution

This section proves various relations for the general error distribution. The density function for the general error distribution is:

$$f(\epsilon_i) = K \exp\left(-\frac{1}{2}\left|\frac{\epsilon_i}{\lambda}\right|^a\right), \quad \text{where} \quad K = \frac{a}{\lambda 2^{(1+1/a)}\Gamma(1/a)} \tag{I.1}$$

I.1 VALUE OF λ FOR VARIANCE h_i

Calculation of the scale factor λ required for a general error distribution with mean zero and variance h_i.

The variance of the distribution, $E(\epsilon_i^2)$, is given by:

$$E(\epsilon_i^2) = K \int_{-\infty}^{\infty} \epsilon_i^2 \exp\left(-\frac{1}{2}\left|\frac{\epsilon_i}{\lambda}\right|^a\right) d\epsilon_i = 2K \int_{0}^{\infty} \epsilon_i^2 \exp\left(-\frac{1}{2}\left(\frac{\epsilon_i}{\lambda}\right)^a\right) d\epsilon_i$$

Using the standard integrals in Appendix K.1 with $n = 2$, $p = a$ and $b = 1/2(1/\lambda)^a$ gives:

$$h_i = \frac{2K}{a}\Gamma\left(\frac{3}{a}\right)\left\{\frac{1}{2}\left(\frac{1}{\lambda}\right)^a\right\}^{-3/a}$$

Which after some simplification yields:

$$h_i = \frac{2K 2^{3/a}\lambda^3}{a}\Gamma\left(\frac{3}{a}\right)$$

Substituting for K and simplifying then gives:

$$h_i = \lambda^2 2^{2/a}\frac{\Gamma(3/a)}{\Gamma(1/a)}$$

The required value of λ is therefore:

$$\lambda = \left\{h_i 2^{-2/a}\frac{\Gamma(1/a)}{\Gamma(3/a)}\right\}^{1/2}$$

I.2 THE KURTOSIS

$$E(\epsilon_i^4) = K \int_{-\infty}^{\infty} \epsilon_i^4 \exp\left(-\frac{1}{2}\left|\frac{\epsilon_i}{\lambda}\right|^a\right) d\epsilon_i$$

$$= 2K \int_{0}^{\infty} \epsilon_i^4 \exp\left(-\frac{1}{2}\left(\frac{\epsilon_i}{\lambda}\right)^a\right) d\epsilon_i$$

However from standard mathematical tables:

$$\int_0^\infty \epsilon_i^4 \exp(-b\epsilon_i^p) = \frac{\Gamma(k)}{pb^k}$$

where $p = a$, $b = (1/2)(1/\lambda)^a$ and $k = 5/a$ which gives:

$$E[\epsilon_i^4] = \frac{2\mathcal{K}2^{5/a}\lambda^5}{a}\Gamma\left(\frac{5}{a}\right) = 2^{2/a}\lambda^2 h_i \frac{\Gamma(5/a)}{\Gamma(3/a)}$$

From Appendix I.1 we have:

$$E[\epsilon_i^2] = h_i = \frac{2\mathcal{K}2^{3/a}\lambda^3}{a}\Gamma\left(\frac{3}{a}\right) \quad \text{and} \quad \lambda^2 = \frac{h_i 2^{-2/a}\Gamma(1/a)}{\Gamma(3/a)}$$

Therefore:

$$E[\epsilon_i^4] = h_i^2 \frac{\Gamma(5/a)\Gamma(1/a)}{\Gamma(3/a)\Gamma(3/a)}$$

Which gives the kurtosis as:

$$\aleph = \frac{E[\epsilon_i^4]}{(E[\epsilon_i^2])^2} = \frac{h_i^2}{h_i^2}\frac{\Gamma(5/a)\Gamma(1/a)}{\Gamma(3/a)\Gamma(3/a)} = \frac{\Gamma(5/a)\Gamma(1/a)}{\Gamma(3/a)\Gamma(3/a)}$$

I.3   THE DISTRIBUTION WHEN THE SHAPE PARAMETER, a IS VERY LARGE

If the distribution has variance h_i then, from Appendix I.1:

$$\lambda = \left(\frac{2^{-2/a}\Gamma(1/a)h_i}{\Gamma(3/a)}\right)^{1/2}$$

Now for $0 < x < 1$ we have $\Gamma(1 + x) = 1 + a_1 x + a_2 x^2 + a_3 x^3 + \cdots +$, where the coefficients are $|a_i| < 1$, see Abramowitz and Stegun (1968).

Since $x\Gamma(x) = \Gamma(1 + x)$ we have, so to third order in x:

$$x\Gamma(x) = 1 + a_1 x + a_2 x^2 + a_3 x^3$$

This gives $\Gamma(x) = (1/x) + a_1 + a_2 x + a_3 x^2$, and $\Gamma(x) \approx 1/x$ as $x \longrightarrow 0$.
So as $a \longrightarrow \infty$ we have the following:

$$2^{(1+1/a)} \approx 2, \quad 2^{-2/a} \approx 1, \quad \frac{1}{\Gamma(1/a)} \approx \frac{1}{a}, \quad \frac{\Gamma(1/a)}{\Gamma(3/a)} \approx \frac{3a}{a} = 3, \quad \text{and} \quad \frac{\Gamma(5/a)}{\Gamma(3/a)} \approx \frac{3a}{5a} = \frac{3}{5}$$

The kurtosis is then:

$$\aleph = \frac{\Gamma(5/a)\Gamma(1/a)}{\Gamma(3/a)\Gamma(3/a)} = \frac{9}{5}$$

Also as $a \longrightarrow \infty$ $\lambda \approx (3h_i)^{1/2}$, and for the range $-(3h_i)^{1/2} < \epsilon_i < (3h_i)^{1/2}$, we have:

$$\left|\frac{\epsilon_i}{\lambda}\right|^a \approx \left|\frac{\epsilon_i}{(3h_i)^{1/2}}\right| \approx 0 \quad \text{and therefore} \quad \exp\left(-\frac{1}{2}\left|\frac{\epsilon_i}{\lambda}\right|^a\right) \approx 1$$

Substituting the above results into Equation I.1 the probability density function reduces to:

$$f(\epsilon_i) \approx \frac{1}{2(3h_i)^{1/2}}$$

which is a uniform distribution $\mathcal{U}(-(3h_i)^{1/2}, (3h_i)^{1/2})$, with lower limit $-(3h_i)^{1/2}$ and upper limit $-(3h_i)^{1/2}$.

Appendix J

The Student's t distribution

J.1 THE KURTOSIS

This section derives an expression for the kurtosis of the Student's t distribution. Since the Student's t distribution density function is:

$$f(\epsilon_i) = K\left[1 + \frac{\epsilon_i^2}{h_i(\nu - 2)}\right]^{-(\nu+1)/2}$$

where

$$K = \frac{\Gamma((\nu + 1)/2)(\nu - 2)^{-1/2}h_i^{-1/2}}{\pi^{1/2}\Gamma(\nu/2)}$$

we have:

$$E[\epsilon_i^2] = 2K \int_0^\infty \frac{\epsilon_i^2 d\epsilon_i}{(1 + \epsilon_i^2/(h_i(\nu - 2)))^{(\nu+1)/2}}$$

$$= 2K(h_i(\nu - 2))^{(\nu+1)/2} \int_0^\infty \frac{\epsilon_i^2 d\epsilon_i}{(h_i(\nu - 2) + \epsilon_i^2)^{(\nu+1)/2}}$$

Using the standard integrals in Appendix K with $a = 2$, $b = 2$, $c = (\nu + 1)/2$ and $m = (\nu - 2)h_i$ gives:

$$\frac{m^{(a+1-bc)/b}}{b} = \frac{(h_i(\nu - 2))^{(2-\nu)/2}}{2}, \quad \Gamma\left(\frac{a+1}{b}\right) = \Gamma(3/2),$$

$$\Gamma\left(c - \frac{a+1}{b}\right) = \Gamma\left(\frac{\nu - 2}{2}\right), \quad \Gamma(c) = \Gamma\left(\frac{\nu + 1}{2}\right)$$

This gives

$$E[\epsilon_i^2] = 2K(h_i(\nu - 2))^{(\nu+1)/2}\left\{\frac{(h_i(\nu - 2))^{(2-\nu)/2}\sqrt{\pi}\Gamma((\nu - 2)/2)}{4\Gamma((\nu + 1)/2)}\right\}$$

Substituting for K and simplifying we obtain:

$$E[\epsilon_i^2] = \frac{h_i(\nu - 2)\Gamma((\nu - 1)/2)}{\Gamma(\nu/2)}$$

But

$$\left(\frac{\nu-2}{2}\right)\Gamma\left(\frac{\nu-2}{2}\right) = \Gamma\left(\frac{\nu-1}{2}+1\right) = \Gamma\left(\frac{\nu}{2}\right)$$

So

$$E[\epsilon_i^2] = \frac{h_i(\nu-2)\Gamma(\nu/2)}{2(\nu-2)\Gamma(\nu/2)} = h_i$$

Similarly we have:

$$E[\epsilon_i^4] = 2\mathcal{K}\int_0^\infty \frac{\epsilon_i^4 d\epsilon_i}{(1+\epsilon_i^2/(h_i(\nu-2)))^{(\nu+1)/2}}$$

$$= 2\mathcal{K}(h_i(\nu-2))^{\frac{(\nu+1)}{2}}\int_0^\infty \frac{\epsilon_i^4 d\epsilon_i}{(h_i(\nu-2)+\epsilon_i^2)^{(\nu+1)/2}}$$

Using the standard integrals in Appendix K with: $a = 4$, $b = 2$, $c = (\nu+1)/2$ and $m = (\nu-2)h_i$ gives:

$$\frac{m^{(a+1-bc)/b}}{b} = \frac{(h_i(\nu-2))^{(4-\nu)/2}}{2}, \quad \Gamma\left(\frac{a+1}{b}\right) = \Gamma(5/2),$$

$$\Gamma\left(c-\frac{a+1}{b}\right) = \Gamma\left(\frac{\nu-4}{2}\right), \quad \Gamma(c) = \Gamma\left(\frac{\nu+1}{2}\right)$$

and

$$E[\epsilon_i^4] = 2\mathcal{K}(h_i(\nu-2))^{(\nu+1)/2}\left\{\frac{(h_i(\nu-2))^{(4-\nu)/2}3\sqrt{\pi}\Gamma((\nu-4)/2)}{8\Gamma((\nu+1)/2)}\right\}$$

Substituting for $\mathcal{K}$ and simplifying we obtain:

$$E[\epsilon_i^4] = \frac{3h_i(\nu-2)^2\Gamma((\nu-4)/2)h_i^2}{4\Gamma(\nu/2)}$$

But

$$\left(\frac{\nu-4}{2}\right)\Gamma\left(\frac{\nu-4}{2}\right) = \Gamma\left(\frac{\nu-2}{2}\right)$$

and

$$\left(\frac{\nu-2}{2}\right)\Gamma\left(\frac{\nu-2}{2}\right) = \Gamma\left(\frac{\nu}{2}\right)$$

Therefore:

$$\Gamma\left(\frac{\nu-4}{2}\right) = \frac{4\Gamma(\nu/2)}{(\nu-4)(\nu-2)}$$

So

$$E[\epsilon_i^4] = \frac{3(\nu-2)^2 4\Gamma(\nu/2)h_i^2}{4\Gamma(\nu/2)(\nu-4)(\nu-2)} = \frac{3(\nu-2)h_i^2}{(\nu-4)}$$

The kurtosis is then:

$$\aleph = \frac{E[e_i^4]}{(E[e_i^2])^2} = \frac{3(\nu-2)h_i^2}{(\nu-4)h_i^2} = \frac{3(\nu-2)}{(\nu-4)} \tag{J.1}$$

Appendix K

Mathematical reference

K.1 STANDARD INTEGRALS

Here we quote some useful standard integrals, see for example Beyer (1982).

$$\int_0^\infty y \exp(-ay^2)\,dy = \frac{1}{2}$$

$$\int_0^\infty y^2 \exp(-ay^2)\,dy = \frac{1}{4a}\sqrt{\frac{\pi}{a}}$$

$$\int_0^\infty y^4 \exp(-ay^2)\,dy = \frac{3}{8a^2}\sqrt{\frac{\pi}{a}}$$

$$\int_0^\infty y^{2n} \exp(-ay^2)\,dy = \frac{1 \times 3 \times 5 \cdots (2n-1)}{2^{n+1}a^n}\sqrt{\frac{\pi}{a}}$$

$$\int_0^\infty \epsilon_i^n \exp(-b\,\epsilon_i^p) = \frac{\Gamma(k)}{pb^k}, \quad \text{where } n > -1,\ p > 0,\ b > 0 \quad \text{and} \quad k = \frac{(n+1)}{p}$$

$$\int_0^\infty \frac{\epsilon_i^a\,d\epsilon_i}{(m + \epsilon_i^b)^c} = \frac{m^{(a+1-bc)/b}}{b}\frac{\Gamma((a+1)/b)\Gamma(c - (a+1)/b)}{\Gamma(c)}$$

where $a > -1$, $b > 0$, $m > 0$, and $c > (a+1)/b$.

K.2 GAMMA FUNCTION

$$\Gamma(1 + x) = x!$$

$$x\Gamma(x) = \Gamma(x + 1)$$

$$\Gamma\left(\frac{1}{2}\right) = \sqrt{\pi}$$

$$\Gamma\left(\frac{3}{2}\right) = \frac{\sqrt{\pi}}{2}$$

$$\Gamma\left(\frac{5}{2}\right) = \frac{3\sqrt{\pi}}{4}$$

$$\frac{\partial\Gamma(x)}{\partial x} = \psi(x)$$

For $0 \le x \le 1$ we have

$$\Gamma(1 + x) = 1 + a_1 x + a_2 x^2 + a_3 x^3 + a_4 x^4 + a_5 x^5$$

where $a_1 = -0.5748$, $a_2 = 0.9512$, $a_3 = -0.6998$, $a_4 = 0.4245$, and $a_5 = -0.1010$.

K.3   THE CUMULATIVE NORMAL DISTRIBUTION FUNCTION

In this section we show that the cumulative normal distribution function, $N_1(x)$, is related to the complementary error function, erfc(x), by the following equation:

$$N_1(x) = \frac{1}{2}\text{erfc}(-x/\sqrt{2}) \tag{K.1}$$

If we let the error function be represented by erf(x) then we have:

$$\text{erf}(x) = \frac{2}{\sqrt{\pi}} \int_0^\infty \exp(-t^2)dt$$

Now we have the following:

$$\text{erfc}(x) = 1 - \text{erf}(x), \quad \text{erf}(-x) = -\text{erf}(x),$$

$$\text{erf}(\infty) = 1 \quad \text{and} \quad \text{erfc}(-x) = 2 - \text{erfc}(x)$$

We will consider the integral

$$I(x) = \frac{2}{\sqrt{\pi}} \int_{-\infty}^x \exp(-t^2)dt = \frac{2}{\sqrt{\pi}} \int_{-\infty}^0 \exp(-t^2)dt + \frac{2}{\sqrt{\pi}} \int_0^x \exp(-t^2)dt$$

Since

$$\frac{2}{\sqrt{\pi}} \int_{-\infty}^0 \exp(-t^2)dt = 1$$

We therefore have

$$I(x) = 1 + \text{erf}(x) = 1 + \{1 - \text{erfc}(x)\} = 2 - \text{erfc}(x)$$

Substituting for erfc(x) we obtain:

$$I(x) = 2 - \{2 - \text{erfc}(-x)\} = \text{erfc}(-x)$$

So we have

$$\text{erfc}(-x) = \frac{2}{\sqrt{\pi}} \int_{-\infty}^x \exp(-t^2)dt \tag{K.2}$$

Now the cumulative normal distribution is defined as

$$N_1(x) = \frac{1}{\sqrt{2\pi}} \int_{-\infty}^x \exp(-t^2)dt$$

Letting $u = t\sqrt{2}$, we have $du = \sqrt{2}dt$ and for the upper limit we have $x = t\sqrt{2}$ or $t = x/\sqrt{2}$.

This integral becomes

$$N_1(x) = \frac{1}{\sqrt{2\pi}} \int_{\infty}^{t=x/\sqrt{2}} \exp(-t^2)\sqrt{2}dt \tag{K.3}$$

So from Equation K.2 we have

$$N_1(x) = \frac{1}{2}\mathrm{erfc}(-x/\sqrt{2}) \qquad QED$$

K.4 ARITHMETIC AND GEOMETRIC PROGRESSIONS

K.4.1 Arithmetic progression

The sum of the first n terms of an arithmetic progression is:

$$s_n = \frac{n}{2}\{2a_1 + (n-1)d\} \tag{K.4}$$

where a_1 is the first term, and d is the common difference; that is the terms in the sequence are: $a_1, a_1 + d, a_1 + 2d, a_1 + 3d, \ldots$

K.4.2 Geometric progression

The sum of the first n terms of geometric progression is:

$$s_n = \frac{a_1(1-r^n)}{1-r} \tag{K.5}$$

where a_1 is the first term, and r is the common ratio; that is the terms in sequence are: $a_1, a_1 r, a_1 r^2, a_1 r^3, \ldots$

Appendix L

The stability of the Black–Scholes finite-difference schemes

L.1 THE GENERAL CASE

In this section we consider the stability of the finite-difference schemes described in Part II Section 10.6.4. It is assumed that the grid contains n_s asset points, and we will denote the time dependent option values at the ith and $(i + 1)$th time instants by the n_{s-2} element vectors X^i and X^{i+1} respectively. We can therefore write:

$$T_1 X^i = T_2 X^{i+1} \tag{L.1}$$

where T_1 and T_2 are $n_{s-2} \times n_{s-2}$ tridiagonal matrices, and x_k^i, $k = 1, \ldots, n_{s-2}$ will be used to denote the elements of the vector X^i.

The option values at the ith time instant are computed from those at the $(i + 1)$th time instant by using

$$X^i = T_1^{-1} T_2 X^{i+1} \tag{L.2}$$

However Equation L.2 is only *stable* if the eigenvalues of the $n_{s-2} \times n_{s-2}$ matrix $T_1^{-1} T_2$ all have modulus less than one, see Smith (1985).

L.2 THE LOG TRANSFORMATION AND A UNIFORM GRID

We will now prove that the *implicit* finite-difference method, $\theta_m = 0$, when used on the log transformed Black–Scholes equation with a uniform grid is *unconditionally stable*; which means that the stability does not depend on the values of σ, Δt, ΔZ, etc.

From Part II Section 10.6.4 the finite-difference scheme is described by the following tridiagonal system:

$$
\begin{pmatrix}
B & C & 0 & 0 & 0 & 0 \\
A & B & C & 0 & 0 & 0 \\
0 & 0 & . & . & 0 & 0 \\
0 & 0 & 0 & . & . & 0 \\
0 & 0 & 0 & A & B & C \\
0 & 0 & 0 & 0 & A & B
\end{pmatrix}
\begin{pmatrix}
x_1^i \\
x_2^i \\
. \\
. \\
x_{s-1}^i \\
x_{s-2}^i
\end{pmatrix}
=
\begin{pmatrix}
\bar{B} & \bar{C} & 0 & 0 & 0 & 0 \\
\bar{A} & \bar{B} & \bar{C} & 0 & 0 & 0 \\
0 & 0 & . & . & 0 & 0 \\
0 & 0 & 0 & . & . & 0 \\
0 & 0 & 0 & \bar{A} & \bar{B} & \bar{C} \\
0 & 0 & 0 & 0 & \bar{A} & \bar{B}
\end{pmatrix}
\begin{pmatrix}
x_1^{i+1} \\
x_2^{i+1} \\
. \\
. \\
x_{s-3}^{i+1} \\
x_{s-2}^{i+1}
\end{pmatrix}
$$

where

$$A = \frac{(1 - \Theta_m)\Delta t}{2\Delta Z^2}\{b\Delta Z - \sigma^2\} \tag{L.3}$$

$$B = 1 + (1 - \Theta_m)\Delta t\left\{r + \frac{\sigma^2}{\Delta Z^2}\right\} \tag{L.4}$$

$$C = -\frac{(1 - \Theta_m)\Delta t}{2\Delta Z^2}\{b\Delta Z + \sigma^2\} \tag{L.5}$$

$$\bar{A} = -\frac{\Theta_m \Delta t}{2\Delta Z^2}\{b\Delta Z - \sigma^2\} \tag{L.6}$$

$$\bar{B} = 1 - \Theta_m \Delta t\left\{r + \frac{\sigma^2}{\Delta Z^2}\right\} \tag{L.7}$$

$$\bar{C} = \frac{\Theta_m \Delta t}{2\Delta Z^2}\{b\Delta Z + \sigma^2\} \tag{L.8}$$

As in Part II Section 10.6, $b = r - q - (\sigma^2/2)$ and $r > 0$.

Substituting $\theta_m = 0$ into Equations L.3 to L.8 we have $\bar{A} = \bar{C} = 0$, $\bar{B} = 1$ and

$$A = \frac{\Delta t}{2\Delta Z^2}\{b\Delta Z - \sigma^2\}, \quad B = 1 + \Delta t\left\{r + \frac{\sigma^2}{\Delta Z^2}\right\},$$

$$C = -\frac{\Delta t}{2\Delta Z^2}\{b\Delta Z + \sigma^2\}$$

The finite-difference scheme is thus represented by the equations

$$\begin{pmatrix} B & C & 0 & 0 & 0 & 0 \\ A & B & C & 0 & 0 & 0 \\ 0 & 0 & . & . & 0 & 0 \\ 0 & 0 & 0 & . & . & 0 \\ 0 & 0 & 0 & A & B & C \\ 0 & 0 & 0 & 0 & A & B \end{pmatrix}\begin{pmatrix} x_1^i \\ x_2^i \\ . \\ . \\ x_{s-1}^i \\ x_{s-2}^i \end{pmatrix} = \begin{pmatrix} 1 & & 0 & 0 & 0 & 0 \\ 0 & 1 & & 0 & 0 & 0 \\ 0 & 0 & . & . & 0 & 0 \\ 0 & 0 & 0 & . & . & 0 \\ 0 & 0 & 0 & 0 & 1 & 0 \\ 0 & 0 & 0 & 0 & 0 & 1 \end{pmatrix}\begin{pmatrix} x_1^{i+1} \\ x_2^{i+1} \\ . \\ . \\ x_{s-3}^{i+1} \\ x_{s-2}^{i+1} \end{pmatrix}$$

or in matrix notation

$$X^i = T_1^{-1}X^{i+1} \tag{L.9}$$

where $T_2 = I$ in Equation L.2.

As mentioned in Section L.1, Equation L.9 is stable if the modulus of all the eigenvalues of T_1^{-1} are less than one. We will now show that this is in fact the case.

If the eigenvalues of T_1 are λ_k, $k = 1, \ldots, n_{s-2}$, then the eigenvalues of T_1^{-1} are λ_k^{-1}, $k = 1, \ldots, n_{s-2}$. This means that the system is stable if all the eigenvalues of T_1 have a modulus *greater* than one. This result can be proved by considering the eigenvalue with the smallest modulus, $\lambda_{\min}$. If $|\lambda_{\min}| > 1$ then the result is proved.

Now the eigenvalues of T_1, see Smith (1985), are given by:

$$\lambda_k = 1 + \Delta t \left(r + \frac{\sigma^2}{\Delta Z^2} \right) + 2\sqrt{AC} \cos \left(\frac{k\pi}{n_{s-2}+1} \right), \quad k = 1, \ldots, n_{s-2} \qquad \text{(L.10)}$$

where the term

$$2\sqrt{AC} = \sqrt{\frac{\Delta t^2 (\sigma^4 - b^2 \Delta Z^2)}{\Delta Z^4}} \qquad \text{(L.11)}$$

It can be seen that if $b^2 \Delta Z^2 > \sigma^4$ then the eigenvalues are complex and if $\sigma^4 \geq b^2 \Delta Z^2$ then eigenvalues are real. We will consider each of these cases in turn.

L.2.1   Complex eigenvalues: $b^2 \Delta Z^2 > \sigma^4$

We will represent the kth complex eigenvalue as:

$$\lambda_k = R + iY$$

where the real part is $R = 1 + \Delta t \left(r + \frac{\sigma^2}{\Delta Z^2} \right)$

and the imaginary part is $Y = 2\sqrt{AC} \cos \left(\frac{k\pi}{n_{s-2}+1} \right)$

Since $|\lambda_k| > |R| + |Y|$ and $|R| > 1$

we conclude that $|\lambda_{\min}| > 1$

L.2.2   Real eigenvalues: $\sigma^4 \geq b^2 \Delta Z^2$

In this case the kth eigenvalue is real, and from Equation L.10 we have:

$$\lambda_k > 1 + \Delta t \left(r + \frac{\sigma^2}{\Delta Z^2} \right) - 2\sqrt{AC}$$

Since $b^2 \Delta^2 > 0$ from Equation L.11 we have

$$2\sqrt{AC} < \sqrt{\frac{\sigma^4 \Delta t^2}{\Delta Z^4}} \quad \text{or} \quad \left| 2\sqrt{AC} \right| < \frac{\sigma^2 \Delta t}{\Delta Z^2}$$

So $\lambda_{\min} > 1 + \Delta t \left(r + \frac{\sigma^2}{\Delta Z^2} \right) - \frac{\sigma^2 \Delta t}{\Delta Z^2}$

Therefore we have $|\lambda_{\min}| > 1 + r\Delta t$

and since $r > 0$, we have: $|\lambda_{\min}| > 1$

Glossary of terms

The notation used is as follows:

$\psi(x)$	The psi function, also called the digamma function, $(\partial(\log \Gamma(x)))/\partial x = \psi(x)$
$\Gamma(x)$	The gamma function. If x is an integer then $\Gamma(x) = (n-1)!$
$\log(x)$	The natural logarithm of x.
$E(x)$	The conditional expectation value of x.
$E[x]$	The unconditional expectation value of x.
$NID(a,b)$	Normally and independently distributed variates, with mean a and variance b.
$\mathcal{R}(a,b)$	An arbitrary distribution, with mean a and variance b.
$IID(a,b)$	Independently and identically distributed, with lower limit a and upper limit b.
$\mathcal{U}(a,b)$	The uniform distribution, with lower limit a and upper limit b.
OLS	Ordinary least squares.
$|x|$	The absolute value of the variable x.
PDF	The probability density function of a given distribution.
$\mathcal{DL}(\theta)$	$(\partial \mathcal{L}(\theta))/\partial \theta$
$\mathcal{D}^2\mathcal{L}(\theta)$	$(\partial^2 \mathcal{L}(\theta))/\partial \theta^2$
Leptokurtic	The distribution has a kurtosis greater than 3. This implies that the tails of the distribution are thicker than those of a Gaussian.
Platykurtic	The distribution has a kurtosis less than 3. This implies that the tails of the distribution are thinner than those of a Gaussian.
$\hat{\theta}$	The vector of estimated GARCH model parameters.
$\hat{\theta}_i$	The estimated value of the ith GARCH model parameter.

Computing reading list

Ammeraal, L. (2001) *C++ for Programmers*, Third Edition, Wiley.

Barwell, F. *et al.* (2002) *Professional VB.NET*, Second Edition, Wrox Press.

Birbeck, M. (2001) *Professional XML*, Second Edition, Wrox Press Ltd.

Black, F. and Scholes, M. (1973) The pricing of corporate liabilities, *Journal of Political Economy*, **81**, 637–657.

Box, D. (1998) *Essential COM*, Addison-Wesley.

Brockschmidt, K. (1995) *Inside OLE*, Microsoft Press.

Cagle, K. *et al.* (2001) *Professional XSL*, Wrox Press Ltd.

Challa, S. and Laksberg, A. (2002) *Essential Guide to Managed Extensions for C++*, Apress.

Conard, J. *et al.* (2000) *Introducing .NET*, Wrox Press Ltd.

Darnell, R. *et al.* (1998) *HTML 4 Unleashed*, Sams.net.

Denning, A. (1997) *ActiveX Controls Inside Out*, Microsoft Press.

Ellis, M. A. and Stroustrup, B. (1990) *The Annotated C++ Reference Manual*, Addison-Wesley.

Flowers, B. H. (1995) *An Introduction to Numerical Methods in C++*, Clarendon Press, Oxford.

Hull, J. C. (1997) *Options Futures and Other Derivatives*, Prentice Hall.

Inprise Corporation (1998) *Delphi 4*, Inprise Corporation.

Koenig, A. and Moo, B. E. (2000) *Accelerated C++*, Addison-Welsey.

Kruglinski, D., Shepherd, G. and Wingo, S. (1998) *Programming Microsoft Visual C++*, Microsoft Press.

Levy, G. F. (1997) Mathematics, *Visual Systems Journal*, **3**, 28–36.

Levy, G. F. (1997) Mathematics part II, *Visual Systems Journal*, **4**, 26–35.

Levy, G. F. (1997) Summing up, *Visual Systems Journal*, **6**, 6–8.

Levy, G. F. (1998) *Calling 32-bit NAG C DLL Functions from Visual Basic 5 and Microsoft Office*, NAG Technical Report, TR2/98.

Levy, G. F. (2001) Numeric ActiveX components, *Software – Practice and Experience*, **31**, 1–43; **31**(2), 147–189.

Levy, G. F. (2003) *Wrapping C with C++ in .NET*, C/C++ Users Journal.

Markowitz, H. M. (1994) The general mean-variance portfolio selection problem, *Phil. Trans. R. Soc. Lond. A*, **347**, 543–549.

Meyers, S. (1996) *More Effective C++*, Addison-Wesley.

Meyers, S. (1998) *Effective C++*, Second Edition, Addison-Wesley.

Meyers, S. (2001) *Effective STL*, Addison-Wesley.

Microsoft Corporation (1995) *Excel/Visual Basic Programmers Guide*, Microsoft Corporation.

Microsoft Corporation (1996) *ActiveX Control Pad*, Microsoft Corporation.

Microsoft Corporation (1997) *Visual Basic 5, Component Tools Guide*, Microsoft Corporation.

NAG Ltd (2001) *The Fortran 77 Library Mark 20*, NAG Ltd, Oxford.

NAG Ltd (2002) *The C Library Mark 7*, NAG Ltd, Oxford.

NAG Ltd (2003) *The NAG C Library Mark 7*, NAG Ltd.

O'Brien, T. M., Pogge, S. J. and White, G. E. (1997) *Microsoft Access 97 Developer's Handbook*, Microsoft Press.

Petroutsos, B., Schongar, E. *et al.* (1997) *VBScript Unleashed*, Sams.net.

Rebonato, R. (1998) *Interest-rate Option Models*, Second Edition, John Wiley.

Robinson, S. *et al.* (2001) *Professional C#*, Wrox Press Ltd.

Rogerson, D. (1997) *Inside COM*, Microsoft Press.

Stroustrup, B. (1991) *The C++ Programming Language*, Second Edition, Addison-Wesley.

Mathematics and finance references

REFERENCES

Abramowitz, M. and Stegun, I. A. (1968) *Handbook of Mathematical Functions*, Dover Publications.

Aitchison, J. and Brown, J. A. C. (1966) *The Lognormal Distribution*, Cambridge University Press.

Alexander, C. O. (2000) *A Primer on the Orthogonal GARCH Model*, ISMA Centre, University of Reading.

Andersen, L. B. G. and Brotherton-Ratcliffe, R. (1998) The equity option volatility smile: an implicit finite-difference approach, *Journal of Computational Finance*, **1**(2), 5–37.

Anderson, H. M., Nam, K. and Vahid, F. (1999) Asymmetric nonlinear smooth transition GARCH models, in *Nonlinear Time Series Analysis of Economic and Financial Data*, P. Rothman (ed.), Kluwer, Boston, 191–201.

Anderson, T. W. (1984) *An Introduction to Multivariate Statistical Analysis*, Second Edition, Wiley, New York.

Bachelier, L. (1900) Theory de la speculation, *Ann. Sci. Ecole. Norm. Sup.*, **17**, 21–86.

Barle, S. and Cakici, N. (1995) Growing a smiling tree, *Risk*, **8**(10), October, 76–81.

Barndorff-Nielsen, O. E. (1977) Exponentially decreasing distributions for the logarithm of particle size, *Proceedings of the Royal Society of London A*, **353**, 401–419.

Barndorff-Nielsen, O. E. (1998) Processes of normal inverse Gaussian type, *Finance and Stochastics*, **2**, 41–68.

Barndorff-Nielsen, O. E. and Halgreen, O. (1977) Infinite divisibility of the hyperbolic and generalized inverse Gaussian distributions, *Zeitschrift fur Wahrscheinlichkeitstheorie und verwandte Gebiete*, **38**, 309–312.

Barone-Adesi, G. and Whaley, R. E. (1987) Efficient analytic approximation of American option values, *The Journal of Finance*, **42**(2), 301–320.

Barraquand, J. and Martineau, D. (1995) Numerical valuation of high dimensional multivariate American securities, *Journal of Financial and Quantitative Analysis*, **30**, 383–405.

Beale, E. M. L. and Little, R. J. A. (1975) Missing values in multivariate analysis, *J. R. Stat. Soc.*, **37**, 129–145.

Berndt, E. K., Hall, B. H., Hall, R. E. and Hausman, J. A. (1974) Estimation and inference in nonlinear structural models, *Annals of Economic and Social Measurement*, **3**(4), 653–665.

Beyer, W. H. (1982) *CRC Standard Mathematical Tables*, CRC Press, Florida.

Black, F. (1975) Fact and fantasy in the use of options and corporate liabilities, *Financial Analysts Journal*, **31**, 36–41, 61–72.

Black, F. (1976) Studies in stock price volatility changes, *Proceedings of the 1976 Business Meeting of Business and Economics Statistics Section*, American Statistical Association, 177–181.

Black, F. and Scholes, M. (1973) The pricing of corporate liabilities, *Journal of Political Economy*, **81**, 637–657.

Bollerslev, T. P. (1987) A conditionally heteroskedastic time series model for speculative prices and rates of return, *Review of Economics and Statistics*, **69**, 542–547.

Box, G. E. P. and Jenkins, G. M. (1976) *Time Series Analysis: Forecasting and Control*, Holden-Day, San Francisco.

Box, G. E. P. and Muller, M. E. (1958) A note on the generation of random normal deviates, *Ann. Math. Stat.*, **29**, 610–611.

Boyle, P. P. and Tian, Yisong (1998) An explicit finite difference approach to the pricing of barrier options, *Applied Mathematical Finance*, **5**, 17–43.

Boyle, P. P., Broadie, M. and Glasserman, P. (1997) Monte Carlo methods for security pricing, *Journal of Economic Dynamics and Control*, **21**, 1267–1321.

Boyle, P. P., Evnine, J. and Gibbs, S. (1989) Numerical evaluation of multivariate contingent claims, *The Review of Management Studies*, **2**(2), 241–250.

Broadie, M. and DeTemple, J. (1996) American option valuation: new bounds, approximations, and a comparison of existings methods, *The Review of Financial Studies*, **9**(4), 1211–1250.

Broadie, M. and Glasserman, P. (1997) Pricing American-style securities using simulation, *Journal of Economic Dynamics and Control*, **21**, 1323–1352.

Brotherton-Ratcliffe, R. (1994) Monte Carlo Motoring, *Risk*, **7**(12), 53–58.

Bunch, J. R. and Kaufman, L. C. (1980) A computational method for the indefinite quadratic programming problem, *Linear Algebra and its Applications*, **34**, 341–370.

Caflisch, R. E., Morokoff, W. and Owen, A. (1997) Valuation of mortgage-backed securities using Brownian bridges to reduce effective dimension, *The Journal of Computational Finance*, **1**(1), 27–46.

Campbell, J. Y., Lo, A. W. and MacKinlay, A. C. (1997) *The Econometrics of Financial Markets*, Princeton University Press.

Chan, T. F., Golub, G. H. and Leveque, R. J. (1982) *Updating Formulae and a Pairwise Algorithm for Computing Sample Variances*, Compstat 1982, Physica-Verlag.

Chesney, M. and Scott, L. O. (1989) Pricing European currency options: a comparison of the modified Black–Scholes model and a random variance model, *J. Financial Quant. Anal.*, **24**, 267–284.

Chriss, N. (1996) Transatlantic trees, *Risk*, **9**(7), 45–48.

Chriss, N. (1997) *Black–Scholes and Beyond*, IRWIN.

Clewlow, L. and Strickland, C. (1999) *Implementing Derivative Models*, John Wiley.

Cox, D. R. and Hinkley, D. V. (1979) *Theoretical Statistics*, Chapman and Hall.

Cox, J. C., Ross, S. A. and Rubinstein, M. (1979) Option pricing: a simplified approach, *Journal of Financial Economics*, **7**, 229–263.

Crank, J. and Nicolson, P. (1947) A practical method for numerical evaluation of solutions of partial differential equations of the heat conduction type, *Proc. Camb. Phil. Soc.*, **43**, 50–67.

DeGroot, M. H. (1970) *Optimal Statistical Decisions*, McGraw-Hill, New York.

Dempster, A. P., Laird, N. M. and Rubin, D. B. (1977) Maximum likelihood from incomplete data via the EM algorithm, *J. R. Statist Soc. Series B, Methodological*, **39**, 1–22.

Derman, E. and Kani, I. (1994) Riding on a smile, *Risk*, **7**(2), 32–39.

Dickey, J. M. (1967) Matricvariate generalizations of the multivariate t distribution and the inverted t distribution, *Ann. Math. Stat.*, **38**(2), 511–518.

Ding, Z. (1994) *Time Series Analysis of Speculative Returns*, PhD dissertation, University of California San Diego.

Dueker, M. J. (1997) Markov switching in GARCH processes and mean-reverting stock market volatility, *Journal of Business and Economic Statistics*, **15**, 26–34.

Duffie, D. and Singleton, K. J. (1989) *Simulated Moment Estimation of Markov Models of Asset Prices*, Stanford Graduate School of Business.

Eberlein, E. (2001) Applications of generalized hyperbolic levy motion to finance, in *Levy Processes, Theory and Applications*, O. E. Barndorff-Nielsen, T. Mikosch and S. I. Resnick (eds), Birkhauser.

Einstein, A. (1905) On the movement of small particles suspended in a stationary liquid demanded by the molecular-kinetic theory of meat, *Ann. Physik*, **17**.

Engle, R. F. (1982) Autoregressive conditional heteroskedasticity with estimates of the variance of United Kingdom inflation, *Econometrica*, **50**, 987–1008.

Engle, R. F. (1995) ARCH selected readings, *Advanced Texts in Econometrics*, Oxford University Press.

Engle, R. F. and Bollerslev, T. P. (1986) Modelling the persistence of conditional variances, *Econometric Reviews*, **5**, 1–50.

Engle, R. F. and Gonzalez-Rivera (1991) Semiparametric ARCH models, *Journal of Business and Economics*, **9**, 345–360.

Engle, R. F. and Ng, V. (1993) Measuring and testing the impact of news on volatility, *Journal of Finance*, **48**, 1749–1777.

Engle, R. F., Lilien, D. M. and Robins, P. R. (1987) Estimating time varying risk premia in the term structure: The ARCH-M model, *Econometrica*, **55**, 391–407.

Evans, M., Hastings, N. and Peacock, B. (2000) *Statistical Distributions*, John Wiley, Third Edition.

Faure, H. (1982) Discrepance de suites associees a un systeme de numeration (en dimensions), *Acta Arith.*, **41**, 337–351.

Feller, W. (1971) *An Introduction to Probability Theory and its Applications*, **II**, John Wiley and Sons.

Fiorentini, G., Calzolari, G. and Panattoni, L. (1996) Analytic derivatives and the computation of GARCH estimates, *Journal of Applied Econometrics*, **11**, 399–417.

Fisher, R. A. (1925) Theory of statistical estimation, *Proc. Cambridge Philos. Soc.*, **22**, 700–725.

Forsberg, L. and Bollerslev, T. (2002) Bridging the GAP between distribution of realised (ECU) volatility and ARCH modelling (of the EURO): the GARCH-NIG model, *Journal of Applied Econometrics*, **17**, 535–548.

Freedman, D. (1983) *Brownian Motion and Diffusion*, Springer-Verlag, New York.

Fu, M. C., Laprise, S. B., Madan, D. B., Su, Y. and Wu, R. (2001) Pricing American options: a comparison of Monte Carlo simulation approaches, *Journal of Computational Finance*, **4**(3), 39–88.

Geske, R. (1979) A note on an analytic valuation formulae for unprotected American call options on stocks with known dividends, *Journal of Econometrics*, **7**, 375–380.

Geske, R. and Johnson, H. E. (1984) The American put options valued analytically, *Journal of Finance*, **39**, 1511–1524.

Ghysels, E., Harvey, A. C. and Renault, E. (1996) Stochastic volatility, *Handbook of Statistics 14:Statistic Methods in Finance*, North-Holland, 119–191.

Gill, P. E., Murray, W. and Wright, M. H. (1981) *Practical Optimization*, Academic Press.

Glasserman, R. P., Heidelberger, P. and Shahabuddin, P. (2000) Variance reduction techniques for value-at-risk with heavy-tailed risk factors, in *Proceedings of the 2000 Winter Simulation Conference*, J. A. Joines, R. R. Barton, K. Kang and P. A. Fishwick (eds).

Glosten, L. and Milgrom, P. (1985) Bid, ask and transaction prices in a specialist market with heterogeneously informed traders, *Journal of Financial Economics* **14**, 71–100.

Glosten, L., Jagannathan, R. and Runkle, D. (1993) Relationship between the expected value and the volatility of nominal excess return on stocks, *Journal of Finance*, **48**, 1779–1801.

Goldberger, A. S. (1997) *A Course in Econometrics*, Havard University Press.

Golub, G. H. and Van Loan, C. F. (1989) *Matrix Computation*, The John Hopkins University Press.

Good, I. J. (1979) Computer generation of the exponential power distribution, *Journal of Statistical Computation and Simulation*, **9**(3), 239–240.

Granger, C. W. J. (2002) Some comments on risk, *Journal of Applied Econometrics*, **15**, 447–456.

Hager, W. (1988) *Applied Numerical Linear Algebra*, Prentice Hall.

Hamilton, J. (1994) *Time Series Analysis*, Princeton University Press.

Harvey, A. (1990) *The Econometric Analysis of Time Series*, Philip Allan.

Harvey, A. C., Ruiz, E. and Shephard, N. (1994) Multivariate stochastic variance models, *Review of Economic Studies*, **61**, 247–264.

Hentschel, L. F. (1995) All in the family: nesting linear and nonlinear GARCH models, *Journal of Financial Economics*, **39**, 139–164.

Hull, J. C. (1997) *Options Futures and Other Derivatives*, Prentice Hall.

Hull, J. C. and White, A. (1994) Numerical procedures for implementing term structure models I, *The Journal of Derivatives*, **2**, 7–16.

Johnson, H. (1987) Options on the maximum or the minimum of several assets, *Journal of Financial and Quantitative Analysis*, **22**(3), 277–283.

Kamrad, B. and Ritchken, P. (1991) Multinomial approximating models for options with k state variables, *Management Science*, **37**(12), 1640–1652.

Karatzas, I. and Shreve, S. (1988) *Brownian Motion and Stochastic Calculus*, Springer-Verlag, New York.

Levi, F. W. (1942) *Algebra*, University of Calcutta.

Levy, G. F. (2000) *Software implementation and testing of GARCH models*, NAG Technical Report, TR4/2000, NAG Ltd, Oxford.

Levy, G. F. (2003) Analytic derivatives of asymmetric GARCH models, *Journal of Computational Finance*, **6**(3).

Levy, P. (1939) Sur certain processus stochastiques homogenes, *Compositio Math.*, **7**, 283–339.

Levy, P. (1948) *Processus Stochastiques et Mouvement Brownian*, Gauthier-Villar, Paris.

Little, R. J. A. and Rubin, D. B. (1987) *Statistical Analysis with Missing Data*, John Wiley.

Lo, A. W. and MacKinlay, A. C. (1990) An econometric analysis of nonsynchronous-Trading, *Journal of Econometrics*, **45**, 181–212.

McIntyre, R. (1999) Black–Scholes will do, *Energy & Power Risk Management*, November, 26–27.

McKenzie, M. D., Mitchell, H., Brooks, R. D. and Faff, R. W. (2001) Power ARCH modelling of commodities futures data on the London Metal Exchange, *The European Journal of Finance*, **7**, 22–28.

MacMillan, L. W. (1986) Analytic approximation for the American put option, *Advances in Futures and Options Research*, **1**, 119–139.

Marchuk, G. I. and Shaidurov, V. V. (1983) *Difference Methods and their Extrapolations*, Springer-Verlag.

Mardia, K. V., Kent, J. T. and Bibby, J. (1988) Multivariate analysis, *Probability and Mathematical Statistics*, Academic Press, London.

Markowitz, H. M. (1989) *Mean Variance Analysis in Portfolio Choice and Capital Markets*, Basil Blackwell.

Markowitz, H. M. (1994) The general mean-variance portfolio selection problem, *Phil. Trans. R. Soc. Lond. A.*, **347**, 543–549.

Melino, A. and Turnbill, S. M. (1990) Pricing Foreign Currency Options with Stochastic Volatility, *J. Econometrics*, **45**, 239–265.

Merton, R. C. (1973) The theory of rational option pricing, *The Bell Journal of Economy and Management Science*, **4**(1), 141–181.

Morgan, J. P. (1996) *Risk Metrics – Technical Document*, Fourth Edition, New York.

Murtagh, B. A. and Saunders, M. A. (1983) *MINOS 5.0 user's guide*, Report SOL 83-20, Department of Operations Research, Stanford University.

Musiela, M. and Rutkowski, M. (1998) *Martingale Methods in Financial Modelling*, Springer-Verlag.

Nelson, D. B. (1990) Stationarity and persistence in the GARCH(1,1) model, *Econometric Theory*, **6**, 318–334.

Nelson, D. B. (1991) Conditional heteroskedasticity in asset returns: a new approach, *Econometrica*, **59**, 347–370.

Niederreiter, H. (1992) *Random Number Generation and Quasi-Monte Carlo Methods*, SIAM.

Orchard, T. and Woodbury, M. A. (1972) A missing information principle: theory and applications, *Proc. 6th Berkeley Symp. Math. Statist. Prob.*, **I**, 697–715.

Perrin, J. B. (1909) in *Annales de Chimie et de Physique, 8me series*, September 1909. Translated by F. Soddy, as *Brownian Movement and Molecular Reality*, Taylor and Francis, London, 1910.

Prause, K. (1999) *The Generalized Hyperbolic Model: Estimation, Financial Derivatives, and Risk Measures*, Dissertation zur Erlangung des Doctorgrades, Albert-Ludwigs-Universitat Freiburg i. Br.

Press, W. H., Teukolsky, S. A., Vetterling, W. T. and Flannery, B. P. (1992) *Numerical Recipes in C: The Art of Scientific Computing*, Second Edition, Cambridge University Press.

Raible, S. (2000) *Levy Processes in Finance: Theory, Numerics, and Empirical Facts*, Dissertation zur Erlangung des Doctorgrades, Albert-Ludwigs-Universitat Freiburg i. Br.

Ramsbottom, J. (1932) Centenary of Robert Brown's Discovery of the Nucleus – Exhibit at natural history museum, *The Journal of Botany British and Foreign*, January, 13–16.

Richardson, L. F. (1910) The approximate arithmetical solution by finite differences of physical problems involving differential equations, with an application to the stresses in a masonry dam, *Philos. Trans. R. Soc. Lond. A*, **210**, 307–357.

Richardson, L. F. and Gaunt, G. A. (1927) The deferred approach to the limit, *Philos. Trans. R. Soc. A*, **226**, 299–361.

Roll, R. (1977) An analytic valuation formulae for unprotected American call options on stocks with known dividends, *Journal of Econometrics*, **5**, 251–258.

Roll, R. (1984) A simple implicit measure of the effective bid-ask spread in an efficient market, *Journal of Finance*, **39**, 1127–1140.

Scott, L. O. (1991) Random variance option pricing: empirical tests of the model and delta-sigma hedging, *Adv. Futures Options Res.*, **5**, 113–135.

Shreve, S., Chalasani, P. and Jha, S. (1997) *Stochastic Calculus and Finance*.

Silvey, S. D. (1975) Statistical inference, *Monographs on Applied Probability*, Chapman and Hall.

Smith, G. D. (1985) *Numerical Solution of Partial Differential Equations: Finite Difference Methods*, Oxford University Press.

Sobol, I. M. (1967) The distribution of points in a cube and the approximate evaluation of integrals, *USSR Comput. Math. Math. Phys.*, **7**(4), 86–112.

Stulz, R. M. (1982) Options on the minimum or maximum of two risky assets, *Journal of Financial Economics*, **10**, 161–185.

Tadikamalla, P. R. (1980) Random sampling from the exponential power distribution, *Journal of the Statistical Association*, **75**(371), 683–686.

Taylor, S. (1986) *Modelling Financial Time Series*, Wiley, Chichester, UK.

Taylor, S. (1994) Modelling stochastic volatility: a review and comparative study, *Mathematical Finance*, **4**(2), 183–204.

Tilley, J. A. (1993) Valuing American options in a path simulation model, *Transaction of the Society of Actuaries*, **45**, 83–104.

Van der Weide, R. (2002) GO-GARCH: A multivariate generalized orthogonal GARCH model, *Journal of Applied Econometrics*, **17**, 549–564.

West, D. H. D. (1979) Updating mean and variance estimates: an improved method, *Communications of the ACM*, **22**(9), 532–535.

Whaley, R. E. (1981) On the valuation of American Call options on Stocks with Known Dividends, *Journal of Financial Economics*, **9**, 207–211.

Wiener, N. (1923) Differential spaces, *J. Math. Physics*, **2**, 131–174.

Wiener, N. (1924) Un problem de probabilities denombrables, *Bull. Soc. Math. France*, **52**, 569–578.

BIBLIOGRAPHY

Baxter, M. and Rennie, A. (1996) *Financial Calculus, An Introduction to Derivative Pricing*, Cambridge University Press.

Bollerslev, T. P. (1986) Generalised autoregressive conditional heteroskedasticity, *Journal of Econometrics*, **31**, 307–327.

Bratley, P. (1986) Algorithm 647: implementation and relative efficiency of quasirandom sequence generators, *ACM Transactions on Mathematical Software*, **12**(4), 362–376.

Bratley, P. and Fox, B. L. (1988) Algorithm 659: implementing Sobol's quasirandom sequence generator, *ACM Transactions on Mathematical Software*, **14**(1), 88–100.

Bratley, P., Fox, B. L. and Niederreiter, H. (1992) Implementation and Tests of Low-Discrepancy Sequences, *ACM Transactions on Modeling and Computer Simulation*, **2**(3), March, 195–213.

Brennan, M. J. and Schwartz, E. S. (1978) Finite difference methods and jump processes arising in the pricing of contingent claims: a synthesis, *Journal of Financial and Quantitative Analysis*, **13**, 462–474.

Cotton, I. W. (1975) Remark on Stably Updating Mean and Standard Deviation of Data, *Communications of the ACM*, **18**(8), 458.

Duffie, D. (1996) *Dynamic Asset Pricing Theory*, Princeton University Press, Second Edition.

Enders, W. (1995) *Applied Econometric Time Series*, John Wiley and Sons.

Engle, R. F. (2000) Dynamic conditional correlation – a simple class of multivariate GARCH models, Discussion Paper 2000–9, University of California, San Diego.

Franses, P. H. and Van Dijk, D. (2000) *Non-Linear Time Series Models in Empirical Finance*, Cambridge University Press.

Gourieroux, C. (1997) ARCH models and financial applications, *Springer Series in Statistics*, New York: Springer-Verlag.

Hanson, R. J. (1975) Stably updating mean and standard deviation of data, *Communications of the ACM*, **18**(1), 57–58.

James, J. and Webber, N. (2000) *Interest Rate Modelling*, John Wiley.

Johnson, N. L. and Kotz, S. (1992) *Distributions in Statistics: Continuous Multivariate Distributions*, Wiley.

Johnson, N. L., Kotz, S. and Balakvishnam, N. (1994) *Continuous Univariate Distributions*, Second Edition, Wiley.

Johnson, N. L., Kotz, S. and Kemp, A. (1992) *Univariate Discrete Distributions*, Wiley.

Johnson, R. A. and Wichern, D. W. (1999) *Applied Multivariate Statistical Analysis*, Prentice Hall.

Jorion, P. (1997) *Value at Risk*, Mc Graw Hill.

Kim, C. J. and Nelson, C. R. (1999) *State-Space Models with Regime Switching*, MIT Press.

Kloeden, P. E. and Platen, E. (1999) *Numerical Solution of Stochastic Differential Equations*, Springer.

Knight, J. and Satchell, S. (1998) *Forecasting Volatility in the Financial Markets*, Butterworth Heinemann.

Martellini, L. and Priaulet, P. (2001) *Fixed-Income Securities, Dynamic Methods for Interest Rate Risk Pricing and Hedging*, John Wiley.

Morokoff, W. (1999) The Brownian bridge E-M algorithm for covariance estimation with missing data, *Journal of Computational Finance*, **2**(2), 75–100.

Rebonato, R. (1998) *Interest-rate Option Models*, Second Edition, John Wiley.

Rogers, L. C. G. and Talay, D. (1997) *Numerical Methods in Finance*, Cambridge University Press.

Roy, A. D. (1952) Safety first and the holding of assets, *Econometrica*, **20**, 431–449.

Sentana, E. (1995) Quadratic ARCH models, *Review of Economic Studies*, **62**, 639–661.

Stuart, A. and Ord, J. K. (1987) *Kendall's Advanced Theory of Statistics*, Fifth Edition, Griffin.

Wilmott, P., Howison, S. and Dewynne, J. (1997) *The Mathematics of Financial Derivatives*, Cambridge University Press.

Index